Microsoft® Visual C#® 2010 Step by Step

John Sharp

PUBLISHED BY
Microsoft Press
A Division of Microsoft Corporation
One Microsoft Way
Redmond, Washington 98052-6399

Library of Congress Control Number: 2009939912

Printed and bound in the United States of America.

ISBN: 978-0-7356-2670-6

4 5 6 7 8 9 10 11 12 QGT 7 6 5 4 3 2

Distributed in Canada by H.B. Fenn and Company Ltd.

A CIP catalogue record for this book is available from the British Library.

Microsoft Press books are available through booksellers and distributors worldwide. For further information about international editions, contact your local Microsoft Corporation office or contact Microsoft Press International directly at fax (425) 936-7329. Visit our Web site at www.microsoft.com/mspress. Send comments to mspinput@microsoft.com.

Acquisitions Editor: Ben Ryan
Developmental Editor: Devon Musgrave
Project Editor: Rosemary Caperton
Editorial Production: Waypoint Press, www.waypointpress.com
Technical Reviewer: Per Blomqvist; Technical Review services provided by Content Master, a member of CM Group, Ltd.
Cover: Tom Draper Design

Body Part No. X16-81630

[2012-01-20]

Contents at a Glance

Table of Contents

What do you think of this book? We want to hear from you!

Microsoft is interested in hearing your feedback so we can continually improve our books and learning resources for you. To participate in a brief online survey, please visit:

www.microsoft.com/learning/booksurvey/

v

Part IV   Building Windows Presentation Foundation Applications

What do you think of this book? We want to hear from you!

Microsoft is interested in hearing your feedback so we can continually improve our books and learning resources for you. To participate in a brief online survey, please visit:

www.microsoft.com/learning/booksurvey/

Acknowledgments

An oft-repeated fable is that the workmen who paint the Forth Railway Bridge, a large Victorian cantilever structure that spans the Firth of Forth just north of Edinburgh, have a job for life. According to the myth, it takes them several years to paint it from one end to the other, and when they have finished they have to start over again. I am not sure whether this is due to the ferocity of the Scottish weather, or the sensitivity of the paint that is used, although my daughter insists it is simply that the members of Edinburgh City Council have yet to decide on a color scheme that they really like for the bridge. I sometimes feel that this book has similar attributes. No sooner have I completed an edition and seen it published, then Microsoft announces another cool update for Visual Studio and C#, and my friends at Microsoft Press contact me and say, "What are your plans for the next edition?" However, unlike painting the Forth Railway Bridge, working on a new edition of this text is always an enjoyable task with a lot more scope for inventiveness than trying to work out new ways to hold a paint brush. There is always something novel to learn and innovative technology to play with. In this edition, I cover the new features of C# 4.0 and the .NET Framework 4.0, which developers will find invaluable for building applications that can take advantage of the increasingly powerful hardware now becoming available. Hence, although this work appears to be a never-ending task, it is always fruitful and pleasurable.

A large part of the enjoyment when working on a project such as this is the opportunity to collaborate with a highly motivated group of talented people within Microsoft Press, the developers at Microsoft working on Visual Studio 2010, and the people who review each chapter and make suggestions for various improvements. I would especially like to single out Rosemary Caperton and Stephen Sagman who have worked tirelessly to keep the project on track, to Per Blomqvist who reviewed (and corrected) each chapter, and to Roger LeBlanc who had the thankless task of copy-editing the manuscript and converting my prose into English. I must also make special mention of Michael Blome who provided me with early access to software and answered the many questions that I had concerning the Task Parallal Library. Several members of Content Master were kept gainfully employed reviewing and testing the code for the exercises—thanks Mike Sumsion, Chris Cully, James Millar, and Louisa Perry. Of course, I must additionally thank Jon Jagger who co-authored the first edition of this book with me back in 2001.

Last but by no means least, I must thank my family. My wife Diana is a wonderful source of inspiration. When writing Chapter 28 on the Task Parallel Library I had a mental block and had to ask her how she would explain Barrier methods. She looked at me quizzically, and gave a reply that although anatomically correct if I was in a doctor's surgery, indicated that either I had not phrased the question very carefully or that she had completely misunderstood what I was asking! James has now grown up and will soon have to learn what real work entails if he is to keep Diana and myself in the manner to which we would like to become accustomed in our dotage. Francesca has also grown up, and seems to have refined a strategy for getting all she wants without doing anything other than looking at me with wide, bright eyes, and smiling.

Finally, "Up the Gills!"

—John Sharp

Introduction

Microsoft Visual C# is a powerful but simple language aimed primarily at developers creating applications by using the Microsoft .NET Framework. It inherits many of the best features of C++ and Microsoft Visual Basic, but few of the inconsistencies and anachronisms, resulting in a cleaner and more logical language. C# 1.0 made its public debut in 2001. The advent of C# 2.0 with Visual Studio 2005 saw several important new features added to the language, including Generics, Iterators, and anonymous methods. C# 3.0 which was released with Visual Studio 2008, added extension methods, lambda expressions, and most famously of all, the Language Integrated Query facility, or LINQ. The latest incarnation of the language, C# 4.0, provides further enhancements that improve its interoperability with other languages and technologies. These features include support for named and optional arguments, the *dynamic* type which indicates that the language runtime should implement late binding for an object, and variance which resolves some issues in the way in which generic interfaces are defined. C# 4.0 takes advantage of the latest version of the .NET Framework, also version 4.0. There are many additions to the .NET Framework in this release, but arguably the most significant are the classes and types that constitute the Task Parallel Library (TPL). Using the TPL, you can now build highly scalable applications that can take full advantage of multi-core processors quickly and easily. The support for Web services and Windows Communication Foundation (WCF) has also been extended; you can now build services that follow the REST model as well as the more traditional SOAP scheme.

The development environment provided by Microsoft Visual Studio 2010 makes all these powerful features easy to use, and the many new wizards and enhancements included in Visual Studio 2010 can greatly improve your productivity as a developer.

Who This Book Is For

This book assumes that you are a developer who wants to learn the fundamentals of programming with C# by using Visual Studio 2010 and the .NET Framework version 4.0. In this book, you will learn the features of the C# language, and then use them to build applications running on the Microsoft Windows operating system. By the time you complete this book, you will have a thorough understanding of C# and will have used it to build Windows Presentation Foundation applications, access Microsoft SQL Server databases by using ADO.NET and LINQ, build responsive and scalable applications by using the TPL, and create REST and SOAP Web services by using WCF.

Finding Your Best Starting Point in This Book

This book is designed to help you build skills in a number of essential areas. You can use this book if you are new to programming or if you are switching from another programming language such as C, C++, Java, or Visual Basic. Use the following table to find your best starting point.

If you are	Follow these steps
New to object-oriented programming	1. Install the practice files as described in the next section, "Installing and Using the Practice Files." 2. Work through the chapters in Parts I, II, and III sequentially. 3. Complete Parts IV, V, and VI as your level of experience and interest dictates.
Familiar with procedural programming languages such as C, but new to C#	1. Install the practice files as described in the next section, "Installing and Using the Practice Files." Skim the first five chapters to get an overview of C# and Visual Studio 2010, and then concentrate on Chapters 6 through 21. 2. Complete Parts IV, and V, and VI as your level of experience and interest dictates.
Migrating from an object-oriented language such as C++, or Java	1. Install the practice files as described in the next section, "Installing and Using the Practice Files." 2. Skim the first seven chapters to get an overview of C# and Visual Studio 2010, and then concentrate on Chapters 8 through 21. 3. For information about building Windows applications and using a database, read Parts IV and V. 4. For information about building scalable applications and Web services, read Part VI.

If you are	Follow these steps
Switching from Visual Basic 6	1. Install the practice files as described in the next section, "Installing and Using the Practice Files."
	2. Work through the chapters in Parts I, II, and III sequentially.
	3. For information about building Windows applications, read Part IV.
	4. For information about accessing a database, read Part V.
	5. For information about building scalable applications and Web services, read Part VI.
	6. Read the Quick Reference sections at the end of the chapters for information about specific C# and Visual Studio 2010 constructs.
Referencing the book after working through the exercises	1. Use the index or the Table of Contents to find information about particular subjects.
	2. Read the Quick Reference sections at the end of each chapter to find a brief review of the syntax and techniques presented in the chapter.

Conventions and Features in This Book

This book presents information using conventions designed to make the information readable and easy to follow. Before you start, read the following list, which explains conventions you'll see throughout the book and points out helpful features that you might want to use.

Conventions

- Each exercise is a series of tasks. Each task is presented as a series of numbered steps (1, 2, and so on). A round bullet (•) indicates an exercise that has only one step.

- Notes labeled "tip" provide additional information or alternative methods for completing a step successfully.

- Notes labeled "important" alert you to information you need to check before continuing.

- Text that you type appears in bold.

- A plus sign (+) between two key names means that you must press those keys at the same time. For example, "Press Alt+Tab" means that you hold down the Alt key while you press the Tab key.

Other Features

- Sidebars throughout the book provide more in-depth information about the exercise. The sidebars might contain background information, design tips, or features related to the information being discussed.

- Each chapter ends with a Quick Reference section. The Quick Reference section contains quick reminders of how to perform the tasks you learned in the chapter.

Prerelease Software

This book was written and tested against Visual Studio 2010 Beta 2. We did review and test our examples against the final release of the software. However, you might find minor differences between the production release and the examples, text, and screenshots in this book.

Hardware and Software Requirements

You'll need the following hardware and software to complete the practice exercises in this book:

- Microsoft Windows 7 Home Premium, Windows 7 Professional, Windows 7 Enterprise, or Windows 7 Ultimate. The exercises will also run using Microsoft Windows Vista with Service Pack 2 or later.

- Microsoft Visual Studio 2010 Standard, Visual Studio 2010 Professional, or Microsoft Visual C# 2010 Express and Microsoft Visual Web Developer 2010 Express.

- Microsoft SQL Server 2008 Express (this is provided with all editions of Visual Studio 2010, Visual C# 2010 Express, and Visual Web Developer 2010 Express).

- 1.6 GHz processor, or faster. Chapters 27 and 28 require a dual-core or better processor.

- 1 GB for x32 processor, 2 GB for an x64 processor, of available, physical RAM.

- Video (1024 ×768 or higher resolution) monitor with at least 256 colors.

- CD-ROM or DVD-ROM drive.

- Microsoft mouse or compatible pointing device

You will also need to have Administrator access to your computer to configure SQL Server 2008 Express Edition.

Code Samples

The companion CD inside this book contains the code samples that you'll use as you perform the exercises. By using the code samples, you won't waste time creating files that aren't relevant to the exercise. The files and the step-by-step instructions in the lessons also let you learn by doing, which is an easy and effective way to acquire and remember new skills.

Installing the Code Samples

Follow these steps to install the code samples and required software on your computer so that you can use them with the exercises.

1. Remove the companion CD from the package inside this book and insert it into your CD-ROM drive.

> **Note** An end user license agreement should open automatically. If this agreement does not appear, open My Computer on the desktop or Start menu, double-click the icon for your CD-ROM drive, and then double-click StartCD.exe.

2. Review the end user license agreement. If you accept the terms, select the accept option and then click **Next**.

   A menu will appear with options related to the book.

3. Click **Install Code Samples**.

4. Follow the instructions that appear.

   The code samples are installed to the following location on your computer:

   Documents\Microsoft Press\Visual CSharp Step By Step

Using the Code Samples

Each chapter in this book explains when and how to use any code samples for that chapter. When it's time to use a code sample, the book will list the instructions for how to open the files.

For those of you who like to know all the details, here's a list of the code sample Visual Studio 2010 projects and solutions, grouped by the folders where you can find them. In many cases, the exercises provide starter files and completed versions of the same projects which you can use as a reference. The completed projects are stored in folders with the suffix "- Complete".

Project	Description
Chapter 1	
TextHello	This project gets you started. It steps through the creation of a simple program that displays a text-based greeting.
WPFHello	This project displays the greeting in a window by using Windows Presentation Foundation.
Chapter 2	
PrimitiveDataTypes	This project demonstrates how to declare variables by using each of the primitive types, how to assign values to these variables, and how to display their values in a window.
MathsOperators	This program introduces the arithmetic operators (+ − * / %).
Chapter 3	
Methods	In this project, you'll re-examine the code in the previous project and investigate how it uses methods to structure the code.
DailyRate	This project walks you through writing your own methods, running the methods, and stepping through the method calls by using the Visual Studio 2010 debugger.
DailyRate Using Optional Parameters	This project shows you how to define a method that takes optional parameters, and call the method by using named arguments.
Chapter 4	
Selection	This project shows how to use a cascading *if* statement to implement complex logic, such as comparing the equivalence of two dates.
SwitchStatement	This simple program uses a *switch* statement to convert characters into their XML representations.
Chapter 5	
WhileStatement	This project demonstrates a *while* statement that reads the contents of a source file one line at a time and displays each line in a text box on a form.
DoStatement	This project uses a *do* statement to convert a decimal number to its octal representation.

Project	Description
Chapter 6	
MathsOperators	This project revisits the MathsOperators project from Chapter 2, "Working with Variables, Operators, and Expressions," and shows how various unhandled exceptions can make the program fail. The *try* and *catch* keywords then make the application more robust so that it no longer fails.
Chapter 7	
Classes	This project covers the basics of defining your own classes, complete with public constructors, methods, and private fields. It also shows how to create class instances by using the *new* keyword and how to define static methods and fields.
Chapter 8	
Parameters	This program investigates the difference between value parameters and reference parameters. It demonstrates how to use the *ref* and *out* keywords.
Chapter 9	
StructsAndEnums	This project defines a *struct* type to represent a calendar date.
Chapter 10	
Cards Using Arrays	This project shows how to use arrays to model hands of cards in a card game.
Cards Using Collections	This project shows how to restructure the card game program to use collections rather than arrays.
Chapter 11	
ParamsArrays	This project demonstrates how to use the *params* keyword to create a single method that can accept any number of *int* arguments.
Chapter 12	
Vehicles	This project creates a simple hierarchy of vehicle classes by using inheritance. It also demonstrates how to define a virtual method.
ExtensionMethod	This project shows how to create an extension method for the *int* type, providing a method that converts an integer value from base 10 to a different number base.

Project	Description
Chapter 13	
Drawing Using Interfaces	This project implements part of a graphical drawing package. The project uses interfaces to define the methods that drawing shapes expose and implement.
Drawing	This project extends the Drawing Using Interfaces project to factor common functionality for shape objects into abstract classes.
Chapter 14	
UsingStatement	This project revisits a small piece of code from Chapter 5, "Using Compound Assignment and Iteration Statements" and reveals that it is not exception-safe. It shows you how to make the code exception-safe with a *using* statement.
Chapter 15	
WindowProperties	This project presents a simple Windows application that uses several properties to display the size of its main window. The display updates automatically as the user resizes the window.
AutomaticProperties	This project shows how to create automatic properties for a class, and use them to initialize instances of the class.
Chapter 16	
Indexers	This project uses two indexers: one to look up a person's phone number when given a name, and the other to look up a person's name when given a phone number.
Chapter 17	
Clock Using Delegates	This project displays a World clock showing the local time as well as the times in London, New York, and Tokyo. The application uses delegates to start and stop the clock displays.
Clock Using Events	This version of the World clock application uses events to start and stop the clock display.
Chapter 18	
BinaryTree	This solution shows you how to use Generics to build a *type-safe* structure that can contain elements of any type.
BuildTree	This project demonstrates how to use Generics to implement a *typesafe* method that can take parameters of any type.
BinaryTreeTest	This project is a test harness that creates instances of the *Tree* type defined in the BinaryTree project.

Project	Description
Chapter 19	
BinaryTree	This project shows you how to implement the generic *IEnumerator<T>* interface to create an enumerator for the generic *Tree* class.
IteratorBinaryTree	This solution uses an Iterator to generate an enumerator for the generic *Tree* class.
EnumeratorTest	This project is a test harness that tests the enumerator and iterator for the *Tree* class.
Chapter 20	
QueryBinaryTree	This project shows how to use LINQ queries to retrieve data from a binary tree object.
Chapter 21	
ComplexNumbers	This project defines a new type that models complex numbers, and implements common operators for this type.
Chapter 22	
BellRingers	This project is a Windows Presentation Foundation application demonstrating how to define styles and use basic WPF controls.
Chapter 23	
BellRingers	This project is an extension of the application created in Chapter 22, "Introducing Windows Presentation Foundation," but with drop-down and pop-up menus added to the user interface.
Chapter 24	
OrderTickets	This project demonstrates how to implement business rules for validating user input in a WPF application, using customer order information as an example.
Chapter 25	
ReportOrders	This project shows how to access a database by using ADO. NET code. The application retrieves information from the Orders table in the Northwind database.
LINQOrders	This project shows how to use LINQ to SQL to access a database and retrieve information from the Orders table in the Northwind database.

Project	Description
Chapter 26	
Suppliers	This project demonstrates how to use data binding with a WPF application to display and format data retrieved from a database in controls on a WPF form. The application also enables the user to modify information in the Products table in the Northwind database.
Chapter 27	
GraphDemo	This project generates and displays a complex graph on a WPF form. It uses a single thread to perform the calculations.
GraphDemo Using Tasks	This version of the GraphDemo project creates multiple tasks to perform the calculations for the graph in parallel.
GraphDemo Using Tasks that Return Results	This is an extended version of the GraphDemo Using Tasks project that shows how to return data from a task.
GraphDemo Using the Parallel Class	This version of the GraphDemo project uses the *Parallel* class to abstract out the process of creating and managing tasks.
GraphDemo Canceling Tasks	This project shows how to implement cancelation to halt tasks in a controlled manner before they have completed
ParallelLoop	This application provides an example showing when you should not use the *Parallel* class to create and run tasks.
Chapter 28	
CalculatePI	This project uses a statistical sampling algorithm to calculate an approximation for PI. It uses parallel tasks.
PLINQ	This project shows some examples of using PLINQ to query data by using parallel tasks.

Project	Description
Chapter 29	
ProductInformationService	This project implements a SOAP Web service built by using WCF. The Web service exposes a method that returns pricing information for products from the Northwind database.
ProductDetailsService	This projects implements a REST Web service built by using WCF. The Web service provides a method that returns the details of a specified product from the Northwind database.
ProductDetailsContracts	This project contains the service and data contracts implemented by the ProductDetailsService Web service.
ProductClient	This project shows how to create a WPF application that consumes a Web service. It shows how to invoke the Web methods in the ProductInformationService and ProductDetailsService Web services.

Uninstalling the Code Samples

Follow these steps to remove the code samples from your computer.

1. In **Control Panel**, under **Programs**, click **Uninstall a program**.

2. From the list of currently installed programs, select Microsoft Visual C# 2010 Step By Step.

3. Click **Uninstall**.

4. Follow the instructions that appear to remove the code samples.

Find Additional Content Online

As new or updated material becomes available that complements your book, it will be posted online on the Microsoft Press Online Developer Tools Web site. The type of material you might find includes updates to book content, articles, links to companion content, errata, sample chapters, and more. This Web site is available at www.microsoft.com/learning/ books/online/developer, and is updated periodically.

> **Digital Content for Digital Book Readers:** If you bought a digital-only edition of this book, you can enjoy select content from the print edition's companion CD.
> Visit **http://go.microsoft.com/fwlink/?LinkId=184386** to get your downloadable content. This content is always up-to-date and available to all readers.

Support for This Book

Every effort has been made to ensure the accuracy of this book and the contents of the companion CD. As corrections or changes are collected, they will be added to a Microsoft Knowledge Base article.

Microsoft Press provides support for books and companion CDs at the following Web site:

http://www.microsoft.com/learning/support/books/.

Questions and Comments

If you have comments, questions, or ideas regarding the book or the companion CD, or questions that are not answered by visiting the sites above, please send them to Microsoft Press via e-mail to

mspinput@microsoft.com.

Please note that Microsoft software product support is not offered through the above address.

Part I
Introducing Microsoft Visual C# and Microsoft Visual Studio 2010

Chapter 1
Welcome to C#

After completing this chapter, you will be able to:

- Use the Microsoft Visual Studio 2010 programming environment.

- Create a C# console application.

- Explain the purpose of namespaces.

- Create a simple graphical C# application.

Microsoft Visual C# is Microsoft's powerful component-oriented language. C# plays an important role in the architecture of the Microsoft .NET Framework, and some people have compared it to the role that C played in the development of UNIX. If you already know a language such as C, C++, or Java, you'll find the syntax of C# reassuringly familiar. If you are used to programming in other languages, you should soon be able to pick up the syntax and feel of C#; you just need to learn to put the braces and semicolons in the right place. I hope this is just the book to help you!

In Part I, you'll learn the fundamentals of C#. You'll discover how to declare variables and how to use arithmetic operators such as the plus sign (+) and minus sign (–) to manipulate the values in variables. You'll see how to write methods and pass arguments to methods. You'll also learn how to use selection statements such as *if* and iteration statements such as *while*. Finally, you'll understand how C# uses exceptions to handle errors in a graceful, easy-to-use manner. These topics form the core of C#, and from this solid foundation, you'll progress to more advanced features in Part II through Part VI.

Beginning Programming with the Visual Studio 2010 Environment

Visual Studio 2010 is a tool-rich programming environment containing the functionality that you need to create large or small C# projects. You can even construct projects that seamlessly combine modules written by using different programming languages such as C++, Visual Basic, and F#. In the first exercise, you will open the Visual Studio 2010 programming environment and learn how to create a console application.

 Note A console application is an application that runs in a command prompt window rather than providing a graphical user interface.

Create a console application in Visual Studio 2010

- If you are using Visual Studio 2010 Standard or Visual Studio 2010 Professional, perform the following operations to start Visual Studio 2010:

   1. On the Microsoft Windows task bar, click the *Start* button, point to *All Programs*, and then point to the *Microsoft Visual Studio 2010* program group.

   2. In the Microsoft Visual Studio 2010 program group, click *Microsoft Visual Studio 2010*.

   Visual Studio 2010 starts, like this:

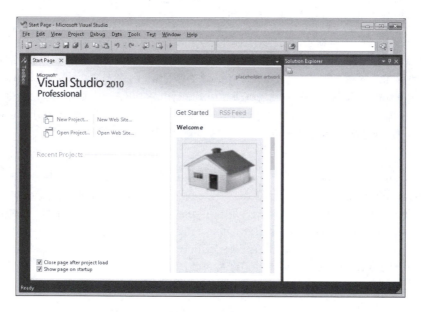

 Note If this is the first time you have run Visual Studio 2010, you might see a dialog box prompting you to choose your default development environment settings. Visual Studio 2010 can tailor itself according to your preferred development language. The various dialog boxes and tools in the integrated development environment (IDE) will have their default selections set for the language you choose. Select *Visual C# Development Settings* from the list, and then click the *Start Visual Studio* button. After a short delay, the Visual Studio 2010 IDE appears.

- If you are using Visual C# 2010 Express, on the Microsoft Windows task bar, click the *Start* button, point to *All Programs*, and then click *Microsoft Visual C# 2010 Express*.

   Visual C# 2010 Express starts, like this:

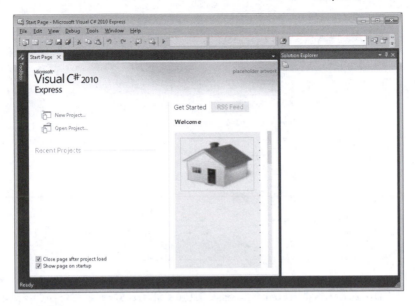

Note If this is the first time you have run Visual C# 2010 Express, you might see a dialog box prompting you to choose your default development environment settings. Select *Expert Settings* from the list, and then click the *Start Visual Studio* button. After a short delay, the Visual C# 2010 IDE appears.

Note To avoid repetition, throughout this book I simply state, "Start Visual Studio" when you need to open Visual Studio 2010 Standard, Visual Studio 2010 Professional, or Visual C# 2010 Express. Additionally, unless explicitly stated, all references to Visual Studio 2010 apply to Visual Studio 2010 Standard, Visual Studio 2010 Professional, and Visual C# 2010 Express.

- If you are using Visual Studio 2010 Standard or Visual Studio 2010 Professional, perform the following tasks to create a new console application:

  1. On the *File* menu, point to *New*, and then click *Project*.

     The *New Project* dialog box opens. This dialog box lists the templates that you can use as a starting point for building an application. The dialog box categorizes templates according to the programming language you are using and the type of application.

  2. In the left pane, under *Installed Templates*, click *Visual C#*. In the middle pane, verify that the combo box at the top of the pane displays the text *.NET Framework 4.0*, and then click the *Console Application* icon. You might need to scroll the middle pane to see the *Console Application* icon.

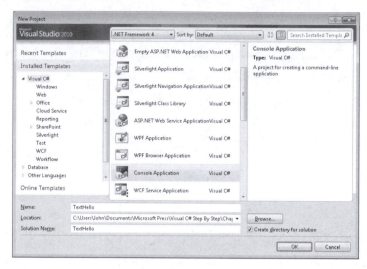

3. In the *Location* field, if you are using Windows Vista type **C:\Users*YourName*\\Documents\Microsoft Press\Visual CSharp Step By Step\Chapter 1**. If you are using Windows 7, type **C:\Users*YourName*\My Documents\Microsoft Press\\Visual CSharp Step By Step\Chapter 1**. Replace the text *YourName* in these paths with your Windows user name.

Note To save space throughout the rest of this book, I will simply refer to the path "C:\Users*YourName*\Documents" or "C:\Users*YourName*\My Documents" as your Documents folder.

Tip If the folder you specify does not exist, Visual Studio 2010 creates it for you.

4. In the *Name* field, type **TextHello**.

5. Ensure that the *Create directory for solution* check box is selected, and then click *OK*.

■ If you are using Visual C# 2010 Express, perform the following tasks to create a new console application:

1. On the *File* menu, click *New Project*.

2. In the *New Project* dialog box, in the middle pane click the *Console Application* icon.

3. In the *Name* field, type **TextHello**.

4. Click *OK*.

   Visual C# 2010 Express saves solutions to the C:\Users*YourName*\AppData\Local\ Temporary Projects folder by default. You can specify an alternative location when you save the solution.

5. On the *File* menu, click *Save TextHello As*.

6. In the *Save Project* dialog box, in the *Location* field specify the **Microsoft Press\ Visual CSharp Step By Step\Chapter 1** folder under your Documents folder.

7. Click *Save*.

Visual Studio creates the project using the Console Application template and displays the starter code for the project, like this:

The *menu bar* at the top of the screen provides access to the features you'll use in the programming environment. You can use the keyboard or the mouse to access the menus and commands exactly as you can in all Windows-based programs. The *toolbar* is located beneath the menu bar and provides button shortcuts to run the most frequently used commands.

The *Code and Text Editor* pane occupying the main part of the IDE displays the contents of source files. In a multifile project, when you edit more than one file, each source file has its own tab labeled with the name of the source file. You can click the tab to bring the named source file to the foreground in the *Code and Text Editor* window. The *Solution Explorer* pane (on the right side of the dialog box) displays the names of the files associated with the project, among other items. You can also double-click a file name in the *Solution Explorer* pane to bring that source file to the foreground in the *Code and Text Editor* window.

Before writing the code, examine the files listed in *Solution Explorer*, which Visual Studio 2010 has created as part of your project:

- **Solution 'TextHello'**   This is the top-level solution file, of which there is one per application. If you use Windows Explorer to look at your Documents\Microsoft Press\Visual CSharp Step By Step\Chapter 1\TextHello folder, you'll see that the actual name of this file is TextHello.sln. Each solution file contains references to one or more project files.

- **TextHello**   This is the C# project file. Each project file references one or more files containing the source code and other items for the project. All the source code in a single project must be written in the same programming language. In Windows Explorer, this file is actually called TextHello.csproj, and it is stored in the \Microsoft Press\Visual CSharp Step By Step\Chapter 1\TextHello\TextHello folder under your Documents folder.

- **Properties**   This is a folder in the TextHello project. If you expand it, you will see that it contains a file called AssemblyInfo.cs. AssemblyInfo.cs is a special file that you can use to add attributes to a program, such as the name of the author, the date the program was written, and so on. You can specify additional attributes to modify the way in which the program runs. Learning how to use these attributes is outside the scope of this book.

- **References**   This is a folder that contains references to compiled code that your application can use. When code is compiled, it is converted into an assembly and given a unique name. Developers use assemblies to package useful bits of code they have written so that they can distribute it to other developers who might want to use the code in their applications. Many of the features that you will be using when writing applications using this book make use of assemblies provided by Microsoft with Visual Studio 2010.

- **App.config**   This is the application configuration file. You can specify settings that your application can use at runtime to modify its behavior, such as the version of the .NET Framework to use to run the application. You will learn more about this file in later chapters in this book.

- **Program.cs**   This is a C# source file and is the one currently displayed in the Code and Text Editor window when the project is first created. You will write your code for the console application in this file. It also contains some code that Visual Studio 2010 provides automatically, which you will examine shortly.

Writing Your First Program

The Program.cs file defines a class called *Program* that contains a method called *Main*. All methods must be defined inside a class. You will learn more about classes in Chapter 7, "Creating and Managing Classes and Objects." The *Main* method is special—it designates the program's entry point. It must be a static method. (You will look at methods in detail in Chapter 3, "Writing Methods and Applying Scope," and Chapter 7 describes static methods.)

Important C# is a case-sensitive language. You must spell *Main* with a capital *M*.

In the following exercises, you write the code to display the message "Hello World" in the console; you build and run your Hello World console application; and you learn how namespaces are used to partition code elements.

Write the code by using Microsoft IntelliSense

1. In the *Code and Text Editor* window displaying the Program.cs file, place the cursor in the *Main* method immediately after the opening brace, {, and then press Enter to create a new line. On the new line, type the word **Console**, which is the name of a built-in class. As you type the letter *C* at the start of the word *Console*, an IntelliSense list appears. This list contains all of the C# keywords and data types that are valid in this context. You can either continue typing or scroll through the list and double-click the *Console* item with the mouse. Alternatively, after you have typed *Con*, the IntelliSense list automatically homes in on the *Console* item and you can press the Tab or Enter key to select it.

   Main should look like this:

   ```
   static void Main(string[] args)
   {
       Console
   }
   ```

 Note *Console* is a built-in class that contains the methods for displaying messages on the screen and getting input from the keyboard.

2. Type a period immediately after *Console*. Another IntelliSense list appears, displaying the methods, properties, and fields of the *Console* class.

3. Scroll down through the list, select *WriteLine*, and then press Enter. Alternatively, you can continue typing the characters *W, r, i, t, e, L* until *WriteLine* is selected, and then press Enter.

   The IntelliSense list closes, and the word *WriteLine* is added to the source file. *Main* should now look like this:

   ```
   static void Main(string[] args)
   {
       Console.WriteLine
   }
   ```

4. Type an opening parenthesis, (. Another IntelliSense tip appears.

   This tip displays the parameters that the *WriteLine* method can take. In fact, *WriteLine* is an *overloaded method*, meaning that the *Console* class contains more than one method named *WriteLine*—it actually provides 19 different versions of this method. Each version of the *WriteLine* method can be used to output different types of data. (Chapter 3 describes overloaded methods in more detail.) *Main* should now look like this:

```
static void Main(string[] args)
{
    Console.WriteLine(
}
```

 Tip You can click the up and down arrows in the tip to scroll through the different overloads of *WriteLine*.

5. Type a closing parenthesis,) followed by a semicolon, ;.

   Main should now look like this:

```
static void Main(string[] args)
{
    Console.WriteLine();
}
```

6. Move the cursor, and type the string **"Hello World"**, including the quotation marks, between the left and right parentheses following the *WriteLine* method.

   Main should now look like this:

```
static void Main(string[] args)
{
    Console.WriteLine("Hello World");
}
```

 Tip Get into the habit of typing matched character pairs, such as (and) and { and }, before filling in their contents. It's easy to forget the closing character if you wait until after you've entered the contents.

IntelliSense Icons

When you type a period after the name of a class, IntelliSense displays the name of every member of that class. To the left of each member name is an icon that depicts the type of member. Common icons and their types include the following:

Icon	Meaning
	method (discussed in Chapter 3)
	property (discussed in Chapter 15, "Implementing Properties to Access Fields")

Icon	Meaning
class (discussed in Chapter 7)	
	struct (discussed in Chapter 9, "Creating Value Types with Enumerations and Structures")
	enum (discussed in Chapter 9)
	interface (discussed in Chapter 13, "Creating Interfaces and Defining Abstract Classes")
	delegate (discussed in Chapter 17, "Interrupting Program Flow and Handling Events")
	extension method (discussed in Chapter 12, "Working with Inheritance")

You will also see other IntelliSense icons appear as you type code in different contexts.

Note You will frequently see lines of code containing two forward slashes followed by ordinary text. These are comments. They are ignored by the compiler but are very useful for developers because they help document what a program is actually doing. For example:

```
Console.ReadLine(); // Wait for the user to press the Enter key
```

The compiler skips all text from the two slashes to the end of the line. You can also add multiline comments that start with a forward slash followed by an asterisk (/*). The compiler skips everything until it finds an asterisk followed by a forward slash sequence (*/), which could be many lines lower down. You are actively encouraged to document your code with as many meaningful comments as necessary.

Build and run the console application

1. On the *Build* menu, click *Build Solution*.

   This action compiles the C# code, resulting in a program that you can run. The *Output* window appears below the *Code and Text Editor* window.

   Tip If the *Output* window does not appear, on the *View* menu, click *Output* to display it.

In the *Output* window, you should see messages similar to the following indicating how the program is being compiled:

```
------ Build started: Project: TextHello, Configuration: Debug x86 ----
CopyFilesToOutputDirectory:
  TextHello -> C:\Users\John\My Documents\Microsoft Press\Visual CSharp Step By Step\
Chapter 1\TextHello\TextHello\bin\Debug\TextHello.exe
========== Build: 1 succeeded or up-to-date, 0 failed, 0 skipped ========
```

If you have made some mistakes, they will appear in the *Error List* window. The following image shows what happens if you forget to type the closing quotation marks after the text Hello World in the *WriteLine* statement. Notice that a single mistake can sometimes cause multiple compiler errors.

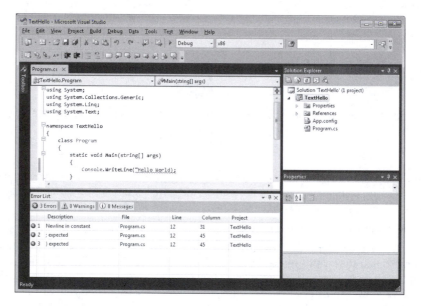

 Tip You can double-click an item in the *Error List* window, and the cursor will be placed on the line that caused the error. You should also notice that Visual Studio displays a wavy red line under any lines of code that will not compile when you enter them.

If you have followed the previous instructions carefully, there should be no errors or warnings, and the program should build successfully.

 Tip There is no need to save the file explicitly before building because the *Build Solution* command automatically saves the file.

An asterisk after the file name in the tab above the *Code and Text Editor* window indicates that the file has been changed since it was last saved.

2. On the *Debug* menu, click *Start Without Debugging*.

A command window opens, and the program runs. The message "Hello World" appears, and then the program waits for you to press any key, as shown in the following graphic:

 Note The prompt "Press any key to continue . . ." is generated by Visual Studio; you did not write any code to do this. If you run the program by using the *Start Debugging* command on the *Debug* menu, the application runs, but the command window closes immediately without waiting for you to press a key.

3. Ensure that the command window displaying the program's output has the focus, and then press Enter.

The command window closes, and you return to the Visual Studio 2010 programming environment.

4. In *Solution Explorer*, click the TextHello project (not the solution), and then click the *Show All Files* toolbar button on the *Solution Explorer* toolbar—this is the second left-most button on the toolbar in the Solution Explorer window.

Show All Files

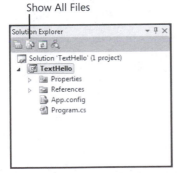

Entries named *bin* and *obj* appear above the Program.cs file. These entries correspond directly to folders named *bin* and *obj* in the project folder (Microsoft Press\Visual CSharp Step By Step\Chapter 1\TextHello\TextHello). Visual Studio creates these folders when you build your application, and they contain the executable version of the program together with some other files used to build and debug the application.

5. In *Solution Explorer*, expand the *bin* entry.

Another folder named *Debug* appears.

Note You might also see a folder called *Release*.

6. In *Solution Explorer*, expand the *Debug* folder.

   Four more items appear, named TextHello.exe, TextHello.pdb, TextHello.vshost.exe, and TextHello.vshost.exe.manifest.

   The file TextHello.exe is the compiled program, and it is this file that runs when you click *Start Without Debugging* on the *Debug* menu. The other files contain information that is used by Visual Studio 2010 if you run your program in *Debug* mode (when you click *Start Debugging* on the *Debug* menu).

Using Namespaces

The example you have seen so far is a very small program. However, small programs can soon grow into much bigger programs. As a program grows, two issues arise. First, it is harder to understand and maintain big programs than it is to understand and maintain smaller programs. Second, more code usually means more names, more methods, and more classes. As the number of names increases, so does the likelihood of the project build failing because two or more names clash (especially when a program also uses third-party libraries written by developers who have also used a variety of names).

In the past, programmers tried to solve the name-clashing problem by prefixing names with some sort of qualifier (or set of qualifiers). This solution is not a good one because it's not scalable; names become longer, and you spend less time writing software and more time typing (there is a difference) and reading and rereading incomprehensibly long names.

Namespaces help solve this problem by creating a named container for other identifiers, such as classes. Two classes with the same name will not be confused with each other if they live in different namespaces. You can create a class named *Greeting* inside the namespace named *TextHello*, like this:

```
namespace TextHello
{
    class Greeting
    {
        ...
    }
}
```

You can then refer to the *Greeting* class as *TextHello.Greeting* in your programs. If another developer also creates a *Greeting* class in a different namespace, such as *NewNamespace*, and installs it on your computer, your programs will still work as expected because they are using the *TextHello.Greeting* class. If you want to refer to the other developer's *Greeting* class, you must specify it as *NewNamespace.Greeting*.

It is good practice to define all your classes in namespaces, and the Visual Studio 2010 environment follows this recommendation by using the name of your project as the top-level namespace. The .NET Framework class library also adheres to this recommendation; every class in the .NET Framework lives inside a namespace. For example, the *Console* class lives inside the *System* namespace. This means that its full name is actually *System.Console*.

Of course, if you had to write the full name of a class every time you used it, the situation would be no better than prefixing qualifiers or even just naming the class with some globally unique name such *SystemConsole* and not bothering with a namespace. Fortunately, you can solve this problem with a *using* directive in your programs. If you return to the TextHello program in Visual Studio 2010 and look at the file Program.cs in the *Code and Text Editor* window, you will notice the following statements at the top of the file:

```
using System;
using System.Collections.Generic;
using System.Linq;
using System.Text;
```

A *using* statement brings a namespace into scope. In subsequent code in the same file, you no longer have to explicitly qualify objects with the namespace to which they belong. The four namespaces shown contain classes that are used so often that Visual Studio 2010 automatically adds these *using* statements every time you create a new project. You can add further *using* directives to the top of a source file.

The following exercise demonstrates the concept of namespaces in more depth.

Try longhand names

1. In the *Code and Text Editor* window displaying the Program.cs file, comment out the first *using* directive at the top of the file, like this:

   ```
   //using System;
   ```

2. On the *Build* menu, click *Build Solution*.

   The build fails, and the *Error List* window displays the following error message:

   ```
   The name 'Console' does not exist in the current context.
   ```

3. In the *Error List* window, double-click the error message.

   The identifier that caused the error is highlighted in the Program.cs source file.

4. In the *Code and Text Editor* window, edit the *Main* method to use the fully qualified name *System.Console*.

   Main should look like this:

   ```
   static void Main(string[] args)
   {
       System.Console.WriteLine("Hello World");
   }
   ```

> **Note** When you type *System*, the names of all the items in the *System* namespace are displayed by IntelliSense.

5. On the *Build* menu, click *Build Solution*.

   The build should succeed this time. If it doesn't, make sure that *Main* is exactly as it appears in the preceding code, and then try building again.

6. Run the application to make sure it still works by clicking *Start Without Debugging* on the *Debug* menu.

Namespaces and Assemblies

A *using* statement simply brings the items in a namespace into scope and frees you from having to fully qualify the names of classes in your code. Classes are compiled into *assemblies*. An assembly is a file that usually has the *.dll* file name extension, although strictly speaking, executable programs with the *.exe* file name extension are also assemblies.

An assembly can contain many classes. The classes that the .NET Framework class library comprises, such as *System.Console,* are provided in assemblies that are installed on your computer together with Visual Studio. You will find that the .NET Framework class library contains many thousands of classes. If they were all held in the same assembly, the assembly would be huge and difficult to maintain. (If Microsoft updated a single method in a single class, it would have to distribute the entire class library to all developers!)

For this reason, the .NET Framework class library is split into a number of assemblies, partitioned by the functional area to which the classes they contain relate. For example, there is a "core" assembly that contains all the common classes, such as *System. Console*, and there are further assemblies that contain classes for manipulating databases, accessing Web services, building graphical user interfaces, and so on. If you want to make use of a class in an assembly, you must add to your project a reference to that assembly. You can then add *using* statements to your code that bring the items in namespaces in that assembly into scope.

You should note that there is not necessarily a 1:1 equivalence between an assembly and a namespace; a single assembly can contain classes for multiple namespaces, and a single namespace can span multiple assemblies. This all sounds very confusing at first, but you will soon get used to it.

When you use Visual Studio to create an application, the template you select automatically includes references to the appropriate assemblies. For example, in *Solution*

Explorer for the TextHello project, expand the *References* folder. You will see that a Console application automatically includes references to assemblies called *Microsoft. CSharp, System, System.Core, System.Data, System.Data.DataExtensions, System.Xml,* and *System.Xml.Linq.* You can add references for additional assemblies to a project by right-clicking the *References* folder and clicking *Add Reference*—you will perform this task in later exercises.

Creating a Graphical Application

So far, you have used Visual Studio 2010 to create and run a basic Console application. The Visual Studio 2010 programming environment also contains everything you need to create graphical Windows-based applications. You can design the forms-based user interface of a Windows application interactively. Visual Studio 2010 then generates the program statements to implement the user interface you've designed.

Visual Studio 2010 provides you with two views of a graphical application: the *design view* and the *code view.* You use the *Code and Text Editor* window to modify and maintain the code and logic for a graphical application, and you use the *Design View* window to lay out your user interface. You can switch between the two views whenever you want.

In the following set of exercises, you'll learn how to create a graphical application by using Visual Studio 2010. This program will display a simple form containing a text box where you can enter your name and a button that displays a personalized greeting in a message box when you click the button.

 Note Visual Studio 2010 provides two templates for building graphical applications—the Windows Forms Application template and the WPF Application template. Windows Forms is a technology that first appeared with the .NET Framework version 1.0. WPF, or Windows Presentation Foundation, is an enhanced technology that first appeared with the .NET Framework version 3.0. It provides many additional features and capabilities over Windows Forms, and you should consider using it in preference to Windows Forms for all new development.

Create a graphical application in Visual Studio 2010

- If you are using Visual Studio 2010 Standard or Visual Studio 2010 Professional, perform the following operations to create a new graphical application:

  1. On the *File* menu, point to *New*, and then click *Project.*

     The *New Project* dialog box opens.

2. In the left pane, under *Installed Templates*, click *Visual C#*.

3. In the middle pane, click the *WPF Application* icon.

4. Ensure that the *Location* field refers to the *\Microsoft Press\Visual CSharp Step By Step\Chapter 1* folder under your *Documents* folder.

5. In the *Name* field, type **WPFHello**.

6. In the *Solution* field, ensure that *Create new solution* is selected.

   This action creates a new solution for holding the project. The alternative, *Add to Solution*, adds the project to the TextHello solution.

7. Click *OK*.

■ If you are using Visual C# 2010 Express, perform the following tasks to create a new graphical application:

1. On the *File* menu, click *New Project*.

2. If the *New Project* message box appears, click *Save* to save your changes to the TextHello project. In the *Save Project* dialog box, verify that the *Location* field is set to *Microsoft Press\Visual CSharp Step By Step\Chapter 1* under your Documents folder, and then click *Save*.

3. In the *New Project* dialog box, click the *WPF Application* icon.

4. In the *Name* field, type **WPFHello**.

5. Click *OK*.

Visual Studio 2010 closes your current application and creates the new WPF application. It displays an empty WPF form in the *Design View* window, together with another window containing an XAML description of the form, as shown in the following graphic:

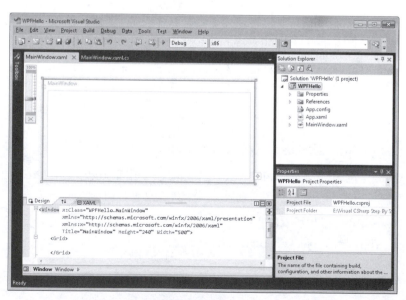

> **Tip** Close the *Output* and *Error List* windows to provide more space for displaying the *Design View* window.

XAML stands for Extensible Application Markup Language and is an XML-like language used by WPF applications to define the layout of a form and its contents. If you have knowledge of XML, XAML should look familiar. You can actually define a WPF form completely by writing an XAML description if you don't like using the Design View window of Visual Studio or if you don't have access to Visual Studio; Microsoft provides a XAML editor called XAMLPad that is installed with the Windows Software Development Kit (SDK).

In the following exercise, you use the Design View window to add three controls to the Windows form and examine some of the C# code automatically generated by Visual Studio 2010 to implement these controls.

Create the user interface

1. Click the *Toolbox* tab that appears to the left of the form in the Design View window.

    The *Toolbox* appears, partially obscuring the form, and displays the various components and controls that you can place on a Windows form. Expand the *Common WPF Controls* section. This section displays a list of controls that are used by most WPF applications. The *All Controls* section displays a more extensive list of controls.

2. In the *Common WPF Controls* section, click *Label*, and then drag the label control onto the visible part of the form.

    A label control is added to the form (you will move it to its correct location in a moment), and the *Toolbox* disappears from view.

> **Tip** If you want the *Toolbox* to remain visible but not to hide any part of the form, click the *Auto Hide* button to the right in the *Toolbox* title bar. (It looks like a pin.) The *Toolbox* appears permanently on the left side of the Visual Studio 2010 window, and the *Design View* window shrinks to accommodate it. (You might lose a lot of space if you have a low-resolution screen.) Clicking the *Auto Hide* button once more causes the *Toolbox* to disappear again.

3. The label control on the form is probably not exactly where you want it. You can click and drag the controls you have added to a form to reposition them. Using this technique, move the label control so that it is positioned toward the upper left corner of the form. (The exact placement is not critical for this application.)

> **Note** The XAML description of the form in the lower pane now includes the label control, together with properties such as its location on the form, governed by the *Margin* property. The *Margin* property consists of four numbers indicating the distance of each edge of the label from the edges of the form. If you move the control around the form, the value of the *Margin* property changes. If the form is resized, the controls anchored to the form's edges that move are resized to preserve their margin values. You can prevent this by setting the *Margin* values to zero. You learn more about the *Margin* and also the *Height* and *Width* properties of WPF controls in Chapter 22, "Introducing Windows Presentation Foundation."

4. On the *View* menu, click *Properties Window*.

   If it was not already displayed, the *Properties* window appears on the lower right side of the screen, under *Solution Explorer*. You can specify the properties of controls by using the XAML pane under the *Design View* window. However, the *Properties* window provides a more convenient way for you to modify the properties for items on a form, as well as other items in a project. It is context sensitive in that it displays the properties for the currently selected item. If you click the title bar of the form displayed in the *Design View* window, you can see that the *Properties* window displays the properties for the form itself. If you click the label control, the window displays the properties for the label instead. If you click anywhere else on the form, the *Properties* window displays the properties for a mysterious item called a *grid*. A grid acts as a container for items on a WPF form, and you can use the grid, among other things, to indicate how items on the form should be aligned and grouped together.

5. Click the label control on the form. In the *Properties* window, locate the *FontSize* property. Change the *FontSize* property to **20**, and then in the *Design View* window click the title bar of the form.

   The size of the text in the label changes.

6. In the XAML pane below the *Design View* window, examine the text that defines the label control. If you scroll to the end of the line, you should see the text *FontSize="20"*. Any changes that you make by using the *Properties* window are automatically reflected in the XAML definitions and vice versa.

   Overtype the value of the *FontSize* property in the XAML pane, and change it back to **12**. The size of the text in the label in the *Design View* window changes back.

7. In the XAML pane, examine the other properties of the label control.

   The properties that are listed in the XAML pane are only the ones that do not have default values. If you modify any property values by using the *Properties Window*, they appear as part of the label definition in the XAML pane.

8. Change the value of the *Content* property from **Label** to **Please enter your name**.

   Notice that the text displayed in the label on the form changes, although the label is too small to display it correctly.

9. In the *Design View* window, click the label control. Place the mouse over the right edge of the label control. It should change into a double-headed arrow to indicate that you can use the mouse to resize the control. Click the mouse and drag the right edge of the label control further to the right, until you can see the complete text for the label.

10. Click the form in the *Design View* window, and then display the *Toolbox* again.

11. In the *Toolbox*, click and drag the *TextBox* control onto the form. Move the text box control so that it is directly underneath the label control.

> **Tip** When you drag a control on a form, alignment indicators appear automatically when the control becomes aligned vertically or horizontally with other controls. This gives you a quick visual cue for making sure that controls are lined up neatly.

12. While the text box control is selected, in the *Properties* window, change the value of the *Name* property displayed at the top of the window to **userName**.

> **Note** You will learn more about naming conventions for controls and variables in Chapter 2, "Working with Variables, Operators, and Expressions."

13. Display the *Toolbox* again, and then click and drag a *Button* control onto the form. Place the button control to the right of the text box control on the form so that the bottom of the button is aligned horizontally with the bottom of the text box.

14. Using the *Properties* window, change the *Name* property of the button control to **ok**. And change the *Content* property from Button to **OK**. Verify that the caption of the button control on the form changes.

15. Click the title bar of the MainWindow.xaml form in the *Design View* window. In the *Properties* window, change the *Title* property to **Hello**.

16. In the *Design View* window, notice that a resize handle (a small square) appears on the lower right corner of the form when it is selected. Move the mouse pointer over the resize handle. When the pointer changes to a diagonal double-headed arrow, click and drag the pointer to resize the form. Stop dragging and release the mouse button when the spacing around the controls is roughly equal.

> **Important** Click the title bar of the form and not the outline of the grid inside the form before resizing it. If you select the grid, you will modify the layout of the controls on the form but not the size of the form itself.

The form should now look similar to the following figure.

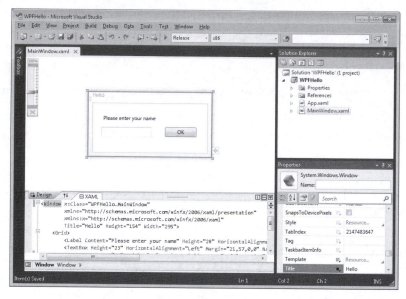

17. On the *Build* menu, click *Build Solution*, and verify that the project builds successfully.

18. On the *Debug* menu, click *Start Without Debugging*.

    The application should run and display your form. You can type your name in the text box and click *OK*, but nothing happens yet. You need to add some code to process the *Click* event for the *OK* button, which is what you will do next.

19. Click the *Close* button (the *X* in the upper-right corner of the form) to close the form and return to Visual Studio.

You have managed to create a graphical application without writing a single line of C# code. It does not do much yet (you will have to write some code soon), but Visual Studio actually generates a lot of code for you that handles routine tasks that all graphical applications must perform, such as starting up and displaying a form. Before adding your own code to the application, it helps to have an understanding of what Visual Studio has generated for you.

In *Solution Explorer*, expand the MainWindow.xaml node. The file MainWindow.xaml.cs appears. Double-click the file MainWindow.xaml.cs. The code for the form is displayed in the *Code and Text Editor* window. It looks like this:

```
using System;
using System.Collections.Generic;
using System.Linq;
using System.Text;
using System.Windows;
using System.Windows.Controls;
using System.Windows.Data;
```

```
using System.Windows.Documents;
using System.Windows.Input;
using System.Windows.Media;
using System.Windows.Media.Imaging;
using System.Windows.Navigation;
using System.Windows.Shapes;

namespace WPFHello
{
    /// <summary>
    /// Interaction logic for MainWindow.xaml
    /// </summary>

    public partial class MainWindow : Window
    {

        public MainWindow()
        {
            InitializeComponent();
        }

    }
}
```

In addition to a good number of *using* statements bringing into scope some namespaces that most WPF applications use, the file contains the definition of a class called *MainWindow* but not much else. There is a little bit of code for the *MainWindow* class known as a constructor that calls a method called *InitializeComponent*, but that is all. (A *constructor* is a special method with the same name as the class. It is executed when an instance of the class is created and can contain code to initialize the instance. You will learn about constructors in Chapter 7.) In fact, the application contains a lot more code, but most of it is generated automatically based on the XAML description of the form, and it is hidden from you. This hidden code performs operations such as creating and displaying the form, and creating and positioning the various controls on the form.

The purpose of the code that you *can* see in this class is so that you can add your own methods to handle the logic for your application, such as determining what happens when the user clicks the *OK* button.

Tip You can also display the C# code file for a WPF form by right-clicking anywhere in the *Design View* window and then clicking *View Code*.

At this point, you might be wondering where the *Main* method is and how the form gets displayed when the application runs; remember that *Main* defines the point at which the program starts. In *Solution Explorer*, you should notice another source file called App.xaml. If you double-click this file, the XAML description of this item appears. One property in the XAML code is called *StartupUri*, and it refers to the MainWindow.xaml file as shown in bold in the following code example:

```
<Application x:Class="WPFHello.App"
            xmlns="http://schemas.microsoft.com/winfx/2006/xaml/presentation"
            xmlns:x="http://schemas.microsoft.com/winfx/2006/xaml"
            StartupUri="MainWindow.xaml">
    <Application.Resources>

    </Application.Resources>
</Application>
```

If you click the *Design* tab at the bottom of the XAML pane, the *Design View* window for App. xaml appears and displays the text "Intentionally left blank. The document root element is not supported by the visual designer". This occurs because you cannot use the *Design View* window to modify the App.xaml file. Click the *XAML* tab to return to the XAML pane.

If you expand the App.xaml node in *Solution Explorer*, you will see that there is also an App. xaml.cs file. If you double-click this file, you will find it contains the following code:

```
using System;
using System.Collections.Generic;
using System.Configuration;
using System.Data;
using System.Linq;
using System.Windows;

namespace WPFHello
{
    /// <summary>
    /// Interaction logic for App.xaml
    /// </summary>

    public partial class App : Application
    {
    }
}
```

Once again, there are a number of *using* statements but not a lot else, not even a *Main* method. In fact, *Main* is there, but it is also hidden. The code for *Main* is generated based on the settings in the App.xaml file; in particular, *Main* will create and display the form specified by the *StartupUri* property. If you want to display a different form, you edit the App.xaml file.

The time has come to write some code for yourself!

Write the code for the OK button

1. Click the *MainWindow.xaml* tab above the *Code and Text Editor* window to display MainWindow in the *Design View* window.

2. Double-click the *OK* button on the form.

The MainWindow.xaml.cs file appears in the *Code and Text Editor* window, but a new method has been added called *ok_Click*. Visual Studio automatically generates code to call this method whenever the user clicks the *OK* button. This is an example of an event. You will learn much more about how events work as you progress through this book.

3. Add the following code shown in bold to the *ok_Click* method:

```
void ok_Click(object sender, RoutedEventArgs e)
{
    MessageBox.Show("Hello " + userName.Text);
}
```

This is the code that will run when the user clicks the *OK* button. Do not worry too much about the syntax of this code just yet (just make sure you copy it exactly as shown) because you will learn all about methods in Chapter 3. The interesting part is the *MessageBox.Show* statement. This statement displays a message box containing the text "Hello" with whatever name the user typed into the username text box on the appended form.

4. Click the *MainWindow.xaml* tab above the *Code and Text Editor* window to display MainWindow in the *Design View* window again.

5. In the lower pane displaying the XAML description of the form, examine the *Button* element, but be careful not to change anything. Notice that it contains an element called *Click* that refers to the *ok_Click* method:

```
<Button Height="23" … Click="ok_Click" />
```

6. On the *Debug* menu, click *Start Without Debugging*.

7. When the form appears, type your name in the text box and then click *OK*. A message box appears, welcoming you by name:

8. Click *OK* in the message box.

The message box closes.

9. Close the form.

In this chapter, you have seen how to use Visual Studio 2010 to create, build, and run applications. You have created a console application that displays its output in a console window, and you have created a WPF application with a simple graphical user interface.

- If you want to continue to the next chapter

  Keep Visual Studio 2010 running, and turn to Chapter 2.

- If you want to exit Visual Studio 2010 now

  On the *File* menu, click *Exit*. If you see a *Save* dialog box, click *Yes* and save the project.

Chapter 1 Quick Reference

To	Do this
Create a new console application using Visual Studio 2010 Standard or Professional	On the *File* menu, point to *New*, and then click *Project* to open the *New Project* dialog box. In the left pane, under Installed Templates, click *Visual C#*. In the middle pane, click *Console Application*. Specify a directory for the project files in the *Location* box. Type a name for the project. Click *OK*.
Create a new console application using Visual C# 2010 Express	On the *File* menu, click *New Project* to open the *New Project* dialog box. For the template, select *Console Application*. Choose a name for the project. Click *OK*.
Create a new graphical application using Visual Studio 2010 Standard or Professional	On the *File* menu, point to *New*, and then click *Project* to open the *New Project* dialog box. In the left pane, under Installed Templates, click *Visual C#*. In the middle pane, click *WPF Application*. Specify a directory for the project files in the *Location* box. Type a name for the project. Click *OK*.
Create a new graphical application using Visual C# 2010 Express	On the *File* menu, click *New Project* to open the *New Project* dialog box. For the template, select *WPF Application*. Choose a name for the project. Click *OK*.
Build the application	On the *Build* menu, click *Build Solution*.
Run the application	On the *Debug* menu, click *Start Without Debugging*.

Chapter 2
Working with Variables, Operators, and Expressions

After completing this chapter, you will be able to:

- Understand statements, identifiers, and keywords.

- Use variables to store information.

- Work with primitive data types.

- Use arithmetic operators such as the plus sign (+) and the minus sign (–).

- Increment and decrement variables.

In Chapter 1, "Welcome to C#," you learned how to use the Microsoft Visual Studio 2010 programming environment to build and run a Console program and a Windows Presentation Foundation (WPF) application. This chapter introduces you to the elements of Microsoft Visual C# syntax and semantics, including statements, keywords, and identifiers. You'll study the primitive types that are built into the C# language and the characteristics of the values that each type holds. You'll also see how to declare and use local variables (variables that exist only in a method or other small section of code), learn about the arithmetic operators that C# provides, find out how to use operators to manipulate values, and learn how to control expressions containing two or more operators.

Understanding Statements

A *statement* is a command that performs an action. You combine statements to create methods. You'll learn more about methods in Chapter 3, "Writing Methods and Applying Scope," but for now, think of a method as a named sequence of statements. *Main*, which was introduced in the previous chapter, is an example of a method. Statements in C# follow a well-defined set of rules describing their format and construction. These rules are collectively known as *syntax*. (In contrast, the specification of what statements *do* is collectively known as *semantics*.) One of the simplest and most important C# syntax rules states that you must terminate all statements with a semicolon. For example, without its terminating semicolon, the following statement won't compile:

```
Console.WriteLine("Hello World");
```

> **Tip** C# is a "free format" language, which means that white space, such as a space character or a newline, is not significant except as a separator. In other words, you are free to lay out your statements in any style you choose. However, you should adopt a simple, consistent layout style and keep to it to make your programs easier to read and understand.

The trick to programming well in any language is learning the syntax and semantics of the language and then using the language in a natural and idiomatic way. This approach makes your programs more easily maintainable. In the chapters throughout this book, you'll see examples of the most important C# statements.

Using Identifiers

Identifiers are the names you use to identify the elements in your programs, such as namespaces, classes, methods, and variables. (You will learn about variables shortly.) In C#, you must adhere to the following syntax rules when choosing identifiers:

- You can use only letters (uppercase and lowercase), digits, and underscore characters.

- An identifier must start with a letter or an underscore.

For example, *result*, *_score*, *footballTeam*, and *plan9* are all valid identifiers, whereas *result%*, *footballTeam$*, and *9plan* are not.

> **Important** C# is a case-sensitive language: *footballTeam* and *FootballTeam* are not the same identifier.

Identifying Keywords

The C# language reserves 77 identifiers for its own use, and you cannot reuse these identifiers for your own purposes. These identifiers are called *keywords*, and each has a particular meaning. Examples of keywords are *class*, *namespace*, and *using*. You'll learn the meaning of most of the C# keywords as you proceed through this book. The keywords are listed in the following table.

abstract	*do*	*in*	*protected*	*true*
as	*double*	*int*	*public*	*try*
base	*else*	*interface*	*readonly*	*typeof*
bool	*enum*	*internal*	*ref*	*uint*
break	*event*	*is*	*return*	*ulong*

byte	explicit	lock	sbyte	unchecked
case	extern	long	sealed	unsafe
catch	false	namespace	short	ushort
char	finally	new	sizeof	using
checked	fixed	null	stackalloc	virtual
class	float	object	static	void
const	for	operator	string	volatile
continue	foreach	out	struct	while
decimal	goto	override	switch	
default	if	params	this	
delegate	implicit	private	throw	

> **Tip** In the Visual Studio 2010 *Code and Text Editor* window, keywords are colored blue when you type them.

C# also uses the following identifiers. These identifiers are not reserved by C#, which means that you can use these names as identifiers for your own methods, variables, and classes, but you should really avoid doing so if at all possible.

dynamic	join	set
from	let	value
get	orderby	var
group	partial	where
into	select	yield

Using Variables

A *variable* is a storage location that holds a value. You can think of a variable as a box in the computer's memory holding temporary information. You must give each variable in a program an unambiguous name that uniquely identifies it in the context in which it is used. You use a variable's name to refer to the value it holds. For example, if you want to store the value of the cost of an item in a store, you might create a variable simply called *cost* and store the item's cost in this variable. Later on, if you refer to the *cost* variable, the value retrieved will be the item's cost that you stored there earlier.

Naming Variables

You should adopt a naming convention for variables that helps you avoid confusion concerning the variables you have defined. The following list contains some general recommendations:

- Don't start an identifier with an underscore.

- Don't create identifiers that differ only by case. For example, do not create one variable named *myVariable* and another named *MyVariable* for use at the same time because it is too easy to get them confused.

> **Note** Using identifiers that differ only by case can limit the ability to reuse classes in applications developed using other languages that are not case sensitive, such as Microsoft Visual Basic.

- Start the name with a lowercase letter.

- In a multiword identifier, start the second and each subsequent word with an uppercase letter. (This is called *camelCase notation*.)

- Don't use Hungarian notation. (Microsoft Visual C++ developers reading this book are probably familiar with Hungarian notation. If you don't know what Hungarian notation is, don't worry about it!)

> **Important** You should treat the first two of these recommendations as compulsory because they relate to Common Language Specification (CLS) compliance. If you want to write programs that can interoperate with other languages, such as Microsoft Visual Basic, you must comply with these recommendations.

For example, *score*, *footballTeam*, *_score*, and *FootballTeam* are all valid variable names, but only the first two are recommended.

Declaring Variables

Variables hold values. C# has many different types of values that it can store and process—integers, floating-point numbers, and strings of characters, to name three. When you declare a variable, you must specify the type of data it will hold.

You declare the type and name of a variable in a declaration statement. For example, the following statement declares that the variable named *age* holds *int* (integer) values. As always, the statement must be terminated with a semicolon.

```
int age;
```

The variable type *int* is the name of one of the *primitive* C# types, *integer*, which is a whole number. (You'll learn about several primitive data types later in this chapter.)

> **Note** Microsoft Visual Basic programmers should note that C# does not allow implicit variable declarations. You must explicitly declare all variables before you use them.

After you've declared your variable, you can assign it a value. The following statement assigns *age* the value 42. Again, you'll see that the semicolon is required.

```
age = 42;
```

The equal sign (=) is the *assignment* operator, which assigns the value on its right to the variable on its left. After this assignment, the *age* variable can be used in your code to refer to the value it holds. The next statement writes the value of the *age* variable, 42, to the console:

```
Console.WriteLine(age);
```

> **Tip** If you leave the mouse pointer over a variable in the Visual Studio 2010 *Code and Text Editor* window, a ScreenTip appears, telling you the type of the variable.

Working with Primitive Data Types

C# has a number of built-in types called *primitive data types*. The following table lists the most commonly used primitive data types in C# and the range of values that you can store in each.

Data type	Description	Size (bits)	Range	Sample usage
int	Whole numbers	32	-2^{31} through $2^{31} - 1$	```int count; count = 42;```
long	Whole numbers (bigger range)	64	-2^{63} through $2^{63} - 1$	```long wait; wait = 42L;```
float	Floating-point numbers	32	$\pm 1.5 \times 10^{-45}$ through $\pm 3.4 \times 10^{38}$	```float away; away = 0.42F;```
double	Double-precision (more accurate) floating-point numbers	64	$\pm 5.0 \times 10^{-324}$ through $\pm 1.7 \times 10^{308}$	```double trouble; trouble = 0.42;```
decimal	Monetary values	128	28 significant figures	```decimal coin; coin = 0.42M;```

Data type	Description	Size (bits)	Range	Sample usage
string	Sequence of characters	16 bits per character	Not applicable	`string vest;` `vest = "fortytwo";`
char	Single character	16	0 through $2^{16} - 1$	`char grill;` `grill = 'x';`
bool	Boolean	8	True or false	`bool teeth;` `teeth = false;`

Unassigned Local Variables

When you declare a variable, it contains a random value until you assign a value to it. This behavior was a rich source of bugs in C and C++ programs that created a variable and accidentally used it as a source of information before giving it a value. C# does not allow you to use an unassigned variable. You must assign a value to a variable before you can use it; otherwise, your program might not compile. This requirement is called the *Definite Assignment Rule*. For example, the following statements generate a compile-time error because *age* is unassigned:

```
int age;
Console.WriteLine(age); // compile-time error
```

Displaying Primitive Data Type Values

In the following exercise, you use a C# program named *PrimitiveDataTypes* to demonstrate how several primitive data types work.

Display primitive data type values

1. Start Visual Studio 2010 if it is not already running.

2. If you are using Visual Studio 2010 Standard or Visual Studio 2010 Professional, on the *File* menu, point to *Open*, and then click *Project/Solution*.

   If you are using Visual C# 2010 Express, on the *File* menu, click *Open Project*.

   The *Open Project* dialog box appears.

3. Move to the \Microsoft Press\Visual CSharp Step By Step\Chapter 2\PrimitiveDataTypes folder in your Documents folder. Select the PrimitiveDataTypes solution file, and then click *Open*.

   The solution loads, and *Solution Explorer* displays the PrimitiveDataTypes project.

Note Solution file names have the .sln suffix, such as PrimitiveDataTypes.sln. A solution can contain one or more projects. Project files have the .csproj suffix. If you open a project rather than a solution, Visual Studio 2010 automatically creates a new solution file for it. If you build the solution, Visual Studio 2010 automatically saves any new or updated files, so you will be prompted to provide a name and location for the new solution file.

4. On the *Debug* menu, click *Start Without Debugging*.

   You might see some warnings in Visual Studio. You can safely ignore them. (You will correct them in the next exercise.) The following application window appears:

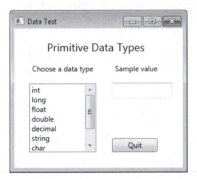

5. In the *Choose a data type* list, click the *string* type.

   The value "forty two" appears in the *Sample value* box.

6. Click the *int* type in the list.

   The value "to do" appears in the *Sample value* box, indicating that the statements to display an *int* value still need to be written.

7. Click each data type in the list. Confirm that the code for the *double* and *bool* types is not yet implemented.

8. Click *Quit* to close the window and stop the program.

   Control returns to the Visual Studio 2010 programming environment.

Use primitive data types in code

1. In *Solution Explorer*, double-click *MainWindow.xaml*.

   The WPF form for the application appears in the *Design View* window.

2. Right-click anywhere in the *Design View* window displaying the MainWindow.xaml form, and then click *View Code*.

   The *Code and Text Editor* window opens, displaying the MainWindow.xaml.cs file.

Note Remember that you can also use *Solution Explorer* to access the code; click the plus sign, +, to the left of the MainWindow.xaml file, and then double-click *MainWindow.xaml.cs*.

3. In the *Code and Text Editor* window, find the *showFloatValue* method.

Tip To locate an item in your project, on the *Edit* menu, point to *Find and Replace*, and then click *Quick Find*. A dialog box opens, asking what you want to search for. Type the name of the item you're looking for, and then click *Find Next*. By default, the search is not case sensitive. If you want to perform a case-sensitive search, click the plus button, +, next to the *Find Options* label to display additional options, and select the *Match Case* check box. If you have time, you can experiment with the other options as well.

You can also press Ctrl+F (press the Control key, and then press F) to display the *Quick Find* dialog box rather than using the *Edit* menu. Similarly, you can press Ctrl+H to display the *Quick Replace* dialog box.

As an alternative to using the *Quick Find* functionality, you also locate the methods in a class by using the class members drop-down list box above the *Code and Text Editor* window, on the right. The class members drop-down list box displays all the methods in the class, together with the variables and other items that the class contains. (You will learn more about these items in later chapters.) In the drop-down list box, click *showFloatValue()*, and the cursor will move directly to the *showFloatValue* method in the class.

The *showFloatValue* method runs when you click the *float* type in the list box. This method contains the following three statements:

```
float variable;
variable=0.42F;
value.Text = "0.42F";
```

The first statement declares a variable named *variable* of type *float*.

The second statement assigns *variable* the value 0.42F. (The *F* is a type suffix specifying that 0.42 should be treated as a *float* value. If you forget the *F*, the value 0.42 is treated as a *double* and your program will not compile, because you cannot assign a value of one type to a variable of a different type without writing additional code—C# is very strict in this respect.)

The third statement displays the value of this variable in the *value* text box on the form. This statement requires a little bit of your attention. The way in which you display an item in a text box is to set its *Text* property. Notice that you access the property of an object by using the same "dot" notation that you saw for running a method. (Remember *Console.WriteLine* from Chapter 1?) The data that you put in the *Text* property must be a string (a sequence of characters enclosed in double quotation marks) and not a number. If you try to assign a number to the *Text* property, your program will not compile. In this program, the statement simply displays the text "0.42F" in the text box. In a real-world application, you add statements that convert the value of the variable *variable* into a string and then put this into the *Text* property, but you need to know a little bit more about C# and the Microsoft .NET Framework before you can do that. (Chapter 11, "Understanding Parameter Arrays," and Chapter 21, "Operator Overloading," cover data type conversions.)

4. In the *Code and Text Editor* window, locate the *showIntValue* method. It looks like this:

```
private void showIntValue()
{
    value.Text = "to do";
}
```

The *showIntValue* method is called when you click the *int* type in the list box.

5. Type the following two statements at the start of the *showIntValue* method, on a new line after the opening brace, as shown in bold type in the following code:

```
private void showIntValue()
{
    int variable;
    variable = 42;
    value.Text = "to do";
}
```

6. In the original statement in this method, change the string *"to do"* to *"42"*.

The method should now look exactly like this:

```
private void showIntValue()
{
    int variable;
    variable = 42;
    value.Text = "42";
}
```

Note If you have previous programming experience, you might be tempted to change the third statement to

```
value.Text = variable;
```

This looks like it should display the value of *variable* in the *value* text box on the form. However, C# performs strict type checking; text boxes can display only *string* values, and *variable* is an *int*, so this statement will not compile. You will see some simple techniques for converting between numeric and string values later in this chapter.

7. On the *Debug* menu, click *Start Without Debugging*.

The form appears again.

8. Select the *int* type in the *Choose a data type* list. Confirm that the value 42 is displayed in the *Sample value* text box.

9. Click *Quit* to close the window and return to Visual Studio.

10. In the *Code and Text Editor* window, find the *showDoubleValue* method.

11. Edit the *showDoubleValue* method exactly as shown in bold type in the following code:

```
private void showDoubleValue()
{
    double variable;
    variable = 0.42;
    value.Text = "0.42";
}
```

12. In the *Code and Text Editor* window, locate the *showBoolValue* method.

13. Edit the *showBoolValue* method exactly as follows:

```
private void showBoolValue()
{
    bool variable;
    variable = false;
    value.Text = "false";
}
```

14. On the *Debug* menu, click *Start Without Debugging*.

15. In the *Choose a data type* list, select the *int*, *double*, and *bool* types. In each case, verify that the correct value is displayed in the *Sample value* text box.

16. Click *Quit* to stop the program.

Using Arithmetic Operators

C# supports the regular arithmetic operations you learned in your childhood: the plus sign (+) for addition, the minus sign (–) for subtraction, the asterisk (*) for multiplication, and the forward slash (/) for division. The symbols +, –, *, and / are called *operators* because they "operate" on values to create new values. In the following example, the variable *moneyPaid-ToConsultant* ends up holding the product of 750 (the daily rate) and 20 (the number of days the consultant was employed):

```
long moneyPaidToConsultant;
moneyPaidToConsultant = 750 * 20;
```

Note The values that an operator operates on are called *operands*. In the expression 750 * 20, the * is the operator, and 750 and 20 are the operands.

Operators and Types

Not all operators are applicable to all data types. The operators that you can use on a value depend on the value's type. For example, you can use all the arithmetic operators on values of type *char*, *int*, *long*, *float*, *double*, or *decimal*. However, with the exception of the plus operator, +, you can't use the arithmetic operators on values of type *string* or *bool*. So the following statement is not allowed, because the *string* type does not support the minus operator (thus, subtracting one string from another would be meaningless):

```
// compile-time error
Console.WriteLine("Gillingham" - "Forest Green Rovers");
```

You can use the + operator to concatenate string values. You need to be careful because this can have results you might not expect. For example, the following statement writes "431" (not "44") to the console:

```
Console.WriteLine("43" + "1");
```

> **Tip** The .NET Framework provides a method called *Int32.Parse* that you can use to convert a string value to an integer if you need to perform arithmetic computations on values held as strings.

You should also be aware that the type of the result of an arithmetic operation depends on the type of the operands used. For example, the value of the expression 5.0/2.0 is 2.5; the type of both operands is *double*, so the type of the result is also *double*. (In C#, literal numbers with decimal points are always *double*, not *float*, to maintain as much accuracy as possible.) However, the value of the expression 5/2 is 2. In this case, the type of both operands is *int*, so the type of the result is also *int*. C# always rounds towards zero in circumstances like this. The situation gets a little more complicated if you mix the types of the operands. For example, the expression 5/2.0 consists of an *int* and a *double*. The C# compiler detects the mismatch and generates code that converts the *int* into a *double* before performing the operation. The result of the operation is therefore a *double* (2.5). However, although this works, it is considered poor practice to mix types in this way.

C# also supports one less-familiar arithmetic operator: the remainder, or modulus, operator, which is represented by the percent sign (%). The result of *x % y* is the remainder after dividing *x* by *y*. For example, 9 % 2 is 1 because 9 divided by 2 is 4, remainder 1.

Numeric Types and Infinite Values

There are one or two other features of numbers in C# that you should be aware of. For example, the result of dividing any number by zero is infinity, which is outside the range of the *int*, *long*, and *decimal* types; consequently, evaluating an expression such as 5/0 results in an error. However, the *double* and *float* types actually have a special value that can represent infinity, and the value of the expression 5.0/0.0 is *Infinity*. The one exception to this rule is the value of the expression 0.0/0.0. Usually, if you divide zero by anything, the result is zero, but if you divide anything by zero the result is infinity. The expression 0.0/0.0 results in a paradox—the value must be zero and infinity at the same time. C# has another special value for this situation called *NaN*, which stands for "not a number." So if you evaluate 0.0/0.0, the result is *NaN*. *NaN* and *Infinity* propagate through expressions. If you evaluate 10 + *NaN*, the result is *NaN*, and if you evaluate 10 + *Infinity*, the result is *Infinity*. The one exception to this rule is the case when you multiply *Infinity* by 0; The value of the expression *Infinity* * 0 is 0, although the value of *NaN* * 0 is *NaN*.

 Note If you are familiar with C or C++, you know that you can't use the remainder operator on *float* or *double* values in these languages. However, C# relaxes this rule. The remainder operator is valid with all numeric types, and the result is not necessarily an integer. For example, the result of the expression 7.0 % 2.4 is 2.2.

Examining Arithmetic Operators

The following exercise demonstrates how to use the arithmetic operators on *int* values.

Work with arithmetic operators

1. Open the MathsOperators project, located in the \Microsoft Press\Visual CSharp Step By Step\Chapter 2\MathsOperators folder in your Documents folder.

2. On the *Debug* menu, click *Start Without Debugging*.

   A WPF form appears on the screen.

3. Type **54** in the *left operand* text box.

4. Type **13** in the *right operand* text box.

   You can now apply any of the operators to the values in the text boxes.

5. Click the – *Subtraction* button, and then click *Calculate*.

The text in the *Expression* text box changes to 54 – 13, and the value 41 appears in the *Result* box, as shown in the following image:

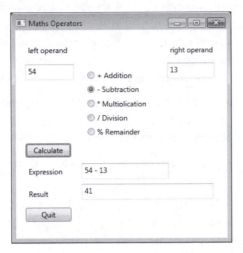

6. Click the */ Division* button, and then click *Calculate*.

   The text in the *Expression* text box changes to 54/13, and the value 4 appears in the *Result* text box. In real life, 54/13 is 4.153846 recurring, but this is not real life; this is C# performing integer division—when you divide one integer by another integer, the answer you get back is an integer, as explained earlier.

7. Click the *% Remainder* button, and then click *Calculate*.

   The text in the *Expression* text box changes to 54 % 13, and the value 2 appears in the *Result* text box. This is because the remainder after dividing 54 by 13 is 2. (54 – ((54/13) * 13)) is 2 if you do the arithmetic, rounding down to an integer at each stage—my old math master at school would be horrified to be told that (54/13) * 13 does not equal 54!

8. Test the other combinations of numbers and operators. When you have finished, click *Quit* to return to the Visual Studio 2010 programming environment.

In the next exercise, you will take a look at the MathsOperators program code.

Examine the MathsOperators program code

1. Display the MainWindow.xaml form in the *Design View* window. (Double-click the file *MainWindow.xaml* in *Solution Explorer*.)

2. On the *View* menu, point to *Other Windows*, and then click *Document Outline*.

   The *Document Outline* window appears, showing the names and types of the controls on the form. The *Document Outline* window provides a simple way to locate and select controls on a complex WPF form. The controls are arranged in a hierarchy, starting with the *Window* that constitutes the WPF form. As mentioned in the previous chapter, a WPF form actually contains a *Grid* control, and the other controls are placed in this *Grid*. If you expand the *Grid* node in the *Document Outline* window, the other controls appear. As you click each of the controls on the form, the name of the control is highlighted in the *Document Outline* window. Similarly, if you select a control in the *Document Outline* window, the corresponding control is selected in the *Design View* window. If you hover the mouse over a control in the *Document Outline* window, an image of the control (and any child controls that the control contains) appears.

3. On the form, click the two *TextBox* controls in which the user types numbers. In the *Document Outline* window, verify that they are named *lhsOperand* and *rhsOperand*. (You can see the name of a control in the parentheses to the right of the control.)

When the form runs, the *Text* property of each of these controls holds the values that the user enters.

4. Toward the bottom of the form, verify that the *TextBox* control used to display the expression being evaluated is named *expression* and that the *TextBox* control used to display the result of the calculation is named *result*.

5. Close the *Document Outline* window.

6. Display the code for the MainWindow.xaml.cs file in the *Code and Text Editor* window.

7. In the *Code and Text Editor* window, locate the *subtractValues* method. It looks like this:

```
private void subtractValues()
{
    int lhs = int.Parse(lhsOperand.Text);
    int rhs = int.Parse(rhsOperand.Text);
    int outcome;
    outcome = lhs - rhs;
    expression.Text = lhsOperand.Text + " - " + rhsOperand.Text;
    result.Text = outcome.ToString();
}
```

The first statement in this method declares an *int* variable called *lhs* and initializes it with the integer corresponding to the value typed by the user in the *lhsOperand* text box. Remember that the *Text* property of a text box control contains a string, so you must convert this string to an integer before you can assign it to an *int* variable. The *int* data type provides the *int.Parse* method, which does precisely this.

The second statement declares an *int* variable called *rhs* and initializes it to the value in the *rhsOperand* text box after converting it to an *int*.

The third statement declares an *int* variable called *outcome*.

The fourth statement subtracts the value of the *rhs* variable from the value of the *lhs* variable and assigns the result to *outcome*.

The fifth statement concatenates three strings indicating the calculation being performed (using the plus operator, +) and assigns the result to the *expression.Text* property. This causes the string to appear in the *expression* text box on the form.

The final statement displays the result of the calculation by assigning it to the *Text* property of the *result* text box. Remember that the *Text* property is a string and that the result of the calculation is an *int*, so you must convert the *int* to a string before assigning it to the *Text* property. This is what the *ToString* method of the *int* type does.

The *ToString* Method

Every class in the .NET Framework has a *ToString* method. The purpose of *ToString* is to convert an object to its string representation. In the preceding example, the *ToString* method of the integer object, *outcome*, is used to convert the integer value of *outcome* to the equivalent string value. This conversion is necessary because the value is displayed in the *Text* property of the *result* text box—the *Text* property can contain only strings. When you create your own classes, you can define your own implementation of the *ToString* method to specify how your class should be represented as a string. You learn more about creating your own classes in Chapter 7, "Creating and Managing Classes and Objects."

Controlling Precedence

Precedence governs the order in which an expression's operators are evaluated. Consider the following expression, which uses the + and * operators:

```
2 + 3 * 4
```

This expression is potentially ambiguous; do you perform the addition first or the multiplication? The order of the operations matters because it changes the result:

- If you perform the addition first, followed by the multiplication, the result of the addition (2 + 3) forms the left operand of the * operator, and the result of the whole expression is 5 * 4, which is 20.

- If you perform the multiplication first, followed by the addition, the result of the multiplication (3 * 4) forms the right operand of the + operator, and the result of the whole expression is 2 + 12, which is 14.

In C#, the multiplicative operators (*, /, and %) have precedence over the additive operators (+ and –), so in expressions such as 2 + 3 * 4, the multiplication is performed first, followed by the addition. The answer to 2 + 3 * 4 is therefore 14.

You can use parentheses to override precedence and force operands to bind to operators in a different way. For example, in the following expression, the parentheses force the 2 and the 3 to bind to the + operator (making 5), and the result of this addition forms the left operand of the * operator to produce the value 20:

```
(2 + 3) * 4
```

Note The term *parentheses* or *round brackets* refers to ( ). The term *braces* or *curly brackets* refers to { }. The term *square brackets* refers to [ ].

Using Associativity to Evaluate Expressions

Operator precedence is only half the story. What happens when an expression contains different operators that have the same precedence? This is where associativity becomes important. *Associativity* is the direction (left or right) in which the operands of an operator are evaluated. Consider the following expression that uses the / and * operators:

```
4 / 2 * 6
```

This expression is still potentially ambiguous. Do you perform the division first or the multiplication? The precedence of both operators is the same (they are both multiplicative), but the order in which the expression is evaluated is important because you get one of two possible results:

- If you perform the division first, the result of the division (4/2) forms the left operand of the * operator, and the result of the whole expression is (4/2) * 6, or 12.

- If you perform the multiplication first, the result of the multiplication (2 * 6) forms the right operand of the / operator, and the result of the whole expression is 4/(2 * 6), or 4/12.

In this case, the associativity of the operators determines how the expression is evaluated. The * and / operators are both left-associative, which means that the operands are evaluated from left to right. In this case, 4/2 will be evaluated before multiplying by 6, giving the result 12.

Note As each new operator is described in subsequent chapters, its associativity is also covered.

Associativity and the Assignment Operator

In C#, the equal sign = is an operator. All operators return a value based on their operands. The assignment operator = is no different. It takes two operands; the operand on its right side is evaluated and then stored in the operand on its left side. The value of the assignment operator is the value that was assigned to the left operand. For example, in the following assignment statement, the value returned by the assignment operator is 10, which is also the value assigned to the variable *myInt*:

```
int myInt;
myInt = 10; // value of assignment expression is 10
```

At this point, you are probably thinking that this is all very nice and esoteric, but so what? Well, because the assignment operator returns a value, you can use this same value with another occurrence of the assignment statement, like this:

```
int myInt;
int myInt2;
myInt2 = myInt = 10;
```

The value assigned to the variable *myInt2* is the value that was assigned to *myInt*. The assignment statement assigns the same value to both variables. This technique is very useful if you want to initialize several variables to the same value. It makes it very clear to anyone reading your code that all the variables must have the same value:

```
myInt5 = myInt4 = myInt3 = myInt2 = myInt = 10;
```

From this discussion, you can probably deduce that the assignment operator associates from right to left. The rightmost assignment occurs first, and the value assigned propagates through the variables from right to left. If any of the variables previously had a value, it is overwritten by the value being assigned.

You should treat this construct with a little caution, however. One frequent mistake that new C# programmers make is to try and combine this use of the assignment operator with variable declarations, like this:

```
int myInt, myInt2, myInt3 = 10;
```

This is legal C# code (because it compiles). What it does is declare the variables *myInt*, *myInt2*, and *myInt3*, and initialize *myInt3* with the value 10. However, it does not initialize *myInt* or *myInt2*. If you try and use *myInt* or *myInt2* in an expressions such as this

```
myInt3 = myInt / myInt2;
```

the compiler generates the following errors:

```
Use of unassigned local variable 'myInt'
Use of unassigned local variable 'myInt2'
```

Incrementing and Decrementing Variables

If you want to add 1 to a variable, you can use the + operator:

```
count = count + 1;
```

However, adding 1 to a variable is so common that C# provides its own operator just for this purpose: the ++ operator. To increment the variable *count* by 1, you can write the following statement:

```
count++;
```

Similarly, C# provides the -- operator that you can use to subtract 1 from a variable, like this:

```
count--;
```

The ++ and -- operators are *unary* operators, meaning that they take only a single operand. They share the same precedence and left associativity as the ! unary operator, which is discussed in Chapter 4, "Using Decision Statements."

Prefix and Postfix

The increment, ++, and decrement, --, operators are unusual in that you can place them either before or after the variable. Placing the operator symbol before the variable is called the *prefix form* of the operator, and using the operator symbol after the variable is called the *postfix form*. Here are examples:

```
count++; // postfix increment
++count; // prefix increment
count--; // postfix decrement
--count; // prefix decrement
```

Whether you use the prefix or postfix form of the ++ or -- operator makes no difference to the variable being incremented or decremented. For example, if you write *count++*, the value of *count* increases by 1, and if you write *++count*, the value of *count* also increases by 1. Knowing this, you're probably wondering why there are two ways to write the same thing. To understand the answer, you must remember that ++ and -- are operators and that all operators are used to evaluate an expression that has a value. The value returned by *count++* is the value of *count* before the increment takes place, whereas the value returned by *++count* is the value of *count* after the increment takes place. Here is an example:

```
int x;
x = 42;
Console.WriteLine(x++); // x is now 43, 42 written out
x = 42;
Console.WriteLine(++x); // x is now 43, 43 written out
```

The way to remember which operand does what is to look at the order of the elements (the operand and the operator) in a prefix or postfix expression. In the expression *x++*, the variable *x* occurs first, so its value is used as the value of the expression before *x* is incremented. In the expression *++x*, the operator occurs first, so its operation is performed before the value of *x* is evaluated as the result.

These operators are most commonly used in *while* and *do* statements, which are presented in Chapter 5, "Using Compound Assignment and Iteration Statements." If you are using the increment and decrement operators in isolation, stick to the postfix form and be consistent.

Declaring Implicitly Typed Local Variables

Earlier in this chapter, you saw that you declare a variable by specifying a data type and an identifier, like this:

```
int myInt;
```

It was also mentioned that you should assign a value to a variable before you attempt to use it. You can declare and initialize a variable in the same statement, like this:

```
int myInt = 99;
```

Or you can even do it like this, assuming that *myOtherInt* is an initialized integer variable:

```
int myInt = myOtherInt * 99;
```

Now, remember that the value you assign to a variable must be of the same type as the variable. For example, you can assign an *int* value only to an *int* variable. The C# compiler can quickly work out the type of an expression used to initialize a variable and tell you if it does not match the type of the variable. You can also ask the C# compiler to infer the type of a variable from an expression and use this type when declaring the variable by using the *var* keyword in place of the type, like this:

```
var myVariable = 99;
var myOtherVariable = "Hello";
```

Variables *myVariable* and *myOtherVariable* are referred to as *implicitly typed* variables. The *var* keyword causes the compiler to deduce the type of the variables from the types of the expressions used to initialize them. In these examples, *myVariable* is an *int*, and *myOtherVariable* is a *string*. Understand that this is a convenience for declaring variables only and that after a variable has been declared, you can assign only values of the inferred type to it—you cannot assign *float*, *double*, or *string* values to *myVariable* at a later point in your program, for example. You should also understand that you can use the *var* keyword only when you supply an expression to initialize a variable. The following declaration is illegal and causes a compilation error:

```
var yetAnotherVariable; // Error - compiler cannot infer type
```

Important If you have programmed with Visual Basic in the past, you might be familiar with the *Variant* type, which you can use to store any type of value in a variable. I emphasize here and now that you should forget everything you ever learned when programming with Visual Basic about *Variant* variables. Although the keywords look similar, *var* and *Variant* mean totally different things. When you declare a variable in C# using the *var* keyword, the type of values that you assign to the variable *cannot change* from that used to initialize the variable.

If you are a purist, you are probably gritting your teeth at this point and wondering why on earth the designers of a neat language such as C# should allow a feature such as *var* to creep in. After all, it sounds like an excuse for extreme laziness on the part of programmers and can make it more difficult to understand what a program is doing or track down bugs (and it can even easily introduce new bugs into your code). However, trust me that *var* has a very valid place in C#, as you will see when you work through many of the following chapters. However, for the time being, we will stick to using explicitly typed variables except for when implicit typing becomes a necessity.

In this chapter, you have seen how to create and use variables, and you have learned about some of the common data types available for variables in C#. You have learned about identifiers. You have used a number of operators to build expressions, and you have learned how the precedence and associativity of operators determine how expressions are evaluated.

■ If you want to continue to the next chapter

Keep Visual Studio 2010 running, and turn to Chapter 3.

■ If you want to exit Visual Studio 2010 now

On the *File* menu, click *Exit*. If you see a *Save* dialog box, click *Yes* and save the project.

Chapter 2 Quick Reference

To	Do this
Declare a variable	Write the name of the data type, followed by the name of the variable, followed by a semicolon. For example: `int outcome;`
Change the value of a variable	Write the name of the variable on the left, followed by the assignment operator, followed by the expression calculating the new value, followed by a semicolon. For example: `outcome = 42;`
Convert a *string* to an *int*	Call the *System.Int32.Parse* method. For example: `System.Int32.Parse("42");`
Override the precedence of an operator	Use parentheses in the expression to force the order of evaluation. For example: `(3 + 4) * 5`
Assign the same value to several variables	Use an assignment statement that lists all the variables. For example: `myInt4 = myInt3 = myInt2 = myInt = 10;`
Increment or decrement a variable	Use the ++ or -- operator. For example: `count++;`

Chapter 3
Writing Methods and Applying Scope

After completing this chapter, you will be able to:

- Declare and call methods.

- Pass information to a method.

- Return information from a method.

- Define local and class scope.

- Use the integrated debugger to step in and out of methods as they run.

In Chapter 2, "Working with Variables, Operators, and Expressions," you learned how to declare variables, how to create expressions using operators, and how precedence and associativity control how expressions containing multiple operators are evaluated. In this chapter, you'll learn about methods. You'll also learn how to use arguments and parameters to pass information to a method and how to return information from a method by using return statements. Finally, you'll see how to step in and out of methods by using the Microsoft Visual Studio 2010 integrated debugger. This information is useful when you need to trace the execution of your methods if they do not work quite as you expected.

Creating Methods

A *method* is a named sequence of statements. If you have previously programmed using languages such as C or Microsoft Visual Basic, you will see that a method is similar to a function or a subroutine. A method has a name and a body. The method name should be a meaningful identifier that indicates the overall purpose of the method (*calculateIncomeTax*, for example). The method body contains the actual statements to be run when the method is called. Additionally, methods can be given some data for processing and can return information, which is usually the result of the processing. Methods are a fundamental and powerful mechanism.

Declaring a Method

The syntax for declaring a C# method is as follows:

```
returnType methodName ( parameterList )
{
    // method body statements go here
}
```

- The *returnType* is the name of a type and specifies the kind of information the method returns as a result of its processing. This can be any type, such as *int* or *string*. If you're writing a method that does not return a value, you must use the keyword *void* in place of the return type.

- The *methodName* is the name used to call the method. Method names follow the same identifier rules as variable names. For example, *addValues* is a valid method name, whereas *add$Values* is not. For now, you should follow the camelCase convention for method names—for example, *displayCustomer*.

- The *parameterList* is optional and describes the types and names of the information that you can pass into the method for it to process. You write the parameters between the opening and closing parentheses as though you're declaring variables, with the name of the type followed by the name of the parameter. If the method you're writing has two or more parameters, you must separate them with commas.

- The method body statements are the lines of code that are run when the method is called. They are enclosed between opening and closing braces { }.

> **Important** C, C++, and Microsoft Visual Basic programmers should note that C# does not support global methods. You must write all your methods inside a class, or your code will not compile.

Here's the definition of a method called *addValues* that returns an *int* result and has two *int* parameters, called *leftHandSide* and *rightHandSide*:

```
int addValues(int leftHandSide, int rightHandSide)
{
    // ...
    // method body statements go here
    // ...
}
```

> **Note** You must explicitly specify the types of any parameters and the return type of a method. You cannot use the *var* keyword.

Here's the definition of a method called *showResult* that does not return a value and has a single *int* parameter, called *answer*:

```
void showResult(int answer)
{
    // ...
}
```

Notice the use of the keyword *void* to indicate that the method does not return anything.

> **Important** Visual Basic programmers should notice that C# does not use different keywords to distinguish between a method that returns a value (a function) and a method that does not return a value (a procedure or subroutine). You must always specify either a return type or *void*.

Returning Data from a Method

If you want a method to return information (that is, its return type is not *void*), you must include a *return* statement at the end of the processing in the method body. A *return* statement consists of the keyword *return* followed by an expression that specifies the returned value, and a semicolon. The type of the expression must be the same as the type specified by the method declaration. For example, if a method returns an *int*, the *return* statement must return an *int*; otherwise, your program will not compile. Here is an example of a method with a *return* statement:

```
int addValues(int leftHandSide, int rightHandSide)
{
    // ...
    return leftHandSide + rightHandSide;
}
```

The *return* statement is usually positioned at the end of your method because it causes the method to finish and control returns to the statement that called the method, as described later in this chapter. Any statements that occur after the *return* statement are not executed (although the compiler warns you about this problem if you place statements after the *return* statement).

If you don't want your method to return information (that is, its return type is *void*), you can use a variation of the *return* statement to cause an immediate exit from the method. You write the keyword *return* immediately followed by a semicolon. For example:

```
void showResult(int answer)
{
    // display the answer
    ...
    return;
}
```

If your method does not return anything, you can also omit the *return* statement because the method finishes automatically when execution arrives at the closing brace at the end of the method. Although this practice is common, it is not always considered good style.

In the following exercise, you will examine another version of the MathsOperators project from Chapter 2. This version has been improved by the careful use of some small methods.

Examine method definitions

1. Start Visual Studio 2010 if it is not already running.

2. Open the *Methods* project in the \Microsoft Press\Visual CSharp Step By Step\ Chapter 3\Methods folder in your Documents folder.

3. On the *Debug* menu, click *Start Without Debugging*.

   Visual Studio 2010 builds and runs the application.

4. Refamiliarize yourself with the application and how it works, and then click *Quit*.

5. Display the code for MainWindow.xaml.cs in the *Code and Text Editor* window.

6. In the *Code and Text Editor* window, locate the *addValues* method.

   The method looks like this:

   ```
   private int addValues(int leftHandSide, int rightHandSide)
   {
       expression.Text = leftHandSide.ToString() + " + " + rightHandSide.ToString();
       return leftHandSide + rightHandSide;
   }
   ```

   The *addValues* method contains two statements. The first statement displays the calculation being performed in the *expression* text box on the form. The values of the parameters *leftHandSide* and *rightHandSide* are converted to strings (using the *ToString* method you met in Chapter 2) and concatenated together with a string representation of the plus operator (+) in the middle.

   The second statement uses the + operator to add the values of the *leftHandSide* and *rightHandSide int* variables together and returns the result of this operation. Remember that adding two *int* values together creates another *int* value, so the return type of the *addValues* method is *int*.

   If you look at the methods *subtractValues*, *multiplyValues*, *divideValues*, and *remainderValues*, you will see that they follow a similar pattern.

7. In the *Code and Text Editor* window, locate the *showResult* method.

   The *showResult* method looks like this:

   ```
   private void showResult(int answer)
   {
       result.Text = answer.ToString();
   }
   ```

This method contains one statement that displays a string representation of the *answer* parameter in the *result* text box. It does not return a value, so the type of this method is *void*.

> **Tip** There is no minimum length for a method. If a method helps to avoid repetition and makes your program easier to understand, the method is useful regardless of how small it is.
>
> There is also no maximum length for a method, but usually you want to keep your method code small enough to get the job done. If your method is more than one screen in length, consider breaking it into smaller methods for readability.

Calling Methods

Methods exist to be called! You call a method by name to ask it to perform its task. If the method requires information (as specified by its parameters), you must supply the information requested. If the method returns information (as specified by its return type), you should arrange to capture this information somehow.

Specifying the Method Call Syntax

The syntax of a C# method call is as follows:

```
result = methodName ( argumentList )
```

- The *methodName* must exactly match the name of the method you're calling. Remember, C# is a case-sensitive language.

- The *result* = clause is optional. If specified, the variable identified by result contains the value returned by the method. If the method is *void* (that is, it does not return a value), you must omit the *result* = clause of the statement. If you don't specify the *result* = clause and the method does return a value, the method runs but the return value is discarded.

- The *argumentList* supplies the optional information that the method accepts. You must supply an argument for each parameter, and the value of each argument must be compatible with the type of its corresponding parameter. If the method you're calling has two or more parameters, you must separate the arguments with commas.

> **Important** You must include the parentheses in every method call, even when calling a method that has no arguments.

To clarify these points, take a look at the *addValues* method again:

```
int addValues(int leftHandSide, int rightHandSide)
{
    // ...
}
```

The *addValues* method has two *int* parameters, so you must call it with two comma-separated *int* arguments:

```
addValues(39, 3);      // okay
```

You can also replace the literal values 39 and 3 with the names of *int* variables. The values in those variables are then passed to the method as its arguments, like this:

```
int arg1 = 99;
int arg2 = 1;
addValues(arg1, arg2);
```

If you try to call *addValues* in some other way, you will probably not succeed for the reasons described in the following examples:

```
addValues;            // compile-time error, no parentheses
addValues();          // compile-time error, not enough arguments
addValues(39);        // compile-time error, not enough arguments
addValues("39", "3"); // compile-time error, wrong types
```

The *addValues* method returns an *int* value. This *int* value can be used wherever an *int* value can be used. Consider these examples:

```
int result = addValues(39, 3);    // on right-hand side of an assignment
showResult(addValues(39, 3));     // as argument to another method call
```

The following exercise continues looking at the Methods application. This time you will examine some method calls.

Examine method calls

1. Return to the Methods project. (This project is already open in Visual Studio 2010 if you're continuing from the previous exercise. If you are not, open it from the \Microsoft Press\Visual CSharp Step By Step\Chapter 3\Methods folder in your Documents folder.)

2. Display the code for MainWindow.xaml.cs in the *Code and Text Editor* window.

3. Locate the *calculateClick* method, and look at the first two statements of this method after the *try* statement and opening brace. (We cover the purpose of *try* statements in Chapter 6, "Managing Errors and Exceptions.")

   The statements are as follows:

```
int leftHandSide = System.Int32.Parse(lhsOperand.Text);
int rightHandSide = System.Int32.Parse(rhsOperand.Text);
```

These two statements declare two *int* variables, called *leftHandSide* and *rightHandSide*. However, the interesting parts are the way in which the variables are initialized. In both cases, the *Parse* method of the *System.Int32* class is called. (*System* is a namespace, and *Int32* is the name of the class in this namespace.) You have seen this method before; it takes a single *string* parameter and converts it to an *int* value. These two lines of code take whatever the user has typed into the *lhsOperand* and *rhsOperand* text box controls on the form and converts them to *int* values.

4. Look at the fourth statement in the *calculateClick* method (after the *if* statement and another opening brace):

   ```
   calculatedValue = addValues(leftHandSide, rightHandSide);
   ```

   This statement calls the *addValues* method, passing the values of the *leftHandSide* and *rightHandSide* variables as its arguments. The value returned by the *addValues* method is stored in the *calculatedValue* variable.

5. Look at the next statement:

   ```
   showResult(calculatedValue);
   ```

   This statement calls the *showResult* method, passing the value in the *calculatedValue* variable as its argument. The *showResult* method does not return a value.

6. In the *Code and Text Editor* window, find the *showResult* method you looked at earlier.

   The only statement of this method is this:

   ```
   result.Text = answer.ToString();
   ```

   Notice that the *ToString* method call uses parentheses even though there are no arguments.

 Tip You can call methods belonging to other objects by prefixing the method with the name of the object. In the preceding example, the expression *answer.ToString()* calls the method named *ToString* belonging to the object called *answer*.

Applying Scope

In some of the examples, you can see that you can create variables inside a method. These variables come into existence at the point where they are defined, and subsequent statements in the same method can then use these variables; a variable can be used only after it has been created. When the method has finished, these variables disappear.

If a variable can be used at a particular location in a program, the variable is said to be in *scope* at that location. To put it another way, the scope of a variable is simply the region of the program in which that variable is usable. Scope applies to methods as well as variables. The scope of an identifier (of a variable or method) is linked to the location of the declaration that introduces the identifier in the program, as you'll now learn.

Defining Local Scope

The opening and closing braces that form the body of a method define a scope. Any variables you declare inside the body of a method are scoped to that method; they disappear when the method ends and can be accessed only by code running in that method. These variables are called *local variables* because they are local to the method in which they are declared; they are not in scope in any other method. This arrangement means that you cannot use local variables to share information between methods. Consider this example:

```
class Example
{
    void firstMethod()
    {
        int myVar;
        ...
    }
    void anotherMethod()
    {
        myVar = 42; // error - variable not in scope
        ...
    }
}
```

This code fails to compile because *anotherMethod* is trying to use the variable *myVar*, which is not in scope. The variable *myVar* is available only to statements in *firstMethod* and that occur after the line of code that declares *myVar*.

Defining Class Scope

The opening and closing braces that form the body of a class also create a scope. Any variables you declare inside the body of a class (but not inside a method) are scoped to that class. The proper C# name for the variables defined by a class is a *field*. In contrast with local variables, you can use fields to share information between methods. Here is an example:

```
class Example
{
    void firstMethod()
    {
        myField = 42; // ok
        ...
    }
```

```
    void anotherMethod()
    {
        myField++; // ok
        ...
    }

    int myField = 0;
}
```

The variable *myField* is defined in the class but outside the methods *firstMethod* and *anotherMethod*. Therefore, *myField* has class scope and is available for use by all methods in the class.

There is one other point to notice about this example. In a method, you must declare a variable before you can use it. Fields are a little different. A method can use a field before the statement that defines the field—the compiler sorts out the details for you!

Overloading Methods

If two identifiers have the same name and are declared in the same scope, they are said to be *overloaded*. Often an overloaded identifier is a bug that gets trapped as a compile-time error. For example, if you declare two local variables with the same name in the same method, the compiler reports an error. Similarly, if you declare two fields with the same name in the same class or two identical methods in the same class, you also get a compile-time error. This fact might seem hardly worth mentioning, given that everything so far has turned out to be a compile-time error. However, there is a way that you can overload an identifier, and that way is both useful and important.

Consider the *WriteLine* method of the *Console* class. You have already used this method for writing a string to the screen. However, when you type *WriteLine* in the *Code and Text Editor* window when writing C# code, you will notice that Microsoft IntelliSense gives you 19 different options! Each version of the *WriteLine* method takes a different set of parameters; one version takes no parameters and simply outputs a blank line, another version takes a *bool* parameter and outputs a string representation of its value (*True* or *False*), yet another implementation takes a *decimal* parameter and outputs it as a string, and so on. At compile time, the compiler looks at the types of the arguments you are passing in and then calls the version of the method that has a matching set of parameters. Here is an example:

```
static void Main()
{
    Console.WriteLine("The answer is ");
    Console.WriteLine(42);
}
```

Overloading is primarily useful when you need to perform the same operation on different data types. You can overload a method when the different implementations have different sets of parameters; that is, when they have the same name but a different number of parameters, or when the types of the parameters differ. This capability is allowed so that, when you call a method, you can supply a comma-separated list of arguments, and the number and type of the arguments are used by the compiler to select one of the overloaded methods. However, note that although you can overload the parameters of a method, you can't overload the return type of a method. In other words, you can't declare two methods with the same name that differ only in their return type. (The compiler is clever, but not that clever.)

Writing Methods

In the following exercises, you'll create a method that calculates how much a consultant would charge for a given number of consultancy days at a fixed daily rate. You will start by developing the logic for the application and then use the Generate Method Stub Wizard to help you write the methods that are used by this logic. Next, you'll run these methods in a Console application to get a feel for the program. Finally, you'll use the Visual Studio 2010 debugger to step in and out of the method calls as they run.

Develop the logic for the application

1. Using Visual Studio 2010, open the DailyRate project in the \Microsoft Press\Visual CSharp Step By Step\Chapter 3\DailyRate folder in your Documents folder.

2. In *Solution Explorer*, double-click the file *Program.cs* to display the code for the program in the *Code and Text Editor* window.

3. Add the following statements to the body of the *run* method, between the opening and closing braces:

```
double dailyRate = readDouble("Enter your daily rate: ");
int noOfDays = readInt("Enter the number of days: ");
writeFee(calculateFee(dailyRate, noOfDays));
```

The *run* method is called by the *Main* method when the application starts. (The way in which it is called requires an understanding of classes, which we look at in Chapter 7, "Creating and Managing Classes and Objects.")

The block of code you have just added to the *run* method calls the *readDouble* method (which you will write shortly) to ask the user for the daily rate for the consultant. The next statement calls the *readInt* method (which you will also write) to obtain the number of days. Finally, the *writeFee* method (to be written) is called to display the results on the screen. Notice that the value passed to *writeFee* is the value returned by the *calculateFee* method (the last one you will need to write), which takes the daily rate and the number of days and calculates the total fee payable.

Note You have not yet written the *readDouble*, *readInt*, *writeFee*, or *calculateFee* method, so IntelliSense does not display these methods when you type this code. Do not try to build the application yet, because it will fail.

Write the methods using the Generate Method Stub Wizard

1. In the *Code and Text Editor* window, right-click the *readDouble* method call in the *run* method.

    A shortcut menu appears that contains useful commands for generating and editing code, as shown here:

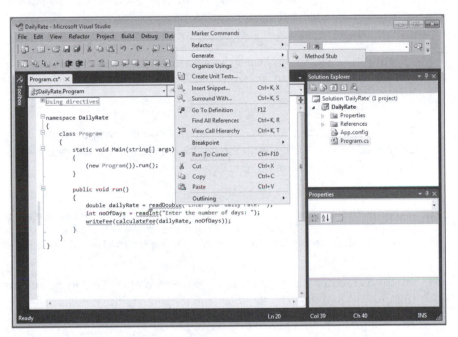

2. On the shortcut menu, point to *Generate* and then click *Method Stub*.

    Visual Studio examines the call to the *readDouble* method, ascertains the type of its parameters and return value, and generates a method with a default implementation, like this:

```
private double readDouble(string p)
{
    throw new NotImplementedException();
}
```

The new method is created with the *private* qualifier, which is described in Chapter 7. The body of the method currently just throws a *NotImplementedException*. (Exceptions are described in Chapter 6.) You will replace the body with your own code in the next step.

3. Delete the *throw new NotImplementedException();* statement from the *readDouble* method, and replace it with the following lines of code:

```
Console.Write(p);
string line = Console.ReadLine();
return double.Parse(line);
```

This block of code displays the string in variable *p* to the screen. This variable is the string parameter passed in when the method is called, and it contains a message prompting the user to type in the daily rate.

> **Note** The *Console.Write* method is similar to the *Console.WriteLine* statement that you have used in earlier exercises, except that it does not output a newline character after the message.

The user types a value, which is read into a *string* by using the *ReadLine* method and converted to a *double* by using the *double.Parse* method. The result is passed back as the return value of the method call.

> **Note** The *ReadLine* method is the companion method to *WriteLine*; it reads user input from the keyboard, finishing when the user presses the Enter key. The text typed by the user is passed back as the return value. The text is returned as a string value.

4. In the *run* method, right-click the call to the *readInt* method in the *run* method, point to *Generate*, and then click *Method Stub* to generate the *readInt* method.

The *readInt* method is generated, like this:

```
private int readInt(string p)
{
    throw new NotImplementedException();
}
```

5. Replace the *throw new NotImplementedException();* statement in the body of the *readInt* method with the following code:

```
Console.Write(p);
string line = Console.ReadLine();
return int.Parse(line);
```

This block of code is similar to the code for the *readDouble* method. The only difference is that the method returns an *int* value, so the *string* typed by the user is converted to a number by using the *int.Parse* method.

6. Right-click the call to the *calculateFee* method in the *run* method, point to *Generate*, and then click *Method Stub*.

The *calculateFee* method is generated, like this:

```
private object calculateFee(double dailyRate, int noOfDays)
{
    throw new NotImplementedException();
}
```

Notice in this case that Visual Studio uses the name of the arguments passed in to generate names for the parameters. (You can of course change the parameter names if they are not suitable.) What is more intriguing is the type returned by the method, which is *object*. Visual Studio is unable to determine exactly which type of value should be returned by the method from the context in which it is called. The *object* type just means a "thing," and you should change it to the type you require when you add the code to the method. You will learn more about the *object* type in Chapter 7.

7. Change the definition of the *calculateFee* method so that it returns a *double*, as shown in bold type here:

```
private double calculateFee(double dailyRate, int noOfDays)
{
    throw new NotImplementedException();
}
```

8. Replace the body of the *calculateFee* method with the following statement, which calculates the fee payable by multiplying the two parameters together and then returns it:

```
return dailyRate * noOfDays;
```

9. Right-click the call to the *writeFee* method in the *run* method, and then click *Generate Method Stub*.

Note that Visual Studio uses the definition of the *calculateFee* method to work out that its parameter should be a *double*. Also, the method call does not use a return value, so the type of the method is *void*:

```
private void writeFee(double p)
{
    ...
}
```

 Tip If you feel sufficiently comfortable with the syntax, you can also write methods by typing them directly into the *Code and Text Editor* window. You do not always have to use the *Generate* menu option.

10. Type the following statements inside the *writeFee* method:

```
Console.WriteLine("The consultant's fee is: {0}", p * 1.1);
```

> **Note** This version of the *WriteLine* method demonstrates the use of a format string. The text *{0}* in the string used as the first argument to the *WriteLine* method is a placeholder that is replaced with the value of the expression following the string (*p * 1.1*) when it is evaluated at run time. Using this technique is preferable to alternatives, such as converting the value of the expression *p * 1.1* to a string and using the + operator to concatenate it to the message.

11. On the *Build* menu, click *Build Solution*.

Refactoring Code

A very useful feature of Visual Studio 2010 is the ability to refactor code.

Occasionally, you will find yourself writing the same (or similar) code in more than one place in an application. When this occurs, highlight the block of code you have just typed, and on the *Refactor* menu, click *Extract Method*. The *Extract Method* dialog box appears, prompting you for the name of a new method to create containing this code. Type a name, and click *OK*. The new method is created containing your code, and the code you typed is replaced with a call to this method. *Extract Method* is also intelligent enough to work out whether the method should take any parameters and return a value.

Test the program

1. On the *Debug* menu, click *Start Without Debugging*.

   Visual Studio 2010 builds the program and then runs it. A console window appears.

2. At the *Enter your daily rate* prompt, type **525** and then press Enter.

3. At the *Enter the number of days* prompt, type **17** and then press Enter.

   The program writes the following message to the console window:

   ```
   The consultant's fee is: 9817.5
   ```

4. Press the Enter key to close the application and return to the Visual Studio 2010 programming environment.

In the next exercise, you'll use the Visual Studio [2010] debugger to run your program in slow motion. You'll see when each method is called (which is referred to as *stepping into the method*) and then see how each *return* statement transfers control back to the caller (also known as *stepping out of the method*). While you are stepping in and out of methods, you use the tools on the *Debug* toolbar. However, the same commands are also available on the *Debug* menu when an application is running in Debug mode.

Step through the methods by using the Visual Studio 2010 debugger

1. In the *Code and Text Editor* window, find the *run* method.

2. Move the mouse to the first statement in the *run* method:

   ```
   double dailyRate = readDouble("Enter your daily rate: ");
   ```

3. Right-click anywhere on this line, and on the shortcut menu, click *Run To Cursor*.

   The program starts and runs until it reaches the first statement in the *run* method, and then it pauses. A yellow arrow in the left margin of the *Code and Text Editor* window indicates the current statement, which is also highlighted with a yellow background.

4. On the *View* menu, point to *Toolbars*, and then make sure that the *Debug* toolbar is selected.

   If it was not already visible, the *Debug* toolbar opens. It might appear docked with the other toolbars. If you cannot see the toolbar, try using the *Toolbars* command on the *View* menu to hide it, and notice which buttons disappear. Then display the toolbar again. The *Debug* toolbar looks like this (although the toolbar differs slightly between Visual Studio 2010 and Microsoft Visual C# 2010 Express—it does not contain the Breakpoints button on the right side):

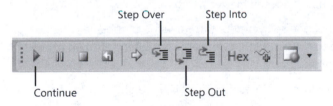

 Tip To make the *Debug* toolbar appear in its own window, use the handle at the left end of the toolbar to drag it over the *Code and Text Editor* window.

5. On the *Debug* toolbar, click the *Step Into* button. (This is the sixth button from the left.)

   This action causes the debugger to step into the method being called. The yellow cursor jumps to the opening brace at the start of the *readDouble* method.

6. Click *Step Into* again. The cursor advances to the first statement:

```
Console.Write(p);
```

> **Tip** You can also press F11 rather than repeatedly clicking *Step Into* on the *Debug* toolbar.

7. On the *Debug* toolbar, click *Step Over*. (This is the seventh button from the left.)

This action causes the method to execute the next statement without debugging it (stepping into it). The yellow cursor moves to the second statement of the method, and the program displays the *Enter your daily rate* prompt in a Console window before returning to Visual Studio 2010. (The Console window might be hidden behind Visual Studio.)

> **Tip** You can also press F10 rather than clicking *Step Over* on the *Debug* toolbar.

8. On the *Debug* toolbar, click *Step Over*.

This time, the yellow cursor disappears and the Console window gets the focus because the program is executing the *Console.ReadLine* method and is waiting for you to type something.

9. Type **525** in the Console window, and then press Enter.

Control returns to Visual Studio 2010. The yellow cursor appears on the third line of the method.

10. Hover the mouse over the reference to the *line* variable on either the second or third line of the method. (It doesn't matter which.)

A ScreenTip appears, displaying the current value of the *line* variable ("525"). You can use this feature to make sure that a variable has been set to an expected value while stepping through methods.

11. On the *Debug* toolbar, click *Step Out*. (This is the eighth button from the left.)

This action causes the current method to continue running uninterrupted to its end. The *readDouble* method finishes, and the yellow cursor is placed back at the first statement of the *run* method.

> **Tip** You can also press Shift+F11 rather than clicking *Step Out* on the *Debug* toolbar.

12. On the *Debug* toolbar, click *Step Into*.

The yellow cursor moves to the second statement in the *run* method:

```
int noOfDays = readInt("Enter the number of days: ");
```

13. On the *Debug* toolbar, click *Step Over*.

This time you have chosen to run the method without stepping through it. The Console window appears again, prompting you for the number of days.

14. In the Console window, type **17** and then press Enter.

Control returns to Visual Studio 2010. The yellow cursor moves to the third statement of the *run* method:

```
writeFee(calculateFee(dailyRate, noOfDays));
```

15. On the *Debug* toolbar, click *Step Into*.

The yellow cursor jumps to the opening brace at the start of the *calculateFee* method. This method is called first, before *writeFee*, because the value returned by this method is used as the parameter to *writeFee*.

16. On the *Debug* toolbar, click *Step Out*.

The yellow cursor jumps back to the third statement of the *run* method.

17. On the *Debug* toolbar, click *Step Into*.

This time, the yellow cursor jumps to the opening brace at the start of the *writeFee* method.

18. Place the mouse over the *p* variable in the method definition.

The value of *p*, 8925.0, is displayed in a ScreenTip.

19. On the *Debug* toolbar, click *Step Out*.

The message *The consultant's fee is: 9817.5* is displayed in the Console window. (You might need to bring the Console window to the foreground to display it if it is hidden behind Visual Studio 2010.) The yellow cursor returns to the third statement in the *run* method.

20. On the *Debug* toolbar, click *Continue* (the first button on the toolbar) to cause the program to continue running without stopping at each statement.

 Tip You can also press F5 to continue execution in the debugger.

The application completes and finishes running.

Using Optional Parameters and Named Arguments

You have seen that by defining overloaded methods you can implement different versions of a method that take different parameters. When you build an application that uses overloaded methods, the compiler determines which specific instances of each method it should use to satisfy each method call. This is a common feature of many object-oriented languages, not just C#.

However, there are other languages and technologies that developers can use for building Windows applications and components that do not follow these rules. A key feature of C# and other languages designed for the .NET Framework is the ability to interoperate with applications and components written by using other technologies. One of the principal technologies used by Microsoft Windows is the Component Object Model, or COM. COM does not support overloaded methods, but instead uses methods that can take optional parameters. To make it easier to incorporate COM libraries and components into a C# solution, C# also supports optional parameters.

Optional parameters are also useful in other situations. They provide a compact and simple solution when it is not possible to use overloading because the types of the parameters do not vary sufficiently to enable the compiler to distinguish between implementations. For example, consider the following method:

```
public void DoWorkWithData(int intData, float floatData, int moreIntData)
{
    ...
}
```

The *DoWorkWithData* method takes three parameters: two *int*s and a *float*. Now suppose you wanted to provide an implementation of *DoWorkWithData* that took only two parameters: *intData* and *floatData*. You can overload the method like this:

```
public void DoWorkWithData(int intData, float floatData)
{
    ...
}
```

If you write a statement that calls the *DoWorkWithData* method, you can provide either two or three parameters of the appropriate types, and the compiler uses the type information to determine which overload to call:

```
int arg1 = 99;
float arg2 = 100.0F;
int arg3 = 101;

DoWorkWithData(arg1, arg2, arg3); // Call overload with three parameters
DoWorkWithData(arg1, arg2);       // Call overload with two parameters
```

However, suppose you want to implement two further versions of *DoWorkWithData* that take only the first parameter and the third parameter. You might be tempted to try this:

```
public void DoWorkWithData(int intData)
{
    ...
}

public void DoWorkWithData(int moreIntData)
{
    ...
}
```

The issue is that to the compiler, these two overloads appear identical and your code will fail to compile and instead generates the error "Type '*typename*' already defines a member called 'DoWorkWithData' with the same parameter types." To understand why this is so, if this code was legal, consider the following statements:

```
int arg1 = 99;
int arg3 = 101;

DoWorkWithData(arg1);
DoWorkWithData(arg3);
```

Which overload or overloads would the calls to *DoWorkWithData* invoke? Using optional parameters and named arguments can help to solve this problem.

Defining Optional Parameters

You specify that a parameter is optional when you define a method by providing a default value for the parameter. You indicate a default value by using the assignment operator. In the *optMethod* method shown next, the *first* parameter is mandatory because it does not specify a default value, but the *second* and *third* parameters are optional:

```
void optMethod(int first, double second = 0.0, string third = "Hello")
{
    ...
}
```

You must specify all mandatory parameters before any optional parameters.

You can call a method that takes optional parameters in the same way that you call any other method; you specify the method name and provide any necessary arguments. The difference with methods that take optional parameters is that you can omit the corresponding arguments, and the method will use the default value when the method runs. In the following example code, the first call to the *optMethod* method provides values for all three parameters. The second call specifies only two arguments, and these values are applied to the *first* and *second* parameters. The *third* parameter receives the default value of "Hello" when the method runs.

```
optMethod(99, 123.45, "World"); // Arguments provided for all three parameters
optMethod(100, 54.321);         // Arguments provided for 1st two parameters only
```

Passing Named Arguments

By default, C# uses the position of each argument in a method call to determine which parameters they apply to. Hence, the second example method shown in the previous section passes the two arguments to the *first* and *second* parameters in the *optMethod* method, because this is the order in which they occur in the method declaration. C# also enables you to specify parameters by name, and this feature lets you pass the arguments in a different sequence. To pass an argument as a named parameter, you provide the name of the parameter, a colon, and the value to use. The following examples perform the same function as those shown in the previous section, except that the parameters are specified by name:

```
optMethod(first : 99, second : 123.45, third : "World");
optMethod(first : 100, second : 54.321);
```

Named arguments give you the ability to pass arguments in any order. You can rewrite the code that calls the *optMethod* method like this:

```
optMethod(third : "World", second : 123.45, first : 99);
optMethod(second : 54.321, first : 100);
```

This feature also enables you to omit arguments. For example, you can call the *optMethod* method and specify values for the *first* and *third* parameters only and use the default value for the *second* parameter like this:

```
optMethod(first : 99, third : "World");
```

Additionally, you can mix positional and named arguments. However, if you use this technique you must specify all the positional arguments before the first named argument:

```
optMethod(99, third : "World");  // First argument is positional
```

Resolving Ambiguities with Optional Parameters and Named Arguments

Using optional parameters and named arguments can result in some possible ambiguities in your code. You need to understand how the compiler resolves these ambiguities; otherwise, you might find your applications behaving in unexpected ways. Suppose that you defined the *optMethod* method as an overloaded method as shown in the following example:

```
void optMethod(int first, double second = 0.0, string third = "Hello")
{
    ...
}

void optMethod(int first, double second = 1.0, string third = "Goodbye", int fourth = 100 )
{
    ...
}
```

This is perfectly legal C# code that follows the rules for overloaded methods. The compiler can distinguish between the methods because they have different parameter lists. However, a problem can arise if you attempt to call the *optMethod* method and omit some of the arguments corresponding to one or more of the optional parameters:

```
optMethod(1, 2.5, "World");
```

Again, this is perfectly legal code, but which version of the *optMethod* method does it run? The answer is that it runs the version that most closely matches the method call, so it invokes the method that takes three parameters and not the version that takes four. That makes good sense, so consider this one:

```
optMethod(1, fourth : 101);
```

In this code, the call to *optMethod* omits arguments for the *second* and *third* parameters, but it specifies the *fourth* parameter by name. Only one version of *optMethod* matches this call, so this is not a problem. The next one will get you thinking though!

```
optMethod(1, 2.5);
```

This time neither version of the *optMethod* method exactly matches the list of arguments provided. Both versions of the *optMethod* method have optional parameters for the second, third, and fourth arguments. So does this statement call the version of *optMethod* that takes three parameters and use the default value for the *third* parameter, or does it call the version of *optMethod* that takes four parameters and use the default value for the *third* and *fourth* parameters? The answer is that it does neither. The compiler decides that this is an ambiguous method call and does not let you compile the application. The same situation arises with the same result if you try and call the *optMethod* method as shown in any of the following statements:

```
optMethod(1, third : "World");
optMethod(1);
optMethod(second : 2.5, first : 1);
```

In the final exercise in this chapter, you will practice implementing methods that take optional parameters and calling them by using named arguments. You will also test common examples of how the C# compiler resolves method calls that involve optional parameters and named arguments.

Define and call a method that takes optional parameters

1. Using Visual Studio 2010, open the DailyRate project in the \Microsoft Press\Visual CSharp Step By Step\Chapter 3\DailyRate Using Optional Parameters folder in your Documents folder.

2. In *Solution Explorer*, double-click the file *Program.cs* to display the code for the program in the *Code and Text Editor* window.

3. In the *Program* class, add the *calculateFee* method below the *run* method. This is the same version of the method that you implemented in the previous set of exercises except that it takes two optional parameters with default values. The method also prints a message indicating the version of the *calculateFee* method that was called. (You add overloaded implementations of this method in the following steps.)

```
private double calculateFee(double dailyRate = 500.0, int noOfDays = 1)
{
    Console.WriteLine("calculateFee using two optional parameters");
    return dailyRate * noOfDays;
}
```

4. Add another implementation of the *calculateFee* method to the *Program* class as shown next. This version takes one optional parameter, called *dailyRate*, of type *double*. The body of the method calculates and returns the fee for a single day.

```
private double calculateFee(double dailyRate = 500.0)
{
    Console.WriteLine("calculateFee using one optional parameter");
    int defaultNoOfDays = 1;
    return dailyRate * defaultNoOfDays;
}
```

5. Add a third implementation of the *calculateFee* method to the *Program* class. This version takes no parameters and uses hardcoded values for the daily rate and number of days.

```
private double calculateFee()
{
    Console.WriteLine("calculateFee using hardcoded values");
    double defaultDailyRate = 400.0;
    int defaultNoOfDays = 1;
    return defaultDailyRate * defaultNoOfDays;
}
```

6. In the *run* method, add the following statements that call *calculateFee* and display the results:

```
public void run()
{
    double fee = calculateFee();
    Console.WriteLine("Fee is {0}", fee);
}
```

7. On the *Debug* menu, click *Start Without Debugging* to build and run the program. The program runs in a console window and displays the following messages:

```
calculateFee using hardcoded values
Fee is 400
```

The *run* method called the version of *calculateFee* that takes no parameters rather than either of the implementations that take optional parameters. This is because this is the version that most closely matches the method call.

Press any key to close the console window and return to Visual Studio.

8. In the *run* method, modify the statement that calls *calculateFee* as shown in bold type in this code sample:

```
public void run()
{
    double fee = calculateFee(650.0);
    Console.WriteLine("Fee is {0}", fee);
}
```

9. On the *Debug* menu, click *Start Without Debugging* to build and run the program. The program displays the following messages:

```
calculateFee using one optional parameter
Fee is 650
```

This time, the *run* method called the version of *calculateFee* that takes one optional parameter. As before, this is because this is the version that most closely matches the method call.

Press any key to close the console window and return to Visual Studio.

10. In the *run* method, modify the statement that calls *calculateFee* again:

```
public void run()
{
    double fee = calculateFee(500.0, 3);
    Console.WriteLine("Fee is {0}", fee);
}
```

11. On the *Debug* menu, click *Start Without Debugging* to build and run the program. The program displays the following messages:

```
calculateFee using two optional parameters
Fee is 1500
```

As you might expect from the previous two cases, the *run* method called the version of *calculateFee* that takes two optional parameters.

Press any key to close the console window and return to Visual Studio.

12. In the *run* method, modify the statement that calls *calculateFee* and specify the *dailyRate* parameter by name:

```
public void run()
{
    double fee = calculateFee(dailyRate : 375.0);
    Console.WriteLine("Fee is {0}", fee);
}
```

13. On the *Debug* menu, click *Start Without Debugging* to build and run the program. The program displays the following messages:

```
calculateFee using one optional parameter
Fee is 375
```

As earlier, the *run* method called the version of *calculateFee* that takes one optional parameter. Changing the code to use a named argument does not change the way in which the compiler resolves the method call in this example.

Press any key to close the console window and return to Visual Studio.

14. In the *run* method, modify the statement that calls *calculateFee* and specify the *noOfDays* parameter by name:

```
public void run()
{
    double fee = calculateFee(noOfDays : 4);
    Console.WriteLine("Fee is {0}", fee);
}
```

15. On the *Debug* menu, click *Start Without Debugging* to build and run the program. The program displays the following messages:

```
calculateFee using two optional parameters
Fee is 2000
```

This time the *run* method called the version of *calculateFee* that takes two optional parameters. The method call has omitted the first parameter (*dailyRate*) and specified the second parameter by name. This is the only version of the *calculateFee* method that matches the call.

Press any key to close the console window and return to Visual Studio.

16. Modify the implementation of the *calculateFee* method that takes two optional parameters. Change the name of the first parameter to *theDailyRate* and update the *return* statement, as shown in bold type in the following code:

```
private double calculateFee(double theDailyRate = 500.0, int noOfDays = 5)
{
    Console.WriteLine("calculateFee using two optional parameters");
    return theDailyRate * noOfDays;
}
```

17. In the *run* method, modify the statement that calls *calculateFee* and specify the *theDailyRate* parameter by name:

```
public void run()
{
    double fee = calculateFee(theDailyRate : 375.0);
    Console.WriteLine("Fee is {0}", fee);
}
```

18. On the *Debug* menu, click *Start Without Debugging* to build and run the program. The program displays the following messages:

```
calculateFee using two optional parameters
Fee is 1875
```

The previous time that you specified the fee but not the daily rate (step 13), the *run* method called the version of *calculateFee* that takes one optional parameter. This time the *run* method called the version of *calculateFee* that takes two optional parameters. In this case, using a named argument has changed the way in which the compiler resolves the method call. If you specify a named argument, the compiler compares the argument name to the names of the parameters specified in the method declarations and selects the method that has a parameter with a matching name.

Press any key to close the console window and return to Visual Studio.

In this chapter, you learned how to define methods to implement a named block of code. You saw how to pass parameters into methods and how to return data from methods. You also saw how to call a method, pass arguments, and obtain a return value. You learned how to define overloaded methods with different parameter lists, and you saw how the scope of a variable determines where it can be accessed. Then you used the Visual Studio 2010 debugger to step through code as it runs. Finally, you learned how to write methods that take optional parameters and how to call methods by using named parameters.

- If you want to continue to the next chapter

  Keep Visual Studio 2010 running, and turn to Chapter 4.

- If you want to exit Visual Studio 2010 now

  On the *File* menu, click *Exit*. If you see a *Save* dialog box, click *Yes* and save the project.

Chapter 3 Quick Reference

To	Do this
Declare a method	Write the method inside a class. For example: ```\nint addValues(int leftHandSide, int rightHandSide)\n{\n ...\n}\n```
Return a value from inside a method	Write a *return* statement inside the method. For example: ```\nreturn leftHandSide + rightHandSide;\n```
Return from a method before the end of the method	Write a *return* statement inside the method. For example: ```\nreturn;\n```
Call a method	Write the name of the method, together with any arguments between parentheses. For example: ```\naddValues(39, 3);\n```
Use the Generate Method Stub Wizard	Right-click a call to the method, and then click *Generate Method Stub* on the shortcut menu.
Display the *Debug* toolbar	On the *View* menu, point to *Toolbars*, and then click *Debug*.
Step into a method	On the *Debug* toolbar, click *Step Into*. or On the *Debug* menu, click *Step Into*.
Step out of a method	On the *Debug* toolbar, click *Step Out*. or On the *Debug* menu, click *Step Out*.
Specify an optional parameter to a method	Provide a default value for the parameter in the method declaration. For example: ```\nvoid optMethod(int first, double second = 0.0,\n string third = "Hello")\n{\n ...\n}\n```
Pass a method argument as a named parameter	Specify the name of the parameter in the method call. For example: ```\noptMethod(first : 100, third : "World");\n```

Chapter 4
Using Decision Statements

After completing this chapter, you will be able to:

- Declare Boolean variables.

- Use Boolean operators to create expressions whose outcome is either true or false.

- Write if statements to make decisions based on the result of a Boolean expression.

- Write switch statements to make more complex decisions.

In Chapter 3, "Writing Methods and Applying Scope," you learned how to group related statements into methods. You also learned how to use parameters to pass information to a method and how to use *return* statements to pass information out of a method. Dividing a program into a set of discrete methods, each designed to perform a specific task or calculation, is a necessary design strategy. Many programs need to solve large and complex problems. Breaking up a program into methods helps you understand these problems and focus on how to solve them one piece at a time. You also need to be able to write methods that selectively perform different actions depending on the circumstances. In this chapter, you'll see how to accomplish this task.

Declaring Boolean Variables

In the world of C# programming (unlike in the real world), everything is black or white, right or wrong, true or false. For example, if you create an integer variable called *x*, assign the value 99 to *x*, and then ask, "Does *x* contain the value 99?", the answer is definitely true. If you ask, "Is *x* less than 10?", the answer is definitely false. These are examples of *Boolean expressions*. A Boolean expression always evaluates to true or false.

> **Note** The answers to these questions are not necessarily definitive for all other programming languages. An unassigned variable has an undefined value, and you cannot, for example, say that it is definitely less than 10. Issues such as this one are a common source of errors in C and C++ programs. The Microsoft Visual C# compiler solves this problem by ensuring that you always assign a value to a variable before examining it. If you try to examine the contents of an unassigned variable, your program will not compile.

Microsoft Visual C# provides a data type called *bool*. A *bool* variable can hold one of two values: *true* or *false*. For example, the following three statements declare a *bool* variable called *areYouReady*, assign *true* to that variable, and then write its value to the console:

```
bool areYouReady;
areYouReady = true;
Console.WriteLine(areYouReady); // writes True to the console
```

Using Boolean Operators

A Boolean operator is an operator that performs a calculation whose result is either true or false. C# has several very useful Boolean operators, the simplest of which is the *NOT* operator, which is represented by the exclamation point, !. The ! operator negates a Boolean value, yielding the opposite of that value. In the preceding example, if the value of the variable *areYouReady* is true, the value of the expression !*areYouReady* is false.

Understanding Equality and Relational Operators

Two Boolean operators that you will frequently use are the equality == and inequality != operators. You use these binary operators to find out whether one value is the same as another value of the same type. The following table summarizes how these operators work, using an *int* variable called *age* as an example.

Operator	Meaning	Example	Outcome if age is 42
==	Equal to	age == 100	false
!=	Not equal to	age != 0	true

Closely related to these two operators are the *relational* operators. You use these operators to find out whether a value is less than or greater than another value of the same type. The following table shows how to use these operators.

Operator	Meaning	Example	Outcome if age is 42
<	Less than	age < 21	false
<=	Less than or equal to	age <= 18	false
>	Greater than	age > 16	true
>=	Greater than or equal to	age >= 30	true

Don't confuse the *equality* operator == with the *assignment* operator =. The expression x==y compares *x* with *y* and has the value *true* if the values are the same. The expression x=y assigns the value of *y* to *x* and returns the value of *y* as its result.

Understanding Conditional Logical Operators

C# also provides two other Boolean operators: the logical AND operator, which is repre-sented by the *&&* symbol, and the logical OR operator, which is represented by the *||* sym-bol. Collectively, these are known as the conditional logical operators. Their purpose is to combine two Boolean expressions or values into a single Boolean result. These binary opera-tors are similar to the equality and relational operators in that the value of the expressions in which they appear is either true or false, but they differ in that the values on which they operate must be either true or false.

The outcome of the *&&* operator is *true* if and only if both of the Boolean expressions it operates on are *true*. For example, the following statement assigns the value *true* to *validPercentage* if and only if the value of *percent* is greater than or equal to 0 and the value of *percent* is less than or equal to 100:

```
bool validPercentage;
validPercentage = (percent >= 0) && (percent <= 100);
```

> **Tip** A common beginner's error is to try to combine the two tests by naming the *percent* variable only once, like this:
>
> ```
> percent >= 0 && <= 100 // this statement will not compile
> ```
>
> Using parentheses helps avoid this type of mistake and also clarifies the purpose of the expression. For example, compare these two expressions:
>
> ```
> validPercentage = percent >= 0 && percent <= 100
> ```
>
> and
>
> ```
> validPercentage = (percent >= 0) && (percent <= 100)
> ```
>
> Both expressions return the same value because the precedence of the *&&* operator is less than that of >= and <=. However, the second expression conveys its purpose in a more readable manner.

The outcome of the *||* operator is *true* if either of the Boolean expressions it operates on is *true*. You use the *||* operator to determine whether any one of a combination of Boolean expressions is *true*. For example, the following statement assigns the value *true* to *invalidPercentage* if the value of *percent* is less than 0 or the value of *percent* is greater than 100:

```
bool invalidPercentage;
invalidPercentage = (percent < 0) || (percent > 100);
```

Short-Circuiting

The *&&* and *||* operators both exhibit a feature called *short-circuiting*. Sometimes it is not necessary to evaluate both operands when ascertaining the result of a conditional logical expression. For example, if the left operand of the *&&* operator evaluates to *false*, the result of the entire expression must be *false* regardless of the value of the right operand. Similarly, if the value of the left operand of the *||* operator evaluates to *true*, the result of the entire expression must be *true*, irrespective of the value of the right operand. In these cases, the *&&* and *||* operators bypass the evaluation of the right operand. Here are some examples:

```
(percent >= 0) && (percent <= 100)
```

In this expression, if the value of *percent* is less than 0, the Boolean expression on the left side of *&&* evaluates to *false*. This value means that the result of the entire expression must be *false*, and the Boolean expression to the right of the *&&* operator is not evaluated.

```
(percent < 0) || (percent > 100)
```

In this expression, if the value of *percent* is less than 0, the Boolean expression on the left side of *||* evaluates to *true*. This value means that the result of the entire expression must be *true* and the Boolean expression to the right of the *||* operator is not evaluated.

If you carefully design expressions that use the conditional logical operators, you can boost the performance of your code by avoiding unnecessary work. Place simple Boolean expressions that can be evaluated easily on the left side of a conditional logical operator, and put more complex expressions on the right side. In many cases, you will find that the program does not need to evaluate the more complex expressions.

Summarizing Operator Precedence and Associativity

The following table summarizes the precedence and associativity of all the operators you have learned about so far. Operators in the same category have the same precedence. The operators in categories higher up in the table take precedence over operators in categories lower down.

Category	Operators	Description	Associativity
Primary	( )	Precedence override	Left
	++	Post-increment	
	--	Post-decrement	
Unary	!	Logical NOT	Left
	+	Addition	
	-	Subtraction	
	++	Pre-increment	
	--	Pre-decrement	

Category	Operators	Description	Associativity
Multiplicative	* / %	Multiply Divide Division remainder (modulus)	Left
Additive	+ –	Addition Subtraction	Left
Relational	< <= > >=	Less than Less than or equal to Greater than Greater than or equal to	Left
Equality	== !=	Equal to Not equal to	Left
Conditional AND	&&	Logical AND	Left
Conditional OR	||	Logical OR	Left
Assignment	=		Right

Using *if* Statements to Make Decisions

When you want to choose between executing two different blocks of code depending on the result of a Boolean expression, you can use an *if* statement.

Understanding *if* Statement Syntax

The syntax of an *if* statement is as follows (*if* and *else* are C# keywords):

```
if ( booleanExpression )
    statement-1;
else
    statement-2;
```

If *booleanExpression* evaluates to *true*, *statement-1* runs; otherwise, *statement-2* runs. The *else* keyword and the subsequent *statement-2* are optional. If there is no *else* clause and the *booleanExpression* is *false*, execution continues with whatever code follows the *if* statement.

For example, here's an *if* statement that increments a variable representing the second hand of a stopwatch. (Minutes are ignored for now.) If the value of the *seconds* variable is 59, it is reset to 0; otherwise, it is incremented using the ++ operator:

```
int seconds;
...
if (seconds == 59)
    seconds = 0;
else
    seconds++;
```

Boolean Expressions Only, Please!

The expression in an *if* statement must be enclosed in parentheses. Additionally, the expression must be a Boolean expression. In some other languages (notably C and C++), you can write an integer expression, and the compiler will silently convert the integer value to *true* (nonzero) or *false* (0). C# does not support this behavior, and the compiler reports an error if you write such an expression.

If you accidentally specify the assignment operator, =, instead of the equality test operator, ==, in an *if* statement, the C# compiler recognizes your mistake and refuses to compile your code. For example:

```
int seconds;
...
if (seconds = 59)  // compile-time error
...
if (seconds == 59) // ok
```

Accidental assignments were another common source of bugs in C and C++ programs, which would silently convert the value assigned (59) to a Boolean expression (with anything nonzero considered to be true), with the result that the code following the *if* statement would be performed every time.

Incidentally, you can use a Boolean variable as the expression for an *if* statement, although it must still be enclosed in parentheses, as shown in this example:

```
bool inWord;
...
if (inWord == true) // ok, but not commonly used
...
if (inWord)         // more common and considered better style
```

Using Blocks to Group Statements

Notice that the syntax of the *if* statement shown earlier specifies a single statement after the *if (booleanExpression)* and a single statement after the *else* keyword. Sometimes, you'll want to perform more than one statement when a Boolean expression is true. You can group the statements inside a new method and then call the new method, but a simpler solution is to group the statements inside a *block*. A block is simply a sequence of statements grouped between an opening brace and a closing brace. A block also starts a new scope. You can define variables inside a block, but they will disappear at the end of the block.

In the following example, two statements that reset the *seconds* variable to 0 and increment the *minutes* variable are grouped inside a block, and the whole block executes if the value of *seconds* is equal to 59:

```
int seconds = 0;
int minutes = 0;
...
if (seconds == 59)
{
    seconds = 0;
    minutes++;
}
else
    seconds++;
```

Important If you omit the braces, the C# compiler associates only the first statement (`seconds = 0;`) with the *if* statement. The subsequent statement (`minutes++;`) will not be recognized by the compiler as part of the *if* statement when the program is compiled. Furthermore, when the compiler reaches the *else* keyword, it will not associate it with the previous *if* statement, and it will report a syntax error instead.

Cascading *if* Statements

You can nest *if* statements inside other *if* statements. In this way, you can chain together a sequence of Boolean expressions, which are tested one after the other until one of them evaluates to *true*. In the following example, if the value of *day* is 0, the first test evaluates to *true* and *dayName* is assigned the string *"Sunday"*. If the value of *day* is not 0, the first test fails and control passes to the *else* clause, which runs the second *if* statement and compares the value of *day* with 1. The second *if* statement is reached only if the first test is *false*. Similarly, the third *if* statement is reached only if the first and second tests are *false*.

```
if (day == 0)
    dayName = "Sunday";
else if (day == 1)
    dayName = "Monday";
else if (day == 2)
    dayName = "Tuesday";
else if (day == 3)
    dayName = "Wednesday";
else if (day == 4)
    dayName = "Thursday";
else if (day == 5)
    dayName = "Friday";
else if (day == 6)
    dayName = "Saturday";
else
    dayName = "unknown";
```

In the following exercise, you'll write a method that uses a cascading *if* statement to compare two dates.

Write *if* statements

1. Start Microsoft Visual Studio 2010 if it is not already running.

2. Open the Selection project, located in the \Microsoft Press\Visual CSharp Step By Step \Chapter 4\Selection folder in your Documents folder.

3. On the *Debug* menu, click *Start Without Debugging*.

   Visual Studio 2010 builds and runs the application. The form contains two *DateTimePicker* controls called *first* and *second*. These controls display a calendar allowing you to select a date when you click the icon. Both controls are initially set to the current date.

4. Click *Compare*.

   The following text appears in the text box:

   ```
   first == second : False
   first != second : True
   first <  second : False
   first <= second : False
   first >  second : True
   first >= second : True
   ```

   The Boolean expression `first == second` should be *true* because both *first* and *second* are set to the current date. In fact, only the less than operator and the greater than or equal to operator seem to be working correctly.

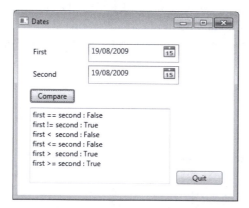

5. Click *Quit* to return to the Visual Studio 2010 programming environment.

6. Display the code for MainWindow.xaml.cs in the *Code and Text Editor* window.

7. Locate the *compareClick* method. It looks like this:

```
private void compareClick(object sender, RoutedEventArgs e)
{
    int diff = dateCompare(first.SelectedDate.Value, second.SelectedDate.Value);
    info.Text = "";
    show("first == second", diff == 0);
    show("first != second", diff != 0);
    show("first < second", diff < 0);
    show("first <= second", diff <= 0);
    show("first > second", diff > 0);
    show("first >= second", diff >= 0);
}
```

This method runs whenever the user clicks the *Compare* button on the form. It retrieves the values of the dates displayed in the *first* and *second DateTimePicker* controls on the form. The date the user selects in each of the *DateTimePicker* controls is available in the *SelectedDate* property. You retrieve the date by using the *Value* property of this prop-erty. (You will learn more about properties in Chapter 15, "Implementing Properties to Access Fields.") The type of this property is *DateTime*. The *DateTime* data type is just another data type, like *int* or *float*, except that it contains subelements that enable you to access the individual pieces of a date, such as the year, month, or day.

The *compareClick* method passes the two *DateTime* values to the *dateCompare* meth-od, which compares them. You will examine the *dateCompare* method in the next step.

The *show* method summarizes the results of the comparison in the *info* text box control on the form.

8. Locate the *dateCompare* method. It looks like this:

```
private int dateCompare(DateTime leftHandSide, DateTime rightHandSide)
{
    // TO DO
    return 42;
}
```

This method currently returns the same value whenever it is called—rather than 0, –1, or +1—depending on the values of its parameters. This explains why the application is not working as expected!

The purpose of this method is to examine its arguments and return an integer value based on their relative values; it should return 0 if they have the same value, –1 if the value of the first argument is less than the value of the second argument, and +1 if the value of the first argument is greater than the value of the second argument. (A date is considered greater than another date if it comes after it chronologically.) You need to implement the logic in this method to compare two dates correctly.

9. Remove the `// TO DO` comment and the *return* statement from the *dateCompare* method.

10. Add the following statements shown in bold type to the body of the *dateCompare* method:

```
private int dateCompare(DateTime leftHandSide, DateTime rightHandSide)
{
    int result;

    if (leftHandSide.Year < rightHandSide.Year)
        result = -1;
    else if (leftHandSide.Year > rightHandSide.Year)
        result = 1;
}
```

If the expression leftHandSide.Year < rightHandSide.Year is *true*, the date in *leftHandSide* must be earlier than the date in *rightHandSide*, so the program sets the *result* variable to –1. Otherwise, if the expression leftHandSide.Year > rightHand-Side.Year is *true*, the date in *leftHandSide* must be later than the date in *rightHand-Side*, and the program sets the result *variable* to 1.

If the expression leftHandSide.Year < rightHandSide.Year is *false* and the expression leftHandSide.Year > rightHandSide.Year is also *false*, the *Year* property of both dates must be the same, so the program needs to compare the months in each date.

11. Add the following statements shown in bold type to the body of the *dateCompare* method, after the code you entered in the preceding step:

```
private int dateCompare(DateTime leftHandSide, DateTime rightHandSide)
{
    ...

    else if (leftHandSide.Month < rightHandSide.Month)
        result = -1;
    else if (leftHandSide.Month > rightHandSide.Month)
        result = 1;
}
```

These statements follow a similar logic for comparing months to that used to compare years in the preceding step.

If the expression leftHandSide.Month < rightHandSide.Month is *false* and the expression leftHandSide.Month > rightHandSide.Month is also *false*, the *Month* property of both dates must be the same, so the program finally needs to compare the days in each date.

12. Add the following statements to the body of the *dateCompare* method, after the code you entered in the preceding two steps:

```
private int dateCompare(DateTime leftHandSide, DateTime rightHandSide)
{
    ...
    else if (leftHandSide.Day < rightHandSide.Day)
        result = -1;
```

```
        else if (leftHandSide.Day > rightHandSide.Day)
            result = 1;
        else
            result = 0;
        return result;
}
```

You should recognize the pattern in this logic by now.

If `leftHandSide.Day < rightHandSide.Day` and `leftHandSide.Day > rightHand-Side.Day` both are *false*, the value in the *Day* properties in both variables must be the same. The *Month* values and the *Year* values must also be identical, respectively, for the program logic to have reached this far, so the two dates must be the same, and the program sets the value of *result* to 0.

The final statement returns the value stored in the *result* variable.

13. On the *Debug* menu, click *Start Without Debugging*.

The application is rebuilt and restarted. Once again, the two *DateTimePicker* controls, *first* and *second*, are set to the current date.

14. Click *Compare*.

The following text appears in the text box:

```
first == second : True
first != second : False
first <  second : False
first <= second : True
first >  second : False
first >= second : True
```

These are the correct results for identical dates.

15. Click the icon for the second *DateTimePicker* control, and then click tomorrow's date in the calendar that appears.

16. Click *Compare*.

The following text appears in the text box:

```
first == second : False
first != second : True
first <  second : True
first <= second : True
first >  second : False
first >= second : False
```

Again, these are the correct results when the first date is earlier than the second date.

17. Test some other dates, and verify that the results are as you would expect. Click *Quit* when you have finished.

Comparing Dates in Real-World Applications

Now that you have seen how to use a rather long and complicated series of *if* and *else* statements, I should mention that this is not the technique you would use to compare dates in a real-world application. In the Microsoft .NET Framework class library, dates are held using a special type called *DateTime*. If you look at the *dateCompare* method you have written in the preceding exercise, you will see that the two parameters, *leftHandSide* and *rightHandSide*, are *DateTime* values. The logic you have written compares only the date part of these variables—there is also a time element. For two *DateTime* values to be considered equal, they should not only have the same date but also the same time. Comparing dates and times is such a common operation that the *DateTime* type has a built-in method called *Compare* for doing just that. The *Compare* method takes two *DateTime* arguments and compares them, returning a value indicating whether the first argument is less than the second, in which case the result will be negative; whether the first argument is greater than the second, in which case the result will be positive; or whether both arguments represent the same date and time, in which case the result will be 0.

Using *switch* Statements

Sometimes when you write a cascading *if* statement, all the *if* statements look similar because they all evaluate an identical expression. The only difference is that each *if* compares the result of the expression with a different value. For example, consider the following block of code that uses an *if* statement to examine the value in the *day* variable and work out which day of the week it is:

```
if (day == 0)
    dayName = "Sunday";
else if (day == 1)
    dayName = "Monday";
else if (day == 2)
    dayName = "Tuesday";
else if (day == 3)
    ...
else
    dayName = "Unknown";
```

In these situations, often you can rewrite the cascading *if* statement as a *switch* statement to make your program more efficient and more readable.

Understanding *switch* Statement Syntax

The syntax of a *switch* statement is as follows (*switch*, *case*, and *default* are keywords):

```
switch ( controllingExpression )
{
    case constantExpression :
        statements
        break;
    case constantExpression :
        statements
        break;
    ...
    default :
        statements
        break;
}
```

The *controllingExpression* is evaluated once. Control then jumps to the block of code identified by the *constantExpression*, whose value is equal to the result of the *controllingExpression*. (The identifier is called a *case label*.) Execution runs as far as the *break* statement, at which point the *switch* statement finishes and the program continues at the first statement after the closing brace of the *switch* statement. If none of the *constantExpression* values are equal to the value of the *controllingExpression*, the statements below the optional *default* label run.

> **Note** Each *constantExpression* value must be unique, so the *controllingExpression* will match only one of them. If the value of the *controllingExpression* does not match any *constantExpression* value and there is no *default* label, program execution continues with the first statement after the closing brace of the *switch* statement.

For example, you can rewrite the previous cascading *if* statement as the following *switch* statement:

```
switch (day)
{
    case 0 :
        dayName = "Sunday";
        break;
    case 1 :
        dayName = "Monday";
        break;
    case 2 :
        dayName = "Tuesday";
        break;
    ...
    default :
        dayName = "Unknown";
        break;
}
```

Following the *switch* Statement Rules

The *switch* statement is very useful, but unfortunately, you can't always use it when you might like to. Any *switch* statement you write must adhere to the following rules:

- You can use switch only on primitive data types, such as *int* or *string*. With any other types (including *float* and *double*), you have to use an *if* statement.

- The case labels must be constant expressions, such as 42 or "42". If you need to calculate your case label values at run time, you must use an *if* statement.

- The case labels must be unique expressions. In other words, two case labels cannot have the same value.

- You can specify that you want to run the same statements for more than one value by providing a list of case labels and no intervening statements, in which case the code for the final label in the list is executed for all cases in that list. However, if a label has one or more associated statements, execution cannot fall through to subsequent labels, and the compiler generates an error. For example:

```
switch (trumps)
{
    case Hearts :
    case Diamonds :        // Fall-through allowed - no code between labels
        color = "Red";     // Code executed for Hearts and Diamonds
        break;
    case Clubs :
        color = "Black";
    case Spades :          // Error - code between labels
        color = "Black";
        break;
}
```

 Note The *break* statement is the most common way to stop fall-through, but you can also use a *return* statement or a *throw* statement. The *throw* statement is described in Chapter 6, "Managing Errors and Exceptions."

switch Fall-Through Rules

Because you cannot accidentally fall through from one *case* label to the next if there is any intervening code, you can freely rearrange the sections of a *switch* statement without affecting its meaning (including the *default* label, which by convention is usually placed as the last label but does not have to be).

C and C++ programmers should note that the *break* statement is mandatory for every case in a *switch* statement (even the default case). This requirement is a good thing; it is common in C or C++ programs to forget the *break* statement, allowing execution to fall through to the next label and leading to bugs that are difficult to spot.

If you really want to, you can mimic C/C++ fall-through in C# by using a *goto* statement to go to the following *case* or *default* label. Using *goto* in general is not recommended, though, and this book does not show you how to do it!

In the following exercise, you will complete a program that reads the characters of a string and maps each character to its XML representation. For example, the left angle bracket character, <, has a special meaning in XML. (It's used to form elements.) If you have data that contains this character, it must be translated into the text "<" so that an XML processor knows that it is data and not part of an XML instruction. Similar rules apply to the right angle bracket (>), ampersand (&), single quotation mark ('), and double quotation mark (") characters. You will write a *switch* statement that tests the value of the character and traps the special XML characters as *case* labels.

Write *switch* statements

1. Start Visual Studio 2010 if it is not already running.

2. Open the SwitchStatement project, located in the \Microsoft Press\Visual CSharp Step By Step\Chapter 4\SwitchStatement folder in your Documents folder.

3. On the *Debug* menu, click *Start Without Debugging*.

   Visual Studio 2010 builds and runs the application. The application displays a form containing two text boxes separated by a *Copy* button.

4. Type the following sample text into the upper text box:

inRange = (lo <= number) && (hi >= number);

5. Click *Copy.*

The statement is copied verbatim into the lower text box, and no translation of the <, &, or > character occurs.

6. Close the form, and return to Visual Studio 2010.

7. Display the code for MainWindow.xaml.cs in the *Code and Text Editor* window, and locate the *copyOne* method.

The *copyOne* method copies the character specified as its input parameter to the end of the text displayed in the lower text box. At the moment, *copyOne* contains a *switch* statement with a single *default* action. In the following few steps, you will modify this *switch* statement to convert characters that are significant in XML to their XML mapping. For example, the "<" character will be converted to the string "<".

8. Add the following statements to the *switch* statement after the opening brace for the statement and directly before the *default* label:

```
case '<' :
    target.Text += "&lt;";
    break;
```

If the current character being copied is a <, this code appends the string "<" to the text being output in its place.

9. Add the following statements to the *switch* statement after the *break* statement you have just added and above the *default* label:

```
case '>' :
    target.Text += "&gt;";
    break;
case '&' :
    target.Text += "&amp;";
    break;
case '\"' :
    target.Text +=   "&#34;";
    break;
case '\'' :
    target.Text += "&#39;";
    break;
```

 Note The single quotation mark (') and double quotation mark (") have a special meaning in C# as well as in XML—they are used to delimit character and string constants. The backslash (\) in the final two *case* labels is an escape character that causes the C# compiler to treat these characters as literals rather than as delimiters.

10. On the *Debug* menu, click *Start Without Debugging*.

11. Type the following text into the upper text box:

inRange = (lo <= number) && (hi >= number);

12. Click *Copy*.

The statement is copied into the lower text box. This time, each character undergoes the XML mapping implemented in the *switch* statement. The target text box displays the following text:

inRange = (lo <= number) && (hi >= number);

13. Experiment with other strings, and verify that all special characters (<, >, &, ", and ') are handled correctly.

14. Close the form.

In this chapter, you learned about Boolean expressions and variables. You saw how to use Boolean expressions with the *if* and *switch* statements to make decisions in your programs, and you combined Boolean expressions by using the Boolean operators.

- If you want to continue to the next chapter

   Keep Visual Studio 2010 running, and turn to Chapter 5.

- If you want to exit Visual Studio 2010 now

   On the *File* menu, click *Exit*. If you see a *Save* dialog box, click *Yes* and save the project.

Chapter 4 Quick Reference

To	Do this	Example
Determine whether two values are equivalent	Use the == or != operator.	`answer == 42`
Compare the value of two expressions	Use the <, <=, >, or >= operator.	`age >= 21`
Declare a Boolean variable	Use the *bool* keyword as the type of the variable.	`bool inRange;`
Create a Boolean expression that is true only if two other conditions are true	Use the && operator.	`inRange = (lo <= number)` `            && (number <= hi);`
Create a Boolean expression that is true if either of two other conditions is true	Use the || operator.	`outOfRange = (number < lo)` `              || (hi < number);`
Run a statement if a condition is true	Use an *if* statement.	`if (inRange)` `    process();`

To	Do this	Example
Run more than one statement if a condition is true	Use an *if* statement and a block.	```csharp\nif (seconds == 59)\n{\n seconds = 0;\n minutes++;\n}\n```
Associate different statements with different values of a controlling expression	Use a *switch* statement.	```csharp\nswitch (current)\n{\n case 0:\n ...\n break;\n\n case 1:\n ...\n break;\n default :\n ...\n break;\n}\n```

Chapter 5
Using Compound Assignment and Iteration Statements

After completing this chapter, you will be able to:

- Update the value of a variable by using compound assignment operators.

- Write *while*, *for*, and *do* iteration statements.

- Step through a *do* statement and watch as the values of variables change.

In Chapter 4, "Using Decision Statements," you learned how to use the *if* and *switch* constructs to run statements selectively. In this chapter, you'll see how to use a variety of iteration (or *looping*) statements to run one or more statements repeatedly. When you write iteration statements, you usually need to control the number of iterations that you perform. You can achieve this by using a variable, updating its value with each iteration, and stopping the process when the variable reaches a particular value. You'll also learn about the special assignment operators that you should use to update the value of a variable in these circumstances.

Using Compound Assignment Operators

You've already seen how to use arithmetic operators to create new values. For example, the following statement uses the plus operator (+) to display to the console a value that is 42 greater than the variable *answer*:

```
Console.WriteLine(answer + 42);
```

You've also seen how to use assignment statements to change the value of a variable. The following statement uses the assignment operator to change the value of *answer* to 42:

```
answer = 42;
```

If you want to add 42 to the value of a variable, you can combine the assignment operator and the addition operator. For example, the following statement adds 42 to *answer*. After this statement runs, the value of *answer* is 42 more than it was before:

```
answer = answer + 42;
```

Although this statement works, you'll probably never see an experienced programmer write code like this. Adding a value to a variable is so common that C# lets you perform this task in shorthand manner by using the operator +=. To add 42 to *answer*, you can write the following statement:

```
answer += 42;
```

You can use this shortcut to combine any arithmetic operator with the assignment operator, as the following table shows. These operators are collectively known as the *compound assignment operators*.

Don't write this	Write this
variable = variable * number;	variable *= number;
variable = variable / number;	variable /= number;
variable = variable % number;	variable %= number;
variable = variable + number;	variable += number;
variable = variable - number;	variable -= number;

> **Tip** The compound assignment operators share the same precedence and right associativity as the simple assignment operators.

The += operator also works on strings; it appends one string to the end of another. For example, the following code displays "Hello John" on the console:

```
string name = "John";
string greeting = "Hello ";
greeting += name;
Console.WriteLine(greeting);
```

You cannot use any of the other compound assignment operators on strings.

> **Note** Use the increment (++) and decrement (−−) operators instead of a compound assignment operator when incrementing or decrementing a variable by 1. For example, replace
>
> ```
> count += 1;
> ```
>
> with
>
> ```
> count++;
> ```

Writing *while* Statements

You use a *while* statement to run a statement repeatedly while some condition is true. The syntax of a *while* statement is as follows:

```
while ( booleanExpression )
    statement
```

The Boolean expression is evaluated, and if it is true, the statement runs and then the Boolean expression is evaluated again. If the expression is still true, the statement is repeated and then the Boolean expression is evaluated again. This process continues until the Boolean expression evaluates to false, when the *while* statement exits. Execution then continues with the first statement after the *while* statement. A *while* statement shares many syntactic similarities with an *if* statement (in fact, the syntax is identical except for the keyword):

- The expression must be a Boolean expression.

- The Boolean expression must be written inside parentheses.

- If the Boolean expression evaluates to false when first evaluated, the statement does not run.

- If you want to perform two or more statements under the control of a *while* statement, you must use braces to group those statements in a block.

Here's a *while* statement that writes the values 0 through 9 to the console:

```
int i = 0;
while (i < 10)
{
    Console.WriteLine(i);
    i++;
}
```

All *while* statements should terminate at some point. A common beginner's mistake is forgetting to include a statement to cause the Boolean expression eventually to evaluate to false and terminate the loop, which results in a program that runs forever. In the example, the i++ statement performs this role.

 Note The variable *i* in the *while* loop controls the number of iterations that it performs. This is a common idiom, and the variable that performs this role is sometimes called the *Sentinel* variable.

In the following exercise, you will write a *while* loop to iterate through the contents of a text file one line at a time and write each line to a text box in a form.

Write a *while* statement

1. Using Microsoft Visual Studio 2010, open the WhileStatement project, located in the \Microsoft Press\Visual CSharp Step By Step\Chapter 5\WhileStatement folder in your Documents folder.

2. On the *Debug* menu, click *Start Without Debugging*.

   Visual Studio 2010 builds and runs the application. The application is a simple text file viewer that you can use to select a text file and display its contents.

3. Click *Open File*.

The *Open* dialog box opens.

4. Move to the \Microsoft Press\Visual CSharp Step By Step\Chapter 5\WhileStatement\ WhileStatement folder in your Documents folder.

5. Select the file MainWindow.xaml.cs, and then click *Open*.

The name of the file, MainWindow.xaml.cs, appears in the small text box on the form, but the contents of the file MainWindow.xaml.cs do not appear in the large text box. This is because you have not yet implemented the code that reads the contents of the file and displays it. You will add this functionality in the following steps.

6. Close the form and return to Visual Studio 2010.

7. Display the code for the file MainWindow.xaml.cs in the *Code and Text Editor* window, and locate the *openFileDialogFileOk* method.

This method runs when the user clicks the *Open* button after selecting a file in the *Open* dialog box. The body of the method is currently implemented as follows:

```
private void openFileDialogFileOk(object sender, System.ComponentModel.
CancelEventArgs e)
{
    string fullPathname = openFileDialog.FileName;
    FileInfo src = new FileInfo(fullPathname);
    filename.Text = src.Name;

    // add while loop here
}
```

The first statement declares a *string* variable called *fullPathname* and initializes it to the *FileName* property of the *openFileDialog* object. This property contains the full name (including the folder) of the source file that the user selected in the *Open* dialog box.

> **Note** The *openFileDialog* object is an instance of the *OpenFileDialog* class. This class pro-vides methods that you can use to display the standard *Windows Open* dialog box, select a file, and retrieve the name and path of the selected file. This is one of a number of classes provided in the .NET Framework Class Library that you can use to perform common tasks that require the user to select a file. These classes are collectively known as the Common Dialog classes. You will learn more about them in Chapter 23, "Gathering User Input."

The second statement declares a *FileInfo* variable called *src* and initializes it to an object that represents the file selected in the *Open* dialog box. (*FileInfo* is a class provided by the Microsoft .NET Framework that you can use to manipulate files.)

The third statement assigns the *Name* property of the *src* variable to the *Text* property of the *filename* control. The *Name* property of the *src* variable holds the name of the file selected in the *Open* dialog box, but without the name of the folder. This statement displays the name of the file in the text box on the form.

8. Replace the *// add while loop here* comment with the following statement:

```
source.Text = "";
```

The *source* variable refers to the large text box on the form. Setting its *Text* property to the empty string ("") clears any text that is currently displayed in this text box.

9. Type the following statement after the line you just added to the *openFileDialogFileOk* method:

```
TextReader reader = src.OpenText();
```

This statement declares a *TextReader* variable called *reader. TextReader* is another class, provided by the .NET Framework, that you can use for reading streams of characters from sources such as files. It is located in the *System.IO* namespace. The *FileInfo* class provides the *OpenText* method for opening a file for reading. This statement opens the file selected by the user in the *Open* dialog box so that the *reader* variable can read the contents of this file.

10. Add the following statement after the previous line you added to the *openFileDialogFileOk* method:

```
string line = reader.ReadLine();
```

This statement declares a *string* variable called *line* and calls the *reader.ReadLine* method to read the first line from the file into this variable. This method returns either the next line of text or a special value called *null* if there are no more lines to read. (If there are no lines initially, the file must be empty.)

11. Add the following statements to the *openFileDialogFileOk* method after the code you have just entered:

```
while (line != null)
{
    source.Text += line + '\n';
    line = reader.ReadLine();
}
```

This is a *while* loop that iterates through the file one line at a time until there are no more lines available.

The Boolean expression at the start of the *while* loop examines the value in the *line* variable. If it is not null, the body of the loop displays the current line of text by appending it to the *Text* property of the *source* text box, together with a newline character ('\n'—the *ReadLine* method of the *TextReader* object strips out the newline characters as it reads each line, so the code needs to add it back in again). The *while* loop then reads in the next line of text before performing the next iteration. The *while* loop finishes when there is no more text in the file and the *ReadLine* method returns a null value.

12. Add the following statement after the closing brace at the end of the *while* loop:

```
reader.Close();
```

This statement closes the file. It is good practice to close any files that you are using when you have finished with them; it enables other applications to use the file and also frees up any memory and other resources required to read the file.

13. On the *Debug* menu, click *Start Without Debugging*.

14. When the form appears, click *Open File*.

15. In the *Open File* dialog box, move to the \Microsoft Press\Visual CSharp Step By Step\ Chapter 5\WhileStatement\WhileStatement folder in your Documents folder. Select the file MainWindow.xaml.cs, and then click *Open*.

This time the contents of the selected file appear in the text box—you should recognize the code that you have just been editing:

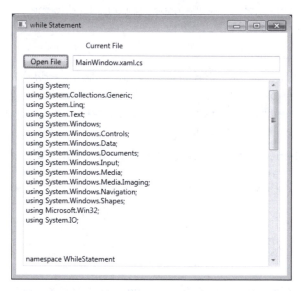

16. Scroll through the text in the text box, and find the *openFileDialogFileOk* method. Verify that this method contains the code you just added.

17. Close the form and return to the Visual Studio 2010 programming environment.

Writing *for* Statements

Most *while* statements have the following general structure:

```
initialization
while (Boolean expression)
{
    statement
    update control variable
}
```

By using a *for* statement, you can write a more formal version of this kind of construct by combining the initialization, Boolean expression, and code that updates the control variable. You'll find the *for* statement useful because it is much harder to forget any one of the three parts. Here is the syntax of a *for* statement:

```
for (initialization; Boolean expression; update control variable)
    statement
```

You can rephrase the *while* loop shown earlier that displays the integers from 0 through 9 as the following *for* loop:

```
for (int i = 0; i < 10; i++)
{
    Console.WriteLine(i);
}
```

The initialization occurs once at the start of the loop. Then, if the Boolean expression evaluates to *true*, the statement runs. The control variable update occurs, and then the Boolean expression is reevaluated. If the condition is still *true*, the statement is executed again, the control variable is updated, the Boolean expression is evaluated again, and so on.

Notice that the initialization occurs only once, that the statement in the body of the loop always executes before the update occurs, and that the update occurs before the Boolean expression reevaluates.

You can omit any of the three parts of a *for* statement. If you omit the Boolean expression, it defaults to *true*. The following *for* statement runs forever:

```
for (int i = 0; ;i++)
{
    Console.WriteLine("somebody stop me!");
}
```

If you omit the initialization and update parts, you have a strangely spelled *while* loop:

```
int i = 0;
for (; i < 10; )
{
    Console.WriteLine(i);
    i++;
}
```

> **Note** The initialization, Boolean expression, and update control variable parts of a *for* statement must always be separated by semicolons, even when they are omitted.

If necessary, you can provide multiple initializations and multiple updates in a *for* loop. (You can have only one Boolean expression.) To achieve this, separate the various initializations and updates with commas, as shown in the following example:

```
for (int i = 0, j = 10; i <= j; i++, j--)
{
    ...
}
```

As a final example, here is the *while* loop from the preceding exercise recast as a *for* loop:

```
for (string line = reader.ReadLine(); line != null; line = reader.ReadLine())
{
    source.Text += line + '\n';
}
```

> **Tip** It's considered good style to use braces to explicitly delineate the statement block for the body of *if*, *while*, and *for* statements even when the block contains only one statement. By writing the block, you make it easier to add statements to the block at a later date. Without the block, to add another statement, you'd have to remember to add both the extra statement *and* the braces, and it's very easy to forget the braces.

Understanding *for* Statement Scope

You might have noticed that you can declare a variable in the initialization part of a *for* statement. That variable is scoped to the body of the *for* statement and disappears when the *for* statement finishes. This rule has two important consequences. First, you cannot use that variable after the *for* statement has ended because it's no longer in scope. Here's an example:

```
for (int i = 0; i < 10; i++)
{
    ...
}
Console.WriteLine(i); // compile-time error
```

Second, you can write next to each other two or more *for* statements that reuse the same variable name because each variable is in a different scope, as shown in the following code:

```
for (int i = 0; i < 10; i++)
{
    ...
}

for (int i = 0; i < 20; i += 2) // okay
{
    ...
}
```

Writing *do* Statements

The *while* and *for* statements both test their Boolean expression at the start of the loop. This means that if the expression evaluates to *false* on the first test, the body of the loop does not run, not even once. The *do* statement is different; its Boolean expression is evaluated after each iteration, so the body always executes at least once.

The syntax of the *do* statement is as follows (don't forget the final semicolon):

```
do
    statement
while (booleanExpression);
```

You must use a *statement* block if the body of the loop comprises more than one statement. Here's a version of the example that writes the values 0 through 9 to the console, this time constructed using a *do* statement:

```
int i = 0;
do
{
    Console.WriteLine(i);
    i++;
}
while (i < 10);
```

The *break* and *continue* Statements

In Chapter 4, you saw the *break* statement being used to jump out of a *switch* statement. You can also use a *break* statement to jump out of the body of an iteration statement. When you break out of a loop, the loop exits immediately and execution continues at the first statement after the loop. Neither the update nor the continuation condition of the loop is rerun.

In contrast, the *continue* statement causes the program to perform the next iteration of the loop immediately (after reevaluating the Boolean expression). Here's another version of the example that writes the values 0 through 9 to the console, this time using *break* and *continue* statements:

```
int i = 0;
while (true)
{
    Console.WriteLine("continue " + i);
    i++;
    if (i < 10)
        continue;
    else
        break;
}
```

This code is absolutely ghastly. Many programming guidelines recommend using *continue* cautiously or not at all because it is often associated with hard-to-understand code. The behavior of *continue* is also quite subtle. For example, if you execute a *continue* statement from inside a *for* statement, the update part runs before performing the next iteration of the loop.

In the following exercise, you will write a *do* statement to convert a positive decimal whole number to its string representation in octal notation. The program is based on the following algorithm, based on a well-known mathematical procedure:

```
store the decimal number in the variable dec
do the following
    divide dec by 8 and store the remainder
    set dec to the quotient from the previous step
while dec is not equal to zero
combine the values stored for the remainder for each calculation in reverse order
```

For example, suppose you want to convert the decimal number 999 to octal. You perform the following steps:

1. Divide 999 by 8. The quotient is 124 and the remainder is 7.

2. Divide 124 by 8. The quotient is 15 and the remainder is 4.

3. Divide 15 by 8. The quotient is 1 and the remainder is 7.

4. Divide 1 by 8. The quotient is 0 and the remainder is 1.

5. Combine the values calculated for the remainder at each step in reverse order. The result is 1747. This is the octal representation of the decimal value 999.

Write a *do* statement

1. Using Visual Studio 2010, open the DoStatement project, located in the \Microsoft Press\Visual CSharp Step By Step\Chapter 5\DoStatement folder in your Documents folder.

2. Display the WPF form *MainWindow.xaml* in the *Design View* window.

   The form contains a text box called *number* that the user can enter a decimal number into. When the user clicks the *Show Steps* button, the octal representation of the number entered is generated. The lower text box, called *steps*, shows the results of each stage of the calculation.

3. Display the code for MainWindow.xaml.cs in the *Code and Text Editor* window. Locate the *showStepsClick* method. This method runs when the user clicks the *Show Steps* button on the form. Currently it is empty.

4. Add the following statements shown in bold to the *showStepsClick* method:

```
private void showStepsClick(object sender, RoutedEventArgs e)
{
    int amount = int.Parse(number.Text);
    steps.Text = "";
    string current = "";
}
```

   The first statement converts the string value in the *Text* property of the *number* text box into an *int* by using the *Parse* method of the *int* type and stores it in a local variable called *amount*.

   The second statement clears the text displayed in the lower text box by setting its *Text* property to the empty string.

   The third statement declares a *string* variable called *current* and initializes it to the empty string. You use this string to store the digits generated at each iteration of the loop used to convert the decimal number to its octal representation.

5. Add the following *do* statement, shown in bold, to the *showStepsClick* method:

```
private void showStepsClick(object sender, RoutedEventArgs e)
{
    int amount = int.Parse(number.Text);
    steps.Text = "";
    string current = "";
    do
    {
        int nextDigit = amount % 8;
        amount /= 8;
        int digitCode = '0' + nextDigit;
        char digit = Convert.ToChar(digitCode);
```

```
            current = digit + current;
            steps.Text += current + "\n";

    }
    while (amount != 0);
}
```

The algorithm used repeatedly performs integer arithmetic to divide the *amount* variable by 8 and determine the remainder; the remainder after each successive division constitutes the next digit in the string being built. Eventually, when *amount* is reduced to 0, the loop finishes. Notice that the body must run at least once. This be-havior is exactly what is required because even the number 0 has one octal digit.

Look more closely at the code, and you will see that the first statement inside the *do* loop is this:

```
int nextDigit = amount % 8;
```

This statement declares an *int* variable called *nextDigit* and initializes it to the remainder after dividing the value in *amount* by 8. This will be a number somewhere between 0 and 7.

The next statement inside the *do* loop is

```
amount /= 8;
```

This is a compound assignment statement and is equivalent to writing amount = amount / 8;. If the value of *amount* is 999, the value of *amount* after this statement runs is 124.

The next statement is this:

```
int digitCode = '0' + nextDigit;
```

This statement requires a little explanation! Characters have a unique code accord-ing to the character set used by the operating system. In the character sets frequently used by the Microsoft Windows operating system, the code for character '0' has in-teger value 48. The code for character '1' is 49, the code for character '2' is 50, and so on up to the code for character '9', which has integer value 57. C# allows you to treat a character as an integer and perform arithmetic on it, but when you do so, C# uses the character's code as the value. So the expression '0' + nextDigit actually results in a value somewhere between 48 and 55 (remember that *nextDigit* will be between 0 and 7), corresponding to the code for the equivalent octal digit.

The fourth statement inside the *do* loop is

```
char digit = Convert.ToChar(digitCode);
```

This statement declares a *char* variable called *digit* and initializes it to the result of the *Convert.ToChar(digitCode)* method call. The *Convert.ToChar* method takes an integer holding a character code and returns the corresponding character. So, for example, if *digitCode* has the value 54, *Convert.ToChar(digitCode)* returns the character '6'.

To summarize, the first four statements in the *do* loop have determined the character representing the least-significant (rightmost) octal digit corresponding to the number the user typed in. The next task is to prepend this digit to the string being output, like this:

```
current = digit + current;
```

The next statement inside the *do* loop is this:

```
steps.Text += current + "\n";
```

This statement adds to the *Steps* text box the string containing the digits produced so far for the octal representation of the number. It also appends a newline character so that each stage of the conversion appears on a separate line in the text box.

Finally, the condition in the *while* clause at the end of the loop is evaluated:

```
while (amount != 0)
```

Because the value of *amount* is not yet 0, the loop performs another iteration.

In the final exercise, you will use the Visual Studio 2010 debugger to step through the previous *do* statement to help you understand how it works.

Step through the *do* statement

1. In the *Code and Text Editor* window displaying the MainWindow.xaml.cs file, move the cursor to the first statement of the *showStepsClick* method:

   ```
   int amount = int.Parse(number.Text);
   ```

2. Right-click anywhere in the first statement, and then click *Run To Cursor*.

3. When the form appears, type **999** in the upper text box and then click *Show Steps*.

   The program stops, and you are placed in Visual Studio 2010 debug mode. A yellow arrow in the left margin of the *Code and Text Editor* window indicates the current statement.

4. Display the *Debug* toolbar if it is not visible. (On the *View* menu, point to *Toolbars*, and then click *Debug*.)

5. If you are using Visual Studio 2010 Professional or Visual Studio 2010 Standard, on the *Debug* toolbar, click the *Breakpoints* drop-down arrow.

   If you are using Visual C# 2010 Express, on the *Debug* toolbar, click the *Output* drop-down arrow.

Note The *Breakpoints* or *Output* drop-down arrow is the rightmost icon in the *Debug* toolbar.

The menu shown in the following image appears:

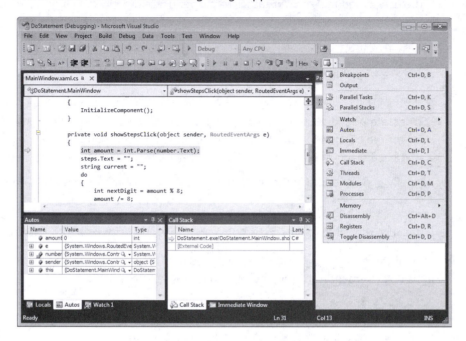

Note If you are using Microsoft Visual C# 2010 Express, the *Output* drop-down menu contains a subset of those shown in this image.

6. On the drop-down menu, click *Locals*.

The *Locals* window appears (if it wasn't already open). This window displays the name, value, and type of the local variables in the current method, including the *amount* local variable. Notice that the value of *amount* is currently 0:

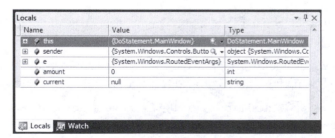

7. On the *Debug* toolbar, click the *Step Into* button.

The debugger runs the statement

```
int amount = int.Parse(number.Text);
```

The value of *amount* in the *Locals* window changes to 999, and the yellow arrow moves to the next statement.

8. Click *Step Into* again.

The debugger runs the statement

```
steps.Text = "";
```

This statement does not affect the *Locals* window because *steps* is a control on the form and not a local variable. The yellow arrow moves to the next statement.

9. Click *Step Into*.

The debugger runs the statement

```
string current = "";
```

The yellow arrow moves to the opening brace at the start of the *do* loop. The *do* loop contains three local variables of its own: *nextDigit*, *digitCode*, and *digit*. Notice that these local variables appear in the *Locals* window, and that the value of all three variables is 0.

10. Click *Step Into*.

The yellow arrow moves to the first statement inside the *do* loop.

11. Click *Step Into*.

The debugger runs the statement

```
int nextDigit = amount % 8;
```

The value of *nextDigit* in the *Locals* window changes to 7. This is the remainder after dividing 999 by 8.

12. Click *Step Into*.

The debugger runs the statement

```
amount /= 8;
```

The value of *amount* changes to 124 in the *Locals* window.

13. Click *Step Into*.

The debugger runs the statement

```
int digitCode = '0' + nextDigit;
```

The value of *digitCode* in the *Locals* window changes to 55. This is the character code of '7' (48 + 7).

14. Click *Step Into*.

The debugger runs the statement

```
char digit = Convert.ToChar(digitCode);
```

The value of *digit* changes to '7' in the *Locals* window. The *Locals* window shows *char* values using both the underlying numeric value (in this case, 55) and also the character representation ('7').

Note that in the *Locals* window, the value of the *current* variable is still "".

15. Click *Step Into*.

The debugger runs the statement

```
current = current + digit;
```

The value of *current* changes to "7" in the *Locals* window.

16. Click *Step Into*.

The debugger runs the statement

```
steps.Text += current + "\n";
```

This statement displays the text "7" in the *steps* text box, followed by a newline character to cause subsequent output to be displayed on the next line in the text box. (The form is currently hidden behind Visual Studio, so you won't be able to see it.) The cursor moves to the closing brace at the end of the *do* loop.

17. Click *Step Into*.

The yellow arrow moves to the *while* statement to evaluate whether the *do* loop has completed or whether it should continue for another iteration.

18. Click *Step Into*.

The debugger runs the statement

```
while (amount != 0);
```

The value of *amount* is 124, and the expression 124 != 0 evaluates to *true*, so the *do* loop performs another iteration. The yellow arrow jumps back to the opening brace at the start of the *do* loop.

19. Click *Step Into*.

The yellow arrow moves to the first statement inside the *do* loop again.

20. Repeatedly click *Step Into* to step through the next three iterations of the *do* loop, and watch how the values of the variables change in the *Locals* window.

21. At the end of the fourth iteration of the loop, the value of *amount* is now 0 and the value of *current* is "1747". The yellow arrow is on the *while* condition at the end of the *do* loop:

```
while (amount != 0);
```

The value of *amount* is now 0, so the expression amount != 0 evaluates to *false*, and the *do* loop should terminate.

22. Click *Step Into*.

The debugger runs the statement

```
while (amount != 0);
```

As predicted, the *do* loop terminates, and the yellow arrow moves to the closing brace at the end of the *showStepsClick* method.

23. Click the *Continue* button on the *Debug* toolbar.

The form appears, displaying the four steps used to create the octal representation of 999: 7, 47, 747, and 1747.

24. Close the form to return to the Visual Studio 2010 programming environment.

In this chapter, you learned how to use the compound assignment operators to update numeric variables. You saw how to use *while*, *for*, and *do* statements to execute code repeatedly while some Boolean condition is *true*.

- If you want to continue to the next chapter

    Keep Visual Studio 2010 running, and turn to Chapter 6.

- If you want to exit Visual Studio 2010 now

    On the *File* menu, click *Exit*. If you see a *Save* dialog box, click *Yes* and save the project.

Chapter 5 Quick Reference

To	Do this
Add an amount to a variable	Use the compound addition operator. For example: ```variable += amount;```
Subtract an amount from a variable	Use the compound subtraction operator. For example: ```variable -= amount;```

Run one or more statements zero or more times while a condition is true	Use a *while* statement. For example:
	
	```int i = 0;```
	```while (i < 10)```
	```{```
	``` Console.WriteLine(i);```
	``` i++;```
	```}```
	
	Alternatively, use a *for* statement. For example:
	
	```for (int i = 0; i < 10; i++)```
	```{```
	``` Console.WriteLine(i);```
	```}```

Repeatedly execute statements one or more times	Use a *do* statement. For example:
	
	```int i = 0;```
	```do```
	```{```
	``` Console.WriteLine(i);```
	``` i++;```
	```}```
	```while (i < 10);```

Chapter 6
Managing Errors and Exceptions

After completing this chapter, you will be able to:

- Handle exceptions by using the *try*, *catch*, and *finally* statements.

- Control integer overflow by using the *checked* and *unchecked* keywords.

- Raise exceptions from your own methods by using the *throw* keyword.

- Ensure that code always runs, even after an exception has occurred, by using a *finally* block.

You have now seen the core Microsoft Visual C# statements you need to know to write methods; declare variables; use operators to create values; write *if* and *switch* statements to run code selectively; and write *while*, *for*, and *do* statements to run code repeatedly. However, the previous chapters haven't considered the possibility (or probability) that things can go wrong. It is very difficult to ensure that a piece of code always works as expected. Failures can occur for a large number of reasons, many of which are beyond your control as a programmer. Any applications that you write must be capable of detecting failures and handling them in a graceful manner. In this final chapter of Part I, "Introducing Microsoft Visual C# and Microsoft Visual Studio 2010," you'll learn how C# uses exceptions to signal that an error has occurred and how to use the *try*, *catch*, and *finally* statements to catch and handle the errors that these exceptions represent. By the end of this chapter, you'll have a solid foundation in C#, on which you will build in Part II, "Understanding the C# Language."

Coping with Errors

It's a fact of life that bad things sometimes happen. Tires get punctured, batteries run down, screwdrivers are never where you left them, and users of your applications behave in an unpredictable manner. In the world of computers, disks fail, other applications running on the same computer as your program run amok and use up all the available memory, and networks disconnect at the most awkward moment. Errors can occur at almost any stage when a program runs, so how do you detect them and attempt to recover?

Over the years, a number of mechanisms have evolved. A typical approach adopted by older systems such as UNIX involved arranging for the operating system to set a special global variable whenever a method failed. Then, after each call to a method, you checked the global variable to see whether the method succeeded. C# and most other modern object-oriented languages don't handle errors in this way. It's just too painful. They use *exceptions* instead. If you want to write robust C# programs, you need to know about exceptions.

Trying Code and Catching Exceptions

Errors can happen at any time, and using traditional techniques to manually add error-detecting code around every statement is cumbersome, time consuming, and error prone in its own right. You can also lose sight of the main flow of an application if each statement requires contorted error-handling logic to manage each possible error that can occur at every stage. Fortunately, C# makes it easy to separate the error-handling code from the code that implements the main flow of the program by using exceptions and exception handlers. To write exception-aware programs, you need to do two things:

1. Write your code inside a *try* block (*try* is a C# keyword). When the code runs, it attempts to execute all the statements inside the *try* block, and if none of the statements generates an exception, they all run, one after the other, to completion. However, if an error condition occurs, execution jumps out of the *try* block and into another piece of code designed to catch and handle the exception—a *catch* handler.

2. Write one or more *catch* handlers (*catch* is another C# keyword) immediately after the *try* block to handle any possible error conditions. A *catch* handler is intended to catch and handle a specific type of exception, and you can have multiple *catch* handlers after a *try* block, each one designed to trap and process a specific exception so that you can provide different handlers for the different errors that could arise in the *try* block. If any one of the statements inside the *try* block causes an error, the runtime generates and throws an exception. The runtime then examines the *catch* handlers after the *try* block and transfers control directly to the first matching handler.

Here's an example of code in a *try* block that attempts to convert strings that a user has typed in some text boxes on a form to integer values, call a method to calculate a value, and write the result to another text box. Converting a string to an integer requires that the string contain a valid set of digits and not some arbitrary sequence of characters. If the string contains invalid characters, the *int.Parse* method automatically throws a *FormatException*, and execution transfers to the corresponding *catch* handler. When the *catch* handler finishes, the program continues with the first statement after the handler:

```
try
{
    int leftHandSide = int.Parse(lhsOperand.Text);
    int rightHandSide = int.Parse(rhsOperand.Text);
    int answer = doCalculation(leftHandSide, rightHandSide);
    result.Text = answer.ToString();
}
catch (FormatException fEx)
{
    // Handle the exception
    ...
}
```

A *catch* handler uses syntax similar to that used by a method parameter to specify the exception to be caught. In the preceding example, when a *FormatException* is thrown, the *fEx* variable is populated with an object containing the details of the exception. The *FormatException* type has a number of properties that you can examine to determine the exact cause of the exception. Many of these properties are common to all exceptions. For example, the *Message* property contains a text description of the error that caused the exception. You can use this information when handling the exception, perhaps recording the details to a log file or displaying a meaningful message to the user and then asking the user to try again.

Unhandled Exceptions

What happens if a *try* block throws an exception and there is no corresponding *catch* handler? In the previous example, it is possible that the *lhsOperand* text box contains the string representation of a valid integer but the integer it represents is outside the range of valid integers supported by C# (for example, "2147483648"). In this case, the *int.Parse* statement throws an *OverflowException*, which will not be caught by the *FormatException catch* handler. If this occurs, if the *try* block is part of a method, the method immediately exits and execution returns to the calling method. If the calling method uses a *try* block, the runtime attempts to locate a matching *catch* handler after the *try* block in the calling method and execute it. If the calling method does not use a *try* block or there is no matching *catch* handler, the calling method immediately exits and execution returns to its caller, where the process is repeated. If a matching *catch* handler is eventually found, the handler runs and execution continues with the first statement after the *catch* handler in the catching method.

> **Important** Notice that after catching an exception, execution continues in the method containing the *catch* block that caught the exception. If the exception occurred in a method other than the one containing the *catch* handler, control does *not* return to the method that caused the exception.

If, after cascading back through the list of calling methods, the runtime is unable to find a matching *catch* handler, the program terminates with an unhandled exception.

You can easily examine exceptions generated by your application. If you are running the application in Microsoft Visual Studio 2010 in debug mode (that is, you selected *Start Debugging* on the *Debug* menu to run the application) and an exception occurs, a dialog box similar to the one shown in the following image appears and the application pauses, helping you to determine the cause of the exception:

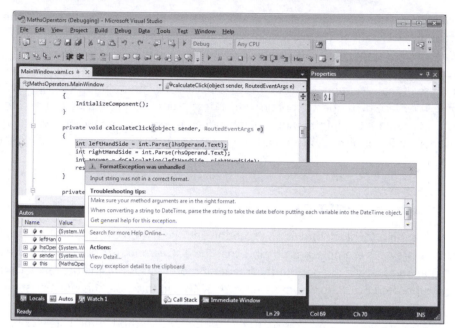

The application stops at the statement that caused the exception and you drop into the debugger. You can examine the values of variables, you can change the values of variables, and you can step through your code from the point at which the exception occurred by using the *Debug* toolbar and the various debug windows.

Using Multiple *catch* Handlers

The previous discussion highlighted how different errors throw different kinds of exceptions to represent different kinds of failures. To cope with these situations, you can supply multiple *catch* handlers, one after the other, like this:

```
try
{
    int leftHandSide = int.Parse(lhsOperand.Text);
    int rightHandSide = int.Parse(rhsOperand.Text);
    int answer = doCalculation(leftHandSide, rightHandSide);
    result.Text = answer.ToString();
}
catch (FormatException fEx)
{
    //...
}
catch (OverflowException oEx)
{
    //...
}
```

If the code in the *try* block throws a *FormatException* exception, the statements in the *catch* block for the *FormatException* exception runs. If the code throws an *OverflowException* exception, the *catch* block for the *OverflowException* exception runs.

> **Note** If the code in the *FormatException catch* block generates an *OverflowException* exception, it does not cause the adjacent *OverflowException* catch block to run. Instead, the exception propagates to the method that invoked this code, as described earlier in this section.

Catching Multiple Exceptions

The exception-catching mechanism provided by C# and the Microsoft .NET Framework is quite comprehensive. The .NET Framework defines many types of exceptions, and any programs you write can throw most of them! It is highly unlikely that you will want to write *catch* handlers for every possible exception that your code can throw. So how do you ensure that your programs catch and handle all possible exceptions?

The answer to this question lies in the way the different exceptions are related to one another. Exceptions are organized into families called inheritance hierarchies. (You will learn about inheritance in Chapter 12, "Working with Inheritance.") *FormatException* and *OverflowException* both belong to a family called *SystemException*, as do a number of other exceptions. *SystemException* is itself a member of a wider family simply called *Exception*, which is the great-granddaddy of all exceptions. If you catch *Exception*, the handler traps every possible exception that can occur.

> **Note** The *Exception* family includes a wide variety of exceptions, many of which are intended for use by various parts of the .NET Framework. Some of these are somewhat esoteric, but it is still useful to understand how to catch them.

The next example shows how to catch all possible exceptions:

```
try
{
    int leftHandSide = int.Parse(lhsOperand.Text);
    int rightHandSide = int.Parse(rhsOperand.Text);
    int answer = doCalculation(leftHandSide, rightHandSide);
    result.Text = answer.ToString();
}
catch (Exception ex) // this is a general catch handler
{
    //...
}
```

> **Tip** If you want to catch *Exception*, you can actually omit its name from the *catch* handler because it is the default exception:
>
> ```
> catch
> {
>     // ...
> }
> ```
>
> However, this is not always recommended. The exception object passed in to the *catch* handler can contain useful information concerning the exception, which is not accessible when using this version of the *catch* construct.

There is one final question you should be asking at this point: What happens if the same exception matches multiple *catch* handlers at the end of a *try* block? If you catch *FormatException* and *Exception* in two different handlers, which one will run (or will both execute)?

When an exception occurs, the first handler found by the runtime that matches the exception is used, and the others are ignored. What this means is that if you place a handler for *Exception* before a handler for *FormatException*, the *FormatException* handler will never run. Therefore, you should place more specific *catch* handlers above a general *catch* handler after a *try* block. If none of the specific *catch* handlers matches the exception, the general *catch* handler will.

In the following exercise, you will write a *try* block and catch an exception.

Write a *try/catch* statement block

1. Start Visual Studio 2010 if it is not already running.

2. Open the MathsOperators solution located in the \Microsoft Press\Visual CSharp Step By Step\Chapter 6\MathsOperators folder in your Documents folder.

   This is a variation on the program that you first saw in Chapter 2, "Working with Variables, Operators, and Expressions." It was used to demonstrate the different arithmetic operators.

3. On the *Debug* menu, click *Start Without Debugging*.

   The form appears. You are now going to enter some text that is deliberately not valid in the left operand text box. This operation will demonstrate the lack of robustness in the current version of the program.

4. Type **John** in the left operand text box, and then click *Calculate*.

This input triggers Windows error handling, and the following dialog box appears:

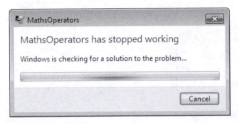

This is followed by another dialog box that reports an unhandled exception:

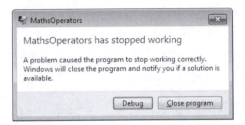

 Note If you are using Visual C# 2010 Express, the *Debug* button does not appear.

You might see a different version of this dialog box depending on how you have configured problem reporting in Control Panel.

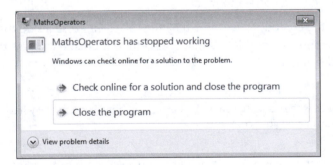

If this dialog box appears, click *Close the program* and continue with the second sentence of step 6 below.

Additionally, you might be presented with a dialog box displaying the message "Do you want to send information about the problem?" Windows can gather information about failing applications and send this information to Microsoft. If this dialog box appears, click *Cancel* and continue at the second sentence of step 6.

5. If you are using Visual Studio 2010 Professional or Visual Studio 2010 Standard, click *Debug*. In the *Visual Studio Just-In-Time Debugger* dialog box, in the *Possible Debuggers*

list box, select *MathsOperators – Microsoft Visual Studio: Visual Studio 2010* and then click *Yes*:

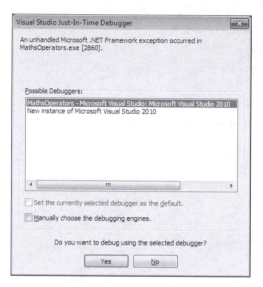

6. If you are using Visual C# 2010 Express, click *Close Program*. On the *Debug* menu, click *Start Debugging*. Type **John** in the left operand text box, and then click *Calculate*.

7. Visual Studio 2010 displays your code and highlights the statement that caused the exception together with a dialog box that describes the exception. In this case, it is "Input string was not in a correct format."

   You can see that the exception was thrown by the call to *int.Parse* inside the *calculateClick* method. The problem is that this method is unable to parse the text "John" into a valid number.

 Note You can view the code that caused an exception only if you actually have the source code available on your computer.

8. In the *Debug* toolbar, click the *Stop Debugging* button. The program terminates.

9. Display the code for the file MainWindow.xaml.cs in the *Code and Text Editor* window, and locate the *calculateClick* method.

10. Add a *try* block (including braces) around the four statements inside this method, as shown in bold type here:

```
try
{
    int leftHandSide = int.Parse(lhsOperand.Text);
    int rightHandSide = int.Parse(rhsOperand.Text);
    int answer = doCalculation(leftHandSide, rightHandSide);
    result.Text = answer.ToString();
}
```

11. Add a *catch* block immediately after the closing brace for this new *try* block, as follows:

```
catch (FormatException fEx)
{
    result.Text = fEx.Message;
}
```

This *catch* handler catches the *FormatException* thrown by *int.Parse* and then displays in the *result* text box at the bottom of the form the text in the exception's *Message* property.

12. On the *Debug* menu, click *Start Without Debugging*.

13. Type **John** in the left operand text box, and then click *Calculate*.

The *catch* handler successfully catches the *FormatException*, and the message "Input string was not in a correct format" is written to the *Result* text box. The application is now a bit more robust.

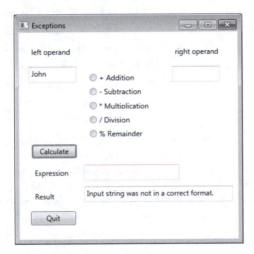

14. Replace John with the number **10**, type **Sharp** in the *right operand* text box, and then click *Calculate*.

The *try* block surrounds the statements that parse both text boxes, so the same exception handler handles user input errors in both text boxes.

15. Replace Sharp with **20** in the *right operand* text box, click the *Addition* button, and then click *Calculate*.

The application works as expected and displays the value 30 in the *Result* text box.

16. Click *Quit* to return to the Visual Studio 2010 programming environment.

Using Checked and Unchecked Integer Arithmetic

In Chapter 2, you learned how to use binary arithmetic operators such as + and * on primitive data types such as *int* and *double*. You also saw that the primitive data types have a fixed size. For example, a C# *int* is 32 bits. Because *int* has a fixed size, you know exactly the range of value that it can hold: it is –2147483648 to 2147483647.

> **Tip** If you want to refer to the minimum or maximum value of *int* in code, you can use the *int.MinValue* or *int.MaxValue* property.

The fixed size of the *int* type creates a problem. For example, what happens if you add 1 to an *int* whose value is currently 2147483647? The answer is that it depends on how the application is compiled. By default, the C# compiler generates code that allows the calculation to overflow silently and you get the wrong answer. (In fact, the calculation wraps around to the largest negative integer value, and the result generated is –2147483648.) The reason for this behavior is performance: integer arithmetic is a common operation in almost every program, and adding the overhead of overflow checking to each integer expression could lead to very poor performance. In many cases, the risk is acceptable because you know (or hope!) that your *int* values won't reach their limits. If you don't like this approach, you can turn on overflow checking.

> **Tip** You can activate and disable overflow checking in Visual Studio 2010 by setting the project properties. In Solution Explorer, click *YourProject* (where *YourProject* is the name of your project). On the *Project* menu, click *YourProject Properties*. In the project properties dialog box, click the *Build* tab. Click the *Advanced* button in the lower-right corner of the page. In the *Advanced Build Settings* dialog box, select or clear the *Check for arithmetic overflow/underflow* check box.

Regardless of how you compile an application, you can use the *checked* and *unchecked* keywords to turn on and off integer arithmetic overflow checking selectively in parts of an application that you think need it. These keywords override the compiler option specified for the project.

Writing Checked Statements

A checked statement is a block preceded by the *checked* keyword. All integer arithmetic in a checked statement always throws an *OverflowException* if an integer calculation in the block overflows, as shown in this example:

```
int number = int.MaxValue;
checked
{
    int willThrow = number++;
    Console.WriteLine("this won't be reached");
}
```

> **Important** Only integer arithmetic directly inside the *checked* block is subject to overflow checking. For example, if one of the checked statements is a method call, checking does not apply to code that runs in the method that is called.

You can also use the *unchecked* keyword to create an *unchecked* block statement. All integer arithmetic in an *unchecked* block is not checked and never throws an *OverflowException*. For example:

```
int number = int.MaxValue;
unchecked
{
    int wontThrow = number++;
    Console.WriteLine("this will be reached");
}
```

Writing Checked Expressions

You can also use the *checked* and *unchecked* keywords to control overflow checking on integer expressions by preceding just the individual parenthesized expression with the *checked* or *unchecked* keyword, as shown in this example:

```
int wontThrow = unchecked(int.MaxValue + 1);
int willThrow = checked(int.MaxValue + 1);
```

The compound operators (such as += and -=) and the increment, ++, and decrement, --, operators are arithmetic operators and can be controlled by using the *checked* and *unchecked* keywords. Remember, x += y; is the same as x = x + y;.

> **Important** You cannot use the *checked* and *unchecked* keywords to control floating-point (noninteger) arithmetic. The *checked* and *unchecked* keywords apply only to integer arithmetic using data types such as *int* and *long*. Floating-point arithmetic never throws *OverflowException*—not even when you divide by 0.0. (The .NET Framework has a representation for infinity.)

In the following exercise, you will see how to perform checked arithmetic when using Visual Studio 2010.

Use checked expressions

1. Return to Visual Studio 2010.

2. On the *Debug* menu, click *Start Without Debugging*.

    You will now attempt to multiply two large values.

3. Type **9876543** in the *left operand* text box, type **9876543** in the *right operand* text box, click the *Multiplication* button, and then click *Calculate*.

    The value –1195595903 appears in the *Result* text box on the form. This is a negative value, which cannot possibly be correct. This value is the result of a multiplication operation that silently overflowed the 32-bit limit of the *int* type.

4. Click *Quit*, and return to the Visual Studio 2010 programming environment.

5. In the *Code and Text Editor* window displaying MainWindow.xaml.cs, locate the *multiplyValues* method. It looks like this:

```
private int multiplyValues(int leftHandSide, int rightHandSide)
{
    expression.Text = leftHandSide.ToString() + " * " + rightHandSide.ToString();
    return leftHandSide * rightHandSide;
}
```

    The *return* statement contains the multiplication operation that is silently overflowing.

6. Edit the *return* statement so that the return value is checked, like this:

```
return checked(leftHandSide * rightHandSide);
```

    The multiplication is now checked and will throw an *OverflowException* rather than silently returning the wrong answer.

7. Locate the *calculateClick* method.

8. Add the following *catch* handler immediately after the existing *FormatException catch* handler in the *calculateClick* method:

```
catch (OverflowException oEx)
{
    result.Text = oEx.Message;
}
```

> **Tip** The logic of this *catch* handler is the same as that for the *FormatException catch* handler. However, it is still worth keeping these handlers separate rather than simply writing a generic *Exception catch* handler because you might decide to handle these exceptions differently in the future.

9. On the *Debug* menu, click *Start Without Debugging* to build and run the application.

10. Type **9876543** in the *left operand* text box, type **9876543** in the *right operand* text box, click the *Multiplication* button, and then click *Calculate*.

    The second *catch* handler successfully catches the *OverflowException* and displays the message "Arithmetic operation resulted in an overflow" in the *Result* text box.

11. Click *Quit* to return to the Visual Studio 2010 programming environment.

Throwing Exceptions

Suppose you are implementing a method called *monthName* that accepts a single *int* argument and returns the name of the corresponding month. For example, *monthName(1)* returns "January", *monthName(2)* returns "February", and so on. The question is: What should the method return if the integer argument is less than 1 or greater than 12? The best answer is that the method shouldn't return anything at all; it should throw an exception. The .NET Framework class libraries contain lots of exception classes specifically designed for situations such as this. Most of the time, you will find that one of these classes describes your exceptional condition. (If not, you can easily create your own exception class, but you need to know a bit more about the C# language before you can do that.) In this case, the existing .NET Framework *ArgumentOutOfRangeException* class is just right. You can throw an exception by using the *throw* statement, as shown in the following example:

```
public static string monthName(int month)
{
   switch (month)
   {
      case 1 :
          return "January";
      case 2 :
          return "February";
      ...
      case 12 :
          return "December";
      default :
          throw new ArgumentOutOfRangeException("Bad month");
   }
}
```

The *throw* statement needs an exception object to throw. This object contains the details of the exception, including any error messages. This example uses an expression that creates a new *ArgumentOutOfRangeException* object. The object is initialized with a string that populates its *Message* property by using a constructor. Constructors are covered in detail in Chapter 7, "Creating and Managing Classes and Objects."

In the following exercises, you will modify the MathsOperators project to throw an exception if the user attempts to perform a calculation without specifying an operation to perform.

Throw an exception

1. Return to Visual Studio 2010.

2. On the *Debug* menu, click *Start Without Debugging*.

3. Type **24** in the *left operand* text box, type **36** in the *right operand* text box, and then click *Calculate*.

   The value *0* appears in the *Result* text box. The fact that you have not selected an operator option is not immediately obvious. It would be useful to write a diagnostic message in the *Result* text box.

4. Click *Quit* to return to the Visual Studio 2010 programming environment.

5. In the *Code and Text Editor* window displaying MainWindow.xaml.cs, locate and examine the *doCalculation* method. It looks like this:

```
private int doCalculation(int leftHandSide, int rightHandSide) {
    int result = 0;

    if (addition.IsChecked.HasValue && addition.IsChecked.Value)
        result = addValues(leftHandSide, rightHandSide);
    else if (subtraction.IsChecked.HasValue && subtraction.IsChecked.Value)
        result = subtractValues(leftHandSide, rightHandSide);
    else if (multiplication.IsChecked.HasValue &&  multiplication.IsChecked.Value)
        result = multiplyValues(leftHandSide, rightHandSide);
    else if (division.IsChecked.HasValue && division.IsChecked.Value)
        result = divideValues(leftHandSide, rightHandSide);
    else if (remainder.IsChecked.HasValue && remainder.IsChecked.Value)
        result = remainderValues(leftHandSide, rightHandSide);

    return result;
}
```

The *addition*, *subtraction*, *multiplication*, *division*, and *remainder* fields are the buttons
that appear on the form. Each button has a property called *IsChecked* that indicates
whether the user has selected it. The *IsChecked* property is an example of a *nullable* value, which means it can either contain a specific value or be in an undefined state. (You
learn more about nullable values in Chapter 8, "Understanding Values and References.")
The *IsChecked.HasValue* property indicates whether the button is in a defined state,
and if it is, the *IsChecked.Value* property indicates what this state is. The *IsChecked.Value*
property is a Boolean that has the value *true* if the button is selected or *false* otherwise.
The cascading *if* statement examines each button in turn to find which one is selected.
(The radio buttons are mutually exclusive, so the user can select only one radio button
at most.) If none of the buttons are selected, none of the *if* statements will be true and
the *result* variable will remain at its initial value (0). This variable holds the value that is
returned by the method.

You could try to solve the problem by adding one more *else* statement to the *if-else*
cascade to write a message to the *result* text box on the form. However, this solution
is not a good idea because it is not really the purpose of this method to output messages. It is better to separate the detection and signaling of an error from the catching
and handling of that error.

6. Add another *else* statement to the list of *if-else* statements (immediately before the
return statement), and throw an *InvalidOperationException* exactly as follows:

```
else
    throw new InvalidOperationException("No operator selected");
```

7. On the *Debug* menu, click *Start Without Debugging* to build and run the application.

8. Type **24** in the *left operand* text box, type **36** in the *right operand* text box, and then
click *Calculate*.

Windows detects that your application has thrown an exception, and an exception dialog box appears (eventually). The application has thrown an exception, but your code does not catch it yet.

9. Click *Close program*.

The application terminates, and you return to Visual Studio 2010.

Now that you have written a *throw* statement and verified that it throws an exception, you will write a *catch* handler to handle this exception.

Catch the exception

1. In the *Code and Text Editor* window displaying MainWindow.xaml.cs, locate the *calculateClick* method.

2. Add the following *catch* handler immediately below the existing two *catch* handlers in the *calculateClick* method:

```
catch (InvalidOperationException ioEx)
{
    result.Text = ioEx.Message;
}
```

This code catches the *InvalidOperationException* that is thrown when no operator button is selected.

3. On the *Debug* menu, click *Start Without Debugging*.

4. Type **24** in the *left operand* text box, type **36** in the *right operand* text box, and then click *Calculate*.

The message "No operator selected" appears in the *Result* text box.

5. Click *Quit*.

The application is now a lot more robust than it was. However, several exceptions could still arise that are not caught and that will cause the application to fail. For example, if you attempt to divide by 0, an unhandled *DivideByZeroException* will be thrown. (Integer division by 0 does throw an exception, unlike floating-point division by 0.) One way to solve this is to write an ever larger number of *catch* handlers inside the *calculateClick* method. However, a better solution is to add a general *catch* handler that catches *Exception* at the end of the list of *catch* handlers. This will trap all unhandled exceptions.

> **Tip** The decision of whether to catch all unhandled exceptions explicitly in a method depends on the nature of the application you are building. In some cases, it makes sense to catch exceptions as close as possible to the point at which they occur. In other situations, it is more useful to let an exception propagate back to the method that invoked the routine that threw the exception and handle the error there.

Catch unhandled exceptions

1. In the *Code and Text Editor* window displaying MainWindow.xaml.cs, locate the *calculateClick* method.

2. Add the following *catch* handler to the end of the list of existing *catch* handlers:

```
catch (Exception ex)
{
    result.Text = ex.Message;
}
```

This *catch* handler will catch all hitherto unhandled exceptions, whatever their specific type.

3. On the *Debug* menu, click *Start Without Debugging*.

You will now attempt to perform some calculations known to cause exceptions and confirm that they are all handled correctly.

4. Type **24** in the *left operand* text box, type **36** in the *right operand* text box, and then click *Calculate*.

Confirm that the diagnostic message "No operator selected" still appears in the *Result* text box. This message was generated by the *InvalidOperationException* handler.

5. Type **John** in the *left operand* text box, and then click *Calculate*.

Confirm that the diagnostic message "Input string was not in a correct format" appears in the *Result* text box. This message was generated by the *FormatException* handler.

6. Type **24** in the *left operand* text box, type **0** in the *right operand* text box, click the *Division* button, and then click *Calculate*.

Confirm that the diagnostic message "Attempted to divide by zero" appears in the *Result* text box. This message was generated by the general *Exception* handler.

7. Click *Quit*.

Using a *finally* Block

It is important to remember that when an exception is thrown, it changes the flow of execution through the program. This means you can't guarantee that a statement will always run when the previous statement finishes because the previous statement might throw an exception. Look at the following example. It's very easy to assume that the call to *reader.Close* will always occur when the *while* loop completes. After all, it's right there in the code:

```
TextReader reader = src.OpenText();
string line;
while ((line = reader.ReadLine()) != null)
{
    source.Text += line + "\n";
}
reader.Close();
```

Sometimes it's not an issue if one particular statement does not run, but on many occasions it can be a big problem. If the statement releases a resource that was acquired in a previous statement, failing to execute this statement results in the resource being retained. This example is just such a case: If the call to *src.OpenText* succeeds, it acquires a resource (a file handle) and you must ensure that you call *reader.Close* to release the resource. If you don't, sooner or later you'll run out of file handles and be unable to open more files. (If you find file handles too trivial, think of database connections instead.)

The way to ensure that a statement is always run, whether or not an exception has been thrown, is to write that statement inside a *finally* block. A *finally* block occurs immediately after a *try* block or immediately after the last *catch* handler after a *try* block. As long as the program enters the *try* block associated with a *finally* block, the *finally* block will always be run, even if an exception occurs. If an exception is thrown and caught locally, the exception handler executes first, followed by the *finally* block. If the exception is not caught locally (that is, the runtime has to search through the list of calling methods to find a handler), the *finally* block runs first. In any case, the *finally* block always executes.

The solution to the *reader.Close* problem is as follows:

```
TextReader reader = null;
try
{
    reader = src.OpenText();
    string line;
    while ((line = reader.ReadLine()) != null)
    {
        source.Text += line + "\n";
    }
}
finally
{
    if (reader != null)
    {
        reader.Close();
    }
}
```

Even if an exception is thrown, the *finally* block ensures that the *reader.Close* statement always executes. You'll see another way to solve this problem in Chapter 14, "Using Garbage Collection and Resource Management."

In this chapter, you learned how to catch and handle exceptions by using the *try* and *catch* constructs. You saw how to enable and disable integer overflow checking by using the *checked* and *unchecked* keywords. You learned how to throw an exception if your code detects an exceptional situation, and you saw how to use a *finally* block to ensure that critical code always runs, even if an exception occurs.

- If you want to continue to the next chapter

  Keep Visual Studio 2010 running, and turn to Chapter 7.

- If you want to exit Visual Studio 2010 now

  On the *File* menu, click *Exit*. If you see a *Save* dialog box, click *Yes* and save the project.

Chapter 6 Quick Reference

To	Do this

Catch a specific exception	Write a *catch* handler that catches the specific exception class. For example:
	
	``
	try
	{
	    ...
	}
	catch (FormatException fEx)
	{
	    ...
	}
	``

Ensure that integer arithmetic is always checked for overflow	Use the *checked* keyword. For example:
	
	``
	int number = Int32.MaxValue;
	checked
	{
	    number++;
	}
	``

Throw an exception	Use a *throw* statement. For example:
	
	``
	throw new FormatException(source);
	``

Catch all exceptions in a single *catch* handler	Write a *catch* handler that catches *Exception*. For example:
	
	``
	try
	{
	    ...
	}
	catch (Exception ex)
	{
	    ...
	}
	``

Ensure that some code will always be run, even if an exception is thrown	Write the code inside a *finally* block. For example:
	
	``
	try
	{
	    ...
	}
	finally
	{
	    // always run
	}
	``

Part II
Understanding the C# Language

In this part:

Chapter 7
Creating and Managing Classes and Objects

After completing this chapter, you will be able to:

- Define a class containing a related set of methods and data items.

- Control the accessibility of members by using the *public* and *private* keywords.

- Create objects by using the *new* keyword to invoke a constructor.

- Write and call your own constructors.

- Create methods and data that can be shared by all instances of the same class by using the *static* keyword.

- Explain how to create anonymous classes.

In Part I, "Introducing Microsoft Visual C# and Microsoft Visual Studio 2010," you learned how to declare variables, use operators to create values, call methods, and write many of the statements you need when implementing a method. You now know enough to progress to the next stage—combining methods and data into your own classes.

The Microsoft .NET Framework contains thousands of classes, and you have used a number of them already, including *Console* and *Exception*. Classes provide a convenient mechanism for modeling the entities manipulated by applications. An *entity* can represent a specific item, such as a customer, or something more abstract, such as a transaction. Part of the design process of any system is concerned with determining the entities that are important to the processes that the system implements, and then performing an analysis to see what information these entities need to hold and what operations they should perform. You store the information that a class holds as fields and use methods to implement the operations that a class can perform.

The chapters in Part II, "Understanding the C# Language," provide you with all you need to know to be able to create your own classes.

Understanding Classification

Class is the root word of the term *classification*. When you design a class, you systematically arrange information and behavior into a meaningful entity. This arranging is an act of classification and is something that everyone does—not just programmers. For example, all cars share common behaviors (they can be steered, stopped, accelerated, and so on) and common attributes (they have a steering wheel, an engine, and so on). People use the word *car* to mean objects that share these common behaviors and attributes. As long as everyone agrees on what a word means, this system works well and you can express complex but precise ideas in a concise form. Without classification, it's hard to imagine how people could think or communicate at all.

Given that classification is so deeply ingrained in the way we think and communicate, it makes sense to try to write programs by classifying the different concepts inherent in a problem and its solution and then modeling these classes in a programming language. This is exactly what you can do with modern object-oriented programming languages, such as Microsoft Visual C#.

The Purpose of Encapsulation

Encapsulation is an important principle when defining classes. The idea is that a program that uses a class should not have to worry how that class actually works internally; the program simply creates an instance of a class and calls the methods of that class. As long as those methods do what they say they will do, the program does not care how they are implemented. For example, when you call the *Console.WriteLine* method, you don't want to be bothered with all the intricate details of how the *Console* class physically arranges for data to be written to the screen. A class might need to maintain all sorts of internal state information to perform its various methods. This additional state information and activity is hidden from the program that is using the class. Therefore, encapsulation is sometimes referred to as information hiding. Encapsulation actually has two purposes:

- To combine methods and data inside a class; in other words, to support classification

- To control the accessibility of the methods and data; in other words, to control the use of the class

Defining and Using a Class

In C#, you use the *class* keyword to define a new class. The data and methods of the class occur in the body of the class between a pair of braces. Here is a C# class called *Circle* that contains one method (to calculate the circle's area) and one piece of data (the circle's radius):

```
class Circle
{
    int radius;

    double Area()
    {
        return Math.PI * radius * radius;
    }
}
```

> **Note** The *Math* class contains methods for performing mathematical calculations and fields containing mathematical constants. The *Math.PI* field contains the value 3.14159265358979323846, which is an approximation of the value of pi.

The body of a class contains ordinary methods (such as *Area*) and fields (such as *radius*)—remember that variables in a class are called *fields*. You've already seen how to declare variables in Chapter 2, "Working with Variables, Operators, and Expressions," and how to write methods in Chapter 3, "Writing Methods and Applying Scope," so there's almost no new syntax here.

You can use the *Circle* class in a similar manner to using the other types that you have already met; you create a variable specifying *Circle* as its type, and then you initialize the variable with some valid data. Here is an example:

```
Circle c;          // Create a Circle variable
c = new Circle();  // Initialize it
```

A point worth highlighting in this code is the use of the *new* keyword. Previously, when you initialized a variable such as an *int* or a *float*, you simply assigned it a value:

```
int i;
i = 42;
```

You cannot do the same with variables of class types. One reason for this is that C# just doesn't provide the syntax for assigning literal class values to variables. You cannot write a statement such as this:

```
Circle c;
c = 42;
```

After all, what is the *Circle* equivalent of 42? Another reason concerns the way in which memory for variables of class types is allocated and managed by the runtime—this is discussed further in Chapter 8, "Understanding Values and References." For now, just accept that the *new* keyword creates a new instance of a class, more commonly called an *object*.

You can, however, directly assign an instance of a class to another variable of the same type, like this:

```
Circle c;
c = new Circle();
Circle d;
d = c;
```

However, this is not as straightforward as it first appears, for reasons that that are described in Chapter 8.

> **Important** Don't get confused between the terms *class* and *object*. A class is the definition of a type. An object is an instance of that type, created when the program runs.

Controlling Accessibility

Surprisingly, the *Circle* class is currently of no practical use. When you encapsulate your methods and data inside a class, the class forms a boundary to the outside world. Fields (such as *radius*) and methods (such as *Area*) defined in the class can be seen by other methods inside the class but not by the outside world—they are private to the class. So, although you can create a *Circle* object in a program, you cannot access its *radius* field or call its *Area* method, which is why the class is not of much use—yet! However, you can modify the definition of a field or method with the *public* and *private* keywords to control whether it is accessible from the outside:

- A method or field is private if it is accessible only from the inside of the class. To declare that a method or field is private, you write the keyword *private* before its declaration. This is actually the default, but it is good practice to state explicitly that fields and methods are private to avoid any confusion.

- A method or field is public if it is accessible from both the inside and outside of the class. To declare that a method or field is public, you write the keyword *public* before its declaration.

Here is the *Circle* class again. This time *Area* is declared as a public method and *radius* is declared as a private field:

```
class Circle
{
    private int radius;

    public double Area()
    {
        return Math.PI * radius * radius;
    }
}
```

> **Note** C++ programmers should note that there is no colon after the *public* and *private* keywords. You must repeat the keyword for every field and method declaration.

Although *radius* is declared as a private field and is not accessible from outside the class, *radius* is accessible from inside the *Circle* class. The *Area* method is inside the *Circle* class, so the body of *Area* has access to *radius*. However, the class is still of limited value because there is no way of initializing the *radius* field. To fix this, you can use a constructor.

> **Tip** Unlike variables declared in a method, which are not initialized by default, the fields in a class are automatically initialized to *0*, *false*, or *null* depending on their type. However, it is still good practice to provide an explicit means of initializing fields.

Naming and Accessibility

The following recommendations relate to the naming conventions for fields and methods based on the accessibility of class members:

- Identifiers that are *public* should start with a capital letter. For example, *Area* starts with "A" (not "a") because it's *public*. This system is known as the *PascalCase* naming scheme (because it was first used in the Pascal language).

- Identifiers that are not *public* (which include local variables) should start with a lowercase letter. For example, *radius* starts with "r" (not "R") because it's *private*. This system is known as the *camelCase* naming scheme.

There's only one exception to this rule: class names should start with a capital letter, and constructors must match the name of their class exactly; therefore, a *private* constructor must start with a capital letter.

> **Important** Don't declare two *public* class members whose names differ only in case. If you do, developers using other languages that are not case sensitive, such as Microsoft Visual Basic, will not be able to use your class.

Working with Constructors

When you use the *new* keyword to create an object, the runtime has to construct that object by using the definition of the class. The runtime has to grab a piece of memory from the operating system, fill it with the fields defined by the class, and then invoke a constructor to perform any initialization required.

A *constructor* is a special method that runs automatically when you create an instance of a class. It has the same name as the class, and it can take parameters, but it cannot return a value (not even *void*). Every class must have a constructor. If you don't write one, the compiler automatically generates a default constructor for you. (However, the compiler-generated default constructor doesn't actually do anything.) You can write your own default constructor quite easily—just add a public method with the same name as the class that does not return a value. The following example shows the *Circle* class with a default constructor that initializes the *radius* field to 0:

```
class Circle
{
    private int radius;

    public Circle()  // default constructor
    {
        radius = 0;
    }

    public double Area()
    {
        return Math.PI * radius * radius;
    }
}
```

 Note In C# parlance, the *default* constructor is a constructor that does not take any parameters. It does not matter whether the compiler generates it or you write it; it is still the default constructor. You can also write non–default constructors (constructors that *do* take parameters), as you will see in the upcoming section titled "Overloading Constructors."

In this example, the constructor is marked as *public*. If this keyword is omitted, the constructor will be private (just like any other methods and fields). If the constructor is private, it cannot be used outside the class, which prevents you from being able to create *Circle* objects from methods that are not part of the *Circle* class. You might therefore think that private constructors are not that valuable. However, they do have their uses, but they are beyond the scope of the current discussion.

You can now use the *Circle* class and exercise its *Area* method. Notice how you use dot notation to invoke the *Area* method on a *Circle* object:

```
Circle c;
c = new Circle();
double areaOfCircle = c.Area();
```

Overloading Constructors

You're almost finished, but not quite. You can now declare a *Circle* variable, point it to a newly created *Circle* object, and then call its *Area* method. However, there is still one last problem. The area of all *Circle* objects will always be 0 because the default constructor sets the radius to 0 and it stays at 0; the *radius* field is private, and there is no easy way of changing its value after it has been initialized. However, you should realize that a constructor is just a special kind of method and that it—like all methods—can be overloaded. Just as there are several versions of the *Console.WriteLine* method, each of which takes different parameters, so too you can write different versions of a constructor. You can add a constructor to the *Circle* class, with the radius as its parameter, like this:

```
class Circle
{
    private int radius;

    public Circle()  // default constructor
    {
        radius = 0;
    }

    public Circle(int initialRadius) // overloaded constructor
    {
        radius = initialRadius;
    }

    public double Area()
    {
        return Math.PI * radius * radius;
    }
}
```

> **Note** The order of the constructors in a class is immaterial; you can define constructors in whatever order you feel most comfortable with.

You can then use this constructor when creating a new *Circle* object, like this:

```
Circle c;
c = new Circle(45);
```

When you build the application, the compiler works out which constructor it should call based on the parameters that you specify to the *new* operator. In this example, you passed an *int*, so the compiler generates code that invokes the constructor that takes an *int* parameter.

You should be aware of a quirk of the C# language: if you write your own constructor for a class, the compiler does not generate a default constructor. Therefore, if you've written your own constructor that accepts one or more parameters and you also want a default constructor, you'll have to write the default constructor yourself.

Partial Classes

A class can contain a number of methods, fields, and constructors, as well as other items discussed in later chapters. A highly functional class can become quite large. With C#, you can split the source code for a class into separate files so that you can organize the definition of a large class into smaller, easier to manage pieces. This feature is used by Microsoft Visual Studio 2010 for Windows Presentation Foundation (WPF) applications, where the source code that the developer can edit is maintained in a separate file from the code that is generated by Visual Studio whenever the layout of a form changes.

When you split a class across multiple files, you define the parts of the class by using the *partial* keyword in each file. For example, if the *Circle* class is split between two files called circ1.cs (containing the constructors) and circ2.cs (containing the methods and fields), the contents of circ1.cs look like this:

```
partial class Circle
{
    public Circle()  // default constructor
    {
        this.radius = 0;
    }

    public Circle(int initialRadius) // overloaded constructor
    {
        this.radius = initialRadius;
    }
}
```

The contents of circ2.cs look like this:

```
partial class Circle
{
    private int radius;

    public double Area()
    {
        return Math.PI * this.radius * this.radius;
    }
}
```

When you compile a class that has been split into separate files, you must provide all the files to the compiler.

> **Note** You can define partial interfaces and structs in the same way.

In the following exercise, you will declare a class that models a point in two-dimensional space. The class will contain two private fields for holding the *x* and *y* coordinates of a point and will provide constructors for initializing these fields. You will create instances of the class by using the *new* keyword and calling the constructors.

Write constructors and create objects

1. Start Visual Studio 2010 if it is not already running.

2. Open the Classes project located in the \Microsoft Press\Visual CSharp Step By Step\ Chapter 7\Classes folder in your Documents folder.

3. In *Solution Explorer*, double-click the file Program.cs to display it in the *Code and Text Editor* window.

4. Locate the *Main* method in the *Program* class.

   The *Main* method calls the *DoWork* method, wrapped in a *try* block and followed by a *catch* handler. With this *try/catch* block, you can write the code that would typically go inside *Main* in the *DoWork* method instead, safe in the knowledge that it will catch and handle any exceptions.

5. Display the file Point.cs in the *Code and Text Editor* window.

   This file defines a class called *Point*, which you will use to represent the location of a point defined by a pair of *x* and *y* coordinates. The *Point* class is currently empty.

6. Return to the Program.cs file, and locate the *DoWork* method of the *Program* class. Edit the body of the *DoWork* method, and replace the // to do comment with the following statement:

   ```
   Point origin = new Point();
   ```

7. On the *Build* menu, click *Build Solution*.

   The code builds without error because the compiler automatically generates the code for a default constructor for the *Point* class. However, you cannot see the C# code for this constructor because the compiler does not generate any source language statements.

8. Return to the *Point* class in the file Point.cs. Replace the // to do comment with a *public* constructor that accepts two *int* arguments called *x* and *y* and that calls the *Console.WriteLine* method to display the values of these arguments to the console, as shown in bold type in the following code example. The *Point* class should look like this:

   ```
   class Point
   {
       public Point(int x, int y)
       {
           Console.WriteLine("x:{0}, y:{1}", x, y);
       }
   }
   ```

> **Note** Remember that the *Console.WriteLine* method uses *{0}* and *{1}* as placeholders. In the statement shown, *{0}* will be replaced with the value of *x*, and *{1}* will be replaced with the value of *y* when the program runs.

9. On the *Build* menu, click *Build Solution*.

The compiler now reports an error:

```
'Classes.Point' does not contain a constructor that takes '0 ' arguments
```

The call to the default constructor in *DoWork* no longer works because there is no longer a default constructor. You have written your own constructor for the *Point* class, so the compiler no longer generates the default constructor. You will now fix this by writing your own default constructor.

10. Edit the *Point* class, and add a *public* default constructor that calls *Console.WriteLine* to write the string *"default constructor called"* to the console, as shown in bold type in the following code example. The *Point* class should now look like this:

```
class Point
{
    public Point()
    {
        Console.WriteLine("Default constructor called");
    }

    public Point(int x, int y)
    {
        Console.WriteLine("x:{0}, y:{1}", x, y);
    }
}
```

11. On the *Build* menu, click *Build Solution*.

The program should now build successfully.

12. In the Program.cs file, edit the body of the *DoWork* method. Declare a variable called *bottomRight* of type *Point*, and initialize it to a new *Point* object by using the constructor with two arguments, as shown in bold type in the following code. Supply the values 1024 and 1280, representing the coordinates at the lower-right corner of the screen based on the resolution 1024 × 1280. The *DoWork* method should now look like this:

```
static void DoWork()
{
    Point origin = new Point();
    Point bottomRight = new Point(1024, 1280);
}
```

13. On the *Debug* menu, click *Start Without Debugging*.

    The program builds and runs, displaying the following messages to the console:

    ```
    Default constructor called
    x:1024, y:1280
    ```

14. Press the Enter key to end the program and return to Visual Studio 2010.

    You will now add two *int* fields to the *Point* class to represent the *x* and *y* coordinates of a point, and you will modify the constructors to initialize these fields.

15. Edit the *Point* class in the Point.cs file, and add two *private* instance fields called *x* and *y* of type *int*, as shown in bold type in the following code. The *Point* class should now look like this:

    ```
    class Point
    {
        private int x, y;

        public Point()
        {
            Console.WriteLine("default constructor called");
        }

        public Point(int x, int y)
        {
            Console.WriteLine("x:{0}, y:{1}", x, y);
        }
    }
    ```

    You will now edit the second *Point* constructor to initialize the *x* and *y* fields to the values of the *x* and *y* parameters. There is a potential trap when you do this. If you are not careful, the constructor will look like this:

    ```
    public Point(int x, int y) // Don't type this!
    {
        x = x;
        y = y;
    }
    ```

    Although this code will compile, these statements appear to be ambiguous. How does the compiler know in the statement x = x; that the first *x* is the field and the second *x* is the parameter? The answer is that it doesn't! A method parameter with the same name as a field hides the field for all statements in the method. All this code actually does is assign the parameters to themselves; it does not modify the fields at all. This is clearly not what you want.

    The solution is to use the *this* keyword to qualify which variables are parameters and which are fields. Prefixing a variable with *this* means "the field in this object."

16. Modify the *Point* constructor that takes two parameters, and replace the *Console.WriteLine* statement with the following code shown in bold type:

```
public Point(int x, int y)
{
    this.x = x;
    this.y = y;
}
```

17. Edit the default *Point* constructor to initialize the *x* and *y* fields to –1, as follows in bold type. Note that although there are no parameters to cause confusion, it is still good practice to qualify the field references with *this*:

```
public Point()
{
    this.x = -1;
    this.y = -1;
}
```

18. On the *Build* menu, click *Build Solution*. Confirm that the code compiles without errors or warnings. (You can run it, but it does not produce any output yet.)

Methods that belong to a class and that operate on the data belonging to a particular instance of a class are called *instance methods*. (There are other types of methods that you will meet later in this chapter.) In the following exercise, you will write an instance method for the *Point* class, called *DistanceTo*, that calculates the distance between two points.

Write and call instance methods

1. In the Classes project in Visual Studio 2010, add the following public instance method called *DistanceTo* to the *Point* class after the constructors. The method accepts a single *Point* argument called *other* and returns a *double*.

   The *DistanceTo* method should look like this:

```
class Point
{
    ...

    public double DistanceTo(Point other)
    {
    }
}
```

   In the following steps, you will add code to the body of the *DistanceTo* instance method to calculate and return the distance between the *Point* object being used to make the call and the *Point* object passed as a parameter. To do this, you must calculate the difference between the *x* coordinates and the *y* coordinates.

2. In the *DistanceTo* method, declare a local *int* variable called *xDiff*, and initialize it to the difference between *this.x* and *other.x*, as shown here in bold type:

```
public double DistanceTo(Point other)
{
    int xDiff = this.x - other.x;
}
```

3. Declare another local *int* variable called *yDiff*, and initialize it to the difference between *this.y* and *other.y*, as shown here in bold type:

```
public double DistanceTo(Point other)
{
    int xDiff = this.x - other.x;
    int yDiff = this.y - other.y;
}
```

To calculate the distance, you can use the Pythagorean theorem and calculate the square root of the sum of the square of *xDiff* and the square of *yDiff*. The *System.Math* class provides the *Sqrt* method that you can use to calculate square roots.

4. Add the *return* statement shown in bold type in the following code to the end of the *DistanceTo* method to perform the calculation:

```
public double DistanceTo(Point other)
{
    int xDiff = this.x - other.x;
    int yDiff = this.y - other.y;
    return Math.Sqrt((xDiff * xDiff) + (yDiff * yDiff));
}
```

You will now test the *DistanceTo* method.

5. Return to the *DoWork* method in the *Program* class. After the statements that declare and initialize the *origin* and *bottomRight Point* variables, declare a variable called *distance* of type *double*. Initialize this *double* variable to the result obtained when you call the *DistanceTo* method on the *origin* object, passing the *bottomRight* object to it as an argument.

The *DoWork* method should now look like this:

```
static void DoWork()
{
    Point origin = new Point();
    Point bottomRight = new Point(1024, 1280);
    double distance = origin.DistanceTo(bottomRight);
}
```

Note Microsoft IntelliSense should display the *DistanceTo* method when you type the period character after *origin*.

6. Add to the *DoWork* method another statement that writes the value of the *distance* variable to the console by using the *Console.WriteLine* method.

The completed *DoWork* method should look like this:

```
static void DoWork()
{
    Point origin = new Point();
    Point bottomRight = new Point(1024, 1280);
    double distance = origin.DistanceTo(bottomRight);
    Console.WriteLine("Distance is: {0}", distance);
}
```

7. On the *Debug* menu, click *Start Without Debugging*.

8. Confirm that the value 1640.60537607311 is written to the console window.

9. Press Enter to close the application and return to Visual Studio 2010.

Understanding *static* Methods and Data

In the preceding exercise, you used the *Sqrt* method of the *Math* class; similarly, when looking at the *Circle* class, you read the *PI* field of the *Math* class. If you think about it, the way in which you called the *Sqrt* method or read the *PI* field was slightly odd. You invoked the method or read the field on the class itself, not on an object of type *Math*. It is like trying to write *Point.DistanceTo* rather than *origin.DistanceTo* in the code you added in the preceding exercise. So what's happening, and how does this work?

You will often find that not all methods naturally belong to an instance of a class; they are utility methods inasmuch as they provide a useful function that is independent of any specific class instance. The *Sqrt* method is just such an example. If *Sqrt* were an instance method of *Math*, you'd have to create a *Math* object to call *Sqrt* on:

```
Math m = new Math();
double d = m.Sqrt(42.24);
```

This would be cumbersome. The *Math* object would play no part in the calculation of the square root. All the input data that *Sqrt* needs is provided in the parameter list, and the result is passed back to the caller by using the method's return value. Objects are not really needed here, so forcing *Sqrt* into an instance straitjacket is just not a good idea. As well as containing the *Sqrt* method and the *PI* field, the *Math* class contains many other mathematical utility methods, such as *Sin*, *Cos*, *Tan*, and *Log*.

In C#, all methods must be declared inside a class. However, if you declare a method or a field as *static*, you can call the method or access the field by using the name of the class. No instance is required. This is how the *Sqrt* method of the real *Math* class is declared:

```
class Math
{
    public static double Sqrt(double d)
    {
        ...
    }
    ...
}
```

When you define a *static* method, it does not have access to any instance fields defined for the class; it can use only fields that are marked as *static*. Furthermore, it can directly invoke only other methods in the class that are marked as *static*; nonstatic (instance) methods require you first to create an object on which to call them.

Creating a Shared Field

As mentioned in the preceding section, you can also use the *static* keyword when defining a field. With this feature, you can create a single field that is shared among all objects created from a single class. (Nonstatic fields are local to each instance of an object.) In the following example, the *static* field *NumCircles* in the *Circle* class is incremented by the *Circle* constructor every time a new *Circle* object is created:

```
class Circle
{
    private int radius;
    public static int NumCircles = 0;

    public Circle()  // default constructor
    {
        radius = 0;
        NumCircles++;
    }

    public Circle(int initialRadius) // overloaded constructor
    {
        radius = initialRadius;
        NumCircles++;
    }
}
```

All *Circle* objects share the same *NumCircles* field, so the statement *NumCircles++;* increments the same data every time a new instance is created. You access the *NumCircles* field by specifying the *Circle* class rather than a *Circle* object. For example:

```
Console.WriteLine("Number of Circle objects: {0}", Circle.NumCircles);
```

> **Tip** Keep in mind that *static* methods are also called *class* methods. However, *static* fields aren't usually called *class* fields; they're just called *static* fields (or sometimes *static* variables).

Creating a *static* Field by Using the *const* Keyword

By prefixing the field with the *const* keyword, you can declare that a field is static but that its value can never change. *const* is short for "constant." A *const* field does not use the *static* keyword in its declaration but is nevertheless static. However, for reasons that are beyond the scope of this book, you can declare a field as *const* only when the field is an enumeration, a numeric type such as *int* or *double*, or a string. (You learn about enumerations in Chapter 9, "Creating Value Types with Enumerations and Structures.") For example, here's how the *Math* class declares *PI* as a *const* field:

```
class Math
{
    ...
    public const double PI = 3.14159265358979323846;
}
```

Static Classes

Another feature of the C# language is the ability to declare a class as *static*. A *static* class can contain only *static* members. (All objects that you create using the class share a single copy of these members.) The purpose of a *static* class is purely to act as a holder of utility methods and fields. A *static* class cannot contain any instance data or methods, and it does not make sense to try to create an object from a *static* class by using the *new* operator. In fact, you can't actually create an instance of an object using a *static* class by using *new* even if you want to. (The compiler will report an error if you try.) If you need to perform any initialization, a *static* class can have a default constructor as long as it is also declared as *static*. Any other types of constructor are illegal and will be reported as such by the compiler.

If you were defining your own version of the *Math* class, one containing only *static* members, it could look like this:

```
public static class Math
{
    public static double Sin(double x) {...}
    public static double Cos(double x) {...}
    public static double Sqrt(double x) {...}
    ...
}
```

Note The real *Math* class is not defined this way because it actually does have some instance methods.

In the final exercise in this chapter, you will add a *private static* field to the *Point* class and initialize the field to 0. You will increment this count in both constructors. Finally, you will write a *public static* method to return the value of this *private static* field. With this field, you can find out how many *Point* objects have been created.

Write *static* members, and call *static* methods

1. Using Visual Studio 2010, display the *Point* class in the *Code and Text Editor* window.

2. Add a *private static* field called *objectCount* of type *int* to the *Point* class, before the constructors. Initialize it to 0 as you declare it, like this:

```
class Point
{
    ...
    private static int objectCount = 0;
    ...
}
```

Note You can write the keywords *private* and *static* in any order. The preferred order is *private* first, *static* second.

3. Add a statement to both *Point* constructors to increment the *objectCount* field, as shown in bold type in the following code example.

Each time an object is created, its constructor is called. As long as you increment the *objectCount* in each constructor (including the default constructor), *objectCount* will hold the number of objects created so far. This strategy works only because *objectCount* is a shared *static* field. If *objectCount* were an instance field, each object would have its own personal *objectCount* field that would be set to 1.

The *Point* class should now look like this:

```
class Point
{
    private int x, y;
    private static int objectCount = 0;

    public Point()
    {
        this.x = -1;
        this.y = -1;
        objectCount++;
    }

    public Point(int x, int y)
    {
        this.x = x;
        this.y = y;
        objectCount++;
    }


    public double DistanceTo(Point other)
    {
        int xDiff = this.x - other.x;
        int yDiff = this.y - other.y;
        return Math.Sqrt((xDiff * xDiff) + (yDiff * yDiff));
    }
}
```

Notice that you cannot prefix *static* fields and methods with the *this* keyword because they do not belong to the current instance of the class. (They do not actually belong to any instance.)

The question now is this: How can users of the *Point* class find out how many *Point* objects have been created? At the moment, the *objectCount* field is *private* and not available outside the class. A poor solution would be to make the *objectCount* field publicly accessible. This strategy would break the encapsulation of the class; you would then have no guarantee that its value was correct because anyone could change the value in the field. A much better idea is to provide a *public static* method that returns the value of the *objectCount* field. This is what you will do now.

4. Add a *public static* method to the *Point* class called *ObjectCount* that returns an *int* but does not take any parameters. In this method, return the value of the *objectCount* field, as follows in bold type:

```
class Point
{
    ...
    public static int ObjectCount()
    {
        return objectCount;
    }
}
```

5. Display the *Program* class in the *Code and Text Editor* window, and locate the *DoWork* method.

6. Add a statement to the *DoWork* method to write the value returned from the *ObjectCount* method of the *Point* class to the screen, as shown in bold type in the following code example. The *DoWork* method should look like this:

```
static void DoWork()
{
    Point origin = new Point();
    Point bottomRight = new Point(600, 800);
    double distance = origin.distanceTo(bottomRight);
    Console.WriteLine("Distance is: {0}", distance);
    Console.WriteLine("No of Point objects: {0}", Point.ObjectCount());
}
```

The *ObjectCount* method is called by referencing *Point*, the name of the class, and not the name of a *Point* variable (such as *origin* or *bottomRight*). Because two *Point* objects have been created by the time *ObjectCount* is called, the method should return the value 2.

7. On the *Debug* menu, click *Start Without Debugging*.

Confirm that the value 2 is written to the console window (after the message displaying the value of the *distance* variable).

8. Press Enter to finish the program and return to Visual Studio 2010.

Anonymous Classes

An *anonymous class* is a class that does not have a name. This sounds rather strange but is actually quite handy in some situations that you will see later in this book, especially when using query expressions. (You learn about query expressions in Chapter 20, "Querying In-Memory Data by Using Query Expressions.") For the time being, just accept the fact that they are useful.

You create an anonymous class simply by using the *new* keyword and a pair of braces defining the fields and values that you want the class to contain, like this:

```
myAnonymousObject = new { Name = "John", Age = 44 };
```

This class contains two public fields called *Name* (initialized to the string *"John"*) and *Age* (initialized to the integer *44*). The compiler infers the types of the fields from the types of the data you specify to initialize them.

When you define an anonymous class, the compiler generates its own name for the class, but it won't tell you what it is. Anonymous classes therefore raise a potentially interesting conundrum: If you don't know the name of the class, how can you create an object of the appropriate type and assign an instance of the class to it? In the code example shown earlier, what should the type of the variable *myAnonymousObject* be? The answer is that you don't know—that is the point of anonymous classes! However, this is not a problem if you declare *myAnonymousObject* as an implicitly typed variable by using the *var* keyword, like this:

```
var myAnonymousObject = new { Name = "John", Age = 44 };
```

Remember that the *var* keyword causes the compiler to create a variable of the same type as the expression used to initialize it. In this case, the type of the expression is whatever name the compiler happens to generate for the anonymous class.

You can access the fields in the object by using the familiar dot notation, like this:

```
Console.WriteLine("Name: {0} Age: {1}", myAnonymousObject.Name, myAnonymousObject.Age};
```

You can even create other instances of the same anonymous class but with different values:

```
var anotherAnonymousObject = new { Name = "Diana", Age = 45 };
```

The C# compiler uses the names, types, number, and order of the fields to determine whether two instances of an anonymous class have the same type. In this case, variables *myAnonymousObject* and *anotherAnonymousObject* have the same number of fields, with the same name and type, in the same order, so both variables are instances of the same anonymous class. This means that you can perform assignment statements such as this:

```
anotherAnonymousObject = myAnonymousObject;
```

> **Note** Be warned that this assignment statement might not accomplish what you expect. You'll learn more about assigning object variables in Chapter 8.

There are quite a lot of restrictions on the contents of an anonymous class. Anonymous classes can contain only public fields, the fields must all be initialized, they cannot be static, and you cannot specify any methods.

In this chapter, you saw how to define new classes. You learned that by default the fields and methods of a class are private and inaccessible to code outside of the class, but that you can use the *public* keyword to expose fields and methods to the outside world. You saw how to use the *new* keyword to create a new instance of a class, and how to define constructors that can initialize class instances. Finally, you saw how to implement static fields and methods to provide data and operations that are independent of any specific instance of a class.

- If you want to continue to the next chapter

  Keep Visual Studio 2010 running, and turn to Chapter 8.

- If you want to exit Visual Studio 2010 now

  On the *File* menu, click *Exit*. If you see a *Save* dialog box, click *Yes* and save the project.

Chapter 7 Quick Reference

To	Do this
Declare a class	Write the keyword *class*, followed by the name of the class, followed by an opening and closing brace. The methods and fields of the class are declared between the opening and closing braces. For example: ```csharp\nclass Point\n{\n ...\n}\n```
Declare a constructor	Write a method whose name is the same as the name of the class and that has no return type (not even *void*). For example: ```csharp\nclass Point\n{\n public Point(int x, int y)\n {\n ...\n }\n}\n```
Call a constructor	Use the *new* keyword, and specify the constructor with an appropriate set of parameters. For example: ```csharp\nPoint origin = new Point(0, 0);\n```
Declare a *static* method	Write the keyword *static* before the declaration of the method. For example: ```csharp\nclass Point\n{\n public static int ObjectCount()\n {\n ...\n }\n}\n```
Call a *static* method	Write the name of the class, followed by a period, followed by the name of the method. For example: ```csharp\nint pointsCreatedSoFar = Point.ObjectCount();\n```
Declare a *static* field	Write the keyword *static* before the declaration of the field. For example: ```csharp\nclass Point\n{\n ...\n private static int objectCount;\n}\n```

To	Do this
Declare a *const* field	Write the keyword *const* before the declaration of the field, and omit the *static* keyword. For example:
| | ```
class Math
{
    ...
    public const double PI = ...;
}
``` |
| Access a *static* field | Write the name of the class, followed by a period, followed by the name of the *static* field. For example: |
| | ```
double area = Math.PI * radius * radius;
``` |

Chapter 8

Understanding Values and References

After completing this chapter, you will be able to:

■ Explain the differences between a value type and a reference type.

■ Modify the way in which arguments are passed as method parameters by using the *ref* and *out* keywords.

■ Box a value by initializing or assigning a variable of type *object*.

■ Unbox a value by casting the object reference that refers to the boxed value.

In Chapter 7, "Creating and Managing Classes and Objects," you learned how to declare your own classes and how to create objects by using the *new* keyword. You also saw how to initialize an object by using a constructor. In this chapter, you will learn about how the characteristics of the primitive types—such as *int*, *double*, and *char*—differ from the characteristics of class types.

Copying Value Type Variables and Classes

Collectively, types such as *int*, *float*, *double*, and *char* are called *value types*. When you declare a variable as a value type, the compiler generates code that allocates a block of memory big enough to hold a corresponding value. For example, declaring an *int* variable causes the compiler to allocate 4 bytes of memory (32 bits). A statement that assigns a value (such as 42) to the *int* causes the value to be copied into this block of memory.

Class types, such as *Circle* (described in Chapter 7), are handled differently. When you declare a *Circle* variable, the compiler *does not* generate code that allocates a block of memory big enough to hold a *Circle*; all it does is allot a small piece of memory that can potentially hold the address of (or a reference to) another block of memory containing a *Circle*. (An address specifies the location of an item in memory.) The memory for the actual *Circle* object is allocated only when the *new* keyword is used to create the object. A class is an example of a *reference type*. Reference types hold references to blocks of memory. To write effective C# programs that make full use of the Microsoft .NET Framework, you need to understand the difference between value types and reference types.

> **Note** Most of the built-in types of the C# language are value types except for *string*, which is a reference type. The description of reference types such as classes in this chapter applies to the *string* type as well. In fact, the *string* keyword in C# is just an alias for the *System.String* class.

Consider the situation in which you declare a variable named *i* as an *int* and assign it the value 42. If you declare another variable called *copyi* as an *int* and then assign *i* to *copyi*, *copyi* will hold the same value as *i* (42). However, even though *copyi* and *i* happen to hold the same value, there are two blocks of memory containing the value 42: one block for *i* and the other block for *copyi*. If you modify the value of *i*, the value of *copyi* does not change. Let's see this in code:

```
int i = 42;     // declare and initialize i
int copyi = i;  // copyi contains a copy of the data in i
i++;            // incrementing i has no effect on copyi
```

The effect of declaring a variable *c* as a *Circle* (the name of a class) is very different. When you declare *c* as a *Circle*, *c* can refer to a *Circle* object. If you declare *refc* as another *Circle*, it can also refer to a *Circle* object. If you assign *c* to *refc*, *refc* will refer to the same *Circle* object that *c* does; there is only one *Circle* object, and *refc* and *c* both refer to it. What has happened here is that the compiler has allocated two blocks of memory, one for *c* and one for *refc*, but the address contained in each block points to the same location in memory that stores the actual *Circle* object. Let's see this in code:

```
Circle c = new Circle(42);
Circle refc = c;
```

The following graphic illustrates both examples. The at sign (@) in the *Circle* objects represents a reference to an address in memory:

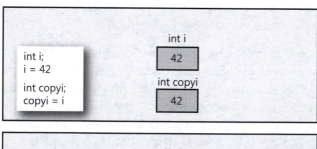

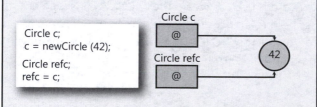

This difference is very important. In particular, it means that the behavior of method parameters depends on whether they are value types or reference types. You'll explore this difference in the following exercise.

> **Note** If you actually want to copy the contents of the *c* variable into *refc* rather than just copying the reference, you must make *refc* refer to a new instance of the *Circle* class and then copy the data field by field from *c* into *refc*, like this:
>
> ```
> Circle refc = new Circle();
> refc.radius = c.radius;       // Don't try this
> ```
>
> However, if any members of the *Circle* class are private (like the *radius* field), you will not be able to copy this data. Instead, you should make the data in the private fields accessible by exposing them as properties. You will learn how to do this in Chapter 15, "Implementing Properties to Access Fields."

Use value parameters and reference parameters

1. Start Microsoft Visual Studio 2010 if it is not already running.

2. Open the Parameters project located in the \Microsoft Press\Visual CSharp Step By Step\Chapter 8\Parameters folder in your Documents folder.

   The project contains three C# code files named Pass.cs, Program.cs, and WrappedInt.cs.

3. Display the Pass.cs file in the *Code and Text Editor* window. Add a *public static* method called *Value* to the *Pass* class, replacing the // to do comment, as shown in bold type in the following code example. This method should accept a single *int* parameter (a value type) called *param* and have the return type *void*. The body of the *Value* method should simply assign 42 to *param*.

   ```
   namespace Parameters
   {
       class Pass
       {
           public static void Value(int param)
           {
               param = 42;
           }
       }
   }
   ```

4. Display the Program.cs file in the *Code and Text Editor* window, and then locate the *DoWork* method of the *Program* class.

   The *DoWork* method is called by the *Main* method when the program starts running. As explained in Chapter 7, the method call is wrapped in a *try* block and followed by a *catch* handler.

5. Add four statements to the *DoWork* method to perform the following tasks:

   1. Declare a local *int* variable called *i*, and initialize it to 0.

   2. Write the value of *i* to the console by using *Console.WriteLine*.

   3. Call *Pass.Value*, passing *i* as an argument.

   4. Write the value of *i* to the console again.

   With the calls to *Console.WriteLine* before and after the call to *Pass.Value*, you can see whether the call to *Pass.Value* actually modifies the value of *i*. The completed *DoWork* method should look exactly like this:

   ```
   static void DoWork()
   {
       int i = 0;
       Console.WriteLine(i);
       Pass.Value(i);
       Console.WriteLine(i);
   }
   ```

6. On the *Debug* menu, click *Start Without Debugging* to build and run the program.

7. Confirm that the value 0 is written to the console window twice.

   The assignment statement inside the *Pass.Value* method that updates the parameter and sets it to 42 uses a copy of the argument passed in, and the original argument *i* is completely unaffected.

8. Press the Enter key to close the application.

   You will now see what happens when you pass an *int* parameter that is wrapped inside a class.

9. Display the WrappedInt.cs file in the *Code and Text Editor* window. Add a *public* instance field called *Number* of type *int* to the *WrappedInt* class, as shown in bold type here:

   ```
   namespace Parameters
   {
       class WrappedInt
       {
           public int Number;
       }
   }
   ```

10. Display the Pass.cs file in the *Code and Text Editor* window. Add a *public static* method called *Reference* to the *Pass* class. This method should accept a single *WrappedInt*

parameter called *param* and have the return type *void*. The body of the *Reference* method should assign 42 to *param.Number*, like this:

```
public static void Reference(WrappedInt param)
{
    param.Number = 42;
}
```

11. Display the Program.cs file in the *Code and Text Editor* window. Comment out the existing code in the *DoWork* method and add four more statements to perform the following tasks:

   a. Declare a local *WrappedInt* variable called *wi*, and initialize it to a new *WrappedInt* object by calling the default constructor.

   b. Write the value of *wi.Number* to the console.

   c. Call the *Pass.Reference* method, passing *wi* as an argument.

   d. Write the value of *wi.Number* to the console again.

As before, with the calls to *Console.WriteLine*, you can see whether the call to *Pass. Reference* modifies the value of *wi.Number*. The *DoWork* method should now look exactly like this (the new statements are shown in bold type):

```
static void DoWork()
{
    // int i = 0;
    // Console.WriteLine(i);
    // Pass.Value(i);
    // Console.WriteLine(i);

    WrappedInt wi = new WrappedInt();
    Console.WriteLine(wi.Number);
    Pass.Reference(wi);
    Console.WriteLine(wi.Number);
}
```

12. On the *Debug* menu, click *Start Without Debugging* to build and run the application.

This time, the two values displayed in the Console window correspond to the value of *wi.Number* before and after *Pass.Reference*. You should see that the values 0 and 42 are output.

13. Press the Enter key to close the application and return to Visual Studio 2010.

To explain what the previous exercise shows, the value of *wi.Number* is initialized to 0 by the compiler-generated default constructor. The *wi* variable contains a reference to the newly created *WrappedInt* object (which contains an *int*). The *wi* variable is then copied as an argument to the *Pass.Reference* method. Because *WrappedInt* is a class (a reference type), *wi* and *param* both refer to the same *WrappedInt* object. Any changes made to the contents of the object through the *param* variable in the *Pass.Reference* method are visible by using the *wi* variable when the method completes. The following diagram illustrates what happens when a *WrappedInt* object is passed as an argument to the *Pass.Reference* method:

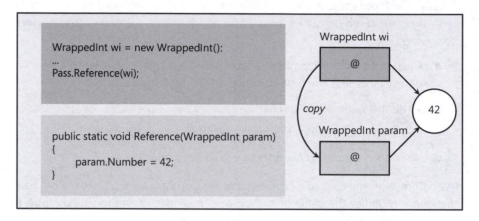

Understanding Null Values and Nullable Types

When you declare a variable, it is always a good idea to initialize it. With value types, it is common to see code such as this:

```
int i = 0;
double d = 0.0;
```

Remember that to initialize a reference variable such as a class, you can create a new instance of the class and assign the reference variable to the new object, like this:

```
Circle c = new Circle(42);
```

This is all very well, but what if you don't actually want to create a new object—perhaps the purpose of the variable is simply to store a reference to an existing object. In the following code example, the *Circle* variable *copy* is initialized, but later it is assigned a reference to another instance of the *Circle* class:

```
Circle c = new Circle(42);
Circle copy = new Circle(99);    // Some random value, for initializing copy
...
copy = c;                        // copy and c refer to the same object
```

After assigning *c* to *copy*, what happens to the original *Circle* object with a radius of 99 that you used to initialize *copy*? Nothing refers to it anymore. In this situation, the runtime can reclaim the memory by performing an operation known as *garbage collection*, which you will learn more about in Chapter 14, "Using Garbage Collection and Resource Management." The important thing to understand for now is that garbage collection is a potentially time-consuming operation.

You could argue that if a variable is going to be assigned a reference to another object at some point in a program, there is no point initializing it. But this is poor programming practice and can lead to problems in your code. For example, you will inevitably meet the situation where you want to refer a variable to an object only if that variable does not already contain a reference, as shown in the following code example:

```
Circle c = new Circle(42);
Circle copy;                    // Uninitialized !!!
...
if (copy == // what goes here?)
    copy = c;                   // copy and c refer to the same object
```

The purpose of the *if* statement is to test the *copy* variable to see whether it is initialized, but to which value should you compare this variable? The answer is to use a special value called *null*.

In C#, you can assign the *null* value to any reference variable. The *null* value simply means that the variable does not refer to an object in memory. You can use it like this:

```
Circle c = new Circle(42);
Circle copy = null;         // Initialized
...
if (copy == null)
    copy = c;                   // copy and c refer to the same object
```

Using Nullable Types

The *null* value is useful for initializing reference types, but *null* is itself a reference, and you cannot assign it to a value type. The following statement is therefore illegal in C#:

```
int i = null; // illegal
```

However, C# defines a modifier that you can use to declare that a variable is a *nullable* value type. A nullable value type behaves in a similar manner to the original value type, but you can assign the *null* value to it. You use the question mark (?) to indicate that a value type is nullable, like this:

```
int? i = null; // legal
```

You can ascertain whether a nullable variable contains *null* by testing it in the same way as a reference type:

```
if (i == null)
    ...
```

You can assign an expression of the appropriate value type directly to a nullable variable. The following examples are all legal:

```
int? i = null;
int j = 99;
i = 100;        // Copy a value type constant to a nullable type
i = j;          // Copy a value type variable to a nullable type
```

You should note that the converse is not true. You cannot assign a nullable value to an ordinary value type variable. So, given the definitions of variables *i* and *j* from the preceding example, the following statement is not allowed:

```
j = i;     // Illegal
```

This makes sense if you consider that the variable *i* might contain *null*, and *j* is a value-type that cannot contain *null*. This also means that you cannot use a nullable variable as a parameter to a method that expects an ordinary value type. If you recall, the *Pass.Value* method from the preceding exercise expects an ordinary *int* parameter, so the following method call will not compile:

```
int? i = 99;
Pass.Value(i);   // Compiler error
```

Understanding the Properties of Nullable Types

Nullable types expose a pair of properties that you can use and that you have already met in Chapter 6, "Managing Errors and Exceptions." The *HasValue* property indicates whether a nullable type contains a value or is *null*, and you can retrieve the value of a non-null nullable type by reading the *Value* property, like this:

```
int? i = null;
...
if (!i.HasValue)
    i = 99;
else
    Console.WriteLine(i.Value);
```

Recall from Chapter 4, "Using Decision Statements," that the NOT operator (!) negates a Boolean value. This code fragment tests the nullable variable *i*, and if it does not have a value (it is *null*), it assigns it the value 99; otherwise, it displays the value of the variable. In this example, using the *HasValue* property does not provide any benefit over testing for a *null* value directly. Additionally, reading the *Value* property is a long-winded way of reading the contents of the variable. However, these apparent shortcomings are caused by the fact that *int?* is a very simple nullable type. You can create more complex value types and use them to declare nullable variables where the advantages of using the *HasValue* and *Value* properties become more apparent. You will see some examples in Chapter 9, "Creating Value Types with Enumerations and Structures."

Note   The *Value* property of a nullable type is read-only. You can use this property to read the value of a variable but not to modify it. To update a nullable variable, use an ordinary assignment statement.

Using *ref* and *out* Parameters

Ordinarily, when you pass an argument to a method, the corresponding parameter is initialized with a copy of the argument. This is true regardless of whether the parameter is a value type (such as an *int*), a nullable type (such as *int?*), or a reference type (such as a *WrappedInt*). This arrangement means it's impossible for any change to the parameter to affect the value of the argument passed in. For example, in the following code, the value output to the console is 42 and not 43. The *DoIncrement* method increments a *copy* of the argument (*arg*) and *not* the original argument:

```
static void DoIncrement(int param)
{
    param++;
}

static void Main()
{
    int arg = 42;
    DoIncrement(arg);
    Console.WriteLine(arg); // writes 42, not 43
}
```

In the preceding exercise, you saw that if the parameter to a method is a reference type, any changes made by using that parameter change the data referenced by the argument passed in. The key point is that, although the data that was referenced changed, the argument passed in as the parameter did not—it still references the same object. In other words, although it is possible to modify the object that the argument refers to through the parameter, it's not possible to modify the argument itself (for example, to set it to refer to a completely different object). Most of the time, this guarantee is very useful and can help to reduce the number of bugs in a program. Occasionally, however, you might want to write a method that actually needs to modify an argument. C# provides the *ref* and *out* keywords so that you can do this.

Creating *ref* Parameters

If you prefix a parameter with the *ref* keyword, the parameter becomes an alias for (or a reference to) the actual argument rather than a copy of the argument. When using a *ref* parameter, anything you do to the parameter you also do to the original argument because the parameter and the argument both reference the same object. When you pass an argument as a *ref* parameter, you must also prefix the argument with the *ref* keyword. This syntax provides a useful visual cue to the programmer that the argument might change. Here's the preceding example again, this time modified to use the *ref* keyword:

```
static void DoIncrement(ref int param) // using ref
{
    param++;
}

static void Main()
{
    int arg = 42;
    DoIncrement(ref arg);     // using ref
    Console.WriteLine(arg);   // writes 43
}
```

This time, you pass to the *DoIncrement* method a reference to the original argument rather than a copy of the original argument, so any changes the method makes by using this reference also change the original argument. That's why the value 43 is displayed on the console.

The rule that you must assign a value to a variable before you can use the variable still applies to *ref* arguments. For example, in the following example, *arg* is not initialized, so this code will not compile. This failure occurs because *param++* inside *DoIncrement* is really *arg++*, and *arg++* is allowed only if *arg* has a defined value:

```
static void DoIncrement(ref int param)
{
    param++;
}

static void Main()
{
    int arg;                   // not initialized
    DoIncrement(ref arg);
    Console.WriteLine(arg);
}
```

Creating *out* Parameters

The compiler checks whether a *ref* parameter has been assigned a value before calling the method. However, there might be times when you want the method to initialize the parameter. You can do this with the *out* keyword.

The *out* keyword is similar to the *ref* keyword. You can prefix a parameter with the *out* keyword so that the parameter becomes an alias for the argument. As when using *ref*, anything you do to the parameter, you also do to the original argument. When you pass an argument to an *out* parameter, you must also prefix the argument with the *out* keyword.

The keyword *out* is short for *output*. When you pass an *out* parameter to a method, the method *must* assign a value to it. The following example does not compile because *DoInitialize* does not assign a value to *param*:

```
static void DoInitialize(out int param)
{
    // Do nothing
}
```

However, the following example does compile because *DoInitialize* now assigns a value to *param*:

```
static void DoInitialize(out int param)
{
    param = 42;
}
```

Because an *out* parameter must be assigned a value by the method, you're allowed to call the method without initializing its argument. For example, the following code calls *DoInitialize* to initialize the variable *arg*, which is then displayed on the console:

```
static void DoInitialize(out int param)
{
    param = 42;
}

static void Main()
{
    int arg;                    // not initialized
    DoInitialize(out arg);
    Console.WriteLine(arg); // writes 42
}
```

You will examine *ref* parameters in the next exercise.

Use *ref* parameters

1. Return to the Parameters project in Visual Studio 2010.

2. Display the Pass.cs file in the *Code and Text Editor* window.

3. Edit the *Value* method to accept its parameter as a *ref* parameter.

   The *Value* method should look like this:

   ```
   class Pass
   {
       public static void Value(ref int param)
       {
           param = 42;
       }
       ...
   }
   ```

4. Display the Program.cs file in the *Code and Text Editor* window.

5. Uncomment the first four statements. Edit the third statement of the *DoWork* method so that the *Pass.Value* method call passes its argument as a *ref* parameter.

> **Note** Leave the four statements that create and test the *WrappedInt* object as they are.

The *DoWork* method should now look like this:

```csharp
class Application
{
    static void DoWork()
    {
        int i = 0;
        Console.WriteLine(i);
        Pass.Value(ref i);
        Console.WriteLine(i);
        ...
    }
}
```

6. On the *Debug* menu, click *Start Without Debugging* to build and run the program.

   This time, the first two values written to the console window are 0 and 42. This result shows that the call to the *Pass.Value* method has successfully modified the argument *i*.

7. Press the Enter key to close the application and return to Visual Studio 2010.

> **Note** You can use the *ref* and *out* modifiers on reference type parameters as well as on value type parameters. The effect is exactly the same. The parameter becomes an alias for the argument. If you reassigned the parameter to a newly constructed object, you would also actually be reassigning the argument to the newly constructed object.

How Computer Memory Is Organized

Computers use memory to hold programs being executed and the data that these programs use. To understand the differences between value and reference types, it is helpful to understand how data is organized in memory.

Operating systems and language runtimes such as that used by C# frequently divide the memory used for holding data in two separate chunks, each of which is managed in a distinct manner. These two chunks of memory are traditionally called *the stack* and *the heap*. The stack and the heap serve very different purposes:

- When you call a method, the memory required for its parameters and its local variables is always acquired from the stack. When the method finishes (because it either returns or throws an exception), the memory acquired for the parameters and local variables is automatically released back to the stack and is available for reuse when another method is called.

- When you create an object (an instance of a class) by using the *new* keyword, the memory required to build the object is always acquired from the heap. You have seen that the same object can be referenced from several places by using reference variables. When the last reference to an object disappears, the memory used by the object becomes available for reuse (although it might not be reclaimed immediately). Chapter 14 includes a more detailed discussion of how heap memory is reclaimed.

> **Note** All value types are created on the stack. All reference types (objects) are created on the heap (although the reference itself is on the stack). Nullable types are actually reference types, and they are created on the heap.

The names *stack* and *heap* come from the way in which the runtime manages the memory:

- Stack memory is organized like a stack of boxes piled on top of one another. When a method is called, each parameter is put in a box that is placed on top of the stack. Each local variable is likewise assigned a box, and these are placed on top of the boxes already on the stack. When a method finishes, all its boxes are removed from the stack.

- Heap memory is like a large pile of boxes strewn around a room rather than stacked neatly on top of each other. Each box has a label indicating whether it is in use. When a new object is created, the runtime searches for an empty box and allocates it to the object. The reference to the object is stored in a local variable on the stack. The runtime keeps track of the number of references to each box. (Remember that two variables can refer to the same object.) When the last reference disappears, the runtime marks the box as not in use, and at some point in the future it will empty the box and make it available for reuse.

Using the Stack and the Heap

Now let's examine what happens when the following method *Method* is called:

```
void Method(int param)
{
    Circle c;
    c = new Circle(param);
    ...
}
```

Suppose the argument passed into *param* is the value 42. When the method is called, a block of memory (just enough for an *int*) is allocated from the stack and initialized with the value 42. As execution moves inside the method, another block of memory big enough to hold a reference (a memory address) is also allocated from the stack but left uninitialized. (This is for the *Circle* variable, *c*.) Next, another piece of memory big enough for a *Circle* object is allocated from the heap. This is what the *new* keyword does. The *Circle* constructor runs to convert this raw heap memory to a *Circle* object. A reference to this *Circle* object is stored in the variable *c*. The following graphic illustrates the situation:

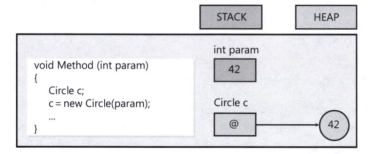

At this point, you should note two things:

- Although the object is stored on the heap, the reference to the object (the variable *c*) is stored on the stack.

- Heap memory is not infinite. If heap memory is exhausted, the *new* operator will throw an *OutOfMemoryException* and the object will not be created.

> **Note** The *Circle* constructor could also throw an exception. If it does, the memory allocated to the *Circle* object will be reclaimed and the value returned by the constructor will be *null*.

When the method ends, the parameters and local variables go out of scope. The memory acquired for *c* and for *param* is automatically released back to the stack. The runtime notes that the *Circle* object is no longer referenced and at some point in the future will arrange for its memory to be reclaimed by the heap. (See Chapter 14.)

The *System.Object* Class

One of the most important reference types in the Microsoft .NET Framework is the *Object* class in the *System* namespace. To fully appreciate the significance of the *System.Object* class requires that you understand inheritance, which is described in Chapter 12, "Working with Inheritance." For the time being, simply accept that all classes are specialized types of *System. Object* and that you can use *System.Object* to create a variable that can refer to any reference type. *System.Object* is such an important class that C# provides the *object* keyword as an alias for *System.Object*. In your code, you can use *object* or you can write *System.Object*; they mean exactly the same thing.

> **Tip** Use the *object* keyword in preference to *System.Object*. It's more direct, and it's consistent with other keywords that are synonyms for classes (such as *string* for *System.String* and some others that you'll discover in Chapter 9).

In the following example, the variables *c* and *o* both refer to the same *Circle* object. The fact that the type of *c* is *Circle* and the type of *o* is *object* (the alias for *System.Object*) in effect provides two different views of the same item in memory:

```
Circle c;
c = new Circle(42);
object o;
o = c;
```

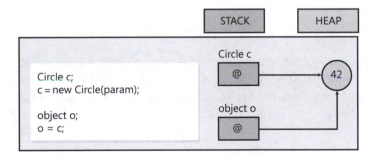

Boxing

As you have just seen, variables of type *object* can refer to any object of any reference type. However, variables of type *object* can also refer to a value type. For example, the following two statements initialize the variable *i* (of type *int*, a value type) to 42 and then initialize the variable *o* (of type *object*, a reference type) to *i*:

```
int i = 42;
object o = i;
```

The second statement requires a little explanation to appreciate what is actually happening. Remember that *i* is a value type and that it lives on the stack. If the reference inside *o* referred directly to *i*, the reference would refer to the stack. However, all references must refer to objects on the heap; creating references to items on the stack could seriously compromise the robustness of the runtime and create a potential security flaw, so it is not allowed. Therefore, the runtime allocates a piece of memory from the heap, copies the value of integer *i* to this piece of memory, and then refers the object *o* to this copy. This automatic copying of an item from the stack to the heap is called *boxing*. The following graphic shows the result:

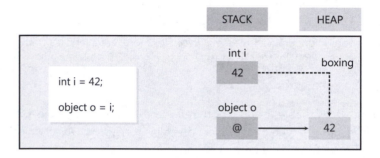

 Important If you modify the original value of a variable, the value on the heap will not change. Likewise, if you modify the value on the heap, the original value of the variable will not change.

Unboxing

Because a variable of type *object* can refer to a boxed copy of a value, it's only reasonable to allow you to get at that boxed value through the variable. You might expect to be able to access the boxed *int* value that a variable *o* refers to by using a simple assignment statement such as this:

```
int i = o;
```

However, if you try this syntax, you'll get a compile-time error. If you think about it, it's pretty sensible that you can't use the `int i = o;` syntax. After all, *o* could be referencing absolutely anything and not just an *int*. Consider what would happen in the following code if this statement were allowed:

```
Circle c = new Circle();
int i = 42;
object o;

o = c;  // o refers to a circle
i = o;  // what is stored in i?
```

To obtain the value of the boxed copy, you must use what is known as a *cast*. This is an operation that checks whether it is safe to convert one type to another before it does the conversion. You prefix the *object* variable with the name of the type in parentheses, as in this example:

```
int i = 42;
object o = i;  // boxes
i = (int)o;    // compiles okay
```

The effect of this cast is subtle. The compiler notices that you've specified the type *int* in the cast. Next, the compiler generates code to check what *o* actually refers to at run time. It could be absolutely anything. Just because your cast says *o* refers to an *int*, that doesn't mean it actually does. If *o* really does refer to a boxed *int* and everything matches, the cast succeeds and the compiler-generated code extracts the value from the boxed *int* and copies it to *i*. (In this example, the boxed value is then stored in *i*.) This is called *unboxing*. The following diagram shows what is happening:

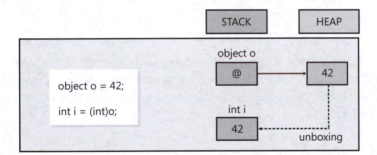

However, if *o* does not refer to a boxed *int*, there is a type mismatch, causing the cast to fail. The compiler-generated code throws an *InvalidCastException* at run time. Here's an example of an unboxing cast that fails:

```
Circle c = new Circle(42);
object o = c;        // doesn't box because Circle is a reference variable
int i = (int)o;      // compiles okay but throws an exception at run time
```

You will use boxing and unboxing in later exercises. Keep in mind that boxing and unboxing are expensive operations because of the amount of checking required and the need to allocate additional heap memory. Boxing has its uses, but injudicious use can severely impair the performance of a program. You will see an alternative to boxing in Chapter 18, "Introducing Generics."

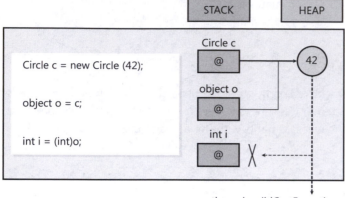

throw InvalidCastException

Casting Data Safely

By using a cast, you can specify that, *in your opinion*, the data referenced by an object has a specific type and that it is safe to reference the object by using that type. The key phrase here is "in your opinion." The C# compiler will trust you when it builds your application, but the runtime is more suspicious and will actually check that this is the case when your application runs. If the type of object in memory does not match the cast, the runtime will throw an *InvalidCastException*, as described in the preceding section. You should be prepared to catch this exception and handle it appropriately if it occurs.

However, catching an exception and attempting to recover in the event that the type of an object is not what you expected it to be is a rather cumbersome approach. C# provides two more very useful operators that can help you perform casting in a much more elegant manner: the *is* and *as* operators.

The *is* Operator

You can use the *is* operator to verify that the type of an object is what you expect it to be, like this:

```
WrappedInt wi = new WrappedInt();
...
object o = wi;
if (o is WrappedInt)
{
    WrappedInt temp = (WrappedInt)o;  // This is safe; o is a WrappedInt
    ...
}
```

The *is* operator takes two operands: a reference to an object on the left and the name of a type on the right. If the type of the object referenced on the heap has the specified type, *is* evaluates to *true*; otherwise, it evaluates to *false*. The preceding code attempts to cast the reference to the *object* variable *o* only if it knows that the cast will succeed.

The *as* Operator

The *as* operator fulfills a similar role to *is* but in a slightly truncated manner. You use the *as* operator like this:

```
WrappedInt wi = new WrappedInt();
...
object o = wi;
WrappedInt temp = o as WrappedInt;
if (temp != null)
    ...   // Cast was successful
```

Like the *is* operator, the *as* operator takes an object and a type as its operands. The runtime attempts to cast the object to the specified type. If the cast is successful, the result is re-turned, and, in this example, it is assigned to the *WrappedInt* variable *temp*. If the cast is un-successful, the *as* operator evaluates to the *null* value and assigns that to *temp* instead.

There is a little more to the *is* and *as* operators than described here, and you will meet them again in Chapter 12.

Pointers and Unsafe Code

This section is purely for your information and is aimed at developers who are familiar with C or C++. If you are new to programming, feel free to skip this section!

If you have already written programs in languages such as C or C++, much of the dis-cussion in this chapter concerning object references might be familiar. Although neither C nor C++ has explicit reference types, both languages have a construct that provides similar functionality—pointers.

A *pointer* is a variable that holds the address of, or a reference to, an item in memory (on the heap or on the stack). A special syntax is used to identify a variable as a pointer. For example, the following statement declares the variable *pi* as a pointer to an integer:

```
int *pi;
```

Although the variable *pi* is declared as a pointer, it does not actually point anywhere until you initialize it. For example, to use *pi* to point to the integer variable *i*, you can use the following statements and the address operator (&), which returns the address of a variable:

```
int *pi;
int i = 99;
...
pi = &i;
```

You can access and modify the value held in the variable *i* through the pointer variable *pi* like this:

```
*pi = 100;
```

This code updates the value of the variable *i* to 100 because *pi* points to the same memory location as the variable *i*.

One of the main problems that developers learning C and C++ have is understanding the syntax used by pointers. The * operator has at least two meanings (in addition to being the arithmetic multiplication operator), and there is often great confusion about when to use & rather than *. The other issue with pointers is that it is easy to point somewhere invalid, or to forget to point somewhere at all, and then try to reference the data pointed to. The result will be either garbage or a program that fails with an error because the operating system detects an attempt to access an illegal address in memory. There is also a whole range of security flaws in many existing systems resulting from the mismanagement of pointers; some environments (not Microsoft Windows) fail to enforce checks that a pointer does not refer to memory that belongs to another process, opening up the possibility that confidential data could be compromised.

Reference variables were added to C# to avoid all these problems. If you really want to, you can continue to use pointers in C#, but you must mark the code as *unsafe*. The *unsafe* keyword can be used to mark a block of code, or an entire method, as shown here:

```
public static void Main(string [] args)
{
    int x = 99, y = 100;
    unsafe
    {
        swap (&x, &y);
    }
    Console.WriteLine("x is now {0}, y is now {1}", x, y);
}

public static unsafe void swap(int *a, int *b)
{
    int temp;
    temp = *a;
    *a = *b;
    *b = temp;
}
```

When you compile programs containing unsafe code, you must specify the */unsafe* option.

Unsafe code also has a bearing on how memory is managed; objects created in unsafe code are said to be unmanaged. We discuss this issue in more detail in Chapter 14.

In this chapter, you learned about some important differences between value types that hold their value directly on the stack and reference types that refer indirectly to their objects on the heap. You also learned how to use the *ref* and *out* keywords on method parameters to gain access to the arguments. You saw how assigning a value (such as the *int* 42) to a variable of the *System.Object* class creates a boxed copy of the value on the heap and then causes the *System.Object* variable to refer to this boxed copy. You also saw how assigning a variable of a value type (such as an *int*) to a variable of the *System.Object* class copies (or unboxes) the value in the *System.Object* class to the memory used by the *int*.

- If you want to continue to the next chapter

    Keep Visual Studio 2010 running, and turn to Chapter 9.

- If you want to exit Visual Studio 2010 now

    On the *File* menu, click *Exit*. If you see a *Save* dialog box, click *Yes* and save the project.

Chapter 8 Quick Reference

To	Do this
Copy a value type variable	Simply make the copy. Because the variable is a value type, you will have two copies of the same value. For example: ```\nint i = 42;\nint copyi = i;\n```
Copy a reference type variable	Simply make the copy. Because the variable is a reference type, you will have two references to the same object. For example: ```\nCircle c = new Circle(42);\nCircle refc = c;\n```
Declare a variable that can hold a value type or the *null* value	Declare the variable using the ? modifier with the type. For example: ```\nint? i = null;\n```
Pass an argument to a *ref* parameter	Prefix the argument with the *ref* keyword. This makes the parameter an alias for the actual argument rather than a copy of the argument. The method may change the value of the parameter, and this change is made to the actual argument rather than a local copy. For example: ```\nstatic void Main()\n{\n int arg = 42;\n DoWork(ref arg);\n Console.WriteLine(arg);\n}\n```

To	Do this
| Pass an argument to an *out* parameter | Prefix the argument with the *out* keyword. This makes the parameter an alias for the actual argument rather than a copy of the argument. The method **must** assign a value to the parameter, and this value is made to the actual argument. For example:<br><br>```csharp
static void Main()
{
    int arg;
    DoWork(out arg);
    Console.WriteLine(arg);
}
``` |
| Box a value | Initialize or assign a variable of type object to the value. For example:<br><br>```csharp
object o = 42;
``` |
| Unbox a value | Cast the object reference that refers to the boxed value to the type of the value variable. For example:<br><br>```csharp
int i = (int)o;
``` |
| Cast an object safely | Use the *is* operator to test whether the cast is valid. For example:<br><br>```csharp
WrappedInt wi = new WrappedInt();
...
object o = wi;
if (o is WrappedInt)
{
    WrappedInt temp = (WrappedInt)o;
    ...
}
```<br><br>Alternatively, use the *as* operator to perform the cast, and test whether the result is *null*. For example:<br><br>```csharp
WrappedInt wi = new WrappedInt();
...
object o = wi;
WrappedInt temp = o as WrappedInt;
if (temp != null)
    ...
``` |
```

Chapter 9
Creating Value Types with Enumerations and Structures

After completing this chapter, you will be able to:

- Declare an enumeration type.

- Create and use an enumeration type.

- Declare a structure type.

- Create and use a structure type.

- Explain the differences in behavior between a structure and a class.

In Chapter 8, "Understanding Values and References," you learned about the two fundamental types that exist in Microsoft Visual C#: *value types* and *reference types*. A value type variable holds its value directly on the stack, whereas a reference type variable holds a reference to an object on the heap. In Chapter 7, "Creating and Managing Classes and Objects," you learned how to create your own reference types by defining classes. In this chapter, you'll learn how to create your own value types.

C# supports two kinds of value types: *enumerations* and *structures*. We'll look at each of them in turn.

Working with Enumerations

Suppose you want to represent the seasons of the year in a program. You could use the integers 0, 1, 2, and 3 to represent spring, summer, fall, and winter, respectively. This system would work, but it's not very intuitive. If you used the integer value 0 in code, it wouldn't be obvious that a particular 0 represented spring. It also wouldn't be a very robust solution. For example, if you declare an *int* variable named *season*, there is nothing to stop you from assigning it any legal integer value apart from 0, 1, 2, or 3. C# offers a better solution. You can create an enumeration (sometimes called an *enum* type), whose values are limited to a set of symbolic names.

Declaring an Enumeration

You define an enumeration by using the *enum* keyword, followed by a set of symbols identifying the legal values that the type can have, enclosed between braces. Here's how to declare an enumeration named *Season* whose literal values are limited to the symbolic names *Spring*, *Summer*, *Fall*, and *Winter*:

```
enum Season { Spring, Summer, Fall, Winter }
```

Using an Enumeration

After you have declared an enumeration, you can use it in exactly the same way as any other type. If the name of your enumeration is *Season*, you can create variables of type *Season*, fields of type *Season*, and parameters of type *Season*, as shown in this example:

```
enum Season { Spring, Summer, Fall, Winter }

class Example
{
    public void Method(Season parameter)
    {
        Season localVariable;
        ...
    }

    private Season currentSeason;
}
```

Before you can read the value of an enumeration variable, it must be assigned a value. You can assign a value that is defined by the enumeration only to an enumeration variable. For example:

```
Season colorful = Season.Fall;
Console.WriteLine(colorful);  // writes out 'Fall'
```

> **Note** As you can with all value types, you can create a nullable version of an enumeration variable by using the ? modifier. You can then assign the *null* value, as well the values defined by the enumeration, to the variable:
>
> ```
> Season? colorful = null;
> ```

Notice that you have to write *Season.Fall* rather than just *Fall*. All enumeration literal names are scoped by their enumeration type. This is useful because it allows different enumerations to coincidentally contain literals with the same name.

Also, notice that when you display an enumeration variable by using *Console.WriteLine*, the compiler generates code that writes out the name of the literal whose value matches the value of the variable. If needed, you can explicitly convert an enumeration variable to a string that represents its current value by using the built-in *ToString* method that all enumerations automatically contain. For example:

```
string name = colorful.ToString();
Console.WriteLine(name);       // also writes out 'Fall'
```

Many of the standard operators you can use on integer variables can also be used on enumeration variables (except the *bitwise* and *shift* operators, which are covered in Chapter 16, "Using Indexers"). For example, you can compare two enumeration variables of the same type for equality by using the equality operator (==), and you can even perform arithmetic on an enumeration variable (although the result might not always be meaningful!).

Choosing Enumeration Literal Values

Internally, an enumeration type associates an integer value with each element of the enumeration. By default, the numbering starts at 0 for the first element and goes up in steps of 1. It's possible to retrieve the underlying integer value of an enumeration variable. To do this, you must cast it to its underlying type. Remember from the discussion of unboxing in Chapter 8 that casting a type converts the data from one type to another as long as the conversion is valid and meaningful. The following code example writes out the value *2* and not the word *Fall* (in the *Season* enumeration *Spring* is *0*, *Summer 1*, *Fall 2*, and *Winter 3*):

```
enum Season { Spring, Summer, Fall, Winter }
...
Season colorful = Season.Fall;
Console.WriteLine((int)colorful); // writes out '2'
```

If you prefer, you can associate a specific integer constant (such as 1) with an enumeration literal (such as *Spring*), as in the following example:

```
enum Season { Spring = 1, Summer, Fall, Winter }
```

 Important The integer value with which you initialize an enumeration literal must be a compile-time constant value (such as 1).

If you don't explicitly give an enumeration literal a constant integer value, the compiler gives it a value that is 1 greater than the value of the previous enumeration literal except for the very first enumeration literal, to which the compiler gives the default value *0*. In the preceding example, the underlying values of *Spring, Summer, Fall,* and *Winter* are now 1, 2, 3, and 4.

You are allowed to give more than one enumeration literal the same underlying value. For example, in the United Kingdom, *Fall* is referred to as *Autumn*. You can cater to both cultures as follows:

```
enum Season { Spring, Summer, Fall, Autumn = Fall, Winter }
```

Choosing an Enumeration's Underlying Type

When you declare an enumeration, the enumeration literals are given values of type *int*. You can also choose to base your enumeration on a different underlying integer type. For example, to declare that *Season*'s underlying type is a *short* rather than an *int*, you can write this:

```
enum Season : short { Spring, Summer, Fall, Winter }
```

The main reason for doing this is to save memory; an *int* occupies more memory than a *short*, and if you do not need the entire range of values available to an *int*, using a smaller data type can make sense.

You can base an enumeration on any of the eight integer types: *byte, sbyte, short, ushort, int, uint, long,* or *ulong*. The values of all the enumeration literals must fit inside the range of the chosen base type. For example, if you base an enumeration on the *byte* data type, you can have a maximum of 256 literals (starting at 0).

Now that you know how to declare an enumeration, the next step is to use it. In the following exercise, you will work with a Console application to declare and use an enumeration that represents the months of the year.

Create and use an enumeration

1. Start Microsoft Visual Studio 2010 if it is not already running.

2. Open the *StructsAndEnums* project, located in the \Microsoft Press\Visual CSharp Step By Step\Chapter 9\StructsAndEnums folder in your Documents folder.

3. In the *Code and Text Editor* window, display the Month.cs file.

   The source file contains an empty namespace named *StructsAndEnums*.

4. Add an enumeration named *Month* for modeling the months of the year inside the *StructsAndEnums* namespace, as shown in bold here. The 12 enumeration literals for *Month* are *January* through *December*.

```
namespace StructsAndEnums
{
    enum Month
    {
        January, February, March, April,
        May, June, July, August,
        September, October, November, December
    }
}
```

5. Display the Program.cs file in the *Code and Text Editor* window.

   As in the exercises in previous chapters, the *Main* method calls the *DoWork* method and traps any exceptions that occur.

6. In the *Code and Text Editor* window, add a statement to the *DoWork* method to declare a variable named *first* of type *Month* and initialize it to *Month.January*. Add another statement to write the value of the first variable to the Console.

   The *DoWork* method should look like this:

```
static void DoWork()
{
    Month first = Month.January;
    Console.WriteLine(first);
}
```

 Note When you type the period following *Month*, Microsoft IntelliSense will automatically display all the values in the *Month* enumeration.

7. On the *Debug* menu, click *Start Without Debugging*.

   Visual Studio 2010 builds and runs the program. Confirm that the word *January* is written to the console.

8. Press Enter to close the program and return to the Visual Studio 2010 programming environment.

9. Add two more statements to the *DoWork* method to increment the *first* variable and display its new value to the console, as shown in bold here:

```
static void DoWork()
{
    Month first = Month.January;
    Console.WriteLine(first);
    first++;
    Console.WriteLine(first);
}
```

10. On the *Debug* menu, click *Start Without Debugging*.

    Visual Studio 2010 builds and runs the program. Confirm that the words *January* and *February* are written to the console.

    Notice that performing a mathematical operation (such as the increment operation) on an enumeration variable changes the internal integer value of the variable. When the variable is written to the console, the corresponding enumeration value is displayed.

11. Press Enter to close the program and return to the Visual Studio 2010 programming environment.

12. Modify the first statement in the *DoWork* method to initialize the *first* variable to *Month.December*, as shown in bold here:

```
static void DoWork()
{
    Month first = Month.December;
    Console.WriteLine(first);
    first++;
    Console.WriteLine(first);
}
```

13. On the *Debug* menu, click *Start Without Debugging*.

Visual Studio 2010 builds and runs the program. This time the word *December* is written to the console, followed by the number *12*. Although you can perform arithmetic on an enumeration, if the results of the operation are outside the range of values defined for the enumerator, all the runtime can do is interpret the value of the variable as the corresponding integer value.

14. Press Enter to close the program and return to the Visual Studio 2010 programming environment.

Working with Structures

You saw in Chapter 8 that classes define reference types that are always created on the heap. In some cases, the class can contain so little data that the overhead of managing the heap becomes disproportionate. In these cases, it is better to define the type as a structure. A structure is a value type. Because structures are stored on the stack, as long as the structure is reasonably small, the memory management overhead is often reduced.

Like a class, a structure can have its own fields, methods, and (with one important exception discussed later in this chapter) constructors.

Common Structure Types

You might not have realized it, but you have already used structures in previous exercises in this book. In C#, the primitive numeric types *int*, *long*, and *float* are aliases for the structures *System.Int32*, *System.Int64*, and *System.Single*, respectively. These structures have fields and methods, and you can actually call methods on variables and literals of these types. For example, all of these structures provide a *ToString* method that can convert a numeric value to its string representation. The following statements are all legal statements in C#:

```
int i = 99;
Console.WriteLine(i.ToString());
Console.WriteLine(55.ToString());
float f = 98.765F;
Console.WriteLine(f.ToString());
Console.WriteLine(98.765F.ToString());
```

You don't see this use of the *ToString* method often, because the *Console.WriteLine* method calls it automatically when it is needed. Use of the static methods exposed by these structures is much more common. For example, in earlier chapters you used the static *int.Parse* method to convert a string to its corresponding integer value. What you are actually doing is invoking the *Parse* method of the *Int32* structure:

```
string s = "42";
int i = int.Parse(s);   // exactly the same as Int32.Parse
```

These structures also include some useful static fields. For example, *Int32.MaxValue* is the maximum value that an *int* can hold, and *Int32.MinValue* is the smallest value you can store in an *int*.

The following table shows the primitive types in C# and their equivalent types in the Microsoft .NET Framework. Notice that the string and object types are classes (reference types) rather than structures.

Keyword	Type equivalent	Class or structure
bool	*System.Boolean*	Structure
byte	*System.Byte*	Structure
decimal	*System.Decimal*	Structure
double	*System.Double*	Structure
float	*System.Single*	Structure
int	*System.Int32*	Structure
long	*System.Int64*	Structure
object	*System.Object*	Class
sbyte	*System.SByte*	Structure
short	*System.Int16*	Structure
string	*System.String*	Class
uint	*System.UInt32*	Structure
ulong	*System.UInt64*	Structure
ushort	*System.UInt16*	Structure

Declaring a Structure

To declare your own structure type, you use the *struct* keyword followed by the name of the type, followed by the body of the structure between opening and closing braces. For example, here is a structure named *Time* that contains three *public int* fields named *hours*, *minutes*, and *seconds*:

```
struct Time
{
    public int hours, minutes, seconds;
}
```

As with classes, making the fields of a structure *public* is not advisable in most cases; there is no way to control the values held in *public* fields. For example, anyone could set the value of *minutes* or *seconds* to a value greater than 60. A better idea is to make the fields *private* and provide your structure with constructors and methods to initialize and manipulate these fields, as shown in this example:

```
struct Time
{
    public Time(int hh, int mm, int ss)
    {
        hours = hh % 24;
        minutes = mm % 60;
        seconds = ss % 60;
    }

    public int Hours()
    {
        return hours;
    }
    ...
    private int hours, minutes, seconds;
}
```

> **Note** By default, you cannot use many of the common operators on your own structure types. For example, you cannot use operators such as the equality operator (==) and the inequality operator (!=) on your own structure type variables. However, you can explicitly declare and implement operators for your own structure types. The syntax for doing this is covered in Chapter 21, "Operator Overloading."

Use structures to implement simple concepts whose main feature is their value. When you copy a value type variable, you get two copies of the value. In contrast, when you copy a reference type variable, you get two references to the same object. In summary, use structures for small data values where it's just as or nearly as efficient to copy the value as it would be to copy an address. Use classes for more complex data that is too big to copy efficiently.

Understanding Structure and Class Differences

A structure and a class are syntactically similar, but there are a few important differences. Let's look at some of these differences:

- You can't declare a default constructor (a constructor with no parameters) for a structure. The following example would compile if *Time* were a class, but because *Time* is a structure, it does not:

```
struct Time
{
    public Time() { ... } // compile-time error
    ...
}
```

The reason you can't declare your own default constructor for a structure is that the compiler *always* generates one. In a class, the compiler generates the default constructor only if you don't write a constructor yourself. The compiler-generated default constructor for a structure always sets the fields to *0*, *false*, or *null*—just as for a class. Therefore, you should ensure that a structure value created by the default constructor behaves logically and makes sense with these default values. If you don't want to use these default values, you can initialize fields to different values by providing a nondefault constructor. However, if you don't initialize a field in your nondefault structure constructor, the compiler won't initialize it for you. This means that you must explicitly initialize all the fields in all your nondefault structure constructors or you'll get a compile-time error. For example, although the following example would compile and silently initialize *seconds* to *0* if *Time* were a class, because *Time* is a structure, it fails to compile:

```
struct Time
{
    private int hours, minutes, seconds;
    ...
    public Time(int hh, int mm)
    {
        this.hours = hh;
        this.minutes = mm;
    }  // compile-time error: seconds not initialized
}
```

- In a class, you can initialize instance fields at their point of declaration. In a structure, you cannot. The following example would compile if *Time* were a class, but because *Time* is a structure, it causes a compile-time error:

```
struct Time
{
    private int hours = 0; // compile-time error
    private int minutes;
    private int seconds;
    ...
}
```

The following table summarizes the main differences between a structure and a class.

Question	Structure	Class
Is this a value type or a reference type?	A structure is a value type.	A class is a reference type.
Do instances live on the stack or the heap?	Structure instances are called *values* and live on the stack.	Class instances are called *objects* and live on the heap.
Can you declare a default constructor?	No	Yes
If you declare your own constructor, will the compiler still generate the default constructor?	Yes	No
If you don't initialize a field in your own constructor, will the compiler automatically initialize it for you?	No	Yes
Are you allowed to initialize instance fields at their point of declaration?	No	Yes

There are other differences between classes and structures concerning inheritance. These differences are covered in Chapter 12.

Declaring Structure Variables

After you have defined a structure type, you can use it in exactly the same way as any other type. For example, if you have defined the *Time* structure, you can create variables, fields, and parameters of type *Time*, as shown in this example:

```
struct Time
{
    private int hours, minutes, seconds;
    ...
}

class Example
{
    private Time currentTime;

    public void Method(Time parameter)
    {
        Time localVariable;
        ...
    }
}
```

 Note You can create a nullable version of a structure variable by using the ? modifier. You can then assign the *null* value to the variable:

```
Time? currentTime = null;
```

Understanding Structure Initialization

Earlier in this chapter, you saw how the fields in a structure can be initialized by using a constructor. If you call a constructor, the various rules described earlier guarantee that all the fields in the structure will be initialized:

```
Time now = new Time();
```

The following graphic depicts the state of the fields in this structure:

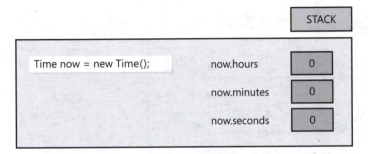

However, because structures are value types, you can create structure variables without calling a constructor, as shown in the following example:

```
Time now;
```

This time, the variable is created but its fields are left in their uninitialized state. The following graphic depicts the state of the fields in the *now* variable. Any attempt to access the values in these fields will result in a compiler error:

STACK

Time now;	now.hours	?
	now.minutes	?
	now.seconds	?

Note that in both cases, the *Time* variable is created on the stack.

If you've written your own structure constructor, you can also use that to initialize a structure variable. As explained earlier in this chapter, a structure constructor must always explicitly initialize all its fields. For example:

```
struct Time
{
    private int hours, minutes, seconds;
    ...
```

```
        public Time(int hh, int mm)
        {
            hours = hh;
            minutes = mm;
            seconds = 0;
        }
}
```

The following example initializes *now* by calling a user-defined constructor:

```
Time now = new Time(12, 30);
```

The following graphic shows the effect of this example:

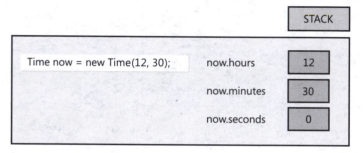

It's time to put this knowledge into practice. In the following exercise, you will create and use a structure to represent a date.

Create and use a structure type

1. In the *StructsAndEnums* project, display the Date.cs file in the *Code and Text Editor* window.

2. Add a structure named *Date* inside the *StructsAndEnums* namespace.

   This structure should contain three private fields: one named *year* of type *int*, one named *month* of type *Month* (using the enumeration you created in the preceding exercise), and one named *day* of type *int*. The *Date* structure should look exactly as follows:

   ```
   struct Date
   {
       private int year;
       private Month month;
       private int day;
   }
   ```

   Consider the default constructor that the compiler will generate for *Date*. This constructor sets the *year* to *0*, the *month* to *0* (the value of January), and the *day* to *0*. The *year* value 0 is not valid (because there was no year 0), and the *day* value 0 is also not valid (because each month starts on day 1). One way to fix this problem is to translate the *year* and *day* values by implementing the *Date* structure so that when the *year* field holds the value *Y*, this value represents the year *Y* + 1900 (or you can pick a different century if you prefer), and when the *day* field holds the value *D*, this value represents the day *D* + 1. The default constructor will then set the three fields to values that represent the date 1 January 1900.

3. Add a *public* constructor to the *Date* structure. This constructor should take three parameters: an *int* named *ccyy* for the *year*, a *Month* named *mm* for the *month*, and an *int* named *dd* for the *day*. Use these three parameters to initialize the corresponding fields. A *year* field with the value *Y* represents the year *Y* + 1900, so you need to initialize the *year* field to the value *ccyy* – 1900. A *day* field with the value *D* represents the day *D* + 1, so you need to initialize the *day* field to the value *dd* – 1.

   The *Date* structure should now look like this (with the constructor shown in bold):

```
struct Date
{
    private int year;
    private Month month;
    private int day;

    public Date(int ccyy, Month mm, int dd)
    {
        this.year = ccyy - 1900;
        this.month = mm;
        this.day = dd - 1;
    }
}
```

4. Add a *public* method named *ToString* to the *Date* structure after the constructor. This method takes no arguments and returns a string representation of the date. Remember, the value of the *year* field represents *year* + 1900, and the value of the *day* field represents *day* + 1.

> **Note** The *ToString* method is a little different from the methods you have seen so far. Every type, including structures and classes that you define, automatically has a *ToString* method whether or not you want it. Its default behavior is to convert the data in a variable to a string representation of that data. Sometimes, the default behavior is meaningful; other times, it is less so. For example, the default behavior of the *ToString* method generated for the *Date* class simply generates the string "StructsAndEnums.Date". To quote Zaphod Beeblebrox in *The Restaurant at the End of the Universe* by Douglas Adams (Pan Macmillan, 1980), this is "shrewd, but dull." You need to define a new version of this method that overrides the default behavior by using the *override* keyword. Overriding methods are discussed in more detail in Chapter 12.

The *ToString* method should look like this:

```
public override string ToString()
{
    string data = String.Format("{0} {1} {2}", this.month, this.day + 1, this.year +
1900);
    return data;
}
```

The *Format* method of the *String* class enables you to format data. It operates in a similar manner to the *Console.WriteLine* method, except that rather than displaying data to the console it returns the formatted result as a string. In this example, the positional parameters are replaced with the text representations of the values of the *month* field, the expression *this.day + 1*, and the expression *this.year + 1900*. The *ToString* method returns the formatted string as its result.

5. Display the Program.cs file in the *Code and Text Editor* window.

6. In the *DoWork* method, comment out the existing four statements. Add code to the *DoWork* method to declare a local variable named *defaultDate*, and initialize it to a *Date* value constructed by using the default *Date* constructor. Add another statement to *DoWork* to write the *defaultDate* variable to the console by calling *Console.WriteLine*.

 Note The *Console.WriteLine* method automatically calls the *ToString* method of its argument to format the argument as a string.

The *DoWork* method should now look like this:

```
static void DoWork()
{
    ...
    Date defaultDate = new Date();
    Console.WriteLine(defaultDate);
}
```

7. On the *Debug* menu, click *Start Without Debugging* to build and run the program. Verify that the date *January 1 1900* is written to the console.

8. Press the Enter key to return to the Visual Studio 2010 programming environment.

9. In the *Code and Text Editor* window, return to the *DoWork* method, and add two more statements. In the first statement, declare a local variable named *weddingAnniversary* and initialize it to July 4 2010. (In an example of supreme irony, I actually did get married on Independence Day and hence lost my independence!) In the second statement, write the value of *weddingAnniversary* to the console.

The *DoWork* method should now look like this:

```
static void DoWork()
{
    ...
    Date weddingAnniversary = new Date(2010, Month.July, 4);
    Console.WriteLine(weddingAnniversary);
}
```

 Note When you type the *new* keyword, IntelliSense automatically detects that there are two constructors available for the *Date* type.

10. On the *Debug* menu, click *Start Without Debugging*. Confirm that the date *July 4 2010* is written to the console below the previous information.

11. Press Enter to close the program.

Copying Structure Variables

You're allowed to initialize or assign one structure variable to another structure variable, but only if the structure variable on the right side is completely initialized (that is, if all its fields are populated with valid data rather than undefined values). The following example compiles because *now* is fully initialized. The graphic shows the results of performing the assignment.

```
Time now = new Time(12, 30);
Time copy = now;
```

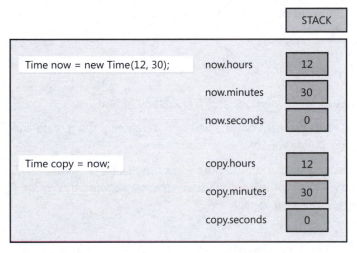

The following example fails to compile because *now* is not initialized:

```
Time now;
Time copy = now; // compile-time error: now has not been assigned
```

When you copy a structure variable, each field on the left side is set directly from the corresponding field on the right side. This copying is done as a fast, single operation that copies the contents of the entire structure and that never throws an exception. Compare this behavior with the equivalent action if *Time* were a class, in which case both variables (*now* and *copy*) would end up referencing the *same* object on the heap.

> **Note** C++ programmers should note that this copy behavior cannot be customized.

In the final exercise in this chapter, you will contrast the copy behavior of a structure with that of a class.

Compare the behavior of a structure and a class

1. In the *StructsAndEnums* project, display the Date.cs file in the *Code and Text Editor* window.

2. Add the following method to the *Date* structure. This method advances the date in the structure by one month. If, after advancing the month, the value of the *month* field has moved beyond December, this code resets the month to January and advances the value of the *year* field by 1.

```csharp
public void AdvanceMonth()
{
    this.month++;
    if (this.month == Month.December + 1)
    {
        this.month = Month.January;
        this.year++;
    }
}
```

3. Display the Program.cs file in the *Code and Text Editor* window.

4. In the *DoWork* method, comment out the first two statements that create and display the value of the *defaultDate* variable.

5. Add the following code shown in bold to the end of the *DoWork* method. This code creates a copy of the *weddingAnniversary* variable called *weddingAnniversaryCopy* and prints out the value of this new variable.

```csharp
static void DoWork()
{
    ...
    Date weddingAnniversaryCopy = weddingAnniversary;
    Console.WriteLine("Value of copy is {0}", weddingAnniversaryCopy);
}
```

6. Add the following statements to the end of the *DoWork* method that call the *AdvanceMonth* method of the *weddingAnniversary* variable, and then display the value of the *weddingAnniversary* and *weddingAnniversaryCopy* variables:

```csharp
static void DoWork()
{
    ...
    weddingAnniversaryCopy.AdvanceMonth();
    Console.WriteLine("New value of weddingAnniversary is {0}", weddingAnniversary);
    Console.WriteLine("Value of copy is {0}", weddingAnniversaryCopy);
}
```

7. On the *Debug* menu, click *Start Without Debugging* to build and run the application. Verify that the console window displays the following messages:

```
July 4 2010
Value of copy is July 4 2010
New value of weddingAnniversary is July 4 2010
Value of copy is August 4 2010
```

The first message displays the initial value of the *weddingAnniversary* variable (July 4 2010). The second message displays the value of the *weddingAnniversaryCopy* variable. You can see that it contains a copy of the date held in the *weddingAnniversary* variable (July 4 2010). The third message displays the value of the *weddingAnniversary* variable after changing the month of the *weddingAnniversaryCopy* variable to August 4 2010. Notice that it has not changed from its original value of July 4 2010. The final message displays the value of the *weddingAnniversaryCopy* variable. You can see that this has changed to August 4 2010.

8. Press Enter and return to Visual Studio 2010.

9. Display the Date.cs file in the *Code and Text Editor* window.

10. Change the *Date* structure into a class, as shown in bold in the following code example:

```
class Date
{
    ...
}
```

11. On the *Debug* menu, click *Start Without Debugging* to build and run the application again. Verify that the console window displays the following messages:

```
July 4 2010
Value of copy is July 4 2010
New value of weddingAnniversary is August 4 2010
Value of copy is August 4 2010
```

The first two messages and the fourth message are the same as before. However, the third message shows that the value of the *weddingAnniversary* variable has changed to August 4 2010. Remember that a structure is a value type, and when you copy a value type variable you make a copy of all the data in the variable. However, a class is a reference type, and when you copy a reference type variable you copy a reference to the original variable. If the data in a class variable changes, all references to this variable see the changes.

12. Press Enter and return to Visual Studio 2010.

In this chapter, you have seen how to create and use enumerations and structures. You have learned some of the similarities and differences between a structure and a class, and you have seen how to define constructors to initialize the fields in a structure. You have also learned how to represent a structure as a string by overriding the *ToString* method.

- If you want to continue to the next chapter

    Keep Visual Studio 2010 running, and turn to Chapter 10.

- If you want to exit Visual Studio 2010 now

    On the *File* menu, click *Exit*. If you see a *Save* dialog box, click *Yes* and save the project.

Chapter 9 Quick Reference

To	Do this
Declare an enumeration	Write the keyword *enum*, followed by the name of the type, followed by a pair of braces containing a comma-separated list of the enumeration literal names. For example: `enum Season { Spring, Summer, Fall, Winter }`
Declare an enumeration variable	Write the name of the enumeration on the left followed by the name of the variable, followed by a semicolon. For example: `Season currentSeason;`

Assign an enumeration variable to a value	Write the name of the enumeration literal in combination with the name of the enumeration to which it belongs. For example:
	
	`currentSeason = Spring;       // error`
	`currentSeason = Season.Spring; // correct`

Declare a structure type	Write the keyword *struct*, followed by the name of the structure type, followed by the body of the structure (the constructors, methods, and fields). For example:
	
	`struct Time`
	`{`
	`    public Time(int hh, int mm, int ss)`
	`    { ... }`
	`    ...`
	`    private int hours, minutes, seconds;`
	`}`

Declare a structure variable	Write the name of the structure type, followed by the name of the variable, followed by a semicolon. For example: `Time now;`
Initialize a structure variable to a value	Initialize the variable to a structure value created by calling the structure constructor. For example: `Time lunch = new Time(12, 30, 0);`

Chapter 10
Using Arrays and Collections

After completing this chapter, you will be able to:

- Declare, initialize, and use array variables.

- Declare, initialize, and use variables of various collection types.

You have already seen how to create and use variables of many different types. However, all the examples of variables you have seen so far have one thing in common—they hold information about a single item (an *int*, a *float*, a *Circle*, a *Date*, and so on). What happens if you need to manipulate a set of items? One solution is to create a variable for each item in the set, but this leads to a number of further questions: How many variables do you need? How should you name them? If you need to perform the same operation on each item in the set (such as increment each variable in a set of integers), how would you avoid very repetitive code? This solution assumes that you know, when you write the program, how many items you will need, but how often is this the case? For example, if you are writing an application that reads and processes records from a database, how many records are in the database, and how likely is this number to change?

Arrays and collections provide mechanisms that solve the problems posed by these questions.

What Is an Array?

An *array* is an unordered sequence of elements. All the elements in an array have the same type (unlike the fields in a structure or class, which can have different types). The elements of an array live in a contiguous block of memory and are accessed by using an integer index (unlike fields in a structure or class, which are accessed by name).

Declaring Array Variables

You declare an array variable by specifying the name of the element type, followed by a pair of square brackets, followed by the variable name. The square brackets signify that the variable is an array. For example, to declare an array of *int* variables named *pins*, you write

```
int[] pins; // Personal Identification Numbers
```

Microsoft Visual Basic programmers should note that you use square brackets and not parentheses. C and C++ programmers should note that the size of the array is not part of the declaration. Java programmers should note that you must place the square brackets *before* the variable name.

> **Note** You are not restricted to primitive types as array elements. You can also create arrays of structures, enumerations, and classes. For example, you can create an array of *Time* structures like this:
>
> ```
> Time[] times;
> ```

> **Tip** It is often useful to give array variables plural names, such as *places* (where each element is a *Place*), *people* (where each element is a *Person*), or *times* (where each element is a *Time*).

Creating an Array Instance

Arrays are reference types, regardless of the type of their elements. This means that an array variable *refers* to a contiguous block of memory holding the array elements on the heap, just as a class variable refers to an object on the heap, and this contiguous block of memory does not hold its array elements directly on the stack as a structure does. (To review values and references and the differences between the stack and the heap, see Chapter 8, "Understanding Values and References.") Remember that when you declare a class variable, memory is not allocated for the object until you create the instance by using *new*. Arrays follow the same rules—when you declare an array variable, you do not declare its size. You specify the size of an array only when you actually create an array instance.

To create an array instance, you use the *new* keyword followed by the element type, followed by the size of the array you're creating between square brackets. Creating an array also initializes its elements by using the now familiar default values (*0*, *null*, or *false*, depending on whether the type is numeric, a reference, or a Boolean, respectively). For example, to create and initialize a new array of four integers for the *pins* variable declared earlier, you write this:

```
pins = new int[4];
```

The following graphic illustrates the effects of this statement:

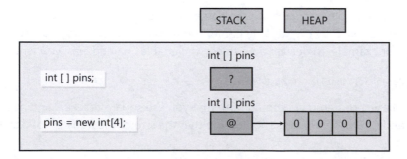

The size of an array instance does not have to be a constant; it can be calculated at run time, as shown in this example:

```
int size = int.Parse(Console.ReadLine());
int[] pins = new int[size];
```

You're allowed to create an array whose size is 0. This might sound bizarre, but it's useful in situations where the size of the array is determined dynamically, and could even be 0. An array of size 0 is not a *null* array.

Initializing Array Variables

When you create an array instance, all the elements of the array instance are initialized to a default value depending on their type. You can modify this behavior and initialize the elements of an array to specific values if you prefer. You achieve this by providing a comma-separated list of values between a pair of braces. For example, to initialize *pins* to an array of four *int* variables whose values are *9, 3, 7,* and *2,* you write this:

```
int[] pins = new int[4]{ 9, 3, 7, 2 };
```

The values between the braces do not have to be constants. They can be values calculated at run time, as shown in this example:

```
Random r = new Random();
int[] pins = new int[4]{ r.Next() % 10, r.Next() % 10,
                         r.Next() % 10, r.Next() % 10 };
```

 Note The *System.Random* class is a pseudorandom number generator. The *Next* method returns a nonnegative random integer in the range *0* to *Int32.MaxValue* by default. The *Next* method is overloaded, and other versions enable you to specify the minimum value and maximum value of the range. The default constructor for the *Random* class seeds the random number generator with a time-dependent seed value, which reduces the possibility of the class duplicating a sequence of random numbers. An overloaded version of the constructor enables you to provide your own seed value. That way, you can generate a repeatable sequence of random numbers for testing purposes.

The number of values between the braces must exactly match the size of the array instance being created:

```
int[] pins = new int[3]{ 9, 3, 7, 2 }; // compile-time error
int[] pins = new int[4]{ 9, 3, 7 };    // compile-time error
int[] pins = new int[4]{ 9, 3, 7, 2 }; // OK
```

When you're initializing an array variable, you can actually omit the *new* expression and the size of the array. The compiler calculates the size from the number of initializers and generates code to create the array. For example:

```
int[] pins = { 9, 3, 7, 2 };
```

If you create an array of structures, you can initialize each structure in the array by calling the structure constructor, as shown in this example:

```
Time[] schedule = { new Time(12,30), new Time(5,30) };
```

Creating an Implicitly Typed Array

The element type when you declare an array must match the type of elements that you attempt to store in the array. For example, if you declare *pins* to be an array of *int*, as shown in the preceding examples, you cannot store a *double*, *string*, *struct*, or anything that is not an *int* in this array. If you specify a list of initializers when declaring an array, you can let the C# compiler infer the actual type of the elements in the array for you, like this:

```
var names = new[]{"John", "Diana", "James", "Francesca"};
```

In this example, the C# compiler determines that the *names* variable is an array of strings. It is worth pointing out a couple of syntactic quirks in this declaration. First, you omit the square brackets from the type; the *names* variable in this example is declared simply as *var*, and not *var[]*. Second, you must specify the *new* operator and square brackets before the initializer list.

If you use this syntax, you must ensure that all the initializers have the same type. This next example causes the compile-time error "No best type found for implicitly typed array":

```
var bad = new[]{"John", "Diana", 99, 100};
```

However, in some cases, the compiler will convert elements to a different type if doing so makes sense. In the following code, the *numbers* array is an array of *double* because the constants *3.5* and *99.999* are both *double*, and the C# compiler can convert the integer values *1* and *2* to *double* values:

```
var numbers = new[]{1, 2, 3.5, 99.999};
```

Generally, it is best to avoid mixing types and hoping that the compiler will convert them for you.

Implicitly typed arrays are most useful when you are working with anonymous types, described in Chapter 7, "Creating and Managing Classes and Objects." The following code creates an array of anonymous objects, each containing two fields specifying the name and age of the members of my family (yes, I am younger than my wife):

```
var names = new[] { new { Name = "John", Age = 44 },
                    new { Name = "Diana", Age = 45 },
                    new { Name = "James", Age = 17 },
                    new { Name = "Francesca", Age = 15 } };
```

The fields in the anonymous types must be the same for each element of the array.

Accessing an Individual Array Element

To access an individual array element, you must provide an index indicating which element you require. For example, you can read the contents of element 2 of the *pins* array into an *int* variable by using the following code:

```
int myPin;
myPin = pins[2];
```

Similarly, you can change the contents of an array by assigning a value to an indexed element:

```
myPin = 1645;
pins[2] = myPin;
```

Array indexes are zero-based. The initial element of an array lives at index 0 and not index 1. An index value of *1* accesses the second element.

All array element access is bounds-checked. If you specify an index that is less than 0 or greater than or equal to the length of the array, the compiler throws an *IndexOutOfRangeException*, as in this example:

```
try
{
    int[] pins = { 9, 3, 7, 2 };
    Console.WriteLine(pins[4]); // error, the 4th and last element is at index 3
}
catch (IndexOutOfRangeException ex)
{
    ...
}
```

Iterating Through an Array

All arrays are instances of the *System.Array* class in the Microsoft .NET Framework, and this class defines a number of useful properties and methods. For example, you can query the *Length* property to discover how many elements an array contains and iterate through all the elements of an array by using a *for* statement. The following sample code writes the array element values of the *pins* array to the console:

```
int[] pins = { 9, 3, 7, 2 };
for (int index = 0; index < pins.Length; index++)
{
    int pin = pins[index];
    Console.WriteLine(pin);
}
```

> **Note** *Length* is a property and not a method, which is why there are no parentheses when you call it. You will learn about properties in Chapter 15, "Implementing Properties to Access Fields."

It is common for new programmers to forget that arrays start at element 0 and that the last element is numbered *Length* – 1. C# provides the *foreach* statement to enable you to iterate through the elements of an array without worrying about these issues. For example, here's the preceding *for* statement rewritten as an equivalent *foreach* statement:

```
int[] pins = { 9, 3, 7, 2 };
foreach (int pin in pins)
{
    Console.WriteLine(pin);
}
```

The *foreach* statement declares an iteration variable (in this example, *int pin*) that automatically acquires the value of each element in the array. The type of this variable must match the type of the elements in the array. The *foreach* statement is the preferred way to iterate through an array; it expresses the intention of the code directly, and all of the *for* loop scaffolding drops away. However, in a few cases, you'll find that you have to revert to a *for* statement:

- A *foreach* statement always iterates through the whole array. If you want to iterate through only a known portion of an array (for example, the first half) or to bypass certain elements (for example, every third element), it's easier to use a *for* statement.

- A *foreach* statement always iterates from index 0 through index *Length* – 1. If you want to iterate backwards or in some other sequence, it's easier to use a *for* statement.

- If the body of the loop needs to know the index of the element rather than just the value of the element, you'll have to use a *for* statement.

- If you need to modify the elements of the array, you'll have to use a *for* statement. This is because the iteration variable of the *foreach* statement is a read-only copy of each element of the array.

You can declare the iteration variable as a *var* and let the C# compiler work out the type of the variable from the type of the elements in the array. This is especially useful if you don't actually know the type of the elements in the array, such as when the array contains anonymous objects. The following example demonstrates how you can iterate through the array of family members shown earlier:

```
var names = new[] { new { Name = "John", Age = 44 },
                    new { Name = "Diana", Age = 45 },
                    new { Name = "James", Age = 17 },
                    new { Name = "Francesca", Age = 15 } };
foreach (var familyMember in names)
{
    Console.WriteLine("Name: {0}, Age: {1}", familyMember.Name, familyMember.Age);
}
```

Copying Arrays

Arrays are reference types (remember that an array is an instance of the *System.Array* class.) An array variable contains a reference to an array instance. This means that when you copy an array variable, you actually end up with two references to the same array instance—for example:

```
int[] pins = { 9, 3, 7, 2 };
int[] alias = pins; //  alias and pins refer to the same array instance
```

In this example, if you modify the value at *pins[1]*, the change will also be visible by reading *alias[1]*.

If you want to make a copy of the array instance (the data on the heap) that an array variable refers to, you have to do two things. First you need to create a new array instance of the same type and the same length as the array you are copying, and then copy the data element by element from the original array to the new array, as in this example:

```
int[] pins = { 9, 3, 7, 2 };
int[] copy = new int[pins.Length];
for (int i = 0; i < copy.Length; i++)
{
    copy[i] = pins[i];
}
```

Note that this code uses the *Length* property of the original array to specify the size of the new array.

Copying an array is actually a common requirement of many applications—so much so that the *System.Array* class provides some useful methods that you can employ to copy an array rather than writing your own code. For example, the *CopyTo* method copies the contents of one array into another array given a specified starting index:

```
int[] pins = { 9, 3, 7, 2 };
int[] copy = new int[pins.Length];
pins.CopyTo(copy, 0);
```

Another way to copy the values is to use the *System.Array* static method named *Copy*. As with *CopyTo*, you must initialize the target array before calling *Copy*:

```
int[] pins = { 9, 3, 7, 2 };
int[] copy = new int[pins.Length];
Array.Copy(pins, copy, copy.Length);
```

Yet another alternative is to use the *System.Array* instance method named *Clone*. You can call this method to create an entire array and copy it in one action:

```
int[] pins = { 9, 3, 7, 2 };
int[] copy = (int[])pins.Clone();
```

 Note The *Clone* method actually returns an *object*, which is why you must cast it to an array of the appropriate type when you use it. Furthermore, all four ways of copying shown earlier create a *shallow* copy of an array—if the elements in the array being copied contain references, the *for* loop as coded and the three preceding methods simply copy the references rather than the objects being referred to. After copying, both arrays refer to the same set of objects. If you need to create a deep copy of such an array, you must use appropriate code in a *for* loop.

Using Multidimensional Arrays

The arrays shown so far have comprised a single dimension, and you can think of them as a simple list of values. You can create arrays with more than one dimension. For example, to create a two-dimensional array, you specify an array that requires two integer indexes. The following code creates a two-dimensional array of 24 integers called *items*. If it helps, you can visualize a two-dimensional array as a table, where the first dimension specifies the number of rows and the second specifies the number of columns.

```
int[,] items = new int[4, 6];
```

To access an element in the array, you provide two index values to specify the "cell" holding the element. (A cell is the intersection of a row and a column.) The following code shows some examples using the *items* array:

```
items[2, 3] = 99;          // set the element at cell(2,3) to 99
items[2, 4] = items [2,3]; // copy the element in cell(2, 3) to cell(2, 4)
items[2, 4]++;             // increment the integer value at cell(2, 4)
```

There is no limit on the number of dimensions that you can specify for an array. The next code example creates and uses an array called *cube* that contains three dimensions. Notice that you must specify three indexes to access each element in the array.

```
int[, ,] cube = new int[5, 5, 5];
cube[1, 2, 1] = 101;
cube[1, 2, 2] = cube[1, 2, 1] * 3;
```

At this point, it is worth giving a word of caution about creating arrays with more than three dimensions. Specifically, arrays can be very memory hungry. The *cube* array contains 125 elements (5 * 5 * 5). A four-dimensional array where each dimension has a size of 5 contains 625 elements. Generally, you should always be prepared to catch and handle *OutOfMemoryException* exceptions when you use multidimensional arrays.

Using Arrays to Play Cards

In the following exercise, you will use arrays to implement an application that deals playing cards as part of a card game. The application displays a Windows Presentation Foundation (WPF) form with four hands of cards dealt at random from a regular (52-card) pack of playing cards. You will complete the code that deals the cards for each hand.

Use arrays to implement a card game

1. Start Microsoft Visual Studio 2010 if it is not already running.

2. Open the *Cards* project, located in the \Microsoft Press\Visual CSharp Step By Step\ Chapter 10\Cards Using Arrays folder in your Documents folder.

3. On the *Debug* menu, click *Start Without Debugging* to build and run the application.

   A WPF form appears with the caption *Card Game*, four text boxes (labeled *North*, *South*, *East* and *West*), and a button with the caption *Deal*.

4. Click *Deal*.

   A message box appears with the text "DealCardFromPack – TBD". You have not yet implemented the code that deals the cards.

5. Click *OK*, and then close the *Card Game* window to return to Visual Studio 2010.

6. In the *Code and Text Editor* window, display the Value.cs file.

   This file contains an enumeration called *Value*, which represents the different values that a card can have, in ascending order:

   ```
   enum Value { Two, Three, Four, Five, Six, Seven, Eight, Nine, Ten, Jack, Queen, King,
   Ace }
   ```

7. Display the Suit.cs file in the *Code and Text Editor* window.

   This file contains an enumeration called *Suit*, which represents the suits of cards in a regular pack:

   ```
   enum Suit { Clubs, Diamonds, Hearts, Spades }
   ```

8. Display the PlayingCard.cs file in the *Code and Text Editor* window.

   This file contains the *PlayingCard* class. This class models a single playing card.

```
class PlayingCard
{
    private readonly Suit suit;
    private readonly Value value;

    public PlayingCard(Suit s, Value v)
    {
        this.suit = s;
        this.value = v;
    }

    public override string ToString()
    {
        string result = string.Format("{0} of {1}", this.value, this.suit);
        return result;
    }

    public Suit CardSuit()
    {
        return this.suit;
    }

    public Value CardValue()
    {
        return this.value;
    }
}
```

This class has two *readonly* fields that represent the value and suit of the card. The constructor initializes these fields.

> **Note** A *readonly* field is useful for modeling data that should not change after it has been initialized. You can assign a value to a *readonly* field by using an initializer when you declare it, or in a constructor, but thereafter you cannot change it.

The class contains a pair of methods called *CardValue* and *CardSuit* that return this information, and it overrides the *ToString* method to return a string representation of the card.

> **Note** The *CardValue* and *CardSuit* methods are actually better implemented as properties. You will learn how to do this in Chapter 15, "Implementing Properties to Access Fields."

9. Open the Pack.cs file in the *Code and Text Editor* window.

This file contains the *Pack* class, which models a pack of playing cards. At the top of the *Pack* class are two public *const int* fields called *NumSuits* and *CardsPerSuit*. These two fields specify the number of suits in a pack of cards, and the number of cards in each suit. The private *cardPack* variable is a two-dimensional array of *PlayingCard* objects. (You will use the first dimension to specify the suit and the second to specify the value of the card in the suit.) The *randomCardSelector* variable is a *Random* object. The *Random* class is a random number generator, and you will use the *randomCardSelector* to shuffle the cards before they are dealt to each hand.

```
class Pack
{
    public const int NumSuits = 4;
    public const int CardsPerSuit = 13;
    private PlayingCard[,] cardPack;
    private Random randomCardSelector = new Random();
    ...
}
```

10. Locate the default constructor for the *Pack* class. Currently, this constructor is empty apart from a *to do* comment. Delete the comment, and add the statement shown in bold to instantiate the *cardPack* array with the correct number of elements:

```
public Pack()
{
    this.cardPack = new PlayingCard[NumSuits, CardsPerSuit];
}
```

11. Add the following code shown in bold to the *Pack* constructor. The outer *for* loop iterates through the list of values in the *Suit* enumeration, and the inner loop iterates through the values each card can have in each suit. The inner loop creates a new *PlayingCard* object of the specified suit and value and adds it to the appropriate element in the *cardPack* array.

```
for (Suit suit = Suit.Clubs; suit <= Suit.Spades; suit++)
{
    for (Value value = Value.Two; value <= Value.Ace; value++)
    {
        this.cardPack[(int)suit, (int)value] = new PlayingCard(suit, value);
    }
}
```

> **Note** You must use one of the integer types as indexes into an array. The *suit* and *value* variables are enumeration variables. However, enumerations are based on the integer types, so it is safe to cast them to *int* as shown in the code.

12. Find the *DealCardFromPack* method in the *Pack* class. The purpose of this method is to pick a random card from the pack, return it, and then remove the card from the pack to prevent it being selected again.

The first task in this method is to pick a suit at random. Delete the comment and the statement that throws the *NotImplementedException* exception from this method, and replace it with the following statement shown in bold:

```
public PlayingCard DealCardFromPack()
{
    Suit suit = (Suit)randomCardSelector.Next(NumSuits);
}
```

This statement uses the *Next* method of the *randomCardSelector* random number generator object to return a random number corresponding to a suit. The parameter to the *Next* method specifies the exclusive upper bound of the range to use; the value selected is between 0 and this value minus one. Note that the value returned is an *int*, so it has to be cast before you can assign it a *Suit* variable.

There is always the possibility that there are no more cards left in the pack of the selected suit. You need to handle this situation and pick another suit if necessary.

13. Locate the *IsSuitEmpty* method. The purpose of this method is to take a *Suit* parameter and return a Boolean value indicating whether there are any more cards of this suit left in the pack. Delete the comment and the statement that throws the *NotImplementedException* exception from this method, and add the following code shown in bold:

```
private bool IsSuitEmpty(Suit suit)
{
    bool result = true;

    for (Value value = Value.Two; value <= Value.Ace; value++)
    {
        if (!IsCardAlreadyDealt(suit, value))
        {
            result = false;
            break;
        }
    }

    return result;
}
```

This code iterates through the possible card values and determines whether there is a card left in the *cardPack* array that has the specified suit and value by using the *IsCardAlreadyDealt* method, which you will complete in the next step. If the loop finds a card, the value in the *result* variable is set to *false* and the *break* statement causes the loop to terminate. If the loop completes without finding a card, the result variable remains set to its initial value of *true*. The value of the *result* variable is passed back as the return value of the method.

14. Find the *IsCardAlreadyDealt* method. The purpose of this method is to determine whether the card with the specified suit and value has already been dealt and removed from the pack. You will see later that when the *DealFromPack* method deals a card, it removes it from the *cardPack* array and sets the corresponding element to null. Replace the comment and the statement that throws the *NotImplementedException* exception in this method with the code shown in bold:

```
private bool IsCardAlreadyDealt(Suit suit, Value value)
{
    return (this.cardPack[(int)suit, (int)value] == null);
}
```

This statement returns *true* if the element in the *cardPack* array corresponding to the suit and value is null, and it returns *false* otherwise.

15. Return to the *DealCardFromPack* method. After the code that selects a suit at random, add the following *while* loop. This loop calls the *IsSuitEmpty* method to determine whether there are any cards of the specified suit left in the pack. If not, it picks another suit at random (it might actually pick the same suit again) and checks again. The loop repeats the process until it finds a suit with at least one card left.

```
public PlayingCard DealCardFromPack()
{
    Suit suit = (Suit)randomCardSelector.Next(NumSuits);
    while (this.IsSuitEmpty(suit))
    {
        suit = (Suit)randomCardSelector.Next(NumSuits);
    }
}
```

16. You have now selected a suit at random with at least one card left. The next task is to pick a card at random in this suit. You can use the random number generator to select a card value, but as before there is no guarantee that the card with the chosen value has not already been dealt. However, you can use the same idiom as before; call the *IsCardAlreadyDealt* method to determine whether the card has been dealt before, and if so pick another card at random and try again, repeating the process until a card is found. Add the following statements to the *DealCardFromPack* method to do this:

```
public PlayingCard DealCardFromPack()
{
    ...
    Value value = (Value)randomCardSelector.Next(CardsPerSuit);
    while (this.IsCardAlreadyDealt(suit, value))
    {
        value = (Value)randomCardSelector.Next(CardsPerSuit);
    }
}
```

17. You have now selected a random playing card that has not been dealt previously. Add the following code to return this card and set the corresponding element in the *cardPack* array to null:

```
public PlayingCard DealCardFromPack()
{
    ...
    PlayingCard card = this.cardPack[(int)suit, (int)value];
    this.cardPack[(int)suit, (int)value] = null;
    return card;
}
```

18. The next step is to add the selected playing card to a hand. Open the Hand.cs file, and display it in the *Code and Text Editor* window. This file contains the *Hand* class, which implements a hand of cards (that is, all cards dealt to one player).

This file contains a *public const int* field called *HandSize*, which is set to the size of a hand of cards (13). It also contains an array of *PlayingCard* objects, which is initialized by using the *HandSize* constant. The *playingCardCount* field is used by your code to keep track of how many cards the hand currently contains as it is being populated.

```
class Hand
{
    public const int HandSize = 13;
    private PlayingCard[] cards = new PlayingCard[HandSize];
    private int playingCardCount = 0;
    ...
}
```

The *ToString* method generates a string representation of the cards in the hand. It uses a *foreach* loop to iterate through the items in the cards array and calls the *ToString* method on each *PlayingCard* object it finds. These strings are concatenated together with a newline character in between (the '\n' character) for formatting purposes.

```
public override string ToString()
{
    string result = "";
    foreach (PlayingCard card in this.cards)
    {
        result += card.ToString() + "\n";
    }

    return result;
}
```

19. Locate the *AddCardToHand* method in the *Hand* class. The purpose of this method is to add the playing card specified as the parameter to the hand. Add the statements shown in bold to this method:

```
public void AddCardToHand(PlayingCard cardDealt)
{
    if (this.playingCardCount >= HandSize)
    {
        throw new ArgumentException("Too many cards");
    }
    this.cards[this.playingCardCount] = cardDealt;
    this.playingCardCount++;
}
```

This code first checks to make sure that the hand is not already full and throws an *ArgumentException* exception if it is. Otherwise, the card is added to the *cards* array at the index specified by the *playingCardCount* variable, and this variable is then incremented.

20. In Solution Explorer, expand the Game.xaml node and then open the Game.xaml.cs file in the *Code and Text Editor* window. This is the code for the *Card Game* window. Locate the *dealClick* method. This method runs when the user clicks the *Deal* button. The code looks like this:

```
private void dealClick(object sender, RoutedEventArgs e)
{
    try
    {
        pack = new Pack();

        for (int handNum = 0; handNum < NumHands; handNum++)
        {
            hands[handNum] = new Hand();
            for (int numCards = 0; numCards < Hand.HandSize; numCards++)
            {
                PlayingCard cardDealt = pack.DealCardFromPack();
                hands[handNum].AddCardToHand(cardDealt);
            }
        }

        north.Text = hands[0].ToString();
        south.Text = hands[1].ToString();
        east.Text = hands[2].ToString();
        west.Text = hands[3].ToString();
    }
    catch (Exception ex)
    {
        MessageBox.Show(ex.Message, "Error", MessageBoxButton.OK, MessageBoxImage.
Error);
    }
}
```

The first statement in the *try* block creates a new pack of cards. The outer *for* loop creates four hands from this pack of cards and stores them in an array called *hands*. The inner *for* loop populates each hand by using the *DealCardFromPack* method to retrieve a card at random from the pack and the *AddCardToHand* method to add this card to a hand.

When all the cards have been dealt, each hand is displayed in the text boxes on the form. These text boxes are called *north*, *south*, *east*, and *west*. The code uses the *ToString* method of each hand to format the output.

If an exception occurs at any point, the catch handler displays a message box with the error message for the exception.

21. On the *Debug* menu, click *Start Without Debugging*. When the *Card Game* window appears, click *Deal*. The card in the pack should be dealt at random to each hand, and the cards in each hand should be displayed on the form as shown in the following image:

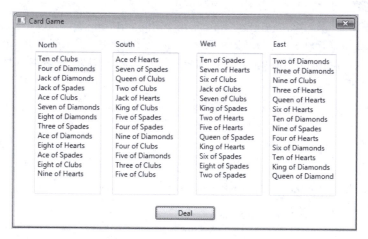

22. Click *Deal* again. A new set of hands is dealt and the cards in each hand change.

23. Close the *Card Game* window and return to Visual Studio.

What Are Collection Classes?

Arrays are useful, but they have their limitations—one of the most obvious being that you have to use an integer index to access elements in an array. Fortunately, arrays are only one way to collect elements of the same type. The Microsoft .NET Framework provides several classes that also collect elements together in other specialized ways. These are the collection classes, and they live in the *System.Collections* namespace and sub-namespaces.

Aside from the issue with indexes, there is one other fundamental difference between an array and a collection. An array can hold value types. The basic collection classes accept, hold, and return their elements as *object* types—that is, the element type of a collection class is an *object*. To understand the implications of this, it is helpful to contrast an array of *int* variables (*int* is a value type) with an array of objects (*object* is a reference type). Because *int* is a value type, an array of *int* variables holds its *int* values directly, as shown in the following image:

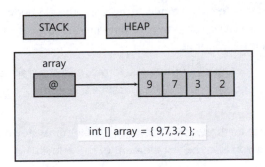

Now consider the effect when the array is an array of objects. You can still add integer values to this array. (In fact, you can add values of any type to it.) When you add an integer value, it is automatically boxed, and the array element (an *object* reference) refers to the boxed copy of the integer value. Similarly, when you remove a value from an array of objects, you must unbox it by using a cast. (For a refresher on boxing, refer to Chapter 8.) The following picture shows an *object* array populated with integer values:

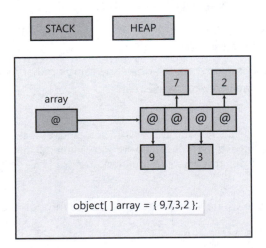

The following sections provide a very quick overview of four of the most useful collection classes. Refer to the Microsoft .NET Framework Class Library documentation for more details on each class.

> **Note** There are other collection classes that don't always use *object* as their element type and that can hold value types as well as references, but you need to know a bit more about C# before learning about them. You will meet these collection classes in Chapter 18, "Introducing Generics."

The *ArrayList* Collection Class

ArrayList is a useful class for shuffling elements around in an array. There are certain occasions when an ordinary array can be too restrictive:

- If you want to resize an array, you have to create a new array, copy the elements (leaving out some if the new array is smaller), and then update any references to the original array so that they refer to the new array.

- If you want to remove an element from an array, you have to move all the trailing elements up by one place. Even this doesn't quite work, because you end up with two copies of the last element.

- If you want to insert an element into an array, you have to move elements down by one place to make a free slot. However, you lose the last element of the array!

The *ArrayList* collection class provides the following features to help overcome these limitations:

- You can remove an element from an *ArrayList* by using its *Remove* method. The *ArrayList* automatically reorders its elements.

- You can add an element to the end of an *ArrayList* by using its *Add* method. You supply the element to be added. The *ArrayList* resizes itself if necessary.

- You can insert an element into the middle of an *ArrayList* by using its *Insert* method. Again, the *ArrayList* resizes itself if necessary.

- You can reference an existing element in an *ArrayList* object by using ordinary array notation, with square brackets and the index of the element.

> **Note** As with arrays, if you use *foreach* to iterate through an *ArrayList*, you cannot use the iteration variable to modify the contents of the *ArrayList*. Additionally, you cannot call the *Remove*, *Add*, or *Insert* method in a *foreach* loop that iterates through an *ArrayList*.

Here's an example that shows how you can create, manipulate, and iterate through the contents of an *ArrayList*:

```
using System;
using System.Collections;
...
ArrayList numbers = new ArrayList();
...
// fill the ArrayList
foreach (int number in new int[12]{10, 9, 8, 7, 7, 6, 5, 10, 4, 3, 2, 1})
{
    numbers.Add(number);
}
...
```

```csharp
// insert an element in the penultimate position in the list, and move the last item up
// (the first parameter is the position;
// the second parameter is the value being inserted)
numbers.Insert(numbers.Count-1, 99);

// remove first element whose value is 7 (the 4th element, index 3)
numbers.Remove(7);
// remove the element that's now the 7th element, index 6 (10)
numbers.RemoveAt(6);
...
// iterate remaining 11 elements using a for statement
for (int i = 0; i < numbers.Count; i++)
{
    int number = (int)numbers[i]; // notice the cast, which unboxes the value
    Console.WriteLine(number);
}
...
// iterate remaining 11 elements using a foreach statement
foreach (int number in numbers)  // no cast needed
{
    Console.WriteLine(number);
}
```

The output of this code is shown here:

```
10
9
8
7
6
5
4
3
2
99
1
10
9
8
7
6
5
4
3
2
99
1
```

Note The way you determine the number of elements for an *ArrayList* is different from querying the number of items in an array. When using an *ArrayList*, you examine the *Count* property, and when using an array, you examine the *Length* property.

The *Queue* Collection Class

The *Queue* class implements a first-in, first-out (FIFO) mechanism. An element is inserted into the queue at the back (the enqueue operation) and is removed from the queue at the front (the dequeue operation).

Here's an example of a queue and its operations:

```
using System;
using System.Collections;
...
Queue numbers = new Queue();
...
// fill the queue
foreach (int number in new int[4]{9, 3, 7, 2})
{
    numbers.Enqueue(number);
    Console.WriteLine(number + " has joined the queue");
}
...
// iterate through the queue
foreach (int number in numbers)
{
    Console.WriteLine(number);
}
...
// empty the queue
while (numbers.Count > 0)
{
    int number = (int)numbers.Dequeue(); // cast required to unbox the value
    Console.WriteLine(number + " has left the queue");
}
```

The output from this code is shown here:

```
9 has joined the queue
3 has joined the queue
7 has joined the queue
2 has joined the queue
9
3
7
2
9 has left the queue
3 has left the queue
7 has left the queue
2 has left the queue
```

The *Stack* Collection Class

The *Stack* class implements a last-in, first-out (LIFO) mechanism. An element joins the stack at the top (the push operation) and leaves the stack at the top (the pop operation). To visualize this, think of a stack of dishes: new dishes are added to the top and dishes are removed from the top, making the last dish to be placed on the stack the first one to be removed. (The dish at the bottom is rarely used and will inevitably require washing before you can put any food on it as it will be covered in grime!) Here's an example:

```
using System;
using System.Collections;
...
Stack numbers = new Stack();
...
// fill the stack
foreach (int number in new int[4]{9, 3, 7, 2})
{
    numbers.Push(number);
    Console.WriteLine(number + " has been pushed on the stack");
}
...
// iterate through the stack
foreach (int number in numbers)
{
    Console.WriteLine(number);
}
...
// empty the stack
while (numbers.Count > 0)
{
    int number = (int)numbers.Pop();
    Console.WriteLine(number +  " has been popped off the stack");
}
```

The output from this program is shown here:

```
9 has been pushed on the stack
3 has been pushed on the stack
7 has been pushed on the stack
2 has been pushed on the stack
2
7
3
9
2 has been popped off the stack
7 has been popped off the stack
3 has been popped off the stack
9 has been popped off the stack
```

The *Hashtable* Collection Class

The array and *ArrayList* types provide a way to map an integer index to an element. You provide an integer index inside square brackets (for example, [4]), and you get back the element at index 4 (which is actually the fifth element). However, sometimes you might want to provide a mapping where the type you map from is not an *int* but rather some other type, such as *string*, *double*, or *Time*. In other languages, this is often called an *associative array*. The *Hashtable* class provides this functionality by internally maintaining two *object* arrays, one for the *keys* you're mapping from and one for the *values* you're mapping to. When you insert a key/value pair into a *Hashtable*, it automatically tracks which key belongs to which value and enables you to retrieve the value that is associated with a specified key quickly and easily. There are some important consequences of the design of the *Hashtable* class:

- A *Hashtable* cannot contain duplicate keys. If you call the *Add* method to add a key that is already present in the keys array, you'll get an exception. You can, however, use the square brackets notation to add a key/value pair (as shown in the following example), without danger of an exception, even if the key has already been added. You can test whether a *Hashtable* already contains a particular key by using the *ContainsKey* method.

- Internally, a *Hashtable* is a sparse data structure that operates best when it has plenty of memory to work in. The size of a *Hashtable* in memory can grow quite quickly as you insert more elements.

- When you use a *foreach* statement to iterate through a *Hashtable*, you get back a *DictionaryEntry*. The *DictionaryEntry* class provides access to the key and value elements in both arrays through the *Key* property and the *Value* properties.

Here is an example that associates the ages of members of my family with their names and then prints the information:

```
using System;
using System.Collections;
...
Hashtable ages = new Hashtable();
...
// fill the Hashtable
ages["John"] = 44;
ages["Diana"] = 45;
ages["James"] = 17;
ages["Francesca"] = 15;
...
// iterate using a foreach statement
// the iterator generates a DictionaryEntry object containing a key/value pair
foreach (DictionaryEntry element in ages)
{
    string name = (string)element.Key;
    int age = (int)element.Value;
    Console.WriteLine("Name: {0}, Age: {1}", name, age);
}
```

The output from this program is shown here:

```
Name: Diana, Age: 45
Name: James, Age: 17
Name: Francesca, Age: 15
Name: John, Age: 44
```

The *SortedList* Collection Class

The *SortedList* class is very similar to the *Hashtable* class in that it enables you to associate keys with values. The main difference is that the keys array is always sorted. (It is called a *SortedList*, after all.)

When you insert a key/value pair into a *SortedList*, the key is inserted into the keys array at the correct index to keep the keys array sorted. The value is then inserted into the values array at the same index. The *SortedList* class automatically ensures that keys and values are kept synchronized, even when you add and remove elements. This means that you can insert key/value pairs into a *SortedList* in any sequence; they are always sorted based on the value of the keys.

Like the *Hashtable* class, a *SortedList* cannot contain duplicate keys. When you use a *foreach* statement to iterate through a *SortedList*, you get back a *DictionaryEntry*. However, the *DictionaryEntry* objects will be returned sorted by the *Key* property.

Here is the same example that associates the ages of members of my family with their names and then prints the information, but this version has been adjusted to use a *SortedList* rather than a *Hashtable*:

```
using System;
using System.Collections;
...
SortedList ages = new SortedList();
...
// fill the SortedList
ages["John"] = 44;
ages["Diana"] = 45;
ages["James"] = 17;
ages["Francesca"] = 15;
...
// iterate using a foreach statement
// the iterator generates a DictionaryEntry object containing a key/value pair
foreach (DictionaryEntry element in ages)
{
    string name = (string)element.Key;
    int age = (int)element.Value;
    Console.WriteLine("Name: {0}, Age: {1}", name, age);
}
```

The output from this program is sorted alphabetically by the names of my family members:

```
Name: Diana, Age: 45
Name: Francesca, Age: 15
Name: James, Age: 17
Name: John, Age: 44
```

Using Collection Initializers

The examples in the preceding subsections have shown you how to add individual elements to a collection by using the method most appropriate to that collection (*Add* for an *ArrayList*, *Enqueue* for a *Queue*, *Push* for a *Stack*, and so on). You can also initialize *some* collection types when you declare them, using a syntax similar to that supported by arrays. For example, the following statement creates and initializes the *numbers ArrayList* object shown earlier, demonstrating an alternative technique to repeatedly calling the *Add* method:

```
ArrayList numbers = new ArrayList(){10, 9, 8, 7, 7, 6, 5, 10, 4, 3, 2, 1};
```

Internally, the C# compiler actually converts this initialization to a series of calls to the *Add* method. Consequently, you can use this syntax only for collections that actually support the *Add* method. (The *Stack* and *Queue* classes do not.)

For more complex collections such as *Hashtable* that take key/value pairs, you can specify each key/value pair as an anonymous type in the initializer list, like this:

```
Hashtable ages =
    new Hashtable(){{"John", 44}, {"Diana", 45}, {"James", 17}, {"Francesca", 15}};
```

The first item in each pair is the key, and the second is the value.

Comparing Arrays and Collections

Here's a summary of the important differences between arrays and collections:

- An array declares the type of the elements that it holds, whereas a collection doesn't. This is because the collections store their elements as objects.

- An array instance has a fixed size and cannot grow or shrink. A collection can dynamically resize itself as required.

- An array can have more than one dimension. A collection is linear. However, the items in a collection can be collections themselves, so you can imitate a multidimensional array as a collection of collections.

Using Collection Classes to Play Cards

In the next exercise, you will convert the card game you developed in the previous exercise to use collections rather than arrays.

Use collections to implement a card game

1. Return to the *Cards* project from the previous exercise.

Note A completed version of the project for the previous exercise is available in the \Microsoft Press\Visual CSharp Step By Step\Chapter 10\Cards Using Arrays – Complete folder in your Documents folder.

2. Display the Pack.cs file in the *Code and Text Editor* window. Notice the following *using* statement near the top of the file:

```
using System.Collections;
```

The collection classes are located in this namespace.

3. In the *Pack* class, change the definition of the *cardPack* two-dimensional array to a *Hashtable* object, as shown here in bold:

```
class Pack
{
    ...
    private Hashtable cardPack;
    ...
}
```

Remember that the *Hashtable* class defines a collection of *object* types, and you do not specify the *PlayingCard* type. Also, the original array had two dimensions whereas a *Hashtable* only has one. You will emulate a two-dimensional array by using *SortedList* collection objects as elements in the *Hashtable*.

4. Locate the *Pack* constructor. Modify the first statement in this constructor to instantiate the *cardPack* variable as a new *Hashtable* object rather than an array, as shown here in bold.

```
public Pack()
{
    this.cardPack = new Hashtable();
    ...
}
```

5. In the outer *for* loop, declare a *SortedList* collection object called *cardsInSuit*. Change the code in the inner *for* loop to add the new *PlayingCard* object to this collection rather than the array. After the inner *for* loop, add the *SortedList* object to the *card-Pack Hashtable*, specifying the value of the *suit* variable as the key to this item. (The *SortedList* contains all the cards in the pack for the specified suit, and the *Hashtable* contains a collection of these *SortedList* objects.)

The following code shows the completed constructor with the changes highlighted in bold:

```
public Pack()
{
    this.cardPack = new Hashtable();

    for (Suit suit = Suit.Clubs; suit <= Suit.Spades; suit++)
    {
```

```
SortedList cardsInSuit = new SortedList();
for (Value value = Value.Two; value <= Value.Ace; value++)
{
    cardsInSuit.Add(value, new PlayingCard(suit, value));
}
this.cardPack.Add(suit, cardsInSuit);
    }
}
```

6. Find the *DealCardFromPack* method. Recall that this method picks a card at random from the pack, removes the card from the pack, and returns this card. The logic for selecting the card does not require any changes, but the statements at the end of the method that retrieve the card and remove it from the array must be updated to use the *Hashtable* collection instead.

Modify the code after the closing brace of the second *while* loop as shown in the following code in bold.

```
public PlayingCard DealCardFromPack()
{
    Suit suit = (Suit)randomCardSelector.Next(NumSuits);
    while (this.IsSuitEmpty(suit))
    {
        suit = (Suit)randomCardSelector.Next(NumSuits);
    }

    Value value = (Value)randomCardSelector.Next(CardsPerSuit);
    while (this.IsCardAlreadyDealt(suit, value))
    {
        value = (Value)randomCardSelector.Next(CardsPerSuit);
    }

    SortedList cardsInSuit = (SortedList) cardPack[suit];
    PlayingCard card = (PlayingCard)cardsInSuit[value];
    cardsInSuit.Remove(value);
    return card;
}
```

The *Hashtable* contains a collection of *SortedList* objects, one for each suit of cards. This new code retrieves the *SortedList* for the card of the suit selected at random from the *Hashtable*, and then it retrieves the card with the selected value from this *SortedList*. The final new statement removes the card from the *SortedList*.

7. Locate the *IsCardAlreadyDealt* method. This method determines whether a card has already been dealt by seeing whether the corresponding element in the array has been set to null. You need to modify this method to determine whether a card with the specified value is present in the *SortedList* for the suit in the *cardPack Hashtable*. Update the method as shown in bold:

```
private bool IsCardAlreadyDealt(Suit suit, Value value)
{
    SortedList cardsInSuit = (SortedList)this.cardPack[suit];
    return (!cardsInSuit.ContainsKey(value));
}
```

8. Display the Hand.cs file in the *Code and Text Editor* window. This class uses an array to hold the playing cards for the hand. Modify the definition of the *cards* array to use an *ArrayList* collection, as shown in bold:

```
class Hand
{
    public const int HandSize = 13;
    private ArrayList cards = new ArrayList();
    ...
}
```

9. Find the *AddCardToHand* method. This method currently checks to see whether the hand is full, and if not it adds the card provided as the parameter to the cards array, at the index specified by the *playingCardCount* variable.

Update this method to use the *Add* method of the *ArrayList* class instead. This change also removes the need to explicitly keep track of how many cards the collection holds because you can use the *Count* property instead. Modify the *if* statement that checks whether the hand is full to reference this property and delete the *playingCardCount* variable from the class.

The completed method should look like this.

```
public void AddCardToHand(PlayingCard cardDealt)
{
    if (this.cards.Count >= HandSize)
    {
        throw new ArgumentException("Too many cards");
    }
    this.cards.Add(cardDealt);
}
```

10. On the *Debug* menu, click *Start Without Debugging* to build and run the application.

11. When the *Card Game* window appears, click *Deal*. Verify that the cards are dealt and that the populated hands appear as before. Click *Deal* again to generate another random set of hands.

12. Close the form and return to Visual Studio 2010.

In this chapter, you have learned how to create and use arrays to manipulate sets of data. You have also seen how to use some of the common collection classes to store and access data.

- If you want to continue to the next chapter

  Keep Visual Studio 2010 running, and turn to Chapter 11.

- If you want to exit Visual Studio 2010 now

  On the *File* menu, click *Exit*. If you see a *Save* dialog box, click *Yes* and save the project.

Chapter 10 Quick Reference

To	Do this
Declare an array variable	Write the name of the element type, followed by square brackets, followed by the name of the variable, followed by a semicolon. For example: ```bool[] flags;```
Create an instance of an array	Write the keyword *new*, followed by the name of the element type, followed by the size of the array enclosed in square brackets. For example: ```bool[] flags = new bool[10];```

Initialize the elements of an array (or of a collection that supports the *Add* method) to specific values	For an array, write the specific values in a comma-separated list enclosed in braces. For example:
	
	```bool[] flags = { true, false, true, false };```
	
	For a collection, use the *new* operator and the collection type with the specific values in a comma-separated list enclosed in braces. For example:
	
	```ArrayList numbers = new ArrayList(){10, 9, 8, 7, 6, 5};```

Find the number of elements in an array	Use the *Length* property. For example:
	
	```int [] flags = ...;```
	```...```
	```int noOfElements = flags.Length;```

Find the number of elements in a collection	Use the *Count* property. For example:
	
	```ArrayList flags = new ArrayList();```
	```...```
	```int noOfElements = flags.Count;```

Access a single array element	Write the name of the array variable, followed by the integer index of the element enclosed in square brackets. Remember, array indexing starts at 0, not 1. For example: ```bool initialElement = flags[0];```

Iterate through the elements of an array or a collection	Use a *for* statement or a *foreach* statement. For example:
	
	```bool[] flags = { true, false, true, false };```
	```for (int i = 0; i < flags.Length; i++)```
	```{```
	``` Console.WriteLine(flags[i]);```
	```}```
	
	```foreach (bool flag in flags)```
	```{```
	``` Console.WriteLine(flag);```
	```}```

Chapter 11
Understanding Parameter Arrays

After completing this chapter, you will be able to:

- Write a method that can accept any number of arguments by using the *params* keyword.

- Write a method that can accept any number of arguments of any type by using the *params* keyword in combination with the *object* type.

- Explain the differences between methods that take parameter arrays and methods that take optional parameters.

Parameter arrays are useful if you want to write methods that can take any number of arguments, possibly of different types, as parameters. If you are familiar with object-oriented concepts, you might well be grinding your teeth in frustration at this sentence. After all, the object-oriented approach to solving this problem is to define overloaded methods.

Overloading is the technical term for declaring two or more methods with the same name in the same scope. Being able to overload a method is very useful in cases where you want to perform the same action on arguments of different types. The classic example of overloading in Microsoft Visual C# is *Console.WriteLine*. The *WriteLine* method is overloaded numerous times so that you can pass any primitive type argument:

```
class Console
{
    public static void WriteLine(int parameter)
    ...
    public static void WriteLine(double parameter)
    ...
    public static void WriteLine(decimal parameter)
    ...
}
```

As useful as overloading is, it doesn't cover every case. In particular, overloading doesn't easily handle a situation in which the type of parameters doesn't vary but the number of parameters does. For example, what if you want to write many values to the console? Do you have to provide versions of *Console.WriteLine* that can take two parameters, other versions that can take three parameters, and so on? That would quickly get tedious. And doesn't the massive duplication of all these overloaded methods worry you? It should. Fortunately, there is a way to write a method that takes a variable number of arguments (a *variadic method*): you can use a parameter array (a parameter declared with the *params* keyword).

To understand how *params* arrays solve this problem, it helps to first understand the uses and shortcomings of ordinary arrays.

Using Array Arguments

Suppose you want to write a method to determine the minimum value in a set of values passed as parameters. One way is to use an array. For example, to find the smallest of several *int* values, you could write a static method named *Min* with a single parameter representing an array of *int* values:

```
class Util
{
    public static int Min(int[] paramList)
    {
        if (paramList == null || paramList.Length == 0)
        {
            throw new ArgumentException("Util.Min: not enough arguments");
        }
        int currentMin = paramList [0];
        foreach (int i in paramList)
        {
            if (i < currentMin)
            {
                currentMin = i;
            }
        }
        return currentMin;
    }
}
```

Note The *ArgumentException* class is specifically designed to be thrown by a method if the arguments supplied do not meet the requirements of the method.

To use the *Min* method to find the minimum of two *int* values, you write this:

```
int[] array = new int[2];
array[0] = first;
array[1] = second;
int min = Util.Min(array);
```

And to use the *Min* method to find the minimum of three *int* values, you write this:

```
int[] array = new int[3];
array[0] = first;
array[1] = second;
array[2] = third;
int min = Util.Min(array);
```

You can see that this solution avoids the need for a large number of overloads, but it does so at a price: you have to write additional code to populate the array that you pass in. However, you can get the compiler to write some of this code for you by using the *params* keyword to declare a *params* array.

Declaring a *params* Array

You use the *params* keyword as an array parameter modifier. For example, here's *Min* again—this time with its array parameter declared as a *params* array:

```
class Util
{
    public static int Min(params int[] paramList)
    {
        // code exactly as before
    }
}
```

The effect of the *params* keyword on the *Min* method is that it allows you to call it by using any number of integer arguments. For example, to find the minimum of two integer values, you write this:

```
int min = Util.Min(first, second);
```

The compiler translates this call into code similar to this:

```
int[] array = new int[2];
array[0] = first;
array[1] = second;
int min = Util.Min(array);
```

To find the minimum of three integer values, you write the code shown here, which is also converted by the compiler to the corresponding code that uses an array:

```
int min = Util.Min(first, second, third);
```

Both calls to *Min* (one call with two arguments and another with three arguments) resolve to the same *Min* method with the *params* keyword. And as you can probably guess, you can call this *Min* method with any number of *int* arguments. The compiler just counts the number of *int* arguments, creates an *int* array of that size, fills the array with the arguments, and then calls the method by passing the single array parameter.

> **Note** C and C++ programmers might recognize *params* as a type-safe equivalent of the *varargs* macros from the header file stdarg.h.

There are several points worth noting about *params* arrays:

- You can't use the *params* keyword on multidimensional arrays. The code in the following example will not compile:

    ```
    // compile-time error
    public static int Min(params int[,] table)
    ...
    ```

- You can't overload a method based solely on the *params* keyword. The *params* keyword does not form part of a method's signature, as shown in this example:

```
// compile-time error: duplicate declaration
public static int Min(int[] paramList)
...
public static int Min(params int[] paramList)
...
```

- You're not allowed to specify the *ref* or *out* modifier with *params* arrays, as shown in this example:

```
// compile-time errors
public static int Min(ref params int[] paramList)
...
public static int Min(out params int[] paramList)
...
```

- A *params* array must be the last parameter. (This means that you can have only one *params* array per method.) Consider this example:

```
// compile-time error
public static int Min(params int[] paramList, int i)
...
```

- A non-*params* method always takes priority over a *params* method. This means that if you want to, you can still create an overloaded version of a method for the common cases. For example:

```
public static int Min(int leftHandSide, int rightHandSide)
...
public static int Min(params int[] paramList)
...
```

The first version of the *Min* method is used when called using two *int* arguments. The second version is used if any other number of *int* arguments is supplied. This includes the case where the method is called with no arguments.

Adding the non-*params* array method might be a useful optimization technique because the compiler won't have to create and populate so many arrays.

Using *params object[ ]*

A parameter array of type *int* is very useful because it enables you to pass any number of *int* arguments in a method call. However, what if not only the number of arguments varies but also the argument type? C# has a way to solve this problem, too. The technique is based on the facts that *object* is the root of all classes and that the compiler can generate code that converts value types (things that aren't classes) to objects by using boxing, as described in Chapter 8, "Understanding Values and References." You can use a parameters array of type *object* to declare a method that accepts any number of *object* arguments, allowing the arguments passed in to be of any type. Look at this example:

```
class Black
{
    public static void Hole(params object [] paramList)
    ...
}
```

I've called this method *Black.Hole*, because no argument can escape from it:

- You can pass the method no arguments at all, in which case the compiler will pass an object array whose length is 0:

  ```
  Black.Hole();
  // converted to Black.Hole(new object[0]);
  ```

> **Tip** It's perfectly safe to attempt to iterate through a zero-length array by using a *foreach* statement.

- You can call the *Black.Hole* method by passing *null* as the argument. An array is a reference type, so you're allowed to initialize an array with *null*:

  ```
  Black.Hole(null);
  ```

- You can pass the *Black.Hole* method an actual array. In other words, you can manually create the array normally created by the compiler:

  ```
  object[] array = new object[2];
  array[0] = "forty two";
  array[1] = 42;
  Black.Hole(array);
  ```

- You can pass the *Black.Hole* method any other arguments of different types, and these arguments will automatically be wrapped inside an *object* array:

  ```
  Black.Hole("forty two", 42);
  //converted to Black.Hole(new object[]{"forty two", 42});
  ```

The *Console.WriteLine* Method

The *Console* class contains many overloads for the *WriteLine* method. One of these overloads looks like this:

```
public static void WriteLine(string format, params object[] arg);
```

This overload enables the *WriteLine* method to support a format string argument that contains placeholders, each of which can be replaced at run time with a variable of any type. Here's an example of a call to this method:

```
Console.WriteLine("Forename:{0}, Middle Initial:{1}, Last name:{2}, Age:{3}", fname,
mi, lname, age);
```

The compiler resolves this call into the following:

```
Console.WriteLine("Forename:{0}, Middle Initial:{1}, Last name:{2}, Age:{3}", new
object[4]{fname, mi, lname, age});
```

Using a *params* Array

In the following exercise, you will implement and test a *static* method named *Util.Sum*. The purpose of this method is to calculate the sum of a variable number of *int* arguments passed to it, returning the result as an *int*. You will do this by writing *Util.Sum* to take a *params int[]* parameter. You will implement two checks on the *params* parameter to ensure that the *Util. Sum* method is completely robust. You will then call the *Util.Sum* method with a variety of different arguments to test it.

Write a *params* array method

1. Start Microsoft Visual Studio 2010 if it is not already running.

2. Open the *ParamsArray* project, located in the \Microsoft Press\Visual CSharp Step By Step\Chapter 11\ ParamArrays folder in your Documents folder.

3. Display the Util.cs file in the *Code and Text Editor* window.

   The Util.cs file contains an empty class named *Util* in the *ParamsArray* namespace.

4. Add a public static method named *Sum* to the *Util* class.

   The *Sum* method returns an *int* and accepts a *params* array of *int* values. The *Sum* method should look like this:

```
public static int Sum(params int[] paramList)
{
}
```

   The first step in implementing the *Sum* method is to check the *paramList* parameter. Apart from containing a valid set of integers, it can also be *null* or it can be an array of zero length. In both of these cases, it is difficult to calculate the sum, so the best option is to throw an *ArgumentException*. (You could argue that the sum of the integers in a zero-length array is 0, but we will treat this situation as an exception in this example.)

5. Add code to *Sum* that throws an *ArgumentException* if *paramList* is *null*.

The *Sum* method should now look like this:

```
public static int Sum(params int[] paramList)
{
    if (paramList == null)
    {
        throw new ArgumentException("Util.Sum: null parameter list");
    }
}
```

6. Add code to the *Sum* method that throws an *ArgumentException* if the length of *array* is 0, as shown in bold here:

```
public static int Sum(params int[] paramList)
{
    if (paramList == null)
    {
        throw new ArgumentException("Util.Sum: null parameter list");
    }

    if (paramList.Length == 0)
    {
        throw new ArgumentException("Util.Sum: empty parameter list");
    }
}
```

If the array passes these two tests, the next step is to add all the elements inside the array together.

7. You can use a *foreach* statement to add all the elements together. You will need a local variable to hold the running total. Declare an integer variable named *sumTotal*, and initialize it to 0 following the code from the preceding step. Add a *foreach* statement to the *Sum* method to iterate through the *paramList* array. The body of this *foreach* loop should add each element in the array to *sumTotal*. At the end of the method, return the value of *sumTotal* by using a *return* statement, as shown in bold here:

```
class Util
{
    public static int Sum(params int[] paramList)
    {
        ...
        int sumTotal = 0;
        foreach (int i in paramList)
        {
            sumTotal += i;
        }
        return sumTotal;
    }
}
```

8. On the *Build* menu, click *Build Solution*. Confirm that your solution builds without any errors.

Test the *Util.Sum* method

1. Display the Program.cs file in the *Code and Text Editor* window.

2. In the *Code and Text Editor* window, locate the *DoWork* method in the *Program* class.

3. Add the following statement to the *DoWork* method:

```
Console.WriteLine(Util.Sum(null));
```

4. On the *Debug* menu, click *Start Without Debugging*.

   The program builds and runs, writing the following message to the console:

```
Exception: Util.Sum: null parameter list
```

   This confirms that the first check in the method works.

5. Press the Enter key to close the program and return to Visual Studio 2010.

6. In the *Code and Text Editor* window, change the call to *Console.WriteLine* in *DoWork* as shown here:

```
Console.WriteLine(Util.Sum());
```

   This time, the method is called without any arguments. The compiler translates the empty argument list into an empty array.

7. On the *Debug* menu, click *Start Without Debugging*.

   The program builds and runs, writing the following message to the console:

```
Exception: Util.Sum: empty parameter list
```

   This confirms that the second check in the method works.

8. Press the Enter key to close the program and return to Visual Studio 2010.

9. Change the call to *Console.WriteLine* in *DoWork* as follows:

```
Console.WriteLine(Util.Sum(10, 9, 8, 7, 6, 5, 4, 3, 2, 1));
```

10. On the *Debug* menu, click *Start Without Debugging*.

    Verify that the program builds, runs, and writes the value *55* to the console.

11. Press Enter to close the application and return to Visual Studio 2010.

Comparing Parameters Arrays and Optional Parameters

In Chapter 3, "Writing Methods and Applying Scope", you saw how to define methods that take optional parameters. At first glance, it appears there is a degree of overlap between methods that use parameter arrays and methods that take optional parameters. However, there are fundamental differences between them:

■ A method that takes optional parameters still has a fixed parameter list, and you cannot pass an arbitrary list of arguments. The compiler generates code that inserts the default values onto the stack for any missing arguments before the method runs, and the method is not aware of which arguments the caller provided and which are the compiler-generated defaults.

■   A method that uses a parameter array effectively has a completely arbitrary list of parameters, and none of them have default values. Furthermore, the method can determine exactly how many arguments the caller provided.

Generally, you use parameter arrays for methods that can take any number of parameters (including none), whereas you use optional parameters only where it is not convenient to force a caller to provide an argument for every parameter.

There is one final question worth pondering. If you define a method that takes a parameter list and provide an overload that takes optional parameters, it is not always immediately apparent which version of the method will be called if the argument list in the calling statement matches both method signatures. You will investigate this scenario in the final exercise in this chapter.

Compare a params array and optional parameters

1. Return to the ParamsArray solution in Visual Studio 2010, and display the Util.cs file in the *Code and Text Editor* window.

2. Add the following *Console.WriteLine* statement shown in bold to the start of the *Sum* method in the *Util* class:

```
public static int Sum(params int[] paramList)
{
    Console.WriteLine("Using parameter list");
    ...
}
```

3. Add another implementation of the *Sum* method to the *Util* class. This version should take four optional *int* parameters with a default value of 0. In the body of the method, output the message "Using optional parameters", and then calculate and return the sum of the four parameters. The completed method should look like this:

```
public static int Sum(int param1 = 0, int param2 = 0, int param3 = 0, int param4 = 0)
{
    Console.WriteLine("Using optional parameters");
    int sumTotal = param1 + param2 + param3 + param4;
    return sumTotal;
}
```

4. Display the Program.cs file in the *Code and Text Editor* window.

5. In the *DoWork* method, comment out the existing code and add the following statement:

```
Console.WriteLine(Util.Sum(2, 4, 6, 8));
```

This statement calls the *Sum* method, passing four *int* parameters. This call matches both overloads of the *Sum* method.

6. On the *Debug* menu, click *Start Without Debugging* to build and run the application.

When the application runs, it displays the following messages:

```
Using optional parameters
20
```

In this case, the compiler generated code that called the method that takes four optional parameters. This is the version of the method that most closely matches the method call.

7. Press Enter and return to Visual Studio.

8. In the *DoWork* method, change the statement that calls the *Sum* method, as shown here:

```
Console.WriteLine(Util.Sum(2, 4, 6));
```

9. On the *Debug* menu, click *Start Without Debugging* to build and run the application.

When the application runs, it displays the following messages:

```
Using optional parameters
12
```

The compiler still generated code that called the method that takes optional parameters, even though the method signature does not exactly match the call. Given a choice between a method that takes optional parameters and a method that takes a parameter list, the C# compiler will use the method that takes optional parameters.

10. Press Enter and return to Visual Studio.

11. In the *DoWork* method, change the statement that calls the *Sum* method again.

```
Console.WriteLine(Util.Sum(2, 4, 6, 8, 10));
```

12. On the *Debug* menu, click *Start Without Debugging* to build and run the application.

When the application runs, it displays the following messages:

```
Using parameter list
30
```

This time, there are more parameters than the method that takes optional parameters specifies, so the compiler generated code that calls the method that takes a parameter array.

13. Press Enter and return to Visual Studio.

In this chapter, you have learned how to use a *params* array to define a method that can take any number of arguments. You have also seen how to use a *params* array of *object* types to create a method that accepts any number of arguments of any type. You have also seen how the compiler resolves method calls when it has a choice between calling a method that takes a parameter array and a method that takes optional parameters.

- If you want to continue to the next chapter

    Keep Visual Studio 2010 running, and turn to Chapter 12.

- If you want to exit Visual Studio 2010 now

    On the *File* menu, click *Exit*. If you see a *Save* dialog box, click *Yes* and save the project.

Chapter 11 Quick Reference

To	Do this

Write a method that accepts any number of arguments of a given type	Write a method whose parameter is a *params* array of the given type. For example, a method that accepts any number of *bool* arguments is declared like this:
	
	``someType Method(params bool[] flags)
	{
	    . . .
	}```

Write a method that accepts any number of arguments of any type	Write a method whose parameter is a *params* array whose elements are of type *object*. For example:
	
	``someType Method(params object[] paramList)
	{
	    . . .
	}```

Chapter 12
Working with Inheritance

After completing this chapter, you will be able to:

- Create a derived class that inherits features from a base class.

- Control method hiding and overriding by using the *new*, *virtual*, and *override* keywords.

- Limit accessibility within an inheritance hierarchy by using the *protected* keyword.

- Define extension methods as an alternative mechanism to using inheritance.

Inheritance is a key concept in the world of object orientation. You can use inheritance as a tool to avoid repetition when defining different classes that have a number of features in common and are quite clearly related to each other. Perhaps they are different classes of the same type, each with its own distinguishing feature—for example, *managers*, *manual workers*, and *all employees* of a factory. If you were writing an application to simulate the factory, how would you specify that managers and manual workers have a number of features that are the same but also have other features that are different? For example, they all have an employee reference number, but managers have different responsibilities and perform different tasks than manual workers.

This is where inheritance proves useful.

What Is Inheritance?

If you ask several experienced programmers what they understand by the term *inheritance*, you will typically get different and conflicting answers. Part of the confusion stems from the fact that the word *inheritance* itself has several subtly different meanings. If someone bequeaths something to you in a will, you are said to inherit it. Similarly, we say that you inherit half of your genes from your mother and half of your genes from your father. Both of these uses of the word *inheritance* have very little to do with inheritance in programming.

Inheritance in programming is all about classification—it's a relationship between classes. For example, when you were at school, you probably learned about mammals, and you learned that horses and whales are examples of mammals. Each has every attribute that a mammal does (it breathes air, it suckles its young, it is warm-blooded, and so on), but each also has its own special features (a horse has hooves, a whale has flippers and a fluke).

How can you model a horse and a whale in a program? One way would be to create two distinct classes named *Horse* and *Whale*. Each class can implement the behaviors that are unique to that type of mammal, such as *Trot* (for a horse) or *Swim* (for a whale), in its own way. How do you handle behaviors that are common to a horse and a whale, such as *Breathe* or *SuckleYoung*? You can add duplicate methods with these names to both classes, but this situation becomes a maintenance nightmare, especially if you also decide to start modeling other types of mammal, such as *Human* or *Aardvark*.

In C#, you can use class inheritance to address these issues. A horse, a whale, a human, and an aardvark are all types of mammals, so create a class named *Mammal* that provides the common functionality exhibited by these types. You can then declare that the *Horse*, *Whale*, *Human*, and *Aardvark* classes all inherit from *Mammal*. These classes then automatically provide the functionality of the *Mammal* class (*Breathe*, *SuckleYoung*, and so on), but you can also add the functionality peculiar to a particular type of mammal to the corresponding class—the *Trot* method for the *Horse* class and the *Swim* method for the *Whale* class. If you need to modify the way in which a common method such as *Breathe* works, you need to change it in only one place, the *Mammal* class.

Using Inheritance

You declare that a class inherits from another class by using the following syntax:

```
class DerivedClass : BaseClass {
    ...
}
```

The derived class inherits from the base class, and the methods in the base class also become part of the derived class. In C#, a class is allowed to derive from, at most, one base class; a class is *not allowed* to derive from two or more classes. However, unless *DerivedClass* is declared as *sealed,* you can create further derived classes that inherit from *DerivedClass* using the same syntax. (You will learn about sealed classes in Chapter 13, "Creating Interfaces and Defining Abstract Classes.")

```
class DerivedSubClass : DerivedClass {
    ...
}
```

 Important All structures inherit from an abstract class called System.ValueType. (You will learn about abstract classes in Chapter 13.) This is purely an implementation detail of the way in which the .NET Framework defines the common behavior for stack-based value types. You cannot define your own inheritance hierarchy with structures—and you cannot define a structure that derives from a class or another structure.

In the example described earlier, you could declare the *Mammal* class as shown here. The methods *Breathe* and *SuckleYoung* are common to all mammals.

```
class Mammal
{
    public void Breathe()
    {
        ...
    }

    public void SuckleYoung()
    {
        ...
    }
    ...
}
```

You could then define classes for each different type of mammal, adding more methods as necessary. For example:

```
class Horse : Mammal
{
    ...
    public void Trot()
    {
        ...
    }
}

class Whale : Mammal
{
    ...
    public void Swim()
    {
        ...
    }
}
```

> **Note** C++ programmers should notice that you do not and cannot explicitly specify whether the inheritance is public, private, or protected. C# inheritance is always implicitly public. Java programmers should note the use of the colon and that there is no *extends* keyword.

Remember that the *System.Object* class is the root class of all classes. All classes implicitly derive from the *System.Object* class. Consequently, the C# compiler silently rewrites the *Mammal* class as the following code (which you can write explicitly if you really want to):

```
class Mammal : System.Object
{
    ...
}
```

Any methods in the *System.Object* class are automatically passed down the chain of inheritance to classes that derive from *Mammal*, such as *Horse* and *Whale*. What this means in practical terms is that all classes that you define automatically inherit all the features of the *System.Object* class. This includes methods such as *ToString* (first discussed in Chapter 2, "Working with Variables, Operators, and Expressions"), which is used to convert an object to a string, typically for display purposes.

Calling Base Class Constructors

In addition to the methods that it inherits, a derived class automatically contains all fields from the base class. These fields usually require initialization when an object is created. You typically perform this kind of initialization in a constructor. Remember that all classes have at least one constructor. (If you don't provide one, the compiler generates a default constructor for you.) It is good practice for a constructor in a derived class to call the constructor for its base class as part of the initialization. You can specify the *base* keyword to call a base class constructor when you define a constructor for an inheriting class, as shown in this example:

```
class Mammal // base class
{
    public Mammal(string name)  // constructor for base class
    {
        ...
    }
    ...
}

class Horse : Mammal // derived class
{
    public Horse(string name)
            : base(name) // calls Mammal(name)
    {
        ...
    }
    ...
}
```

If you don't explicitly call a base class constructor in a derived class constructor, the compiler attempts to silently insert a call to the base class's default constructor before executing the code in the derived class constructor. Taking the earlier example, the compiler rewrites this:

```
class Horse : Mammal
{
    public Horse(string name)
    {
        ...
    }
    ...
}
```

as this:

```
class Horse : Mammal
{
    public Horse(string name)
        : base()
    {
        ...
    }
    ...
}
```

This works if *Mammal* has a public default constructor. However, not all classes have a public default constructor (for example, remember that the compiler generates only a default constructor if you don't write any nondefault constructors), in which case forgetting to call the correct base class constructor results in a compile-time error.

Assigning Classes

In previous examples in this book, you have seen how to declare a variable by using a class type and then how to use the *new* keyword to create an object. You have also seen how the type-checking rules of C# prevent you from assigning an object of one type to a variable declared as a different type. For example, given the definitions of the *Mammal*, *Horse*, and *Whale* classes shown here, the code that follows these definitions is illegal:

```
class Mammal
{
    ...
}
class Horse : Mammal
{
    ...
}

class Whale : Mammal
{
    ...
}
...
Horse myHorse = new Horse("Neddy");  // constructor shown earlier expects a name!
Whale myWhale = myHorse;             // error - different types
```

However, it is possible to refer to an object from a variable of a different type as long as the type used is a class that is higher up the inheritance hierarchy. So the following statements are legal:

```
Horse myHorse = new Horse("Neddy");
Mammal myMammal = myHorse; // legal, Mammal is the base class of Horse
```

If you think about it in logical terms, all *Horse*s are *Mammal*s, so you can safely assign an object of type *Horse* to a variable of type *Mammal*. The inheritance hierarchy means that you can think of a *Horse* simply as a special type of *Mammal*; it has everything that a *Mammal* has with a few extra bits defined by any methods and fields you add to the *Horse* class. You can also make a *Mammal* variable refer to a *Whale* object. There is one significant limitation, however—when referring to a *Horse* or *Whale* object by using a *Mammal* variable, you can access only methods and fields that are defined by the *Mammal* class. Any additional methods defined by the *Horse* or *Whale* class are not visible through the *Mammal* class:

```
Horse myHorse = new Horse("Neddy");
Mammal myMammal = myHorse;
myMammal.Breathe();         // OK - Breathe is part of the Mammal class
myMammal.Trot();            // error - Trot is not part of the Mammal class
```

> **Note** This explains why you can assign almost anything to an *object* variable. Remember that *object* is an alias for *System.Object* and all classes inherit from *System.Object* either directly or indirectly.

Be warned that the converse situation is not true. You cannot unreservedly assign a *Mammal* object to a *Horse* variable:

```
Mammal myMammal = newMammal("Mammalia");
Horse myHorse = myMammal;    // error
```

This looks like a strange restriction, but remember that not all *Mammal* objects are *Horses*— some might be *Whale*s. You can assign a *Mammal* object to a *Horse* variable as long as you check that the *Mammal* is really a *Horse* first, by using the *as* or *is* operator or by using a cast. The following code example uses the *as* operator to check that *myMammal* refers to a *Horse*, and if it does, the assignment to *myHorseAgain* results in *myHorseAgain* referring to the same *Horse* object. If *myMammal* refers to some other type of *Mammal*, the *as* operator returns *null* instead.

```
Horse myHorse = new Horse("Neddy");
Mammal myMammal = myHorse;                  // myMammal refers to a Horse
...
Horse myHorseAgain = myMammal as Horse;  // OK - myMammal was a Horse
...
Whale myWhale = new Whale("Moby Dick");
myMammal = myWhale;
...
myHorseAgain = myMammal as Horse;           // returns null - myMammal was a Whale
```

Declaring *new* Methods

One of the hardest problems in the realm of computer programming is the task of thinking up unique and meaningful names for identifiers. If you are defining a method for a class and that class is part of an inheritance hierarchy, sooner or later you are going to try to reuse a name that is already in use by one of the classes higher up the hierarchy. If a base class and a derived class happen to declare two methods that have the same signature, you will receive a warning when you compile the application.

> **Note** The method signature refers to the name of the method and the number and types of its parameters, but not its return type. Two methods that have the same name and that take the same list of parameters have the same signature, even if they return different types.

The method in the derived class masks (or hides) the method in the base class that has the same signature. For example, if you compile the following code, the compiler generates a warning message telling you that *Horse.Talk* hides the inherited method *Mammal.Talk*:

```
class Mammal
{
    ...
    public void Talk() // assume that all mammals can talk
    {
        ...
    }
}

class Horse : Mammal
{
    ...
    public void Talk()   // horses talk in a different way from other mammals!
    {
        ...
    }
}
```

Although your code will compile and run, you should take this warning seriously. If another class derives from *Horse* and calls the *Talk* method, it might be expecting the method implemented in the *Mammal* class to be called. However, the *Talk* method in the *Horse* class hides the *Talk* method in the *Mammal* class, and the *Horse.Talk* method will be called instead. Most of the time, such a coincidence is at best a source of confusion, and you should consider renaming methods to avoid clashes. However, if you're sure that you want the two methods to have the same signature, thus hiding the *Mammal.Talk* method, you can silence the warning by using the *new* keyword as follows:

```
class Mammal
{
    ...
    public void Talk()
    {
        ...
    }
}

class Horse : Mammal
{
    ...
    new public void Talk()
    {
        ...
    }
}
```

Using the *new* keyword like this does not change the fact that the two methods are completely unrelated and that hiding still occurs. It just turns the warning off. In effect, the *new* keyword says, "I know what I'm doing, so stop showing me these warnings."

Declaring Virtual Methods

Sometimes you do want to hide the way in which a method is implemented in a base class. As an example, consider the *ToString* method in *System.Object*. The purpose of *ToString* is to convert an object to its string representation. Because this method is very useful, it is a member of the *System.Object* class, thereby automatically providing all classes with a *ToString* method. However, how does the version of *ToString* implemented by *System.Object* know how to convert an instance of a derived class to a string? A derived class might contain any number of fields with interesting values that should be part of the string. The answer is that the implementation of *ToString* in *System.Object* is actually a bit simplistic. All it can do is convert an object to a string that contains the name of its type, such as "Mammal" or "Horse." This is not very useful after all. So why provide a method that is so useless? The answer to this second question requires a bit of detailed thought.

Obviously, *ToString* is a fine idea in concept, and all classes should provide a method that can be used to convert objects to strings for display or debugging purposes. It is only the implementation that is problematic. In fact, you are not expected to call the *ToString* method defined by *System.Object*—it is simply a placeholder. Instead, you should provide your own version of the *ToString* method in each class you define, overriding the default implementation in *System.Object*. The version in *System.Object* is there only as a safety net, in case a class does not implement its own *ToString* method. In this way, you can be confident that you can call *ToString* on any object, and the method will return a string containing something.

A method that is intended to be overridden is called a *virtual* method. You should be clear on the difference between *overriding* a method and *hiding* a method. Overriding a method is a mechanism for providing different implementations of the same method—the methods are all related because they are intended to perform the same task, but in a class-specific manner. Hiding a method is a means of replacing one method with another—the methods are usually unrelated and might perform totally different tasks. Overriding a method is a useful programming concept; hiding a method is usually an error.

You can mark a method as a virtual method by using the *virtual* keyword. For example, the *ToString* method in the *System.Object* class is defined like this:

```
namespace System
{
    class Object
    {
        public virtual string ToString()
        {
            ...
        }
        ...
    }
    ...
}
```

 Note Java developers should note that C# methods are not virtual by default.

Declaring *override* Methods

If a base class declares that a method is *virtual*, a derived class can use the *override* keyword to declare another implementation of that method. For example:

```
class Horse : Mammal
{
    ...
    public override string ToString()
    {
        ...
    }
}
```

The new implementation of the method in the derived class can call the original implementation of the method in the base class by using the *base* keyword, like this:

```
public override string ToString()
{
    base.ToString();
    ...
}
```

There are some important rules you must follow when declaring polymorphic methods (as discussed in the following sidebar, "Virtual Methods and Polymorphism") by using the *virtual* and *override* keywords:

- You're not allowed to declare a private method when using the *virtual* or *override* keyword. If you try, you'll get a compile-time error. Private really is private.

- The two method signatures must be identical—that is, they must have the same name, number, and type of parameters. In addition, both methods must return the same type.

- The two methods must have the same level of access. For example, if one of the two methods is public, the other must also be public. (Methods can also be protected, as you will find out in the next section.)

- You can override only a virtual method. If the base class method is not virtual and you try to override it, you'll get a compile-time error. This is sensible; it should be up to the designer of the base class to decide whether its methods can be overridden.

- If the derived class does not declare the method by using the override keyword, it does not override the base class method. In other words, it becomes an implementation of a completely different method that happens to have the same name. As before, this will cause a compile-time hiding warning, which you can silence by using the *new* keyword as previously described.

- An *override* method is implicitly virtual and can itself be overridden in a further derived class. However, you are not allowed to explicitly declare that an override method is virtual by using the *virtual* keyword.

Virtual Methods and Polymorphism

Virtual methods enable you to call different versions of the same method, based on the type of the object determined dynamically at run time. Consider the following example classes that define a variation on the *Mammal* hierarchy described earlier:

```
class Mammal
{
    ...
    public virtual string GetTypeName()
    {
        return "This is a mammal";
    }
}

class Horse : Mammal
{
    ...
    public override string GetTypeName()
    {
        return "This is a horse";
    }
```

```
}

class Whale : Mammal
{
    ...
    public override string GetTypeName ()
    {
        return "This is a whale";
    }
}

class Aardvark : Mammal
{
    ...
}
```

Notice two things: first, the *override* keyword used by the *GetTypeName* method in the *Horse* and *Whale* classes, and second, the fact that the *Aardvark* class does not have a *GetTypeName* method.

Now examine the following block of code:

```
Mammal myMammal;
Horse myHorse = new Horse(...);
Whale myWhale = new Whale(...);
Aardvark myAardvark = new Aardvark(...);

myMammal = myHorse;
Console.WriteLine(myMammal.GetTypeName()); // Horse
myMammal = myWhale;
Console.WriteLine(myMammal.GetTypeName()); // Whale
myMammal = myAardvark;
Console.WriteLine(myMammal.GetTypeName()); // Aardvark
```

What will be output by the three different *Console.WriteLine* statements? At first glance, you would expect them all to print "This is a mammal," because each statement calls the *GetTypeName* method on the *myMammal* variable, which is a *Mammal*. However, in the first case, you can see that *myMammal* is actually a reference to a *Horse*. (Remember, you are allowed to assign a *Horse* to a *Mammal* variable because the *Horse* class inherits from the *Mammal* class.) Because the *GetTypeName* method is defined as *virtual*, the runtime works out that it should call the *Horse.GetTypeName* method, so the statement actually prints the message "This is a horse." The same logic applies to the second *Console.WriteLine* statement, which outputs the message "This is a whale." The third statement calls *Console.WriteLine* on an *Aardvark* object. However, the *Aardvark* class does not have a *GetTypeName* method, so the default method in the *Mammal* class is called, returning the string "This is a mammal."

This phenomenon of the same statement invoking a different method depending on its context is called *polymorphism*, which literally means "many forms."

Understanding *protected* Access

The *public* and *private* access keywords create two extremes of accessibility: public fields and methods of a class are accessible to everyone, whereas private fields and methods of a class are accessible to only the class itself.

These two extremes are sufficient when considering classes in isolation. However, as all experienced object-oriented programmers know, isolated classes cannot solve complex problems. Inheritance is a powerful way of connecting classes, and there is clearly a special and close relationship between a derived class and its base class. Frequently, it is useful for a base class to allow derived classes to access some of its members while hiding these same members from classes that are not part of the hierarchy. In this situation, you can use the *protected* keyword to tag members:

- If a class A is derived from another class B, it can access the protected class members of class B. In other words, inside the derived class A, a protected member of class B is effectively public.

- If a class A is not derived from another class B, it cannot access any protected members of class B. In other words, within class A, a protected member of class B is effectively private.

C# gives programmers complete freedom to declare methods and fields as protected. However, most object-oriented programming guidelines recommend keeping your fields strictly private. Public fields violate encapsulation because all users of the class have direct, unrestricted access to the fields. Protected fields maintain encapsulation for users of a class, for whom the protected fields are inaccessible. However, protected fields still allow encapsulation to be violated by classes that inherit from the class.

> **Note** You can access a protected base class member not only in a derived class but also in classes derived from the derived class. A protected base class member retains its protected accessibility in a derived class and is accessible to further derived classes.

In the following exercise, you will define a simple class hierarchy for modeling different types of vehicles. You will define a base class named *Vehicle* and derived classes named *Airplane* and *Car*. You will define common methods named *StartEngine* and *StopEngine* in the *Vehicle* class, and you will add some methods to both of the derived classes that are specific to those classes. Last you will add a virtual method named *Drive* to the *Vehicle* class and override the default implementation of this method in both of the derived classes.

Create a hierarchy of classes

1. Start Microsoft Visual Studio 2010 if it is not already running.

2. Open the *Vehicles* project, located in the \Microsoft Press\Visual CSharp Step By Step\ Chapter 12\Vehicles folder in your Documents folder.

   The *Vehicles* project contains the file Program.cs, which defines the *Program* class with the *Main* and *DoWork* methods that you have seen in previous exercises.

3. In *Solution Explorer*, right-click the *Vehicles* project, point to *Add*, and then click *Class*.

   The *Add New Item—Vehicles* dialog box appears, enabling you to add a new file defining a class to the project.

4. In the *Add New Item—Vehicles* dialog box, verify that the Class template is highlighted in the middle pane, type **Vehicle.cs** in the *Name* box, and then click *Add*.

   The file Vehicle.cs is created and added to the project and appears in the *Code and Text Editor* window. The file contains the definition of an empty class named *Vehicle*.

5. Add the *StartEngine* and *StopEngine* methods to the *Vehicle* class as shown next in bold:

```
class Vehicle
{
    public void StartEngine(string noiseToMakeWhenStarting)
    {
        Console.WriteLine("Starting engine: {0}", noiseToMakeWhenStarting);
    }

    public void StopEngine(string noiseToMakeWhenStopping)
    {
        Console.WriteLine("Stopping engine: {0}", noiseToMakeWhenStopping);
    }
}
```

   All classes that derive from the *Vehicle* class will inherit these methods. The values for the *noiseToMakeWhenStarting* and *noiseToMakeWhenStopping* parameters will be different for each different type of vehicle and will help you to identify which vehicle is being started and stopped later.

6. On the *Project* menu, click *Add Class*.

   The *Add New Item—Vehicles* dialog box appears again.

7. In the *Name* box, type **Airplane.cs** and then click *Add*.

   A new file containing a class named *Airplane* is added to the project and appears in the *Code and Text Editor* window.

8. In the *Code and Text Editor* window, modify the definition of the *Airplane* class so that it inherits from the *Vehicle* class, as shown in bold here:

```
class Airplane : Vehicle
{
}
```

9. Add the *TakeOff* and *Land* methods to the *Airplane* class, as shown in bold here:

```
class Airplane : Vehicle
{
    public void TakeOff()
    {
        Console.WriteLine("Taking off");
    }

    public void Land()
    {
        Console.WriteLine("Landing");
    }
}
```

10. On the *Project* menu, click *Add Class*.

The *Add New Item—Vehicles* dialog box appears again.

11. In the *Name* box, type **Car.cs** and then click *Add*.

A new file containing a class named *Car* is added to the project and appears in the *Code and Text Editor* window.

12. In the *Code and Text Editor* window, modify the definition of the *Car* class so that it derives from the *Vehicle* class, as shown here in bold:

```
class Car : Vehicle
{
}
```

13. Add the *Accelerate* and *Brake* methods to the *Car* class, as shown in bold here:

```
class Car : Vehicle
{
    public void Accelerate()
    {
        Console.WriteLine("Accelerating");
    }

    public void Brake()
    {
        Console.WriteLine("Braking");
    }
}
```

14. Display the Vehicle.cs file in the *Code and Text Editor* window.

15. Add the virtual *Drive* method to the *Vehicle* class, as shown here in bold:

```
class Vehicle
{
    ...
    public virtual void Drive()
    {
        Console.WriteLine("Default implementation of the Drive method");
    }
}
```

16. Display the Program.cs file in the *Code and Text Editor* window.

17. In the *DoWork* method, create an instance of the *Airplane* class and test its methods by simulating a quick journey by airplane, as follows:

```
static void DoWork()
{
    Console.WriteLine("Journey by airplane:");
    Airplane myPlane = new Airplane();
    myPlane.StartEngine("Contact");
    myPlane.TakeOff();
    myPlane.Drive();
    myPlane.Land();
    myPlane.StopEngine("Whirr");
}
```

18. Add the following statements shown in bold to the *DoWork* method after the code you have just written. These statements create an instance of the *Car* class and test its methods.

```
static void DoWork()
{
    ...
    Console.WriteLine("\nJourney by car:");
    Car myCar = new Car();
    myCar.StartEngine("Brm brm");
    myCar.Accelerate();
    myCar.Drive();
    myCar.Brake();
    myCar.StopEngine("Phut phut");
}
```

19. On the *Debug* menu, click *Start Without Debugging*.

In the console window, verify that the program outputs messages simulating the different stages of performing a journey by airplane and by car, as shown in the following image:

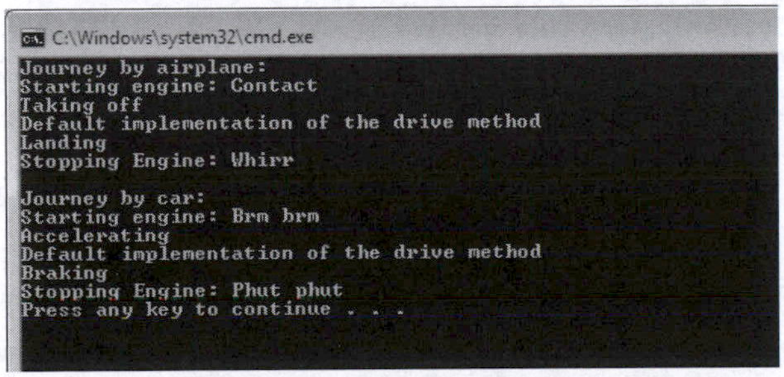

Notice that both modes of transport invoke the default implementation of the virtual *Drive* method because neither class currently overrides this method.

20. Press Enter to close the application and return to Visual Studio 2010.

21. Display the *Airplane* class in the *Code and Text Editor* window. Override the *Drive* method in the *Airplane* class, as follows:

```
public override void Drive()
{
    Console.WriteLine("Flying");
}
```

> **Note** IntelliSense displays a list of available virtual methods. If you select the *Drive* method from the IntelliSense list, Visual Studio automatically inserts into your code a statement that calls the *base.Drive* method. If this happens, delete the statement, as this exercise does not require it.

22. Display the *Car* class in the *Code and Text Editor* window. Override the *Drive* method in the *Car* class as follows:

```
public override void Drive()
{
    Console.WriteLine("Motoring");
}
```

23. On the *Debug* menu, click *Start Without Debugging*.

In the console window, notice that the *Airplane* object now displays the message *Flying* when the application calls the *Drive* method and the *Car* object displays the message *Motoring*.

24. Press Enter to close the application and return to Visual Studio 2010.

25. Display the Program.cs file in the *Code and Text Editor* window.

26. Add the statements shown here in bold to the end of the *DoWork* method:

```
static void DoWork()
{
    ...
    Console.WriteLine("\nTesting polymorphism");
    Vehicle v = myCar;
    v.Drive();
    v = myPlane;
    v.Drive();
}
```

This code tests the polymorphism provided by the virtual *Drive* method. The code creates a reference to the *Car* object using a *Vehicle* variable (which is safe, because all *Car* objects are *Vehicle* objects) and then calls the *Drive* method using this *Vehicle* variable. The final two statements refer the *Vehicle* variable to the *Airplane* object and call what seems to be the same *Drive* method again.

27. On the *Debug* menu, click *Start Without Debugging*.

In the console window, verify that the same messages appear as before, followed by this text:

```
Testing polymorphism
Motoring
Flying
```

The *Drive* method is virtual, so the runtime (not the compiler) works out which version of the *Drive* method to call when invoking it through a *Vehicle* variable based on the real type of the object referenced by this variable. In the first case, the *Vehicle* object refers to a *Car*, so the application calls the *Car.Drive* method. In the second case, the *Vehicle* object refers to an *Airplane*, so the application calls the *Airplane.Drive* method.

28. Press Enter to close the application and return to Visual Studio 2010.

Understanding Extension Methods

Inheritance is a powerful feature, enabling you to extend the functionality of a class by creating a new class that derives from it. However, sometimes using inheritance is not the most appropriate mechanism for adding new behaviors, especially if you need to quickly extend a type without affecting existing code.

For example, suppose you want to add a new feature to the *int* type—a method named *Negate* that returns the negative equivalent value that an integer currently contains. (I know that you could simply use the unary minus operator [–] to perform the same task, but bear with me.) One way to achieve this is to define a new type named *NegInt32* that inherits from *System.Int32* (*int* is an alias for *System.Int32*) and that adds the *Negate* method:

```
class NegInt32 : System.Int32  // don't try this!
{
    public int Negate()
    {
        ...
    }
}
```

The theory is that *NegInt32* will inherit all the functionality associated with the *System.Int32* type in addition to the *Negate* method. There are two reasons why you might not want to follow this approach:

- This method applies only to the *NegInt32* type, and if you want to use it with existing *int* variables in your code, you have to change the definition of every *int* variable to the *NegInt32* type.

- The *System.Int32* type is actually a structure, not a class, and you cannot use inheritance with structures.

This is where extension methods become very useful.

An extension method enables you to extend an existing type (a class or a structure) with additional static methods. These static methods become immediately available to your code in any statements that reference data of the type being extended.

You define an extension method in a *static* class and specify the type that the method applies to as the first parameter to the method, along with the *this* keyword. Here's an example showing how you can implement the *Negate* extension method for the *int* type:

```
static class Util
{
    public static int Negate(this int i)
    {
        return -i;
    }
}
```

The syntax looks a little odd, but it is the *this* keyword prefixing the parameter to *Negate* that identifies it as an extension method, and the fact that the parameter that *this* prefixes is an *int* means that you are extending the *int* type.

To use the extension method, bring the *Util* class into scope. (If necessary, add a *using* statement specifying the namespace to which the *Util* class belongs.) Then you can simply use "." notation to reference the method, like this:

```
int x = 591;
Console.WriteLine("x.Negate {0}", x.Negate());
```

Notice that you do not need to reference the *Util* class anywhere in the statement that calls the *Negate* method. The C# compiler automatically detects all extension methods for a given type from all the static classes that are in scope. You can also invoke the *Utils.Negate* method passing an *int* as the parameter, using the regular syntax you have seen before, although this use obviates the purpose of defining the method as an extension method:

```
int x = 591;
Console.WriteLine("x.Negate {0}", Util.Negate(x));
```

In the following exercise, you will add an extension method to the *int* type. This extension method enables you to convert the value an *int* variable contains from base 10 to a representation of that value in a different number base.

Create an extension method

1. In Visual Studio 2010, open the *ExtensionMethod* project, located in the \Microsoft Press\Visual CSharp Step By Step\Chapter 12\ExtensionMethod folder in your Documents folder.

2. Display the Util.cs file in the *Code and Text Editor* window.

   This file contains a static class named *Util* in a namespace named *Extensions*. The class is empty apart from the *// to do* comment. Remember that you must define extension methods inside a static class.

3. Add a public static method to the *Util* class, named *ConvertToBase*. The method should take two parameters: an *int* parameter named *i*, prefixed with the *this* keyword to indicate that the method is an extension method for the *int* type, and another ordinary *int* parameter named *baseToConvertTo*. The method will convert the value in *i* to the base indicated by *baseToConvertTo*. The method should return an *int* containing the converted value.

   The *ConvertToBase* method should look like this:

   ```
   static class Util
   {
       public static int ConvertToBase(this int i, int baseToConvertTo)
       {
       }
   }
   ```

4. Add an *if* statement to the *ConvertToBase* method that checks that the value of the *baseToConvertTo* parameter is between 2 and 10. The algorithm used by this exercise does not work reliably outside this range of values. Throw an *ArgumentException* with a suitable message if the value of *baseToConvertTo* is outside this range.

   The *ConvertToBase* method should look like this:

   ```
   public static int ConvertToBase(this int i, int baseToConvertTo)
   {
       if (baseToConvertTo < 2 || baseToConvertTo > 10)
           throw new ArgumentException("Value cannot be converted to base " +
   baseToConvertTo.ToString());
   }
   ```

5. Add the following statements shown in bold to the *ConvertToBase* method, after the statement that throws the *ArgumentException*. This code implements a well-known algorithm that converts a number from base 10 to a different number base. (You saw a version of this algorithm for converting a decimal number to octal in Chapter 5, "Using Compound Assignment and Iteration Statements.")

   ```
   public static int ConvertToBase(this int i, int baseToConvertTo)
   {
       ...
       int result = 0;
       int iterations = 0;
       do
   ```

```
        {
            int nextDigit = i % baseToConvertTo;
            i /= baseToConvertTo;
            result += nextDigit * (int)Math.Pow(10, iterations);
            iterations++;
        }
        while (i != 0);

        return result;
    }
```

6. Display the Program.cs file in the *Code and Text Editor* window.

7. Add the following *using* statement after the *using System;* statement at the top of the file:

```
using Extensions;
```

This statement brings the namespace containing the *Util* class into scope. The *ConvertToBase* extension method will not be visible in the Program.cs file if you do not perform this task.

8. Add the following statements to the *DoWork* method of the *Program* class:

```
int x = 591;
for (int i = 2; i <= 10; i++)
{
    Console.WriteLine("{0} in base {1} is {2}", x, i, x.ConvertToBase(i));
}
```

This code creates an *int* named *x* and sets it to the value *591*. (You can pick any integer value you want.) The code then uses a loop to print out the value 591 in all number bases between 2 and 10. Notice that *ConvertToBase* appears as an extension method in IntelliSense when you type the period (.) after *x* in the *Console.WriteLine* statement.

9. On the *Debug* menu, click *Start Without Debugging*. Confirm that the program displays messages showing the value 591 in the different number bases to the console, like this:

10. Press Enter to close the program.

In this chapter, you have seen how to use inheritance to define a hierarchy of classes, and you should now understand how to override inherited methods and implement virtual methods. You have also seen how to add an extension method to an existing type.

- If you want to continue to the next chapter

    Keep Visual Studio 2010 running, and turn to Chapter 13.

- If you want to exit Visual Studio 2010 now

    On the *File* menu, click *Exit*. If you see a *Save* dialog box, click *Yes* and save the project.

Chapter 12 Quick Reference

To	Do this
Create a derived class from a base class	Declare the new class name followed by a colon and the name of the base class. For example: ```\nclass Derived : Base\n{\n ...\n}\n```
Call a base class constructor as part of the constructor for an inheriting class	Supply a constructor parameter list before the body of the derived class constructor. For example: ```\nclass Derived : Base\n{\n ...\n public Derived(int x) : Base(x)\n {\n ...\n }\n ...\n}\n```
Declare a virtual method	Use the *virtual* keyword when declaring the method. For example: ```\nclass Mammal\n{\n public virtual void Breathe()\n {\n ...\n }\n ...\n}\n```

Implement a method in a derived class that overrides an inherited *virtual* method	Use the *override* keyword when declaring the method in the derived class. For example:

```
class Whale : Mammal
{
    public override void Breathe()
    {
        ...
    }
    ...
}
```

Define an extension method for a type	Add a static public method to a static class. The first parameter must be of the type being extended, preceded by the *this* keyword. For example:

```
static class Util
{
    public static int Negate(this int i)
    {
        return -i;
    }
}
```

Chapter 13
Creating Interfaces and Defining Abstract Classes

After completing this chapter, you will be able to:

- Define an interface specifying the signatures and return types of methods.

- Implement an interface in a structure or class.

- Reference a class through an interface.

- Capture common implementation details in an abstract class.

- Implement sealed classes that cannot be used to derive new classes.

Inheriting from a class is a powerful mechanism, but the real power of inheritance comes from inheriting from an interface. An interface does not contain any code or data; it just specifies the methods and properties that a class that inherits from the interface must provide. Using an interface enables you to completely separate the names and signatures of the methods of a class from the method's implementation.

Abstract classes are similar in many ways to interfaces except that they can contain code and data. However, you can specify that certain methods of an abstract class are virtual so that a class that inherits from the abstract class must provide its own implementation of these methods. You frequently use abstract classes with interfaces, and together they provide a key technique for enabling you to build extensible programming frameworks, as you will discover in this chapter.

Understanding Interfaces

Suppose you want to define a new collection class that enables an application to store objects in a sequence that depends on the type of objects the collection contains. For example, if the collection holds alphanumeric objects such as strings, the collection should sort the objects according to the collating sequence of the computer, and if the collection holds numeric objects such as integers, the collection should sort the objects numerically.

When you define the collection class, you do not want to restrict the types of objects that it can hold (the objects can even be class or structure types), and consequently you don't know how to order these objects. The question is, how do you provide a method in the collection class that sorts objects whose types you do not know when you write the collection class? At first glance, this problem seems similar to the *ToString* problem described in Chapter 12,

"Working with Inheritance," which could be resolved by declaring a virtual method that subclasses of your collection class can override. However, this is not the case. There is not usually any form of inheritance relationship between the collection class and the objects that it holds, so a virtual method would not be of much use. If you think for a moment, the problem is that the way in which the objects in the collection should be ordered is dependent on the type of the objects themselves, and not on the collection. The solution, therefore, is to require that all the objects provide a method such as the *CompareTo* method shown here that the collection can call, enabling the collection to compare these objects with one another:

```
int CompareTo(object obj)
{
    // return 0 if this instance is equal to obj
    // return < 0 if this instance is less than obj
    // return > 0 if this instance is greater than obj
    ...
}
```

The collection class can make use of this method to sort the objects that it contains.

You can define an interface for collectable objects that includes the *CompareTo* method and specify that the collection class can collect only classes that implement this interface. In this way, an interface is similar to a contract. If a class implements an interface, the interface guarantees that the class contains all the methods specified in the interface. This mechanism ensures that you will be able to call the *CompareTo* method on all objects in the collection and sort them.

Interfaces enable you to truly separate the "what" from the "how." The interface tells you only the name, return type, and parameters of the method. Exactly how the method is implemented is not a concern of the interface. The interface describes the functionality that a class should implement but not how this functionality is implemented.

Defining an Interface

To define an interface, you use the *interface* keyword instead of the *class* or *struct* keyword. Inside the interface, you declare methods exactly as in a class or a structure except that you never specify an access modifier (*public*, *private*, or *protected*), and you replace the method body with a semicolon. Here is an example:

```
interface IComparable
{
    int CompareTo(object obj);
}
```

> **Tip** The Microsoft .NET Framework documentation recommends that you preface the name of your interfaces with the capital letter *I*. This convention is the last vestige of Hungarian notation in C#. Incidentally, the *System* namespace already defines the *IComparable* interface as shown above.

Implementing an Interface

To implement an interface, you declare a class or structure that inherits from the interface and that implements *all* the methods specified by the interface. For example, suppose you are defining the *Mammal* hierarchy described in Chapter 12 but you need to specify that land-bound mammals provide a method named *NumberOfLegs* that returns as an *int* the number of legs that a mammal has. (Sea-bound mammals do not implement this interface.) You could define the *ILandBound* interface that contains this method as follows:

```
interface ILandBound
{
    int NumberOfLegs();
}
```

You could then implement this interface in the *Horse* class. You inherit from the interface and provide an implementation of every method defined by the interface.

```
class Horse : ILandBound
{
    ...
    public int NumberOfLegs()
    {
        return 4;
    }
}
```

When you implement an interface, you must ensure that each method matches its corresponding interface method exactly, according to the following rules:

- The method names and return types match exactly.

- Any parameters (including *ref* and *out* keyword modifiers) match exactly.

- The method name is prefaced by the name of the interface. This is known as *explicit interface implementation* and is a good habit to cultivate.

- All methods implementing an interface must be publicly accessible. However, if you are using explicit interface implementation, the method should not have an access qualifier.

If there is any difference between the interface definition and its declared implementation, the class will not compile.

A class can extend another class and implement an interface at the same time. In this case, C# does not denote the base class and the interface by using specific keywords as, for example, Java does. Instead, C# uses a positional notation. The base class is named first, followed by a comma, followed by the interface. The following example defines *Horse* as a class that is a *Mammal* but that additionally implements the *ILandBound* interface:

```
interface ILandBound
{
    ...
}

class Mammal
{
    ...
}

class Horse : Mammal , ILandBound
{
    ...
}
```

Referencing a Class Through Its Interface

In the same way that you can reference an object by using a variable defined as a class that is higher up the hierarchy, you can reference an object by using a variable defined as an interface that its class implements. Taking the preceding example, you can reference a *Horse* object by using an *ILandBound* variable, as follows:

```
Horse myHorse = new Horse(...);
ILandBound iMyHorse = myHorse; // legal
```

This works because all horses are land-bound mammals, although the converse is not true, and you cannot assign an *ILandBound* object to a *Horse* variable without casting it first to verify that it does actually reference a *Horse* object and not some other class that also happens to implement the *ILandBound* interface.

The technique of referencing an object through an interface is useful because it enables you to define methods that can take different types as parameters, as long as the types implement a specified interface. For example, the *FindLandSpeed* method shown here can take any argument that implements the *ILandBound* interface:

```
int FindLandSpeed(ILandBound landBoundMammal)
{
    ...
}
```

Note that when referencing an object through an interface, you can invoke only methods that are visible through the interface.

Working with Multiple Interfaces

A class can have at most one base class, but it is allowed to implement an unlimited number of interfaces. A class must still implement all the methods it inherits from all its interfaces.

If an interface, structure, or class inherits from more than one interface, you write the interfaces in a comma-separated list. If a class also has a base class, the interfaces are listed *after* the base class. For example, suppose you define another interface named *IGrazable* that contains the *ChewGrass* method for all grazing animals. You can define the *Horse* class like this:

```
class Horse : Mammal, ILandBound, IGrazable
{
    ...
}
```

Explicitly Implementing an Interface

The examples you have seen so far have shown classes that implicitly implement an interface. If you revisit the *ILandBound* interface and the *Horse* class (shown next), although the *Horse* class implements from the *ILandBound* interface, there is nothing in the implementation of the *NumberOfLegs* method in the *Horse* class that says it is part of the *ILandBound* interface:

```
interface ILandBound
{
    int NumberOfLegs();
}

class Horse : ILandBound
{
    ...
    public int NumberOfLegs()
    {
        return 4;
    }
}
```

This might not be an issue in a simple situation, but suppose the *Horse* class implemented multiple interfaces. There is nothing to prevent multiple interfaces specifying a method with the same name, although they might have different semantics. For example, suppose you wanted to implement a transportation system based on horse-drawn coaches. A lengthy journey might be broken down into several stages, or "legs." If you wanted to keep track of how many legs each horse had pulled the coach for, you might define the following interface:

```
interface IJourney
{
    int NumberOfLegs();
}
```

Now, if you implement this interface in the *Horse* class you have an interesting problem:

```
class Horse : ILandBound, IJourney
{
    ...
    public int NumberOfLegs()
    {
        return 4;
    }
}
```

This is legal code, but does the horse have four legs, or has it pulled the coach for four legs of the journey? The answer as far as C# is concerned is both of these! By default, C# does not distinguish which interface the method is implementing, so the same method actually implements both interfaces.

To solve this problem and disambiguate which method is part of which interface implementation, you can implement interfaces explicitly. To do this, you specify which interface a method belongs to when you implement it, like this:

```
class Horse : ILandBound, IJourney
{
    ...
    int ILandBound.NumberOfLegs()
    {
        return 4;
    }

    int IJourney.NumberOfLegs()
    {
        return 3;
    }
}
```

Now you can see that the horse has four legs, and has pulled the coach for three legs of the journey.

Apart from prefixing the name of the method with the interface name, there is one other subtle difference in this syntax; the methods are not marked as *public*. You cannot specify the protection for methods that are part of an explicit interface implementation. This leads to another interesting phenomenon. If you create a *Horse* variable in code, you cannot actually invoke either of the *NumberOfLegs* methods because they are not visible. As far as the *Horse* class is concerned, they are both private. In fact, this makes sense. If the methods were visible through the *Horse* class, which method would the following code actually invoke—the one for the *ILandBound* interface or the one for the *IJourney* interface?

```
Horse horse = new Horse();
...
int legs = horse.NumberOfLegs();
```

So, how do you access these methods? The answer is that you reference the *Horse* object through the appropriate interface, like this:

```
Horse horse = new Horse();
...
IJourney journeyHorse = horse;
int legsInJourney = journeyHorse.NumberOfLegs();
ILandBound landBoundHorse = horse;
int legsOnHorse = landBoundHorse.NumberOfLegs();
```

I recommend explicitly implementing interfaces when possible.

Interface Restrictions

The essential idea to remember is that an interface never contains any implementation. The following restrictions are natural consequences of this:

- You're not allowed to define any fields in an interface, not even static ones. A field is an implementation detail of a class or structure.

- You're not allowed to define any constructors in an interface. A constructor is also considered to be an implementation detail of a class or structure.

- You're not allowed to define a destructor in an interface. A destructor contains the statements used to destroy an object instance. (Destructors are described in Chapter 14, "Using Garbage Collection and Resource Management.")

- You cannot specify an access modifier for any method. All methods in an interface are implicitly public.

- You cannot nest any types (such as enumerations, structures, classes, or interfaces) inside an interface.

- An interface is not allowed to inherit from a structure or a class, although an interface can inherit from another interface. Structures and classes contain implementation; if an interface were allowed to inherit from either, it would be inheriting some implementation.

Defining and Using Interfaces

In the following exercises, you will define and implement interfaces that constitute part of a simple graphical drawing package. You will define two interfaces called *IDraw* and *IColor*, and you will define classes that implement them. Each class will define a shape that can be drawn on a canvas on a Windows Presentation Foundation (WPF) form. (A canvas is a WPF control that enables you to draw lines, text, and shapes.)

The *IDraw* interface defines the following methods:

- **SetLocation**   This method enables you to specify the position as X and Y coordinates of the shape on the canvas.

- **Draw**   This method actually draws the shape on the canvas at the location specified by using the *SetLocation* method.

The *IColor* interface defines the following method:

- **SetColor**   This method lets you specify the color of the shape. When the shape is drawn on the canvas, it will appear in this color.

Define the *IDraw* and *IColor* interfaces

1. Start Microsoft Visual Studio 2010 if it is not already running.

2. Open the *Drawing* project, located in the \Microsoft Press\Visual CSharp Step By Step\ Chapter 13\Drawing folder in your Documents folder.

   The *Drawing* project is a WPF application. It contains a WPF form called *DrawingPad*. This form contains a canvas control called *drawingCanvas*. You will use this form and canvas to test your code.

3. On the *Project* menu, click *Add New Item*.

   The *Add New Item – Drawing* dialog box appears.

4. In the left pane of the *Add New Item – Drawing* dialog box, click *Visual C#*. If you are using Visual Studio 2010 Professional or Visual Studio 2010 Standard, click *Code*. (Visual C# 2010 Express has fewer templates and does not break them up into groups in the same way that Visual Studio does.) In the middle pane, click the *Interface* template. In the *Name* text box, type **IDraw.cs**, and then click *Add*.

   Visual Studio creates the IDraw.cs file and adds it to your project. The IDraw.cs file appears in the *Code and Text Editor* window. It should look like this:

```
using System;
using System.Collections.Generic;
using System.Linq;
using System.Text;

namespace Drawing
{
    interface IDraw
    {
    }
}
```

5. In the IDraw.cs file, add the following *using* statement to the list at the top of the file:

```
using System.Windows.Controls;
```

You will reference the *Canvas* class in this interface. The *Canvas* class is located in the *System.Windows.Controls* namespace.

6. Add the methods shown here in bold to the *IDraw* interface:

```
interface IDraw
{
    void SetLocation(int xCoord, int yCoord);
    void Draw(Canvas canvas);
}
```

7. On the *Project* menu, click *Add New Item* again.

8. In the middle pane of the *Add New Item – Drawing* dialog box, click the *Interface* template. In the *Name* text box, type **IColor.cs**, and then click *Add*.

Visual Studio creates the IColor.cs file and adds it to your project. The IColor.cs file appears in the *Code and Text Editor* window.

9. In the IColor.cs file, add the following *using* statement to the list at the top of the file:

```
using System.Windows.Media;
```

You will reference the *Color* class in this interface, which is located in the *System. Windows.Media* namespace.

10. Add the following method shown in bold to the *IColor* interface definition:

```
interface IColor
{
    void SetColor(Color color);
}
```

You have now defined the *IDraw* and *IColor* interfaces. The next step is to create some classes that implement them. In the following exercise, you will create two new shape classes called *Square* and *Circle*. These classes will implement both interfaces.

Create the *Square* and *Circle* classes, and implement the interfaces

1. On the *Project* menu, click *Add Class*.

2. In the *Add New Item – Drawing* dialog box, verify that the *Class* template is selected in the middle pane, type **Square.cs** in the *Name* text box, and then click *Add*.

Visual Studio creates the Square.cs file and displays it in the *Code and Text Editor* window.

3. Add the following *using* statements to the list at the top of the Square.cs file:

```
using System.Windows;
using System.Windows.Media;
using System.Windows.Shapes;
using System.Windows.Controls;
```

4. Modify the definition of the *Square* class so that it implements the *IDraw* and *IColor* interfaces as shown here in bold:

```
class Square : IDraw, IColor
{
}
```

5. Add the following private variables shown in bold to the *Square* class. These variables will hold the position and size of the *Square* object on the canvas. The *Rectangle* class is a WPF class located in the *System.Windows.Shapes* namespace. You will use this class to draw the square:

```
class Square : IDraw, IColor
{
    private int sideLength;
    private int locX = 0, locY = 0;
    private Rectangle rect = null;
}
```

6. Add the constructor shown in bold to the *Square* class. This constructor initializes the *sideLength* field and specifies the length of each side of the square.

```
class Square : IDraw, IColor
{
    ...
    public Square(int sideLength)
    {
        this.sideLength = sideLength;
    }
}
```

7. In the definition of the *Square* class, right-click the *IDraw* interface. A shortcut menu appears. In the shortcut menu, point to *Implement Interface*, and then click *Implement Interface Explicitly*, as shown in the following image:

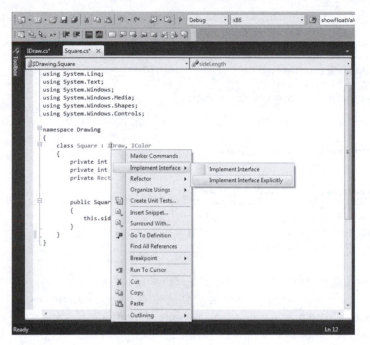

This feature causes Visual Studio to generate default implementations of the methods in the *IDraw* interface. You can also add the methods to the *Square* class manually if you prefer. The following example shows the code generated by Visual Studio:

```
void IDraw.SetLocation(int xCoord, int yCoord)
{
    throw new NotImplementedException();
}

void IDraw.Draw(Canvas canvas)
{
    throw new NotImplementedException();
}
```

Each of these methods currently throws a *NotImplementedException* exception. You are expected to replace the body of these methods with your own code.

8. In the *SetLocation* method, replace the existing code with the statements shown in bold. This code stores the values passed in through the parameters in the *locX* and *locY* fields in the *Square* object.

```
void IDraw.SetLocation(int xCoord, int yCoord)
{
    this.locX = xCoord;
    this.locY = yCoord;
}
```

9. Replace the code in the *Draw* method with the statements shown here in bold:

```
void IDraw.Draw(Canvas canvas)
{
    if (this.rect != null)
    {
        canvas.Children.Remove(this.rect);
    }
    else
    {
        this.rect = new Rectangle();
    }

    this.rect.Height = this.sideLength;
    this.rect.Width = this.sideLength;
    Canvas.SetTop(this.rect, this.locY);
    Canvas.SetLeft(this.rect, this.locX);
    canvas.Children.Add(rect);
}
```

This method renders the *Square* object by drawing a *Rectangle* shape on the canvas. (A square is simply a rectangle where all four sides have the same length.) If the *Rectangle* has been drawn previously (possibly at a different location and with a different color), it is removed from the canvas. The height and width of the *Rectangle* are set by using the value of the *sideLength* field. The position of the *Rectangle* on the canvas is set by using the static *SetTop* and *SetLeft* methods of the *Canvas* class, and then the *Rectangle* is added to the canvas. (This causes it to appear.)

10. Add the *SetColor* method from the *IColor* interface to the *Square* class, as shown here:

```
void IColor.SetColor(Color color)
{
    if (rect != null)
    {
        SolidColorBrush brush = new SolidColorBrush(color);
        rect.Fill = brush;
    }
}
```

This method checks that the *Square* object has actually been displayed. (The *rect* field will be null if it has not yet been rendered.) The code sets the *Fill* property of the *rect* field with the specified color by using a *SolidColorBrush* object. (The details of the *SolidBrushClass* are outside the scope of this discussion.)

11. On the *Project* menu, click *Add Class*. In the *Add New Item – Drawing* dialog box, type **Circle.cs** in the *Name* text box, and then click *Add*.

Visual Studio creates the Circle.cs file and displays it in the *Code and Text Editor* window.

12. Add the following *using* statements to the list at the top of the Circle.cs file:

```
using System.Windows;
using System.Windows.Media;
using System.Windows.Shapes;
using System.Windows.Controls;
```

13. Modify the definition of the *Circle* class so that it implements the *IDraw* and *IColor* interfaces as shown here in bold:

```
class Circle : IDraw, IColor
{
}
```

14. Add the following private variables shown in bold to the *Circle* class. These variables will hold the position and size of the *Circle* object on the canvas. The *Ellipse* class is another WPF class that you will use to draw the circle.

```
class Circle : IDraw, IColor
{
    private int radius;
    private int locX = 0, locY = 0;
    private Ellipse circle = null;
}
```

15. Add the constructor shown in bold to the *Circle* class. This constructor initializes the *radius* field.

```
class Circle : IDraw, IColor
{
    ...
    public Circle(int radius)
    {
        this.radius = radius;
    }
}
```

16. Add the *SetLocation* method shown below to the *Circle* class. This method implements part of the *IDraw* interface, and the code is exactly the same as that in the *Square* class.

```
void IDraw.SetLocation(int xCoord, int yCoord)
{
    this.locX = xCoord;
    this.locY = yCoord;
}
```

17. Add the *Draw* method shown below to the *Circle* class. This method is also part of the *IDraw* interface.

```
void IDraw.Draw(Canvas canvas)
{
    if (this.circle != null)
    {
        canvas.Children.Remove(this.circle);
    }
    else
    {
        this.circle = new Ellipse();
    }

    this.circle.Height = this.radius;
    this.circle.Width = this.radius;
    Canvas.SetTop(this.circle, this.locY);
    Canvas.SetLeft(this.circle, this.locX);
    canvas.Children.Add(circle);
}
```

This method is similar to the *Draw* method in the *Square* class, except that it renders the *Circle* object by drawing an *Ellipse* shape on the canvas. (A circle is an ellipse where the width and height are the same.)

18. Add the *SetColor* method to the *Circle* class. This method is part of the *IColor* interface. As before, this method is similar to that of the *Square* class.

```
void IColor.SetColor(Color color)
{
    if (circle != null)
    {
        SolidColorBrush brush = new SolidColorBrush(color);
        circle.Fill = brush;
    }
}
```

You have completed the *Square* and *Circle* classes. You can now use the WPF form to test them.

Test the *Square* and *Circle* classes

1. Display the DrawingPad.xaml file in the *Design View* window.

2. Click the shaded area in the middle of the WPF form.

The shaded area of the form is the *Canvas* object, and this action sets the focus to this object.

3. In *Properties* window, click the *Events* button. (This button has an icon that looks like a bolt of lightning.)

4. In the list of events, locate the *MouseLeftButtonDown* event and then double-click it.

Visual Studio creates a method called *drawingCanvas_MouseLeftButtonDown* for the *DrawingPadWindow* class that implements the WPF form and displays it in the *Code and Text Editor* window. This is an event handler that runs when the user clicks the left mouse button over the canvas. (You will learn more about event handlers in Chapter 17, "Interrupting Program Flow and Handling Events.")

5. Add the code shown in bold to the *drawingCanvas_MouseLeftButtonDown* method:

```
private void drawingCanvas_MouseLeftButtonDown(object sender, MouseButtonEventArgs e)
{
    Point mouseLocation = e.GetPosition(this.drawingCanvas);
    Square mySquare = new Square(100);


    if (mySquare is IDraw)
    {
        IDraw drawSquare = mySquare;
        drawSquare.SetLocation((int)mouseLocation.X, (int)mouseLocation.Y);
        drawSquare.Draw(drawingCanvas);
    }
}
```

The *MouseButtonEventArgs* parameter, *e*, to this method provides useful information about the position of the mouse. In particular, the *GetPosition* method returns a *Point* structure that contains the X and Y coordinates of the mouse. The code that you have added creates a new *Square* object. It then checks to verify that this object implements the *IDraw* interface (which is good practice) and creates a reference to the object by using the *IDraw* interface. Remember that when you explicitly implement an interface, the methods defined by the interface are available only by creating a reference to that interface. (The *SetLocation* and *Draw* methods are private to the *Square* class and are available only through the *IDraw* interface.) The code then sets the location of the *Square* to the position of the mouse. Note that the X and Y coordinates in the *Point* structure are actually *double* values, so this code casts them to *ints*. The code then calls the *Draw* method to display the *Square* object.

6. Add the following code shown in bold to the end of the *drawingCanvas_ MouseLeftButtonDown* method:

```
private void drawingCanvas_MouseLeftButtonDown(object sender, MouseButtonEventArgs e)
{
    ...

    if (mySquare is IColor)
    {
        IColor colorSquare = mySquare;
        colorSquare.SetColor(Colors.BlueViolet);
    }
}
```

This code tests the *Square* class to verify that it implements the *IColor* interface; if it does, it creates a reference to the *Square* class through this interface and calls the

SetColor method to set the color of the *Square* object to *Colors.BlueViolet*. (The *Colors* enumeration is provided as part of the .NET Framework.)

> **Important** You must call *Draw* before you call *SetColor*. This is because the *SetColor* method sets the color of the *Square* only if it has already been rendered. If you invoke *SetColor* before *Draw*, the color will not be set and the *Square* object will not appear.

7. Return to the DrawingPad.xaml file in the *Design View* window, and click the *Canvas* object in the middle of the form. In the list of events in the *Properties* window, double-click the *MouseRightButtonDown* event.

   Visual Studio creates another method called *drawingCanvas_MouseRightButtonDown*. This method runs when the user clicks the right mouse button on the canvas.

8. Add the code shown next in bold to the *drawingCanvas_MouseRightButtonDown* method. The logic in this code is similar to the method that handles the left mouse button, except that it displays a *Circle* object in *HotPink*.

```
private void drawingCanvas_MouseRightButtonDown(object sender, MouseButtonEventArgs e)
{
    Point mouseLocation = e.GetPosition(this.drawingCanvas);
    Circle myCircle = new Circle(100);

    if (myCircle is IDraw)
    {
        IDraw drawCircle = myCircle;
        drawCircle.SetLocation((int)mouseLocation.X, (int)mouseLocation.Y);
        drawCircle.Draw(drawingCanvas);
    }

    if (myCircle is IColor)
    {
        IColor colorCircle = myCircle;
        colorCircle.SetColor(Colors.HotPink);
    }
}
```

9. On the *Debug* menu, click *Start Without Debugging* to build and run the application.

10. When the *Drawing Pad* window appears, left-click anywhere in the window. A violet square should appear.

11. Right-click anywhere in the window. A pink circle should appear. You can click the left and right mouse buttons any number of times, and each click will draw a square or circle at the mouse position, as shown in the following image:

12. Close the window and return to Visual Studio.

Abstract Classes

You can implement the *ILandBound* and *IGrazable* interfaces discussed in the previous section in many different classes, depending on how many different types of mammals you want to model in your C# application. In situations such as this, it's quite common for parts of the derived classes to share common implementations. For example, the duplication in the following two classes is obvious:

```
class Horse : Mammal, ILandBound, IGrazable
{
    ...
    void IGrazable.ChewGrass()
    {
        Console.WriteLine("Chewing grass");
        // code for chewing grass
    }
}

class Sheep : Mammal, ILandBound, IGrazable
{
    ...
    void IGrazable.ChewGrass()
    {
        Console.WriteLine("Chewing grass");
        // same code as horse for chewing grass
    }
}
```

Duplication in code is a warning sign. If possible, you should refactor the code to avoid this duplication and reduce any maintenance costs. One way to achieve this refactoring is to put the common implementation into a new class created specifically for this purpose. In effect, you can insert a new class into the class hierarchy. For example:

```
class GrazingMammal : Mammal, IGrazable
{
    ...
    void IGrazable.ChewGrass()
    {
        Console.WriteLine("Chewing grass");
        // common code for chewing grass
    }
}

class Horse : GrazingMammal, ILandBound
{
    ...
}

class Sheep : GrazingMammal, ILandBound
{
    ...
}
```

This is a good solution, but there is one thing that is still not quite right: you can actually create instances of the *GrazingMammal* class (and the *Mammal* class for that matter). This doesn't really make sense. The *GrazingMammal* class exists to provide a common default implementation. Its sole purpose is to be inherited from. The *GrazingMammal* class is an abstraction of common functionality rather than an entity in its own right.

To declare that creating instances of a class is not allowed, you must explicitly declare that the class is abstract, by using the *abstract* keyword. For example:

```
abstract class GrazingMammal : Mammal, IGrazable
{
    ...
}
```

If you try to instantiate a *GrazingMammal* object, the code will not compile:

```
GrazingMammal myGrazingMammal =  new GrazingMammal(...);  // illegal
```

Abstract Methods

An abstract class can contain abstract methods. An abstract method is similar in principle to a virtual method (which you met in Chapter 12) except that it does not contain a method body.

A derived class *must* override this method. The following example defines the *DigestGrass* method in the *GrazingMammal* class as an abstract method; grazing mammals might use the same code for chewing grass, but they must provide their own implementation of the *DigestGrass* method. An abstract method is useful if it does not make sense to provide a default implementation in the abstract class and you want to ensure that an inheriting class provides its own implementation of that method.

```
abstract class GrazingMammal : Mammal, IGrazable
{
    abstract void DigestGrass();
    ...
}
```

Sealed Classes

Using inheritance is not always easy and requires forethought. If you create an interface or an abstract class, you are knowingly writing something that will be inherited from in the future. The trouble is that predicting the future is a difficult business. With practice and experience, you can develop the skills to craft a flexible, easy-to-use hierarchy of interfaces, abstract classes, and classes, but it takes effort and you also need a solid understanding of the problem you are modeling. To put it another way, unless you consciously design a class with the intention of using it as a base class, it's extremely unlikely that it will function very well as a base class. C# allows you to use the *sealed* keyword to prevent a class from being used as a base class if you decide that it should not be. For example:

```
sealed class Horse : GrazingMammal, ILandBound
{
    ...
}
```

If any class attempts to use *Horse* as a base class, a compile-time error will be generated. Note that a sealed class cannot declare any virtual methods and that an abstract class cannot be sealed.

> **Note** A structure is implicitly sealed. You can never derive from a structure.

Sealed Methods

You can also use the *sealed* keyword to declare that an individual method in an unsealed class is sealed. This means that a derived class cannot then override the sealed method. You can seal only an *override* method, and you declare the method as *sealed override*, which means that you cannot seal a method that is directly implementing a method in an interface. (You cannot override a method inherited directly from an interface, only from a class.) You can think of the *interface*, *virtual*, *override*, and *sealed* keywords as follows:

- An interface introduces the name of a method.

- A virtual method is the first implementation of a method.

- An override method is another implementation of a method.

- A sealed method is the last implementation of a method.

Implementing and Using an Abstract Class

The following exercises use an abstract class to rationalize some of the code that you developed in the previous exercise. The *Square* and *Circle* classes contain a high propor-tion of duplicate code. It makes sense to factor this code out into an abstract class called *DrawingShape* because this will ease maintenance of the *Square* and *Circle* classes in the future.

Create the *DrawingShape* abstract class

1. Return to the Drawing project in Visual Studio.

 Note A finished working copy of the previous exercise is available in the Drawing project located in the \Microsoft Press\Visual CSharp Step By Step\Chapter 13\Drawing Using Interfaces - Complete folder in your Documents folder.

2. On the *Project* menu, click *Add Class*.

    The *Add New Item – Drawing* dialog box appears.

3. In the *Name* text box, type *DrawingShape.cs*, and then click *Add*.

    Visual Studio creates the file and displays it in the *Code and Text Editor* window.

4. In the DrawingShape.cs file, add the following *using* statements to the list at the top:

```
using System.Windows;
using System.Windows.Media;
using System.Windows.Shapes;
using System.Windows.Controls;
```

5. The purpose of this class is to contain the code common to the *Circle* and *Square* class-es. A program should not be able to instantiate a *DrawingShape* object directly. Modify the definition of the *DrawingShape* class, and declare it as *abstract*, as shown here in bold:

```
abstract class DrawingShape
{
}
```

6. Add the private variables shown in bold to the *DrawingShape* class:

```
abstract class DrawingShape
{
    protected int size;
    protected int locX = 0, locY = 0;
    protected Shape shape = null;
}
```

The *Square* and *Circle* classes both use the *locX* and *locY* fields to specify the location of the object on the canvas, so you can move these fields to the abstract class. Similarly, the *Square* and *Circle* classes both used a field to indicate the size of the object when it was rendered; although it has a different name in each class (*sideLength* and *radius*), semantically the field performed the same task in both classes. The name "size" is a good abstraction of the purpose of this field.

Internally, the *Square* class uses a *Rectangle* object to render itself on the canvas, and the *Circle* class uses an *Ellipse* object. Both of these classes are part of a hierarchy based on the abstract *Shape* class in the .NET Framework. The *DrawingShape* class uses a *Shape* field to represent both of these types.

7. Add the following constructor to the *DrawingShape* class:

```
public DrawingShape(int size)
{
    this.size = size;
}
```

This code initializes the *size* field in the *DrawingShape* object.

8. Add the *SetLocation* and *SetColor* methods to the *DrawingShape* class, as shown in bold. These methods provide implementations that are inherited by all classes that derive from the *DrawingShape* class. Notice that they are not marked as *virtual*, and a derived class is not expected to override them. Also, the *DrawingShape* class is not declared as implementing the *IDraw* or *IColor* interfaces (interface implementation is a feature of the *Square* and *Circle* classes and not this abstract class), so these methods are simply declared as *public*.

```
abstract class DrawingShape
{
    ...
    public void SetLocation(int xCoord, int yCoord)
    {
        this.locX = xCoord;
        this.locY = yCoord;
    }
```

```
public void SetColor(Color color)
{
    if (shape != null)
    {
        SolidColorBrush brush = new SolidColorBrush(color);
        shape.Fill = brush;
    }
}
}
```

9. Add the *Draw* method to the *DrawingShape* class. Unlike the previous methods, this method is declared as *virtual*, and any derived classes are expected to override it to extend the functionality. The code in this method verifies that the *shape* field is not null, and then draws it on the canvas. The classes that inherit this method must provide their own code to instantiate the *shape* object. (Remember that the *Square* class creates a *Rectangle* object and the *Circle* class creates an *Ellipse* object.)

```
abstract class DrawingShape
{
    ...
    public virtual void Draw(Canvas canvas)
    {
        if (this.shape == null)
        {
            throw new ApplicationException("Shape is null");
        }

        this.shape.Height = this.size;
        this.shape.Width = this.size;
        Canvas.SetTop(this.shape, this.locY);
        Canvas.SetLeft(this.shape, this.locX);
        canvas.Children.Add(shape);
    }
}
```

You have now completed the *DrawingShape* abstract class. The next step is to change the *Square* and *Circle* classes so that they inherit from this class, and remove the duplicated code from the *Square* and *Circle* classes.

Modify the *Square* and *Circle* classes to inherit from the *DrawingShape* class

1. Display the code for the *Square* class in the *Code and Text Editor* window. Modify the definition of the *Square* class so that it inherits from the *DrawingShape* class as well as implementing the *IDraw* and *IColor* interfaces.

```
class Square : DrawingShape, IDraw, IColor
{
    ...
}
```

Notice that you must specify the class that the *Square* class inherits from before any interfaces.

2. In the *Square* class, remove the definitions of the *sideLength*, *rect*, *locX*, and *locY* fields.

3. Replace the existing constructor with the following code, which calls the constructor in the base class. Notice that the body of this constructor is empty because the base class constructor performs all the initialization required.

```
class Square : DrawingShape, IDraw, IColor
{
    public Square(int sideLength) : base(sideLength)
    {
    }
    ...
}
```

4. Remove the *SetLocation* and *SetColor* methods from the *Square* class. The *DrawingShape* class now provides the implementation of these methods.

5. Modify the definition of the *Draw* method. Declare it as *public override*, and remove the reference to the *IDraw* interface. Again, the *DrawingShape* class already provides the base functionality for this method, but you will extend it with specific code required by the *Square* class.

```
public override void Draw(Canvas canvas)
{
    ...
}
```

6. Replace the body of the *Draw* method with the code shown in bold. These statements instantiate the *shape* field inherited from the *DrawingShape* class as a new instance of the *Rectangle* class if it has not already been instantiated, and then they call the *Draw* method in the *DrawingShape* class.

```
public override void Draw(Canvas canvas)
{
    if (this.shape != null)
    {
        canvas.Children.Remove(this.shape);
    }
    else
    {
        this.shape = new Rectangle();
    }

    base.Draw(canvas);
}
```

7. Repeat steps 2 through 6 for the *Circle* class, except that the constructor should be called *Circle* with a parameter called *radius*, and in the *Draw* method you should

instantiate the *shape* field as a new *Ellipse* object. The complete code for the *Circle* class should look like this:

```
class Circle : DrawingShape, IDraw, IColor
{
    public Circle(int radius) : base(radius)
    {
    }

    public override void Draw(Canvas canvas)
    {
        if (this.shape != null)
        {
            canvas.Children.Remove(this.shape);
        }
        else
        {
            this.shape = new Ellipse();
        }

        base.Draw(canvas);
    }
}
```

8. On the *Debug* menu, click *Start Without Debugging*. When the *Drawing Pad* window appears, verify that *Square* objects appear when you left-click in the window and *Circle* objects appear when you right-click in the window.

9. Close the *Drawing Pad* window, and return to Visual Studio.

In this chapter, you have seen how to define and implement interfaces and abstract classes. The following table summarizes the various valid (*yes*), invalid (*no*), and mandatory (*required*) keyword combinations when defining methods for interfaces and classes.

Keyword	Interface	Abstract class	Class	Sealed class	Structure
abstract	no	yes	no	no	no
new	yes[1]	yes	yes	yes	yes
override	no	yes	yes	yes	yes
private	no	yes	yes	yes	yes
protected	no	yes	yes	yes	no[2]
public	no	yes	yes	yes	yes
sealed	no	yes	yes	required	no
virtual	no	yes	yes	no	no

[1] An interface can extend another interface and introduce a new method with the same signature.

[2] A structure is implicitly sealed and cannot be derived from.

- If you want to continue to the next chapter

  Keep Visual Studio 2010 running, and turn to Chapter 14.

- If you want to exit Visual Studio 2010 now

  On the *File* menu, click *Exit*. If you see a *Save* dialog box, click *Yes* and save the project.

Chapter 13 Quick Reference

To	Do this
Declare an interface	Use the *interface* keyword. For example: ```\ninterface IDemo\n{\n string Name();\n string Description();\n}\n```
Implement an interface	Declare a class using the same syntax as class inheritance, and then implement all the member functions of the interface. For example: ```\nclass Test : IDemo\n{\n public string IDemo.Name()\n {\n ...\n }\n\n public string IDemo.Description()\n {\n ...\n }\n}\n```
Create an abstract class that can be used only as a base class, containing abstract methods	Declare the class using the *abstract* keyword. For each abstract method, declare the method with the *abstract* keyword and without a method body. For example: ```\nabstract class GrazingMammal\n{\n abstract void DigestGrass();\n ...\n}\n```
Create a sealed class that cannot be used as a base class	Declare the class using the *sealed* keyword. For example: ```\nsealed class Horse\n\n{\n ...\n}\n```

Chapter 14

Using Garbage Collection and Resource Management

After completing this chapter, you will be able to:

- Manage system resources by using garbage collection.

- Write code that runs when an object is finalized by using a destructor.

- Release a resource at a known point in time in an exception-safe manner by writing a *try/finally* statement.

- Release a resource at a known point in time in an exception-safe manner by writing a *using* statement.

You have seen in earlier chapters how to create variables and objects, and you should understand how memory is allocated when you create variables and objects. (In case you don't remember, value types are created on the stack, and reference types are allocated memory from the heap.) Computers do not have infinite amounts of memory, so memory must be reclaimed when a variable or an object no longer needs it. Value types are destroyed and their memory reclaimed when they go out of scope. That's the easy bit. How about reference types? You create an object by using the *new* keyword, but how and when is an object destroyed? That's what this chapter is all about.

The Life and Times of an Object

First, let's recap what happens when you create an object.

You create an object by using the *new* operator. The following example creates a new instance of the *Square* class that you met in Chapter 13, "Creating Interfaces and Defining Abstract Classes":

```
Square mySquare = new Square(); // Square is a reference type
```

From your point of view, the *new* operation is atomic, but underneath, object creation is really a two-phase process:

1. The *new* operation allocates a chunk of *raw* memory from the heap. You have no control over this phase of an object's creation.

2. The *new* operation converts the chunk of raw memory to an object; it has to initialize the object. You can control this phase by using a constructor.

Note C++ programmers should note that in C#, you cannot overload *new* to control allocation.

After you have created an object, you can access its members by using the dot operator (.). For example, the *Square* class includes a method named *Draw* that you can run:

```
mySquare.Draw();
```

Note This code is based on the version of the *Square* class that inherits from the *DrawingShape* abstract class and that does not implement the *IDraw* interface explicitly. For more information, please refer back to Chapter 13.

You can make other reference variables refer to the same object:

```
Square referenceToMySquare = mySquare;
```

How many references can you create to an object? As many as you want! This has an impact on the lifetime of an object. The runtime has to keep track of all these references. If the variable *mySquare* disappears (by going out of scope), other variables (such as *referenceToMySquare*) might still exist. The lifetime of an object cannot be tied to a particular reference variable. An object can be destroyed and its memory reclaimed only when *all* the references to it have disappeared.

Like object creation, object destruction is a two-phase process. The two phases of destruction exactly mirror the two phases of creation:

1. The runtime has to perform some tidying up. You can control this by writing a *destructor*.

2. The runtime has to return the memory previously belonging to the object back to the heap; the memory that the object lived in has to be deallocated. You have no control over this phase.

The process of destroying an object and returning memory back to the heap is known as *garbage collection*.

Note C++ programmers should note that C# does not have a delete operator. The runtime controls when an object is destroyed.

Writing Destructors

You can use a destructor to perform any tidying up required when an object is garbage collected. A destructor is a special method, a little like a constructor, except that the runtime calls it after the last reference to an object has disappeared. The syntax for writing a destructor is a tilde (~) followed by the name of the class. For example, here's a simple class that counts the number of existing instances by incrementing a static variable in the constructor and decrementing the same static variable in the destructor:

```
class Tally
{
    public Tally()
    {
        this.instanceCount++;
    }

    ~Tally()
    {
        this.instanceCount--;
    }

    public static int InstanceCount()
    {
        return this.instanceCount;
    }
    ...
    private static int instanceCount = 0;
}
```

There are some very important restrictions that apply to destructors:

- Destructors apply only to reference types. You cannot declare a destructor in a value type, such as a *struct*.

  ```
  struct Tally
  {
      ~Tally() { ... } // compile-time error
  }
  ```

- You cannot specify an access modifier (such as *public*) for a destructor. You never call the destructor in your own code—part of the runtime called the *garbage collector* does this for you.

  ```
  public ~Tally() { ... } // compile-time error
  ```

- A destructor cannot take any parameters. Again, this is because you never call the destructor yourself.

  ```
  ~Tally(int parameter) { ... } // compile-time error
  ```

Internally, the C# compiler automatically translates a destructor into an override of the *Object.Finalize* method. The compiler converts the following destructor:

```
class Tally
{
    ~Tally() { // your code goes here }
}
```

into this:

```
class Tally
{
    protected override void Finalize()
    {
        try { // your code goes here }
        finally { base.Finalize(); }
    }
}
```

The compiler-generated *Finalize* method contains the destructor body inside a *try* block, followed by a *finally* block that calls the *Finalize* method in the base class. (The *try* and *finally* keywords are described in Chapter 6, "Managing Errors and Exceptions.") This ensures that a destructor always calls its base class destructor, even if an exception occurs during your destructor code.

It's important to understand that only the compiler can make this translation. You can't write your own method to override *Finalize*, and you can't call *Finalize* yourself.

Why Use the Garbage Collector?

You should now understand that you can never destroy an object yourself by using C# code. There just isn't any syntax to do it. The runtime does it for you, and there are good reasons why the designers of C# decided to prevent you from doing it. If it were *your* responsibility to destroy objects, sooner or later one of the following situations would arise:

- You'd forget to destroy the object. This would mean that the object's destructor (if it had one) would not be run, tidying up would not occur, and memory would not be deallocated back to the heap. You could quite easily run out of memory.

- You'd try to destroy an active object. Remember, objects are accessed by reference. If a class held a reference to a destroyed object, it would be a *dangling reference*. The dangling reference would end up referring either to unused memory or possibly to a completely different object in the same piece of memory. Either way, the outcome of using a dangling reference would be undefined at best or a security risk at worst. All bets would be off.

- You'd try and destroy the same object more than once. This might or might not be disastrous, depending on the code in the destructor.

These problems are unacceptable in a language like C#, which places robustness and security high on its list of design goals. Instead, the garbage collector is responsible for destroying objects for you. The garbage collector makes the following guarantees:

- Every object will be destroyed, and its destructors will be run. When a program ends, all outstanding objects will be destroyed.

- Every object will be destroyed exactly once.

- Every object will be destroyed only when it becomes unreachable—that is, when there are no references to the object in the process running your application.

These guarantees are tremendously useful and free you, the programmer, from tedious housekeeping chores that are easy to get wrong. They allow you to concentrate on the logic of the program itself and be more productive.

When does garbage collection occur? This might seem like a strange question. After all, surely garbage collection occurs when an object is no longer needed. Well, it does, but not necessarily immediately. Garbage collection can be an expensive process, so the runtime collects garbage only when it needs to (when it thinks available memory is starting to run low), and then it collects as much as it can. Performing a few large sweeps of memory is more efficient than performing lots of little dustings!

> **Note** You can invoke the garbage collector in a program by calling the static method *Collect* of the *GC* class located in the *System* namespace However, except in a few cases, this is not recommended. The *System.GC.Collect* method starts the garbage collector, but the process runs asynchronously; the *System.GC.Collect* method does not wait for garbage collection to be complete before it returns, so you still don't know whether your objects have been destroyed. Let the runtime decide when it is best to collect garbage!

One feature of the garbage collector is that you don't know, and should not rely upon, the order in which objects will be destroyed. The final point to understand is arguably the most important: destructors do not run until objects are garbage collected. If you write a destructor, you know it will be executed, but you just don't know when. Consequently, you should never write code that depends on destructors running in a particular sequence or at a specific point in your application.

How Does the Garbage Collector Work?

The garbage collector runs in its own thread and can execute only at certain times—typically, when your application reaches the end of a method. While it runs, other threads running in your application will temporarily halt. This is because the garbage collector might need to move objects around and update object references; it cannot do this while objects are in use.

> **Note** A thread is a separate path of execution in an application. Windows uses threads to enable an application to perform multiple operations concurrently.

The steps that the garbage collector takes are as follows:

1. It builds a map of all reachable objects. It does this by repeatedly following reference fields inside objects. The garbage collector builds this map very carefully and makes sure that circular references do not cause an infinite recursion. Any object *not* in this map is deemed to be unreachable.

2. It checks whether any of the unreachable objects has a destructor that needs to be run (a process called *finalization*). Any unreachable object that requires finalization is placed in a special queue called the *freachable queue* (pronounced "F-reachable").

3. It deallocates the remaining unreachable objects (those that don't require finalization) by moving the *reachable* objects down the heap, thus defragmenting the heap and freeing memory at the top of the heap. When the garbage collector moves a reachable object, it also updates any references to the object.

4. At this point, it allows other threads to resume.

5. It finalizes the unreachable objects that require finalization (now in the *freachable* queue) by its own thread.

Recommendations

Writing classes that contain destructors adds complexity to your code and to the garbage collection process and makes your program run more slowly. If your program does not contain any destructors, the garbage collector does not need to place unreachable objects in the *freachable* queue and finalize them. Clearly, not doing something is faster than doing it. Therefore, try to avoid using destructors except when you really need them. For example, consider a *using* statement instead. (See the section "The *using* Statement" later in this chapter.)

You need to be very careful when you write a destructor. In particular, you need to be aware that, if your destructor calls other objects, those other objects might have *already* had their destructor called by the garbage collector. Remember that the order of finalization is not guaranteed. Therefore, ensure that destructors do not depend on one another or overlap with one another. (Don't have two destructors that try to release the same resource, for example.)

Resource Management

Sometimes it's inadvisable to release a resource in a destructor; some resources are just too valuable to lie around waiting for an arbitrary length of time until the garbage collector actually releases them. Scarce resources need to be released, and they need to be released as soon as possible. In these situations, your only option is to release the resource yourself. You can achieve this by creating a *disposal* method. A disposal method is a method that explicitly disposes of a resource. If a class has a disposal method, you can call it and control when the resource is released.

> **Note** The term *disposal method* refers to the purpose of the method rather than its name. A disposal method can be named using any valid C# identifier.

Disposal Methods

An example of a class that implements a disposal method is the *TextReader* class from the *System.IO* namespace. This class provides a mechanism to read characters from a sequential stream of input. The *TextReader* class contains a virtual method named *Close*, which closes the stream. The *StreamReader* class (which reads characters from a stream, such as an open file) and the *StringReader* class (which reads characters from a string) both derive from *TextReader,* and both override the *Close* method. Here's an example that reads lines of text from a file by using the *StreamReader* class and then displays them on the screen:

```
TextReader reader = new StreamReader(filename);
string line;
while ((line = reader.ReadLine()) != null)
{
    Console.WriteLine(line);
}
reader.Close();
```

The *ReadLine* method reads the next line of text from the stream into a string. The *ReadLine* method returns *null* if there is nothing left in the stream. It's important to call *Close* when you have finished with *reader* to release the file handle and associated resources. However, there is a problem with this example: it's not exception-safe. If the call to *ReadLine* or *WriteLine* throws an exception, the call to *Close* will not happen; it will be bypassed. If this happens often enough, you will run out of file handles and be unable to open any more files.

Exception-Safe Disposal

One way to ensure that a disposal method (such as *Close*) is always called, regardless of whether there is an exception, is to call the disposal method inside a *finally* block. Here's the preceding example coded using this technique:

```
TextReader reader = new StreamReader(filename);
try
{
    string line;
    while ((line = reader.ReadLine()) != null)
```

```
    {
        Console.WriteLine(line);
    }
}
finally
{
    reader.Close();
}
```

Using a *finally* block like this works, but it has several drawbacks that make it a less than ideal solution:

- It quickly gets unwieldy if you have to dispose of more than one resource. (You end up with nested *try* and *finally* blocks.)

- In some cases, you might have to modify the code. (For example, you might need to reorder the declaration of the resource reference, remember to initialize the reference to *null*, and remember to check that the reference isn't *null* in the *finally* block.)

- It fails to create an abstraction of the solution. This means that the solution is hard to understand and you must repeat the code everywhere you need this functionality.

- The reference to the resource remains in scope after the *finally* block. This means that you can accidentally try to use the resource after it has been released.

The *using* statement is designed to solve all these problems.

The *using* Statement

The *using* statement provides a clean mechanism for controlling the lifetimes of resources. You can create an object, and this object will be destroyed when the *using* statement block finishes.

 Important Do not confuse the *using* statement shown in this section with the *using* directive that brings a namespace into scope. It is unfortunate that the same keyword has two different meanings.

The syntax for a *using* statement is as follows:

```
using ( type variable = initialization )
{
    StatementBlock
}
```

Here is the best way to ensure that your code always calls *Close* on a *TextReader*:

```
using (TextReader reader = new StreamReader(filename))
{
    string line;
    while ((line = reader.ReadLine()) != null)
    {
        Console.WriteLine(line);
    }
}
```

This *using* statement is precisely equivalent to the following transformation:

```
{
    TextReader reader = new StreamReader(filename);
    try
    {
        string line;
        while ((line = reader.ReadLine()) != null)
        {
            Console.WriteLine(line);
        }
    }
    finally
    {
        if (reader != null)
        {
            ((IDisposable)reader).Dispose();
        }
    }
}
```

The variable you declare in a *using* statement must be of a type that implements the *IDisposable* interface.

> **Note** The *using* statement introduces its own block for scoping purposes. This arrangement means that the variable you declare in a *using* statement automatically goes out of scope at the end of the embedded statement and you cannot accidentally attempt to access a disposed resource.

The *IDisposable* interface lives in the *System* namespace and contains just one method, named *Dispose*:

```
namespace System
{
    interface IDisposable
    {
        void Dispose();
    }
}
```

It just so happens that the *StreamReader* class implements the *IDisposable* interface, and its *Dispose* method calls *Close* to close the stream. You can employ a *using* statement as a clean, exception-safe, and robust way to ensure that a resource is always released. This approach solves all of the problems that existed in the manual *try/finally* solution. You now have a solution that

- Scales well if you need to dispose of multiple resources.

- Doesn't distort the logic of the program code.

- Abstracts away the problem and avoids repetition.

- Is robust. You can't use the variable declared inside the *using* statement (in this case, *reader*) after the *using* statement has ended because it's not in scope anymore—you'll get a compile-time error.

Calling the *Dispose* Method from a Destructor

When writing a class, should you write a destructor or implement the *IDisposable* interface? A call to a destructor *will* happen, but you just don't know when. On the other hand, you know exactly when a call to the *Dispose* method happens, but you just can't be sure that it will actually happen, because it relies on the programmer remembering to write a *using* statement. However, it is possible to ensure that the *Dispose* method always runs by calling it from the destructor. This acts as a useful backup. You might forget to call the *Dispose* method, but at least you can be sure that it will be called, even if it's only when the program shuts down. Here's an example of how to do this:

```
class Example : IDisposable
{
    private Resource scarce;       // scarce resource to manage and dispose of
    private bool disposed = false; // flag to indicate whether the resource
                                   // has already been disposed of
    ...
    ~Example()
    {
        Dispose();
    }

    public virtual void Dispose()
    {
        if (!this.disposed)
        {
            try {
                // release scarce resource here
            }
            finally {
                this.disposed = true;
                GC.SuppressFinalize(this);
            }
        }
    }
}
```

```
    public void SomeBehavior() // example method
    {
        checkIfDisposed();
        ...
    }
    ...
    private void checkIfDisposed()
    {
        if (this.disposed)
        {
            throw new ObjectDisposedException("Example: object has been disposed of");
        }
    }
}
```

Notice the following features of the *Example* class:

- The class implements the *IDisposable* interface.

- The destructor calls *Dispose*.

- The *Dispose* method is public and can be called at any time.

- The *Dispose* method can safely be called multiple times. The variable *disposed* indicates whether the method has already been run. The scarce resource is released only the first time the method runs.

- The *Dispose* method calls the static *GC.SuppressFinalize* method. This method stops the garbage collector from calling the destructor on this object, because the object has now been finalized.

- All the regular methods of the class (such as *SomeBehavior*) check to see whether the object has already been disposed of. If it has, they throw an exception.

Implementing Exception-Safe Disposal

In the following exercise, you will rewrite a small piece of code to make the code exception safe. The code opens a text file, reads its contents one line at a time, writes these lines to a text box on a form on the screen, and then closes the text file. However, if an exception arises as the file is read or as the lines are written to the text box, the call to close the text file will be bypassed. You will rewrite the code to use a *using* statement instead, ensuring that the code is exception safe.

Write a *using* statement

1. Start Microsoft Visual Studio 2010 if it is not already running.

2. Open the *UsingStatement* project, located in the \Microsoft Press\Visual CSharp Step By Step\Chapter 14\UsingStatement folder in your Documents folder.

3. On the *Debug* menu, click *Start Without Debugging*.

A Windows Presentation Foundation (WPF) form appears.

4. On the form, click *Open File*.

5. In the *Open* dialog box, move to the \Microsoft Press\Visual CSharp Step By Step\ Chapter 14\UsingStatement\UsingStatement folder in your Documents folder, and select the MainWindow.xaml.cs source file.

This is the source file for the application itself.

6. Click *Open*.

The contents of the file are displayed in the form, as shown here:

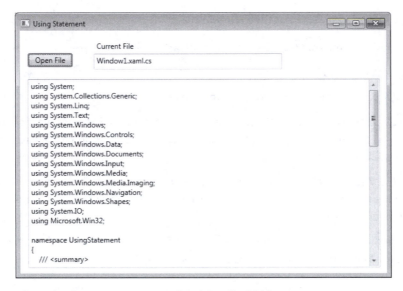

7. Close the form to return to Visual Studio 2010.

8. Open the MainWindow.xaml.cs file in the *Code and Text Editor* window, and then locate the *openFileDialogFileOk* method.

The method looks like this:

```
private void openFileDialogFileOk(object sender,
System.ComponentModel.CancelEventArgs e)
{
    string fullPathname = openFileDialog.FileName;
    FileInfo src = new FileInfo(fullPathname);
    fileName.Text = src.Name;
    source.Clear();

    TextReader reader = new StreamReader(fullPathname);
    string line;
    while ((line = reader.ReadLine()) != null)
```

```
    {
        source.Text += line + "\n";
    }
    reader.Close();
}
```

The variables *fileName*, *openFileDialog*, and *source* are three private fields of the *MainWindow* class. This code uses a *TextReader* object called *reader* to open the file specified by the user. (The details of how the user selects the file are described in Chapter 23, "Gathering User Input.") The *while* statement contains the key functionality in this method; it iterates through the file a line at a time by using the *ReadLine* method of the *reader* object and displays each line by appending it to the *Text* property of the *Source* text field on the form. When the *ReadLine* method returns null, there is no more data left in the file, the *while* loop finishes, and the *Close* method of the *reader* object closes the file.

The problem with this code is that the call to *reader.Close* is not guaranteed to execute. If an exception occurs after opening the file, the method will terminate with an exception, but the file will remain open until the application itself finishes.

9. Modify the *openFileDialogFileOk* method, and wrap the code that processes the file in a *using* statement (including opening and closing braces), as shown in bold here. Remove the statement that closes the *TextReader* object.

```
private void openFileDialogFileOk(object sender,
System.ComponentModel.CancelEventArgs e)
{
    string fullPathname = openFileDialog.FileName;
    FileInfo src = new FileInfo(fullPathname);
    fileName.Text = src.Name;
    source.Clear();
    using (TextReader reader = new StreamReader(fullPathname))
    {
        string line;
        while ((line = reader.ReadLine()) != null)
        {
            source.Text += line + "\n";
        }
    }
}
```

You no longer need to call *reader.Close* because it will be invoked automatically by the *Dispose* method of the *StreamReader* class when the *using* statement completes. This applies whether the *using* statement finishes naturally or terminates because of an exception.

10. On the *Debug* menu, click *Start Without Debugging*.

11. Verify that the application still works as before, and then close the form.

In this chapter, you saw how the garbage collector works and how the .NET Framework uses it to dispose of objects and reclaim memory. You have learned how to write a destructor to clean up the resources used by an object when memory is recycled by the garbage collector. You have also seen how to use the *using* statement to implement exception-safe disposal of resources.

- If you want to continue to the next chapter

  Keep Visual Studio 2010 running, and turn to Chapter 15.

- If you want to exit Visual Studio 2010 now

  On the *File* menu, click *Exit*. If you see a *Save* dialog box, click *Yes* and save the project.

Chapter 14 Quick Reference

To	Do this
| Write a destructor | Write a method whose name is the same as the name of the class and is prefixed with a tilde (~). The method must not have an access modifier (such as *public*) and cannot have any parameters or return a value. For example:<br><br>```csharp
class Example
{
    ~Example()
    {
        ...
    }
}
``` |
| Call a destructor | You can't call a destructor. Only the garbage collector can call a destructor. |
| Force garbage collection (not recommended) | Call *System.GC.Collect*. |
| Release a resource at a known point in time (but at the risk of memory leaks if an exception interrupts the execution) | Write a disposal method (a method that disposes of a resource) and call it explicitly from the program. For example:<br><br>```csharp
class TextReader
{
    ...
    public virtual void Close()
    {
        ...
    }
}

class Example
{
    void Use()
    {
        TextReader reader = ...;
        // use reader
        reader.Close();
    }
}
``` |

Part III
Creating Components

Chapter 15
Implementing Properties to Access Fields

After completing this chapter, you will be able to:

- Encapsulate logical fields by using properties.

- Control read access to properties by declaring *get* accessors.

- Control write access to properties by declaring *set* accessors.

- Create interfaces that declare properties.

- Implement interfaces containing properties by using structures and classes.

- Generate properties automatically based on field definitions.

- Use properties to initialize objects.

The first two parts of this book have introduced the core syntax of the C# language and have shown you how to use C# to build new types by using structures, enumerations, and classes. You have also seen how the runtime manages the memory used by variables and objects when a program runs, and you should now understand the life cycle of C# objects. The chapters in Part III, "Creating Components," build on this information, showing you how to use C# to create reusable components—functional classes that you can reuse in many different applications.

This chapter looks at how to define and use properties to encapsulate fields and data in a class. Previous chapters have emphasized that you should make the fields in a class private and provide methods to store values in them and to retrieve their values. This approach provides safe and controlled access to fields and enables you to encapsulate additional logic and rules concerning the values that are permitted. However, the syntax for accessing a field in this way is unnatural. When you want to read or write a variable, you normally use an assignment statement, so calling a method to achieve the same effect on a field (which is, after all, just a variable) feels a little clumsy. Properties are designed to alleviate this awkwardness.

Implementing Encapsulation by Using Methods

First let's recap the original motivation for using methods to hide fields.

Consider the following structure that represents a position on a computer screen as a pair of coordinates, *x* and *y*. Assume that the range of valid values for the *x*-coordinate lies between 0 and 1280 and the range of valid values for the *y*-coordinate lies between 0 and 1024:

```
struct ScreenPosition
{
    public int X;
    public int Y;

    public ScreenPosition(int x, int y)
    {
        this.X = rangeCheckedX(x);
        this.Y = rangeCheckedY(y);
    }

    private static int rangeCheckedX(int x)
    {
        if (x < 0 || x > 1280)
        {
            throw new ArgumentOutOfRangeException("X");
        }
        return x;
    }

    private static int rangeCheckedY(int y)
    {
        if (y < 0 || y > 1024)
        {
            throw new ArgumentOutOfRangeException("Y");
        }
        return y;
    }
}
```

One problem with this structure is that it does not follow the golden rule of encapsulation—that is, it does not keep its data private. Public data is often a bad idea because the class cannot control the values that an application specifies. For example, the *ScreenPosition* constructor range checks its parameters to make sure that they are in a specified range, but no such check can be done on the "raw" access to the public fields. Sooner or later (probably sooner), an error or misunderstanding on the part of a developer using this class in an application can cause either *X* or *Y* to stray out of this range:

```
ScreenPosition origin = new ScreenPosition(0, 0);
...
int xpos = origin.X;
origin.Y = -100; // oops
```

The common way to solve this problem is to make the fields private and add an accessor method and a modifier method to respectively read and write the value of each private field. The modifier methods can then range-check new field values. For example, the following code contains an accessor (*GetX*) and a modifier (*SetX*) for the *X* field. Notice that *SetX* checks its parameter value.

```
struct ScreenPosition
{
    ...
    public int GetX()
    {
        return this.x;
    }

    public void SetX(int newX)
    {
        this.x = rangeCheckedX(newX);
    }
    ...
    private static int rangeCheckedX(int x) { ... }
    private static int rangeCheckedY(int y) { ... }
    private int x, y;
}
```

The code now successfully enforces the range constraints, which is good. However, there is a price to pay for this valuable guarantee—*ScreenPosition* no longer has a natural field-like syntax; it uses awkward method-based syntax instead. The following example increases the value of *X* by 10. To do so, it has to read the value of *X* by using the *GetX* accessor method and then write the value of *X* by using the *SetX* modifier method.

```
int xpos = origin.GetX();
origin.SetX(xpos + 10);
```

Compare this with the equivalent code if the *X* field were public:

```
origin.X += 10;
```

There is no doubt that, in this case, using public fields is syntactically cleaner, shorter, and easier. Unfortunately, using public fields breaks encapsulation. Properties enable you to combine the best of both worlds (fields and methods) to retain encapsulation while providing a field-like syntax.

What Are Properties?

A *property* is a cross between a field and a method—it looks like a field but acts like a method. You access a property by using exactly the same syntax that you use to access a field. However, the compiler automatically translates this field-like syntax into calls to accessor methods.

The syntax for a property declaration looks like this:

```
AccessModifier Type PropertyName
{
    get
    {
        // read accessor code
    }

    set
    {
        // write accessor code
    }
}
```

A property can contain two blocks of code, starting with the *get* and *set* keywords. The *get* block contains statements that execute when the property is read, and the *set* block contains statements that run when the property is written to. The type of the property specifies the type of data read and written by the *get* and *set* accessors.

The next code example shows the *ScreenPosition* structure rewritten by using properties. When reading this code, notice the following:

- Lowercase *x* and *y* are *private* fields.

- Uppercase *X* and *Y* are *public* properties.

- All *set* accessors are passed the data to be written by using a hidden, built-in parameter named *value*.

 Tip The fields and properties follow the standard Microsoft Visual C# *public/private* naming convention. Public fields and properties should start with an uppercase letter, but private fields and properties should start with a lowercase letter.

```
struct ScreenPosition
{
    private int x, y;

    public ScreenPosition(int X, int Y)
    {
        this.x = rangeCheckedX(X);
        this.y = rangeCheckedY(Y);
    }

    public int X
    {
        get { return this.x; }
        set { this.x = rangeCheckedX(value); }
    }
```

```
public int Y
{
    get { return this.y; }
    set { this.y = rangeCheckedY(value); }
}

private static int rangeCheckedX(int x) { ... }
private static int rangeCheckedY(int y) { ... }
}
```

In this example, a private field directly implements each property, but this is only one way to implement a property. All that is required is that a *get* accessor returns a value of the specified type. Such a value can easily be calculated dynamically rather than being simply retrieved from stored data, in which case there would be no need for a physical field.

> **Note** Although the examples in this chapter show how to define properties for a structure, they are equally applicable to classes; the syntax is the same.

Using Properties

When you use a property in an expression, you can use it in a read context (when you are reading its value) and in a write context (when you are modifying its value). The following example shows how to read values from the *X* and *Y* properties of a *ScreenPosition* structure:

```
ScreenPosition origin = new ScreenPosition(0, 0);
int xpos = origin.X;      // calls origin.X.get
int ypos = origin.Y;      // calls origin.Y.get
```

Notice that you access properties and fields by using the same syntax. When you use a property in a read context, the compiler automatically translates your field-like code into a call to the *get* accessor of that property. Similarly, if you use a property in a write context, the compiler automatically translates your field-like code into a call to the *set* accessor of that property:

```
origin.X = 40;       // calls origin.X.set, with value set to 40
origin.Y = 100;      // calls origin.Y.Set, with value set to 100
```

The values being assigned are passed in to the *set* accessors by using the *value* variable, as described in the preceding section. The runtime does this automatically.

It's also possible to use a property in a read/write context. In this case, both the *get* accessor and the *set* accessor are used. For example, the compiler automatically translates statements such as the following into calls to the *get* and *set* accessors:

```
origin.X += 10;
```

Tip You can declare *static* properties in the same way that you can declare *static* fields and methods. Static properties are accessed by using the name of the class or structure rather than an instance of the class or structure.

Read-Only Properties

You can declare a property that contains only a *get* accessor. In this case, you can use the property only in a read context. For example, here's the *X* property of the *ScreenPosition* structure declared as a read-only property:

```
struct ScreenPosition
{
    ...
    public int X
    {
        get { return this.x; }
    }
}
```

The *X* property does not contain a *set* accessor; therefore, any attempt to use *X* in a write context will fail. For example:

```
origin.X = 140; // compile-time error
```

Write-Only Properties

Similarly, you can declare a property that contains only a *set* accessor. In this case, you can use the property only in a write context. For example, here's the *X* property of the *ScreenPosition* structure declared as a write-only property:

```
struct ScreenPosition
{
    ...
    public int X
    {
        set { this.x = rangeCheckedX(value); }
    }
}
```

The *X* property does not contain a *get* accessor; any attempt to use *X* in a read context will fail. For example:

```
Console.WriteLine(origin.X);    // compile-time error
origin.X = 200;                 // compiles OK
origin.X += 10;                 // compile-time error
```

> **Note** Write-only properties are useful for secure data such as passwords. Ideally, an application that implements security should allow you to set your password but should never allow you to read it back. When a user attempts to log in, he can provide the password. A login method can compare this password with the stored password and return only an indication of whether they match.

Property Accessibility

You can specify the accessibility of a property (*public*, *private*, or *protected*) when you declare it. However, it is possible within the property declaration to override the property accessibility for the *get* and *set* accessors. For example, the version of the *ScreenPosition* structure shown here defines the *set* accessors of the *X* and *Y* properties as *private*. (The *get* accessors are *public*, because the properties are *public*.)

```
struct ScreenPosition
{
    ...
    public int X
    {
        get { return this.x; }
        private set { this.x = rangeCheckedX(value); }
    }

    public int Y
    {
        get { return this.y; }
        private set { this.y = rangeCheckedY(value); }
    }
    ...
    private int x, y;
}
```

You must observe some rules when defining accessors with different accessibility from one another:

- You can change the accessibility of only one of the accessors when you define it. It wouldn't make much sense to define a property as *public* only to change the accessibility of both accessors to *private* anyway!

- The modifier must not specify an accessibility that is less restrictive than that of the property. For example, if the property is declared as *private*, you cannot specify the read accessor as *public*. (Instead, you would make the property *public* and make the write accessor *private*.)

Properties and Field Names: A Warning

Although it is a commonly accepted practice to give properties and private fields the same name that differs only in the case of the initial letter, you should be aware of one drawback. Examine the following code, which implements a class named *Employee*. The *employeeID* field is private, but the *EmployeeID* property provides public access to this field.

```
class Employee
{
    private int employeeID;

    public int EmployeeID;
    {
        get { return this.EmployeeID; }
        set { this.EmployeeID = value; }
    }
}
```

This code will compile perfectly well, but it results in a program raising a *StackOverflowException* whenever the *EmployeeID* property is accessed. This is because the *get* and *set* accessors reference the property (uppercase *E*) rather than the private field (lowercase *e*), which causes an endless recursive loop that eventually causes the process to exhaust the available memory. This sort of bug is very difficult to spot!

Understanding the Property Restrictions

Properties look, act, and feel like fields. However, they are not true fields, and certain restrictions apply to them:

- You can assign a value through a property of a structure or class only after the structure or class has been initialized. The following code example is illegal because the location variable has not been initialized (by using *new*):

```
ScreenPosition location;
location.X = 40; // compile-time error, location not assigned
```

 Note This might seem trivial, but if *X* were a field rather than a property, the code would be legal. What this really means is that there are some differences between fields and properties. You should define structures and classes by using properties from the start, rather than by using fields that you later migrate to properties—code that uses your classes and structures might no longer work after you change fields into properties. We will return to this matter in the section "Generating Automatic Properties" later in this chapter.

- You can't use a property as a *ref* or an *out* argument to a method (although you can use a writable field as a *ref* or an *out* argument). This makes sense because the property doesn't really point to a memory location but rather to an accessor method. For example:

```
MyMethod(ref location.X); // compile-time error
```

- A property can contain at most one *get* accessor and one *set* accessor. A property cannot contain other methods, fields, or properties.

- The *get* and *set* accessors cannot take any parameters. The data being assigned is passed to the *set* accessor automatically by using the *value* variable.

- You can't declare *const* properties. For example:

```
const int X { get { ... } set { ... } } // compile-time error
```

Using Properties Appropriately

Properties are a powerful feature, and used in the correct manner they can help to make code easier to understand and maintain. However, they are no substitute for careful object-oriented design that focuses on the behavior of objects rather than on the properties of objects. Accessing private fields through regular methods or through properties does not, by itself, make your code well-designed. For example, a bank account holds a balance. You might therefore be tempted to create a *Balance* property on a *BankAccount* class, like this:

```
class BankAccount
{
    ...
    public money Balance
    {
        get { ... }
        set { ... }
    }

    private money balance;
}
```

This is a poor design. It fails to represent the functionality required when withdrawing money from and depositing money into an account. (If you know of a bank that allows you to change the balance of your account directly without depositing money, please let me know!) When you're programming, try to express the problem you are solving in the solution and don't get lost in a mass of low-level syntax:

```
class BankAccount
{
    ...
    public money Balance { get { ... } }
    public void Deposit(money amount) { ... }
    public bool Withdraw(money amount) { ... }
    private money balance;
}
```

Declaring Interface Properties

You encountered interfaces in Chapter 13, "Creating Interfaces and Defining Abstract Classes." Interfaces can define properties as well as methods. To do this, you specify the *get* or *set* keyword, or both, but replace the body of the *get* or *set* accessor with a semicolon. For example:

```
interface IScreenPosition
{
    int X { get; set; }
    int Y { get; set; }
}
```

Any class or structure that implements this interface must implement the *X* and *Y* properties with *get* and *set* accessor methods. For example:

```
struct ScreenPosition : IScreenPosition
{
    ...
    public int X
    {
        get { ... }
        set { ... }
    }

    public int Y
    {
        get { ... }
        set { ... }
    }
    ...
}
```

If you implement the interface properties in a class, you can declare the property implementations as *virtual*, which enables derived classes to override the implementations. For example:

```
class ScreenPosition : IScreenPosition
{
    ...
    public virtual int X
    {
        get { ... }
        set { ... }
    }

    public virtual int Y
    {
        get { ... }
        set { ... }
    }
    ...
}
```

Note This example shows a *class*. Remember that the *virtual* keyword is not valid when creating a *struct* because structures are implicitly sealed.

You can also choose to implement a property by using the explicit interface implementation syntax covered in Chapter 13. An explicit implementation of a property is nonpublic and nonvirtual (and cannot be overridden). For example:

```
struct ScreenPosition : IScreenPosition
{
    ...
    int IScreenPosition.X
    {
        get { ... }
        set { ... }
    }

    int IScreenPosition.Y
    {
        get { ... }
        set { ... }
    }
    ...
    private int x, y;
}
```

Using Properties in a Windows Application

When you set property values of objects such as *TextBox* controls, *Windows*, and *Button* controls by using the Properties window in Microsoft Visual Studio 2010, you are actually generating code that sets the values of these properties at run time. Some components have a large number of properties, although some properties are more commonly used than others. You can write your own code to modify many of these properties at run time by using the same syntax you have seen throughout this chapter.

In the following exercise, you will use some predefined properties of the *TextBox* controls and the *Window* class to create a simple application that continually displays the size of its main window, even when the window is resized.

Use properties

1. Start Visual Studio 2010 if it is not already running.

2. Open the *WindowProperties* project, located in the \Microsoft Press\Visual CSharp Step By Step\Chapter 15\WindowProperties folder in your Documents folder.

3. On the *Debug* menu, click *Start Without Debugging*.

   The project builds and runs. A Windows Presentation Foundation (WPF) form appears, displaying two empty text boxes labeled *Width* and *Height*.

   In the program, the text box controls are named *width* and *height*. They are currently empty. You will add code to the application that displays the current size of the window and that updates the values in these text boxes if the window is resized.

4. Close the form, and return to the Visual Studio 2010 programming environment.

5. Display the MainWindow.xaml.cs file in the *Code and Text Editor* window, and locate the *sizeChanged* method.

   This method is called by the *MainWindow* constructor. You will use it to display the current size of the form in the *width* and *height* text boxes. You will make use of the *ActualWidth* and *ActualHeight* properties of the *Window* class. These properties return the current width and height of the form as *double* values.

6. Add two statements to the *sizeChanged* method to display the size of the form. The first statement should read the value of the *ActualWidth* property of the form, convert it to a string, and assign this value to the *Text* property of the *width* text box. The second statement should read the value of the *ActualHeight* property of the form, convert it to a string, and assign this value to the *Text* property of the *height* text box.

   The *sizeChanged* method should look like this:

   ```
   private void sizeChanged()
   {
       width.Text = this.ActualWidth.ToString();
       height.Text = this.ActualHeight.ToString();
   }
   ```

7. Locate the *mainWindowSizeChanged* method.

   This method runs whenever the size of the window changes when the application is running. Notice that this method calls the *sizeChanged* method to display the new size of the window in the text boxes.

8. On the *Debug* menu, click *Start Without Debugging* to build and run the project.

   The form displays the two text boxes containing the values *305* and *155*. These are the default dimensions of the form, specified when the form was designed.

9. Resize the form. Notice that the text in the text boxes changes to reflect the new size.

10. Close the form, and return to the Visual Studio 2010 programming environment.

Generating Automatic Properties

This chapter mentioned earlier that the principal purpose of properties is to hide the implementation of fields from the outside world. This is fine if your properties actually perform some useful work, but if the *get* and *set* accessors simply wrap operations that just read or assign a value to a field, you might be questioning the value of this approach. There are at least two good reasons why you should define properties rather than exposing data as public fields:

- **Compatibility with applications**   Fields and properties expose themselves by using different metadata in assemblies. If you develop a class and decide to use public fields, any applications that use this class will reference these items as fields. Although you use the same C# syntax for reading and writing a field that you use when reading and writing a property, the compiled code is actually quite different—the C# compiler just hides the differences from you. If you later decide that you really do need to change these fields to properties (maybe the business requirements have changed, and you need to perform additional logic when assigning values), existing applications will not be able to use the updated version of the class without being recompiled. This is awkward if you have deployed the application on a large number of users' desktops throughout an organization. There are ways around this, but it is generally better to avoid getting into this situation in the first place.

- **Compatibility with interfaces**   If you are implementing an interface and the interface defines an item as a property, you must write a property that matches the specification in the interface, even if the property just reads and writes data in a private field. You cannot implement a property simply by exposing a public field with the same name.

The designers of the C# language recognized that programmers are busy people who should not have to waste their time writing more code than they need to. To this end, the C# compiler can generate the code for properties for you automatically, like this:

```
class Circle
{
    public int Radius{ get; set; }
    ...
}
```

In this example, the *Circle* class contains a property named *Radius*. Apart from the type of this property, you have not specified how this property works—the *get* and *set* accessors are empty. The C# compiler converts this definition to a private field and a default implementation that looks similar to this:

```csharp
class Circle
{
    private int _radius;
    public int Radius{
        get
        {
            return this._radius;
        }
        set
        {
            this._radius = value;
        }
    }
    ...
}
```

So for very little effort, you can implement a simple property by using automatically generated code, and if you need to include additional logic later, you can do so without breaking any existing applications. You should note, however, that you must specify both a *get* and a *set* accessor with an automatically generated property—an automatic property cannot be read-only or write-only.

Note The syntax for defining an automatic property is almost identical to the syntax for defining a property in an interface. The exception is that an automatic property can specify an access modifier, such as *private*, *public*, or *protected*.

Initializing Objects by Using Properties

In Chapter 7, "Creating and Managing Classes and Objects," you learned how to define constructors to initialize an object. An object can have multiple constructors, and you can define constructors with varying parameters to initialize different elements in an object. For example, you could define a class that models a triangle like this:

```csharp
public class Triangle
{
    private int side1Length;
    private int side2Length;
    private int side3Length;

    // default constructor - default values for all sides
    public Triangle()
    {
        this.side1Length = this.side2Length = this.side3Length = 10;
    }
```

```
// specify length for side1Length, default values for the others
public Triangle(int length1)
{
    this.side1Length = length1;
    this.side2Length = this.side3Length = 10;
}

// specify length for side1Length and side2Length,
// default value for side3Length
public Triangle(int length1, int length2)
{
    this.side1Length = length1;
    this.side2Length = length2;
    this.side3Length = 10;
}

// specify length for all sides
public Triangle(int length1, int length2, int length3)
{
    this.side1Length = length1;
    this.side2Length = length2;
    this.side3Length = length3;
}
}
```

Depending on how many fields a class contains and the various combinations you want to enable for initializing the fields, you could end up writing a lot of constructors. There are also potential problems if many of the fields have the same type: you might not be able to write a unique constructor for all combinations of fields. For example, in the preceding *Triangle* class, you could not easily add a constructor that initializes only the *side1Length* and *side3Length* fields because it would not have a unique signature; it would take two *int* parameters, and the constructor that initializes *side1Length* and *side2Length* already has this signature. One possible solution is to define a constructor that takes optional parameters, and specify values for the parameters as named arguments when you create a *Triangle* object. However, a better and more transparent solution is to initialize the private fields to their default values and to define properties, like this:

```
public class Triangle
{
    private int side1Length = 10;
    private int side2Length = 10;
    private int side3Length = 10;

    public int Side1Length
    {
        set { this.side1Length = value; }
    }

    public int Side2Length
    {
        set { this.side2Length = value; }
    }
}
```

```
public int Side3Length
{
    set { this.side3Length = value; }
}
}
```

When you create an instance of a class, you can initialize it by specifying values for any public properties that have *set* accessors. This means that you can create *Triangle* objects and initialize any combination of the three sides, like this:

```
Triangle tri1 = new Triangle { Side3Length = 15 };
Triangle tri2 = new Triangle { Side1Length = 15, Side3Length = 20 };
Triangle tri3 = new Triangle { Side2Length = 12, Side3Length = 17 };
Triangle tri4 = new Triangle { Side1Length = 9, Side2Length = 12,
                               Side3Length = 15 };
```

This syntax is known as an *object initializer*. When you invoke an object initializer in this way, the C# compiler generates code that calls the default constructor and then calls the *set* accessor of each named property to initialize it with the value specified. You can specify object initializers in combination with non–default constructors as well. For example, if the *Triangle* class also provided a constructor that took a single string parameter describing the type of triangle, you could invoke this constructor and initialize the other properties like this:

```
Triangle tri5 = new Triangle("Equilateral triangle") { Side1Length = 3,
                                                        Side2Length = 3,
                                                        Side3Length = 3 };
```

The important point to remember is that the constructor runs first and the properties are set afterward. Understanding this sequencing is important if the constructor sets fields in an object to specific values and the properties that you specify change these values.

You can also use object initializers with automatic properties, as you will see in the next exercise. In this exercise, you will define a class for modeling regular polygons, which contains automatic properties for providing access to information about the number of sides the polygon contains and the length of these sides.

Define automatic properties, and use object initializers

1. In Visual Studio 2010, open the *AutomaticProperties* project, located in the \Microsoft Press\Visual CSharp Step By Step\Chapter 15\AutomaticProperties folder in your Documents folder.

   The *AutomaticProperties* project contains the Program.cs file, defining the *Program* class with the *Main* and *DoWork* methods that you saw in previous exercises.

2. In *Solution Explorer*, right-click the *AutomaticProperties* project, point to *Add*, and then click *Class*. In the *Add New Item—AutomaticProperties* dialog box, in the *Name* text box, type **Polygon.cs** and then click *Add*.

   The Polygon.cs file, holding the *Polygon* class, is created and added to the project and appears in the *Code and Text Editor* window.

3. Add the automatic properties *NumSides* and *SideLength*, shown here in bold, to the *Polygon* class:

   ```
   class Polygon
   {
       public int NumSides { get; set; }
       public double SideLength { get; set; }
   }
   ```

4. Add the following default constructor to the *Polygon* class:

   ```
   class Polygon
   {
       ...

       public Polygon()
       {
           this.NumSides = 4;
           this.SideLength = 10.0;
       }
   }
   ```

   In this exercise, the default polygon is a square with sides 10 units long.

5. Display the Program.cs file in the *Code and Text Editor* window.

6. Add the statements shown here in bold to the *DoWork* method:

   ```
   static void DoWork()
   {
       Polygon square = new Polygon();
       Polygon triangle = new Polygon { NumSides = 3 };
       Polygon pentagon = new Polygon { SideLength = 15.5, NumSides = 5 };
   }
   ```

   These statements create *Polygon* objects. The *square* variable is initialized by using the default constructor. The *triangle* and *pentagon* variables are also initialized by using the default constructor, and then this code changes the value of the properties exposed by the *Polygon* class. In the case of the *triangle* variable, the *NumSides* property is set to 3, but the *SideLength* property is left at its default value of *10.0*. For the *pentagon* variable, the code changes the values of the *SideLength* and *NumSides* properties.

7. Add the following code to the end of the *DoWork* method:

```
static void DoWork()
{
    ...

        Console.WriteLine("Square: number of sides is {0}, length of each side is {1}",
            square.NumSides, square.SideLength);
        Console.WriteLine("Triangle: number of sides is {0}, length of each side is {1}",
            triangle.NumSides, triangle.SideLength);
        Console.WriteLine("Pentagon: number of sides is {0}, length of each side is {1}",
            pentagon.NumSides, pentagon.SideLength);
}
```

These statements display the values of the *NumSides* and *SideLength* properties for each *Polygon* object.

8. On the *Debug* menu, click *Start Without Debugging*.

Verify that the program builds and runs, writing the message shown here to the console:

```
C:\Windows\system32\cmd.exe
Square: number of sides is 4, length of each side is 10
Triangle: number of sides is 3, length of each side is 10
Pentagon: number of sides is 5, length of each side is 15.5
Press any key to continue . . .
```

9. Press the Enter key to close the application and return to Visual Studio 2010.

In this chapter, you saw how to create and use properties to provide controlled access to data in an object. You also saw how to create automatic properties and how to use properties when initializing objects.

- If you want to continue to the next chapter

    Keep Visual Studio 2010 running, and turn to Chapter 16.

- If you want to exit Visual Studio 2010 now

    On the *File* menu, click *Exit*. If you see a *Save* dialog box, click *Yes* and save the project.

Chapter 15 Quick Reference

To	Do this

Declare a read/write property for a structure or class	Declare the type of the property, its name, a *get* accessor, and a *set* accessor. For example:
	
	``csharp
	struct ScreenPosition
	{
	    ...
	    public int X
	    {
	        get { ... }
	        set { ... }
	    }
	    ...
	}
	``

Declare a read-only property for a structure or class	Declare a property with only a *get* accessor. For example:
	
	``csharp
	struct ScreenPosition
	{
	    ...
	    public int X
	    {
	        get { ... }
	    }
	    ...
	}
	``

Declare a write-only property for a structure or class	Declare a property with only a *set* accessor. For example:
	
	``csharp
	struct ScreenPosition
	{
	    ...
	    public int X
	    {
	        set { ... }
	    }
	    ...
	}
	``

Declare a property in an interface	Declare a property with just the *get* or *set* keyword, or both. For example:
	
	``csharp
	interface IScreenPosition
	{
	    int X { get; set; } // no body
	    int Y { get; set; } // no body
	}
	``

To	Do this
Implement an interface property in a structure or class	In the class or structure that implements the interface, declare the property and implement the accessors. For example:

```
struct ScreenPosition : IScreenPosition
{
    public int X
    {
        get { ... }
        set { ... }
    }

    public int Y
    {
        get { ... }
        set { ... }
    }
}
```

Create an automatic property	In the class or structure that contains the property, define the property with empty *get* and *set* accessors. For example:

```
class Polygon
{
    public int NumSides { get; set; }
}
```

Use properties to initialize an object	Specify the properties and their values as a list enclosed in braces when constructing the object. For example:

```
Triangle tri3 =
    new Triangle { Side2Length = 12, Side3Length = 17 };
```

Chapter 16
Using Indexers

After completing this chapter, you will be able eto:

- Encapsulate logical array-like access to an object by using indexers.

- Control read access to indexers by declaring *get* accessors.

- Control write access to indexers by declaring *set* accessors.

- Create interfaces that declare indexers.

- Implement indexers in structures and classes that inherit from interfaces.

The preceding chapter described how to implement and use properties as a means of providing controlled access to the fields in a class. Properties are useful for mirroring fields that contain a single value. However, indexers are invaluable if you want to provide access to items that contain multiple values by using a natural and familiar syntax.

What Is an Indexer?

You can think of an *indexer* as a smart array in much the same way that you can think of a property as a smart field. Where a property encapsulates a single value in a class, an indexer encapsulates a set of values. The syntax that you use for an indexer is exactly the same as the syntax that you use for an array.

The best way to understand indexers is to work through an example. First we'll examine a problem and examine a solution that doesn't use indexers. Then we'll work through the same problem and look at a better solution that does use indexers. The problem concerns integers, or more precisely, the *int* type.

An Example That Doesn't Use Indexers

You normally use an *int* to hold an integer value. Internally, an *int* stores its value as a sequence of 32 bits, where each bit can be either 0 or 1. Most of the time, you don't care about this internal binary representation; you just use an *int* type as a container that holds an integer value. However, sometimes programmers use the *int* type for other purposes: some programs use an *int* as a set of binary flags and manipulate the individual bits within an *int*. If you are an old C hack like I am, what follows should have a very familiar feel!

> **Note** Some older programs used *int* types to try to save memory. Such programs typically date back to when the size of computer memory was measured in kilobytes rather than the gigabytes available these days and memory was at an absolute premium. A single *int* holds 32 bits, each of which can be 1 or 0. In some cases, programmers assigned 1 to indicate the value *true* and 0 to indicate *false* and then employed an *int* as a set of Boolean values.

C# provides a set of operators that you can use to access and manipulate the individual bits in an *int*. These operators are

- **The NOT (~) operator**   This is a unary operator that performs a bitwise complement. For example, if you take the 8-bit value *11001100* (*204* decimal) and apply the ~ operator to it, you obtain the result *00110011* (*51* decimal)—all the 1s in the original value become 0s, and all the 0s become 1s.

- **The left-shift (<<) operator**   This is a binary operator that performs a left shift. The expression *204 << 2* returns the value *48*. (In binary, *204* decimal is *11001100*, and left-shifting it by two places yields *00110000*, or *48* decimal.) The far-left bits are discarded, and zeros are introduced from the right. There is a corresponding right-shift operator >>.

- **The OR (|) operator**   This is a binary operator that performs a bitwise OR operation, returning a value containing a 1 in each position in which either of the operands has a 1. For example, the expression *204 | 24* has the value *220* (*204* is *11001100*, *24* is *00011000*, and *220* is *11011100*).

- **The AND (&) operator**   This operator performs a bitwise AND operation. AND is similar to the bitwise OR operator, except that it returns a value containing a 1 in each position where both of the operands have a 1. So *204 & 24* is *8* (*204* is *11001100*, *24* is *00011000*, and *8* is *00001000*).

- **The XOR (^) operator**   This operator performs a bitwise exclusive OR operation, returning a 1 in each bit where there is a 1 in one operand or the other but not both. (Two 1s yield a 0—this is the "exclusive" part of the operator.) So *204 ^ 24* is *212* (*11001100 ^ 00011000* is *11010100*).

You can use these operators together to determine the values of the individual bits in an *int*. As an example, the following expression uses the left-shift (<<) and bitwise AND (&) operators to determine whether the sixth bit of the *int* named *bits* is set to *0* or to *1*:

```
(bits & (1 << 5)) != 0
```

Suppose the *bits* variable contains the decimal value 42. In binary, this is 00101010. The decimal value 1 is 00000001 in binary, so the expression 1 << 5 has the value 00100000. In binary, the expression *bits & (1 << 5)* is 00101010 & 00100000, and the value of this expression is binary 00100000, which is non-zero. If the variable *bits* contains the value 65, or 01000001 in binary, the value of the expression is 01000001 & 00100000, which yields the binary result 00000000, or zero.

This is a fairly complicated example, but it's trivial in comparison to the following expression, which uses the compound assignment operator *&=* to set the bit at position 4 to *0*:

```
bits &= ~(1 << 4)
```

> **Note** The bitwise operators count the positions of bits from right to left, so bit 0 is the rightmost bit, and the bit at position 6 is the bit seven places from the right.

Similarly, if you want to set the bit at position 4 to *1*, you can use a bitwise OR (|) operator. The following complicated expression is based on the compound assignment operator |=:

```
bits |= (1 << 4)
```

The trouble with these examples is that although they work, they are fiendishly difficult to understand. They're complicated, and the solution is a very low-level one: it fails to create an abstraction of the problem that it solves.

The Same Example Using Indexers

Let's pull back from the preceding low-level solution for a moment and stop to remind ourselves what the problem is. We'd like to use an *int* not as an *int* but as an array of bits. Therefore, the best way to solve this problem is to use an *int* as if it were an array of bits! In other words, what we'd like to be able to write to access the bit at index 6 of the *bits* variable is something like this:

```
bits[6]
```

And to set the bit at index 4 to *true*, we'd like to be able to write this:

```
bits[4] = true
```

> **Note** To seasoned C developers, the Boolean value *true* is synonymous with the binary value 1, and the Boolean value *false* is synonymous with the binary value 0. Consequently, the expression `bits[4] = true` means "set bit 4 of the *bits* variable to 1".

Unfortunately, you can't use the square bracket notation on an *int*—it works only on an array or on a type that behaves like an array. So the solution to the problem is to create a new type that acts like, feels like, and is used like an array of *bool* variables but is implemented by using an *int*. You can achieve this feat by defining an indexer. Let's call this new type *IntBits*. *IntBits* will contain an *int* value (initialized in its constructor), but the idea is that we'll use *IntBits* as an array of *bool* variables.

> **Tip** The *IntBits* type is small and lightweight, so it makes sense to create it as a structure rather than as a class.

```
struct IntBits
{
    public IntBits(int initialBitValue)
    {
        bits = initialBitValue;
    }

    // indexer to be written here

    private int bits;
}
```

To define the indexer, you use a notation that is a cross between a property and an array. You introduce the indexer with the *this* keyword, specify the type of the value returned by the indexer, and also specify the type of the value to use as the index into the indexer between square brackets. The indexer for the *IntBits* struct uses an integer as its index type and returns a Boolean value. It looks like this:

```
struct IntBits
{
    ...
    public bool this [ int index ]
    {
        get
        {
            return (bits & (1 << index)) != 0;
        }

        set
        {
            if (value)  // turn the bit on if value is true; otherwise, turn it off
                bits |=  (1 << index);
            else
                bits &= ~(1 << index);
        }
    }
    ...
}
```

Notice the following points:

- An indexer is not a method—there are no parentheses containing a parameter, but there are square brackets that specify an index. This index is used to specify which element is being accessed.

- All indexers use the *this* keyword. A class or structure can define at most one indexer, and it is always named *this*.

- Indexers contain *get* and *set* accessors just like properties. In this example, the *get* and *set* accessors contain the complicated bitwise expressions previously discussed.

- The index specified in the indexer declaration is populated with the index value specified when the indexer is called. The *get* and *set* accessor methods can read this argument to determine which element should be accessed.

Note You should perform a range check on the index value in the indexer to prevent any unexpected exceptions from occurring in your indexer code.

After you have declared the indexer, you can use a variable of type *IntBits* instead of an *int* and apply the square bracket notation, as shown in the next example:

```
int adapted = 126;       // 126 has the binary representation 1111110
IntBits bits = new IntBits(adapted);
bool peek = bits[6];  // retrieve bool at index 6; should be true (1)
bits[0] = true;       // set the bit at index 0 to true (1)
bits[3] = false;      // set the bit at index 3 to false (0)
                      // the value in adapted is now 110111, or 55 in decimal
```

This syntax is certainly much easier to understand. It directly and succinctly captures the essence of the problem.

Understanding Indexer Accessors

When you read an indexer, the compiler automatically translates your array-like code into a call to the *get* accessor of that indexer. Consider the following example:

```
bool peek = bits[6];
```

This statement is converted to a call to the *get* accessor for *bits*, and the *index* argument is set to 6.

Similarly, if you write to an indexer, the compiler automatically translates your array-like code into a call to the *set* accessor of that indexer, setting the *index* argument to the value enclosed in the square brackets. For example:

```
bits[4] = true;
```

This statement is converted to a call to the *set* accessor for *bits* where *index* is 4. As with ordinary properties, the data you are writing to the indexer (in this case, *true*) is made available inside the *set* accessor by using the *value* keyword. The type of *value* is the same as the type of indexer itself (in this case, *bool*).

It's also possible to use an indexer in a combined read/write context. In this case, the *get* and *set* accessors are both used. Look at the following statement, which uses the XOR operator (^) to invert the value of bit 6 in the *bits* variable:

```
bits[6] ^= true;
```

This code is automatically translated into the following:

```
bits[6] = bits[6] ^ true;
```

This code works because the indexer declares both a *get* and a *set* accessor.

> **Note** You can declare an indexer that contains only a *get* accessor (a read-only indexer) or only a *set* accessor (a write-only accessor).

Comparing Indexers and Arrays

When you use an indexer, the syntax is deliberately very array-like. However, there are some important differences between indexers and arrays:

- Indexers can use non-numeric subscripts, such as a string as shown in the following example. Arrays can use only integer subscripts:

```
public int this [ string name ] { ... } // OK
```

> **Tip** Many collection classes, such as *Hashtable*, that implement an associative lookup based on key/value pairs implement indexers to provide a convenient alternative to using the *Add* method to add a new value and as an alternative to iterating through the *Values* property to locate a value in your code. For example, instead of this:
>
> ```
> Hashtable ages = new Hashtable();
> ages.Add("John", 42);
> ```
>
> you can use this:
>
> ```
> Hashtable ages = new Hashtable();
> ages["John"] = 42;
> ```

- Indexers can be overloaded (just like methods), whereas arrays cannot:

```
public Name        this [ PhoneNumber number ] { ... }
public PhoneNumber this [ Name name ] { ... }
```

- Indexers cannot be used as *ref* or *out* parameters, whereas array elements can:

```
IntBits bits;        // bits contains an indexer
Method(ref bits[1]); // compile-time error
```

Properties, Arrays, and Indexers

It is possible for a property to return an array, but remember that arrays are reference types, so exposing an array as a property makes it possible to accidentally overwrite a lot of data. Look at the following structure that exposes an array property named *Data*:

```
struct Wrapper
{
    private int[] data;
    ...
    public int[] Data
    {
```

```
        get { return this.data; }
        set { this.data = value; }
    }
}
```

Now consider the following code that uses this property:

```
Wrapper wrap = new Wrapper();
...
int[] myData = wrap.Data;
myData[0]++;
myData[1]++;
```

This looks pretty innocuous. However, because arrays are reference types, the variable *myData* refers to the same object as the private *data* variable in the *Wrapper* structure. Any changes you make to elements in *myData* are made to the *data* array; the expression *myData[0]++* has exactly the same effect as *data[0]++*. If this is not the intention, you should use the *Clone* method in the *get* and *set* accessors of the *Data* property to return a copy of the data array, or make a copy of the value being set, as shown here. (The *Clone* method returns an object, which you must cast to an integer array.)

```
struct Wrapper
{
    private int[] data;
    ...
    public int[] Data
    {
        get { return this.data.Clone() as int[]; }
        set { this.data = value.Clone() as int[]; }
    }
}
```

However, this approach can become very messy and expensive in terms of memory use. Indexers provide a natural solution to this problem—don't expose the entire array as a property; just make its individual elements available through an indexer:

```
struct Wrapper
{
    private int[] data;
    ...
    public int this [int i]
    {
        get { return this.data[i]; }
        set { this.data[i] = value; }
    }
}
```

The following code uses the indexer in a similar manner to the property shown earlier:

```
Wrapper wrap = new Wrapper();
...
int[] myData = new int[2];
myData[0] = wrap[0];
```

```
myData[1] = wrap[1];
myData[0]++;
myData[1]++;
```

This time, incrementing the values in the *MyData* array has no effect on the original array in the *Wrapper* object. If you really want to modify the data in the *Wrapper* object, you must write statements such as this:

```
wrap[0]++;
```

This is much clearer, and safer!

Indexers in Interfaces

You can declare indexers in an interface. To do this, specify the *get* keyword, the *set* keyword, or both, but replace the body of the *get* or *set* accessor with a semicolon. Any class or structure that implements the interface must implement the *indexer* accessors declared in the interface. For example:

```
interface IRawInt
{
    bool this [ int index ] { get; set; }
}

struct RawInt : IRawInt
{
    ...
    public bool this [ int index ]
    {
        get { ... }
        set { ... }
    }
    ...
}
```

If you implement the interface indexer in a class, you can declare the indexer implementations as *virtual*. This allows further derived classes to override the *get* and *set* accessors. For example:

```
class RawInt : IRawInt
{
    ...
    public virtual bool this [ int index ]
    {
        get { ... }
        set { ... }
    }
    ...
}
```

You can also choose to implement an indexer by using the explicit interface implementation syntax covered in Chapter 12, "Working with Inheritance." An explicit implementation of an indexer is nonpublic and nonvirtual (and so cannot be overridden). For example:

```
struct RawInt : IRawInt
{
    ...
    bool IRawInt.this [ int index ]
    {
        get { ... }
        set { ... }
    }
    ...
}
```

Using Indexers in a Windows Application

In the following exercise, you will examine a simple phone book application and complete its implementation. You will write two indexers in the *PhoneBook* class: one that accepts a *Name* parameter and returns a *PhoneNumber* and another that accepts a *PhoneNumber* parameter and returns a *Name*. (The *Name* and *PhoneNumber* structures have already been written.) You will also need to call these indexers from the correct places in the program.

Familiarize yourself with the application

1. Start Microsoft Visual Studio 2010 if it is not already running.

2. Open the *Indexers* project, located in the \Microsoft Press\Visual CSharp Step By Step\ Chapter 16\Indexers folder in your Documents folder.

   This is a Windows Presentation Foundation (WPF) application that enables a user to search for the telephone number for a contact and also find the name of a contact that matches a given telephone number.

3. On the *Debug* menu, click *Start Without Debugging*.

   The project builds and runs. A form appears, displaying two empty text boxes labeled *Name* and *Phone Number*. The form also contains three buttons—one to add a name/ phone number pair to a list of names and phone numbers held by the application, one to find a phone number when given a name, and one to find a name when given a phone number. These buttons currently do nothing. Your task is to complete the application so that these buttons work.

4. Close the form, and return to Visual Studio 2010.

5. Display the Name.cs file in the *Code and Text Editor* window. Examine the *Name* structure. Its purpose is to act as a holder for names.

The name is provided as a string to the constructor. The name can be retrieved by using the read-only string property named *Text*. (The *Equals* and *GetHashCode* methods are used for comparing *Name*s when searching through an array of *Name* values—you can ignore them for now.)

6. Display the PhoneNumber.cs file in the *Code and Text Editor* window, and examine the *PhoneNumber* structure. It is similar to the *Name* structure.

7. Display the PhoneBook.cs file in the *Code and Text Editor* window, and examine the *PhoneBook* class.

   This class contains two private arrays: an array of *Name* values named *names*, and an array of *PhoneNumber* values named *phoneNumbers*. The *PhoneBook* class also contains an *Add* method that adds a phone number and name to the phone book. This method is called when the user clicks the *Add* button on the form. The *enlargeIfFull* method is called by *Add* to check whether the arrays are full when the user adds another entry. This method creates two new bigger arrays, copies the contents of the existing arrays to them, and then discards the old arrays.

Write the indexers

1. In the PhoneBook.cs file, add a *public* read-only indexer to the *PhoneBook* class, as shown in bold in the following code. The indexer should return a *Name* and take a *PhoneNumber* item as its index. Leave the body of the *get* accessor blank.

   The indexer should look like this:

   ```
   sealed class PhoneBook
   {
       ...
       public Name this [PhoneNumber number]
       {
           get
           {
           }
       }
       ...
   }
   ```

2. Implement the *get* accessor as shown in bold in the following code. The purpose of the accessor is to find the name that matches the specified phone number. To do this, you need to call the static *IndexOf* method of the *Array* class. The *IndexOf* method performs a search through an array, returning the index of the first item in the array that matches the specified value. The first argument to *IndexOf* is the array to search through (*phoneNumbers*). The second argument to *IndexOf* is the item you are searching for. *IndexOf* returns the integer index of the element if it finds it; otherwise, *IndexOf* returns –1. If the indexer finds the phone number, it should return it; otherwise, it should return an empty *Name* value. (Note that *Name* is a structure and so the default constructor sets its private *name* field to *null*.)

```
sealed class PhoneBook
{
    ...
    public Name this [PhoneNumber number]
    {
        get
        {
            int i = Array.IndexOf(this.phoneNumbers, number);
            if (i != -1)
            {
                return this.names[i];
            }
            else
            {
                return new Name();
            }
        }
    }
    ...
}
```

3. Add a second *public* read-only indexer to the *PhoneBook* class that returns a *PhoneNumber* and accepts a single *Name* parameter. Implement this indexer in the same way as the first one. (Again note that *PhoneNumber* is a structure and therefore always has a default constructor.)

The second indexer should look like this:

```
sealed class PhoneBook
{
    ...
    public PhoneNumber this [Name name]
    {
        get
        {
            int i = Array.IndexOf(this.names, name);
            if (i != -1)
            {
                return this.phoneNumbers[i];
            }
            else
            {
                return new PhoneNumber();
            }
        }
    }
    ...
}
```

Notice that these overloaded indexers can coexist because they return different types, which means that their signatures are different. If the *Name* and *PhoneNumber* structures were replaced by simple strings (which they wrap), the overloads would have the same signature and the class would not compile.

4. On the *Build* menu, click *Build Solution*. Correct any syntax errors, and then rebuild if necessary.

Call the indexers

1. Display the MainWindow.xaml.cs file in the *Code and Text Editor* window, and then locate the *findPhoneClick* method.

   This method is called when the *Search by Name* button is clicked. This method is currently empty. Add the code shown in bold in the following example to perform these tasks:

   1.1. Read the value of the *Text* property from the *name* text box on the form. This is a string containing the contact name that the user has typed in.

   1.2. If the string is not empty, search for the phone number corresponding to that name in the *PhoneBook* by using the indexer. (Notice that the *MainWindow* class contains a private *PhoneBook* field named *phoneBook*.) Construct a *Name* object from the string, and pass it as the parameter to the *PhoneBook* indexer.

   1.3. Write the *Text* property of the *PhoneNumber* structure returned by the indexer to the *phoneNumber* text box on the form.

   The *findPhoneClick* method should look like this:

   ```
   private void findPhoneClick(object sender, RoutedEventArgs e)
   {
       string text = name.Text;
       if (!String.IsNullOrEmpty(text))
       {
           Name personsName = new Name(text);
           PhoneNumber personsPhoneNumber = this.phoneBook[personsName];
           phoneNumber.Text = personsPhoneNumber.Text;
       }
   }
   ```

    Tip Notice the use of the static *String* method *IsNullOrEmpty* to determine whether a string is empty or contains a null value. This is the preferred method for testing whether a string contains a value. It returns *true* if the string has a non-null value and *false* otherwise.

2. Locate the *findNameClick* method in the MainWindow.xaml.cs file. It is below the *findPhoneClick* method.

   The *findName_Click* method is called when the *Search by Phone* button is clicked. This method is currently empty, so you need to implement it as follows. (The code is shown in bold in the following example.)

   2.1. Read the value of the *Text* property from the *phoneNumber* text box on the form. This is a string containing the phone number that the user has typed.

   2.2. If the string is not empty, search for the name corresponding to that phone number in the *PhoneBook* by using the indexer.

   2.3. Write the *Text* property of the *Name* structure returned by the indexer to the *name* text box on the form.

The completed method should look like this:

```
private void findNameClick(object sender, RoutedEventArgs e)
{
    string text = phoneNumber.Text;
    if (!String.IsNullOrEmpty(text))
    {
        PhoneNumber personsPhoneNumber = new PhoneNumber(text);
        Name personsName = this.phoneBook[personsPhoneNumber];
        name.Text = personsName.Text;
    }
}
```

3. On the *Build* menu, click *Build Solution*. Correct any errors that occur.

Run the application

1. On the *Debug* menu, click *Start Without Debugging*.

2. Type your name and phone number in the text boxes, and then click *Add*.

   When you click the *Add* button, the *Add* method stores the information in the phone book and clears the text boxes so that they are ready to perform a search.

3. Repeat step 2 several times with some different names and phone numbers so that the phone book contains a selection of entries. Note that the application performs no checking of the names and telephone numbers that you enter, and you can input the same name and telephone number more than once. To avoid confusion, please make sure that you provide different names and telephone numbers.

4. Type a name that you used in step 2 into the *Name* text box, and then click *Search by Name*.

   The phone number you added for this contact in step 2 is retrieved from the phone book and is displayed in the *Phone Number* text box.

5. Type a phone number for a different contact in the *Phone Number* text box, and then click *Search by Phone*.

   The contact name is retrieved from the phone book and is displayed in the *Name* text box.

6. Type a name that you did not enter in the phone book into the *Name* text box, and then click *Search by Name*.

   This time the *Phone Number* text box is empty, indicating that the name could not be found in the phone book.

7. Close the form, and return to Visual Studio 2010.

In this chapter, you have seen how to use indexers to provide array-like access to data in a class. You have learned how to create indexers that can take an index and return the corresponding value by using logic defined by the *get* accessor, and you have seen how to use the *set* accessor with an index to populate a value in an indexer.

- If you want to continue to the next chapter

    Keep Visual Studio 2010 running, and turn to Chapter 17.

- If you want to exit Visual Studio 2010 now

    On the *File* menu, click *Exit*. If you see a *Save* dialog box, click *Yes* and save the project.

Chapter 16 Quick Reference

To	Do this
Create an indexer for a class or structure	Declare the type of the indexer, followed by the keyword *this* and then the indexer arguments in square brackets. The body of the indexer can contain a *get* and/or *set* accessor. For example:

```
struct RawInt
{
    ...
    public bool this [ int index ]
    {
        get { ... }
        set { ... }
    }
    ...
}
```

To	Do this
Define an indexer in an interface	Define an indexer with the *get* and/or *set* keywords. For example:

```
interface IRawInt
{
    bool this [ int index ] { get;  set; }
}
```

To	Do this
Implement an interface indexer in a class or structure	In the class or structure that implements the interface, define the indexer and implement the accessors. For example:

```
struct RawInt : IRawInt
{
    ...
    public bool this [ int index  ]
    {
        get { ... }
        set { ... }
    }
    ...
}
```

To	Do this
Implement an indexer defined by an interface by using explicit interface implementation in a class or structure	In the class or structure that implements the interface, specify the interface, but do not specify the indexer accessibility. For example:

```
struct RawInt : IRawInt
{
    ...
    bool IRawInt.this [ int index  ]
    {
        get { ... }
        set { ... }
    }
    ...
}
```

Chapter 17
Interrupting Program Flow and Handling Events

After completing this chapter, you will be able to:

- Declare a delegate type to create an abstraction of a method signature.

- Create an instance of a delegate to refer to a specific method.

- Call a method through a delegate.

- Define a lambda expression to specify the code for a delegate.

- Declare an event field.

- Handle an event by using a delegate.

- Raise an event.

Much of the code you have written in the various exercises in this book has assumed that statements execute sequentially. Although this is a common scenario, you will find that it is sometimes necessary to interrupt the current flow of execution and perform another, more important, task. When the task has completed, the program can continue where it left off. The classic example of this style of program is the Microsoft Windows Presentation Foundation (WPF) form. A WPF form displays controls such as buttons and text boxes. When you click a button or type text in a text box, you expect the form to respond immediately. The application has to temporarily stop what it is doing and handle your input. This style of operation applies not just to graphical user interfaces but to any application where an operation must be performed urgently—shutting down the reactor in a nuclear power plant if it is getting too hot, for example.

To handle this type of application, the runtime has to provide two things: a means of indicating that something urgent has happened and a way of specifying the code that should be run when it happens. This is the purpose of events and delegates.

We start by looking at delegates.

Declaring and Using Delegates

A delegate is a pointer to a method. You can call a method through a delegate by specifying the name of the delegate. When you invoke a delegate, the runtime actually executes the method to which the delegate refers. You can dynamically change the method that a delegate references so that code that calls a delegate might actually run a different method each time it executes. The best way to understand delegates is to see them in action, so let's work through an example.

> **Note** If you are familiar with C++, a delegate is similar to a function pointer. However, delegates are type-safe; you can make a delegate refer to only a method that matches the signature of the delegate, and you cannot call a delegate that does not refer to a valid method.

The Automated Factory Scenario

Suppose you are writing the control systems for an automated factory. The factory contains a large number of different machines, each performing distinct tasks in the production of the articles manufactured by the factory—shaping and folding metal sheets, welding sheets together, painting sheets, and so on. Each machine was built and installed by a specialist vendor. The machines are all computer controlled, and each vendor has provided a set of APIs that you can use to control its machine. Your task is to integrate the different systems used by the machines into a single control program. One aspect on which you have decided to concentrate is to provide a means of shutting down all the machines, quickly if needed!

> **Note** The term *API* stands for application programming interface. It is a method, or set of methods, exposed by a piece of software that you can use to control that software. You can think of the Microsoft .NET Framework as a set of APIs because it provides methods that you can use to control the .NET common language runtime and the Microsoft Windows operating system.

Each machine has its own unique computer-controlled process (and API) for shutting down safely. These are summarized here:

```
StopFolding();     // Folding and shaping machine
FinishWelding();   // Welding machine
PaintOff();        // Painting machine
```

Implementing the Factory Without Using Delegates

A simple approach to implementing the shutdown functionality in the control program is as follows:

```
class Controller
{
    // Fields representing the different machines
    private FoldingMachine folder;
    private WeldingMachine welder;
    private PaintingMachine painter;
    ...
    public void ShutDown()
    {
        folder.StopFolding();
        welder.FinishWelding();
        painter.PaintOff();
    }
    ...
}
```

Although this approach works, it is not very extensible or flexible. If the factory buys a new machine, you must modify this code; the *Controller* class and code for managing the machines is tightly coupled.

Implementing the Factory by Using a Delegate

Although the names of each method are different, they all have the same "shape": They take no parameters, and they do not return a value. (We consider what happens if this isn't the case later, so bear with me!) The general format of each method, therefore, is this:

```
void methodName();
```

This is where a delegate is useful. A delegate that matches this shape can be used to refer to any of the machinery shutdown methods. You declare a delegate like this:

```
delegate void stopMachineryDelegate();
```

Note the following points:

- Use the *delegate* keyword when declaring a delegate.

- A delegate defines the shape of the methods it can refer to. You specify the return type (*void* in this example), a name for the delegate (*stopMachineryDelegate*), and any parameters. (There are none in this case.)

After you have defined the delegate, you can create an instance and make it refer to a matching method by using the += compound assignment operator. You can do this in the constructor of the controller class like this:

```
class Controller
{
    delegate void stopMachineryDelegate();
    private stopMachineryDelegate stopMachinery; // an instance of the delegate
    ...
    public Controller()
    {
        this.stopMachinery += folder.StopFolding;
    }
    ...
}
```

This syntax takes a bit of getting used to. You *add* the method to the delegate; you are not actually calling the method at this point. The + operator is overloaded to have this new meaning when used with delegates. (You will learn more about operator overloading in Chapter 21, "Operator Overloading.") Notice that you simply specify the method name and do not include any parentheses or parameters.

It is safe to use the += operator on an uninitialized delegate. It will be initialized automatically. Alternatively, you can also use the *new* keyword to initialize a delegate explicitly with a single specific method, like this:

```
this.stopMachinery = new stopMachineryDelegate(folder.StopFolding);
```

You can call the method by invoking the delegate, like this:

```
public void ShutDown()
{
    this.stopMachinery();
    ...
}
```

You use the same syntax to invoke a delegate as you use to make a method call. If the method that the delegate refers to takes any parameters, you should specify them at this time, between parentheses.

> **Note** If you attempt to invoke a delegate that is uninitialized and does not refer to any methods, you will get a *NullReferenceException*.

The principal advantage of using a delegate is that it can refer to more than one method; you simply use the += operator to add methods to the delegate, like this:

```
public Controller()
{
    this.stopMachinery += folder.StopFolding;
    this.stopMachinery += welder.FinishWelding;
    this.stopMachinery += painter.PaintOff;
}
```

Invoking *this.stopMachinery()* in the *Shutdown* method of the *Controller* class automatically calls each of the methods in turn. The *Shutdown* method does not need to know how many machines there are or what the method names are.

You can remove a method from a delegate by using the −= compound assignment operator:

```
this.stopMachinery -= folder.StopFolding;
```

The current scheme adds the machine methods to the delegate in the *Controller* constructor. To make the *Controller* class totally independent of the various machines, you need to make *stopMachineryDelegate* type public and supply a means of enabling classes outside *Controller* to add methods to the delegate. You have several options:

- Make the delegate variable, *stopMachinery*, public:

  ```
  public stopMachineryDelegate stopMachinery;
  ```

- Keep the *stopMachinery* delegate variable private, but provide a read/write property to provide access to it:

  ```
  public delegate void stopMachineryDelegate();
  ...
  public stopMachineryDelegate StopMachinery
  {
      get
  ```

```
    {
        return this.stopMachinery;
    }

    set
    {
        this.stopMachinery = value;
    }
}
```

- Provide complete encapsulation by implementing separate *Add* and *Remove* methods.
  The *Add* method takes a method as a parameter and adds it to the delegate, while
  the *Remove* method removes the specified method from the delegate (notice that you
  specify a method as a parameter by using a delegate type):

```
public void Add(stopMachineryDelegate stopMethod)
{
    this.stopMachinery += stopMethod;
}

public void Remove(stopMachineryDelegate stopMethod)
{
    this.stopMachinery -= stopMethod;
}
```

If you are an object-oriented purist, you will probably opt for the *Add/Remove* approach.
However, the others are viable alternatives that are frequently used, which is why they are
shown here.

Whichever technique you choose, you should remove the code that adds the machine
methods to the delegate from the *Controller* constructor. You can then instantiate a
Controller and objects representing the other machines like this (this example uses the
Add/Remove approach):

```
Controller control = new Controller();
FoldingMachine folder = new FoldingMachine();
WeldingMachine welder = new WeldingMachine();
PaintingMachine painter = new PaintingMachine();
...
control.Add(folder.StopFolding);
control.Add(welder.FinishWelding);
control.Add(painter.PaintOff);
...
control.ShutDown();
...
```

Using Delegates

In the following exercise, you will complete an application that implements a world clock.
The application contains a WPF form that displays the local time, as well as the current time
in London, New York, and Tokyo. Each of the displays is controlled by a clock object. Each of
the clocks are implemented differently, to simulate the earlier scenario of controlling a set of

independent machines operating in a factory. However, each clock exposes a pair of methods that enable you to start and stop the clock. When you start a clock, its display is updated every second with the time. When you stop a clock, the display is no longer updated. You will add functionality to the application that starts and stops the clocks by using delegates.

Complete the World Clock application

1. Start Microsoft Visual Studio 2010 if it is not already running.

2. Open the Clock project located in the \Microsoft Press\Visual CSharp Step By Step\ Chapter 17\Clock folder in your Documents folder.

3. On the *Debug* menu, click *Start Without Debugging*.

   The project builds and runs. A form appears, displaying the local time as well as the times in London, New York, and Tokyo. The clock displays the current times as "00:00:00".

4. Click *Start* to start the clocks.

   Nothing happens. The *Start* method has not been written yet, and the *Stop* button is disabled by default. Your task is to implement the code behind these buttons.

5. Close the form, and return to the Visual Studio 2010 environment.

6. Examine the list of files in Solution Explorer. The project contains a number of files, including AmericanClock.cs, EuropeanClock.cs, JapaneseClock.cs, and LocalClock.cs. These files contain the classes that implement the different clocks. You don't need to be concerned with how these clocks work just yet (although you are welcome to examine the code). However, the key information that you need is the names of the methods that start and stop each type of clock. The following list summarizes them by clock type (they are all very similar):

   - **AmericanClock**. The start method is called *StartAmericanClock*, and the stop method is called *StopAmericanClock*. Neither method takes any parameters, and both methods have a *void* return type.

   - **EuropeanClock**. The start method is called *StartEuropeanClock*, and the stop method is called *StopEuropeanClock*. Neither method takes any parameters, and both methods have a *void* return type.

   - **JapaneseClock**. The start method is called *StartJapaneseClock*, and the stop method is called *StopJapaneseClock*. Neither method takes any parameters, and both methods have a *void* return type.

   - **LocalClock**. The start method is called *StartLocalClock*, and the stop method is called *StopLocalClock*. Neither method takes any parameters, and both methods have a *void* return type.

7. Open the ClockWindow.xaml.cs file in the *Code and Text Editor* window. This is the code for the WPF form, and it looks like this:

```
public partial class ClockWindow : Window
{
    private LocalClock localClock = null;
    private EuropeanClock londonClock = null;
    private AmericanClock newYorkClock = null;
    private JapaneseClock tokyoClock = null;

    public ClockWindow()
    {
        InitializeComponent();
        localClock = new LocalClock(localTimeDisplay);
        londonClock = new EuropeanClock(londonTimeDisplay);
        newYorkClock = new AmericanClock(newYorkTimeDisplay);
        tokyoClock = new JapaneseClock(tokyoTimeDisplay);
    }

    private void startClick(object sender, RoutedEventArgs e)
    {

    }

    private void stopClick(object sender, RoutedEventArgs e)
    {

    }
}
```

The four private fields represent the four clock objects used by the application. The constructor initializes each of these clock objects. The parameter to the constructor in each case specifies the text field on the form that the clock object will update when it starts running. The *startClick* method runs when the user clicks the *Start* button on the form, and its purpose is to start each of the clocks. Similarly, the *stopClick* method runs when the user clicks the *Stop* button and is intended to stop the clocks. You can see that both of these methods are currently empty.

A naïve approach would simply be to call the appropriate start methods for each clock in the *startClick* method and the stop methods for each clock in the *stopClick* method. However, as you saw earlier in this chapter, that approach ties the application very closely to the way in which each clock is implemented and is not very extensible. Instead, you are going to create a *Controller* object to start and stop the clocks, and you will use a pair of delegates to specify the methods that the *Controller* object should use.

8. On the *Project* menu, click *Add Class*. In the *Add New Item - Delegates* dialog box, in the *Name* text box, type **Controller.cs** and then click *Add*.

Visual Studio creates the *Controller* class and displays the Controller.cs file in the *Code and Text Editor* window.

9. In the *Controller* class, add the delegate types *startClocksDelegate* and *stopClocksDelegate*, as shown below in bold. These delegate types can refer to methods that take no parameters and that have a *void* return type. This signature and return type matches the various start and stop methods for the clock classes.

```
class Controller
{
    public delegate void StartClocksDelegate();
    public delegate void StopClocksDelegate();
}
```

10. Add two public delegates called *StartClocks* and *StopClocks* to the *Controller* class by using these delegate types, as shown next in bold.

```
class Controller
{
    public delegate void StartClocksDelegate();
    public delegate void StopClocksDelegate();

    public StartClocksDelegate StartClocks;
    public StopClocksDelegate StopClocks;
}
```

11. Add the *StartClocksRunning* method to the *Controller* class. This method simply invokes the *StartClocks* delegate. Any methods attached to this delegate will be run.

```
class Controller
{
    ...
    public void StartClocksRunning()
    {
        this.StartClocks();
    }
}
```

12. Add the *StopClocksRunning* method to the *Controller* class. This method is similar to the *StartClocksRunning* method, except that it invokes the *StopClocks* delegate.

```
class Controller
{
    ...
    public void StopClocksRunning()
    {
        this.StopClocks();
    }
}
```

13. Return to the ClockWindow.xaml.cs file in the *Code and Text Editor* window. Add a private *Controller* variable called *controller* to the *ClockWindow* class and instantiate it, like this:

```
public partial class ClockWindow : Window
{
    ...
    private Controller controller = new Controller();
    ...
}
```

14. In the *ClockWindow* constructor, add the statements shown next in bold. These
statements add the methods that start and stop the clocks to the delegates exposed by
the *Controller* class.

```
public ClockWindow()
{
    InitializeComponent();
    localClock = new LocalClock(localTimeDisplay);
    londonClock = new EuropeanClock(londonTimeDisplay);
    newYorkClock = new AmericanClock(newYorkTimeDisplay);
    tokyoClock = new JapaneseClock(tokyoTimeDisplay);

    controller.StartClocks += localClock.StartLocalClock;
    controller.StartClocks += londonClock.StartEuropeanClock;
    controller.StartClocks += newYorkClock.StartAmericanClock;
    controller.StartClocks += tokyoClock.StartJapaneseClock;

    controller.StopClocks += localClock.StopLocalClock;
    controller.StopClocks += londonClock.StopEuropeanClock;
    controller.StopClocks += newYorkClock.StopAmericanClock;
    controller.StopClocks += tokyoClock.StopJapaneseClock;
}
```

15. In the *startClick* method, invoke the *StartClocks* delegate of the *controller* object,
disable the *Start* button, and enable the *Stop* button, like this:

```
private void startClick(object sender, RoutedEventArgs e)
{
    controller.StartClocks();
    start.IsEnabled = false;
    stop.IsEnabled = true;
}
```

Remember that when you invoke a delegate, all the methods attached to that delegate
run. In this case, the call to *StartClocks* will call the start method of each of the clocks.

Many WPF controls expose the Boolean property *IsEnabled*. By default, controls are
enabled when you add them to a form. This means that you can click them and they
will do something. However, in this application, the *IsEnabled* property of the *Stop* button is set to *false* because it does not make sense to try and stop the clocks until they
have been started. The last two statements in this method disable the *Start* button and
enable the *Stop* button.

16. In the *stopClick* method, call the *StopClocks* delegate of the *controller* object, enable the
Start button, and disable the *Stop* button:

```
private void stopClick(object sender, RoutedEventArgs e)
{
    controller.StopClocks();
    start.IsEnabled = true;
    stop.IsEnabled = false;
}
```

17. On the *Debug* menu, click *Start Without Debugging*.

18. On the WPF form, click *Start*.

The form now displays the correct times and updates every second, as shown in the following image. (I am based in the UK, so my local time is the same as London time.)

19. Click *Stop*.

The display stops updating the clocks.

20. Click *Start* again.

The display resumes processing, corrects the time, and updates the time every second.

21. Close the form, and return to Visual Studio 2010.

Lambda Expressions and Delegates

All the examples of adding a method to a delegate that you have seen so far use the method's name. For example, returning to the automated factory scenario described earlier, you add the *StopFolding* method of the *folder* object to the *stopMachinery* delegate like this:

```
this.stopMachinery += folder.StopFolding;
```

This approach is very useful if there is a convenient method that matches the signature of the delegate, but what if this is not the case? Suppose that the *StopFolding* method actually had the following signature:

```
void StopFolding(int shutDownTime); // Shut down in the specified number of seconds
```

This signature is now different from that of the *FinishWelding* and *PaintOff* methods, and therefore you cannot use the same delegate to handle all three methods. So, what do you do?

Creating a Method Adapter

One way around this problem is to create another method that calls *StopFolding* but that takes no parameters itself, like this:

```
void FinishFolding()
{
    folder.StopFolding(0); // Shut down immediately
}
```

You can then add the *FinishFolding* method to the *stopMachinery* delegate in place of the *StopFolding* method, using the same syntax as before:

```
this.stopMachinery += folder.FinishFolding;
```

When the *stopMachinery* delegate is invoked, it calls *FinishFolding*, which in turn calls the *StopFolding* method, passing in the parameter of 0.

> **Note** The *FinishFolding* method is a classic example of an adapter: a method that converts (or adapts) a method to give it a different signature. This pattern is very common and is one of the set of patterns documented in the book *Design Patterns: Elements of Reusable Object-Oriented Software* by Gamma, Helm, Johnson, and Vlissides (Addison-Wesley Professional, 1994).

In many cases, adapter methods such as this are small, and it is easy to lose them in a sea of methods, especially in a large class. Furthermore, apart from using it to adapt the *StopFolding* method for use by the delegate, it is unlikely to be called elsewhere. C# provides lambda expressions for situations such as this.

Using a Lambda Expression as an Adapter

A lambda expression is an expression that returns a method. This sounds rather odd because most expressions that you have met so far in C# actually return a value. If you are familiar with functional programming languages such as Haskell, you are probably comfortable with this concept. For the rest of you, fear not: lambda expressions are not particularly complicated, and after you have gotten used to a new bit of syntax, you will see that they are very useful.

You saw in Chapter 3, "Writing Methods and Applying Scope," that a typical method consists of four elements: a return type, a method name, a list of parameters, and a method body. A lambda expression contains two of these elements: a list of parameters and a method body. Lambda expressions do not define a method name, and the return type (if any) is inferred from the context in which the lambda expression is used. In the *StopFolding* method of the *FoldingMachine* class, the problem is that this method now takes a parameter, so you need to create an adapter that takes no parameters that you can add to the *stopMachinery* delegate. You can use the following statement to do this:

```
this.stopMachinery += (() => { folder.StopFolding(0); });
```

All of the text to the right of the += operator is a lambda expression, which defines the method to be added to the *stopMachinery* delegate. It has the following syntactic items:

- A list of parameters enclosed in parentheses. As with a regular method, if the method you are defining (as in the preceding example) takes no parameters, you must still provide the parentheses.

- The => operator, which indicates to the C# compiler that this is a lambda expression.

- The body of the method. The example shown here is very simple, containing a single statement. However, a lambda expression can contain multiple statements, and you can format it in whatever way you feel is most readable. Just remember to add a semicolon after each statement as you would in an ordinary method.

Strictly speaking, the body of a lambda expression can be a method body containing multiple statements, or it can actually be a single expression. If the body of a lambda expression contains only a single expression, you can omit the braces and the semicolon (but you still need a semicolon to complete the entire statement), like this:

```
this.stopMachinery += (() => folder.StopFolding(0));
```

When you invoke the *stopMachinery* delegate, it will run the code defined by the lambda expression.

The Form of Lambda Expressions

Lambda expressions can take a number of subtly different forms. Lambda expressions were originally part of a mathematical notation called the Lambda Calculus, which provides a no-tation for describing functions. (You can think of a function as a method that returns a value.) Although the C# language has extended the syntax and semantics of the Lambda Calculus in its implementation of lambda expressions, many of the original principles still apply. Here are some examples showing the different forms of lambda expression available in C#:

```
x => x * x  // A simple expression that returns the square of its parameter
            // The type of parameter x is inferred from the context.

x => { return x * x ; } // Semantically the same as the preceding
                        // expression, but using a C# statement block as
                        // a body rather than a simple expression

(int x) => x / 2  // A simple expression that returns the value of the
                  // parameter divided by 2
                  // The type of parameter x is stated explicitly.

() => folder.StopFolding(0) // Calling a method
                            // The expression takes no parameters.
                            // The expression might or might not
                            // return a value.
```

```
(x, y) => { x++; return x / y; } // Multiple parameters; the compiler
                                 // infers the parameter types.
                                 // The parameter x is passed by value, so
                                 // the effect of the ++ operation is
                                 // local to the expression.


(ref int x, int y) => { x++; return x / y; } // Multiple parameters
                                             // with explicit types
                                             // Parameter x is passed by
                                             // reference, so the effect of
                                             // the ++ operation is permanent.
```

To summarize, here are some features of lambda expressions that you should be aware of:

- If a lambda expression takes parameters, you specify them in the parentheses to the left of the => operator. You can omit the types of parameters, and the C# compiler will infer their types from the context of the lambda expression. You can pass parameters by reference (by using the *ref* keyword) if you want the lambda expression to be able to change their values other than locally, but this is not recommended.

- Lambda expressions can return values, but the return type must match that of the delegate they are being added to.

- The body of a lambda expression can be a simple expression or a block of C# code made up of multiple statements, method calls, variable definitions, and other code items.

- Variables defined in a lambda expression method go out of scope when the method finishes.

- A lambda expression can access and modify all variables outside the lambda expression that are in scope when the lambda expression is defined. Be very careful with this feature!

You will learn more about lambda expressions and see further examples that take parameters and return values in later chapters in this book.

Lambda Expressions and Anonymous Methods

Lambda expressions are a new addition to the C# language in version 3.0. C# version 2.0 introduced anonymous methods that can perform a similar task but that are not as flexible. Anonymous methods were added primarily so that you can define delegates without having to create a named method; you simply provide the definition of the method body in place of the method name, like this:

```
this.stopMachinery += delegate { folder.StopFolding(0); };
```

You can also pass an anonymous method as a parameter in place of a delegate, like this:

```
control.Add(delegate { folder.StopFolding(0); } );
```

> Notice that whenever you introduce an anonymous method, you must prefix it with the *delegate* keyword. Also, any parameters needed are specified in parentheses following the *delegate* keyword. For example:
>
> ```
> control.Add(delegate(int param1, string param2) { /* code that uses param1 and param2
> */ ... });
> ```
>
> After you are used to them, you will notice that lambda expressions provide a more succinct syntax than anonymous methods do and they pervade many of the more advanced aspects of C#, as you will see later in this book. Generally speaking, you should use lambda expressions rather than anonymous methods in your code.

Enabling Notifications with Events

You have now seen how to declare a delegate type, call a delegate, and create delegate instances. However, this is only half the story. Although by using delegates you can invoke any number of methods indirectly, you still have to invoke the delegate explicitly. In many cases, it would be useful to have the delegate run automatically when something significant happens. For example, in the automated factory scenario, it could be vital to be able to invoke the *stopMachinery* delegate and halt the equipment if the system detects that a machine is overheating.

The .NET Framework provides *events*, which you can use to define and trap significant actions and arrange for a delegate to be called to handle the situation. Many classes in the .NET Framework expose events. Most of the controls that you can place on a WPF form, and the *Windows* class itself, use events so that you can run code when, for example, the user clicks a button or types something in a field. You can also declare your own events.

Declaring an Event

You declare an event in a class intended to act as an event source. An event source is usually a class that monitors its environment and raises an event when something significant happens. In the automated factory, an event source could be a class that monitors the temperature of each machine. The temperature-monitoring class would raise a "machine overheating" event if it detects that a machine has exceeded its thermal radiation boundary (that is, it has become too hot). An event maintains a list of methods to call when it is raised. These methods are sometimes referred to as *subscribers*. These methods should be prepared to handle the "machine overheating" event and take the necessary corrective action: shut down the machines.

You declare an event similarly to how you declare a field. However, because events are intended to be used with delegates, the type of an event must be a delegate, and you must prefix the declaration with the *event* keyword. Use the following syntax to declare an event:

```
event delegateTypeName eventName
```

As an example, here's the *StopMachineryDelegate* delegate from the automated factory. It has been relocated to a new class called *TemperatureMonitor*, which provides an interface to the various electronic probes monitoring the temperature of the equipment (this is a more logical place for the event than the *Controller* class is):

```
class TemperatureMonitor
{
    public delegate void StopMachineryDelegate();
    ...
}
```

You can define the *MachineOverheating* event, which will invoke the *stopMachineryDelegate*, like this:

```
class TemperatureMonitor
{
    public delegate void StopMachineryDelegate();
    public event StopMachineryDelegate MachineOverheating;
    ...
}
```

The logic (not shown) in the *TemperatureMonitor* class raises the *MachineOverheating* event as necessary. You will see how to raise an event in the upcoming "Raising an Event" section. Also, you add methods to an event (a process known as *subscribing* to the event) rather than adding them to the delegate that the event is based on. You will look at this aspect of events next.

Subscribing to an Event

Like delegates, events come ready-made with a += operator. You subscribe to an event by using this += operator. In the automated factory, the software controlling each machine can arrange for the shutdown methods to be called when the *MachineOverheating* event is raised, like this:

```
class TemperatureMonitor
{
    public delegate void StopMachineryDelegate();
    public event StopMachineryDelegate MachineOverheating;
    ...
}
...
TemperatureMonitor tempMonitor = new TemperatureMonitor();
...
tempMonitor.MachineOverheating += (() => { folder.StopFolding(0); });
```

```
tempMonitor.MachineOverheating += welder.FinishWelding;
tempMonitor.MachineOverheating += painter.PaintOff;
```

Notice that the syntax is the same as for adding a method to a delegate. You can even subscribe by using a lambda expression. When the *tempMonitor.MachineOverheating* event runs, it will call all the subscribing methods and shut down the machines.

Unsubscribing from an Event

Knowing that you use the += operator to attach a delegate to an event, you can probably guess that you use the −= operator to detach a delegate from an event. Calling the −= operator removes the method from the event's internal delegate collection. This action is often referred to as unsubscribing from the event.

Raising an Event

An event can be raised, just like a delegate, by calling it like a method. When you raise an event, all the attached delegates are called in sequence. For example, here's the *TemperatureMonitor* class with a private *Notify* method that raises the *MachineOverheating* event:

```
class TemperatureMonitor
{
    public delegate void StopMachineryDelegate();
    public event StopMachineryDelegate MachineOverheating;
    ...
    private void Notify()
    {
        if (this.MachineOverheating != null)
        {
            this.MachineOverheating();
        }
    }
    ...
}
```

This is a common idiom. The *null* check is necessary because an event field is implicitly *null* and only becomes non-*null* when a method subscribes to it by using the += operator. If you try to raise a *null* event, you will get a *NullReferenceException*. If the delegate defining the event expects any parameters, the appropriate arguments must be provided when you raise the event. You will see some examples of this later.

 Important Events have a very useful built-in security feature. A public event (such as *MachineOverheating*) can be raised only by methods in the class that defines it (the *TemperatureMonitor* class). Any attempt to raise the method outside the class results in a compiler error.

Understanding WPF User Interface Events

As mentioned earlier, the .NET Framework classes and controls used for building graphical user interfaces (GUIs) employ events extensively. You'll see and use GUI events on many occasions in the second half of this book. For example, the WPF *Button* class derives from the *ButtonBase* class, inheriting a public event called *Click* of type *RoutedEventHandler*. The *RoutedEventHandler* delegate expects two parameters: a reference to the object that caused the event to be raised and a *RoutedEventArgs* object that contains additional information about the event:

```
public delegate void RoutedEventHandler(Object sender, RoutedEventArgs e);
```

The *Button* class looks like this:

```
public class ButtonBase: ...
{
    public event RoutedEventHandler Click;
    ...
}

public class Button: ButtonBase
{
    ...
}
```

The *Button* class automatically raises the *Click* event when you click the button on-screen. (How this actually happens is beyond the scope of this book.) This arrangement makes it easy to create a delegate for a chosen method and attach that delegate to the required event. The following example shows the code for a WPF form that contains a button called *okay* and the code to connect the *Click* event of the *okay* button to the *okayClick* method:

```
public partial class Example : System.Windows.Window, System.Windows.Markup.
IComponentConnector
{
    internal System.Windows.Controls.Button okay;
    ...
    void System.Windows.Markup.IComponentConnector.Connect(...)
    {
        ...
        this.okay.Click += new System.Windows.RoutedEventHandler(this.okayClick);
        ...
    }
    ...
}
```

This code is usually hidden from you. When you use the *Design View* window in Visual Studio 2010 and set the *Click* property of the *okay* button to *okayClick* in the Extensible Application Markup Language (XAML) description of the form, Visual Studio 2010 generates this code for you. All you have to do is write your application logic in the event handling method, *okayClick*, in the part of the code that you do have access to, in the Example.xaml.cs file in this case:

```
public partial class Example : System.Windows.Window
{
    ...
    private void okayClick(object sender, RoutedEventArgs args)
    {
        // your code to handle the Click event
    }
}
```

The events that the various GUI controls generate always follow the same pattern. The events are of a delegate type whose signature has a *void* return type and two arguments. The first argument is always the sender (the source) of the event, and the second argument is always an *EventArgs* argument (or a class derived from *EventArgs*).

With the *sender* argument, you can reuse a single method for multiple events. The delegated method can examine the *sender* argument and respond accordingly. For example, you can use the same method to subscribe to the *Click* event for two buttons. (You add the same method to two different events.) When the event is raised, the code in the method can examine the *sender* argument to ascertain which button was clicked.

You learn more about how to handle events for WPF controls in Chapter 22, "Introducing Windows Presentation Foundation."

Using Events

In the previous exercise, you completed a World Clock application that displays the local time as well as the time in London, New York, and Tokyo. You used delegates to start and stop the clocks. You might recall that each of the clocks had a constructor that expected the name of the field on the form in which to display the time. However, a clock should really concentrate on being a clock and should not necessarily be concerned with how to display the time—this functionality is best left to the logic in the WPF form itself. In this exercise, you will modify the local clock to raise an event every second. You will subscribe to this event in the WPF form and invoke an event handler that displays the new local time.

Modify the World Clock application to use events

1. Return to the Visual Studio 2010 window displaying the Clock project.

2. Display the LocalClock.cs file in the *Code and Text Editor* window.

This file contains the *LocalClock* class that implements the local clock. Here are key elements of this class:

❑ A *DispatcherTimer* object called *ticker*. The *DispatcherTimer* class is provided as part of the .NET Framework. Its purpose is to raise events at specified time intervals.

❑ A *TextBox* field called *display*. The constructor initializes this field with the *TextBox* object passed in as the parameter. The *LocalClock* class sets the *Text* property of this object to display the time in the *RefreshTime* method.

❑ A *TimeZoneInfo* object called *timeZoneForThisClock*. The *TimeZoneInfo* class is also part of the .NET Framework. You use this class to obtain the time in a specified time zone. The constructor initializes this object to *TimeZone.Local*, which is the local time zone for the computer running the application.

❑ The *StartLocalClock* method, which starts the *DispatcherTimer* running. The *DispatcherTimer* class provides the *Tick* event, which you use to specify a method to run each time a tick event occurs, and the *Interval* property, which you use to specify how frequently *Tick* events occur. The code in the *LocalClock* class raises an event every second. The *Start* method of the *DispatcherTimer* class actually starts the timer running. Remember from the previous exercise that you called this method by using the *StartClocksDelegate* delegate in the *Controller* class.

❑ The *StopLocalClock* method, which calls the *Stop* method of the *DispatcherTimer* object. This stops the timer running, and it will not raise any more events until you call the *Start* method again. You called this method in the previous exercise by using the *StopClocksDelegate* in the *Controller* class.

❑ The *OnTimedEvent* method. The *StartLocalClock* method adds this method to the *Tick* event of the *DispatcherTimer* object, so when a *Tick* event occurs, this method runs. The parameters to this method are required by the definition of the delegate used by the *Tick* event, but they are not used in this example so you can ignore them. This method retrieves the current date and time by using the static *Now* property of the *DateTime* class. It then converts the time retrieved to the local time by using the *TimeZoneInfo.ConvertTime* method. The hours, minutes, and seconds are extracted from the time, and they are passed as parameters to the *RefreshTime* method.

Note It is not actually necessary to convert from the value returned by *DateTime.Now* to local time because the value of *DateTime.Now* is expressed as local time by default. However, this is good practice, and you can convert the value of *DateTime.Now* to the time in any time zone by using this technique—you simply specify the target time zone as the second parameter to the *TimeZoneInfo.ConvertTime* method. This is what the *AmericanClock*, *EuropeanClock*, and *JapaneseClock* classes do.

❏ The *RefreshTime* method, which formats the hours, minutes, and seconds passed in as parameters into a string and then displays this string in the *TextBox* referenced by the *display* field.

3. The purpose of this exercise is to remove the responsibility for displaying the time from the *LocalClock* class, so comment out the definition of the *display* field:

```
class LocalClock
{
    ...
    // private TextBox display = null;
    ...
}
```

4. Remove the parameter from the *LocalClock* constructor, and comment out the statement that sets the *display* field with this parameter. The amended constructor should look like this:

```
public LocalClock()
{
    this.timeZoneForThisClock = TimeZoneInfo.Local;
    // this.display = displayBox;
}
```

5. Add a public delegate called *DisplayTime* to the *LocalClock* class, before the constructor. This delegate should specify a method that takes a string parameter and that returns a *void*. The WPF form will provide a method that matches this delegate. This method will update the time displayed on the form with the string passed in as the parameter.

```
class LocalClock
{
    ...
    public delegate void DisplayTime(string time);
    ...
}
```

6. Add a public event called *LocalClockTick* to the *LocalClock* class after the *DisplayTime* delegate. This event should be based on the *DisplayTime* delegate.

```
class LocalClock
{
    ...
    public delegate void DisplayTime(string time);
    public event DisplayTime LocalClockTick;
    ...
}
```

7. Locate the *RefreshTime* method at the end of the *LocalClock* class. This method currently sets the *Text* property of the *display* field with a formatted string containing the current time. Change this method so that it raises the *LocalClockTick* event instead, and passes the formatted string as the parameter to any methods that subscribe to this event.

```
private void RefreshTime(int hh, int mm, int ss)
{
    if (this.LocalClockTick != null)
    {
        this.LocalClockTick(String.Format("{0:D2}:{1:D2}:{2:D2}". hh, mm, ss));
    }
}
```

 Note The format string in this example specifies that each digit should be displayed as a two-digit decimal value, with a leading zero if necessary.

8. Display the ClockWindow.xaml.cs file in the *Code and Text Editor* window. In the *ClockWindow* constructor, modify the statement that instantiates the *localClock* variable and remove the parameter from the call to the constructor.

```
public ClockWindow()
{
    ...
    localClock = new LocalClock();
    ...
}
```

9. On the *Debug* menu, click *Start Without Debugging*. When the WPF form appears, click *Start*. You should see that the clocks for London, New York, and Tokyo function as before, but the display for the local time remains stuck at 00:00:00. This is because although the *LocalClock* object is raising events every second, you have not subscribed to them yet. Close the WPF form and return to Visual Studio.

10. In the ClockWindow.xaml.cs file, add the following method to the end of the *ClockWindow* class:

```
private void displayLocalTime(string time)
{
    localTimeDisplay.Text = time;
}
```

This method displays the string passed in as the parameter in the *localTimeDisplay TextBox* on the form.

11. In the *startClick* method, add the statement shown next in bold that subscribes the *displayLocalTime* method to the *LocalClockTick* event of the *localClock* object:

```
private void startClick(object sender, RoutedEventArgs e)
{
    controller.StartClocks();
    localClock.LocalClockTick += displayLocalTime;
    start.IsEnabled = false;
    stop.IsEnabled = true;
}
```

12. In the *stopClick* method, unsubscribe the *displayLocalTime* method from the *LocalClockTick* event.

```
private void stopClick(object sender, RoutedEventArgs e)
{
    controller.StopClocks();
    localClock.LocalClockTick -= displayLocalTime;
    start.IsEnabled = true;
    stop.IsEnabled = false;
}
```

13. On the *Debug* menu, click *Start Without Debugging*.

14. Click *Start*. This time, the local clock displays the correct time and is updated every second.

15. Click *Stop*, and verify that the local clock stops. Then close the form, and return to Visual Studio 2010.

In this exercise, you updated the local clock to signal to the form that it should update its display by using events but that the other clocks should still display the time themselves. If you have time, you might like to modify the remaining clock classes in the same manner.

In this chapter, you learned how to use delegates to reference methods and invoke those methods. You saw how to define anonymous methods and lambda expressions that can be run by using a delegate. Finally, you learned how to define and use events to trigger execution of a method.

- If you want to continue to the next chapter

    Keep Visual Studio 2010 running, and turn to Chapter 18.

- If you want to exit Visual Studio 2010 now

    On the *File* menu, click *Exit*. If you see a *Save* dialog box, click *Yes* and save the project.

Chapter 17 Quick Reference

To	Do this
Declare a delegate type	Write the keyword *delegate*, followed by the return type, followed by the name of the delegate type, followed by any parameter types. For example: `delegate void myDelegate();`

Create an instance of a delegate initialized with a single specific method	Use the same syntax you use for a class or structure: write the keyword *new*, followed by the name of the type (the name of the delegate), followed by the argument between parentheses. The argument must be a method whose signature exactly matches the signature of the delegate. For example:
	
	`delegate void myDelegate();`
	`private void myMethod() { ... }`
	`...`
	`myDelegate del = new myDelegate(this.myMethod);`

To	Do this
Invoke a delegate	Use the same syntax as a method call. For example: ```\nmyDelegate del;\n...\ndel();\n```
Declare an event	Write the keyword *event*, followed by the name of the type (the type must be a delegate type), followed by the name of the event. For example: ```\ndelegate void myDelegate();\n\nclass MyClass\n{\n public event myDelegate MyEvent;\n}\n```

Subscribe to an event	Create a delegate instance (of the same type as the event), and attach the delegate instance to the event by using the += operator. For example:
	
	```\nclass MyEventHandlingClass\n{\n private MyClass myClass = new MyClass();\n ...\n public void Start()\n {\n myClass.MyEvent += new myDelegate\n (this.eventHandlingMethod);\n }\n\n private void eventHandlingMethod()\n {\n ...\n }\n}\n```
	
	You can also get the compiler to generate the new delegate automatically simply by specifying the subscribing method:
	
	```\npublic void Start()\n{\n myClass.MyEvent += this.eventHandlingMethod;\n}\n```

To	Do this
| Unsubscribe from an event | Create a delegate instance (of the same type as the event), and detach the delegate instance from the event by using the −= operator. For example:<br><br>```csharp
class MyEventHandlingClass
{
    private MyClass myClass = new MyClass();
    ...
    public void Stop()
    {
        myClass.MyEvent -= new myDelegate
            (this.eventHandlingMethod);
    }
    ...
}
```<br>Or:<br><br>```csharp
public void Stop()
{
    myClass.MyEvent -= this.eventHandlingMethod;
}
``` |
| Raise an event | Use the same syntax as a method call. You must supply arguments to match the type of the parameters expected by the delegate referenced by the event. Don't forget to check whether the event is *null*. For example:<br><br>```csharp
class MyClass
{
    public event myDelegate MyEvent;
    ...
    private void RaiseEvent()
    {
        if (this.MyEvent != null)
        {
            this.MyEvent();
        }
    }
    ...
}
``` |
```

Chapter 18
Introducing Generics

After completing this chapter, you will be able to:

- Define a type-safe class by using generics.

- Create instances of a generic class based on types specified as type parameters.

- Implement a generic interface.

- Define a generic method that implements an algorithm independent of the type of data on which it operates.

In Chapter 8, "Understanding Values and References," you learned how to use the *object* type to refer to an instance of any class. You can use the *object* type to store a value of any type, and you can define parameters by using the *object* type when you need to pass values of any type into a method. A method can also return values of any type by specifying *object* as the return type. Although this practice is very flexible, it puts the onus on the programmer to remember what sort of data is actually being used and can lead to run-time errors if the programmer makes a mistake. In this chapter, you will learn about generics, a feature that has been designed to help you prevent this kind of mistake.

The Problem with *objects*

To understand generics, it is worth looking in detail at the problems they are designed to solve, specifically when using the *object* type.

You can use the *object* type to refer to a value or variable of any type. All reference types automatically inherit (either directly or indirectly) from the *System.Object* class in the Microsoft .NET Framework. You can use this information to create highly generalized classes and methods. For example, many of the classes in the *System.Collections* namespace exploit this fact, so you can create collections holding almost any type of data. (You have already been introduced to the collection classes in Chapter 10, "Using Arrays and Collections.") By homing in on one particular collection class as a detailed example, you will also notice in the *System.Collections.Queue* class that you can create queues containing practically anything. The following code example shows how to create and manipulate a queue of *Circle* objects:

```
using System.Collections;
...
Queue myQueue = new Queue();
Circle myCircle = new Circle();
myQueue.Enqueue(myCircle);
...
myCircle = (Circle)myQueue.Dequeue();
```

The *Enqueue* method adds an *object* to the head of a queue, and the *Dequeue* method removes the *object* at the other end of the queue. These methods are defined like this:

```
public void Enqueue( object item );
public object Dequeue();
```

Because the *Enqueue* and *Dequeue* methods manipulate *object*s, you can operate on queues of *Circle*s, *PhoneBook*s, *Clock*s, or any of the other classes you have seen in earlier exercises in this book. However, it is important to notice that you have to cast the value returned by the *Dequeue* method to the appropriate type because the compiler will not perform the conversion from the *object* type automatically. If you don't cast the returned value, you will get the compiler error "Cannot implicitly convert type 'object' to 'Circle'."

This need to perform an explicit cast denigrates much of the flexibility afforded by the *object* type. It is very easy to write code such as this:

```
Queue myQueue = new Queue();
Circle myCircle = new Circle();
myQueue.Enqueue(myCircle);
...
Clock myClock = (Clock)myQueue.Dequeue(); // run-time error
```

Although this code will compile, it is not valid and throws a *System.InvalidCastException* at run time. The error is caused by trying to store a reference to a *Circle* in a *Clock* variable, and the two types are not compatible. This error is not spotted until run time because the compiler does not have enough information to perform this check at compile time. The real type of the object being dequeued becomes apparent only when the code runs.

Another disadvantage of using the *object* approach to create generalized classes and methods is that it can use additional memory and processor time if the runtime needs to convert an *object* to a value type and back again. Consider the following piece of code that manipulates a queue of *int* variables:

```
Queue myQueue = new Queue();
int myInt = 99;
myQueue.Enqueue(myInt);        // box the int to an object
...
myInt = (int)myQueue.Dequeue(); // unbox the object to an int
```

The *Queue* data type expects the items it holds to be reference types. Enqueueing a value type, such as an *int*, requires it to be boxed to convert it to a reference type. Similarly, dequeueing into an *int* requires the item to be unboxed to convert it back to a value type. See the sections titled "Boxing" and "Unboxing" in Chapter 8 for more details. Although boxing and unboxing happen transparently, they add performance overhead because they involve dynamic memory allocations. This overhead is small for each item, but it adds up when a program creates queues of large numbers of value types.

The Generics Solution

C# provides generics to remove the need for casting, improve type safety, reduce the amount of boxing required, and make it easier to create generalized classes and methods. Generic classes and methods accept *type parameters*, which specify the type of objects that they operate on. The .NET Framework class library includes generic versions of many of the collection classes and interfaces in the *System.Collections.Generic* namespace. The following code example shows how to use the generic *Queue* class found in this namespace to create a queue of *Circle* objects:

```
using System.Collections.Generic;
...
Queue<Circle> myQueue = new Queue<Circle>();
Circle myCircle = new Circle();
myQueue.Enqueue(myCircle);
...
myCircle = myQueue.Dequeue();
```

There are two new things to note about the code in the preceding example:

- The use of the type parameter between the angle brackets, *<Circle>*, when declaring the *myQueue* variable

- The lack of a cast when executing the *Dequeue* method

The type parameter in angle brackets specifies the type of objects accepted by the queue. All references to methods in this queue automatically expect to use this type rather than *object*, rendering unnecessary the cast to the *Circle* type when invoking the *Dequeue* method. The compiler checks to ensure that types are not accidentally mixed and generates an error at compile time rather than at run time if you try to dequeue an item from *circleQueue* into a *Clock* object, for example.

If you examine the description of the generic *Queue* class in the Microsoft Visual Studio 2010 documentation, you will notice that it is defined as follows:

```
public class Queue<T> : ...
```

The *T* identifies the type parameter and acts as a placeholder for a real type at compile time. When you write code to instantiate a generic *Queue*, you provide the type that should be substituted for *T* (*Circle* in the preceding example). Furthermore, if you then look at the methods of the *Queue<T>* class, you will observe that some of them, such as *Enqueue* and *Dequeue*, specify *T* as a parameter type or return value:

```
public void Enqueue( T item );
public T Dequeue();
```

The type parameter, *T*, is replaced with the type you specify when you declare the queue. Additionally, the compiler now has enough information to perform strict type checking when you build the application and can trap any type mismatch errors early.

You should also be aware that this substitution of *T* for a specified type is not simply a textual replacement mechanism. Instead, the compiler performs a complete semantic substitution so that you can specify any valid type for *T*. Here are more examples:

```
struct Person
{
    ...
}
...
Queue<int> intQueue = new Queue<int>();
Queue<Person> personQueue = new Queue<Person>();
Queue<Queue<int>> queueQueue = new Queue<Queue<int>>();
```

The first two examples create queues of value types, while the third creates a queue of queues (of *int*s). For example, for the *intQueue* variable the compiler also generates the following versions of the *Enqueue* and *Dequeue* methods:

```
public void Enqueue( int item );
public int Dequeue();
```

Contrast these definitions with those of the nongeneric *Queue* class shown in the preceding section. In the methods derived from the generic class, the *item* parameter to *Enqueue* is passed as a value type that does not require boxing. Similarly, the value returned by *Dequeue* is also a value type that does not need to be unboxed.

It is also possible for a generic class to have multiple type parameters. For example, the generic *System.Collections.Generic.Dictionary* class expects two type parameters: one type for keys and another for the values. The following definition shows how to specify multiple type parameters:

```
public class Dictionary<TKey, TValue>
```

A dictionary provides a collection of key/value pairs. You store values (type *TValue*) with an associated key (type *TKey*) and then retrieve them by specifying the key to look up. The *Dictionary* class provides an indexer that allows you to access items by using array notation. It is defined like this:

```
public virtual TValue this[ TKey key ] { get; set; }
```

Notice that the indexer accesses values of type *TValue* by using a key of type *TKey*. To create and use a dictionary called *directory* containing *Person* values identified by *string* keys, you could use the following code:

```
struct Person
{
    ...
}
...
Dictionary<string, Person> directory = new Dictionary<string, Person>();
Person john = new Person();
directory["John"] = john;
...
Person author = directory["John"];
```

As with the generic *Queue* class, the compiler detects attempts to store values other than *Person* structures in the directory, as well as ensures that the key is always a *string* value. For more information about the *Dictionary* class, you should read the Visual Studio 2010 documentation.

> **Note** You can also define generic structures and interfaces by using the same type–parameter syntax as generic classes.

Generics vs. Generalized Classes

It is important to be aware that a generic class that uses type parameters is different from a *generalized* class designed to take parameters that can be cast to different types. For example, the *System.Collections.Queue* class is a generalized class. There is a *single* implementation of this class, and its methods take *object* parameters and return *object* types. You can use this class with *ints*, *strings*, and many other types, but in each case, you are using instances of the same class and you have to cast the data you are using to and from the *object* type.

Compare this with the *System.Collections.Generic.Queue<T>* class. Each time you use this class with a type parameter (such as *Queue<int>* or *Queue<string>*), you actually cause the compiler to generate an entirely new class that happens to have functionality defined by the generic class. What this means is that *Queue<int>* is a completely different type from *Queue<string>*, but they both happen to have the same behavior. You can think of a generic class as one that defines a template that is then used by the compiler to generate new type-specific classes on demand. The type-specific versions of a generic class (*Queue<int>*, *Queue<string>*, and so on) are referred to as *constructed types*, and you should treat them as distinctly different types (albeit ones that have a similar set of methods and properties).

Generics and Constraints

Occasionally, you will want to ensure that the type parameter used by a generic class identifies a type that provides certain methods. For example, if you are defining a *PrintableCollection* class, you might want to ensure that all objects stored in the class have a *Print* method. You can specify this condition by using a *constraint*.

By using a constraint, you can limit the type parameters of a generic class to those that implement a particular set of interfaces, and therefore provide the methods defined by those interfaces. For example, if the *IPrintable* interface defined the *Print* method, you could create the *PrintableCollection* class like this:

```
public class PrintableCollection<T> where T : IPrintable
```

When you build this class with a type parameter, the compiler checks to ensure that the type used for *T* actually implements the *IPrintable* interface and it stops with a compilation error if the type doesn't.

Creating a Generic Class

The .NET Framework class library contains a number of generic classes readily available for you. You can also define your own generic classes, which is what you will do in this section. Before you do this, I provide a bit of background theory.

The Theory of Binary Trees

In the following exercises, you will define and use a class that represents a binary tree. This is a practical exercise because this class happens to be one that is missing from the *System. Collections.Generic* namespace. A binary tree is a useful data structure used for a variety of operations, including sorting and searching through data very quickly. There are volumes written on the minutiae of binary trees, but it is not the purpose of this book to cover binary trees in detail. Instead, we just look at the pertinent details. If you are interested, you should consult a book such as *The Art of Computer Programming, Volume 3: Sorting and Searching* by Donald E. Knuth (Addison-Wesley Professional, 2nd edition, 1998).

A binary tree is a recursive (self-referencing) data structure that can either be empty or contain three elements: a datum, which is typically referred to as the *node*, and two subtrees, which are themselves binary trees. The two subtrees are conventionally called the *left subtree* and the *right subtree* because they are typically depicted to the left and right of the node, respectively. Each left subtree or right subtree is either empty or contains a node and other subtrees. In theory, the whole structure can continue ad infinitum. The following image shows the structure of a small binary tree.

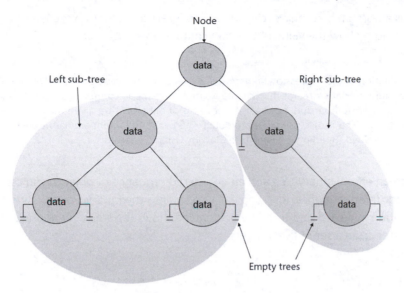

The real power of binary trees becomes evident when you use them for sorting data. If you start with an unordered sequence of objects of the same type, you can construct an ordered binary tree and then walk through the tree to visit each node in an ordered sequence. The algorithm for inserting an item I into an ordered binary tree T is shown here:

```
If the tree, T, is empty
Then
   Construct a new tree T with the new item I as the node, and empty left and
   right subtrees
Else
   Examine the value of the current node, N, of the tree, T
   If the value of N is greater than that of the new item, I
   Then
     If the left subtree of T is empty
     Then
       Construct a new left subtree of T with the item I as the node, and
       empty left and right subtrees
     Else
       Insert I into the left subtree of T
     End If
   Else
     If the right subtree of T is empty
     Then
       Construct a new right subtree of T with the item I as the node, and
       empty left and right subtrees
     Else
       Insert I into the right subtree of T
     End If
   End If
End If
```

Notice that this algorithm is recursive, calling itself to insert the item into the left or right subtree depending on how the value of the item compares with the current node in the tree.

> **Note** The definition of the expression *greater than* depends on the type of data in the item and node. For numeric data, greater than can be a simple arithmetic comparison, and for text data it can be a string comparison; however, other forms of data must be given their own means of comparing values. This is discussed in more detail when you implement a binary tree in the upcoming section titled "Building a Binary Tree Class by Using Generics."

If you start with an empty binary tree and an unordered sequence of objects, you can iterate through the unordered sequence, inserting each object into the binary tree by using this algorithm, resulting in an ordered tree. The next image shows the steps in the process for constructing a tree from a set of five integers.

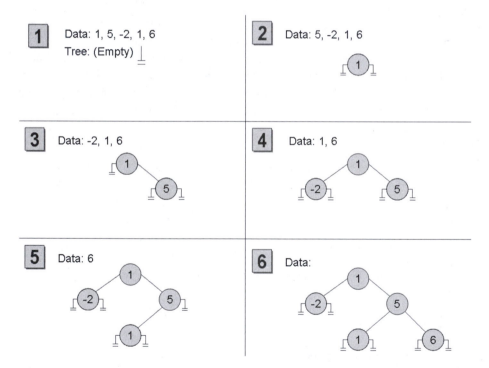

After you have built an ordered binary tree, you can display its contents in sequence by visiting each node in turn and printing the value found. The algorithm for achieving this task is also recursive:

```
If the left subtree is not empty
Then
  Display the contents of the left subtree
End If
Display the value of the node
```

```
If the right subtree is not empty
Then
  Display the contents of the right subtree
End If
```

The following image shows the steps in the process for outputting the tree. Notice that the integers are now displayed in ascending order.

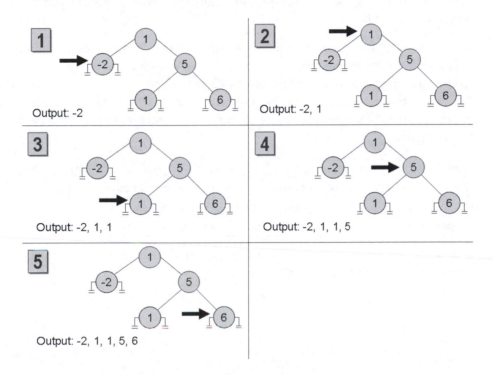

Building a Binary Tree Class by Using Generics

In the following exercise, you will use generics to define a binary tree class capable of holding almost any type of data. The only restriction is that the data type must provide a means of comparing values between different instances.

The binary tree class is a class that you might find useful in many different applications. Therefore, you will implement it as a class library rather than as an application in its own right. You can then reuse this class elsewhere without having to copy the source code and recompile it. A class library is a set of compiled classes (and other types such as structures and delegates) stored in an assembly. An assembly is a file that usually has the .dll suffix. Other projects and applications can make use of the items in a class library by adding a reference to its assembly and then bringing its namespaces into scope with *using* statements. You will do this when you test the binary tree class.

The *System.IComparable* and *System.IComparable<T>* Interfaces

The algorithm for inserting a node into a binary tree requires you to compare the value of the node that you are inserting against nodes already in the tree. If you are using a numeric type, such as int, you can use the <, >, and == operators. However, if you are using some other type, such as Mammal or Circle described in previous chapters, how do you compare objects?

If you need to create a class that requires you to be able to compare values according to some natural (or possibly unnatural) ordering, you should implement the *IComparable* interface. This interface contains a method called *CompareTo*, which takes a single parameter specifying the object to be compared with the current instance and returns an integer that indicates the result of the comparison as summarized by the following table.

Value	Meaning
Less than 0	The current instance is less than the value of the parameter.
0	The current instance is equal to the value of the parameter.
Greater than 0	The current instance is greater than the value of the parameter.

As an example, consider the *Circle* class that was described in Chapter 7, "Creating and Managing Classes and Objects," and is reproduced here:

```
class Circle
{
    public Circle(int initialRadius)
    {
        radius = initialRadius;
    }

    public double Area()
    {
        return Math.PI * radius * radius;
    }

    private double radius;
}
```

You can make the *Circle* class "comparable" by implementing the *System.IComparable* interface and providing the *CompareTo* method. In this example, the *CompareTo* method compares *Circle* objects based on their areas. A circle with a larger area is considered to be greater than a circle with a smaller area.

```
class Circle : System.IComparable
{
    ...
```

```
    public int CompareTo(object obj)
    {
        Circle circObj = (Circle)obj;  // cast the parameter to its real type
        if (this.Area() == circObj.Area())
            return 0;

        if (this.Area() > circObj.Area())
            return 1;

        return -1;
    }
}
```

If you examine the *System.IComparable* interface, you will see that its parameter is defined as an *object*. However, this approach is not type-safe. To understand why this is so, consider what happens if you try to pass something that is not a *Circle* to the *CompareTo* method. The *System.IComparable* interface requires the use of a cast to be able to access the *Area* method. If the parameter is not a *Circle* but some other type of object, this cast will fail. However, the *System* namespace also defines the generic *IComparable<T>* interface, which contains the following methods:

```
int CompareTo(T other);
```

Notice that this method takes a type parameter (*T*) rather than an *object* and, therefore, is much safer than the nongeneric version of the interface. The following code shows how you can implement this interface in the *Circle* class:

```
class Circle : System.IComparable<Circle>
{
    ...
    public int CompareTo(Circle other)
    {
        if (this.Area() == other.Area())
            return 0;

        if (this.Area() > other.Area())
            return 1;

        return -1;
    }
}
```

The parameter for the *CompareTo* method must match the type specified in the interface, *IComparable<Circle>*. In general, it is preferable to implement the *System. IComparable<T>* interface rather than the *System.IComparable* interface. You can also implement both, just as many of the types in the .NET Framework do.

Create the *Tree<TItem>* class

1. Start Visual Studio 2010 if it is not already running.

2. If you are using Visual Studio 2010 Standard or Visual Studio 2010 Professional, perform the following tasks to create a new class library project:

    2.1. On the *File* menu, point to *New*, and then click *Project*.

    2.2. In the *New Project* dialog box, in the middle pane, select the *Class Library* template.

    2.3. In the *Name* text box, type **BinaryTree**.

    2.4. In the *Location* text box, specify *Microsoft Press\Visual CSharp Step By Step\Chapter 18* under your Documents folder.

    2.5. Click *OK*.

3. If you are using Microsoft Visual C# 2010 Express, perform the following tasks to create a new class library project:

    3.1. On the *Tools* menu, click *Options*.

    3.2. In the *Options* dialog box, select the *Show all settings* check box.

    3.3. Click *Projects and Solutions* in the tree view in the left pane.

    3.4. In the right pane, in the *Visual Studio projects location* text box, specify the location as the *\Microsoft Press\Visual CSharp Step By Step\Chapter 18* folder under your Documents folder.

    3.5. Click *OK*.

    3.6. On the *File* menu, click *New Project*.

    3.7. In the *New Project* dialog box, click the *Class Library* icon.

    3.8. In the *Name* field, type **BinaryTree**.

    3.9. Click *OK*.

4. In *Solution Explorer*, right-click *Class1.cs*, click *Rename*, and change the name of the file to **Tree.cs**. Allow Visual Studio to change the name of the class as well as the name of the file when prompted.

5. In the *Code and Text Editor* window, change the definition of the *Tree* class to *Tree<TItem>*, as shown in bold type in the following code:

```
public class Tree<TItem>
{
}
```

6. In the *Code and Text Editor* window, modify the definition of the *Tree<TItem>* class as follows in bold type to specify that the type parameter *TItem* must denote a type that implements the generic *IComparable<TItem>* interface.

   The modified definition of the *Tree<TItem>* class should look like this:

   ```
   public class Tree<TItem> where TItem : IComparable<TItem>
   {
   }
   ```

7. Add three public, automatic properties to the *Tree<TItem>* class: a *TItem* property called *NodeData* and two *Tree<TItem>* properties called *LeftTree* and *RightTree*, as follows in bold type:

   ```
   public class Tree<TItem> where TItem : IComparable<TItem>
   {
       public TItem NodeData { get; set; }
       public Tree<TItem> LeftTree { get; set; }
       public Tree<TItem> RightTree { get; set; }
   }
   ```

8. Add a constructor to the *Tree<TItem>* class that takes a single *TItem* parameter called *nodeValue*. In the constructor, set the *NodeData* property to *nodeValue*, and initialize the *LeftTree* and *RightTree* properties to *null*, as shown in bold type in the following code:

   ```
   public class Tree<TItem> where TItem : IComparable<TItem>
   {
       public Tree(TItem nodeValue)
       {
           this.NodeData = nodeValue;
           this.LeftTree = null;
           this.RightTree = null;
       }
       ...
   }
   ```

 Note Notice that the name of the constructor does not include the type parameter; it is called *Tree*, and not *Tree<TItem>*.

9. Add a public method called *Insert* to the *Tree<TItem>* class as shown in bold type in the following code. This method inserts a *TItem* value into the tree.

   The method definition should look like this:

   ```
   public class Tree<TItem> where TItem: IComparable<TItem>
   {
       ...
       public void Insert(TItem newItem)
       {
       }
       ...
   }
   ```

The *Insert* method implements the recursive algorithm described earlier for creating an ordered binary tree. The programmer will have used the constructor to create the initial node of the tree (there is no default constructor), so the *Insert* method can assume that the tree is not empty. The part of the algorithm after checking whether the tree is empty is reproduced here to help you understand the code you will write for the *Insert* method in the following steps:

```
...
Examine the value of the node, N, of the tree, T
If the value of N is greater than that of the new item, I
Then
  If the left subtree of T is empty
  Then
    Construct a new left subtree of T with the item I as the node, and empty
    left and right subtrees
  Else
    Insert I into the left subtree of T
End If
...
```

10. In the *Insert* method, add a statement that declares a local variable of type *TItem*, called *currentNodeValue*. Initialize this variable to the value of the *NodeData* property of the tree, as shown here:

```
public void Insert(TItem newItem)
{
    TItem currentNodeValue = this.NodeData;
}
```

11. Add the following *if-else* statement shown in bold type to the *Insert* method after the definition of the *currentNodeValue* variable. This statement uses the *CompareTo* method of the *IComparable<T>* interface to determine whether the value of the current node is greater than the new item is:

```
public void Insert(TItem newItem)
{
    TItem currentNodeValue = this.NodeData;
    if (currentNodeValue.CompareTo(newItem) > 0)
    {
        // Insert the new item into the left subtree
    }
    else
    {
        // Insert the new item into the right subtree
    }
}
```

12. Replace the `// Insert the new item into the left subtree` comment with the following block of code:

```
if (this.LeftTree == null)
{
    this.LeftTree = new Tree<TItem>(newItem);
}
else
{
    this.LeftTree.Insert(newItem);
}
```

These statements check whether the left subtree is empty. If so, a new tree is created using the new item and it is attached as the left subtree of the current node; otherwise, the new item is inserted into the existing left subtree by calling the *Insert* method recursively.

13. Replace the `// Insert the new item into the right subtree` comment with the equivalent code that inserts the new node into the right subtree:

```
if (this.RightTree == null)
{
    this.RightTree = new Tree<TItem>(newItem);
}
else
{
    this.RightTree.Insert(newItem);
}
```

14. Add another public method called *WalkTree* to the *Tree<TItem>* class after the *Insert* method. This method walks through the tree, visiting each node in sequence and printing out its value.

    The method definition should look like this:

```
public void WalkTree()
{
}
```

15. Add the following statements to the *WalkTree* method. These statements implement the algorithm described earlier for printing the contents of a binary tree:

```
if (this.LeftTree != null)
{
    this.LeftTree.WalkTree();
}

Console.WriteLine(this.NodeData.ToString());

if (this.RightTree != null)
{
    this.RightTree.WalkTree();
}
```

16. On the *Build* menu, click *Build Solution*. The class should compile cleanly, but correct any errors that are reported and rebuild the solution if necessary.

> **Note** If you are using Visual C# 2010 Express and the *Build* menu is not visible, on the *Tools* menu click *Settings*, and then click *Expert Settings*.

17. If you are using Visual C# 2010 Express, on the *File* menu, click *Save All*. If the *Save Project* dialog box appears, click *Save*.

In the next exercise, you will test the *Tree<TItem>* class by creating binary trees of integers and strings.

Test the *Tree<TItem>* class

1. In *Solution Explorer*, right-click the BinaryTree solution, point to *Add*, and then click *New Project*.

> **Note** Make sure you right-click the BinaryTree solution rather than the BinaryTree project.

2. Add a new project using the Console Application template. Name the project *BinaryTreeTest*. Set the *Location* to *\Microsoft Press\Visual CSharp Step By Step\Chapter 18* under your Documents folder, and then click *OK*.

> **Note** Remember that a Visual Studio 2010 solution can contain more than one project. You are using this feature to add a second project to the BinaryTree solution for testing the *Tree<TItem>* class. This is the recommended way of testing class libraries.

3. Ensure that the BinaryTreeTest project is selected in *Solution Explorer*. On the *Project* menu, click *Set as Startup Project*.

The BinaryTreeTest project is highlighted in *Solution Explorer*. When you run the application, this is the project that will actually execute.

4. Ensure that the BinaryTreeTest project is still selected in *Solution Explorer*. On the *Project* menu, click *Add Reference*. In the *Add Reference* dialog box, click the *Projects* tab. Select the *BinaryTree* project, and then click *OK*.

The BinaryTree assembly appears in the list of references for the BinaryTreeTest project in *Solution Explorer*. You will now be able to create *Tree<TItem>* objects in the BinaryTreeTest project.

Note If the class library project is not part of the same solution as the project that uses it, you must add a reference to the assembly (the .dll file) and not to the class library project. You do this by selecting the assembly from the *Browse* tab in the *Add Reference* dialog box. You will use this technique in the final set of exercises in this chapter.

5. In the *Code and Text Editor* window displaying the *Program* class, add the following *using* directive to the list at the top of the class:

```
using BinaryTree;
```

6. Add the statements in bold type in the following code to the *Main* method:

```
static void Main(string[] args)
{
    Tree<int> tree1 = new Tree<int>(10);
    tree1.Insert(5);
    tree1.Insert(11);
    tree1.Insert(5);
    tree1.Insert(-12);
    tree1.Insert(15);
    tree1.Insert(0);
    tree1.Insert(14);
    tree1.Insert(-8);
    tree1.Insert(10);
    tree1.Insert(8);
    tree1.Insert(8);
    tree1.WalkTree();
}
```

These statements create a new binary tree for holding *int*s. The constructor creates an initial node containing the value 10. The *Insert* statements add nodes to the tree, and the *WalkTree* method prints out the contents of the tree, which should appear sorted in ascending order.

Note Remember that the *int* keyword in C# is actually just an alias for the *System.Int32* type; whenever you declare an *int* variable, you are actually declaring a *struct* variable of type *System.Int32*. The *System.Int32* type implements the *IComparable* and *IComparable<T>* interfaces, which is why you can create *Tree<int>* objects. Similarly, the *string* keyword is an alias for *System.String*, which also implements *IComparable* and *IComparable<T>*.

7. On the *Build* menu, click *Build Solution*. Verify that the solution compiles, and correct any errors if necessary.

8. Save the project, and then on the *Debug* menu, click *Start Without Debugging*.

   The program runs and displays the values in the following sequence:

   –12, –8, 0, 5, 5, 8, 8, 10, 10, 11, 14, 15

9. Press the Enter key to return to Visual Studio 2010.

10. Add the following statements shown in bold type to the end of the *Main* method in the *Program* class, after the existing code:

```
static void Main(string[] args)
{
    ...
    Tree<string> tree2 = new Tree<string>("Hello");
    tree2.Insert("World");
    tree2.Insert("How");
    tree2.Insert("Are");
    tree2.Insert("You");
    tree2.Insert("Today");
    tree2.Insert("I");
    tree2.Insert("Hope");
    tree2.Insert("You");
    tree2.Insert("Are");
    tree2.Insert("Feeling");
    tree2.Insert("Well");
    tree2.Insert("!");
    tree2.WalkTree();
}
```

These statements create another binary tree for holding *strings*, populate it with some test data, and then print the tree. This time, the data is sorted alphabetically.

11. On the *Build* menu, click *Build Solution*. Verify that the solution compiles, and correct any errors if necessary.

12. On the *Debug* menu, click *Start Without Debugging*.

The program runs and displays the integer values as before, followed by the strings in the following sequence:

!, Are, Are, Feeling, Hello, Hope, How, I, Today, Well, World, You, You

13. Press the Enter key to return to Visual Studio 2010.

Creating a Generic Method

As well as defining generic classes, you can also use the .NET Framework to create generic methods.

With a generic method, you can specify parameters and the return type by using a type parameter in a manner similar to that used when defining a generic class. In this way, you can define generalized methods that are type-safe and avoid the overhead of casting (and boxing in some cases). Generic methods are frequently used in conjunction with generic classes—you need them for methods that take a generic class as a parameter or that have a return type that is a generic class.

You define generic methods by using the same type parameter syntax that you use when creating generic classes. (You can also specify constraints.) For example, you can call the following generic *Swap<T>* method to swap the values in its parameters. Because this functionality is useful regardless of the type of data being swapped, it is helpful to define it as a generic method:

```
static void Swap<T>(ref T first, ref T second)
{
    T temp = first;
    first = second;
    second = temp;
}
```

You invoke the method by specifying the appropriate type for its type parameter. The following examples show how to invoke the *Swap<T>* method to swap over two *int*s and two *string*s:

```
int a = 1, b = 2;
Swap<int>(ref a, ref b);
...
string s1 = "Hello", s2 = "World";
Swap<string>(ref s1, ref s2);
```

Note Just as instantiating a generic class with different type parameters causes the compiler to generate different types, each distinct use of the *Swap<T>* method causes the compiler to generate a different version of the method. *Swap<int>* is not the same method as *Swap<string>*; both methods just happen to have been generated from the same generic method, so they exhibit the same behavior, albeit over different types.

Defining a Generic Method to Build a Binary Tree

The preceding exercise showed you how to create a generic class for implementing a binary tree. The *Tree<TItem>* class provides the *Insert* method for adding data items to the tree. However, if you want to add a large number of items, repeated calls to the *Insert* method are not very convenient. In the following exercise, you will define a generic method called *InsertIntoTree* that you can use to insert a list of data items into a tree with a single method call. You will test this method by using it to insert a list of characters into a tree of characters.

Write the *InsertIntoTree* method

1. Using Visual Studio 2010, create a new project by using the Console Application template. In the *New Project* dialog box, name the project **BuildTree**. If you are using Visual Studio 2010 Standard or Visual Studio 2010 Professional, set the *Location* to \ *Microsoft Press\Visual CSharp Step By Step\Chapter 18* under your Documents folder, and select *Create a new Solution* from the *Solution* drop-down list. Click *OK*.

2. On the *Project* menu, click *Add Reference*. In *the Add Reference* dialog box, click the *Browse* tab. Move to the folder *\Microsoft Press\Visual CSharp Step By Step\Chapter 18\ BinaryTree\BinaryTree\bin\Debug*, click *BinaryTree.dll*, and then click *OK*.

The *BinaryTree* assembly is added to the list of references shown in *Solution Explorer*.

3. In the *Code and Text Editor* window displaying the Program.cs file, add the following *using* directive to the top of the Program.cs file:

```
using BinaryTree;
```

This namespace contains the *Tree<TItem>* class.

4. Add a method called *InsertIntoTree* to the *Program* class after the *Main* method. This should be a *static* method that takes a *Tree<TItem>* variable and a *params* array of *TItem* elements called *data*.

The method definition should look like this:

```
static void InsertIntoTree<TItem>(Tree<TItem> tree, params TItem[] data)
{
}
```

> **Tip** An alternative way of implementing this method is to create an extension method of the *Tree<TItem>* class by prefixing the *Tree<TItem>* parameter with the *this* keyword and defining the *InsertIntoTree* method in a static class, like this:
>
> ```
> public static class TreeMethods
> {
>   public static void InsertIntoTree<TItem>(this Tree<TItem> tree,
>                                            params TItem[] data)
>   {
>     ...
>   }
>   ...
> }
> ```
>
> The principal advantage of this approach is that you can invoke the *InsertIntoTree* method directly on a *Tree<TItem>* object rather than pass the *Tree<TItem>* in as a parameter. However, for this exercise, we will keep things simple.

5. The *TItem* type used for the elements being inserted into the binary tree must implement the *IComparable<TItem>* interface. Modify the definition of the *InsertIntoTree* method and add the appropriate *where* clause, as shown in bold type in the following code:

```
static void InsertIntoTree<TItem>(Tree<TItem> tree, params TItem[] data) where TItem :
IComparable<TItem>
{
}
```

6. Add the following statements shown in bold type to the *InsertIntoTree* method. These statements check to make sure that the user has actually passed some parameters into the method (the *data* array might be empty), and then they iterate through the *params* list, adding each item to the tree by using the *Insert* method.

```
static void InsertIntoTree<TItem>(Tree<TItem> tree, params TItem[] data) where TItem :
IComparable<TItem>
{
    if (data.Length == 0)
        throw new ArgumentException("Must provide at least one data value");

    foreach (TItem datum in data)
    {
        tree.Insert(datum);
    }
}
```

Test the *InsertIntoTree* method

1. In the *Main* method of the *Program* class, add the following statements shown in bold type that create a new *Tree* for holding character data, populate it with some sample data by using the *InsertIntoTree* method, and then display it by using the *WalkTree* method of *Tree*:

```
static void Main(string[] args)
{
    Tree<char> charTree = new Tree<char>('M');
    InsertIntoTree<char>(charTree, 'X', 'A', 'M', 'Z', 'Z', 'N');
    charTree.WalkTree();
}
```

2. On the *Build* menu, click *Build Solution*. Verify that the solution compiles, and correct any errors if necessary.

3. On the *Debug* menu, click *Start Without Debugging*.

   The program runs and displays the character values in the following order:

   A, M, M, N, X, Z, Z

4. Press the Enter key to return to Visual Studio 2010.

Variance and Generic Interfaces

In Chapter 8, you learned that you can use the *object* type to hold a value or reference of any other type. For example, the following code is completely legal:

```
string myString = "Hello";
object myObject = myString;
```

Remember that in inheritance terms, the *String* class is derived from the *Object* class, so all strings are objects.

Now consider the following generic interface and class:

```
interface IWrapper<T>
{
    void SetData(T data);
    T GetData();
}

class Wrapper<T> : IWrapper<T>
{
    private T storedData;

    void IWrapper<T>.SetData(T data)
    {
        this.storedData = data;
    }

    T IWrapper<T>.GetData()
    {
        return this.storedData;
    }
}
```

The *Wrapper<T>* class provides a simple wrapper around a specified type. The *IWrapper* interface defines the *SetData* method that the *Wrapper<T>* class implements to store the data, and the *GetData* method that the *Wrapper<T>* class implements to retrieve the data. You can create an instance of this class and use it to wrap a string like this:

```
Wrapper<string> stringWrapper = new Wrapper<string>();
IWrapper<string> storedStringWrapper = stringWrapper;
storedStringWrapper.SetData("Hello");
Console.WriteLine("Stored value is {0}", storedStringWrapper.GetData());
```

The code creates an instance of the *Wrapper<string>* type. It references the object through the *IWrapper<string>* interface to call the *SetData* method. (The *Wrapper<T>* type implements its interfaces explicitly, so you must call the methods through an appropriate interface reference.) The code also calls the *GetData* method through the *IWrapper<string>* interface. If you run this code, it outputs the message "Stored value is Hello".

Now look at the following line of code:

```
IWrapper<object> storedObjectWrapper = stringWrapper;
```

This statement is similar to the one that creates the *IWrapper<string>* reference in the previous code example, the difference being that the type parameter is *object* rather than *string*. Is this code legal? Remember that all strings are objects (you can assign a *string* value to an *object* reference, as shown earlier), so in theory this statement looks promising.

However, if you try it, the statement will fail to compile with the message "Cannot implicitly convert type 'Wrapper<string>' to 'IWrapper<object>'."

You can try an explicit cast such as this:

```
IWrapper<object> storedObjectWrapper = (IWrapper<object>)stringWrapper;
```

This code compiles, but will fail at runtime with an *InvalidCastException* exception. The problem is that although all strings are objects, the converse is not true. If this statement was allowed, you could write code like this, which ultimately attempts to store a *Circle* object in a *string* field:

```
IWrapper<object> storedObjectWrapper = (IWrapper<object>)stringWrapper;
Circle myCircle = new Circle();
storedObjectWrapper.SetData(myCircle);
```

The *IWrapper<T>* interface is said to be *invariant*. You cannot assign an *IWrapper<A>* object to a reference of type *IWrapper<B>*, even if type *A* is derived from type *B*. By default, C# implements this restriction to ensure the type-safety of your code.

Covariant Interfaces

Suppose you defined the *IStoreWrapper<T>* and *IRetrieveWrapper<T>* interfaces shown next in place of *IWrapper<T>* and implemented these interfaces in the *Wrapper<T>* class, like this:

```
interface IStoreWrapper<T>
{
    void SetData(T data);
}

interface IRetrieveWrapper<T>
{
    T GetData();
}

class Wrapper<T> : IStoreWrapper<T>, IRetrieveWrapper<T>
{
    private T storedData;

    void IStoreWrapper<T>.SetData(T data)
    {
        this.storedData = data;
    }

    T IRetrieveWrapper<T>.GetData()
    {
        return this.storedData;
    }
}
```

Functionally, the *Wrapper<T>* class is the same as before, except that you access the *SetData* and *GetData* methods through different interfaces:

```
Wrapper<string> stringWrapper = new Wrapper<string>();
IStoreWrapper<string> storedStringWrapper = stringWrapper;
storedStringWrapper.SetData("Hello");
IRetrieveWrapper<string> retrievedStringWrapper = stringWrapper;
Console.WriteLine("Stored value is {0}", retrievedStringWrapper.GetData());
```

Now, is the following code legal?

```
IRetrieveWrapper<object> retrievedObjectWrapper = stringWrapper;
```

The quick answer is "no", and it fails to compile with the same error as before. But if you think about it, although the C# compiler has deemed that this statement is not type-safe, the reasons for assuming this are no longer valid. The *IRetrieveWrapper<T>* interface only allows you to read the data held in the *IWrapper<T>* object by using the *GetData* method, and it does not provide any way to change the data. In situations such as this where the type parameter occurs only as the return value of the methods in a generic interface, you can inform the compiler that some implicit conversions are legal and that it does not have to enforce strict type-safety. You do this by specifying the *out* keyword when you declare the type parameter, like this:

```
interface IRetrieveWrapper<out T>
{
    T GetData();
}
```

This feature is called *covariance*. You can assign an *IRetrieveWrapper<A>* object to an *IRetrieveWrapper<B>* reference as long as there is a valid conversion from type *A* to type *B*, or type *A* derives from type *B*. The following code now compiles and runs as expected:

```
// string derives from object, so this is now legal
IRetrieveWrapper<object> retrievedObjectWrapper = stringWrapper;
```

You can specify the *out* qualifier with a type parameter only if the type parameter occurs as the return type of methods. If you use the type parameter to specify the type of any method parameters, the *out* qualifier is illegal and your code will not compile. Also, covariance works only with reference types. This is because value types cannot form inheritance hierarchies. The following code will not compile because *int* is a value type:

```
Wrapper<int> intWrapper = new Wrapper<int>();
IStoreWrapper<int> storedIntWrapper = intWrapper; // this is legal
...
// the following statement is not legal - ints are not objects
IRetrieveWrapper<object> retrievedObjectWrapper = intWrapper;
```

Several of the interfaces defined by the .NET Framework exhibit covariance, including the *IEnumerable<T>* interface that you will meet in Chapter 19, "Enumerating Collections."

Contravariant Interfaces

Contravariance is the corollary of covariance. It enables you to use a generic interface to reference an object of type *B* through a reference to type *A* as long as type *B* derives type *A*. This sounds complicated, so it is worth looking at an example from the .NET Framework class library.

The *System.Collections.Generic* namespace in the .NET Framework provides an interface called *IComparer*, which looks like this:

```
public interface IComparer<in T>
{
    int Compare(T x, T y);
}
```

A class that implements this interface has to define the *Compare* method, which is used to compare two objects of the type specified by the *T* type parameter. The *Compare* method is expected to return an integer value: zero if the parameters *x* and *y* have the same value, negative if *x* is less than *y*, and positive if *x* is greater than *y*. The following code shows an example that sorts objects according to their hash code. (The *GetHashCode* method is implemented by the *Object* class. It simply returns an integer value that identifies the object. All reference types inherit this method and can override it with their own implementations.)

```
class  ObjectComparer : IComparer<Object>
{
    int IComparer<Object>.Compare(Object x, Object y)
    {
        int xHash = x.GetHashCode();
        int yHash = y.GetHashCode();

        if (xHash == yHash)
            return 0;

        if (xHash < yHash)
            return -1;

        return 1;
    }
}
```

You can create an *ObjectComparer* object and call the *Compare* method through the *IComparer<Object>* interface to compare two objects, like this:

```
Object x = ...;
Object y = ...;
ObjectComparer objectComparer = new ObjectComparer();
IComparer<object> objectComparator = objectComparer;
int result = objectComparator.Compare(x, y);
```

That's the boring bit. What is more interesting is that you can reference this same object through a version of the *IComparer* interface that compares strings, like this:

```
IComparer<String> stringComparator = objectComparer;
```

At first glance, this statement seems to break every rule of type-safety that you can imagine. However, if you think about what the *IComparer<T>* interface does, this makes some sense. The purpose of the *Compare* method is to return a value based on a comparison between the parameters passed in. If you can compare *Objects*, you certainly should be able to compare *Strings*, which are just specialized types of *Objects*. After all, a *String* should be able to do anything that an *Object* can do—that is the purpose of inheritance.

This still sounds a little presumptive, however. How does the C# compiler know that you are not going to perform any type-specific operations in the code for the *Compare* method that might fail if you invoke the method through an interface based on a different type? If you revisit the definition of the *IComparer* interface, you can see the *in* qualifier prior to the type parameter:

```
public interface IComparer<in T>
{
    int Compare(T x, T y);
}
```

The *in* keyword tells the C# compiler that either you can pass the type *T* as the parameter type to methods or you can pass any type that derives from *T*. You cannot use *T* as the return type from any methods. Essentially, this enables you to reference an object either through a generic interface based on the object type or through a generic interface based on a type that derives from the object type. Basically, if a type *A* exposes some operations, properties, or fields, then if type *B* derives from type *A* it must also expose the same operations (which might behave differently if they have been overridden), properties, and fields. Consequently, it should be safe to substitute an object of type *B* for an object of type *A*.

Covariance and contravariance might seem like fringe topics in the world of generics, but they are useful. For example, the *List<T>* generic collection class uses *IComparer<T>* objects to implement the *Sort* and *BinarySearch* methods. A *List<Object>* object can contain a collection of objects of any type, so the *Sort* and *BinarySearch* methods need to be able to sort objects of any type. Without using contravariance, the *Sort* and *BinarySearch* methods would need to include logic that determines the real types of the items being sorted or searched and then implement a type-specific sort or search mechanism. However, unless you are a mathematician it can be quite difficult to recall what covariance and contravariance actually do. The way I remember, based on the examples in this section, is as follows:

- **Covariance**   If the methods in a generic interface can return strings, they can also return objects. (All strings are objects.)

- **Contravariance**   If the methods in a generic interface can take object parameters, they can take string parameters. (If you can perform an operation by using an object, you can perform the same operation by using a string because all strings are objects.)

 Note Only interface and delegate types can be declared as covariant or contravariant. You cannot use the *in* or *out* modifiers with generic classes.

In this chapter, you learned how to use generics to create type-safe classes. You saw how to instantiate a generic type by specifying a type parameter. You also saw how to implement a generic interface and define a generic method. Finally, you learned how to define covariant and contravariant generic interfaces that can operate with a hierarchy of types.

- If you want to continue to the next chapter

  Keep Visual Studio 2010 running, and turn to Chapter 19.

- If you want to exit Visual Studio 2010 now

  On the *File* menu, click *Exit*. If you see a *Save* dialog box, click *Yes* and save the project.

Chapter 18 Quick Reference

To	Do this
Instantiate an object by using a generic type	Specify the appropriate generic type parameter. For example: ```Queue<int> myQueue = new Queue<int>();```
Create a new generic type	Define the class using a type parameter. For example: ```\npublic class Tree<TItem>\n{\n ...\n}\n```
Restrict the type that can be substituted for the generic type parameter	Specify a constraint by using a *where* clause when defining the class. For example: ```\npublic class Tree<TItem>\nwhere TItem : IComparable<TItem>\n{\n ...\n}\n```
Define a generic method	Define the method by using type parameters. For example: ```\nstatic void InsertIntoTree<TItem>\n(Tree<TItem> tree, params TItem[] data)\n{\n ...\n}\n```

To	Do this
Invoke a generic method	Provide types for each of the type parameters. For example: `InsertIntoTree<char>(charTree, 'Z', 'X');`

Define a covariant interface	Specify the *out* qualifier for covariant type parameters. Reference the covariant type parameters only as the return types from methods and not as the types for method parameters:
	`interface IRetrieveWrapper<`**out** `T>`
	`{`
	`    T GetData();`
	`}`

Define a contravariant interface	Specify the *in* qualifier for contravariant type parameters. Reference the contravariant type parameters only as the types of method parameters and not as return types:
	`public interface IComparer<`**in** `T>`
	`{`
	`    int Compare(T x, T y);`
	`}`

Chapter 19
Enumerating Collections

After completing this chapter, you will be able to:

- Manually define an enumerator that can be used to iterate over the elements in a collection.

- Implement an enumerator automatically by creating an iterator.

- Provide additional iterators that can step through the elements of a collection in different sequences.

In Chapter 10, "Using Arrays and Collections," you learned about arrays and collection classes for holding sequences or sets of data. Chapter 10 also introduced the *foreach* statement that you can use for stepping through, or iterating over, the elements in a collection. At the time, you just used the *foreach* statement as a quick and convenient way of accessing the contents of a collection, but now it is time to learn a little more about how this statement actually works. This topic becomes important when you start defining your own collection classes. Fortunately, C# provides iterators to help you automate much of the process.

Enumerating the Elements in a Collection

In Chapter 10, you saw an example of using the *foreach* statement to list the items in a simple array. The code looked like this:

```
int[] pins = { 9, 3, 7, 2 };
foreach (int pin in pins)
{
    Console.WriteLine(pin);
}
```

The *foreach* construct provides an elegant mechanism that greatly simplifies the code you need to write, but it can be exercised only under certain circumstances—you can use *foreach* only to step through an *enumerable* collection. So, what exactly is an enumerable collection? The quick answer is that it is a collection that implements the *System.Collections.IEnumerable* interface.

 Note Remember that all arrays in C# are actually instances of the *System.Array* class. The *System.Array* class is a collection class that implements the *IEnumerable* interface.

The *IEnumerable* interface contains a single method called *GetEnumerator*:

```
IEnumerator GetEnumerator();
```

The *GetEnumerator* method should return an enumerator object that implements the *System.Collections.IEnumerator* interface. The enumerator object is used for stepping through (enumerating) the elements of the collection. The *IEnumerator* interface specifies the following property and methods:

```
object Current { get; }
bool MoveNext();
void Reset();
```

Think of an enumerator as a pointer pointing to elements in a list. Initially, the pointer points *before* the first element. You call the *MoveNext* method to move the pointer down to the next (first) item in the list; the *MoveNext* method should return *true* if there actually is another item and *false* if there isn't. You use the *Current* property to access the item currently pointed to, and you use the *Reset* method to return the pointer back to *before* the first item in the list. By creating an enumerator by using the *GetEnumerator* method of a collection and repeatedly calling the *MoveNext* method and retrieving the value of the *Current* property by using the enumerator, you can move forward through the elements of a collection one item at a time. This is exactly what the *foreach* statement does. So if you want to create your own enumerable collection class, you must implement the *IEnumerable* interface in your collection class and also provide an implementation of the *IEnumerator* interface to be returned by the *GetEnumerator* method of the collection class.

> **Important** At first glance, it is easy to confuse the *IEnumerable<T>* and *IEnumerator<T>* interfaces because of the similarity of their names. Don't get them mixed up.

If you are observant, you will have noticed that the *Current* property of the *IEnumerator* interface exhibits non–type-safe behavior in that it returns an *object* rather than a specific type. However, you should be pleased to know that the Microsoft .NET Framework class library also provides the generic *IEnumerator<T>* interface, which has a *Current* property that returns a *T* instead. Likewise, there is also an *IEnumerable<T>* interface containing a *GetEnumerator* method that returns an *Enumerator<T>* object. If you are building applications for the .NET Framework version 2.0 or later, you should make use of these generic interfaces when defining enumerable collections rather than using the nongeneric definitions.

> **Note** The *IEnumerator<T>* interface has some further differences from the *IEnumerator* interface; it does not contain a *Reset* method but extends the *IDisposable* interface.

Manually Implementing an Enumerator

In the next exercise, you will define a class that implements the generic *IEnumerator<T>* interface and create an enumerator for the binary tree class that you built in Chapter 18, "Introducing Generics." In Chapter 18, you saw how easy it is to traverse a binary tree and display its contents. You would therefore be inclined to think that defining an enumerator that retrieves each element in a binary tree in the same order would be a simple matter. Sadly, you would be mistaken. The main problem is that when defining an enumerator you need to remember where you are in the structure so that subsequent calls to the *MoveNext* method can update the position appropriately. Recursive algorithms, such as that used when walking a binary tree, do not lend themselves to maintaining state information between method calls in an easily accessible manner. For this reason, you will first preprocess the data in the binary tree into a more amenable data structure (a queue) and actually enumerate this data structure instead. Of course, this deviousness is hidden from the user iterating through the elements of the binary tree!

Create the *TreeEnumerator* class

1. Start Microsoft Visual Studio 2010 if it is not already running.

2. Open the BinaryTree solution located in the \Microsoft Press\Visual CSharp Step By Step\Chapter 19\BinaryTree folder in your Documents folder. This solution contains a working copy of the BinaryTree project you created in Chapter 18.

3. Add a new class to the project: On the *Project* menu, click *Add Class*. In the middle pane of the *Add New Item – BinaryTree* dialog box, select the *Class* template, type **TreeEnumerator.cs** in the *Name* text box, and then click *Add*.

4. The *TreeEnumerator* class generates an enumerator for a *Tree<TItem>* object. To ensure that the class is type-safe, you must provide a type parameter and implement the *IEnumerator<T>* interface. Also, the type parameter must be a valid type for the *Tree<TItem>* object that the class enumerates, so it must be constrained to implement the *IComparable<TItem>* interface.

   In the *Code and Text Editor* window displaying the TreeEnumerator.cs file, modify the definition of the *TreeEnumerator* class to satisfy these requirements, as shown in bold in the following example:

   ```
   class TreeEnumerator<TItem> : IEnumerator<TItem> where TItem : IComparable<TItem>
   {
   }
   ```

5. Add the following three private variables shown next in bold to the *TreeEnumerator<TItem>* class:

```
class TreeEnumerator<TItem> : IEnumerator<TItem> where TItem : IComparable<TItem>
{
    private Tree<TItem> currentData = null;
    private TItem currentItem = default(TItem);
    private Queue<TItem> enumData = null;
}
```

The *currentData* variable will be used to hold a reference to the tree being enumerated, and the *currentItem* variable will hold the value returned by the *Current* property. You will populate the *enumData* queue with the values extracted from the nodes in the tree, and the *MoveNext* method will return each item from this queue in turn. The *default* keyword is explained in the section titled "Initializing a Variable Defined with a Type Parameter" later in this chapter.

6. Add a *TreeEnumerator* constructor that takes a single *Tree<TItem>* parameter called *data*. In the body of the constructor, add a statement that initializes the *currentData* variable to *data*:

```
class TreeEnumerator<TItem> : IEnumerator<TItem> where TItem : IComparable<TItem>
{
    public TreeEnumerator(Tree<TItem> data)
    {
        this.currentData = data;
    }
    ...
}
```

7. Add the following private method, called *populate*, to the *TreeEnumerator<TItem>* class immediately after the constructor:

```
private void populate(Queue<TItem> enumQueue, Tree<TItem> tree)
{
    if (tree.LeftTree != null)
    {
        populate(enumQueue, tree.LeftTree);
    }

    enumQueue.Enqueue(tree.NodeData);

    if (tree.RightTree != null)
    {
        populate(enumQueue, tree.RightTree);
    }
}
```

This method walks a binary tree, adding the data it contains to the queue. The algorithm used is similar to that used by the *WalkTree* method in the *Tree<TItem>* class, which was described in Chapter 18. The main difference is that rather than the method outputting *NodeData* values to the screen, it stores these values in the queue.

8. Return to the definition of the *TreeEnumerator<TItem>* class. Right-click anywhere in the *IEnumerator<TItem>* interface in the class declaration, point to *Implement Interface*, and then click *Implement Interface Explicitly*.

   This action generates stubs for the methods of the *IEnumerator<TItem>* interface and the *IEnumerator* interface and adds them to the end of the class. It also generates the *Dispose* method for the *IDisposable* interface.

> **Note** The *IEnumerator<TItem>* interface inherits from the *IEnumerator* and *IDisposable* interfaces, which is why their methods also appear. In fact, the only item that belongs to the *IEnumerator<TItem>* interface is the generic *Current* property. The *MoveNext* and *Reset* methods belong to the nongeneric *IEnumerator* interface. The *IDisposable* interface was described in Chapter 14, "Using Garbage Collection and Resource Management."

9. Examine the code that has been generated. The bodies of the properties and methods contain a default implementation that simply throws a *NotImplementedException*. You will replace this code with a real implementation in the following steps.

10. Replace the body of the *MoveNext* method with the code shown in bold here:

```
bool System.Collections.IEnumerator.MoveNext()
{
    if (this.enumData == null)
    {
        this.enumData = new Queue<TItem>();
        populate(this.enumData, this.currentData);
    }

    if (this.enumData.Count > 0)
    {
        this.currentItem = this.enumData.Dequeue();
        return true;
    }

    return false;
}
```

The purpose of the *MoveNext* method of an enumerator is actually twofold. The first time it is called, it should initialize the data used by the enumerator and advance to the first piece of data to be returned. (Prior to *MoveNext* being called for the first time, the value returned by the *Current* property is undefined and should result in an exception.) In this case, the initialization process consists of instantiating the queue and then calling the *populate* method to fill the queue with data extracted from the tree.

Subsequent calls to the *MoveNext* method should just move through data items until there are no more left, dequeuing items from the queue until the queue is empty in this example. It is important to bear in mind that *MoveNext* does not actually return data items—that is the purpose of the *Current* property. All *MoveNext* does is update the internal state in the enumerator (that is, the value of the *currentItem* variable is set to the data item extracted from the queue) for use by the *Current* property, returning *true* if there is a next value and *false* otherwise.

11. Modify the definition of the *get* accessor of the generic *Current* property as follows:

```
TItem IEnumerator<TItem>.Current
{
    get
    {
        if (this.enumData == null)
            throw new InvalidOperationException
                ("Use MoveNext before calling Current");

        return this.currentItem;
    }
}
```

> **Important** Be sure to add the code to the correct implementation of the *Current* property. Leave the nongeneric version, *System.Collections.IEnumerator.Current*, with its default implementation.

The *Current* property examines the *enumData* variable to ensure that *MoveNext* has been called. (This variable will be null prior to the first call to *MoveNext*.) If this is not the case, the property throws an *InvalidOperationException*—this is the conventional mechanism used by .NET Framework applications to indicate that an operation cannot be performed in the current state. If *MoveNext* has been called beforehand, it will have updated the *currentItem* variable, so all the *Current* property needs to do is return the value in this variable.

12. Locate the *IDisposable.Dispose* method. Comment out the `throw new NotImplementedException();` statement as follows in bold below. The enumerator does not use any resources that require explicit disposal, so this method does not need to do anything. It must still be present, however. For more information about the *Dispose* method, refer to Chapter 14.

```
void IDisposable.Dispose()
{
    // throw new NotImplementedException();
}
```

13. Build the solution, and fix any errors that are reported.

Initializing a Variable Defined with a Type Parameter

You should have noticed that the statement that defines and initializes the *currentItem* variable uses the *default* keyword. The *currentItem* variable is defined by using the type parameter *TItem*. When the program is written and compiled, the actual type that will be substituted for *TItem* might not be known—this issue is resolved only when the code is executed. This makes it difficult to specify how the variable should be initialized. The temptation is to set it to *null*. However, if the type substituted for *TItem* is a value type, this is an illegal assignment. (You cannot set value types to *null*, only reference types.) Similarly, if you set it to 0 in the expectation that the type will be numeric, this will be illegal if the type used is actually a reference type. There are other possibilities as well—*TItem* could be a *boolean*, for example. The *default* keyword solves this problem. The value used to initialize the variable will be determined when the statement is executed; if *TItem* is a reference type, *default(TItem)* returns *null*; if *TItem* is numeric, *default(TItem)* returns 0; if *TItem* is a *boolean*, *default(TItem)* returns *false*. If *TItem* is a *struct*, the individual fields in the *struct* are initialized in the same way. (Reference fields are set to *null*, numeric fields are set to 0, and *boolean* fields are set to *false*.)

Implementing the *IEnumerable* Interface

In the following exercise, you will modify the binary tree class to implement the *IEnumerable* interface. The *GetEnumerator* method will return a *TreeEnumerator<TItem>* object.

Implement the *IEnumerable<TItem>* interface in the *Tree<TItem>* class

1. In *Solution Explorer*, double-click the file Tree.cs to display the *Tree<TItem>* class in the *Code and Text Editor* window.

2. Modify the definition of the *Tree<TItem>* class so that it implements the *IEnumerable<TItem>* interface, as shown in bold in the following code:

   ```
   public class Tree<TItem> : IEnumerable<TItem> where TItem : IComparable<TItem>
   ```

   Notice that constraints are always placed at the end of the class definition.

3. Right-click the *IEnumerable<TItem>* interface in the class definition, point to *Implement Interface*, and then click *Implement Interface Explicitly*.

   This action generates implementations of the *IEnumerable<TItem>.GetEnumerator* and *IEnumerable.GetEnumerator* methods and adds them to the class. The non-generic *IEnumerable* interface method is implemented because the generic *IEnumerable<TItem>* interface inherits from *IEnumerable*.

4. Locate the generic *IEnumerable<TItem>.GetEnumerator* method near the end of the class. Modify the body of the *GetEnumerator()* method, replacing the existing *throw* statement as shown in bold here:

```
IEnumerator<TItem> IEnumerable<TItem>.GetEnumerator()
{
    return new TreeEnumerator<TItem>(this);
}
```

The purpose of the *GetEnumerator* method is to construct an enumerator object for iterating through the collection. In this case, all you need to do is build a new *TreeEnumerator<TItem>* object by using the data in the tree.

5. Build the solution.

The project should compile cleanly, but correct any errors that are reported and rebuild the solution if necessary.

You will now test the modified *Tree<TItem>* class by using a *foreach* statement to iterate through a binary tree and display its contents.

Test the enumerator

1. In *Solution Explorer*, right-click the BinaryTree solution, point to *Add*, and then click *New Project*. Add a new project by using the Console Application template. Name the project **EnumeratorTest**, set the *Location* to *\Microsoft Press\Visual CSharp Step By Step\ Chapter 19* in your Documents folder, and then click *OK*.

2. Right-click the EnumeratorTest project in *Solution Explorer*, and then click *Set as Startup Project*.

3. On the *Project* menu, click *Add Reference*. In the *Add Reference* dialog box, click the *Projects* tab. Select the BinaryTree project, and then click *OK*.

The BinaryTree assembly appears in the list of references for the EnumeratorTest project in *Solution Explorer*.

4. In the *Code and Text Editor* window displaying the *Program* class, add the following *using* directive to the list at the top of the file:

```
using BinaryTree;
```

5. Add to the *Main* method the following statements shown in bold that create and populate a binary tree of integers:

```
static void Main(string[] args)
{
    Tree<int> tree1 = new Tree<int>(10);
    tree1.Insert(5);
    tree1.Insert(11);
    tree1.Insert(5);
```

```
        tree1.Insert(-12);
        tree1.Insert(15);
        tree1.Insert(0);
        tree1.Insert(14);
        tree1.Insert(-8);
        tree1.Insert(10);
    }
```

6. Add a *foreach* statement, as follows in bold, that enumerates the contents of the tree and displays the results:

```
static void Main(string[] args)
{
    ...
    foreach (int item in tree1)
        Console.WriteLine(item);
}
```

7. Build the solution, correcting any errors if necessary.

8. On the *Debug* menu, click *Start Without Debugging*.

   The program runs and displays the values in the following sequence:

   –12, –8, 0, 5, 5, 10, 10, 11, 14, 15

9. Press Enter to return to Visual Studio 2010.

Implementing an Enumerator by Using an Iterator

As you can see, the process of making a collection enumerable can become complex and potentially error prone. To make life easier, C# includes iterators that can automate much of this process.

An *iterator* is a block of code that yields an ordered sequence of values. Additionally, an iterator is not actually a member of an enumerable class. Rather, it specifies the sequence that an enumerator should use for returning its values. In other words, an iterator is just a description of the enumeration sequence that the C# compiler can use for creating its own enumerator. This concept requires a little thought to understand it properly, so consider a basic example before returning to binary trees and recursion.

A Simple Iterator

The following *BasicCollection<T>* class illustrates the principles of implementing an iterator. The class uses a *List<T>* object for holding data and provides the *FillList* method for populating this list. Notice also that the *BasicCollection<T>* class implements the *IEnumerable<T>* interface. The *GetEnumerator* method is implemented by using an iterator:

```
using System;
using System.Collections.Generic;
using System.Collections;

class BasicCollection<T> : IEnumerable<T>
{
    private List<T> data = new List<T>();

    public void FillList(params T [] items)
    {
        foreach (var datum in items)
            data.Add(datum);
    }

    IEnumerator<T> IEnumerable<T>.GetEnumerator()
    {
        foreach (var datum in data)
            yield return datum;
    }

    IEnumerator IEnumerable.GetEnumerator()
    {
        // Not implemented in this example
    }
}
```

The *GetEnumerator* method appears to be straightforward, but it warrants closer examination. The first thing you should notice is that it doesn't appear to return an *IEnumerator<T>* type. Instead, it loops through the items in the *data* array, returning each item in turn. The key point is the use of the *yield* keyword. The *yield* keyword indicates the value that should be returned by each iteration. If it helps, you can think of the *yield* statement as calling a temporary halt to the method, passing back a value to the caller. When the caller needs the next value, the *GetEnumerator* method continues at the point it left off, looping around and then yielding the next value. Eventually, the data is exhausted, the loop finishes, and the *GetEnumerator* method terminates. At this point, the iteration is complete.

Remember that this is not a normal method in the usual sense. The code in the *GetEnumerator* method defines an *iterator*. The compiler uses this code to generate an implementation of the *IEnumerator<T>* class containing a *Current* method and a *MoveNext* method. This implementation exactly matches the functionality specified by the *GetEnumerator* method. You don't actually get to see this generated code (unless you decompile the assembly containing the compiled code), but that is a small price to pay for the convenience and reduction in code that you need to write. You can invoke the enumerator generated by the iterator in the usual manner, as shown in this block of code:

```
BasicCollection<string> bc = new BasicCollection<string>();
bc.FillList("Twas", "brillig", "and", "the", "slithy", "toves");
foreach (string word in bc)
    Console.WriteLine(word);
```

This code simply outputs the contents of the *bc* object in this order:

Twas, brillig, and, the, slithy, toves

If you want to provide alternative iteration mechanisms presenting the data in a different sequence, you can implement additional properties that implement the *IEnumerable* interface and that use an iterator for returning data. For example, the *Reverse* property of the *BasicCollection<T>* class, shown here, emits the data in the list in reverse order:

```
public IEnumerable<T> Reverse
{
    get
    {
        for (int i = data.Count - 1; i >= 0; i--)
            yield return data[i];
    }
}
```

You can invoke this property as follows:

```
BasicCollection<string> bc = new BasicCollection<string>();
bc.FillList("Twas", "brillig", "and", "the", "slithy", "toves");
foreach (string word in bc.Reverse)
    Console.WriteLine(word);
```

This code outputs the contents of the *bc* object in reverse order:

toves, slithy, the, and, brillig, Twas

Defining an Enumerator for the *Tree<TItem>* Class by Using an Iterator

In the next exercise, you will implement the enumerator for the *Tree<TItem>* class by using an iterator. Unlike the preceding set of exercises, which required the data in the tree to be preprocessed into a queue by the *MoveNext* method, you can define an iterator that traverses the tree by using the more natural recursive mechanism, similar to the *WalkTree* method discussed in Chapter 18.

Add an enumerator to the *Tree<TItem>* class

1. Using Visual Studio 2010, open the BinaryTree solution located in the \Microsoft Press\ Visual CSharp Step By Step\Chapter 19\IteratorBinaryTree folder in your Documents folder. This solution contains another copy of the BinaryTree project you created in Chapter 18.

2. Display the file Tree.cs in the *Code and Text Editor* window. Modify the definition of the *Tree<TItem>* class so that it implements the *IEnumerable<TItem>* interface, as shown in bold here:

```
public class Tree<TItem> : IEnumerable<TItem> where TItem : IComparable<TItem>
{
    ...
}
```

3. Right-click the *IEnumerable<TItem>* interface in the class definition, point to *Implement Interface*, and then click *Implement Interface Explicitly*.

The *IEnumerable<TItem>.GetEnumerator* and *IEnumerable.GetEnumerator* methods are added to the class.

4. Locate the generic *IEnumerable<TItem>.GetEnumerator* method. Replace the contents of the *GetEnumerator* method as shown in bold in the following code:

```
IEnumerator<TItem> IEnumerable<TItem>.GetEnumerator()
{
    if (this.LeftTree != null)
    {
        foreach (TItem item in this.LeftTree)
        {
            yield return item;
        }
    }

    yield return this.NodeData;

    if (this.RightTree != null)
    {
        foreach (TItem item in this.RightTree)
        {
            yield return item;
        }
    }
}
```

It might not look like it at first glance, but this code follows the same recursive algorithm that you used in Chapter 18 for printing the contents of a binary tree. If *LeftTree* is not empty, the first *foreach* statement implicitly calls the *GetEnumerator* method (which you are currently defining) over it. This process continues until a node is found that has no left subtree. At this point, the value in the *NodeData* property is yielded, and the right subtree is examined in the same way. When the right subtree is exhausted, the process unwinds to the parent node, outputting the parent's *NodeData* property and examining the right subtree of the parent. This course of action continues until the entire tree has been enumerated and all the nodes have been output.

Test the new enumerator

1. In *Solution Explorer*, right-click the BinaryTree solution, point to *Add*, and then click *Existing Project*. In the *Add Existing Project* dialog box, move to the folder \Microsoft Press\Visual CSharp Step By Step\Chapter 19\EnumeratorTest, select the EnumeratorTest project file, and then click *Open*.

   This is the project that you created to test the enumerator you developed manually earlier in this chapter.

2. Right-click the EnumeratorTest project in *Solution Explorer*, and then click *Set as Startup Project*.

3. Expand the References node for the EnumeratorTest project in *Solution Explorer*. Right-click the BinaryTree assembly, and then click *Remove*.

   This action removes the reference to the old BinaryTree assembly (from Chapter 18) from the project.

4. On the *Project* menu, click *Add Reference*. In the *Add Reference* dialog box, click the *Projects* tab. Select the BinaryTree project, and then click *OK*.

   The new BinaryTree assembly appears in the list of references for the EnumeratorTest project in *Solution Explorer*.

> **Note** These two steps ensure that the EnumeratorTest project references the version of the *BinaryTree* assembly that uses the iterator to create its enumerator rather than the earlier version.

5. Display the Program.cs file for the EnumeratorTest project in the *Code and Text Editor* window. Review the *Main* method in the Program.cs file. Recall from testing the earlier enumerator that this method instantiates a *Tree<int>* object, fills it with some data, and then uses a *foreach* statement to display its contents.

6. Build the solution, correcting any errors if necessary.

7. On the *Debug* menu, click *Start Without Debugging*.

   The program runs and displays the values in the same sequence as before:

   −12, −8, 0, 5, 5, 10, 10, 11, 14, 15

8. Press Enter and return to Visual Studio 2010.

In this chapter, you saw how to implement the *IEnumerable* and *IEnumerator* interfaces with a collection class to enable applications to iterate through the items in the collection. You also saw how to implement an enumerator by using an iterator.

- If you want to continue to the next chapter

    Keep Visual Studio 2010 running, and turn to Chapter 20.

- If you want to exit Visual Studio 2010 now

    On the *File* menu, click *Exit*. If you see a *Save* dialog box, click *Yes* and save the project.

Chapter 19 Quick Reference

To	Do this
| Make a class enumerable, allowing it to support the *foreach* construct | Implement the *IEnumerable* interface, and provide a *GetEnumerator* method that returns an *IEnumerator* object. For example:<br><br>```csharp
public class Tree<TItem> : IEnumerable<TItem>
{
    ...
    IEnumerator<TItem> GetEnumerator()
    {
        ...
    }
}
``` |
| Implement an enumerator not by using an iterator | Define an enumerator class that implements the *IEnumerator* interface and that provides the *Current* property and the *MoveNext* method (and optionally the *Reset* method). For example:<br><br>```csharp
public class TreeEnumerator<TItem> : IEnumerator<TItem>
{
    ...
    TItem Current
    {
        get
        {
            ...
        }
    }

    bool MoveNext()
    {
        ...
    }
}
``` |
| Define an enumerator by using an iterator | Implement the enumerator to indicate which items should be returned (using the *yield* statement) and in which order. For example:<br><br>```csharp
IEnumerator<TItem> GetEnumerator()
{
    for (...)
        yield return ...
}
``` |
```

Chapter 20
Querying In-Memory Data by Using Query Expressions

After completing this chapter, you will be able to:

- Define Language Integrated Query (LINQ) queries to examine the contents of enumerable collections.

- Use LINQ extension methods and query operators.

- Explain how LINQ defers evaluation of a query and how you can force immediate execution and cache the results of a LINQ query.

You have now met most of the features of the C# language. However, we have glossed over one important aspect of the language that is likely to be used by many applications—the support that C# provides for querying data. You have seen that you can define structures and classes for modeling data and that you can use collections and arrays for temporarily storing data in memory. However, how do you perform common tasks such as searching for items in a collection that match a specific set of criteria? For example, if you have a collection of *Customer* objects, how do you find all customers that are located in London, or how can you find out which town has the most customers for your services? You can write your own code to iterate through a collection and examine the fields in each object, but these types of tasks occur so often that the designers of C# decided to include features to minimize the amount of code you need to write. In this chapter, you will learn how to use these advanced C# language features to query and manipulate data.

What Is Language Integrated Query?

All but the most trivial of applications need to process data. Historically, most applications provided their own logic for performing these operations. However, this strategy can lead to the code in an application becoming very tightly coupled to the structure of the data that it processes; if the data structures change, you might need to make a significant number of changes to the code that handles the data. The designers of the Microsoft .NET Framework thought long and hard about these issues and decided to make the life of an application developer easier by providing features that abstract the mechanism that an application uses to query data from application code itself. These features are called Language Integrated Query, or LINQ.

The designers of LINQ took an unabashed look at the way in which relational database management systems, such as Microsoft SQL Server, separate the language used to query a database from the internal format of the data in the database. Developers accessing a SQL Server database issue Structured Query Language (SQL) statements to the database management system. SQL provides a high-level description of the data that the developer wants to retrieve but does not indicate exactly how the database management system should retrieve this data. These details are controlled by the database management system itself. Consequently, an application that invokes SQL statements does not care how the database management system physically stores or retrieves data. The format used by the database management system can change (for example, if a new version is released) without the application developer needing to modify the SQL statements used by the application.

LINQ provides syntax and semantics very reminiscent of SQL, and with many of the same advantages. You can change the underlying structure of the data being queried without needing to change the code that actually performs the queries. You should be aware that although LINQ looks similar to SQL, it is far more flexible and can handle a wider variety of logical data structures. For example, LINQ can handle data organized hierarchically, such as that found in an XML document. However, this chapter concentrates on using LINQ in a relational manner.

Using LINQ in a C# Application

Perhaps the easiest way to explain how to use the C# features that support LINQ is to work through some simple examples based on the following sets of customer and address information:

Customer Information

CustomerID	FirstName	LastName	CompanyName
1	Orlando	Gee	A Bike Store
2	Keith	Harris	Bike World
3	Donna	Carreras	A Bike Store
4	Janet	Gates	Fitness Hotel
5	Lucy	Harrington	Grand Industries
6	David	Liu	Bike World
7	Donald	Blanton	Grand Industries
8	Jackie	Blackwell	Fitness Hotel
9	Elsa	Leavitt	Grand Industries
10	Eric	Lang	Distant Inn

Address Information

CompanyName	City	Country
A Bike Store	New York	United States
Bike World	Chicago	United States
Fitness Hotel	Ottawa	Canada
Grand Industries	London	United Kingdom
Distant Inn	Tetbury	United Kingdom

LINQ requires the data to be stored in a data structure that implements the *IEnumerable* interface, as described in Chapter 19, "Enumerating Collections." It does not matter what structure you use (an array, a *HashTable*, a *Queue*, or any of the other collection types, or even one that you define yourself) as long as it is enumerable. However, to keep things straightforward, the examples in this chapter assume that the customer and address information is held in the *customers* and *addresses* arrays shown in the following code example.

 Note In a real-world application, you would populate these arrays by reading the data from a file or a database. You will learn more about the features provided by the .NET Framework for retrieving information from a database in Part V of this book, "Managing Data".

```
var customers = new[] {
    new { CustomerID = 1, FirstName = "Orlando", LastName = "Gee",
        CompanyName = "A Bike Store" },
    new { CustomerID = 2, FirstName = "Keith", LastName = "Harris",
        CompanyName = "Bike World" },
    new { CustomerID = 3, FirstName = "Donna", LastName = "Carreras",
        CompanyName = "A Bike Store" },
    new { CustomerID = 4, FirstName = "Janet", LastName = "Gates",
        CompanyName = "Fitness Hotel" },
    new { CustomerID = 5, FirstName = "Lucy", LastName = "Harrington",
        CompanyName = "Grand Industries" },
    new { CustomerID = 6, FirstName = "David", LastName = "Liu",
        CompanyName = "Bike World" },
    new { CustomerID = 7, FirstName = "Donald", LastName = "Blanton",
        CompanyName = "Grand Industries" },
    new { CustomerID = 8, FirstName = "Jackie", LastName = "Blackwell",
        CompanyName = "Fitness Hotel" },
    new { CustomerID = 9, FirstName = "Elsa", LastName = "Leavitt",
        CompanyName = "Grand Industries" },
    new { CustomerID = 10, FirstName = "Eric", LastName = "Lang",
        CompanyName = "Distant Inn" }
};

var addresses = new[] {
    new { CompanyName = "A Bike Store", City = "New York", Country = "United States"},
    new { CompanyName = "Bike World", City = "Chicago", Country = "United States"},
    new { CompanyName = "Fitness Hotel", City = "Ottawa", Country = "Canada"},
```

```
        new { CompanyName = "Grand Industries", City = "London",
            Country = "United Kingdom"},
        new { CompanyName = "Distant Inn", City = "Tetbury", Country = "United Kingdom"}
};
```

> **Note** The following sections—"Selecting Data," "Filtering Data," "Ordering, Grouping, and
> Aggregating Data," and "Joining Data"—show you the basic capabilities and syntax for querying
> data by using LINQ methods. The syntax can become a little complex at times, and you will see
> when you reach the section "Using Query Operators" that it is not actually necessary to remem-
> ber how the syntax all works. However, it is useful for you to at least take a look at the following
> sections so that you can fully appreciate how the query operators provided with C# perform
> their tasks.

Selecting Data

Suppose you want to display a list comprising the first name of each customer in the
customers array. You can achieve this task with the following code:

```
IEnumerable<string> customerFirstNames =
    customers.Select(cust => cust.FirstName);
foreach (string name in customerFirstNames)
{
    Console.WriteLine(name);
}
```

Although this block of code is quite short, it does a lot, and it requires a degree of
explanation, starting with the use of the *Select* method of the *customers* array.

The *Select* method enables you to retrieve specific data from the array—in this case, just the
value in the *FirstName* field of each item in the array. How does it work? The parameter to
the *Select* method is actually another method that takes a row from the *customers* array and
returns the selected data from that row. You can define your own custom method to perform
this task, but the simplest mechanism is to use a lambda expression to define an anonymous
method, as shown in the preceding example. There are three important things that you need
to understand at this point:

- The variable *cust* is the parameter passed in to the method. You can think of *cust* as an
  alias for each row in the *customers* array. The compiler deduces this from the fact that
  you are calling the *Select* method on the *customers* array. You can use any legal C#
  identifier in place of *cust*.

- The *Select* method does not actually retrieve the data at this time; it simply returns
  an enumerable object that will fetch the data identified by the *Select* method when
  you iterate over it later. We will return to this aspect of LINQ in the section "LINQ and
  Deferred Evaluation" later in this chapter.

- The *Select* method is not actually a method of the *Array* type. It is an extension method of the *Enumerable* class. The *Enumerable* class is located in the *System.Linq* namespace and provides a substantial set of static methods for querying objects that implement the generic *IEnumerable<T>* interface.

The preceding example uses the *Select* method of the *customers* array to generate an *IEnumerable<string>* object named *customerFirstNames*. (It is of type *IEnumerable<string>* because the *Select* method returns an enumerable collection of customer first names, which are strings.) The *foreach* statement iterates through this collection of strings, printing out the first name of each customer in the following sequence:

```
Orlando
Keith
Donna
Janet
Lucy
David
Donald
Jackie
Elsa
Eric
```

You can now display the first name of each customer. How do you fetch the first and last name of each customer? This task is slightly trickier. If you examine the definition of the *Enumerable.Select* method in the *System.Linq* namespace in the documentation supplied with Microsoft Visual Studio 2010, you will see that it looks like this:

```
public static IEnumerable<TResult> Select<TSource, TResult> (
        this IEnumerable<TSource> source,
        Func<TSource, TResult> selector
)
```

What this actually says is that *Select* is a generic method that takes two type parameters named *TSource* and *TResult*, as well as two ordinary parameters named *source* and *selector*. *TSource* is the type of the collection that you are generating an enumerable set of results for (*customer* objects in our example), and *TResult* is the type of the data in the enumerable set of results (*string* objects in our example). Remember that *Select* is an extension method, so the *source* parameter is actually a reference to the type being extended (a generic collection of *customer* objects that implements the *IEnumerable* interface in our example). The *selector* parameter specifies a generic method that identifies the fields to be retrieved. (*Func* is the name of a generic delegate type in the .NET Framework that you can use for encapsulating a generic method.) The method referred to by the *selector* parameter takes a *TSource* (in this case, *customer*) parameter and yields a *TResult* (in this case, *string*) object. The value returned by the *Select* method is an enumerable collection of *TResult* (again *string*) objects.

> **Note** If you need to review how extension methods work and the role of the first parameter to an extension method, revisit Chapter 12, "Working with Inheritance."

The important point to understand from the preceding paragraph is that the *Select* method returns an enumerable collection based on a single type. If you want the enumerator to return multiple items of data, such as the first and last name of each customer, you have at least two options:

- You can concatenate the first and last names together into a single string in the *Select* method, like this:

```
IEnumerable<string> customerFullName =
    customers.Select(cust => cust.FirstName + " " + cust.LastName);
```

- You can define a new type that wraps the first and last names and use the *Select* method to construct instances of this type, like this:

```
class Names
{
    public string FirstName{ get; set; }
    public string LastName{ get; set; }
}
...
IEnumerable<Names> customerName =
    customers.Select(cust => new Names
    {
        FirstName = cust.FirstName,
        LastName = cust.LastName
    } );
```

The second option is arguably preferable, but if this is the only use that your application makes of the *Names* type, you might prefer to use an anonymous type instead of defining a new type specifically for a single operation, like this:

```
var customerName =
    customers.Select(cust => new { FirstName = cust.FirstName, LastName = cust.LastName } );
```

Notice the use of the *var* keyword here to define the type of the enumerable collection. The type of objects in the collection is anonymous, so you do not know the specific type for the objects in the collection.

Filtering Data

The *Select* method enables you to specify, or *project*, the fields that you want to include in the enumerable collection. However, you might also want to restrict the rows that the enumerable collection contains. For example, suppose you want to list the names of all companies in the *addresses* array that are located in the United States only. To do this, you can use the *Where* method, as follows:

```
IEnumerable<string> usCompanies =
    addresses.Where(addr => String.Equals(addr.Country, "United States"))
            .Select(usComp => usComp.CompanyName);

foreach (string name in usCompanies)
{
    Console.WriteLine(name);
}
```

Syntactically, the *Where* method is similar to *Select*. It expects a parameter that defines a method that filters the data according to whatever criteria you specify. This example makes use of another lambda expression. The type *addr* is an alias for a row in the *addresses* array, and the lambda expression returns all rows where the *Country* field matches the string *"United States"*. The *Where* method returns an enumerable collection of rows containing every field from the original collection. The *Select* method is then applied to these rows to project only the *CompanyName* field from this enumerable collection to return another enumerable collection of *string* objects. (The type *usComp* is an alias for the type of each row in the enumerable collection returned by the *Where* method.) The type of the result of this complete expression is therefore *IEnumerable<string>*. It is important to understand this sequence of operations—the *Where* method is applied first to filter the rows, followed by the *Select* method to specify the fields. The *foreach* statement that iterates through this collection displays the following companies:

```
A Bike Store
Bike World
```

Ordering, Grouping, and Aggregating Data

If you are familiar with SQL, you are aware that SQL enables you to perform a wide variety of relational operations besides simple projection and filtering. For example, you can specify that you want data to be returned in a specific order, you can group the rows returned according to one or more key fields, and you can calculate summary values based on the rows in each group. LINQ provides the same functionality.

To retrieve data in a particular order, you can use the *OrderBy* method. Like the *Select* and *Where* methods, *OrderBy* expects a method as its argument. This method identifies the expressions that you want to use to sort the data. For example, you can display the names of each company in the *addresses* array in ascending order, like this:

```
IEnumerable<string> companyNames =
    addresses.OrderBy(addr => addr.CompanyName).Select(comp => comp.CompanyName);

foreach (string name in companyNames)
{
    Console.WriteLine(name);
}
```

This block of code displays the companies in the addresses table in alphabetical order:

```
A Bike Store
Bike World
Distant Inn
Fitness Hotel
Grand Industries
```

If you want to enumerate the data in descending order, you can use the *OrderByDescending* method instead. If you want to order by more than one key value, you can use the *ThenBy* or *ThenByDescending* method after *OrderBy* or *OrderByDescending*.

To group data according to common values in one or more fields, you can use the *GroupBy* method. The next example shows how to group the companies in the *addresses* array by country:

```
var companiesGroupedByCountry =
    addresses.GroupBy(addrs => addrs.Country);

foreach (var companiesPerCountry in companiesGroupedByCountry)
{
    Console.WriteLine("Country: {0}\t{1} companies",
            companiesPerCountry.Key, companiesPerCountry.Count());
    foreach (var companies in companiesPerCountry)
    {
        Console.WriteLine("\t{0}", companies.CompanyName);
    }
}
```

By now, you should recognize the pattern! The *GroupBy* method expects a method that specifies the fields to group the data by. There are some subtle differences between the *GroupBy* method and the other methods that you have seen so far, though.

The main point of interest is that you don't need to use the *Select* method to project the fields to the result. The enumerable set returned by *GroupBy* contains all the fields in the original source collection, but the rows are ordered into a set of enumerable collections based on the field identified by the method specified by *GroupBy*. In other words, the result of the *GroupBy* method is an enumerable set of groups, each of which is an enumerable set of rows. In the example just shown, the enumerable set *companiesGroupedByCountry* is a set of countries. The items in this set are themselves enumerable collections containing the companies for each country in turn. The code that displays the companies in each country uses a *foreach* loop to iterate through the *companiesGroupedByCountry* set to yield and display each country in turn, and then it uses a nested *foreach* loop to iterate through the set of companies in each country. Notice in the outer *foreach* loop that you can access the value you are grouping by using the *Key* field of each item, and you can also calculate summary data for each group by using methods such as *Count, Max, Min*, and many others. The output generated by the example code looks like this:

```
Country: United States    2 companies
        A Bike Store
        Bike World
Country: Canada 1 companies
        Fitness Hotel
Country: United Kingdom   2 companies
        Grand Industries
        Distant Inn
```

You can use many of the summary methods such as *Count, Max*, and *Min* directly over the results of the *Select* method. If you want to know how many companies there are in the *addresses* array, you can use a block of code such as this:

```
int numberOfCompanies = addresses.Select(addr => addr.CompanyName).Count();
Console.WriteLine("Number of companies: {0}", numberOfCompanies);
```

Notice that the result of these methods is a single scalar value rather than an enumerable collection. The output from this block of code looks like this:

```
Number of companies: 5
```

I should utter a word of caution at this point. These summary methods do not distinguish between rows in the underlying set that contain duplicate values in the fields you are projecting. What this means is that, strictly speaking, the preceding example shows you only how many rows in the *addresses* array contain a value in the *CompanyName* field. If you wanted to find out how many different countries are mentioned in this table, you might be tempted to try this:

```
int numberOfCountries = addresses.Select(addr => addr.Country).Count();
Console.WriteLine("Number of countries: {0}", numberOfCountries);
```

The output looks like this:

```
Number of countries: 5
```

In fact, there are only three different countries in the *addresses* array; it just so happens that United States and United Kingdom both occur twice. You can eliminate duplicates from the calculation by using the *Distinct* method, like this:

```
int numberOfCountries =
    addresses.Select(addr => addr.Country).Distinct().Count();
Console.WriteLine("Number of countries: {0}", numberOfCountries);
```

The *Console.WriteLine* statement will now output the expected result:

```
Number of countries: 3
```

Joining Data

Just like SQL, LINQ enables you to join multiple sets of data together over one or more common key fields. The following example shows how to display the first and last names of each customer, together with the names of the countries where they are located:

```
var companiesAndCustomers = customers
  .Select(c => new { c.FirstName, c.LastName, c.CompanyName })
  .Join(addresses, custs => custs.CompanyName, addrs => addrs.CompanyName,
  (custs, addrs) => new {custs.FirstName, custs.LastName, addrs.Country });

foreach (var row in companiesAndCustomers)
{
    Console.WriteLine(row);
}
```

The customers' first and last names are available in the *customers* array, but the country for each company that customers work for is stored in the *addresses* array. The common key between the *customers* array and the *addresses* array is the company name. The *Select* method specifies the fields of interest in the *customers* array (*FirstName* and *LastName*), together with the field containing the common key (*CompanyName*). You use the *Join* method to join the data identified by the *Select* method with another enumerable collection. The parameters to the *Join* method are as follows:

- The enumerable collection with which to join

- A method that identifies the common key fields from the data identified by the *Select* method

- A method that identifies the common key fields on which to join the selected data

- A method that specifies the columns you require in the enumerable result set returned by the *Join* method

In this example, the *Join* method joins the enumerable collection containing the *FirstName*, *LastName*, and *CompanyName* fields from the *customers* array with the rows in the *addresses* array. The two sets of data are joined where the value in the *CompanyName* field in the *customers* array matches the value in the *CompanyName* field in the *addresses* array. The result set comprises rows containing the *FirstName* and *LastName* fields from the *customers* array with the *Country* field from the *addresses* array. The code that outputs the data from the *companiesAndCustomers* collection displays the following information:

```
{ FirstName = Orlando, LastName = Gee, Country = United States }
{ FirstName = Keith, LastName = Harris, Country = United States }
{ FirstName = Donna, LastName = Carreras, Country = United States }
{ FirstName = Janet, LastName = Gates, Country = Canada }
{ FirstName = Lucy, LastName = Harrington, Country = United Kingdom }
{ FirstName = David, LastName = Liu, Country = United States }
{ FirstName = Donald, LastName = Blanton, Country = United Kingdom }
```

```
{ FirstName = Jackie, LastName = Blackwell, Country = Canada }
{ FirstName = Elsa, LastName = Leavitt, Country = United Kingdom }
{ FirstName = Eric, LastName = Lang, Country = United Kingdom }
```

> **Note** Remember that collections in memory are not the same as tables in a relational database and that the data they contain is not subject to the same data integrity constraints. In a relational database, it could be acceptable to assume that every customer had a corresponding company and that each company had its own unique address. Collections do not enforce the same level of data integrity, meaning that you could quite easily have a customer referencing a company that does not exist in the *addresses* array, and you might even have the same company occurring more than once in the *addresses* array. In these situations, the results that you obtain might be accurate but unexpected. Join operations work best when you fully understand the relationships between the data you are joining.

Using Query Operators

The preceding sections have shown you many of the features available for querying in-memory data by using the extension methods for the *Enumerable* class defined in the *System.Linq* namespace. The syntax makes use of several advanced C# language features, and the resultant code can sometimes be quite hard to understand and maintain. To relieve you of some of this burden, the designers of C# added query operators to the language to enable you to employ LINQ features by using a syntax more akin to SQL.

As you saw in the examples shown earlier in this chapter, you can retrieve the first name for each customer like this:

```
IEnumerable<string> customerFirstNames =
    customers.Select(cust => cust.FirstName);
```

You can rephrase this statement by using the *from* and *select* query operators, like this:

```
var customerFirstNames = from cust in customers
                         select cust.FirstName;
```

At compile time, the C# compiler resolves this expression into the corresponding *Select* method. The *from* operator defines an alias for the source collection, and the *select* operator specifies the fields to retrieve by using this alias. The result is an enumerable collection of customer first names. If you are familiar with SQL, notice that the *from* operator occurs before the *select* operator.

Continuing in the same vein, to retrieve the first and last name for each customer, you can use the following statement. (You might want to refer to the earlier example of the same statement based on the *Select* extension method.)

```
var customerNames = from cust in customers
                    select new { cust.FirstName, cust.LastName };
```

You use the *where* operator to filter data. The following example shows how to return the names of the companies based in the United States from the *addresses* array:

```
var usCompanies = from a in addresses
                  where String.Equals(a.Country, "United States")
                  select a.CompanyName;
```

To order data, use the *orderby* operator, like this:

```
var companyNames = from a in addresses
                   orderby a.CompanyName
                   select a.CompanyName;
```

You can group data by using the *group* operator:

```
var companiesGroupedByCountry = from a in addresses
                                group a by a.Country;
```

Notice that, as with the earlier example showing how to group data, you do not provide the *select* operator, and you can iterate through the results by using exactly the same code as the earlier example, like this:

```
foreach (var companiesPerCountry in companiesGroupedByCountry)
{
    Console.WriteLine("Country: {0}\t{1} companies",
            companiesPerCountry.Key, companiesPerCountry.Count());
    foreach (var companies in companiesPerCountry)
    {
        Console.WriteLine("\t{0}", companies.CompanyName);
    }
}
```

You can invoke the summary functions, such as *Count*, over the collection returned by an enumerable collection, like this:

```
int numberOfCompanies = (from a in addresses
                         select a.CompanyName).Count();
```

Notice that you wrap the expression in parentheses. If you want to ignore duplicate values, use the *Distinct* method, like this:

```
int numberOfCountries = (from a in addresses
                         select a.Country).Distinct().Count();
```

Tip In many cases, you probably want to count just the number of rows in a collection rather than the number of values in a field across all the rows in the collection. In this case, you can invoke the *Count* method directly over the original collection, like this:

```
int numberOfCompanies = addresses.Count();
```

You can use the *join* operator to combine two collections across a common key. The following example shows the query returning customers and addresses over the *CompanyName* column in each collection, this time rephrased using the *join* operator. You use the *on* clause with the *equals* operator to specify how the two collections are related. (LINQ currently supports equi-joins only.)

```
var citiesAndCustomers = from a in addresses
                         join c in customers
                         on a.CompanyName equals c.CompanyName
                         select new { c.FirstName, c.LastName, a.Country };
```

> **Note** In contrast with SQL, the order of the expressions in the *on* clause of a LINQ expression is important. You must place the item you are joining from (referencing the data in the collection in the *from* clause) to the left of the *equals* operator and the item you are joining with (referencing the data in the collection in the *join* clause) to the right.

LINQ provides a large number of other methods for summarizing information, joining, grouping, and searching through data; this section has covered just the most common features. For example, LINQ provides the *Intersect* and *Union* methods, which you can use to perform setwide operations. It also provides methods such as *Any* and *All* that you can use to determine whether at least one item in a collection or every item in a collection matches a specified predicate. You can partition the values in an enumerable collection by using the *Take* and *Skip* methods. For more information, see the documentation provided with Visual Studio 2010.

Querying Data in *Tree<TItem>* Objects

The examples you've seen so far in this chapter have shown how to query the data in an array. You can use exactly the same techniques for any collection class that implements the generic *IEnumerable<T>* interface. In the following exercise, you will define a new class for modeling employees for a company. You will create a *BinaryTree* object containing a collection of *Employee* objects, and then you will use LINQ to query this information. You will initially call the LINQ extension methods directly, but then you will modify your code to use query operators.

Retrieve data from a *BinaryTree* by using the extension methods

1. Start Visual Studio 2010 if it is not already running.

2. Open the *QueryBinaryTree* solution, located in the \Microsoft Press\Visual CSharp Step By Step\Chapter 20\QueryBinaryTree folder in your Documents folder. The project contains the Program.cs file, which defines the *Program* class with the *Main* and *DoWork* methods that you saw in previous exercises.

3. In *Solution Explorer*, right-click the *QueryBinaryTree* project, point to *Add*, and then click *Class*. In the *Add New Item—Query BinaryTree* dialog box, type **Employee.cs** in the *Name* box and then click *Add*.

4. Add the automatic properties shown here in bold to the *Employee* class:

```
class Employee
{
    public string FirstName { get; set; }
    public string LastName { get; set; }
    public string Department { get; set; }
    public int Id { get; set; }
}
```

5. Add the *ToString* method shown here in bold to the *Employee* class. Classes in the .NET Framework use this method when converting the object to a string representation, such as when displaying it by using the *Console.WriteLine* statement.

```
class  Employee
{
    ...
    public override string ToString()
    {
        return String.Format("Id: {0}, Name: {1} {2}, Dept: {3}",
                            this.Id, this.FirstName, this.LastName,
                            this.Department);
    }
}
```

6. Modify the definition of the *Employee* class in the Employee.cs file to implement the *IComparable<Employee>* interface, as shown here:

```
class Employee : IComparable<Employee>
{
}
```

This step is necessary because the *BinaryTree* class specifies that its elements must be "comparable."

7. Right-click the *IComparable<Employee>* interface in the class definition, point to *Implement Interface*, and then click *Implement Interface Explicitly*.

This action generates a default implementation of the *CompareTo* method. Remember that the *BinaryTree* class calls this method when it needs to compare elements when inserting them into the tree.

8. Replace the body of the *CompareTo* method with the code shown here in bold. This implementation of the *CompareTo* method compares *Employee* objects based on the value of the *Id* field.

```
int IComparable<Employee>.CompareTo(Employee other)
{
    if (other == null)
        return 1;
```

```
    if (this.Id > other.Id)
        return 1;

    if (this.Id < other.Id)
        return -1;

    return 0;
}
```

> **Note** For a description of the *IComparable* interface, refer to Chapter 18, "Introducing Generics."

9. In *Solution Explorer*, right-click the *QueryBinaryTree* solution, point to *Add*, and then click *Existing Project*. In the *Add Existing Project* dialog box, move to the folder Microsoft Press\Visual CSharp Step By Step\Chapter 20\BinaryTree in your Documents folder, click the *BinaryTree* project, and then click *Open*.

   The *BinaryTree* project contains a copy of the enumerable *BinaryTree* class that you implemented in Chapter 19.

10. In *Solution Explorer*, right-click the *QueryBinaryTree* project and then click *Add Reference*. In the *Add Reference* dialog box, click the *Projects* tab, select the *BinaryTree* project, and then click *OK*.

11. Display the Program.cs file for the QueryBinaryTree project in the *Code and Text Editor* window, and verify that the list of *using* statements at the top of the file includes the following line of code:

    ```
    using System.Linq;
    ```

12. Add the following *using* statement to the list at the top of the Program.cs file to bring the *BinaryTree* namespace into scope:

    ```
    using BinaryTree;
    ```

13. In the *DoWork* method in the *Program* class, add the following statements shown in bold type to construct and populate an instance of the *BinaryTree* class:

    ```
    static void DoWork()
    {
      Tree<Employee> empTree = new Tree<Employee>(new Employee
        { Id = 1, FirstName = "Janet", LastName = "Gates", Department = "IT"});
      empTree.Insert(new Employee
        { Id = 2, FirstName = "Orlando", LastName = "Gee", Department = "Marketing"});
      empTree.Insert(new Employee
        { Id = 4, FirstName = "Keith", LastName = "Harris", Department = "IT" });
      empTree.Insert(new Employee
        { Id = 6, FirstName = "Lucy", LastName = "Harrington", Department = "Sales" });
    ```

```
empTree.Insert(new Employee
  { Id = 3, FirstName = "Eric", LastName = "Lang", Department = "Sales" });
empTree.Insert(new Employee
  { Id = 5, FirstName = "David", LastName = "Liu", Department = "Marketing" });
}
```

14. Add the following statements shown in bold to the end of the *DoWork* method. This code invokes the *Select* method to list the departments found in the binary tree.

```
static void DoWork()
{
    ...
    Console.WriteLine("List of departments");
    var depts = empTree.Select(d => d.Department);

    foreach (var dept in depts)
    {
        Console.WriteLine("Department: {0}", dept);
    }
}
```

15. On the *Debug* menu, click *Start Without Debugging*.

The application should output the following list of departments:

```
List of departments
Department: IT
Department: Marketing
Department: Sales
Department: IT
Department: Marketing
Department: Sales
```

Each department occurs twice because there are two employees in each department. The order of the departments is determined by the *CompareTo* method of the *Employee* class, which uses the *Id* property of each employee to sort the data. The first department is for the employee with the *Id* value 1, the second department is for the employee with the *Id* value 2, and so on.

16. Press Enter to return to Visual Studio 2010.

17. Modify the statement that creates the enumerable collection of departments as shown here in bold:

```
var depts = empTree.Select(d => d.Department).Distinct();
```

The *Distinct* method removes duplicate rows from the enumerable collection.

18. On the *Debug* menu, click *Start Without Debugging*.

Verify that the application now displays each department only once, like this:

```
List of departments
Department: IT
Department: Marketing
Department: Sales
```

19. Press Enter to return to Visual Studio 2010.

20. Add the following statements to the end of the *DoWork* method. This block of code uses the *Where* method to filter the employees and return only those in the IT department. The *Select* method returns the entire row rather than projecting specific columns.

```
Console.WriteLine("\nEmployees in the IT department");
var ITEmployees =
    empTree.Where(e => String.Equals(e.Department, "IT"))
    .Select(emp => emp);

foreach (var emp in ITEmployees)
{
    Console.WriteLine(emp);
}
```

21. Add the code shown next to the end of the *DoWork* method, after the code from the preceding step. This code uses the *GroupBy* method to group the employees found in the binary tree by department. The outer *foreach* statement iterates through each group, displaying the name of the department. The inner *foreach* statement displays the names of the employees in each department.

```
Console.WriteLine("\nAll employees grouped by department");
var employeesByDept = empTree.GroupBy(e => e.Department);

foreach (var dept in employeesByDept)
{
    Console.WriteLine("Department: {0}", dept.Key);
    foreach (var emp in dept)
    {
        Console.WriteLine("\t{0} {1}", emp.FirstName, emp.LastName);
    }
}
```

22. On the *Debug* menu, click *Start Without Debugging*. Verify that the output of the application looks like this:

```
List of departments
Department: IT
Department: Marketing
Department: Sales

Employees in the IT department
Id: 1, Name: Janet Gates, Dept: IT
Id: 4, Name: Keith Harris, Dept: IT

All employees grouped by department
Department: IT
        Janet Gates
        Keith Harris
Department: Marketing
        Orlando Gee
        David Liu
```

```
Department: Sales
        Eric Lang
        Lucy Harrington
```

23. Press Enter to return to Visual Studio 2010.

Retrieve data from a *BinaryTree* by using query operators

1. In the *DoWork* method, comment out the statement that generates the enumerable collection of departments, and replace it with the following statement shown in bold, based on the *from* and *select* query operators:

```
//var depts = empTree.Select(d => d.Department).Distinct();
var depts = (from d in empTree
             select d.Department).Distinct();
```

2. Comment out the statement that generates the enumerable collection of employees in the IT department, and replace it with the following code shown in bold:

```
//var ITEmployees =
//    empTree.Where(e => String.Equals(e.Department, "IT"))
//    .Select(emp => emp);
var ITEmployees = from e in empTree
                  where String.Equals(e.Department, "IT")
                  select e;
```

3. Comment out the statement that generates the enumerable collection grouping employees by department, and replace it with the statement shown here in bold:

```
//var employeesByDept = empTree.GroupBy(e => e.Department);
var employeesByDept = from e in empTree
                      group e by e.Department;
```

4. On the *Debug* menu, click *Start Without Debugging*. Verify that the output of the application is the same as before.

5. Press Enter to return to Visual Studio 2010.

LINQ and Deferred Evaluation

When you use LINQ to define an enumerable collection, either by using the LINQ extension methods or by using query operators, you should remember that the application does not actually build the collection at the time that the LINQ extension method is executed; the collection is enumerated only when you iterate over the collection. This means that the data in the original collection can change between executing a LINQ query and retrieving the data that the query identifies; you will always fetch the most up-to-date data. For example, the following query (which you saw earlier) defines an enumerable collection of U.S. companies:

```
var usCompanies = from a in addresses
                  where String.Equals(a.Country, "United States")
                  select a.CompanyName;
```

The data in the *addresses* array is not retrieved, and any conditions specified in the *Where* filter are not evaluated until you iterate through the *usCompanies* collection:

```
foreach (string name in usCompanies)
{
    Console.WriteLine(name);
}
```

If you modify the data in the *addresses* array between defining the *usCompanies* collection and iterating through the collection (for example, if you add a new company based in the United States), you will see this new data. This strategy is referred to as *deferred evaluation*.

You can force evaluation of a LINQ query and generate a static, cached collection. This collection is a copy of the original data and will not change if the data in the collection changes. LINQ provides the *ToList* method to build a static *List* object containing a cached copy of the data. You use it like this:

```
var usCompanies = from a in addresses.ToList()
                  where String.Equals(a.Country, "United States")
                  select a.CompanyName;
```

This time, the list of companies is fixed when you define the query. If you add more U.S. companies to the *addresses* array, you will not see them when you iterate through the *usCompanies* collection. LINQ also provides the *ToArray* method that stores the cached collection as an array.

In the final exercise in this chapter, you will compare the effects of using deferred evaluation of a LINQ query to generating a cached collection.

Examine the effects of deferred and cached evaluation of a LINQ query

1. Return to Visual Studio 2010, displaying the *QueryBinaryTree* project, and edit the Program.cs file.

2. Comment out the contents of the *DoWork* method apart from the statements that construct the *empTree* binary tree, as shown here:

```
static void DoWork()
{
    Tree<Employee> empTree = new Tree<Employee>(new Employee
        { Id = 1, FirstName = "Janet", LastName = "Gates", Department = "IT" });
    empTree.Insert(new Employee
        { Id = 2, FirstName = "Orlando", LastName = "Gee", Department = "Marketing" });
    empTree.Insert(new Employee
        { Id = 4, FirstName = "Keith", LastName = "Harris", Department = "IT" });
    empTree.Insert(new Employee
        { Id = 6, FirstName = "Lucy", LastName = "Harrington", Department = "Sales" });
    empTree.Insert(new Employee
        { Id = 3, FirstName = "Eric", LastName = "Lang", Department = "Sales" });
```

```
empTree.Insert(new Employee
    { Id = 5, FirstName = "David", LastName = "Liu", Department = "Marketing" });

    // comment out the rest of the method
    ...
}
```

> **Tip** You can comment out a block of code by selecting the entire block in the *Code and Text Editor* window and then clicking the *Comment Out The Selected Lines* button on the toolbar or by pressing Ctrl+E and then pressing C.

3. Add the following statements to the *DoWork* method, after building the *empTree* binary tree:

```
Console.WriteLine("All employees");
var allEmployees = from e in empTree
                   select e;

foreach (var emp in allEmployees)
{
    Console.WriteLine(emp);
}
```

This code generates an enumerable collection of employees named *allEmployees* and then iterates through this collection, displaying the details of each employee.

4. Add the following code immediately after the statements you typed in the preceding step:

```
empTree.Insert(new Employee
                {
                    Id = 7,
                    FirstName = "Donald",
                    LastName = "Blanton",
                    Department = "IT"
                });
Console.WriteLine("\nEmployee added");

Console.WriteLine("All employees");
foreach (var emp in allEmployees)
{
    Console.WriteLine(emp);
}
```

These statements add a new employee to the *empTree* tree and then iterate through the *allEmployees* collection again.

5. On the *Debug* menu, click *Start Without Debugging*. Verify that the output of the application looks like this:

```
All employees
Id: 1, Name: Janet Gates, Dept: IT
```

```
Id: 2, Name: Orlando Gee, Dept: Marketing
Id: 3, Name: Eric Lang, Dept: Sales
Id: 4, Name: Keith Harris, Dept: IT
Id: 5, Name: David Liu, Dept: Marketing
Id: 6, Name: Lucy Harrington, Dept: Sales

Employee added
All employees
Id: 1, Name: Janet Gates, Dept: IT
Id: 2, Name: Orlando Gee, Dept: Marketing
Id: 3, Name: Eric Lang, Dept: Sales
Id: 4, Name: Keith Harris, Dept: IT
Id: 5, Name: David Liu, Dept: Marketing
Id: 6, Name: Lucy Harrington, Dept: Sales
Id: 7, Name: Donald Blanton, Dept: IT
```

Notice that the second time the application iterates through the *allEmployees* collection, the list displayed includes Donald Blanton, even though this employee was added only after the *allEmployees* collection was defined.

6. Press Enter to return to Visual Studio 2010.

7. In the *DoWork* method, change the statement that generates the *allEmployees* collection to identify and cache the data immediately, as shown here in bold:

```
var allEmployees = from e in empTree.ToList<Employee>()
                   select e;
```

LINQ provides generic and nongeneric versions of the *ToList* and *ToArray* methods. If possible, it is better to use the generic versions of these methods to ensure the type safety of the result. The data returned by the *select* operator is an *Employee* object, and the code shown in this step generates *allEmployees* as a generic *List<Employee>* collection. If you specify the nongeneric *ToList* method, the *allEmployees* collection will be a *List* of *object* types.

8. On the *Debug* menu, click *Start Without Debugging*. Verify that the output of the application looks like this:

```
All employees
Id: 1, Name: Janet Gates, Dept: IT
Id: 2, Name: Orlando Gee, Dept: Marketing
Id: 3, Name: Eric Lang, Dept: Sales
Id: 4, Name: Keith Harris, Dept: IT
Id: 5, Name: David Liu, Dept: Marketing
Id: 6, Name: Lucy Harrington, Dept: Sales

Employee added
All employees
Id: 1, Name: Janet Gates, Dept: IT
Id: 2, Name: Orlando Gee, Dept: Marketing
Id: 3, Name: Eric Lang, Dept: Sales
Id: 4, Name: Keith Harris, Dept: IT
Id: 5, Name: David Liu, Dept: Marketing
Id: 6, Name: Lucy Harrington, Dept: Sales
```

Notice that this time, the second time the application iterates through the *allEmployees* collection, the list displayed does not include Donald Blanton. This is because the query is evaluated and the results are cached before Donald Blanton is added to the *empTree* binary tree.

9. Press Enter to return to Visual Studio 2010.

In this chapter, you learned how LINQ uses the *IEnumerable<T>* interface and extension methods to provide a mechanism for querying data. You also saw how these features support the query expression syntax in C#.

- If you want to continue to the next chapter

  Keep Visual Studio 2010 running, and turn to Chapter 21.

- If you want to exit Visual Studio 2010 now

  On the *File* menu, click *Exit*. If you see a *Save* dialog box, click *Yes* and save the project.

Chapter 20 Quick Reference

To	Do this
Project specified fields from an enumerable collection	Use the *Select* method, and specify a lambda expression that identifies the fields to project. For example:
	`var customerFirstNames = customers.Select(cust => cust.FirstName);`
	Or use the *from* and *select* query operators. For example:

	`var customerFirstNames =`
	`    from cust in customers`
	`    select cust.FirstName;`

Filter rows from an enumerable collection	Use the *Where* method, and specify a lambda expression containing the criteria that rows should match. For example:

	`var usCompanies =`
	`    addresses.Where(addr =>`
	`        String.Equals(addr.Country, "United States"))`
	`        .Select(usComp => usComp.CompanyName);`

	Or use the *where* query operator. For example:

	`var usCompanies =`
	`    from a in addresses`
	`    where String.Equals(a.Country, "United States")`
	`    select a.CompanyName;`

To	Do this

Enumerate data in a specific order	Use the *OrderBy* method, and specify a lambda expression identifying the field to use to order rows. For example:
	
	```\nvar companyNames =\n addresses.OrderBy(addr => addr.CompanyName)\n .Select(comp => comp.CompanyName);\n```
	
	Or use the *orderby* query operator. For example:
	
	```\nvar companyNames =\n from a in addresses\n orderby a.CompanyName\n select a.CompanyName;\n```

Group data by the values in a field	Use the *GroupBy* method, and specify a lambda expression identifying the field to use to group rows. For example:
	
	```\nvar companiesGroupedByCountry =\n addresses.GroupBy(addrs => addrs.Country);\n```
	
	Or use the *group by* query operator. For example:
	
	```\nvar companiesGroupedByCountry =\n from a in addresses\n group a by a.Country;\n```

Join data held in two different collections	Use the *Join* method specifying the collection to join with, the join criteria, and the fields for the result. For example:
	
	```\nvar citiesAndCustomers =\n customers\n .Select(c => new { c.FirstName, c.LastName, c.CompanyName }).\n Join(addresses, custs => custs.CompanyName,\n addrs => addrs.CompanyName,\n (custs, addrs) => new {custs.FirstName, custs.LastName,\n addrs.Country });\n```
	
	Or use the *join* query operator. For example:
	
	```\nvar citiesAndCustomers =\n from a in addresses\n join c in customers\n on a.CompanyName equals c.CompanyName\n select new { c.FirstName, c.LastName, a.Country };\n```

Force immediate generation of the results for a LINQ query	Use the *ToList* or *ToArray* method to generate a list or an array containing the results. For example: ```\nvar allEmployees =\n from e in empTree.ToList<Employee>()\n select e;\n```

Chapter 21
Operator Overloading

After completing this chapter, you will be able to:

■ Implement binary operators for your own types.

■ Implement unary operators for your own types.

■ Write increment and decrement operators for your own types.

■ Understand the need to implement some operators as pairs.

■ Implement implicit conversion operators for your own types.

■ Implement explicit conversion operators for your own types.

You have made a great deal of use of the standard operator symbols (such as + and –) to perform standard operations (such as addition and subtraction) on types (such as *int* and *double*). Many of the built-in types come with their own predefined behaviors for each operator. You can also define how operators should behave for your own structures and classes, which is the subject of this chapter.

Understanding Operators

It is worth recapping some of the fundamental aspects of operators before delving into the details of how they work and how you can overload them. In summary:

■ You use operators to combine operands together into expressions. Each operator has its own semantics, dependent on the type it works with. For example, the + operator means "add" when used with numeric types or "concatenate" when used with strings.

■ Each operator has a *precedence*. For example, the * operator has a higher precedence than the + operator. This means that the expression *a + b * c* is the same as *a + (b * c)*.

■ Each operator also has an *associativity* to define whether the operator evaluates from left to right or from right to left. For example, the = operator is right-associative (it evaluates from right to left), so *a = b = c* is the same as *a = (b = c)*.

■ A *unary operator* is an operator that has just one operand. For example, the increment operator (++) is a unary operator.

■ A *binary operator* is an operator that has two operands. For example, the multiplication operator (*) is a binary operator.

Operator Constraints

You have seen throughout this book that C# enables you to overload methods when defining your own types. C# also allows you to overload many of the existing operator symbols for your own types, although the syntax is slightly different. When you do this, the operators you implement automatically fall into a well-defined framework with the following rules:

- You cannot change the precedence and associativity of an operator. The precedence and associativity are based on the operator symbol (for example, +) and not on the type (for example, *int*) on which the operator symbol is being used. Hence, the expression *a + b * c* is *always* the same as *a + (b * c)*, regardless of the types of *a*, *b*, and *c*.

- You cannot change the multiplicity (the number of operands) of an operator. For example, * (the symbol for multiplication), is a binary operator. If you declare a * operator for your own type, it must be a binary operator.

- You cannot invent new operator symbols. For example, you can't create a new operator symbol, such as ** for raising one number to the power of another number. You'd have to create a method for that.

- You can't change the meaning of operators when applied to built-in types. For example, the expression *1 + 2* has a predefined meaning, and you're not allowed to override this meaning. If you could do this, things would be too complicated!

- There are some operator symbols that you can't overload. For example, you can't overload the dot (.) operator, which indicates access to a class member. Again, if you could do this, it would lead to unnecessary complexity.

> **Tip** You can use indexers to simulate *[ ]* as an operator. Similarly, you can use properties to simulate assignment (=) as an operator, and you can use delegates to simulate a function call as an operator.

Overloaded Operators

To define your own operator behavior, you must overload a selected operator. You use method-like syntax with a return type and parameters, but the name of the method is the keyword *operator* together with the operator symbol you are declaring. For example, the following code shows a user-defined structure named *Hour* that defines a binary + operator to add together two instances of *Hour*:

```
struct Hour
{
    public Hour(int initialValue)
    {
        this.value = initialValue;
```

```
    }

    public static Hour operator +(Hour lhs, Hour rhs)
    {
        return new Hour(lhs.value + rhs.value);
    }
    ...
    private int value;
}
```

Notice the following:

- The operator is *public*. All operators *must* be public.

- The operator is *static*. All operators *must* be static. Operators are never polymorphic and cannot use the *virtual*, *abstract*, *override*, or *sealed* modifier.

- A binary operator (such as the + operator, shown earlier) has two explicit arguments, and a unary operator has one explicit argument. (C++ programmers should note that operators never have a hidden *this* parameter.)

> **Tip** When declaring highly stylized functionality (such as operators), it is useful to adopt a naming convention for the parameters. For example, developers often use *lhs* and *rhs* (acronyms for left-hand side and right-hand side, respectively) for binary operators.

When you use the + operator on two expressions of type *Hour*, the C# compiler automatically converts your code to a call to your *operator+* method. The C# compiler converts the code

```
Hour Example(Hour a, Hour b)
{
    return a + b;
}
```

to this:

```
Hour Example(Hour a, Hour b)
{
    return Hour.operator +(a,b); // pseudocode
}
```

Note, however, that this syntax is pseudocode and not valid C#. You can use a binary operator only in its standard infix notation (with the symbol between the operands).

There is one final rule that you must follow when declaring an operator (otherwise, your code will not compile): at least one of the parameters must always be of the containing type. In the preceding *operator+* example for the *Hour* class, one of the parameters, *a* or *b*, must be an *Hour* object. In this example, both parameters are *Hour* objects. However, there could be times when you want to define additional implementations of *operator+* that add, for example, an integer (a number of hours) to an *Hour* object—the first parameter could be *Hour*, and the second parameter could be the integer. This rule makes it easier for the compiler to know where to look when trying to resolve an operator invocation, and it also ensures that you can't change the meaning of the built-in operators.

Creating Symmetric Operators

In the preceding section, you saw how to declare a binary + operator to add together two instances of type *Hour*. The *Hour* structure also has a constructor that creates an *Hour* from an *int*. This means that you can add together an *Hour* and an *int*—you just have to first use the *Hour* constructor to convert the *int* to an *Hour*. For example:

```
Hour a = ...;
int b = ...;
Hour sum = a + new Hour(b);
```

This is certainly valid code, but it is not as clear or concise as adding together an *Hour* and an *int* directly, like this:

```
Hour a = ...;
int b = ...;
Hour sum = a + b;
```

To make the expression *(a + b)* valid, you must specify what it means to add together an *Hour* (*a*, on the left) and an *int* (*b*, on the right). In other words, you must declare a binary + operator whose first parameter is an *Hour* and whose second parameter is an *int*. The following code shows the recommended approach:

```
struct Hour
{
    public Hour(int initialValue)
    {
        this.value = initialValue;
    }
    ...
    public static Hour operator +(Hour lhs, Hour rhs)
    {
        return new Hour(lhs.value + rhs.value);
    }

    public static Hour operator +(Hour lhs, int rhs)
    {
        return lhs + new Hour(rhs);
    }
    ...
    private int value;
}
```

Notice that all the second version of the operator does is construct an *Hour* from its *int* argument and then call the first version. In this way, the real logic behind the operator is held in a single place. The point is that the extra *operator +* simply makes existing function-ality easier to use. Also, notice that you should not provide many different versions of this operator, each with a different second parameter type—instead, cater to the common and meaningful cases only, and let the user of the class take any additional steps if an unusual case is required.

This *operator+* declares how to add together an *Hour* as the left-hand operand and an *int* as the right-hand operand. It does not declare how to add together an *int* as the left-hand operand and an *Hour* as the right-hand operand:

```
int a = ...;
Hour b = ...;
Hour sum = a + b; // compile-time error
```

This is counterintuitive. If you can write the expression *a + b*, you expect to also be able to write *b + a*. Therefore, you should provide another overload of *operator+*:

```
struct Hour
{
    public Hour(int initialValue)
    {
        this.value = initialValue;
    }
    ...
    public static Hour operator +(Hour lhs, int rhs)
    {
        return lhs + new Hour(rhs);
    }

    public static Hour operator +(int lhs, Hour rhs)
    {
        return new Hour(lhs) + rhs;
    }
    ...
    private int value;
}
```

> **Note** C++ programmers should notice that you must provide the overload yourself. The compiler won't write the overload for you or silently swap the sequence of the two operands to find a matching operator.

Operators and Language Interoperability

Not all languages that execute using the common language runtime (CLR) support or understand operator overloading. If you are creating classes that you want to be able to use from other languages, if you overload an operator, you should provide an alternative mechanism that supports the same functionality. For example, suppose you implement *operator+* for the *Hour* structure:

```
public static Hour operator +(Hour lhs, int rhs)
{
    . . .
}
```

If you need to be able to use your class from a Visual Basic application, you should also provide an *Add* method that achieves the same thing:

```
public static Hour Add(Hour lhs, int rhs)
{
    . . .
}
```

Understanding Compound Assignment Evaluation

A compound assignment operator (such as +=) is always evaluated in terms of its associated operator (such as +). In other words, the statement

```
a += b;
```

is automatically evaluated like this:

```
a = a + b;
```

In general, the expression *a @= b* (where @ represents any valid operator) is always evaluated as *a = a @ b*. If you have overloaded the appropriate simple operator, the overloaded version is automatically called when you use its associated compound assignment operator. For example:

```
Hour a = ...;
int b = ...;
a += a; // same as a = a + a
a += b; // same as a = a + b
```

The first compound assignment expression *(a += a)* is valid because *a* is of type *Hour*, and the *Hour* type declares a binary *operator+* whose parameters are both *Hour*. Similarly, the second compound assignment expression *(a += b)* is also valid because *a* is of type *Hour* and *b* is of type *int*. The *Hour* type also declares a binary *operator+* whose first parameter is an *Hour* and whose second parameter is an *int*. Note, however, that you cannot write the expression *b += a* because that's the same as *b = b + a*. Although the addition is valid, the assignment is not, because there is no way to assign an *Hour* to the built-in *int* type.

Declaring Increment and Decrement Operators

C# allows you to declare your own version of the increment (++) and decrement (−−) operators. The usual rules apply when declaring these operators: they must be public, they must be static, and they must be unary (they can only take a single parameter). Here is the increment operator for the *Hour* structure:

```
struct Hour
{
    ...
    public static Hour operator ++(Hour arg)
    {
        arg.value++;
        return arg;
    }
    ...
    private int value;
}
```

The increment and decrement operators are unique in that they can be used in prefix and postfix forms. C# cleverly uses the same single operator for both the prefix and postfix versions. The result of a postfix expression is the value of the operand *before* the expression takes place. In other words, the compiler effectively converts the code

```
Hour now = new Hour(9);
Hour postfix = now++;
```

to this:

```
Hour now = new Hour(9);
Hour postfix = now;
now = Hour.operator ++(now); // pseudocode, not valid C#
```

The result of a prefix expression is the return value of the operator. The C# compiler effectively converts the code

```
Hour now = new Hour(9);
Hour prefix = ++now;
```

to this:

```
Hour now = new Hour(9);
now = Hour.operator ++(now); // pseudocode, not valid C#
Hour prefix = now;
```

This equivalence means that the return type of the increment and decrement operators must be the same as the parameter type.

Comparing Operators in Structures and Classes

Be aware that the implementation of the increment operator in the *Hour* structure works only because *Hour* is a structure. If you change *Hour* into a class but leave the implementation of its increment operator unchanged, you will find that the postfix translation won't give the correct answer. If you remember that a class is a reference type and revisit the compiler translations explained earlier, you can see why this occurs:

```
Hour now = new Hour(9);
Hour postfix = now;
now = Hour.operator ++(now); // pseudocode, not valid C#
```

If *Hour* is a class, the assignment statement *postfix = now* makes the variable *postfix* refer to the same object as *now*. Updating *now* automatically updates *postfix*! If *Hour* is a structure, the assignment statement makes a copy of *now* in *postfix*, and any changes to *now* leave *postfix* unchanged, which is what we want.

The correct implementation of the increment operator when *Hour* is a class is as follows:

```
class Hour
{
    public Hour(int initialValue)
    {
        this.value = initialValue;
    }
    ...
    public static Hour operator ++(Hour arg)
    {
        return new Hour(arg.value + 1);
    }
    ...
    private int value;
}
```

Notice that *operator* ++ now creates a new object based on the data in the original. The data in the new object is incremented, but the data in the original is left unchanged. Although this works, the compiler translation of the increment operator results in a new object being created each time it is used. This can be expensive in terms of memory use and garbage collection overhead. Therefore, it is recommended that you limit operator overloads when you define types. This recommendation applies to all operators, and not just to the increment operator.

Defining Operator Pairs

Some operators naturally come in pairs. For example, if you can compare two *Hour* values by using the *!=* operator, you would expect to be able to also compare two *Hour* values by using the *==* operator. The C# compiler enforces this very reasonable expectation by insisting that if you define either *operator ==* or *operator !=*, you must define them both. This neither-or-both rule also applies to the < and > operators and the <= and >= operators. The C# compiler does not write any of these operator partners for you. You must write them all explicitly yourself, regardless of how obvious they might seem. Here are the == and *!=* operators for the *Hour* structure:

```
struct Hour
{
    public Hour(int initialValue)
    {
        this.value = initialValue;
    }
    ...
    public static bool operator ==(Hour lhs, Hour rhs)
    {
        return lhs.value == rhs.value;
    }

    public static bool operator !=(Hour lhs, Hour rhs)
    {
        return lhs.value != rhs.value;
    }
    ...
    private int value;
}
```

The return type from these operators does not actually have to be Boolean. However, you would have to have a very good reason for using some other type, or these operators could become very confusing!

> **Note** If you define *operator* == and *operator* *!=* in a class, you should also override the *Equals* and *GetHashCode* methods inherited from *System.Object* (or *System.ValueType* if you are creating a structure). The *Equals* method should exhibit *exactly* the same behavior as *operator* ==. (You should define one in terms of the other.) The *GetHashCode* method is used by other classes in the Microsoft .NET Framework. (When you use an object as a key in a hash table, for example, the *GetHashCode* method is called on the object to help calculate a hash value. For more information, see the .NET Framework Reference documentation supplied with Visual Studio 2010.) All this method needs to do is return a distinguishing integer value. (Don't return the same integer from the *GetHashCode* method of all your objects, however, because this will nullify the effectiveness of the hashing algorithms.)

Implementing Operators

In the following exercise, you will develop a class that simulates complex numbers.

A complex number has two elements: a real component and an imaginary component. Typically, a complex number is represented in the form (x + yi), where x is the real component and yi is the imaginary component. The values of x and y are regular integers, and *i* represents the square root of –1 (hence the reason why *yi* is imaginary). Despite their rather obscure and theoretical feel, complex numbers have a large number of uses in the fields of electronics, applied mathematics, physics, and many aspects of engineering.

> **Note** The .NET Framework 4.0 now includes a type called *Complex* in the *System.Numerics* namespace that implements complex numbers, so there is no real need to define your own implementation any more. However, it is still instructive to see how to implement some of the common operators for this type.

You will implement complex numbers as a pair of integers that represent the coefficients x and y for the real and imaginary elements. You will also implement the operands necessary for performing simple arithmetic using complex numbers. The following table summarizes how to perform the four primary arithmetic operations on a pair of complex numbers, (a + b*i*) and (c + d*i*).

Operation	Calculation
(a + b*i*) + (c + d*i*)	((a + c) + (b + d)*i*)
(a + b*i*) – (c + d*i*)	((a – c) + (b – d)*i*)
(a + b*i*) * (c + d*i*)	((a * c – b * d) + (b * c + a * d)*i*)
(a + b*i*) / (c + d*i*)	(((a * c + b * d) / (c * c + d * d)) + ((b * c - a * d) / (c * c + d * d))*i*)

Create the *Complex* class, and implement the arithmetic operators

1. Start Microsoft Visual Studio 2010 if it is not already running.

2. Open the ComplexNumbers project, located in the \Microsoft Press\Visual CSharp Step By Step\Chapter 21\ComplexNumbers folder in your Documents folder. This is a console application that you will use to build and test your code. The Program.cs file contains the familiar *DoWork* method.

3. On the *Project* menu, click *Add Class*. In the *Add New Item – Complex Numbers* dialog box, type **Complex.cs** in the *Name* text box and then click *Add*.

   Visual Studio creates the *Complex* class and opens the Complex.cs file in the *Code and Text Editor* window.

4. Add the automatic integer properties *Real* and *Imaginary* to the *Complex* class, as shown next in bold. You will use these two properties to hold the real and imaginary components of a complex number.

```
class Complex
{
    public int Real { get; set; }
    public int Imaginary { get; set; }
}
```

5. Add the constructor shown next in bold to the *Complex* class. This constructor takes two *int* parameters and uses them to populate the *Real* and *Imaginary* properties.

```
class Complex
{
    ...
    public Complex (int real, int imaginary)
    {
        this.Real = real;
        this.Imaginary = imaginary;
    }
}
```

6. Override the *ToString* method as shown next in bold. This method returns a string representing the complex number in the form (x + yi).

```
class Complex
{
    ...
    public override string ToString()
    {
        return String.Format("({0} + {1}i)", this.Real, this.Imaginary);
    }
}
```

7. Add the overloaded + operator shown next in bold to the *Complex* class. This is the binary addition operator. It takes two *Complex* objects and adds them together by performing the calculation shown in the table at the start of the exercise. The operator returns a new *Complex* object containing the results of this calculation.

```
class Complex
{
    ...
    public static Complex operator +(Complex lhs, Complex rhs)
    {
        return new Complex(lhs.Real + rhs.Real, lhs.Imaginary + rhs.Imaginary);
    }
}
```

8. Add the overloaded – operator to the *Complex* class. This operator follows the same form as the overloaded + operator.

```
class Complex
{
    ...
    public static Complex operator -(Complex lhs, Complex rhs)
    {
        return new Complex(lhs.Real - rhs.Real, lhs.Imaginary - rhs.Imaginary);
    }
}
```

9. Implement the * operator and / operator. These two operators follow the same form as the previous two operators, although the calculations are a little more complicated.

(The calculation for the / operator has been broken down into two steps to avoid lengthy lines of code.)

```
class Complex
{
    ...
    public static Complex operator *(Complex lhs, Complex rhs)
    {
        return new Complex(lhs.Real * rhs.Real - lhs.Imaginary * rhs.Imaginary,
                           lhs.Imaginary * rhs.Real + lhs.Real * rhs.Imaginary);
    }


    public static Complex operator /(Complex lhs, Complex rhs)
    {
        int realElement = (lhs.Real * rhs.Real + lhs.Imaginary * rhs.Imaginary) /
                          (rhs.Real * rhs.Real + rhs.Imaginary * rhs.Imaginary);
        int imaginaryElement = (lhs.Imaginary * rhs.Real - lhs.Real * rhs.Imaginary) /
                               (rhs.Real * rhs.Real + rhs.Imaginary * rhs.Imaginary);
        return new Complex(realElement, imaginaryElement);
    }
}
```

10. Display the Program.cs file in the *Code and Text Editor* window. Add the following statements shown in bold to the *DoWork* method of the *Program* class:

```
static void DoWork()
{
    Complex first = new Complex(10, 4);
    Complex second = new Complex(5, 2);

    Console.WriteLine("first is {0}", first);
    Console.WriteLine("second is {0}", second);

    Complex temp = first + second;
    Console.WriteLine("Add: result is {0}", temp);

    temp = first - second;
    Console.WriteLine("Subtract: result is {0}", temp);

    temp = first * second;
    Console.WriteLine("Multiply: result is {0}", temp);

    temp = first / second;
    Console.WriteLine("Divide: result is {0}", temp);
}
```

This code creates two *Complex* objects that represent the complex values (10 + 4i) and (5 + 2i). The code displays them, and then tests each of the operators you have just defined, displaying the results in each case.

11. On the *Debug* menu, click *Start Without Debugging*.

Verify that the application displays the results shown in the following image.

12. Close the application, and return to the Visual Studio 2010 programming environment.

You have now created a type that models complex numbers and supports basic arithmetic operations. In the next exercise, you will extend the *Complex* class and provide the equality operators, == and *!=*. Remember that if you implement these operators you should also override the *Equals* and *GetHashCode* methods that the class inherits from the *Object* type.

Implement the equality operators

1. In Visual Studio 2010, display the Complex.cs file in the *Code and Text Editor* window.

2. Add the == and *!=* operators to the *Complex* class as shown next in bold. Notice that these operators both make use of the *Equal* method. The *Equal* method compares an instance of a class against another instance specified as an argument. It returns *true* if they are equal and *false* otherwise.

```
class Complex
{
    ...
    public static bool operator ==(Complex lhs, Complex rhs)
    {
        return lhs.Equals(rhs);
    }

    public static bool operator !=(Complex lhs, Complex rhs)
    {
        return !(lhs.Equals(rhs));
    }
}
```

3. On the *Build* menu, click *Rebuild Solution*.

The *Error List* window displays the following warning messages:

```
'ComplexNumbers.Complex' defines operator == or operator != but does not override
Object.GetHashCode()
```

```
'ComplexNumbers.Complex' defines operator == or operator != but does not override
Object.Equals(object o)
```

If you define the *!=* and == operators, you should also override the *Equal* and *GetHashCode* methods inherited from *SystemObject*.

Note If the *Error List* window is not displayed, on the *View* menu, click *Error List*.

4. Override the *Equals* method in the *Complex* class as shown next in bold:

```
class Complex
{
    ...
    public override bool Equals(Object obj)
    {
        if (obj is Complex)
        {
            Complex compare = (Complex)obj;
            return (this.Real == compare.Real) &&
                    (this.Imaginary == compare.Imaginary);
        }
        else
        {
            return false;
        }
    }
}
```

The *Equals* method takes an *Object* as a parameter. This code verifies that the type of the parameter is actually a *Complex* object. If it is, this code compares the values in the *Real* and *Imaginary* properties in the current instance and the parameter passed in; if they are the same, the method returns *true*, or it returns *false* otherwise. If the parameter passed in is not a *Complex* object, the method returns *false*.

 Important It is tempting to write the Equals method like this:

```
public override bool Equals(Object obj)
{
    Complex compare = obj as Complex;
    if (compare != null)
    {
        return (this.Real == compare.Real) &&
                (this.Imaginary == compare.Imaginary);
    }
    else
    {
        return false;
    }
}
```

However, the expression `compare != null` invokes the *!=* operator of the *Complex* class, which calls the *Equals* method again, resulting in an infinitely recursive loop.

5. Override the *GetHashCode* method. This implementation simply calls the method inherited from the *Object* class, but you can provide your own mechanism to generate a hash code for an object if you prefer.

```
Class Complex
{
    ...
    public override int GetHashCode()
    {
        return base.GetHashCode();
    }
}
```

6. On the *Build* menu, click *Rebuild Solution*.

   Verify that the solution now builds without reporting any warnings.

7. Display the Program.cs file in the *Code and Text Editor* window. Add the following code to the end of the *DoWork* method:

```
static void DoWork()
{
    ...
    if (temp == first)
    {
        Console.WriteLine("Comparison: temp == first");
    }
    else
    {
        Console.WriteLine("Comparison: temp != first");
    }

    if (temp == temp)
    {
        Console.WriteLine("Comparison: temp == temp");
    }
    else
    {
        Console.WriteLine("Comparison: temp != temp");
    }
}
```

 Note The expression temp == temp generates a warning message "Comparison made to same variable: did you mean to compare to something else?" In this case, you can ignore the warning because this comparison is intentional; it is to verify that the == operator is working as expected.

8. On the *Debug* menu, click *Start Without Debugging*. Verify that the final two messages displayed are these:

```
Comparison: temp != first
Comparison: temp == temp
```

9. Close the application, and return to Visual Studio 2010.

Understanding Conversion Operators

Sometimes you need to convert an expression of one type to another. For example, the following method is declared with a single *double* parameter:

```
class Example
{
    public static void MyDoubleMethod(double parameter)
    {
        ...
    }
}
```

You might reasonably expect that only values of type *double* could be used as arguments when calling *MyDoubleMethod*, but this is not so. The C# compiler also allows *MyDoubleMethod* to be called with an argument whose type is not *double*, but only if that value can be converted to a *double*. For example, you can provide an *int* argument. In that case, the compiler generates code that converts the argument from an *int* to a *double* when the method is called.

Providing Built-in Conversions

The built-in types have some built-in conversions. For example, as mentioned previously, an *int* can be implicitly converted to a *double*. An implicit conversion requires no special syntax and never throws an exception:

```
Example.MyDoubleMethod(42); // implicit int-to-double conversion
```

An implicit conversion is sometimes called a *widening conversion* because the result is *wider* than the original value—it contains at least as much information as the original value, and nothing is lost.

On the other hand, a *double* cannot be implicitly converted to an *int*:

```
class Example
{
    public static void MyIntMethod(int parameter)
    {
        ...
    }
}
...
Example.MyIntMethod(42.0); // compile-time error
```

When you convert a *double* to an *int*, you run the risk of losing information, so the conversion will not be performed automatically. (Consider what would happen if the argument to *MyIntMethod* were 42.5—how should this be converted?) A *double* can be converted to an *int*, but the conversion requires an explicit notation (a cast):

```
Example.MyIntMethod((int)42.0);
```

An explicit conversion is sometimes called a *narrowing conversion* because the result is *narrower* than the original value (that is, it can contain less information) and can throw an *OverflowException*. C# allows you to provide conversion operators for your own user-defined types to control whether it is sensible to convert values to other types and whether these conversions are implicit or explicit.

Implementing User-Defined Conversion Operators

The syntax for declaring a user-defined conversion operator is similar to that for declaring an overloaded operator. A conversion operator must be *public* and must also be *static*. Here's a conversion operator that allows an *Hour* object to be implicitly converted to an *int*:

```
struct Hour
{
    ...
    public static implicit operator int (Hour from)
    {
        return from.value;
    }

    private int value;
}
```

The type you are converting from is declared as the single parameter (in this case, *Hour*), and the type you are converting to is declared as the type name after the keyword *operator* (in this case, *int*). There is no return type specified before the keyword *operator*.

When declaring your own conversion operators, you must specify whether they are implicit conversion operators or explicit conversion operators. You do this by using the *implicit* and *explicit* keywords. For example, the *Hour* to *int* conversion operator mentioned earlier is implicit, meaning that the C# compiler can use it implicitly (without requiring a cast):

```
class Example
{
    public static void MyOtherMethod(int parameter) { ... }
    public static void Main()
    {
        Hour lunch = new Hour(12);
        Example.MyOtherMethod(lunch); // implicit Hour to int conversion
    }
}
```

If the conversion operator had been declared *explicit*, the preceding example would not have compiled, because an explicit conversion operator requires an explicit cast:

```
Example.MyOtherMethod((int)lunch); // explicit Hour to int conversion
```

When should you declare a conversion operator as explicit or implicit? If a conversion is always safe, does not run the risk of losing information, and cannot throw an exception, it can be defined as an *implicit* conversion. Otherwise, it should be declared as an *explicit* conversion. Converting from an *Hour* to an *int* is always safe—every *Hour* has a corresponding *int* value—so it makes sense for it to be implicit. An operator that converts a *string* to an *Hour* should be explicit because not all strings represent valid *Hours*. (The string *"7"* is fine, but how would you convert the string *"Hello, World"* to an *Hour*?)

Creating Symmetric Operators, Revisited

Conversion operators provide you with an alternative way to resolve the problem of providing symmetric operators. For example, instead of providing three versions of *operator+* (*Hour + Hour*, *Hour + int*, and *int + Hour*) for the *Hour* structure, as shown earlier, you can provide a single version of *operator+* (that takes two *Hour* parameters) and an implicit *int* to *Hour* conversion, like this:

```
struct Hour
{
    public Hour(int initialValue)
    {
        this.value = initialValue;
    }

    public static Hour operator +(Hour lhs, Hour rhs)
    {
        return new Hour(lhs.value + rhs.value);
    }

    public static implicit operator Hour (int from)
    {
        return new Hour (from);
    }
    ...
    private int value;
}
```

If you add an *Hour* to an *int* (in either order), the C# compiler automatically converts the *int* to an *Hour* and then calls *operator+* with two *Hour* arguments:

```
void Example(Hour a, int b)
{
    Hour eg1 = a + b; // b converted to an Hour
    Hour eg2 = b + a; // b converted to an Hour
}
```

Writing Conversion Operators

In the following exercise, you will add further operators to the *Complex* class. You will start by writing a pair of conversion operators that convert between the *int* type and the *Complex* type. Converting an *int* to a *Complex* object is always a safe process and never loses information (because an *int* is really just a *Complex* number without an imaginary element). So you will implement this as an implicit conversion operator. However, the converse is not true; to convert a *Complex* object into an *int*, you have to discard the imaginary element. So you will implement this conversion operator as explicit.

Implement the conversion operators

1. Return to Visual Studio 2010 and display the Complex.cs file in the *Code and Text Editor* window. Add the constructor shown next in bold to the *Complex* class. This constructor takes a single *int* parameter which it uses to initialize the *Real* property. The imaginary property is set to 0.

```
class Complex
{
    ...
    public Complex(int real)
    {
        this.Real = real;
        this.Imaginary = 0;
    }
    ...
}
```

2. Add the following implicit conversion operator to the *Complex* class. This operator converts from an *int* to a *Complex* object by returning a new instance of the *Complex* class by using the constructor you created in the previous step.

```
class Complex
{
    ...
    public static implicit operator Complex(int from)
    {
        return new Complex(from);
    }
}
```

3. Add the explicit conversion operator shown next to the *Complex* class. This operator takes a *Complex* object and returns the value of the *Real* property. This conversion discards the imaginary element of the complex number.

```
class Complex
{
    ...
    public static explicit operator int(Complex from)
    {
        return from.Real;
    }
}
```

4. Display the Program.cs file in the *Code and Text Editor* window. Add the following code to the end of the *DoWork* method:

```
static void DoWork()
{
    ...
    Console.WriteLine("Current value of temp is {0}", temp);

    if (temp == 2)
    {
        Console.WriteLine("Comparison after conversion: temp == 2");
    }
    else
    {
        Console.WriteLine("Comparison after conversion: temp != 2");
    }

    temp += 2;
    Console.WriteLine("Value after adding 2: temp = {0}", temp);
}
```

These statements test the implicit operator that converts an *int* to a *Complex* object. The *if* statement compares a *Complex* object to an *int*. The compiler generates code that converts the *int* into a *Complex* object first, and then invokes the == operator of the *Complex* class. The statement that adds 2 to the *temp* variable converts the *int* value 2 into a *Complex* object and then uses the + operator of the *Complex* class.

5. Add the following statements to end of the *DoWork* method:

```
static void DoWork()
{
    ...
    int tempInt = temp;
    Console.WriteLine("Int value after conversion: tempInt = {0}", tempInt);
}
```

The first statement attempts to assign a *Complex* object to an *int* variable.

6. On the *Build* menu, click *Rebuild Solution*.

   The solution fails to build, and the compiler reports the following error in the *Error List* window:

   ```
   Cannot implicitly convert type 'ComplexNumbers.Complex' to 'int'. An explicit
   conversion exists (are you missing a cast?)
   ```

   The operator that converts from a *Complex* object to an *int* is an explicit conversion operator, so you must specify a cast.

7. Modify the statement that attempts to store a *Complex* value in an *int* variable to use a cast, like this:

   ```
   int tempInt = (int)temp;
   ```

8. On the *Debug* menu, click *Start Without Debugging*. Verify that the solution now builds, and that the final four statements output are these:

   ```
   Current value of temp is (2 + 0i)
   Comparison after conversion: temp == 2
   Value after adding 2: temp = (4 + 0i)
   Int value after conversion: tempInt = 4
   ```

9. Close the application, and return to Visual Studio 2010.

In this chapter, you learned how to overload operators and provide functionality specific to a class or structure. You implemented a number of common arithmetic operators, and you also created operators that enable you to compare instances of a class. Finally, you learned how to create implicit and explicit conversion operators.

- If you want to continue to the next chapter

  Keep Visual Studio 2010 running, and turn to Chapter 22.

- If you want to exit Visual Studio 2010 now

  On the *File* menu, click *Exit*. If you see a *Save* dialog box, click *Yes* and save the project.

Chapter 21 Quick Reference

To	Do this
Implement an operator	Write the keywords *public* and *static*, followed by the return type, followed by the *operator* keyword, followed by the operator symbol being declared, followed by the appropriate parameters between parentheses. Implement the logic for the operator in the body of the method. For example:

```
class Complex
{
    ...
    public static bool operator==(Complex lhs, Complex rhs)
    {
        ... // Implement logic for == operator
    }
    ...
}
```

To	Do this
Define a conversion operator	Write the keywords *public* and *static*, followed by the keyword *implicit* or *explicit*, followed by the operator keyword, followed by the type being converted to, followed by the type being converted from as a single parameter between parentheses. For example:

```
class Complex
{
    ...
    public static implicit operator Complex(int from)
    {
        ... // code to convert from an int
    }
    ...
}
```

Part IV

Building Windows Presentation Foundation Applications

Chapter 22
Introducing Windows Presentation Foundation

After completing this chapter, you will be able to:

- Create Microsoft Windows Presentation Foundation (WPF) applications.

- Use common WPF controls such as labels, text boxes, and buttons.

- Define styles for WPF controls.

- Change the properties of WPF forms and controls at design time and through code at run time.

- Handle events exposed by WPF forms and controls.

Now that you have completed the exercises and examined the examples in the first three parts of this book, you should be well versed in the C# language. You have learned how to write programs and create components by using Microsoft C#, and you should understand many of the finer points of the language, such as extension methods, lambda expressions, and the distinction between value and reference types. You now have the essential language skills, and in Part IV you will expand upon them and use C# to take advantage of the graphical user interface (GUI) libraries provided as part of the Microsoft .NET Framework. In particular, you will see how to use the objects in the *System.Windows* namespace to create WPF applications.

In this chapter, you learn how to build a basic WPF application by using the common components that are a feature of most GUI applications. You see how to set the properties of WPF forms and controls by using the *Design View* and *Properties* windows, and also by using Extensible Application Markup Language, or XAML. You also learn how to use WPF styles to build user interfaces that can be easily adapted to conform to your organization's presentation standards. Finally, you learn how to intercept and handle some of the events that WPF forms and controls expose.

Creating a WPF Application

As an example, you are going to create an application that a user can use to input and display details for members of the Middleshire Bell Ringers Association, an esteemed group of the finest campanologists. Initially, you will keep the application very simple, concentrating on laying out the form and making sure that it all works. On the way, you learn about some of the features that WPF provides for building highly adaptable user interfaces. In later chapters, you will provide menus and learn how to implement validation to ensure that the data that is entered makes sense. The following graphic shows what the application will look like after you have completed it. (You can see the completed version by building and running the BellRingers project in the \Microsoft Press\Visual CSharp Step By Step\Chapter 22\BellRingers - Complete\ folder in your Documents folder.)

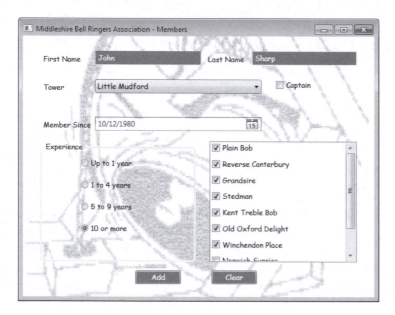

Building the WPF Application

In this exercise, you'll start building the Middleshire Bell Ringers Association application by creating a new project, laying out the form, and adding controls to the form. You have been using existing WPF applications in Microsoft Visual Studio 2010 in previous chapters, so much of the first couple of exercises will be a review for you.

Create the Middleshire Bell Ringers Association project

1. Start Visual Studio 2010 if it is not already running.

2. If you are using Visual Studio 2010 Standard or Visual Studio 2010 Professional, perform the following operations to create a new WPF application:

   2.1. On the *File* menu, point to *New*, and then click *Project*.

   The *New Project* dialog box opens.

   2.2. In the left pane, expand *Installed Templates* (if it is not already expanded) expand *Visual C#*, and then click *Windows*.

   2.3. In the middle pane, click the *WPF Application* icon.

2.4. In the *Location* field, type **\Microsoft Press\Visual CSharp Step By Step\ Chapter 22** under your Documents folder.

2.5. In the *Name* field, type **BellRingers**.

2.6. Click *OK*.

3. If you are using Microsoft Visual C# 2010 Express, perform the following tasks to create a new graphical application:

3.1. On the *File* menu, click *New Project*.

3.2. In the *New Project* dialog box, in the left pane, under *Installed Templates*, click *Visual C#*.

3.3. In the middle pane, click *WPF Application*; in the *Name* field, type **BellRingers**; and then click *OK*.

3.4. When Visual Studio has created the project, on the *File* menu click *Save All*.

3.5. In the *Save Project* dialog box, in the *Location* field specify the location **Microsoft Press\Visual CSharp Step By Step\Chapter 22** under your Documents folder, and then click *Save*.

The new project is created and contains a blank form called MainWindow.

Examine the form and the Grid layout

1. Examine the form in the *XAML* pane underneath the *Design View* window. Notice that the XAML definition of the form looks like this:

```
<Window x:Class="BellRingers.MainWindow"
    xmlns="http://schemas.microsoft.com/winfx/2006/xaml/presentation"
    xmlns:x="http://schemas.microsoft.com/winfx/2006/xaml"
    Title="MainWindow" Height="350" Width="525">
    <Grid>

    </Grid>
</Window>
```

The *Class* attribute specifies the fully qualified name of the class that implements the form. In this case, it is called MainWindow in the *BellRingers* namespace. The WPF Application template uses the name of the application as the default namespace for forms. The *xmlns* attributes specify the XML namespaces that define the schemas used by WPF; all the controls and other items that you can incorporate into a WPF application have definitions that live in these namespaces. (If you are not familiar with XML namespaces, you can ignore these *xmlns* attributes for now.) The *Title* attribute specifies the text that appears in the title bar of the form, and the *Height* and *Width* attributes specify the default height and width of the form. You can modify these values either by changing them in the *XAML* pane or by using the *Properties* window. You can also change the value of these and many other properties dynamically by writing C# code that executes when the form runs.

2. Click the MainWindow form in the *Design View* window. In the *Properties* window, locate and click the *Title* property, type **Middleshire Bell Ringers Association – Members**, and then press Enter to change the text in the title bar of the form.

Notice that the value in the *Title* attribute of the form changes in the *XAML* pane, and the new title is displayed in the title bar of the form in the *Design View* window.

> **Note** The MainWindow form contains a child control that you will examine in the next step. If the *Properties* window displays the properties for a *System.Windows.Controls.Grid* control, click the *MainWindow* text on the MainWindow form. This action selects the form rather than the grid, and the *Properties* window then displays the properties for the *System.Windows.Window* control.

3. In the *XAML* pane, notice that the *Window* element contains a child element called *Grid*.

In a WPF application, you place controls such as buttons, text boxes, and labels in a panel on a form. The panel manages the layout of the controls it contains. The default panel added by the WPF Application template is a *Grid*, which you can use to specify exactly the location of your controls at design time. Other types of panels are available that provide different styles of layout. For example, *StackPanel* automatically places controls in a vertical arrangement, with each control arranged directly beneath its immediate predecessor. Another example is *WrapPanel*, which arranges controls in a row from left to right and then wraps the content to the next line when the current row is full. A primary purpose of a layout panel is to govern how the controls are positioned if the user resizes the window at run time; the controls are automatically resized and repositioned according to the type of the panel.

> **Note** The *Grid* panel is flexible but complex. By default, you can think of the *Grid* panel as defining a single cell into which you can drop controls and set their location. However, you can set the properties of a *Grid* panel to define multiple rows and columns (hence its name), and you can drop controls into each of the cells defined by these rows and columns. In this chapter, we keep things simple and use only a single cell.

4. In the *Design View* window, click the MainWindow form, and then click the *Toolbox* tab.

5. In the *Common WPF Controls* section of the toolbox, click *Button*, and then click in the upper right part of the form.

A button control that displays two connectors anchoring it to the top and left edges of the form is added to the form, like this:

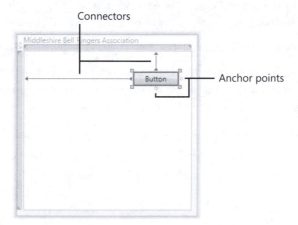

Although you clicked the form, the *Button* control is added to the *Grid* control contained in the form. The grid occupies the entire form apart from the title bar at the top. The connectors show that the button is anchored to the top and left edges of the grid. At run time, if you resize the form, the button moves to maintain these connections and keep the button the same distance from the connected edges. You can anchor the button to different edges of the form by clicking the anchor points of the control or changing the *HorizontalAlignment* and *VerticalAlignment* properties of the button, as described in the next step.

6. Examine the code in the *XAML* pane. The *Grid* element and its contents should now look something like this (although your values for the *Margin* property might vary):

```
<Grid>
    <Button Content="Button" Height="23" HorizontalAlignment="Left"
    Margin="374,40,0,0" Name="button1"
    VerticalAlignment="Top" Width="75"/>
</Grid>
```

> **Note** Throughout this chapter, lines from the *XAML* pane are shown split and indented so that they will fit on the printed page.

When you place a control on a grid, you can connect any or all of the anchor points to the corresponding edge of the grid. If you move the control around, it stays connected to the same edges until you change the alignment properties of the control.

The *HorizontalAlignment* and *VerticalAlignment* properties of the button indicate the edges to which the button is currently connected, and the *Margin* property indicates the distance to those edges. Recall from Chapter 1, "Welcome to C#," that the *Margin* property contains four values specifying the distance from the left, top, right, and bottom edges of the grid, respectively. In the XAML fragment just shown, the button is 84 units from the top edge of the grid and 34 units from the right edge. (Each unit is 1/96th of an inch.) Margin values of 0 indicate that the button is not connected to the corresponding edge. As mentioned in the previous step, when you run the application, the WPF runtime will endeavor to maintain these distances even if you resize the form.

7. On the *Debug* menu, click *Start Without Debugging* to build and run the application.

8. When the form appears, resize the window by clicking and dragging each of the edges in turn. Notice that as you drag the edges of the form around, the distance of the button from the top and left edges of the form remains fixed.

9. Close the form, and return to Visual Studio 2010.

10. In the *Design View* window, click the button control, and then click the right anchor point to attach the control to the right edge of the form, as shown in the following image:

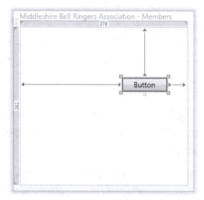

In the *XAML* pane, notice that the *HorizontalAlignment* property is no longer specified. The default value for the *HorizontalAlignment* and *VerticalAlignment* properties is a value called *Stretch*, which indicates that the control is anchored to both opposite edges. Also notice that the *Margin* property now specifies a nonzero value for the right margin.

> **Note** You can also click the anchor point that is connected to the edge of the grid to remove the connection.

11. On the *Debug* menu, click *Start Without Debugging* to build and run the application again.

12. When the form appears, experiment by making the form narrower and wider. Notice that the button no longer moves to the left or right because it is anchored to the left and right edges of the form. Instead, the button gets wider or narrower as the edges move.

13. Close the form, and return to Visual Studio 2010.

14. In the *Design View* window, add a second *Button* control to the form from the *Toolbox*, and position it near the middle of the form.

15. In the *XAML* pane, set the *Margin* property to 0,0,0,0; remove the *VerticalAlignment* and *HorizontalAlignment* properties; and set the *Width* and *Height* properties, as shown here:

```
<Button Content="Button" Margin="0,0,0,0" Name="button2"
 Width="75" Height="23"/>
```

Tip You can also set many of the properties of a control, such as *Margin*, by using the *Properties* window. However, sometimes it is simply easier to type values directly into the *XAML* pane as long as you enter the values carefully.

Note If you don't set the *Width* and *Height* properties of the button control, the button fills the entire form.

16. On the *Debug* menu, click *Start Without Debugging* to build and run the application once more.

17. When the form appears, resize the form. Notice that as the form shrinks or grows the new button relocates itself to try to maintain its relative position on the form with respect to all four sides (that is, it tries to stay in the center of the form). The new button control even travels over the top of the first button control if you shrink the height of the form.

18. Close the form, and return to Visual Studio 2010.

As long as you are consistent in your approach, by using layout panes, such as the *Grid*, you can build forms that look right regardless of the user's screen resolution without having to write complex code to determine when the user has resized a window. Additionally, with WPF, you can modify the look and feel of the controls an application uses—again, without having to write lots of complex code. With these features, you can build applications that can easily be customized to conform to any house style required by your organization. You will examine some of these features in the following exercises.

Add a background image to the form

1. In the *Design View* window, click the MainWindow form.

2. In the *Toolbox*, in the *Common WPF Controls* section, click *Image*, and then click anywhere on the form. You will use this image control to display an image on the background of the form.

Note You can use many other techniques to display an image in the background of a *Grid*. The method shown in this exercise is probably the simplest, although other strategies can provide more flexibility.

3. In the *XAML* pane, set the *Margin* property of the image control and remove any other property values apart from the *Name*, as shown here:

```
<Image Margin="0,0,0,0" Name="image1"/>
```

The image control expands to occupy the grid; the two button controls remain visible.

4. In *Solution Explorer*, right-click the BellRingers project, point to *Add*, and then click *Existing Item*. In the *Add Existing Item – BellRingers* dialog box, move to the folder Microsoft Press\Visual CSharp Step By Step\Chapter 22 under your Documents folder. In the drop-down list box adjacent to the *File name* text box, select *All Files (*.*)*. Select the file *bell.gif*, and then click *Add*.

   This action adds the image file bell.gif as a resource to your application. The bell.gif file contains a sketch of a ringing bell.

5. In the *XAML* pane, modify the definition of the image control as shown here in bold. The *Image.Source* property is an example of a composite property that contains one or more child elements. Notice that you must replace the closing tag delimiter (/>) of the image control with an ordinary tag delimiter character (>) and add a closing *</Image>* tag to enclose the *Image.Source* property:

```
<Image Margin="0,0,0,0" Name="image1" >
    <Image.Source>
        <BitmapImage UriSource="bell.gif" />
    </Image.Source>
</Image>
```

   The purpose of an image control is to display an image. You can specify the source of the image in a variety of ways. The example shown here loads the image from the file bell.gif that you just added as a resource to the project.

   The image should now appear on the form, like this:

There is a problem, however. The image is not in the background, and it totally obscures the two button controls. The issue is that, unless you specify otherwise, all controls placed on a layout panel have an implied z-order that renders controls added lower down in the XAML description over the top of controls added previously.

 Note The term *z-order* refers to the relative depth positions of items on the z-axis of a three-dimensional space (the y-axis being vertical and the x-axis being horizontal). Items with a higher value for the z-order appear in front of those items with a lower value.

There are at least two ways you can move the image control behind the buttons. The first is to move the XAML definitions of the buttons so that they appear after the image control, and the second is to explicitly specify a value for the *ZIndex* property for the control. Controls with a higher *ZIndex* value appear in front of those on the same panel with a lower *ZIndex*. If two controls have the same *ZIndex* value, their relative precedence is determined by the order in which they occur in the XAML description, as before.

6. In the *XAML* pane, set the *ZIndex* properties of the button and image controls as shown in bold type in the following code:

```
<Button Panel.ZIndex="1" Content="Button" Margin="379,84,49,0"
    Name="button1" Height="23" VerticalAlignment="Top" />
<Button Panel.ZIndex="1" Content="Button" Height="23" Margin="0,0,0,0"
    Name="button2" Width="75" />
<Image Panel.ZIndex="0" Margin="0,0,0,0" Name="image1" >
    <Image.Source>
        <BitmapImage UriSource="Bell.gif" />
    </Image.Source>
</Image>
```

The two buttons should now reappear in front of the image.

With WPF, you can create styles to modify the way in which controls such as buttons, text boxes, and labels present themselves on a form. You will investigate this feature in the next exercise.

Create a style to manage the look and feel of controls on the form

1. In the *XAML* pane, modify the definition of the first button on the form, as shown in bold type in the following code. The *Button.Resources* property is another example of a composite property, and you must modify the definition of the *Button* element to wrap this property—by replacing the closing tag delimiter (/>) of the button control with an ordinary tag delimiter character (>) and adding a closing </Button> tag. Notice that it is good practice to split the XAML description of a control that contains composite

child property values such as *Button.Resources* over multiple lines to make the code easier to read and maintain:

```
<Button Panel.ZIndex="1" Content="Button" Margin="169,84,34,0"
 Name="button1" Height="23" VerticalAlignment="Top">
    <Button.Resources>
        <Style x:Key="buttonStyle">
            <Setter Property="Button.Background" Value="Gray"/>
            <Setter Property="Button.Foreground" Value="White"/>
            <Setter Property="Button.FontFamily" Value="Comic Sans MS"/>
        </Style>
    </Button.Resources>
</Button>
```

This example specifies the values for the background and foreground colors of the button as well as the font used for the text on the button. Styles are resources, and you add them to a *Resources* element for the control. You can give each style a unique name by using the *Key* property.

> **Note** When you compile a WPF window, Visual Studio adds any resources included with the window to a collection associated with the window. Strictly speaking, the *Key* property doesn't specify the name of the style but rather an identifier for the resource in this collection. You can specify the *Name* property as well if you want to manipulate the resource in your C# code, but controls reference resources by specifying the *Key* value for that resource. Controls and other items that you add to a form should have their *Name* property set because, as with resources, this is how you reference these items in code.

Although you have defined a style as part of the button definition, the appearance of the button has not changed. You specify the style to apply to a control by using the *Style* property.

2. Modify the definition of the button to reference the *buttonStyle* style, as shown here in bold:

```
<Button Style="{DynamicResource buttonStyle}" Panel.ZIndex="1"
 Content="Button" Margin ="169,84,34,0" Name="button1" Height="23"
 VerticalAlignment="Top">
    <Button.Resources>
        <Style x:Key="buttonStyle">
            ...
        </Style>
    </Button.Resources>
    Button
</Button>
```

The syntax {DynamicResource buttonStyle} creates a new style object based on the named style, and the *Style* property applies this style to the button. The appearance of the button on the form should now change.

Styles have scope. If you attempt to reference the *buttonStyle* style from the second button on the form, it will have no effect. One solution is to create a copy of this style and add it to the *Resources* element of the second button, and then reference it, like this:

```
<Grid>
    <Button Style="{DynamicResource buttonStyle}" Content="Button"
     Panel.ZIndex="1" Margin ="169,84,34,0" Name="button1" Height="23"
     VerticalAlignment="Top">
        <Button.Resources>
            <Style x:Key="buttonStyle">
                <Setter Property="Button.Background" Value="Gray"/>
                <Setter Property="Button.Foreground" Value="White"/>
                <Setter Property="Button.FontFamily" Value="Comic Sans MS"/>
            </Style>
        </Button.Resources>
    </Button>
    <Button Style="{DynamicResource buttonStyle}" Content="Button"
     Panel.ZIndex="1" Height="23" Margin="0,0,0,0" Name="button2"
     Width="76">
        <Button.Resources>
            <Style x:Key="buttonStyle">
                <Setter Property="Button.Background" Value="Gray"/>
                <Setter Property="Button.Foreground" Value="White"/>
                <Setter Property="Button.FontFamily" Value="Comic Sans MS"/>
            </Style>
        </Button.Resources>
    </Button>
    ...
</Grid>
```

However, this approach can get very repetitive and becomes a maintenance nightmare if you need to change the style of buttons. A much better strategy is to define the style as a resource for the window, and then you can reference it from all controls in that window.

3. In the *XAML* pane, add a *<Window.Resources>* element above the grid, move the definition of the *buttonStyle* style to this new element, and then delete the *<Button. Resources>* element from the first button. Add or modify the *Style* property of both buttons to reference this style. The updated code for the entire XAML description of the form is as follows, with the resource definition and references to the resource shown in bold type:

```
<Window x:Class="BellRingers.MainWindow"
    xmlns="http://schemas.microsoft.com/winfx/2006/xaml/presentation"
    xmlns:x="http://schemas.microsoft.com/winfx/2006/xaml"
    Title="Middleshire Bell Ringers Association - Members"
    Height="350" Width="525">
    <Window.Resources>
        <Style x:Key="buttonStyle">
            <Setter Property="Button.Background" Value="Gray"/>
            <Setter Property="Button.Foreground" Value="White"/>
```

```
                <Setter Property="Button.FontFamily" Value="Comic Sans MS"/>
            </Style>
        </Window.Resources>
        <Grid>
            <Button Style="{StaticResource buttonStyle}"  Panel.ZIndex="1"
             Content="Button" Margin ="169,84,34,0" Name="button1" Height="23"
             VerticalAlignment="Top">
            </Button>
            <Button Style="{StaticResource buttonStyle}" Panel.ZIndex="1"
             Content="Button" Height="23" Margin="0,0,0,0" Name="button2"
             Width="76" />
            <Image Panel.ZIndex="0" Margin="0,0,0,0" Name ="image1">
                <Image.Source>
                    <BitmapImage UriSource="Bell.gif" />
                </Image.Source>
            </Image>
        </Grid>
    </Window>
```

Both buttons now appear in the *Design View* window using the same style.

The code you have just entered references the button style by using the *StaticResource* keyword rather than the *DynamicResource* keyword. The scoping rules of static resources are like those of C# in that they require you to define a resource before you can reference it. In step 1 of this exercise, you referenced the *buttonStyle* style above the XAML code that defined it, so the style name was not actually in scope. This out-of-scope reference works because using *DynamicResource* defers until run time the time at which the resource reference is resolved, at which point the resource should have been created.

Generally speaking, static resources are more efficient than dynamic ones because they are resolved when the application is built, but dynamic resources give you more flexibility. For example, if the resource itself changes as the application executes (you can write code to change styles at run time), any controls referencing the style using *StaticResource* will not be updated, but any controls referencing the style using *DynamicResource* will be.

 Note There are many other differences between the behavior of static and dynamic resources and restrictions on when you can reference a resource dynamically. For more information, consult the .NET Framework documentation provided with Visual Studio 2010.

There is still a little bit of repetition involved in the definition of the style; each of the properties (background, foreground, and font family) explicitly state that they are button properties. You can remove this repetition by specifying the *TargetType* attribute in the *Style* tag.

4. Modify the definition of the style to specify the *TargetType* attribute, and remove the *Button* reference from each of the properties, like this:

```
<Style x:Key="buttonStyle" TargetType="Button">
    <Setter Property="Background" Value="Gray"/>
    <Setter Property="Foreground" Value="White"/>
    <Setter Property="FontFamily" Value="Comic Sans MS"/>
</Style>
```

You can add as many buttons as you like to the form, and you can style them all using the *buttonStyle* style. But what about other controls, such as labels and text boxes?

5. In the *Design View* window, click the MainWindow form, and then click the *Toolbox* tab. In the *Common* section, click *TextBox*, and then click anywhere in the lower half of the form.

The *TextBox* control is added to the form.

6. In the *XAML* pane, change the definition of the text box control and specify the *Style* attribute shown in bold type in the following example, attempting to apply the *buttonStyle* style:

```
<TextBox Style="{StaticResource buttonStyle}" Height="21"
 Margin="114,0,44,58" Name="textBox1" VerticalAlignment="Bottom" />
```

Not surprisingly, attempting to set the style of a text box to a style intended for a button fails. The XAML pane displays blue underline below the reference to the style in the *TextBox* control. If you hover the mouse over this element, a tooltip appears and displays the message "'Button' TargetType does not match type of element 'TextBox'." If you attempt to build the application, it will fail with the same error message.

7. To fix this error, in the *XAML* pane, change the *TargetType* to *Control* in the definition of the style, change the *Key* property to *bellRingersStyle* (a more meaningful name), and then modify the references to the style in the button and text box controls as shown in bold type here:

```
<Window x:Class="BellRingers.MainWindow"
    ...>
    <Window.Resources>
        <Style x:Key="bellRingersStyle" TargetType="Control">
            <Setter Property="Background" Value="Gray"/>
            <Setter Property="Foreground" Value="White"/>
            <Setter Property="FontFamily" Value="Comic Sans MS"/>
        </Style>
    </Window.Resources>
    <Grid>
        <Button Style="{StaticResource bellRingersStyle}" ...>
        </Button>
        <Button Style="{StaticResource bellRingersStyle}" ... />
        ...
        <TextBox ... Style="{StaticResource bellRingersStyle}" ... />
    </Grid>
</Window>
```

Setting the *TargetType* attribute of a style to *Control* specifies that the style can be applied to any control that inherits from the *Control* class. In the WPF model, many different types of controls, including text boxes and buttons, inherit from the *Control* class. However, you can provide *Setter* elements only for properties that explicitly belong to the *Control* class. (Buttons have some additional properties that are not part of the *Control* class; if you specify any of these button-only properties, you cannot set the *TargetType* to *Control*.)

8. On the *Debug* menu, click *Start Without Debugging* to build and run the application. Type some text in the text box, and verify that it appears in white using the Comic Sans MS font.

   Unfortunately, the choice of colors makes it a little difficult to see the text caret when you click the text box and type text. You will fix this in a following step.

9. Close the form, and return to Visual Studio 2010.

10. In the *XAML* pane, edit the *bellRingersStyle* style and add the *<Style.Triggers>* element shown in bold type in the following code. (If you get an error message that the *TriggerCollection* is sealed, simply rebuild the solution.)

```
<Style x:Key="bellRingersStyle" TargetType="Control">
    <Setter Property="Background" Value="Gray"/>
    <Setter Property="Foreground" Value="White"/>
    <Setter Property="FontFamily" Value="Comic Sans MS"/>
    <Style.Triggers>
        <Trigger Property="IsMouseOver" Value="True">
            <Setter Property="Background" Value="Blue" />
        </Trigger>
    </Style.Triggers>
</Style>
```

A trigger specifies an action to perform when a property value changes. The *bellRingersStyle* style detects a change in the *IsMouseOver* property to temporarily modify the background color of the control the mouse is over.

> **Note** Don't confuse triggers with events. Triggers respond to transient changes in property values. When the value in the triggering property reverts to its original value, the triggered action is undone. In the example shown previously, when the *IsMouseOver* property is no longer *true* for a control, the *Background* property is set back to its original value. Events specify an action to perform when a significant incident (such as the user clicking a button) occurs in an application; the actions performed by an event are not undone when the incident is finished.

11. On the *Debug* menu, click *Start Without Debugging* to build and run the application again. This time, when you move the mouse over the text box, it turns blue so that you can see the text caret more easily. The text box reverts to its original gray color when you move the mouse away. Notice that the buttons do not behave in quite the same way. Button controls already implement this functionality and turn a paler shade of

blue when you place the mouse over them. This default behavior overrides the trigger specified in the style.

12. Close the form, and return to Visual Studio 2010.

> **Note** An alternative approach that you can use to apply a font globally to all controls on a form is to set the text properties of the window holding the controls. These properties include *FontFamily*, *FontSize*, and *FontWeight*. However, styles provide additional facilities, such as triggers, and you are not restricted to setting font-related properties. If you specify the text properties for a window and apply a style to controls in the window, the controls' style takes precedence over the window's text properties.

How a WPF Application Runs

A WPF application can contain any number of forms—you can add forms to an application by using the *Add Window* command on the *Project* menu in Visual Studio 2010. How does an application know which form to display when an application starts? If you recall from Chapter 1, this is the purpose of the App.xaml file. If you open the App.xaml file for the BellRingers project, you will see that it looks like this:

```
<Application x:Class="BellRingers.App"
    xmlns="http://schemas.microsoft.com/winfx/2006/xaml/presentation"
    xmlns:x="http://schemas.microsoft.com/winfx/2006/xaml"
    StartupUri="MainWindow.xaml">
    <Application.Resources>

    </Application.Resources>
</Application>
```

When you build a WPF application, the compiler converts this XAML definition to an *Application* object. The *Application* object controls the lifetime of the application and is responsible for creating the initial form that the application displays. You can think of the *Application* object as providing the *Main* method for the application. The key property is *StartupUri*, which specifies the XAML file for the window that the *Application* object should create. When you build the application, this property is converted to code that creates and opens the specified WPF form. If you want to display a different form, you simply need to change the value of the *StartupUri* property.

It is important to realize that the *StartupUri* property refers to the name of the XAML file and not the class implementing the window in this XAML file. If you rename the class from the default (*MainWindow*), the file name does not change. (It is still MainWindow.xaml.) Similarly, if you change the name of the file, the name of the window class defined in this file does not change. It can become confusing if the window class and XAML file have different names, so if you do want to rename things, be consistent and change both the file name and the window class name.

Adding Controls to the Form

So far, you have created a form, set some properties, added a few controls, and defined a style. To make the form useful, you need to add some more controls and write some code of your own to implement some meaningful functionality.

The WPF library contains a varied collection of controls. The purposes of some are obvious—for example, *TextBox*, *ListBox*, *CheckBox*, and *ComboBox*—whereas other, more powerful controls might not be so familiar.

Using WPF Controls

In the next exercise, you will add controls to the form that a user can use to input details about members of the bell ringers association. You will use a variety of controls, each suited to a particular type of data entry.

You will use *TextBox* controls for entering the first name and last name of the member. Each member belongs to a "tower" (where bells hang). The Middleshire district has several towers, but the list is static—new towers are not built very often, and hopefully, old towers do not fall down with any great frequency either. The ideal control for handling this type of data is a *ComboBox*. The form also records whether the member is the tower "captain" (the person in charge of the tower who conducts the other ringers). A *CheckBox* is the best sort of control for this; it can be either selected (*True*) or cleared (*False*).

> **Tip** *CheckBox* controls can actually have three states if the *IsThreeState* property is set to *True*. The three states are *true*, *false*, and *null*. These states are useful if you are displaying information that has been retrieved from a relational database. Some columns in a table in a database allow *null* values, indicating that the value held is not defined or is unknown.

The application also gathers statistical information about when members joined the association and how much bell-ringing experience they have (up to 1 year, between 1 and 4 years, between 5 and 9 years, and 10 or more years). You can use a group of options, or radio buttons, to indicate the member's experience—radio buttons provide a mutually exclusive set of values. WPF provides the *DateTimePicker* control for selecting and displaying dates, and this control is ideal for indicating the date that the member joined the association.

Finally, the application records the tunes the member can ring—rather confusingly, these tunes are referred to as "methods" by the bell-ringing fraternity. Although a bell ringer rings only one bell at a time, a group of bell ringers under the direction of the tower captain can ring their bells in different sequences and play simple music. There are a variety of bell-ringing methods, and they have rather quaint-sounding names such as Plain Bob, Reverse Canterbury, Grandsire, Stedman, Kent Treble Bob, and Old Oxford Delight. New methods are being written with alarming regularity, so the list of methods can vary over time. In a real-world application, you would store this list in a database. In this application, you will use a small selection of methods that you will hard-wire into the form. (You will see how to access and retrieve data from a database in Part V of this book, "Managing Data.") A good control for displaying this information and indicating whether a member can ring a method is a *ListBox* containing a list of *CheckBox* controls.

When the user has entered the member's details, the *Add* button will validate and store the data. The user can click *Clear* to reset the controls on the form and cancel any data entered.

Add controls to the form

1. Ensure that MainWindow.xaml is displayed in the *Design View* window. Remove the two button controls and the text box control from the form.

> **Tip** To remove a control from a form, click the control and then press the *Delete* key.

2. In the *XAML* pane, change the *Height* property of the form to **470** and the *Width* property to **600**, as shown in bold type here:

```
<Window x:Class="BellRingers.MainWindow"
    ...
    Title="..." Height="470" Width="600">
    ...
</Window>
```

3. In the *Design View* window, click the MainWindow form. From the *Toolbox*, drag a *Label* control onto the form and place it near the upper left corner. Do not worry about positioning and sizing the label precisely, because you will do this task for several controls later.

4. In the *XAML* pane, change the text for the label to **First Name**, as shown in bold type here:

```
<Label Content="First Name" ... />
```

> **Tip** You can also change the text displayed by a label and many other controls by setting the *Content* property in the *Properties* window.

5. In the *Design View* window, click the MainWindow form. From the *Toolbox*, drag a *TextBox* control onto the form and place it to the right of the label.

> **Tip** You can use the guide lines displayed by the *Design View* window to help align controls. (The guide lines are displayed after you drop the control on the form.)

6. In the *XAML* pane, change the *Name* property of the text box to **firstName**, as shown here in bold type:

```
<TextBox ... Name="firstName" .../>
```

7. Add a second *Label* control to the form. Place it to the right of the *firstName* text box. In the *XAML* pane, modify the *Content* property to change the text for the label to **Last Name**.

8. Add another *TextBox* control to the form, and position it to the right of the *Last Name* label. In the *XAML* pane, change the *Name* property of this text box to **lastName**.

9. Add a third *Label* control to the form, and place it directly under the *First Name* label. In the *XAML* pane, change the text for the label to **Tower**.

10. Add a *ComboBox* control to the form. Place it under the *firstName* text box and to the right of the *Tower* label. In the *XAML* pane, change the *Name* property of this combo box to **towerNames**.

11. Add a *CheckBox* control to the form. Place it under the *lastName* text box and to the right of the *towerNames* combo box. In the *XAML* pane, change the *Name* property of the check box to **isCaptain**, and change the text displayed by this check box to **Captain**.

12. Add a fourth *Label* to the form, and place it under the *Tower* label. In the *XAML* pane, change the text for this label to **Member Since**.

13. In the *Toolbox*, expand the *Controls* section. Add a *DatePicker* control to the form, and place it under the *towerNames* combo box. *Change* the *Name* property of this control to **memberSince**.

14. Add a *GroupBox* control from the *Controls* section of the *Toolbox* to the form, and place it under the *Member Since* label. In the *XAML* pane, change the *Name* property of the group box to **yearsExperience** and change the *Header* property to **Experience**. The *Header* property changes the label that appears on the form for the group box. Set the *Height* property to **200**.

15. Add a *StackPanel* control to the form. In the *XAML* pane, set the *Margin* property of this control to "0,0,0,0". Remove the values for all the other properties apart from the *Name* property. The code for the *StackPanel* control should look like this:

```
<StackPanel Margin="0,0,0,0" Name="stackPanel1" />
```

16. In the *XAML* pane, change the definition of the *yearsExperience GroupBox* control and delete the *<Grid></Grid>* elements. Move the definition of the *StackPanel* control into the XAML code for the *GroupBox* control, like this:

```
<GroupBox Header="Experience" ... Name="yearsExperience" ...>
    <StackPanel Margin="0,0,0,0" Name="stackPanel1" />
</GroupBox>
```

17. Add a *RadioButton* control to the form, and place it inside the *StackPanel* control, at the top. Add three more *RadioButton* controls to the *StackPanel* control. They should automatically be arranged vertically.

18. In the *XAML* pane, change the *Name* property of each radio button and the text it displays in the *Content* property, as shown here in bold type:

```
<GroupBox...>
    <StackPanel ...>
        <RadioButton ... Content="Up to 1 year" ... Name="novice" ... />
        <RadioButton ... Content="1 to 4 years" ... Name="intermediate" ... />
        <RadioButton ... Content="5 to 9 years" ... Name="experienced" ... />
        <RadioButton ... Content="10 or more years" ... Name="accomplished" ... />
    </StackPanel>
</GroupBox>
```

19. Add a *ListBox* control to the form, and place it to the right of the *GroupBox* control. In the *XAML* pane, change the *Name* property of the list box to **methods**.

20. Add a *Button* control to the form, and place it near the bottom on the lower left side of the form, underneath the *GroupBox* control. In the *XAML* pane, change the *Name* property of this button to **add** and change the text displayed by the *Content* property to **Add**.

21. Add another *Button* control to the form, and place it near the bottom to the right of the *Add* button. In the *XAML* pane, change the *Name* property of this button to **clear** and change the text displayed by the *Content* property to **Clear**.

You have now added all the required controls to the form. The next step is to tidy up the layout. The following table lists the layout properties and values you should assign to each of the controls. In the *Design View* window, click each control in turn, and then using the *Properties* window, make these changes. The margins and alignment of the controls are designed to keep the controls in place if the user resizes the form. Also notice that the margin values specified for the radio buttons are relative to each preceding item in the *StackPanel* control containing them; the first radio button is 10 units from the top of the *StackPanel* control, and the remaining radio buttons have a gap between them of 20 units vertically.

Control	Property	Value
label1	*Height*	28
	Margin	29, 25, 0, 0
	VerticalAlignment	Top
	HorizontalAlignment	Left
	Width	75
firstName	*Height*	23
	Margin	121, 25, 0, 0
	VerticalAlignment	Top
	HorizontalAlignment	Left
	Width	175
label2	*Height*	28
	Margin	305, 25, 0, 0
	VerticalAlignment	Top
	HorizontalAlignment	Left
	Width	75
lastName	*Height*	23
	Margin	380, 25, 0, 0
	VerticalAlignment	Top
	HorizontalAlignment	Left
	Width	175
label3	*Height*	28
	Margin	29, 72, 0, 0
	VerticalAlignment	Top
	HorizontalAlignment	Left
	Width	75
towerNames	*Height*	23
	Margin	121, 72, 0, 0
	VerticalAlignment	Top
	HorizontalAlignment	Left
	Width	275
isCaptain	*Height*	23
	Margin	420, 72, 0, 0
	VerticalAlignment	Top
	HorizontalAlignment	Left

Control	Property	Value
	Width	75
label4	*Height*	28
	Margin	29, 134, 0, 0
	VerticalAlignment	Top
	HorizontalAlignment	Left
	Width	90
memberSince	*Height*	23
	Margin	121, 134, 0, 0
	VerticalAlignment	Top
	HorizontalAlignment	Left
	Width	275
yearsExperience	*Height*	200
	Margin	29, 174, 0, 0
	VerticalAlignment	Top
	HorizontalAlignment	Left
	Width	258
stackPanel1	*Margin*	0, 0, 0, 0
novice	*Height*	16
	Margin	0, 10, 0, 0
	Width	120
intermediate	*Height*	16
	Margin	0, 20, 0, 0
	Width	120
experienced	*Height*	16
	Margin	0, 20, 0, 0
	Width	120
accomplished	*Height*	16
	Margin	0, 20, 0, 0
	Width	120
methods	*Height*	200
	Margin	310, 174, 0, 0
	VerticalAlignment	Top
	HorizontalAlignment	Left
	Width	245

Control	Property	Value
add	*Height*	23
	Margin	188, 388, 0, 0
	VerticalAlignment	Top
	HorizontalAlignment	Left
	Width	75
clear	*Height*	23
	Margin	313, 388, 0, 0
	VerticalAlignment	Top
	HorizontalAlignment	Left
	Width	75

As a finishing touch, you will next apply a style to the controls. You can use the *bellRingersStyle* style for controls such as the buttons and text boxes, but the labels, combo box, group box, and radio buttons should probably not be displayed on a gray background.

Apply styles to the controls, and test the form

1. In the *XAML* pane, add the *bellRingersFontStyle* style shown in bold type in the following code to the *<Windows.Resources>* element. Leave the existing *bellRingersStyle* style in place. Notice that this new style only changes the font.

```
<Window.Resources>
    <Style x:Key="bellRingersFontStyle" TargetType="Control">
        <Setter Property="FontFamily" Value="Comic Sans MS"/>
    </Style>
    <Style x:Key="bellRingersStyle" TargetType="Control">
        ...
    </Style>
</Window.Resources>
```

2. On the form, click the *label1 Label* control displaying the text *First Name*. In the *Properties* window, locate the *Style* property for this control. Click the *Resource...* label shown as the value for this property. A list of the styles available as resources in the form appears as shown in the following image.

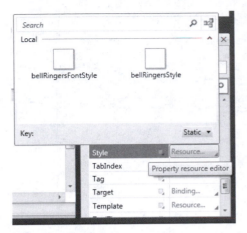

3. Verify that the drop-down list in the bottom right corner of the list box is set to *Static*, and then double-click *bellRingersFontStyle*.

4 In the *XAML* pane, verify that the *bellRingersFontStyle* style has been applied to the *label1* control, as shown in bold type here:

```
<Label Content="First Name" ... Style="{StaticResource bellRingersFontStyle}"/>
```

5. Apply the same style to the following controls. You can either use the property resource editor or add the style manually to each control by editing the XAML definitions:

- label2
- label3
- isCaptain
- towerNames
- label4
- yearsExperience
- methods

Note Applying the style to the *yearsExperience* group box and the *methods* list box automatically causes the style to be used by the items displayed in these controls.

6. Apply the *bellRingersStyle* style to the following controls:

- firstName
- lastName
- add
- clear

7. On the *Debug* menu, click *Start Without Debugging*.

When the form runs, it should look like the following image:

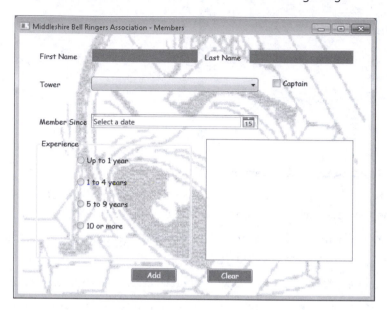

Notice that the *methods* list box is currently empty. You will add code to populate it in a later exercise.

8. Click the drop-down arrow in the *Tower* combo box. The list of towers is currently empty. Again, you will write code to fill this combo box in a later exercise.

9. Close the form, and return to Visual Studio 2010.

Changing Properties Dynamically

You have been using the *Design View* window, *Properties* window, and *XAML* pane to set properties statically. When the form runs, it would be useful to reset the value of each control to an initial default value. To do this, you will need to write some code (at last). In the following exercises, you will create a *private* method called *Reset*. Later, you will invoke the *Reset* method when the form first starts as well as when the user clicks the *Clear* button.

Create the *Reset* method

1. In the *Design View* window, right-click the form, and then click *View Code*. The *Code and Text Editor* window opens and displays the MainWindow.xaml.cs file so that you can add C# code to the form.

2. Add the following *Reset* method, shown in bold type, to the *MainWindow* class:

```
public partial class MainWindow : Window
{
    ...
    public void Reset()
    {
        firstName.Text = String.Empty;
        lastName.Text = String.Empty;
    }
}
```

These two statements in this method ensure that the *firstName* and *lastName* text boxes are blank by assigning an empty string to their *Text* property.

You also need to initialize the properties for the remaining controls on the form and populate the *towerNames* combo box and the *methods* list box.

If you recall, the *towerName* combo box will contain a list of all the bell towers in the Middleshire district. This information would usually be held in a database, and you would write code to retrieve the list of towers and populate the *ComboBox*. For this example, the application will use a hard-coded collection. A *ComboBox* has a property called *Items* that contains a list of the data to be displayed.

3. Add the following string array called *towers*, shown in bold type, which contains a hard-coded list of tower names, to the *MainWindow* class:

```
public partial class MainWindow : Window
{
    private string[] towers = { "Great Shevington", "Little Mudford",
                                "Upper Gumtree", "Downley Hatch" };
    ...
}
```

4. Add the following statements shown in bold type to the end of the *Reset* method. This code clears the *towerNames* combo box (which is important because otherwise you could end up with many duplicate values in the list) and adds the towers found in the *towers* array. A combo box contains a property called *Items* that contains a collection of items to display. The statement after the *foreach* loop causes the first tower to be displayed as the default value:

```
public void Reset()
{
    ...
    towerNames.Items.Clear();
    foreach (string towerName in towers)
    {
        towerNames.Items.Add(towerName);
    }
    towerNames.Text = towerNames.Items[0] as string;
}
```

Note You can also specify hard-coded values at design time in the XAML description of a combo box, like this:

```
<ComboBox Text="towerNames">
    <ComboBox.Items>
        <ComboBoxItem>
            Great Shevington
        </ComboBoxItem>
        <ComboBoxItem>
            Little Mudford
        </ComboBoxItem>
        <ComboBoxItem>
            Upper Gumtree
        </ComboBoxItem>
        <ComboBoxItem>
            Downley Hatch
        </ComboBoxItem>
    </ComboBox.Items>
</ComboBox>
```

5. You must populate the *methods* list box with a list of bell-ringing methods. As with a combo box, a list box has a property called *Items* that contains a collection of values to be displayed. Also, like the *ComboBox*, it can be populated from a database. However, as before, you will simply supply some hard-coded values for this example. Add the following string array shown in bold type, which contains the list of methods, to the *MainWindow* class:

```
public partial class MainWindow : Window
{
    ...
    private string[] ringingMethods = { "Plain Bob", "Reverse Canterbury",
        "Grandsire", "Stedman", "Kent Treble Bob", "Old Oxford Delight",
        "Winchendon Place", "Norwich Surprise", "Crayford Little Court" };
    ...
}
```

6. To enable the user to specify which methods a member can ring, the *methods* list box should display a list of check boxes rather than ordinary text strings. With the flexibility of the WPF model, you can specify different types of content for controls such as list boxes and combo boxes. Add the following code shown in bold type to the *Reset* method to fill the *methods* list box with the methods in the *ringingMethods* array. Notice that this time each item is a check box. You can specify the text displayed by the check box by setting its *Content* property, and you can specify the spacing between items in the list by setting the *Margin* property; this code inserts a spacing of 10 units after each item:

```
public void Reset()
{
    ...
    methods.Items.Clear();
```

```
    CheckBox method = null;
    foreach (string methodName in ringingMethods)
    {
        method = new CheckBox();
        method.Margin = new Thickness(0, 0, 0, 10);
        method.Content = methodName;
        methods.Items.Add(method);
    }
}
```

> **Note** Most WPF controls have a *Content* property that you can use to set and read the value displayed by that control. This property is actually an *object*, so you can set it to almost any type, as long as it makes sense to display it!

7. The *isCaptain* check box should default to *false*. To do this, you need to set the *IsChecked* property. Add the following statement shown in bold type to the *Reset* method:

```
public void Reset()
{
    ...
    isCaptain.IsChecked = false;
}
```

8. The form contains four radio buttons that indicate the number of years of bell-ringing experience the member has. A radio button is similar to a *CheckBox* in that it can contain a *true* or *false* value. However, the power of radio buttons increases when you put them together in a *GroupBox*. In this case, the radio buttons form a mutually exclusive collection—at most, only one radio button in a group can be selected (set to *true*), and all the others will automatically be cleared (set to *false*). By default, none of the buttons will be selected. You should rectify this by setting the *IsChecked* property of the *novice* radio button. Add the following statement shown in bold type to the *Reset* method:

```
public void Reset()
{
    ...
    novice.IsChecked = true;
}
```

9. You should ensure that the *memberSince DatePicker* control defaults to the current date. You can do this by setting the *Text* property of the control. You can obtain the current date from the static *Today* method of the *DateTime* struct.

   Add the following code shown in bold type to the *Reset* method to initialize the *DatePicker* control:

```
public void Reset()
{
    ...
    memberSince.Text = DateTime.Today.ToString();
}
```

10. Finally, you need to arrange for the *Reset* method to be called when the form is first displayed. A good place to do this is in the *MainWindow* constructor. Insert a call to the *Reset* method after the statement that calls the *InitializeComponent* method, as shown in bold type here:

```
public MainWindow()
{
    InitializeComponent();
    this.Reset();
}
```

11. On the *Debug* menu, click *Start Without Debugging* to verify that the project builds and runs.

12. When the form opens, click the *Tower* combo box.

    You will see the list of bell towers, and you can select one of them.

13. Click the icon on the right side of the *Member Since* date/time picker.

    You will be presented with a calendar of dates. The default value will be the current date. You can click a date and use the arrows to select a month. You can also click the month name to display the months as a list, and you can also click the year to display a list of years.

14. Click each of the radio buttons in the *Experience* group box.

    Notice that you cannot select more than one radio button at a time.

15. In the *Methods* list box, click some of the methods to select the corresponding check box. If you click a method a second time, it clears the corresponding check box, just as you would expect.

16. Click the *Add* and *Clear* buttons.

    Currently, these buttons don't do anything. You will add this functionality in the final set of exercises in this chapter.

17. Close the form, and return to Visual Studio 2010.

Handling Events in a WPF Form

If you are familiar with Microsoft Visual Basic, Microsoft Foundation Classes (MFC), or any of the other tools available for building GUI applications for Windows, you are aware that Windows uses an event-driven model to determine when to execute code. In Chapter 17, "Interrupting Program Flow and Handling Events," you saw how to publish your own events and subscribe to them. WPF forms and controls have their own predefined events that you can subscribe to, and these events should be sufficient to handle the requirements of most user interfaces.

Processing Events in Windows Forms

The developer's task is to capture the events that are relevant to the application and write the code that responds to these events. A familiar example is the *Button* control, which raises a "Somebody clicked me" event when a user clicks it with the mouse or presses Enter when the button has the focus. If you want the button to do something, you write code that responds to this event. This is what you will do in the next exercise.

Handle the *Click* events for the *Clear* and *Add* buttons

1. Display the MainWindow.xaml file in the *Design View* window. Double-click the *Clear* button on the form.

 Note When you modify the code behind a WPF form and build the application, the next time you display the form in the *Design View* window it might display the following message at the top of the window: "An assembly or related document has been updated which requires the designer to be reloaded. Click here to reload." If this happens, click the message and allow the form to be reloaded.

The *Code and Text Editor* window appears and creates a method called *clear_Click*. This is an event method that will be invoked when the user clicks the *Clear* button. Notice that the event method takes two parameters: the *sender* parameter (an *object*) and an additional arguments parameter (a *RoutedEventArgs* object). The WPF runtime will populate these parameters with information about the source of the event and with any additional information that might be useful when handling the event. You will not use these parameters in this exercise.

WPF controls can raise a variety of events. When you double-click a control or a form in the *Design View* window, Visual Studio generates the stub of an event method for the default event for the control; for a button, the default event is the *Click* event. (If you double-click a text box control, Visual Studio generates the stub of an event method for handling the *TextChanged* event.)

2. When the user clicks the *Clear* button, you want the form to be reset to its default values. In the body of the *clear_Click* method, call the *Reset* method, as shown here in bold type:

```
private void clear_Click(object sender, RoutedEventArgs e)
{
    this.Reset();
}
```

Users will click the *Add* button when they have filled in all the data for a member and want to store the information. The *Click* event for the *Add* button should validate the information entered to ensure that it makes sense (for example, should you allow a tower captain to have less than one year of experience?) and, if it is okay, arrange for the data to be sent to a database or other persistent store. You will learn more about validation and storing data in later chapters. For now, the code for the *Click* event of the *Add* button will simply display a message box echoing the data input.

3. Return to the *Design View* window displaying the MainWindow.xaml form. In the *XAML* pane, locate the element that defines the *Add* button, and begin entering the following code shown in bold type:

```
<Button Content="Add" ... Click= />
```

Notice that as you type the = character, a shortcut menu appears, displaying two items: *<New Event Handler>* and *clear_Click*. If two buttons perform a common action, you can share the same event handler method between them, such as *clear_Click*. If you want to generate an entirely new event handling method, you can select the *<New Event Handler>* command instead.

4. On the shortcut menu, double-click the *<New Event Handler>* command.

The text *add_Click* appears in the XAML code for the button.

> **Note** You are not restricted to handling the *Click* event for a button. When you edit the XAML code for a control, the IntelliSense list displays the properties and events for the control. To handle an event other than the *Click* event, simply type the name of the event, and then select or type the name of the method that you want to handle this event. For a complete list of events supported by each control, see the Visual Studio 2010 documentation.

5. Switch to the *Code and Text Editor* window displaying the MainWindow.xaml.cs file. Notice that the *add_Click* method has been added to the *MainWindow* class.

> **Tip** You don't have to use the default names generated by Visual Studio 2010 for the event handler methods. Rather than clicking the *<New Event Handler>* command on the shortcut menu, you can just type the name of a method. However, you must then manually add the method to the window class. This method must have the correct signature; it should return a *void* and take two arguments—an *object* parameter and a *RoutedEventArgs* parameter.

> **Important** If you later decide to remove an event method such as *add_Click* from the MainWindow.xaml.cs file, you must also edit the XAML definition of the corresponding control and remove the `Click="add_Click"` reference to the event; otherwise, your application will not compile.

6. Add the following code shown in bold type to the *add_Click* method:

```
private void add_Click(object sender, RoutedEventArgs e)
{
    string nameAndTower = String.Format(
        "Member name: {0} {1} from the tower at {2} rings the following methods:",
        firstName.Text, lastName.Text, towerNames.Text);

    StringBuilder details = new StringBuilder();
    details.AppendLine(nameAndTower);

    foreach (CheckBox cb in methods.Items)
    {
        if (cb.IsChecked.Value)
        {
            details.AppendLine(cb.Content.ToString());
        }
    }

    MessageBox.Show(details.ToString(), "Member Information");
}
```

This block of code creates a *string* variable called *nameAndTower* that it fills with the name of the member and the tower to which the member belongs.

Notice how the code accesses the *Text* property of the text box and combo box controls to read the current values of those controls. Additionally, the code uses the static *String.Format* method to format the result. The *String.Format* method operates in a similar manner to the *Console.WriteLine* method, except that it returns the formatted string as its result rather than displaying it on the screen.

The code then creates a *StringBuilder* object called *details*. The method uses this *StringBuilder* object to build a string representation of the information it will display. The text in the *nameAndTower* string is used to initially populate the *details* object. The code then iterates through the *Items* collection in the *methods* list box. If you recall, this list box contains check box controls. Each check box is examined in turn, and if the user has selected it, the text in the *Content* property of the check box is appended to the *details StringBuilder* object. There is one small quirk here. Remember that a *CheckBox* can be set to *true*, *false*, or *null*. The *IsChecked* property actually returns a nullable *bool?* value. You access the Boolean value of the *IsChecked* property through the *Value* property.

Finally, the *MessageBox* class provides static methods for displaying dialog boxes on the screen. The *Show* method used here displays the contents of the *details* string in the body of the message box and will put the text "Member Information" in the title bar. *Show* is an overloaded method, and there are other variants that you can use to specify icons and buttons to display in the message box.

Note You could use ordinary string concatenation instead of a *StringBuilder* object, but the *StringBuilder* class is far more efficient and is the recommended approach for performing the kind of tasks required in this code. In the .NET Framework and C#, the *string* data type is immutable; when you modify the value in a string, the run time actually creates a new string containing the modified value and then discards the old string. Repeatedly modifying a string can cause your code to become inefficient because a new string must be created in memory at each change. (The old strings will eventually be garbage collected.) The *StringBuilder* class, in the *System.Text* namespace, is designed to avoid this inefficiency. You can add and remove characters from a *StringBuilder* object using the *Append*, *Insert*, and *Remove* methods without creating a new object each time.

7. On the *Debug* menu, click *Start Without Debugging* to build and run the application.

8. Type some sample data for the member's first name and last name, select a tower, and pick a few methods. Click the *Add* button, and verify that the *Member Information* message box appears displaying the details of the new member and the methods he can ring. In the *Member Information* message box, click *OK*.

9. Click the *Clear* button, and verify that the controls on the form are reset to the correct default values.

10. Close the form, and return to Visual Studio 2010.

In the final exercise in this chapter, you will add an event handler to handle the *Closing* event for the window so that users can confirm that they really want to quit the application. The *Closing* event is raised when the user attempts to close the form but before the form actually closes. You can use this event to prompt the user to save any unsaved data or even ask the user whether she really wants to close the form—if not, you can cancel the event in the event handler and prevent the form from closing.

Handle the *Closing* event for the form

1. In the *Design View* window, in the *XAML* pane, begin entering the code shown in bold type to the XAML description of the *MainWindow* window:

```
<Window x:Class="BellRingers.MainWindow"
    ...
    Title="..." ... Closing=>
```

2. When the shortcut menu appears after you type the = character, double-click the *<New Event Handler>* command.

Visual Studio generates an event method called *Window_Closing* and associates it with the *Closing* event for the form, like this:

```
<Window x:Class="BellRingers.MainWindow"
    ...
    Title="..." ... Closing="Window_Closing">
```

3. Switch to the *Code and Text Editor* window displaying the MainWindow.xaml.cs file.

   A stub for the *Window_Closing* event method has been added to the *MainWindow* class:

```
private void Window_Closing(object sender, System.ComponentModel.CancelEventArgs e)
{

}
```

   Observe that the second parameter for this method has the type *CancelEventArgs*. The *CancelEventArgs* class has a Boolean property called *Cancel*. If you set *Cancel* to *true* in the event handler, the form will not close. If you set *Cancel* to *false* (the default value), the form will close when the event handler finishes.

4. Add the following statements shown in bold type to the *Window_Closing* method:

```
private void Window_Closing(object sender, System.ComponentModel.CancelEventArgs e)
{
    MessageBoxResult key = MessageBox.Show(
        "Are you sure you want to quit",
        "Confirm",
        MessageBoxButton.YesNo,
        MessageBoxImage.Question,
        MessageBoxResult.No);
    e.Cancel = (key == MessageBoxResult.No);
}
```

   These statements display a message box asking the user to confirm whether to quit the application. The message box will contain *Yes* and *No* buttons and a question mark icon. The final parameter, *MessageBoxResult.No*, indicates the default button if the user simply presses the Enter key—it is safer to assume that the user does not want to exit the application than to risk accidentally losing the details that the user has just typed. When the user clicks either button, the message box will close and the button clicked will be returned as the value of the method (as a *MessageBoxResult*—an enumeration identifying which button was clicked). If the user clicks *No*, the second statement will set the *Cancel* property of the *CancelEventArgs* parameter (*e*) to *true*, preventing the form from closing.

5. On the *Debug* menu, click *Start Without Debugging* to run the application.

6. Try to close the form. In the message box that appears, click *No*.

   The form should continue running.

7. Try to close the form again. This time, in the message box, click *Yes*.

   The form closes, and the application finishes.

In this chapter, you saw how to use the essential features of WPF to build a functional user interface. WPF contains many more features than we have space to go into here, especially concerning some of its really cool capabilities for handling two-dimensional and three-dimensional graphics and animation. If you want to learn more about WPF, you can consult a book such as *Applications = Code + Markup: A Guide to the Microsoft Windows Presentation Foundation*, by Charles Petzold (Microsoft Press, 2006).

- If you want to continue to the next chapter

    Keep Visual Studio 2010 running, and turn to Chapter 23.

- If you want to exit Visual Studio 2010 now

    On the *File* menu, click *Exit*. If you see a *Save* dialog box, click *Yes* and save the project.

Chapter 22 Quick Reference

To	Do this
Create a WPF application	Use the WPF Application template.
Add controls to a form	Drag the control from the *Toolbox* onto the form.
Change the properties of a form or control	Click the form or control in the *Design View* window. Then do one of the following: ■ In the Properties window, select the property you want to change and enter the new value. ■ In the XAML pane, specify the property and value in the <Window> element or the element defining the control.
View the code behind a form	Do one of the following: ■ On the View menu, click Code. ■ Right-click in the Design View window, and then click View Code. ■ In Solution Explorer, expand the folder corresponding to the .xaml file for the form, and then double-click the .xaml.cs file that appears.
Define a set of mutually exclusive radio buttons.	Add a panel control, such as *StackPanel*, to the form. Add the radio buttons to the panel. All radio buttons in the same panel are mutually exclusive.

Populate a combo box or a list box by using C# code	Use the *Add* method of the *Items* property. For example:
	`towerNames.Items.Add("Upper Gumtree");`
	You might need to clear the *Items* property first, depending on whether you want to retain the existing contents of the list. For example:
	`towerNames.Items.Clear();`

Initialize a check box or radio button control	Set the *IsChecked* property to *true* or *false*. For example: `novice.IsChecked = true;`
Handle an event for a control or form	In the *XAML* pane, add code to specify the event, and then either select an existing method that has the appropriate signature or click the *<Add New Event>* command on the shortcut menu that appears, and then write the code that handles the event in the event method that is created.

Chapter 23
Gathering User Input

After completing this chapter, you will be able to:

- Create menus for Microsoft Windows Presentation Foundation (WPF) applications by using the *Menu* and *MenuItem* classes.

- Perform processing in response to menu events when a user clicks a menu command.

- Create context-sensitive pop-up menus by using the *ContextMenu* class.

- Manipulate menus through code, and create dynamic menus.

- Use Windows common dialog boxes in an application to prompt the user for the name of a file.

- Build WPF applications that can take advantage of multiple threads to improve responsiveness.

In Chapter 22, "Introducing Windows Presentation Foundation," you saw how to create a simple WPF application made up of a selection of controls and events. Many professional Microsoft Windows–based applications also provide menus containing commands and options, giving the user the ability to perform various tasks related to the application. In this chapter, you will learn how to create menus and add them to forms by using the *Menu* control. You will see how to respond when the user clicks a command on a menu. You'll learn how to create pop-up menus whose contents vary according to the current context. Finally, you will find out about the common dialog classes supplied as part of the WPF library. With these dialog classes, you can prompt the user for frequently used items, such as files and printers, in a quick, easy, and familiar manner.

Menu Guidelines and Style

If you look at most Windows-based applications, you'll notice that some items on the menu bar tend to appear repeatedly in the same place, and the contents of these items are often predictable. For example, the *File* menu is typically the first item on the menu strip, and on this menu you typically find commands for creating a new document, opening an existing document, saving the document, printing the document, and exiting the application.

 Note The term *document* means the data that the application manipulates. In Microsoft Office Excel, it is a worksheet; in the BellRingers application that you created in Chapter 22, it could be the details of a new member.

The order in which these commands appear tends to be the same across applications; for example, the *Exit* command is invariably the last command on the *File* menu. There might be other application-specific commands on the *File* menu as well.

An application often has an *Edit* menu containing commands such as *Cut*, *Paste*, *Clear*, and *Find*. There are usually some additional application-specific menus on the menu bar, but again, convention dictates that the final menu is the *Help* menu, which contains access to the Help system for your application as well as "about" information, which contains copyright and licensing details for the application. In a well-designed application, most menus are predictable and help ensure that the application is easy to learn and use.

> **Tip** Microsoft publishes a full set of guidelines for building intuitive user interfaces, including menu design, on the Microsoft Web site at *http://msdn2.microsoft.com/en-us/library/Aa286531.aspx.*

Menus and Menu Events

WPF provides the *Menu* control as a container for menu items. The *Menu* control provides a basic shell for defining a menu. Like most aspects of WPF, the *Menu* control is very flexible so that you can define a menu structure consisting of almost any type of WPF control. You are probably familiar with menus that contain text items that you can click to perform a command. WPF menus can also contain buttons, text boxes, combo boxes, and so on. You can define menus by using the *XAML* pane in the *Design View* window, and you can also construct menus at run time by using Microsoft Visual C# code. Laying out a menu is only half of the story. When a user clicks a command on a menu, the user expects something to happen! Your application acts on the commands by trapping menu events and executing code in much the same way as handling control events.

Creating a Menu

In the following exercise, you will use the *XAML* pane to create menus for the Middleshire Bell Ringers Association application. You will learn how to manipulate and create menus through code later in this chapter.

Create the application menu

1. Start Microsoft Visual Studio 2010 if it is not already running.

2. Open the BellRingers solution located in the \Microsoft Press\Visual CSharp Step By Step\Chapter 23\BellRingers folder in your Documents folder. This is a copy of the application that you built in Chapter 22.

3. Display the MainWindow.xaml file in the *Design View* window.

4. From the *Toolbox*, drag a *DockPanel* control from the *All WPF Controls* section any-where onto the form. (Make sure that you drop it onto the form and not onto one of the controls on the form.) In the *Properties* window, set the *Width* property of the *DockPanel* to **Auto**, set the *HorizontalAlignment* property to *Stretch*, set the *VerticalAlignment* property to **Top**, and set the *Margin* property to **0**.

> **Note** Setting the *Margin* property to 0 is the same as setting it to 0, 0, 0, 0.

The *DockPanel* control should appear at the top of the form, occupying the full width of the form. (It will cover the *First Name*, *Last Name*, *Tower*, and *Captain* user interface elements.)

The *DockPanel* control is a panel control that you can use for controlling the arrange-ment of other controls that you place on it, such as the *Grid* and *StackPanel* controls that you met in Chapter 22. You can add a menu directly to a form, but it is better practice to place it on a *DockPanel* because you can then more easily manipulate the menu and its positioning on the form. For example, if you want to place the menu at the bottom or on one side, you can relocate the entire menu elsewhere on the form simply by moving the panel either at design time or at run time by executing code.

5. From the *Toolbox*, drag a *Menu* control from the *All WPF Controls* section onto the *DockPanel* control. In the *Properties* window, set the *DockPanel.Dock* property to **Top**, set the *Width* property to **Auto**, set the *HorizontalAlignment* property to **Stretch**, and set the *VerticalAlignment* property to **Top**.

The *Menu* control appears as a gray bar across the top of the *DockPanel*. If you examine the code for the *DockPanel* and *Menu* controls in the *XAML* pane, they should look like this:

```
<DockPanel Height="100" HorizontalAlignment="Stretch" Margin="0"
 Name="dockPanel1" VerticalAlignment="Top" Width="Auto">
    <Menu Height="23" Name="menu1" Width="Auto" DockPanel.Dock="Top"
    VerticalAlignment="Top"/>
</DockPanel>
```

The *HorizontalAlignment* property does not appear in the XAML code because the value "Stretch" is the default value for this property.

> **Note** Throughout this chapter, lines from the *XAML* pane are shown split and indented so that they fit on the printed page.

6. Click the *Menu* control on the form. In the *Properties* window, locate the *Items* property. The value of this property is reported as *(Collection)*. A Menu control contains a collection of *MenuItem* elements. Currently, the menu has no menu items, so the collection is empty. Click the ellipses button (...) adjacent to the value.

The *Collection Editor: Items* dialog box appears, as shown in the following image:

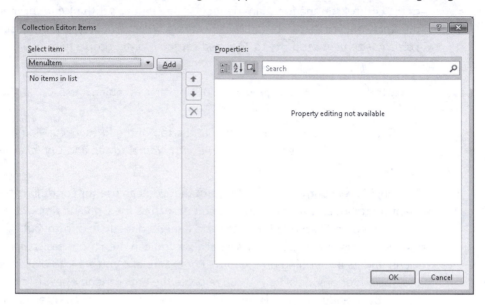

7. In the *Collection Editor: Items* dialog box, click *Add*. A new *MenuItem* element is created and appears in the dialog box. In the *Properties* pane, set the *Header* property to **_File** (including the leading underscore).

   The *Header* attribute of the *MenuItem* element specifies the text that appears for the menu item. The underscore (_) in front of a letter provides fast access to that menu item when the user presses the Alt key and the letter following the underscore (in this case, Alt+F for "File"). This is another common convention. At run time, when the user presses the Alt key, the F at the start of File appears underscored. Do not use the same access key more than once on any menu because you will confuse the user (and probably the application).

8. Click *Add* again. In the *Properties* pane, set the *Header* property of the second *MenuItem* element to **_Help**, and then click **OK** to close the dialog box.

9. In the *XAML* pane, examine the definition of the *Menu* control. It should look like this (the new items are shown in bold):

```
<Menu Height="22" Name="menu1" Width="Auto" DockPanel.Dock="Top"
    VerticalAlignment="Top" HorizontalAlignment="Stretch" >
    <MenuItem Header="_File" />
    <MenuItem Header="_Help" />
</Menu>
```

Notice that *MenuItem* elements appear as child items of the *Menu* control. You can create menu items by typing the code directly into the XAML pane rather than by using the *Collection Editor* dialog box if you prefer.

10. On the *Debug* menu, click *Start Without Debugging* to build and run the application.

 When the form appears, you should see the menu at the top of the window underneath the title bar. Press the Alt key; the menu should get the focus, and the "F" in "File" and the "H" in "Help" should both be underscored, like this:

 If you click either menu item, nothing currently happens because you have not defined the child menus that each of these items will contain.

11. Close the form, and return to Visual Studio 2010.

12. In the *XAML* pane, modify the definition of the *_File* menu item, remove the "/" character from the end of the tag, and add the child menu items together with a closing *</MenuItem>* element as shown here in bold type:

```
<MenuItem Header="_File" >
    <MenuItem Header="_New Member" Name="newMember" />
    <MenuItem Header="_Save Member Details" Name="saveMember" />
    <Separator/>
    <MenuItem Header="E_xit" Name="exit" />
</MenuItem>
```

 This XAML code adds *New Member*, *Save Member Details*, and *Exit* as commands to the *File* menu. The *<Separator/>* element appears as a bar when the menu is displayed and is conventionally used to group related menu items. Apart from the separator, each menu item is also given a name because you will need to refer to them later in your application.

 Tip You can also add child menu items to a *MenuItem* element by using the *Collection Editor: Items* dialog box. Like the *Menu* control, each *MenuItem* element has a property called *Items*, which is a collection of *MenuItem* elements. You can click the ellipses button that appears in the *Items* property in the *Properties* pane for a *MenuItem* element to open another instance of the *Collection Editor: Items* dialog box. Any items that you add appear as child items of the *MenuItem* element.

13. Modify the definition of the *_Help* menu item, and add the child menu item shown next in bold type:

```
<MenuItem Header="_Help" >
    <MenuItem Header="_About Middleshire Bell Ringers" Name="about" />
</MenuItem>
```

14. On the *Debug* menu, click *Start Without Debugging* to build and run the application.

When the form appears, click the *File* menu. You should see the child menu items, like this:

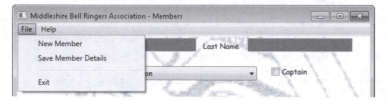

You can also click the *Help* menu to display the *About Middleshire Bell Ringers* child menu item.

None of the child menu items do anything when you click them, though. You will see how to associate menu items with actions in the next section.

15. Close the form, and return to Visual Studio 2010.

As a further touch, you can add icons to menu items. Many applications, including Visual Studio 2010, make use of icons in menus to provide an additional visual cue.

16. In *Solution Explorer*, right-click the BellRingers project, point to *Add*, and then click *Existing Item*. In the *Add Existing Item – BellRingers* dialog box, move to the folder Microsoft Press\Visual CSharp Step By Step\Chapter 23 under your Documents folder. In the drop-down list box adjacent to the *File name* text box, select *All Files (*.*)*. Select the files *Face.bmp*, *Note.bmp*, and *Ring.bmp*, and then click *Add*.

This action adds the three image files as resources to your application.

17. In the *XAML* pane, modify the definitions of the *newMember*, *saveMember*, and *about* menu items and add *MenuItem.Icon* child elements that refer to each of the three icon files you added to the project in the preceding step, as shown in bold type next. Notice that you also need to remove the "/" character from the closing tag for each *MenuItem* element, and add a *</MenuItem>* tag:

```
<Menu Height="22" Name="menu1" ... >
    <MenuItem Header="_File" >
        <MenuItem Header="_New Member" Name="newMember" >
            <MenuItem.Icon>
                <Image Source="Face.bmp"/>
            </MenuItem.Icon>
        </MenuItem>
        <MenuItem Header="_Save Member Details" Name="saveMember" >
            <MenuItem.Icon>
                <Image Source="Note.bmp"/>
            </MenuItem.Icon>
        </MenuItem>
        <Separator/>
        <MenuItem Header="E_xit" Name="exit"/>
    </MenuItem>
```

```
<MenuItem Header="_Help">
    <MenuItem Header="_About Middleshire Bell Ringers" Name="about" >
        <MenuItem.Icon>
            <Image Source="Ring.bmp"/>
        </MenuItem.Icon>
    </MenuItem>
</MenuItem>
</Menu>
```

18. The final tweak is to ensure that the text for the menu items is styled in a consistent manner with the rest of the form. In the *XAML* pane, edit the definition of the top-level *menu1* element and set the *Style* property to the *BellRingersFontStyle* style, as shown in bold type here:

```
<Menu Style="{StaticResource bellRingersFontStyle}" ... Name="menu1" ... >
```

Note that the child menu items automatically inherit the style from the top-level menu item that contains them.

19. On the *Debug* menu, click *Start Without Debugging* to build and run the application again.

When the form appears, click the *File* menu. You should now see that the text of the menu items is displayed in the correct font and that the icons appear with the child menu items, like this:

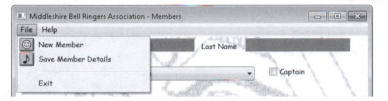

20. Close the form, and return to Visual Studio 2010.

Types of Menu Items

You have been using the *MenuItem* element to add child menu items to a *Menu* control. You have seen that you can specify the items in the top-level menu as *MenuItem* elements and then add nested *MenuItem* elements to define your menu structure. The nested *MenuItem* elements can themselves contain further nested *MenuItem* elements if you want to create cascading menus. In theory, you can continue this process to a very deep level, but in practice you should probably not go beyond two levels of nesting.

However, you are not restricted to using the *MenuItem* element. You can also add combo boxes, text boxes, and most other types of controls to WPF menus. For example, the following menu structure contains a button and a combo box:

```
<Menu ...>
    <MenuItem Header="Miscellaneous">
        <Button Content="Add new member" />
        <ComboBox>
            <ComboBox.Items>
                <ComboBoxItem>
                    Great Shevington
                </ComboBoxItem>
                <ComboBoxItem>
                    Little Mudford
                </ComboBoxItem>
                <ComboBoxItem>
                    Upper Gumtree
                </ComboBoxItem>
                <ComboBoxItem>
                    Downley Hatch
                </ComboBoxItem>
            </ComboBox.Items>
        </ComboBox>
    </MenuItem>
</Menu>
```

At run time, the menu structure looks like this:

Although you have great freedom when designing your menus, you should endeavor to keep things simple and not be too elaborate. A menu such as this is not very intuitive!

Handling Menu Events

The menu that you have built so far looks very pretty, but none of the items do anything when you click them. To make them functional, you have to write code to handle the various menu events. Several different events can occur when a user selects a menu item. Some are more useful than others are. The most frequently used event is the *Click* event, which occurs when the user clicks the menu item. You typically trap this event to perform the tasks associated with the menu item.

In the following exercise, you will learn more about menu events and how to process them. You will create *Click* events for the *newMember* and *exit* menu items.

The purpose of the *New Member* command is so that the user can enter the details of a new member. Therefore, until the user clicks *New Member*, all fields on the form should be disabled, as should the *Save Member Details* command. When the user clicks the *New Member* command, you want to enable all the fields, reset the contents of the form so that the user can start adding information about a new member, and enable the *Save Member Details* command.

Handle the *New Member* and *Exit* menu item events

1. In the *XAML* pane, click the definition of the *firstName* text box. In the *Properties* window, clear the *IsEnabled* property. (This action sets *IsEnabled* to *False* in the XAML definition.)

   Repeat this process for the *lastName*, *towerNames*, *isCaptain*, *memberSince*, *yearsExperience*, *methods*, and *clear* controls and for the *saveMember* menu item.

2. In the *Design View* window, in the *XAML* pane, begin entering the code shown here in bold type in the XAML description of the *_New Member* menu item:

   ```
   <MenuItem Header="_New Member" Name="newMember" Click=>
   ```

3. When the shortcut menu appears after you type the = character, double-click the *<New Event Handler>* command.

   Visual Studio generates an event method called *newMember_Click* and associates it with the *Click* event for the menu item.

> **Tip** Always give a menu item a meaningful name if you are going to define event methods for it. If you don't, Visual Studio generates an event method called *MenuItem_Click* for the *Click* event. If you then create *Click* event methods for other menu items that also don't have names, they are called *MenuItem_Click_1*, *MenuItem_Click_2*, and so on. If you have several of these event methods, it can be difficult to work out which event method belongs to which menu item.

4. Switch to the *Code and Text Editor* window displaying the MainWindow.xaml.cs file. (On the *View* menu, click *Code*.)

The *newMember_Click* event method will have been added to the bottom of the *MainWindow* class definition:

```
private void newMember_Click(object sender, RoutedEventArgs e)
{

}
```

5. Add the following statements shown in bold type to the *newMember_Click* method:

```
private void newMember_Click(object sender, RoutedEventArgs e)
{
    this.Reset();
    saveMember.IsEnabled = true;
    firstName.IsEnabled = true;
    lastName.IsEnabled = true;
    towerNames.IsEnabled = true;
    isCaptain.IsEnabled = true;
    memberSince.IsEnabled = true;
    yearsExperience.IsEnabled = true;
    methods.IsEnabled = true;
    clear.IsEnabled = true;
}
```

This code calls the *Reset* method and then enables all the controls. Recall from Chapter 22 that the *Reset* method resets the controls on the form to their default values. (If you don't recall how the *Reset* method works, scroll the *Code and Text Editor* window to display the method and refresh your memory.)

Next, you need to create a *Click* event method for the *Exit* command. This method should cause the form to close.

6. Return to the *Design View* window displaying the MainWindow.xaml file. Use the technique you followed in step 2 to create a *Click* event method for the *exit* menu item called *exit_Click*. (This is the default name generated by selecting *<New Event Handler>*.)

7. Switch to the *Code and Text Editor* window. In the body of the *exit_Click* method, type the statement shown in bold type in the following code:

```
private void exit_Click(object sender, RoutedEventArgs e)
{
    this.Close();
}
```

The *Close* method of a form *attempts* to close the form. Remember that if the form intercepts the *Closing* event, it can prevent the form from closing. The Middleshire Bell Ringers Association application does precisely this, and it asks the user if he wants to quit. If the user says no, the form does not close and the application continues to run.

The next step is to handle the *saveMember* menu item. When the user clicks this menu item, the data on the form should be saved to a file. For the time being, you will save the information to an ordinary text file called Members.txt in the current folder. Later, you will modify the code so that the user can select an alternative file name and location.

Handle the *Save Member Details* menu item event

1. Return to the *Design View* window displaying the MainWindow.xaml file. In the *XAML* pane, locate the definition of the *saveMember* menu item and use the *<New Event Handler>* command to generate a *Click* event method called *saveMember_Click*. (This is the default name generated by selecting *<New Event Handler>*.)

2. In the *Code and Text Editor* window displaying the MainWindow.xaml.cs file, scroll to the top of the file and add the following *using* statement to the list:

```
using System.IO;
```

3. Locate the *saveMember_Click* event method at the end of the file. Add the following statements shown in bold type to the body of the method:

```
private void saveMember_Click(object sender, RoutedEventArgs e)
{
    using (StreamWriter writer = new StreamWriter("Members.txt"))
    {
        writer.WriteLine("First Name: {0}", firstName.Text);
        writer.WriteLine("Last Name: {0}", lastName.Text);
        writer.WriteLine("Tower: {0}", towerNames.Text);
        writer.WriteLine("Captain: {0}", isCaptain.IsChecked.ToString());
        writer.WriteLine("Member Since: {0}", memberSince.Text);
        writer.WriteLine("Methods: ");
        foreach (CheckBox cb in methods.Items)
        {
            if (cb.IsChecked.Value)
            {
                writer.WriteLine(cb.Content.ToString());
            }
        }

        MessageBox.Show("Member details saved", "Saved");
    }
}
```

This block of code creates a *StreamWriter* object that the method uses for writing text to the Member.txt file. Using the *StreamWriter* class is similar to displaying text in a console application by using the *Console* object—you can simply use the *WriteLine* method.

When the details have all been written out, a message box is displayed giving the user some feedback (always a good idea).

4. The *Add* button and its associated event method are now obsolete, so in the *Design View* window delete the *Add* button. In the *Code and Text Editor* window, comment out the *add_Click* method.

The remaining menu item is the *about* menu item, which should display a dialog box providing information about the version of the application, the publisher, and any other useful information. You will add an event method to handle this event in the next exercise.

Handle the About Middleshire Bell Ringers menu item event

1. On the *Project* menu, click *Add Window*.

2. In the *Add New Item – BellRingers* dialog box, in the middle pane, click *Window (WPF)*. In the *Name* text box, type **About.xaml**, and then click *Add*.

   When you have added the appropriate controls, you will display this window when the user clicks the *About Middleshire Bell Ringers* command on the *Help* menu.

> **Note** Visual Studio provides the *About Box* windows template. However, this template generates a Windows Forms window rather than a WPF window.

3. In the *Design View* window, click the *About.xaml* form. In the *Properties* window, change the *Title* property to **About Middleshire Bell Ringers**, set the *Width* property to **300**, and set the *Height* property to **156**. Set the *ResizeMode* property to **NoResize** to prevent the user from changing the size of the window when it appears. (This is the convention for this type of dialog box.)

4. In the *Name* box at the top of the *Properties* window, type **AboutBellRingers**.

5. From the *Toolbox*, add two label controls and a button control to the form. In the *XAML* pane, modify the properties of these three controls as shown next in bold type (or change the text displayed by the *buildDate* label if you prefer):

```
<Window x:Class="BellRingers.About"
    xmlns="http://schemas.microsoft.com/winfx/2006/xaml/presentation"
    xmlns:x="http://schemas.microsoft.com/winfx/2006/xaml"
    Title="About Middleshire Bell Ringers" Height="156" Width="300"
        Name="AboutBellRingers" ResizeMode="NoResize">
    <Grid>
        <Label Content="Version 1.0" Height="28" HorizontalAlignment="Left"
         Margin="80,20,0,0" Name="version" VerticalAlignment="Top"
         Width="75" />
        <Label Content="Build date: September 2009" Height="28"
         HorizontalAlignment="Left" Margin="80,50,0,0" Name="buildDate"
         VerticalAlignment="Top" Width="160" />
        <Button Content="OK" Height="23" HorizontalAlignment="Left"
         Margin="100,85,0,0" Name="ok" VerticalAlignment="Top"
         Width="78" />
    </Grid>
</Window>
```

The completed form should look like this:

6. In the *Design View* window, double-click the *OK* button.

   Visual Studio generates an event method called *ok_Click* for the *Click* event of the button and adds this method to the About.xaml.cs file.

7. In the *Code and Text Editor* window displaying the About.xaml.cs file, add the statement shown in bold type to the *ok_Click* method:

```
private void ok_Click(object sender, RoutedEventArgs e)
{
    this.Close();
}
```

   When the user clicks the *OK* button, the *About Middleshire Bell Ringers* window will close.

8. Return to the *Design View* window displaying the MainWindow.xaml file. In the *XAML* pane, locate the definition of the *about* menu item and use the *<New Event Handler>* command to specify a *Click* event method called *about_Click*. (This is the default name.)

9. In the *Code and Text Editor* window displaying the MainWindow.xaml.cs file, add the following statements shown in bold to the *about_Click* method:

```
private void about_Click(object sender, RoutedEventArgs e)
{
    About aboutWindow = new About();
    aboutWindow.ShowDialog();
}
```

   WPF forms are really just classes that inherit from the *System.Windows.Windows* class. You can create an instance of a WPF form in the same way as any other class. This code creates a new instance of the *About* window and then calls the *ShowDialog* method to display it. The *ShowDialog* method is inherited from the Windows class and displays the WPF form on the screen. The *ShowDialog* method does not return until the *About* window closes (when the user clicks the *OK* button).

Test the menu events

1. On the *Debug* menu, click *Start Without Debugging* to build and run the application.

   Notice that all the fields on the form are disabled.

2. Click the *File* menu.

The *Save Member Details* command is disabled.

3. On the *File* menu, click *New Member*.

The fields on the form are now available.

4. Input some details for a new member.

5. Click the *File* menu again.

The *Save Member Details* command is now available.

6. On the *File* menu, click *Save Member Details*.

After a short delay, the message "Member details saved" appears. Click *OK* in this message box.

7. Using Windows Explorer, move to the \Microsoft Press\Visual CSharp Step By Step\ Chapter 23\BellRingers\BellRingers\bin\Debug folder under your Documents folder.

You should see a file called Members.txt in this folder.

8. Double-click *Members.txt* to display its contents using Notepad.

This file should contain the details of the new member. The following text shows an example:

```
First Name: John
Last Name: Sharp
Tower: Little Mudford
Captain: False
Member Since: 15/01/2000
Methods:
Plain Bob
Reverse Canterbury
Grandsire
Stedman
Kent Treble Bob
Old Oxford Delight
Winchendon Place
```

9. Close Notepad, and return to the Middleshire Bell Ringers application.

10. On the *Help* menu, click *About Middleshire Bell Ringers*.

The *About* window appears. Notice that you cannot resize this window, and you cannot click any items on the *Members* form while the *About* window is still visible.

11. Click *OK* to return to the *Members* form.

12. On the *File* menu, click *Exit*.

The form tries to close. You are asked if you are sure you want to close the form. If you click *No*, the form remains open; if you click *Yes*, the form closes and the application finishes.

13. Click *Yes* to close the form.

Shortcut Menus

Many Windows-based applications make use of pop-up menus that appear when you right-click a form or control. These menus are usually context-sensitive and display commands that are applicable only to the control or form that currently has the focus. They are usually referred to as *context* or *shortcut* menus. You can easily add shortcut menus to a WPF application by using the *ContextMenu* class.

Creating Shortcut Menus

In the following exercises, you will create two shortcut menus. The first shortcut menu is attached to the *firstName* and *lastName* text box controls and allows the user to clear these controls. The second shortcut menu is attached to the form and contains commands for saving the currently displayed member's information and for clearing the form.

 Note *TextBox* controls are associated with a default shortcut menu that provides *Cut*, *Copy*, and *Paste* commands for performing text editing. The shortcut menu that you will define in the following exercise will override this default menu.

Create the *firstName* and *lastName* shortcut menu

1. In the *Design View* window displaying MainWindow.xaml, add the following *ContextMenu* element shown in bold type to the end of the window resources in the *XAML* pane after the style definitions:

   ```
   <Window.Resources>
       ...
       <ContextMenu x:Key="textBoxMenu" Style="{StaticResource bellRingersFontStyle}" >
       </ContextMenu>
   </Window.Resources>
   ```

   This shortcut menu will be shared by the *firstName* and *lastName* text boxes. Adding the shortcut menu to the window resources makes it available to any controls in the window.

2. Add the following *MenuItem* element shown in bold type to the *textBoxMenu* shortcut menu:

   ```
   <Window.Resources>
       ...
       <ContextMenu x:Key="textBoxMenu" Style="{StaticResource bellRingersFontStyle}">
           <MenuItem Header="Clear Name" Name="clearName" />
       </ContextMenu>
   </Window.Resources>
   ```

   This code adds a menu item called *clearName* with the legend "Clear Name" to the shortcut menu.

3. In the *XAML* pane, modify the definitions of the *firstName* and *lastName* text box controls, and add the *ContextMenu* property, shown here in bold type:

```
<TextBox ... Name="firstName" ContextMenu="{StaticResource textBoxMenu}" ... />
...
<TextBox ... Name="lastName" ContextMenu="{StaticResource textBoxMenu}" ... />
```

The *ContextMenu* property determines which menu (if any) will be displayed when the user right-clicks the control.

4. Return to the definition of the *textBoxMenu* style, and add a *Click* event method called *clearName_Click* to the *clearName* menu item. (This is the default name generated by the *<New Event Handler>* command.)

```
<MenuItem Header="Clear Name" Name="clearName" Click="clearName_Click" />
```

5. In the *Code and Text Editor* window displaying MainWindow.xaml.cs, add the following statements to the *clearName_Click* event method that the *<New Event Handler>* command generated:

```
firstName.Clear();
lastName.Clear();
```

This code clears both text boxes when the user clicks the *Clear Name* command on the shortcut menu.

6. On the *Debug* menu, click *Start Without Debugging* to build and run the application. When the form appears, click *File*, and then click *New Member*.

7. Type a name in the *First Name* and *Last Name* text boxes. Right-click the *First Name* text box. On the shortcut menu, click the *Clear Name* command, and verify that both text boxes are cleared.

8. Type a name in the *First Name* and *Last Name* text boxes. This time, right-click the *Last Name* text box. On the shortcut menu, click the *Clear Name* command and again verify that both text boxes are cleared.

9. Right-click any controls except the *Member Since* control. Right-click anywhere on the form outside the *First Name* and *Last Name* text boxes.

With the exception of the *Member Since* control, only the *First Name* and *Last Name* text boxes have shortcut menus, so no pop-up menu should appear anywhere else.

 Note   The *Member Since* control displays a pop-up menu with *Cut*, *Copy*, and *Paste* commands. This functionality is built into the *DatePicker* control by default.

10. Close the form, and return to Visual Studio 2010.

Now you can add the second shortcut menu, which contains commands that the user can use to save member information and to clear the fields on the form. To provide a bit of variation, and to show you how easy it is to create shortcut menus dynamically, in the following exercise you will create the shortcut menu by using code. The best place to put this code is in the constructor of the form. You will then add code to enable the shortcut menu for the window when the user creates a new member.

Create the window shortcut menu

1. Switch to the *Code and Text Editor* window displaying the MainWindow.xaml.cs file.

2. Add the following private variable shown in bold type to the *MainWindow* class:

```
public partial class MainWindow : Window
{
    ...
    private ContextMenu windowContextMenu = null;
    ...
}
```

3. Locate the constructor for the *MainWindow* class. This is actually the first method in the class and is called *MainWindow*. Add the statements shown in bold type after the code that calls the *Reset* method to create the menu items for saving member details:

```
public MainWindow()
{
    InitializeComponent();
    this.Reset();

    MenuItem saveMemberMenuItem = new MenuItem();
    saveMemberMenuItem.Header = "Save Member Details";
    saveMemberMenuItem.Click += new RoutedEventHandler(saveMember_Click);
}
```

This code sets the *Header* property for the menu item and then specifies that the *Click* event should invoke the *saveMember_Click* event method; this is the same method that you wrote in an earlier exercise in this chapter. The *RoutedEventHandler* type is a delegate that represents methods for handling the events raised by many WPF controls. (For more information about delegates and events, refer to Chapter 17, "Interrupting Program Flow and Handling Events.")

4. In the *MainWindow* constructor, add the following statements shown in bold type to create the menu items for clearing the fields on the form and resetting them to their default values:

```
public MainWindow()
{
    ...
    MenuItem clearFormMenuItem = new MenuItem();
    clearFormMenuItem.Header = "Clear Form";
    clearFormMenuItem.Click += new RoutedEventHandler(clear_Click);
}
```

This menu item invokes the *clear_Click* event method when clicked by the user.

5. In the *MainWindow* constructor, add the following statements shown in bold type to construct the shortcut menu and populate it with the two menu items you have just created:

```
public MainWindow()
{
    . . .
    windowContextMenu = new ContextMenu();
    windowContextMenu.Items.Add(saveMemberMenuItem);
    windowContextMenu.Items.Add(clearFormMenuItem);
}
```

The *ContextMenu* type contains a collection called *Items* that holds the menu items.

6. At the end of the *newMember_Click* event method, add the statement shown in bold type to associate the context menu with the form:

```
private void newMember_Click(object sender, RoutedEventArgs e)
{
    . . .
    this.ContextMenu = windowContextMenu;
}
```

Notice that the application associates the shortcut menu with the form only when the new member functionality is available. If you were to set the *ContextMenu* property of the form in the constructor, the *Save Member Details* and *Clear Details* shortcut menu items would be available even when the controls on the form were disabled, which is not how you want this application to behave.

 Tip You can disassociate a shortcut menu from a form by setting the *ContextMenu* property of the form to *null*.

7. On the *Debug* menu, click *Start Without Debugging* to build and run the application.

8. When the form appears, right-click the form and verify that the shortcut menu does not appear.

9. On the *File* menu, click *New Member*, and then input some details for a new member.

10. Right-click the form. On the shortcut menu, click *Clear Form* and verify that the fields on the form are reset to their default values.

11. Input some more member details. Right-click the form. On the shortcut menu, click *Save Member Details*. Verify that the "Member details saved" message box appears, and then click *OK*.

12. Close the form, and return to Visual Studio 2010.

Windows Common Dialog Boxes

The BellRingers application now lets you save member information, but it always saves data to the same file, overwriting anything that is already there. Now is the time to address this issue.

A number of everyday tasks require the user to specify the same information, regardless of the functionality of the application that the user is running. For example, if the user wants to open or save a file, the user is usually asked which file to open or where to save it. You might have noticed that the same dialog boxes are used by many different applications. This is not a result of a lack of imagination by applications developers; it is just that this functionality is so common that Microsoft has standardized it and made it available as a "common dialog box"—a component supplied with the Microsoft Windows operating system that you can use in your own applications. The Microsoft .NET Framework class library provides the *OpenFileDialog* and *SaveFileDialog* classes, which act as wrappers for these common dialog boxes.

Using the *SaveFileDialog* Class

In the following exercise, you will use the *SaveFileDialog* class. In the BellRingers application, when the user saves details to a file, you will prompt the user for the name and location of the file by displaying the Save File common dialog box.

Use the *SaveFileDialog* class

1. In the *Code and Text Editor* window displaying MainWindow.xaml.cs, add the following *using* statement to the list at the top of the file:

   ```
   using Microsoft.Win32;
   ```

   The *SaveFileDialog* class is in the *Microsoft.Win32* namespace (even on 64-bit versions of the Windows operating system).

2. Locate the *saveMember_Click* method, and add the code shown in bold to the start of this method, replacing *YourName* with the name of your account on your computer:

   ```
   private void saveMember_Click(object sender, RoutedEventArgs e)
   {
       SaveFileDialog saveDialog = new SaveFileDialog();
       saveDialog.DefaultExt = "txt";
       saveDialog.AddExtension = true;
       saveDialog.FileName = "Members";
       saveDialog.InitialDirectory = @"C:\Users\YourName\Documents\";
       saveDialog.OverwritePrompt = true;
       saveDialog.Title = "Bell Ringers";
       saveDialog.ValidateNames = true;
       ...
   }
   ```

This code creates a new instance of the *SaveFileDialog* class and sets its properties. The following table describes the purpose of these properties.

Property	Description
DefaultExt	The default file name extension to use if the user does not specify the extension when providing the file name.
AddExtension	Enables the dialog box to add the file name extension indicated by the *DefaultExt* property to the name of the file specified by the user if the user omits the extension.
FileName	The name of the currently selected file. You can populate this property to specify a default file name or clear it if you don't want a default file name.
InitialDirectory	The default directory to be used by the dialog box.
OverwritePrompt	Causes the dialog box to warn the user when an attempt is made to overwrite an existing file with the same name. For this to work, the *ValidateNames* property must also be set to *true*.
Title	A string that is displayed on the title bar of the dialog box.
ValidateNames	Indicates whether file names are validated. It is used by some other properties, such as *OverwritePrompt*. If the *ValidateNames* property is set to *true*, the dialog box also checks to verify that any file name typed by the user contains only valid characters.

3. Add the following *if* statement (and closing brace) shown in bold type to the *saveMember_Click* method. This statement encloses the previous code that creates the *StreamWriter* object and writes the member details to a file:

```
if (saveDialog.ShowDialog().Value)
{
    using (StreamWriter writer = new StreamWriter("Members.txt"))
    {
        // existing code
        ...
    }
}
```

The *ShowDialog* method displays the *Save File* dialog box. The *Save File* dialog box is modal, which means that the user cannot continue using any other forms in the application until the user has closed this dialog box by clicking one of its buttons. The *Save File* dialog box has a *Save* button and a *Cancel* button. If the user clicks *Save*, the value returned by the *ShowDialog* method is *true*; otherwise, it is *false*.

The *ShowDialog* method prompts the user for the name of a file to save to but does not actually do any saving—you still have to supply that code yourself. All it does is provide the name of the file that the user has selected in the *FileName* property.

4. In the *saveMember_Click* method, modify the statement that creates the *StreamWriter* object as shown in bold type here:

```
using (StreamWriter writer = new StreamWriter(saveDialog.FileName))
{
    ...
}
```

The *saveMember_Click* method will now write to the file specified by the user rather than to Members.txt.

5. On the *Debug* menu, click *Start Without Debugging* to build and run the application.

6. On the *File* menu, click *New Member*, and then add some details for a new member.

7. On the *File* menu, click *Save Member Details*.

The *Save File* dialog box should appear, with the caption "Bell Ringers." The default folder should be your Documents folder, and the default file name should be Members, as shown in the following image:

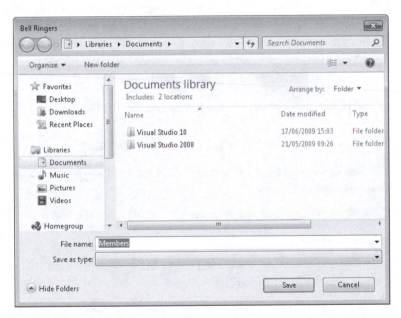

If you omit the file name extension, .txt is added automatically when the file is saved. If you pick an existing file, the dialog box warns you before it closes.

8. Change the value in the *File name* text box to **TestMember**, and then click *Save*.

9. In the BellRingers application, verify that the "Member details saved" message appears, click *OK*, and then close the application.

10. Using Windows Explorer, move to your Documents folder.

Verify that the TestMember.txt file has been created.

11. Double-click the file, and verify that it contains the details of the member that you added. Close Notepad when you have finished.

You can use a similar technique for opening a file: create an *OpenFileDialog* object, activate it by using the *ShowDialog* method, and retrieve the *FileName* property when the method returns if the user has clicked the *Open* button. You can then open the file, read its contents, and populate the fields on the screen. For more details on using the *OpenFileDialog* class, consult the MSDN Library for Visual Studio 2010.

Improving Responsiveness in a WPF Application

The purpose of the WPF libraries is to provide a foundation for building applications that provide graphical user interfaces. Consequently, WPF applications are inherently interactive. When a user runs a WPF application, she might visit the controls that form the user interface in almost any order. You have seen that your application responds to the user performing operations such as clicking buttons, typing text into boxes, or selecting menu items by using code that runs when the corresponding events are triggered. However, what happens if the code that responds to an event takes a long time to run? For example, suppose the BellRingers application saved its data to a remote database located somewhere over the Internet. It might take several seconds to actually transmit this data and store it. What effect might this delay have on the usability of your application?

In the next exercise, you will simulate this scenario and see the results.

Simulate a long-running event handler in a WPF application

1. In Visual Studio, switch to the *Code and Text Editor* window displaying the MainWindow.xaml.cs file.

2. Add the following *using* statement to the list at the top of the file.

```
using System.Threading;
```

3. Add the following statement shown in bold to the *using* statement that writes the member data to the file specified by the user:

```
private void saveMember_Click(object sender, RoutedEventArgs e)
{
    ...
    if (saveDialog.ShowDialog().Value)
    {
        using (StreamWriter writer = new StreamWriter(saveDialog.FileName))
        {
            ...
            Thread.Sleep(10000);
            MessageBox,Show("Member details saved", "Saved");
        }
    }
}
```

The static *Sleep* method of the *Thread* class in the *System.Threading* namespace causes the current thread in the application to stop responding for the specified period of time. This time is specified in milliseconds, so this code causes the thread to stop for 10 seconds.

> **Note** A thread is a path of execution in an application. All applications have at least one thread, and you can create applications that use multiple threads. If a computer has multiple CPUs or a multicore processor, it can execute multiple threads simultaneously. If you create more threads than there are available CPUs or processor cores, the operating system allocates quanta of CPU time to each thread to give the appearance of simultaneous execution. You will learn a lot more about threads and performing operations in parallel in Chapter 27, "Introducing the Task Parallel Library."

4. On the *Debug* menu, click *Start Without Debugging*.

5. When the WPF form appears, on the *File* menu click *New Member* and enter some details for a new member.

6. On the *File* menu, click *Save Member Details*. In the *Bell Ringers* dialog box, accept the default file name and then click *Save* (and overwrite the file if you are prompted).

7. When the *Bell Ringers* dialog box closes, attempt to click any of the controls on the WPF form. Notice that the form fails to respond. (The form might appear blank, and the title bar might display the text "Not Responding.")

8. When the *Saved* dialog box appears, click *OK*.

9. Now click any of the controls on the WPF form. The form now responds properly.

10. Close the form, and return to Visual Studio 2010.

By default, WPF applications are single-threaded. Consequently, a long-running event handler can cause the application to stop responding. This is clearly not acceptable in a professional program. However, the .NET Framework enables you to create multiple threads. You can then execute long-running tasks on these threads. However, you should be aware that there are some restrictions with these threads in a WPF application, as you will see in the next exercise.

Perform a long-running operation on a new thread

1. In Visual Studio, display the MainWindow.xaml.cs file in the *Code and Text Editor* window.

2. Add a new private method to the *MainWindow* class called *saveData*. This method should take a string parameter that specifies a file name and should not return a value, as follows:

```
private void saveData(string fileName)
{
}
```

3. Locate the *saveMember_Click* method. Copy the *using* statement and the enclosing code from this method to the *saveData* method. The *saveData* method should look like this:

```
private void saveData(string fileName)
{
    using (StreamWriter writer = new StreamWriter(saveDialog.FileName))
    {
        writer.WriteLine("First Name: {0}", firstName.Text);
        writer.WriteLine("Last Name: {0}", lastName.Text);
        writer.WriteLine("Tower: {0}", towerNames.Text);
        writer.WriteLine("Captain: {0}", isCaptain.IsChecked.ToString());
        writer.WriteLine("Member Since: {0}", memberSince.Text);
        writer.WriteLine("Methods: ");
        foreach (CheckBox cb in methods.Items)
        {
            if (cb.IsChecked.Value)
            {
                writer.WriteLine(cb.Content.ToString());
            }
        }

        Thread.Sleep(10000);
        MessageBox.Show("Member details saved", "Saved");
    }
}
```

4. In the *using* statement, change the code that calls the constructor for the *StreamWriter* object and replace the reference to *saveDialog.FileName* with the *fileName* parameter, as shown here in bold:

```
using (StreamWriter writer = new StreamWriter(fileName))
{
    ...
}
```

5. In the *saveMember_Click* method, remove the *using* statement and enclosing code block and replace it with the statements shown here in bold:

```
private void saveMember_Click(object sender, RoutedEventArgs e)
{
    ...
    if (saveDialog.ShowDialog().Value)
    {
        Thread workerThread = new Thread(
            () => this.saveData(saveDialog.FileName));
        workerThread.Start();
    }
}
```

This code creates a new *Thread* object called *workerThread*. The constructor for the *Thread* class expects a delegate that references a method to run when the thread executes. This example uses a lambda expression to create an anonymous delegate that invokes the *saveData* method.

The *Start* method of the *Thread* class starts the thread running. The thread executes asynchronously—the *Start* method does not wait for the method run by the thread to complete.

6. On the *Debug* menu, click *Start Debugging*.

> **Important**   Do not run the application without debugging.

7. When the WPF form appears, on the *File* menu, click *New Member*, provide some data for the new member, and then click *Save Member Details*. In the *Bell Ringers* dialog box, select the Members.txt file and then click *Save* (and overwrite the file if you are prompted).

The application stops in the *saveData* method and reports the exception "InvalidOperationException was unhandled" shown in the following image.

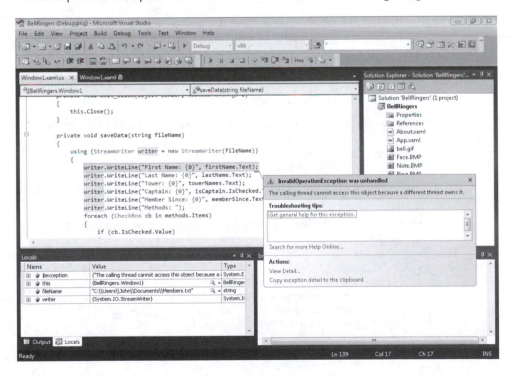

The text of the exception is "The calling thread cannot access this object because a different thread owns it", and the line highlighted is the code that reads the data from the *firstName* text box.

8. On the *Debug* menu, click *Stop Debugging* and return to Visual Studio 2010.

You have attempted to use a thread to perform a long-running task in the background. This is a sound approach. The problem is that the security model implemented by WPF prevents any threads other than the thread that created a user interface object such as a control from accessing that object. This restriction prevents two or more threads from attempting to take control of the user input or modifying the data on the screen because this could result in corruption of your data.

You can work around this restriction in many ways, but the simplest solution is to gather the data to be saved into a structure in the method run by the user-interface thread and then pass this structure to the method run by the background thread. This is what you will do in the next exercise.

Copy data from the user-interface thread to the background thread

1. In Visual Studio, on the *Project* menu, click *Add New Item*.

2. In the *Add New Item – Bell Ringers* dialog box, in the left pane expand *Visual C#* and then click *Code*. In the middle pane, click *Code File*. In the *Name* text box, type **Member.cs** and then click *Add*.

Visual Studio adds a blank code file called Member.cs to your project and displays it in the *Code and Text Editor* window.

3. Add the following *using* statements to the top of the Member.cs file:

```
using System;
using System.Collections.Generic;
```

4. In the Member.cs file, define the *Member* structure as shown next. This structure contains public properties that correspond to each of the fields on the form. The list of methods (tunes) that the member can ring is held as a *List<string>* collection (not a property).

```
struct Member
{
    public string FirstName { get; set; }
    public string LastName { get; set; }
    public string TowerName { get; set; }
    public bool IsCaptain { get; set; }
    public DateTime MemberSince { get; set; }
    public List<string> Methods;
}
```

5. Return to the MainWindow.xaml.cs file in the *Code and Text Editor* window.

6. Modify the *saveData* method to take a *Member* structure as the second parameter. In the body of the *saveData* method, change the code to read the member data from this structure rather than the fields on the WPF form. The following code example shows the completed method. Notice that the *foreach* loop iterates through the *List<string>* collection rather than the check boxes on the form:

```
private void saveData(string fileName, Member member)
{
    using (StreamWriter writer = new StreamWriter(fileName))
    {
        writer.WriteLine("First Name: {0}", member.FirstName);
        writer.WriteLine("Last Name: {0}", member.LastName);
        writer.WriteLine("Tower: {0}", member.TowerName);
        writer.WriteLine("Captain: {0}", member.IsCaptain.ToString());
        writer.WriteLine("Member Since: {0}", member.MemberSince.ToString());
        writer.WriteLine("Methods: ");
        foreach (string method in member.Methods)
        {
            writer.WriteLine(method);
        }

        Thread.Sleep(10000);
        MessageBox.Show("Member details saved", "Saved");
    }
}
```

7. In the *saveMember_Click* method, in the *if* statement block that starts the background thread, create a *Member* variable and populate it with the data from the form. Pass this *Member* variable as the second parameter to the *saveData* method run by the background thread. The following code in bold shows the changes you need to make:

```
private void saveMember_Click(object sender, RoutedEventArgs e)
{
    ...
    if (saveDialog.ShowDialog().Value)
    {
        Member member = new Member();
        member.FirstName = firstName.Text;
        member.LastName = lastName.Text;
        member.TowerName = towerNames.Text;
        member.IsCaptain = isCaptain.IsChecked.Value;
        member.MemberSince = memberSince.SelectedDate.Value;
        member.Methods = new List<string>();
        foreach (CheckBox cb in methods.Items)
        {
            if (cb.IsChecked.Value)
            {
                member.Methods.Add(cb.Content.ToString());
            }
        }

        Thread workerThread = new Thread(
            () => this.saveData(saveDialog.FileName, member));
        workerThread.Start();
    }
}
```

> **Note** The *isCaptain* control on the form is a *CheckBox* control, and the *IsChecked* property is nullable, so you determine whether the control is checked by examining the *Value* property. Similarly, the *SelectedDate* property of the *DatePicker* control is also nullable, so the code uses the *Value* property to retrieve the data related to membership.

8. On the *Debug* menu, click *Start Without Debugging*. On the *File* menu, click *New Member* and add some data. Then, on the *File* menu, click *Save MemberDetails*. In the *Bell Ringers* dialog box, specify the default file name and then click *Save*.

   Notice that the WPF form now functions correctly—it responds when you click any fields or try to enter some data.

9. After 10 seconds, the *Saved* message box appears indicating that the data has been saved. Click *OK*, close the WPF form, and return to Visual Studio 2010.

Threads and the *BackgroundWorker* Class

The example shown in the previous exercise created a *Thread* object to run a method on a new thread. An alternative approach is to create a *BackgroundWorker* object. The *BackgroundWorker* class lives in the *System.ComponentModel* namespace and provides a wrapper around threads. The following code shows how to run the *saveData* method by using a *BackgroundWorker* object.

```
BackgroundWorker workerThread = new BackgroundWorker();
workerThread.DoWork += (x, y) => this.saveData(saveDialog.FileName, member);
workerThread.RunWorkerAsync();
```

You specify the method that a *BackgroundWorker* object runs by subscribing to the *DoWork* event. The *DoWork* event expects you to provide a *DoWorkEventHandler* delegate (specified as a lambda expression in this example). The *DoWorkEventHandler* delegate refers to a method that takes two parameters; an *object* parameter that indicates the item that invoked the *BackgroundWorker* object, and a *DoWorkEventArgs* parameter that contains specific information passed to the *BackgroundWorker* to perform its work. The example code shown does not use these two parameters.

You start a thread running by calling the *RunWorkerAsync* method of the *BackgroundWorker* object.

For performing simple operations in the background, the *Thread* class is ideal. However, in more complex scenarios the *BackgroundWorker* class provides some advantages over the *Thread* class. Specifically, it provides the *ProgressChanged* event that a thread can use to report the progress of a long-running task, and the *RunWorkerCompleted* event that a thread can use to indicate that it has completed its work.

For more information about the *BackgroundWorker* class, consult the documentation provided with Visual Studio.

You have made the application more responsive by using a separate thread to perform a long-running operation and passing the data required by that thread as a parameter. However, there is one final quirk that you need to address. When the user saves the data for a member, the *Saved* message box appears and confirms that the data was saved correctly. This was fine originally when the save operation ran quickly and the user was not able to perform any other tasks at the same time. Now, though, this message box can appear while the user is entering data for another member and can become an annoyance because the message box grabs the focus. The user has to acknowledge the message box before being able to continue entering data, and this action can break the user's concentration, leading to input errors. A better solution is to display the message in a status bar at the bottom of the form. This provides an unobtrusive means of informing the user that the save operation has completed.

There is a problem with this approach, though; the status bar is a control created and owned by the user interface thread. How can the background thread access this control and display a message? The answer lies in the WPF *Dispatcher* object.

You can use the *Dispatcher* object to request that the user interface thread runs a method on behalf of another thread. The *Dispatcher* object queues these requests and runs them on the user interface thread at an appropriate point in time—for example, you can assign a priority to a request telling the *Dispatcher* object to run the request only when the user interface thread is idle. You can access the *Dispatcher* object through the *Dispatcher* property of any control on a WPF form, including the form itself.

You send a request to the *Dispatcher* object by calling the *Invoke* method. This method is overloaded, but all overloads expect a *Delegate* object that wraps a reference to a method that the *Dispatcher* object should run.

In the final exercise in this chapter, you will amend the BellRingers application to display the status of the save operation in a status bar at the bottom of the form, by using the *Dispatcher* object.

Use the *Dispatcher* object to display a status message

1. In Visual Studio, display the MainWindow.xaml file in the *Design View* window.

2. In the *Toolbox*, select the *StatusBar* control in the *Controls* section and add it to the bottom of the WPF form.

3. In the *Properties* window, set the properties of the *StatusBar* control to the values listed in the following table.

Property	Value
Name	status
Height	23
HorizontalAlignment	Stretch
Margin	0, 0, 0, 0
Style	{StaticResource bellRingersFontStyle}
VerticalAlignment	Bottom
Width	Auto

These properties cause the status bar to occupy one line at the bottom of the form.

4. The *Clear* button is partly obscured by the status bar, so it needs to be moved. In the *Properties* window, change the *Margin* property for the *Clear* button to **313,378,0,0**.

5. Display the MainWindow.xaml.cs file in the *Code and Text Editor* window.

6. Add the following *using* statement to the list at the top of the file:

```
using System.Windows.Threading;
```

7. In the *saveData* method, replace the statement that displays the message box with the code shown here in bold:

```
private void saveData(string fileName, Member member)
{
    using (StreamWriter writer = new StreamWriter(fileName))
    {
        ...
        Thread.Sleep(10000);
        Action action = new Action(() => {
            status.Items.Add("Member details saved");
        });
        this.Dispatcher.Invoke(action, DispatcherPriority.ApplicationIdle);
    }
}
```

The *Invoke* method of the *Dispatcher* object expects a request in the form of a *Delegate* parameter that references a method to run. However, *Delegate* is an abstract class. The *Action* class in the *System* namespace is a concrete implementation of the *Delegate* class, designed for referencing a method that takes no parameters and that does not return a result. (In other words, the method simply performs an action.)

Note The *Func<T>* generic type that you met briefly in Chapter 20, "Querying In-Memory Data by Using Query Expressions," is another implementation of the *Delegate* class. A *Func<T>* object references a method that returns an object of type *T*, and it is useful if you need to invoke a method that returns a value through a delegate.

The code shown here uses a lambda expression to define an anonymous method that displays the message "Member details saved" in the status bar. A *StatusBar* object can display multiple pieces of information, and to display an item you add it to the *Items* collection.

The example of the *Invoke* method shown here obtains a reference to the *Dispatcher* object by using the *Dispatcher* property of the form. The second parameter to the *Invoke* method specifies the priority that the *Dispatcher* object should assign to the request. This is a value from the *DispatcherPriority* enumeration in the *System.Windows.Threading* namespace. The value *ApplicationIdle* causes the *Dispatcher* object to run the request when the application is not performing any other work.

8. On the *Debug* menu, click *Start Without Debugging*. When the WPF form appears, on the *File* menu click *New Member* and add some member details. Then, on the *File* menu, click *Save Member Details*. In the *Bell Ringers* dialog box, specify the default file name and then click *Save*.

   Verify that the WPF form still responds while the background thread is running.

9. After 10 seconds, verify that the "Member details saved" message box appears in the status bar at the bottom of the form.

10. Close the WPF form, and return to Visual Studio 2010.

Threads are extremely valuable for maintaining responsiveness in a user interface. However, sometimes threads can be difficult to manage effectively; it can be difficult to synchronize concurrent operations if you need to wait for one or more threads to complete before continuing a process, and if you create too many threads the computer can become overloaded and slow down. The .NET Framework provides an abstraction of threads called *Tasks* that you can use to create and control threads in a manageable manner. You will learn more about *Tasks* in Chapter 27.

In this chapter, you saw how to create menus to enable users to perform operations in an application, and you also created shortcut menus that appear when the user right-clicks on a control or form. You saw how to use the common dialog classes to prompt the user for the name and location of a file. Finally, you learned about the threading model used by WPF applications and how you can use threads to make applications more responsive.

■ If you want to continue to the next chapter

   Keep Visual Studio 2010 running, and turn to Chapter 24.

■ If you want to exit Visual Studio 2010 now

   On the *File* menu, click *Exit*. If you see a *Save* dialog box, click *Yes* and save the project.

Chapter 23 Quick Reference

To	Do this
Create a menu for a form	Add a *DockPanel* control, and place it at the top of the form. Add a *Menu* control to the *DockPanel* control.
Add menu items to a menu	Add *MenuItem* elements to the *Menu* control. Specify the text for a menu item by setting the *Header* property, and give each menu item a name by specifying the *Name* property. You can optionally specify properties so that you can display features such as icons and child menus. You can add an access key to a menu item by prefixing the appropriate letter with an underscore character.
Create a separator bar in a menu	Add a *Separator* element to the menu.
Enable or disable a menu item	Set the *IsEnabled* property to *True* or *False* in the *Properties* window at design time, or write code to set the *IsEnabled* property of the menu item to *true* or *false* at run time.
Perform an action when the user clicks a menu item	Select the menu item, and specify an event method for the *Click* event. Add your code to the event method.
Create a shortcut menu	Add a *ContextMenu* to the window resources. Add items to the shortcut menu just as you add items to an ordinary menu.
Associate a shortcut menu with a form or control	Set the *ContextMenu* property of the form or control to refer to the shortcut menu.
Create a shortcut menu dynamically	Create a *ContextMenu* object. Populate the *Items* collection of this object with *MenuItem* objects defining each of the menu items. Set the *ContextMenu* property of the form or control to refer to the shortcut menu.
Prompt the user for the name of a file to save	Use the *SaveFileDialog* class. Display the dialog box by using the *ShowDialog* method. When the dialog box closes, the *FileName* property of the *SaveFileDialog* instance contains the name of the file selected by the user.

Perform an operation on a background thread	Create a *Thread* object that references a method to run. Call the *Start* method of the *Thread* object to invoke the method. For example:
	
	```Thread workerThread new Thread(```
	``` () => doWork(...));```
	
	```workerThread,Start();```

Enable a background thread to access controls managed by the user interface thread	Create an *Action* delegate that references a method that accesses the controls. Run the method by using the *Invoke* method of the *Dispatcher* object, and optionally specify a priority. For example:
	
	```Action action = new Action(() => {```
	``` status.Items.Add("Member details added");```
	```});```
	
	```this.Dispatcher.Invoke(action,```
	``` DispatcherPriority.ApplicationIdle);```

Chapter 24
Performing Validation

After completing this chapter, you will be able to:

- Verify the information entered by a user to ensure that it does not violate any application or business rules.

- Bind properties of one control on a form to properties of other controls.

- Use data binding validation rules to validate information entered by a user.

- Perform validation effectively but unobtrusively.

In the previous two chapters, you saw how to create a Microsoft Windows Presentation Foundation (WPF) application that uses a variety of controls for data entry. You created menus to make the application easier to use. You learned how to trap events raised by menus, forms, and controls so that your application can actually do something besides just look pretty. You also used threads to make the application responsive.

Although careful design of a form and the appropriate use of controls can help to ensure that the information entered by a user makes sense, you often need to perform additional checks. In this chapter, you will learn how to validate the data entered by a user running an application to ensure that it matches any business rules specified by the application's requirements.

Validating Data

The concept of input validation is simple enough, but it is not always easy to implement, especially if validation involves cross-checking data the user has entered into two or more controls. The underlying business rule might be relatively straightforward, but all too often, the validation is performed at an inappropriate time, making the form difficult (and infuriating) to use.

Strategies for Validating User Input

You can employ many strategies to validate the information entered by the users of your applications. A common technique that many Microsoft Windows developers familiar with previous versions of the Microsoft .NET Framework use is to handle the *LostFocus* event of controls. The *LostFocus* event is raised when the user moves away from a control. You can add code to this event to examine the data in the control that the user is vacating and ensure that it matches the requirements of the application before allowing the cursor to move away. The problem with this strategy is that often you need to cross-check data entered into one control against the values in others, and the validation logic can become quite convoluted; you frequently end up repeating similar logic in the *LostFocus* event handler for several controls. Additionally, you have no power over the sequence in which the user moves from control to control. Users can move through the controls on a form in any order, so you cannot always assume that every control contains a valid value if you are cross-checking a particular control against others on the form.

Another fundamental issue with this strategy is that it can tie the validation logic of the presentation elements of an application too closely to the business logic. If the business requirements change, you might need to modify the validation logic, and maintenance can become a complex task.

With WPF, you can define validation rules as part of the business model used by your applications. You can then reference these rules from the Extensible Application Markup Language (XAML) description of the user interface. To do this, you define the classes required by the business model and then bind properties of the user interface controls to properties exposed by these classes. At run time, WPF can create instances of these classes. When you modify the data in a control, the data can be automatically copied back to the specified property in the appropriate business model class instance and validated. You will learn more about data binding in Part V, "Managing Data." For the purposes of this chapter, I will concentrate on the validation rules you can associate with data binding.

An Example—Order Tickets for Events

Consider a simple scenario. You have been asked to build an application that enables customers to order tickets for events. Part of the application needs to enable a customer to enter her details, specify an event, and select the number of tickets required. A customer has a privilege level (Standard, Premium, Executive, or Premium Executive), and the higher this level the more tickets a customer can order. (Standard customers can order at most two tickets for an event, Premium customers can order four tickets, Executive customers can order eight tickets, and Premium Executive customers can order 10 tickets). You decide to create a prototype form like the one shown in the following graphic.

You need to ensure that the user's input is valid and consistent. Specifically, the customer must do the following:

- Select an event. The prototype application uses a hard-coded set of events. In a production application, you store the set of events in a database and use data binding to retrieve and display these events. You will see how to do this in Chapter 26, "Displaying and Editing Data by Using the Entity Framework and Data Binding."

- Input a customer reference number. The prototype application does not verify this reference number.

- Specify a privilege level. Again, the prototype application does not verify that the customer actually has this privilege level.

- Pick a number of tickets greater than 0 and less than or equal to the value that the customer's privilege level allows.

When the user has completed entering data, the user clicks the *Purchase* item in the *File* menu. The real application takes the user to a screen that enables the user to enter her payment details. In this prototype application, all that happens is that the application displays a message box confirming the user's input.

Performing Validation by Using Data Binding

In the following exercises, you will examine the Ticket Ordering application and add validation rules by using data binding. As a cautionary step, one of the exercises will show you how easy it is to get the validation timing wrong and render an application almost unusable!

Examine the Ticket Orders form

1. Start Microsoft Visual Studio 2010 if it is not already running.

2. Open the OrderTickets project, located in the \Microsoft Press\Visual CSharp Step By Step\Chapter 24\OrderTickets folder in your Documents folder.

3. On the *Debug* menu, click *Start Without Debugging* to build and run the application.

4. When the form appears, do not enter any data, but on the *File* menu click *Purchase* immediately.

   The application displays a message box with the text "Purchasing 0 tickets for customer: for event:". The application currently enables the user to purchase tickets without specifying who they are for, the event, or even the number of tickets required.

5. Click *OK* and return to the *Ticket Orders* form.

6. In the *Event* combo box, click *Little Mudford Festival*.

7. In the *Customer Reference* box, type **C1234**.

8. In the *Privilege Level* combo box, click *Premium*.

9. Using the *Tickets* slider control, click the slider and drag it to the right side of the control. This specifies 10 tickets.

10. On the *File* menu, click *Purchase*.

    The application displays a message box with the text "Purchasing 10 tickets for Premium customer: C1234 for event: Little Mudford Festival." Notice that the application does not check whether the number of tickets exceeds the number allowed by the customer's privilege level.

11. Click *OK*, and then close the form and return to Visual Studio 2010.

Currently, this form is not very useful. It does not validate the data entered by the user, and the slider control makes it difficult to determine exactly how many tickets the user has selected until the user clicks the *Purchase* button. (You have to count the ticks underneath the control.) This second problem is the easiest to fix, so you will start with that. In the next exercise, you will add a *TextBox* control to the form and use data binding to display the current value of the slider in this control.

Use data binding to display the number of tickets requested

1. In *Solution Explorer*, double-click the TicketForm.xaml file.

2. From the *Toolbox*, add a *TextBox* control to the form and place it to the right of the slider control. In the *Properties* window, set the properties of this control to the values shown in the following table.

Property	Value
Name	tickets
Height	23
Width	25
Margin	380, 170, 0, 0
IsReadOnly	True (selected)
TextAlignment	Right
HorizontalAlignment	Left
VerticalAlignment	Top

3. In the XAML pane, edit the definition of the *tickets TextBox* control. Add the *TextBox. Text* child element as shown next in bold type, making sure you replace the closing de-limiter tag (/>) for the *TextBox* control with an ordinary delimiter (>) and that you add a closing </TextBox> tag:

```
<TextBox Height="23" HorizontalAlignment="Left" Margin="380,170,0,0"
    Name="tickets" VerticalAlignment="Top" Width="25" TextAlignment="Right"
    IsReadOnly="True">
    <TextBox.Text>
    </TextBox.Text>
</TextBox>
```

4. In the *TextBox.Text* child element, add the *Binding* element shown here in bold:

```
<TextBox ...>
    <TextBox.Text>
        <Binding ElementName="numberOfTickets" Path="Value" />
    </TextBox.Text>
</TextBox>
```

This *Binding* element associates the *Text* property of the *TextBox* control with the *Value* property of the *Slider* control. (The *Slider* control is named *numberOfTickets*.) When the user changes this value, the *TextBox* will be updated automatically. Notice that the *TextBox* control displays the value 0 in the *Design View* window—this is the default value of the *Slider* control.

5. On the Debug menu, click Start Without Debugging.

6. When the form appears, drag the slider on the *Slider* control and verify that the number of tickets appears in the *TextBox* control to the right.

7. Close the form and return to Visual Studio.

You can now turn your attention to validating the data that the user enters. There are many approaches you can take, but in cases such as this, the recommended approach involves creating a class that can model the entity that you are entering the data for. You can add the validation logic to this class, and then bind the properties in the class to the various fields on the form. If you enter invalid data on the form, the validation rules in the class can throw an exception that you can capture and display on the form.

You will start by creating a class to model a customer's order, and then learning how to use this class to ensure the user always specifies an event and enters a reference number for the customer.

> **Create the *TicketOrder* class with validation logic for specifying an event and enforcing the entry of a customer reference number**

1. In *Solution Explorer*, right-click the OrderTickets project, point to *Add*, and then click *Class*.

2. In the *Add New Item – OrderTickets* dialog box, in the *Name* text box, type **TicketOrder.cs** and then click *Add*.

3. In the *Code and Text Editor* window displaying the TickerOrder.cs file, add the private *eventName* and *customerReference* fields shown here in bold type to the *TicketOrder* class:

```
class TicketOrder
{
    private string eventName;
    private string customerReference;
}
```

4. Add the following public *EventName* property to the *TicketOrder* class as shown in bold type, based on the *eventName* field you added in the previous step:

```
class TicketOrder
{
    ...
    public string EventName
    {
        get { return this.eventName; }
        set
        {
            if (String.IsNullOrEmpty(value))
            {
                throw new ApplicationException
                    ("Specify an event");
            }
            else
            {
                this.eventName = value;
            }
        }
    }
}
```

The property *set* accessor examines the value supplied for the event name, and if it is empty, it raises an exception with a suitable message.

5. Add the following public *CustomerReference* property to the *TicketOrder* class as shown in bold type:

```
class TicketOrder
{
    ...
    public string CustomerReference
    {
```

```
        get { return this.customerReference; }
        set
        {
            if (String.IsNullOrEmpty(value))
            {
                throw new ApplicationException
                    ("Specify the customer reference number");
            }
            else
            {
                this.customerReference = value;
            }
        }
    }
}
```

This property is similar to the *EventName* property. The property *set* accessor examines the value supplied for the customer reference number, and if it is empty, it raises an exception.

Now that you have created the *TicketOrder* class, the next step is to bind the *customerReference* text box on the form to the *CustomerReference* property of the class.

Bind the text box control on the form to the property in the *TicketOrder* class

1. In *Solution Explorer*, double-click the TicketForm.xaml file to display the form in the *Design View* window.

2. In the *XAML* pane, add the XML namespace declaration shown here in bold type to the *Window* definition:

```
<Window x:Class="OrderTickets.TicketForm"
    xmlns="http://schemas.microsoft.com/winfx/2006/xaml/presentation"
    xmlns:x="http://schemas.microsoft.com/winfx/2006/xaml"
    xmlns:ticketOrder="clr-namespace:OrderTickets"
    Title="Ticket Orders" Height="250" Width="480" ResizeMode="NoResize">
...
```

This declaration is similar to a *using* statement in Microsoft C# code. It enables you to reference the types in the *OrderTickets* namespace in the XAML code for the window.

3. Add the following *Window.Resources* element shown in bold type to the window:

```
<Window x:Class=" OrderTickets.TicketForm"
    ...
    ...ResizeMode="NoResize">
<Window.Resources>
    <ticketOrder:TicketOrder x:Key="orderData" />
</Window.Resources>
<Grid>
    ...
```

This resource creates a new instance of the *TicketOrder* class. You can reference this instance by using the key value, *orderData*, elsewhere in the XAML definition of the window.

4. Find the definition of the *customerReference* text box in the *XAML* pane, and modify it as shown here in bold type, making sure you replace the closing delimiter tag (/>) for the *TextBox* control with an ordinary delimiter (>) and that you add a closing </TextBox> tag:

```xml
<TextBox Height="23" HorizontalAlignment="Left" Margin="156,78,0,0"
    Name="customerReference" VerticalAlignment="Top" Width="205">
    <TextBox.Text>
        <Binding Source="{StaticResource orderData}"
            Path="CustomerReference" />
    </TextBox.Text>
</TextBox>
```

This code binds the data displayed in the *Text* property of this text box to the value in the *CustomerReference* property of the *orderData* object. If the user updates the value in the *customerReference* text box on the form, the new data is automatically copied to the *orderData* object. Remember that the *CustomerReference* property in the *TicketOrder* class checks that the user has actually specified a value.

5. Modify the definition of the binding you added in the preceding step, and add a *Binding.ValidationRules* child element, as shown here in bold type:

```xml
<TextBox Height="23" HorizontalAlignment="Left" Margin="156,78,0,0"
    Name="customerReference" VerticalAlignment="Top" Width="205">
    <TextBox.Text>
        <Binding Source="{StaticResource orderData}"
            Path="CustomerReference">
            <Binding.ValidationRules>
                <ExceptionValidationRule/>
            </Binding.ValidationRules>
        </Binding>
    </TextBox.Text>
</TextBox>
```

The *ValidationRules* element of a binding enables you to specify the validation that the application should perform when the user enters data in this control. The *ExceptionValidationRule* element is a built-in rule that checks for any exceptions thrown by the application when the data in this control changes. If it detects any exceptions, it highlights the control so that the user can see there is a problem with the input.

6. Add the equivalent binding and binding rule to the *Text* property of the *eventList* combo box, associating it with the *EventName* property of the *orderData* object, as shown here in bold:

```
<ComboBox Height="23" HorizontalAlignment="Left" Margin="156,29,0,0"
    Name="eventList" VerticalAlignment="Top" Width="205" >
    <ComboBox.Text>
        <Binding Source="{StaticResource orderData}" Path="EventName" >
            <Binding.ValidationRules>
                <ExceptionValidationRule/>
            </Binding.ValidationRules>
        </Binding>
    </ ComboBox.Text>
    <ComboBox.Items>
        . . .
    </ComboBox.Items>
</ComboBox >
```

7. On the *Debug* menu, click *Start Without Debugging* to build and run the application.

8. When the form appears, on the *File* menu click *Purchase* without entering any data.

    The message "Purchasing 0 tickets for customer: for event:" appears.

9. Click *OK*.

10. On the Ticket Orders form, select *Little Mudford Festival* from the *Event* combo box, type **C1234** in the *customerReference* text box, and then select *Premium* in the *Privilege Level* combo box.

    Nothing noteworthy should happen.

11. Click the *customerReference* text box, delete the reference number you entered, and then click the *Privilege Level* combo box again.

    This time, the *customerReference* text box is highlighted with a red border. When the binding attempted to copy the value that the user entered to the *TickerOrder* object, the value was an empty string, so the *CustomerReference* property throws an *ApplicationException* exception. In these circumstances, a control that uses binding indicates that an exception has occurred by displaying a red border.

12. Type **C1234** in the *customerReference* text box again, and then click the *Privilege Level* combo box.

    The red box around the *customerReference* text box disappears.

13. Delete the value in the *customerReference* text box again. On the *File* menu, click *Purchase*.

    Rather surprisingly, no red border appears around the *customerReference* text box.

14. In the message box, click *OK*, and then click the *Privilege Level* combo box.

    The red border now appears around the *customerReference* text box.

15. Close the form, and return to Visual Studio 2010.

There are at least two questions you should be asking yourself at this point:

■ Why doesn't the form always detect when the user has forgotten to enter a value in a text box? The answer is that the validation occurs only when the text box loses its focus. This, in turn, happens only when the user moves the focus to another control on the form. Menus are not actually treated as though they are part of the form. (They are handled differently.) When you select a menu item, you are not moving to another control on the form; therefore, the text box has not yet lost its focus. Only when you click the *Privilege Level* combo box (or some other control) does the focus move and the validation occur. Additionally, the *customerReference* text box and the *Event* combo box are initially empty. If you move away from either of these controls without selecting or typing anything, the validation will not be performed. Only when you select or type something and then delete it does the validation run. You will address these problems later in this chapter.

■ How can I get the form to display a meaningful error message rather than just highlighting that there is a problem with the input in a control? You can capture the message generated by an exception and display it elsewhere on the form. You will see how to do this in the following exercise.

The next exercise answers these questions.

Add a style to display exception messages

1. In the *Design View* window displaying the TicketForm.xaml file, in the *XAML* pane, add the following style shown in bold type to the *Window.Resources* element:

```
<Window.Resources>
    <ticketOrder:TicketOrder x:Key="orderData" />
    <Style x:Key="errorStyle" TargetType="Control">
        <Style.Triggers>
            <Trigger Property="Validation.HasError" Value="True">
                <Setter Property="ToolTip"
                        Value="{Binding RelativeSource={x:Static RelativeSource.Self},
                        Path=(Validation.Errors)[0].ErrorContent}" />
            </Trigger>
        </Style.Triggers>
    </Style>
</Window.Resources>
```

This style contains a trigger that detects when the *Validation.HasError* property of the control is set to *true*. This occurs if a binding validation rule for the control generates an exception. The trigger sets the *ToolTip* property of the current control to display the text of the exception. A detailed explanation of the binding syntax shown here is outside the scope of this book, but the binding source `{Binding RelativeSource={x:Static RelativeSource.Self}` is a reference to the current control, and the binding path (`Validation.Errors`)[0].`ErrorContent` associates the first exception message found in this binding source with the *ToolTip* property. (An exception could throw further exceptions, all of which generate their own messages. The first message is usually the most significant, though.)

2. Apply the *errorStyle* style to the *eventList* and *customerReference* controls, as shown in bold type here:

```
<ComboBox Style="{StaticResource errorStyle}" ... Name="eventList" ... >
   ...
</ComboBox>
<TextBox Style="{StaticResource errorStyle}" ... Name="customerReference" ... >
   ...
</TextBox>
```

3. On the *Debug* menu, click *Start Without Debugging* to build and run the application.

4. When the form appears, in the *Event* combo box select *Little Mudford Festival*, type **C1234** in the *customerReference* text box, and then click the *Privilege Level* combo box.

5. Click the *customerReference* text box, delete the reference number you entered, and then click the *Privilege Level* combo box again.

   The *customerReference* text box is highlighted with a red border.

 Note Make sure you actually delete the contents of the *foreName* text box rather than just overtyping the text with spaces.

6. Rest the mouse pointer on the *customerReference* text box. A ScreenTip should appear, displaying the message "Specify the customer reference number," like this:

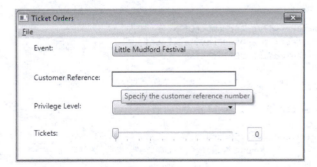

   This is the message from the *ApplicationException* exception raised by the *CustomerReference* property in the *TicketOrder* class.

7. Close the form, and return to Visual Studio 2010.

There are still some issues left to fix, but you will address them after you have seen how to validate the privilege level and number of tickets and ensure that they are consistent.

Add properties to validate the privilege level and number of tickets

1. Switch to the *Code and Text Editor* window displaying the TicketOrder.cs file.

2. Add the *PrivilegeLevel* enumeration shown next in bold type to the file, above the *TicketOrder* class:

```
enum PrivilegeLevel { Standard, Premium, Executive, PremiumExecutive }

class TicketOrder
{
    ...
}
```

You will use this enumeration to specify the type of the *PrivilegeLevel* property in the *TicketOrder* class.

3. Add the *privilegeLevel* and *numberOfTickets* private fields to the *TicketOrder* class, as shown in bold type here:

```
class TicketOrder
{
    private string eventName;
    private string customerReference;
    private PrivilegeLevel privilegeLevel;
    private short numberOfTickets;
    ...
}
```

4. Add the private *checkPrivilegeAndNumberOfTickets* Boolean method to the *TicketOrder* class as shown in bold type here:

```
class TicketOrder
{
    ...
    private bool checkPrivilegeAndNumberOfTickets(
            PrivilegeLevel proposedPrivilegeLevel,
            short proposedNumberOfTickets)
    {
        bool retVal = false;

        switch (proposedPrivilegeLevel)
        {
            case PrivilegeLevel.Standard:
                retVal = (proposedNumberOfTickets <= 2);
                break;

            case PrivilegeLevel.Premium:
                retVal = (proposedNumberOfTickets <= 4);
                break;

            case PrivilegeLevel.Executive:
                retVal = (proposedNumberOfTickets <= 8);
                break;
```

```
            case PrivilegeLevel.PremiumExecutive:
                retVal = (proposedNumberOfTickets <= 10);
                break;
        }

        return retVal;
    }
}
```

This method examines the values in the *proposedPrivilegeLevel* and *proposedNumberOfTickets* parameters and tests them for consistency according to the business rules described earlier in this chapter. If the values are consistent, this method returns *true*; otherwise, it returns *false*.

5. Add the public *PrivilegeLevel* and *NumberOfTickets* properties shown next in bold type to the *TicketOrder* class. Note that the type of the *PrivilegeLevel* property is the *PrivilegeLevel* enumeration:

```
class TicketOrder
{
    ...
    public PrivilegeLevel PrivilegeLevel
    {
        get { return this.privilegeLevel; }
        set
        {
            this.privilegeLevel = value;
            if (!this.checkPrivilegeAndNumberOfTickets(value, this.numberOfTickets))
            {
                throw new ApplicationException(
                    "Privilege level too low for this number of tickets");
            }
        }
    }

    public short NumberOfTickets
    {
        get { return this.numberOfTickets; }
        set
        {
            this.numberOfTickets = value;
            if (!this.checkPrivilegeAndNumberOfTickets(this.privilegeLevel, value))
            {
                throw new ApplicationException(
                    "Too many tickets for this privilege level");
            }

            if (this.numberOfTickets <=0)
            {
                throw new ApplicationException(
                    "You must buy at least one ticket");
            }
        }
    }
}
```

The *set* accessors of these properties call the *CheckPrivilegeAndNumberOfTickets* method to verify that the *privilegeLevel* and the *numberOfTickets* fields match, and they raise an exception if the fields do not match.

Additionally, the *set* accessor for the *NumberOfTickets* property verifies that the user has specified at least one ticket. You do not need to verify that the user has specified a value for the *PrivilegeLevel* property because it defaults to *Standard* (the first item in the *PrivilegeLevel* enumeration).

6. Add the *ToString* method shown next in bold type to the *TicketOrder* class:

```
class TicketOrder
{
    ...
    public override string ToString()
    {
        string formattedString = String.Format("Event: {0}\tCustomer: {1}\tPrivilege:
{2}\tTickets: {3}",
            this.eventName, this.customerReference,
            this.privilegeLevel.ToString(), this.numberOfTickets.ToString());
        return formattedString;
    }
}
```

You will use this method to display the details of ticket orders to verify that the data is correct.

The next step is to bind the *privilegeLevel* combo box and the *numberOfTickets* slider control on the form to these new properties. However, if you stop and think for a moment, you will realize that there is a small problem with the *PrivilegeLevel* property. You need to bind the *Text* property of the *privilegeLevel* combo box to the *PrivilegeLevel* property of the *TicketOrder* object created by the form. The type of the *Text* property is *string*. The type of the *PrivilegeLevel* property is *PrivilegeLevel* (an enumeration). You must convert between *string* and *PrivilegeLevel* values for the binding to work. Fortunately, with the binding mechanism implemented by WPF, you can specify a converter class to perform actions such as this.

> **Note** A WPF binding can automatically convert between an enumeration and a string if the string values are identical to the names of each element in the enumeration. In the *Ticket Order* application, the first three items in the *privilegeLevel* combo box (*Standard*, *Premium*, and *Executive*) correspond directly to elements with the same names in the *PrivilegeLevel* enumeration. However, the final item in the combo box is *Premium Executive* (with a space), but the corresponding element in the enumeration is called *PremiumExecutive* (without a space). The WPF binding cannot convert between these two values, so a converter class is required.

Converter methods reside in their own classes that must implement the *IValueConverter* interface. This interface defines two methods: *Convert*, which converts from the type used by the property in the class that is providing the data for the binding to the type displayed on the form, and *ConvertBack*, which converts the data from the type displayed on the form to the type required by the class.

Create the converter class and methods

1. In the TicketOrder.cs file, add the following *using* statement to the list at the top of the file:

```
using System.Windows.Data;
```

The *IValueConverter* interface is defined in this namespace.

2. Add the *PrivilegeLevelConverter* class shown next to the end of the file, after the *TicketOrder* class:

```
[ValueConversion(typeof(string), typeof(PrivilegeLevel))]
public class PrivilegeLevelConverter : IValueConverter
{
}
```

The text in brackets directly above the class is an example of an attribute. An attribute provides descriptive metadata for a class. The *ValueConversion* attribute is used by tools such as the WPF designer in the *Design View* window to verify that you are applying the class correctly when you reference it. The parameters to the *ValueConversion* attribute specify the type of the value displayed by the form (*string*) and the type of the value in the corresponding property in the class (*PrivilegeLevel*). You will see more examples of attributes in later chapters in this book.

3. In the *PrivilegeLevelConverter* class, add the *Convert* method shown here in bold type:

```
[ValueConversion(typeof(string), typeof(PrivilegeLevel))]
public class PrivilegeLevelConverter: IValueConverter
{
    public object  Convert(object value, Type targetType, object parameter,
                           System.Globalization.CultureInfo culture)
    {
        PrivilegeLevel privilegeLevel = (PrivilegeLevel)value;
        string convertedPrivilegeLevel = String.Empty;

        switch (privilegeLevel)
        {
            case PrivilegeLevel.Standard:
                convertedPrivilegeLevel = "Standard";
                break;

            case PrivilegeLevel.Premium:
                convertedPrivilegeLevel = "Premium";
                break;

            case PrivilegeLevel.Executive:
                convertedPrivilegeLevel = "Executive";
                break;
```

```
                    case PrivilegeLevel.PremiumExecutive:
                        convertedPrivilegeLevel = "Premium Executive";
                        break;
            }

            return convertedPrivilegeLevel;
        }
    }
```

The signature of the *Convert* method is defined by the *IValueConverter* interface. The *value* parameter is the value in the class that you are converting from. (You can ignore the other parameters for now.) The return value from this method is the data bound to the property on the form. In this case, the *Convert* method converts a *PrivilegeLevel* value to a *string*. Notice that the *value* parameter is passed in as an *object*, so you need to cast it to the appropriate type before attempting to use it.

4. Add the *ConvertBack* method shown next in bold type to the *PrivilegeLevelConverter* class:

```
[ValueConversion(typeof(string), typeof(PrivilegeLevel))]
public class PrivilegeLevelConverter: IValueConverter
{
    ...
    public object  ConvertBack(object value, Type targetType, object parameter,
                               System.Globalization.CultureInfo culture)
    {
        PrivilegeLevel privilegeLevel = PrivilegeLevel.Standard;

        switch ((string)value)
        {
            case "Standard":
                privilegeLevel = PrivilegeLevel.Standard;
                break;

            case "Premium":
                privilegeLevel = PrivilegeLevel.Premium;
                break;

            case "Executive":
                privilegeLevel = PrivilegeLevel.Executive;
                break;

            case "Premium Executive":
                privilegeLevel = PrivilegeLevel.PremiumExecutive;
                break;
        }

        return privilegeLevel;
    }
}
```

The *ConvertBack* method is also part of the *IValueConverter* interface. In the *ConvertBack* method, the *value* parameter is now the value from the form that you are converting back to a value of the appropriate type for the class. In this case, the *ConvertBack* method converts the data from a *string* (displayed in the *Text* property in the combo box) to the corresponding *Title* value.

5. On the *Build* menu, click *Build Solution*. Verify that the solution compiles correctly, and correct any errors and rebuild the solution if necessary.

> **Bind the combo box and slider controls on the form to the properties in the *TicketOrder* class**

1. Return to the *Design View* window displaying the TicketForm.xaml file.

2. In the *XAML* pane, add a *PrivilegeLevelConverter* object as a resource to the window, and specify a key value of *privilegeLevelConverter*, as shown in bold type here:

```
<Window.Resources>
    <ticketOrder:TicketOrder x:Key="orderData" />
    <ticketOrder:PrivilegeLevelConverter x:Key="privilegeLevelConverter" />
    ...
</Window.Resources>
```

3. Locate the definition of the *privilegeLevel* combo box control, and style the control by using the *errorStyle* style. Before the list of combo box items, add the XAML code shown next in bold type to bind the *Text* property of the combo box to the *Title* property in the *orderData* object, specifying the *titleConverter* resource as the object providing the converter methods:

```
<ComboBox Style="{StaticResource errorStyle}" ... Name="privilegeLevel" ...>
    <ComboBox.Text>
        <Binding Source="{StaticResource orderData}" Path="PrivilegeLevel"
            Converter="{StaticResource privilegeLevelConverter}" >
            <Binding.ValidationRules>
                <ExceptionValidationRule />
            </Binding.ValidationRules>
        </Binding>
    </ComboBox.Text>
    <ComboBox.Items>
        ...
    </ComboBox.Items>
</ComboBox>
```

4. Modify the definition for the *numberOfTickets* slider control .Apply the *errorStyle* style, and bind the *Value* property to the *NumberOfTickets* property of the *orderData* object, as shown here in bold type:

```
<Slider Style="{StaticResource errorStyle}" Height="22"
    HorizontalAlignment="Left" Margin="156,171,0,0", Name="numberOfTickets"
    VerticalAlignment="Top" Width="205" SmallChange="1"
    TickPlacement="BottomRight" Maximum="10" IsSnapToTickEnabled="True" >
    <Slider.Value>
        <Binding Source="{StaticResource orderData}" Path="NumberOfTickets">
            <Binding.ValidationRules>
```

```
        <ExceptionValidationRule />
      </Binding.ValidationRules>
    </Binding>
  </Slider.Value>
</Slider>
```

5. On the *View* menu, click *Code* to switch to the *Code and Text Editor* window displaying the TicketForm.xaml.cs file.

6. Change the code in the *purchaseTickets_Click* method, as shown here in bold type:

```
private void purchaseTickets_Click(object sender, RoutedEventArgs e)
{
    Binding ticketOrderBinding =
        BindingOperations.GetBinding(privilegeLevel, ComboBox.TextProperty);
    TicketOrder ticketOrder = ticketOrderBinding.Source as TicketOrder;
    MessageBox.Show(ticketOrder.ToString(), "Purchased");
}
```

This code displays the details of the order in the message box. (It still does not actually save the ticket order anywhere.) The static *GetBinding* method of the *BindingOperations* class returns a reference to the object to which the specified property is bound. In this case, the *GetBinding* method retrieves the object bound to the *Text* property of the *title* combo box. This should be the same object referred to by the *orderData* resource. In fact, the code could have queried any of the bound properties of the *eventList*, *customerReference*, *privilegeLevel*, or *numberOfTickets* controls to retrieve the same reference. The reference is returned as a *Binding* object. The code then casts this *Binding* object into a *TicketOrder* object before displaying its details.

You can now run the application again and see how the validation performs.

Run the application, and test the validation

1. On the *Debug* menu, click *Start Without Debugging* to build and run the application.

2. In the *Privilege Level* combo box, click *Premium*.

3. Set the *Tickets* slider to 5.

   The *CheckPrivilegeAndNumberOfTickets* method in the *TicketOrder* class generates an exception because the privilege level and the number of tickets do not match. The *Tickets* slider is highlighted with a red border. Rest the mouse pointer on the *Tickets* slider, and verify that the ScreenTip text "Too many tickets for this privilege level" appears.

4. In the *Privilege Level* combo box, click *Executive*.

   Although the privilege level is now sufficient to enable the customer to order 5 tickets, the slider remains highlighted.

5. Set the *Tickets* slider to 6.

Verify that the red highlighting disappears. The validation occurs only when you change the value in a control, not when you change the value of a different control.

6. In the *Privilege Level* combo box, click *Standard*.

    The combo box is highlighted. If you hover the mouse cursor over the combo box, it should display the message "Privilege level too low for this number of tickets."

7. Set the *Tickets* slider to 5.

    The slider control is now also highlighted.

8. On the *File* menu, click *Purchase*.

    A message box appears, displaying the privilege level (Standard) and the number of tickets (5) for the order. Additionally, the event and customer reference are both blank. Although the form contains erroneous and missing data, you can still make the purchase!

9. Click *OK*, and then type **C1234** in the *customerReference* text box, but do not click away from this text box.

10. On the *File* menu, click *Purchase* again.

    The message box does not include the customer reference. This happens because the *customerReference* text box on the form has not lost the focus. Remember from earlier that data binding validation for a text box occurs only when the user clicks another control on the form. The same applies to the data itself; by default, it is copied to the *orderDetails* object only when the text box loses the focus. In fact, it is the act of copying the data from the form to the *orderDetails* object that triggers the validation.

11. Click *OK*, and then click the *Event* combo box and select *Little Mudford Festival*.

12. On the *File* menu, click *Purchase*.

    This time, the message box displays all the details from the form.

13. Click *OK*, close the application, and return to Visual Studio 2010.

You can see from this exercise that although the validation successfully cross-checks the *Privilege Level* and *Tickets* controls, there is still more work to be done before the application is usable.

Changing the Point at Which Validation Occurs

The issues with the application are that the validation is performed at the wrong time, is inconsistently applied, and does not actually prevent the user from providing inconsistent data. You just need an alternative approach to handling the validation. The solution is to check the user's input only when the user attempts to make the purchase. This way, you can ensure the user has finished entering all the data and that it is consistent. If there are any problems, you can display an error message and prevent the data from being used until the problems have been corrected. In the following exercise, you will modify the application to postpone validation until the user attempts to purchase tickets.

Validate data explicitly

1. Return to the *Design View* window displaying TicketForm.xaml. In the *XAML* pane, modify the binding for the *privilegeLevel* combo box and set the *UpdateSourceTrigger* property to *"Explicit"*, as shown in bold type here:

```
<ComboBox ... Name="privilegeLevel" ...>
...
    <ComboBox.Text>
        <Binding Source="{StaticResource orderData}" Path="PrivilegeLevel"
          Converter="{StaticResource privilegeLevelConverter}"
UpdateSourceTrigger="Explicit" >
            ...
        </Binding>
    </ComboBox.Text>
</ComboBox>
```

The *UpdateSourceTrigger* property governs when the information entered by the user is sent back to the underlying *TicketOrder* object and validated. Setting this property to *"Explicit"* postpones this synchronization until your application explicitly performs it by using code.

2. Modify the bindings for the *eventList, customerReference,* and *numberOfTickets* controls to set the *UpdateSourceTrigger* property to *"Explicit"*:

```
<ComboBox ... Name="eventList" ... >
    <ComboBox.Text>
        <Binding Source="{StaticResource orderData}" Path="EventName"
            UpdateSourceTrigger="Explicit" >
            ...
        </Binding>
    </ComboBox.Text>
    ...
</ComboBox>
...
<TextBox ... Name="customerReference" ... >
    <TextBox.Text>
        <Binding Source="{StaticResource orderData}" Path="CustomerReference"
            UpdateSourceTrigger="Explicit" >
            ...
        </Binding>
    </TextBox.Text>
</TextBox>
...
<Slider ...Name="numberOfTickets" ...>
    <Slider.Value>
        <Binding Source="{StaticResource orderData}" Path="NumberOfTickets"
            UpdateSourceTrigger="Explicit" >
```

```
            ...
        </Binding>
    </Slider.Value>
</Slider>
```

3. Display the TicketForm.xaml.cs file in the *Code and Text Editor* window. In the *purchaseTickets_Click* method, add the statements shown next in bold type to the start of the method:

```
private void purchaseTickets_Click(object sender, RoutedEventArgs e)
{
    BindingExpression eventBe =
        eventList.GetBindingExpression(ComboBox.TextProperty);
    BindingExpression customerReferenceBe =
        customerReference.GetBindingExpression(TextBox.TextProperty);
    BindingExpression privilegeLevelBe =
        privilegeLevel.GetBindingExpression(ComboBox.TextProperty);
    BindingExpression numberOfTicketsBe =
        numberOfTickets.GetBindingExpression(Slider.ValueProperty);
    ...
}
```

These statements create *BindingExpression* objects for each of the four controls with binding validation rules. You will use these objects in the next step to propagate the values on the form to the *TicketOrder* object and trigger the validation rules.

4. Add the statements shown next in bold type to the *purchaseTickets_Click* method after the code you added in the preceding step:

```
private void purchaseTickets_Click(object sender, RoutedEventArgs e)
{
    ...
    eventBe.UpdateSource();
    customerReferenceBe.UpdateSource();
    privilegeLevelBe.UpdateSource();
    numberOfTicketsBe.UpdateSource();
    ...
}
```

The *UpdateSource* method of the *BindingExpression* class synchronizes data in an object with the controls that reference the object through bindings. It sends the values in the bound properties of controls on the form back to the *TicketOrder* object. When this occurs, the data is also validated.

The statements you added in the step update the properties in the *TicketOrder* object with the values entered by the user on the form, and they validate the data as they do so. The *BindingExpression* class provides a property called *HasError* that indicates whether the *UpdateSource* method was successful or whether it caused an exception.

5. Add the code shown next in bold type to the *purchaseTickets_Click* method to test the *HasError* property of each *BindingExpression* object and display a message if the validation fails. Move the original code that displays the customer details to the *else* part of the *if* statement.

```
private void purchaseTickets_Click(object sender, RoutedEventArgs e)
{
    ...
    if (eventBe.HasError || customerReferenceBe.HasError ||
        privilegeLevelBe.HasError || numberOfTicketsBe.HasError)
    {
        MessageBox.Show("Please correct errors", "Purchase aborted");
    }
    else
    {
        Binding ticketOrderBinding =
            BindingOperations.GetBinding(privilegeLevel, ComboBox.TextProperty);
        TicketOrder ticketOrder = ticketOrderBinding.Source as TicketOrder;
        MessageBox.Show(ticketOrder.ToString(), "Purchased");
    }
}
```

Test the application again

1. On the *Debug* menu, click *Start Without Debugging* to build and run the application.

2. When the Ticket Orders form appears, on the *File* menu, click *Purchase*.

   Verify that the *Purchase aborted* message box appears with the text "Please correct errors" and that the *Event*, *Customer Reference*, and *Tickets* controls are highlighted.

> **Note** The *Privilege Level* is not highlighted because it defaults to *Standard*, as described earlier in this chapter.

3. Click *OK* and return to the Ticket Orders form. Hover the mouse cursor over each highlighted control in turn, and verify that the messages thrown by the *ApplicationException* exception for each property in the underlying *TicketOrder* object appear as ToolTips.

4. In the *Event* combo box, select *Little Mudford Festival*. In the Customer Reference text box, type **C1234**. In the *Privilege Level* combo box, select *Premium*. Set the *Tickets* slider to 8, and then on the *File* menu click *Purchase*.

   Verify that the *Purchase aborted* message box appears again, but that this time only the *Tickets* slider is highlighted.

5. Click OK, and hover the mouse cursor over the *Tickets* control.

   Verify that the ToolTip displays the message "Too many tickets for this privilege level".

6. In the *Privilege Level* combo box, select *Premium Executive*, and then on the *File* menu click *Purchase*.

   Verify that a *Purchased* message box now appears displaying the text "Event: Little Mudford Festival   Customer: C1234   Privilege: PremiumExecutiveTickets: 8" and that none of the controls on the form are highlighted. The data is now complete and consistent.

7. Experiment with other combinations of values, and verify that the validation works as expected. When you have finished, close the form and return to Visual Studio.

In this chapter, you saw how to perform basic validation by using the default exception validation rule processing provided by using data binding. You learned how to define your own custom validation rules if you want to perform more complex checks.

- If you want to continue to the next chapter

  Keep Visual Studio 2010 running, and turn to Chapter 25.

- If you want to exit Visual Studio 2010 now

  On the *File* menu, click *Exit*. If you see a *Save* dialog box, click *Yes* and save the project.

Chapter 24 Quick Reference

To	Do this

Use data binding to bind a property of a control on a form to a property of another control on the same form	In the XAML code for the property of the control, create a binding. Reference the control containing the property to bind to by using the *ElementName* tag, and the property to bind to by using the *Path* tag. For example:
	
	``xml
	<TextBox ...>
	    <TextBox.Text>
	        <Binding ElementName="numberOfTickets"
	            Path="Value" />
	    </TextBox.Text>
	</TextBox>
	``

Use data binding to bind a property of a control on a form to a property of an object	In the XAML code for the property of the control, specify a binding source identifying the object and the name of the property in the object to bind to. For example:
	
	``xml
	<TextBox ...>
	    <TextBox.Text>
	        <Binding Source="{StaticResource orderData}"
	            Path="ForeName" />
	    </TextBox.Text>
	</TextBox>
	``

To	Do this

Enable a data binding to validate data entered by the user	Specify the *Binding.ValidationRules* element as part of the binding. For example:
	
	 ``xml
	<Binding Source="{StaticResource orderData}"
	    Path="ForeName" />
	    <Binding.ValidationRules>
	        <ExceptionValidationRule/>
	    </Binding.ValidationRules>
	</Binding>
	``

Display error information in a nonintrusive manner	Define a style that detects a change to the *Validation.HasError* property of the control, and then set the *ToolTip* property of the control to the message returned by the exception. Apply this style to all controls that require validation. For example:
	
	 ``xml
	<Style x:Key="errorStyle" TargetType="Control">
	  <Style.Triggers>
	    <Trigger Property="Validation.HasError"
	    Value="True">
	      <Setter Property="ToolTip"
	        Value="{Binding RelativeSource=
	          {x:Static RelativeSource.Self},
	          Path=(Validation.Errors)[0].ErrorContent}" />
	    </Trigger>
	  </Style.Triggers>
	</Style>
	``

Validate all the controls on a form under programmatic control rather than when the user moves from control to control	In the XAML code for the binding, set the *UpdateSourceTrigger* property of the binding to *"Explicit"* to defer validation until the application requests it. To validate the data for all controls, create a *BindingExpression* object for each bound property of each control and call the *UpdateSource* method. Examine the *HasError* property of each *BindingExpression* object. If this property is *true*, the validation failed.

Part V

Managing Data

Chapter 25
Querying Information in a Database

After completing this chapter, you will be able to:

- Fetch and display data from a Microsoft SQL Server database by using Microsoft ADO.NET.

- Define entity classes for holding data retrieved from a database.

- Use LINQ to SQL to query a database and populate instances of entity classes.

- Create a custom *DataContext* class for accessing a database in a typesafe manner.

In Part IV of this book, "Building Windows Presentation Foundation Applications," you learned how to use Microsoft Visual C# to build user interfaces and present and validate information. In Part V, you will learn about managing data by using the data access functionality available in Microsoft Visual Studio 2010 and the Microsoft .NET Framework. The chapters in this part of the book describe ADO.NET, a library of objects specifically designed to make it easy to write applications that use databases. In this chapter, you will also learn how to query data by using LINQ to SQL—extensions to LINQ based on ADO.NET that are designed for retrieving data from a database. In Chapter 26, "Displaying and Editing Data by Using the Entity Framework and Data Binding," you will learn more about using ADO.NET and LINQ to SQL for updating data.

 Important To perform the exercises in this chapter, you must have installed Microsoft SQL Server 2008 Express. This software is available on the retail DVD with Microsoft Visual Studio 2010 and Visual C# 2010 Express and is installed by default.

 Important It is recommended that you use an account that has Administrator privileges to perform the exercises in this chapter and the remainder of this book.

Querying a Database by Using ADO.NET

The ADO.NET class library contains a comprehensive framework for building applications that need to retrieve and update data held in a relational database. The model defined by ADO.NET is based on the notion of data providers. Each database management system (such as SQL Server, Oracle, IBM DB2, and so on) has its own data provider that implements an abstraction of the mechanisms for connecting to a database, issuing queries, and updating data. By using these abstractions, you can write portable code that is independent of the underlying database management system. In this chapter, you will connect to a database managed by SQL Server 2008 Express, but the techniques that you will learn are equally applicable when using a different database management system.

The Northwind Database

Northwind Traders is a fictitious company that sells edible goods with exotic names. The Northwind database contains several tables with information about the goods that Northwind Traders sells, the customers it sells to, orders placed by customers, suppliers from whom Northwind Traders obtains goods to resell, shippers that it uses to send goods to customers, and employees who work for Northwind Traders. The following image shows all the tables in the Northwind database and how they are related to one another. The tables that you will be using in this chapter are *Orders* and *Products*.

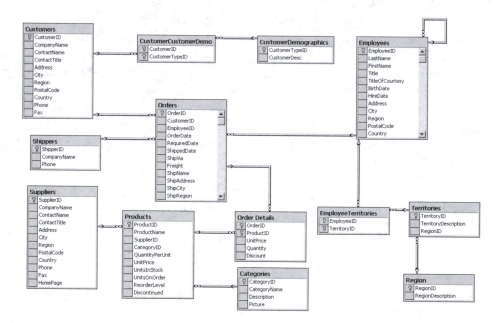

Creating the Database

Before proceeding further, you need to create the Northwind database.

Create the Northwind database

1. On the Windows *Start* menu, click *All Programs*, click *Accessories*, right-click *Command Prompt*, and then click *Run as administrator*.

   If you are logged in using an account that has administrator rights, in the *User Account Control* dialog box, click *Yes*.

If you are logged in using an account that does not have administrator rights, in the *User Account Control* dialog box enter the administrator password and then click *Yes*.

The command prompt window appears, running as Administrator.

2. In the command prompt window, type the following command:

```
sqlcmd -S.\SQLExpress -E
```

This command starts the sqlcmd utility to connect to your local instance of SQL Server 2008 Express. A "1>" prompt should appear.

> **Tip** Ensure that SQL Server 2008 Express is running before you attempt to run the sqlcmd utility. (It is set to start automatically by default. You will simply receive an error message if it is not started when you execute the *sqlcmd* command.) You can check the status of SQL Server 2008 Express, and start it running if necessary, by using the SQL Configuration Manager tool available in the Configuration Tools folder of the Microsoft SQL Server 2008 program group.

3. At the 1> prompt, type the following command including the square brackets, and then press Enter. Replace *computer* with the name of your computer, and replace *login* with the name of the account you used to log in to Windows.

```
CREATE LOGIN [computer\login] FROM WINDOWS
```

A "2>" prompt should appear.

4. At the 2> prompt, type **GO** and then press Enter.

SQL Server attempts to create a login for your user account so that you can create the Northwind database. If the command is successful, the "1>" prompt should reappear. If the command displays the message "The server principal 'computer\login' already exists.", you already have a SQL Server login and you can ignore the message. If the command displays any other message, check that you have specified the correct values for *computer* and *login* and repeat steps 3 and 4.

5. At the 1> prompt, type the following command and the press Enter (and as before, replace *computer* with the name of your computer, and replace *login* with the name of the account you used to log in to Windows):

```
GRANT CREATE DATABASE TO [computer\login]
```

6. At the 2> prompt, type **GO** and then press Enter.

7. At the 1> prompt, type **EXIT** and then press Enter.

This command quits the sqlcmd utility, and you return to the Windows command prompt.

8. Close the command prompt window.

9. On the Windows *Start* menu, click *All Programs,* click *Accessories,* and then click *Command Prompt.*

   This action opens a command prompt window using your own credentials rather than that of an administrator.

10. In the command prompt window, type the following command to go to the \Microsoft Press\Visual CSharp Step By Step\Chapter 25 folder under your Documents folder. Replace *Name* with your user name.

    ```
    cd "\Users\Name\Documents\Microsoft Press\Visual CSharp Step By Step\Chapter 25"
    ```

11. In the command prompt window, type the following command:

    ```
    sqlcmd -S.\SQLExpress -E -iinstnwnd.sql
    ```

    This command uses the sqlcmd utility to run the instnwnd.sql script. This script contains the SQL commands that create the Northwind Traders database and the tables in the database, and it fills them with some sample data.

12. When the script finishes running, close the command prompt window.

> **Note** You can run the command you executed in step 11 at any time if you need to reset the Northwind Traders database. The instnwnd.sql script automatically drops the database if it exists and then rebuilds it. See Chapter 26 for additional information.

Using ADO.NET to Query Order Information

In the following set of exercises, you will write code to access the Northwind database and display information in a simple console application. The aim of the exercise is to help you learn more about ADO.NET and understand the object model it implements. In later exercises, you will use LINQ to SQL to query the database. In Chapter 26, you will see how to use the wizards included with Visual Studio 2010 to generate code that can retrieve and update data and display data graphically in a Windows Presentation Foundation (WPF) application.

The first application you are going to create will produce a simple report displaying information about customers' orders. The program will prompt the user for a customer ID and then display the orders for that customer.

Connect to the database

1. Start Visual Studio 2010 if it is not already running.

2. Create a new project called **ReportOrders** by using the *Console Application* template. Save it in the \Microsoft Press\Visual CSharp Step By Step\Chapter 25 folder under your Documents folder.

> **Note** Remember, if you are using Visual C# 2010 Express, you can specify the location for saving your project when you save your project by using *Save ReportOrders* on the *File* menu.

3. In *Solution Explorer*, right-click the file Program.cs and rename it **Report.cs.** In the *Microsoft Visual Studio* message, click *Yes* to change all references of the *Program* class to *Report*.

4. In the *Code and Text Editor* window, add the following *using* statements to the list at the top of the Report.cs file:

```
using System.Data;
using System.Data.SqlClient;
```

The *System.Data* namespace contains many of the types used by ADO.NET. The *System.Data.SqlClient* namespace contains the SQL Server data provider classes for ADO.NET. These classes are specialized versions of the ADO.NET classes, optimized for working with SQL Server.

5. In the *Main* method of the *Report* class, add the following statement shown in bold type, which creates a *SqlConnection* object:

```
static void Main(string[] args)
{
    SqlConnection dataConnection = new SqlConnection();
}
```

SqlConnection is a subclass of an ADO.NET class called *Connection*. It is designed to handle connections to SQL Server databases.

6. After the variable declaration, add a *try/catch* block to the *Main* method as shown next in bold. All the code that you will write for gaining access to the database goes inside the *try* part of this block. In the *catch* block, add a simple handler that catches *SqlException* exceptions.

```
static void Main(string[] args)
{
    ...
    try
    {
        // You will add your code here in a moment
    }
    catch (SqlException e)
    {
        Console.WriteLine("Error accessing the database: {0}", e.Message);
    }
}
```

A *SqlException* is thrown if an error occurs when accessing a SQL Server database.

7. Replace the comment in the *try* block with the code shown in bold here:

```
try
{
    SqlConnectionStringBuilder builder = new SqlConnectionStringBuilder();
    builder.DataSource = ".\\SQLExpress";
    builder.InitialCatalog = "Northwind";
    builder.IntegratedSecurity = true;
    dataConnection.ConnectionString = builder.ConnectionString;
}
```

To connect to a SQL Server database, you must construct a connection string that specifies the database to connect to, the instance of SQL Server holding this database, and how the application will identify itself as a valid user of the database to SQL Server. The simplest way to do this is to use a *SqlConnectionStringBuilder* object. The *SqlConnectionStringBuilder* class exposes properties for each of the elements of a connection string. You can then read a complete connection string that combines all of these elements in the correct format from the *ConnectionString* property.

This code uses a *SqlConnectionStringBuilder* object to build a connection string for accessing the Northwind database running on the instance of SQL Server Express on your computer. The code specifies that the connection will use Windows Authentication to connect to the database. This is the preferred method of access because you do not have to prompt the user for any form of user name or password, and you are not tempted to hard-code user names and passwords into your application.

The connection string is stored in the *ConnectionString* property of the *SqlConnection* object, which you will use in the next step.

You can also encode many other elements in the connection string by using the *SqlConnectionStringBuilder* class—the properties shown in this example are a minimal but sufficient set. See the documentation supplied with Visual Studio 2010 for more details.

8. Add the following statement shown in bold to the code in the *try* block:

```
try
{
    ...
    dataConnection.Open();
}
```

This statement uses the connection string specified by the *ConnectionString* property of the *dataConnection* object to open a connection to the database. If the connection is successful, you can use the *dataConnection* object to perform database commands and queries. If the connection is unsuccessful, the statement throws a *SqlException* exception.

Using SQL Server Authentication

Windows Authentication is useful for authenticating users who are all members of a Windows domain. However, there might be occasions when the user accessing the database does not have a Windows account—for example, if you are building an application designed to be accessed by remote users over the Internet. In these cases, you can use the *User ID* and *Password* parameters instead, like this:

```
string userName = ...;
string password = ...;
// Prompt the user for his name and password, and fill these variables

string connString = String.Format(
    "User ID={0};Password={1};Initial Catalog=Northwind;" +
    "Data Source=YourComputer\\SQLExpress", username, password);

myConnection.ConnectionString = connString;
```

At this point, I should offer a sentence of advice: never hard-code user names and passwords into your applications. Anyone who obtains a copy of the source code (or who reverse-engineers the compiled code) can see this information, and this renders the whole point of security meaningless.

The next step is to prompt the user for a customer ID and then query the database to find all of the orders for that customer.

Query the *Orders* table

1. Add the statements shown here in bold type to the *try* block after the *dataConnection. Open();* statement:

```
try
{
    ...
    Console.Write("Please enter a customer ID (5 characters): ");
    string customerId = Console.ReadLine();
}
```

   These statements prompt the user for a customer ID and read the user's response in the string variable *customerId*.

2. Type the following statements shown in bold type after the code you just entered:

```
try
{
    . . .
    SqlCommand dataCommand = new SqlCommand();
    dataCommand.Connection = dataConnection;
    dataCommand.CommandType = CommandType.Text;
    dataCommand.CommandText =
        "SELECT OrderID, OrderDate, ShippedDate, ShipName, ShipAddress, " +
        "ShipCity, ShipCountry " +
        "FROM Orders WHERE CustomerID = @CustomerIdParam";
}
```

The first statement creates a *SqlCommand* object. Like *SqlConnection*, this is a special-ized version of an ADO.NET class, *Command*, that has been designed for performing queries against a SQL Server database. An ADO.NET *Command* object is used to ex-ecute a command against a data source. In the case of a relational database, the text of the command is a SQL statement.

The second line of code sets the *Connection* property of the *SqlCommand* object to the database connection you opened in the preceding exercise. The next two statements specify that the *SqlCommand* object contains the text of a SQL statement (you can also specify the name of a stored procedure or the name of a single table in the database) and populate the *CommandText* property with a SQL SELECT statement that retrieves information from the *Orders* table for all orders that have a specified *CustomerID*. The text @*CustomerIdParam* is a placeholder for a SQL parameter. (The @ symbol indicates to the data provider that this is a parameter and not the name of a column in the data-base.) The value for the *CustomerID* will be passed as a *SqlParameter* object in the next step.

3. Add the following statements shown in bold to the *try* block, after the code you en-tered in the previous step:

```
try
{
    . . .
    SqlParameter param = new SqlParameter("@CustomerIdParam", SqlDbType.Char, 5);
    param.Value = customerId;
    dataCommand.Parameters.Add(param);
}
```

These statements create a *SqlParameter* object that can be substituted for the @ *CustomerIdParam* when the *SqlCommand* object is executed. The parameter is marked as a database *Char* type (the SQL Server equivalent of a fixed-length string), and the length of this string is specified as 5 characters. The *SqlParameter* is populated with the string entered by the user in the *customerId* variable and then added to the *Parameter* collection of the *SqlCommand*. When SQL Server runs this command, it will examine the *Parameters* collection of the command for a parameter named @*CustomerIdParam* and then substitute the value of this parameter into the text of the SQL statement.

> **Important** If you are new to building database applications, you might be wondering
> why the code creates a *SqlParameter* object and does not just build a simple SQL state-
> ment that embeds the value of the *customerId* variable, like this:
>
> ```
> dataCommand.CommandText =
>     "SELECT OrderID, OrderDate, ShippedDate, ShipName, ShipAddress, " +
>     "ShipCity, ShipCountry " +
>     "FROM Orders WHERE CustomerID = '" + customerId + "'";
> ```
>
> This approach is phenomenally bad practice because it renders your application vulnerable
> to SQL injection attacks. Do not write code such as this in your production applications.
> For a description of what a SQL injection attack is and how dangerous it can be, see the
> SQL Injection topic in SQL Server Books Online, available at *http://msdn2.microsoft.com/*
> *en-us/library/ms161953.aspx.*

4. Add the following statements shown in bold type after the code you just entered:

```
try
{
    ...
    Console.WriteLine("About to find orders for customer {0}\n\n", customerId);
    SqlDataReader dataReader = dataCommand.ExecuteReader();
}
```

The *ExecuteReader* method of a *SqlCommand* object constructs a *SqlDataReader* object
that you can use to fetch the rows identified by the SQL statement. The *SqlDataReader*
class provides the fastest mechanism available (as fast as your network allows) for retrieving data from a SQL Server.

The next task is to iterate through all the orders (if there are any) and display them.

Fetch data and display orders

1. In the Report.cs file, add the *while* loop shown next in bold type after the statement
that creates the *SqlDataReader* object:

```
try
{
    ...
    while (dataReader.Read())
    {
        // Code to display the current row
    }
}
```

The *Read* method of the *SqlDataReader* class fetches the next row from the database. It
returns *true* if another row was retrieved successfully; otherwise, it returns *false*, usually
because there are no more rows. The *while* loop you have just entered keeps reading
rows from the *dataReader* variable and finishes when there are no more rows available.

2. Add the statements shown in bold type here to the body of the *while* loop you created in the preceding step:

```
while (dataReader.Read())
{
    int orderId = dataReader.GetInt32(0);
    DateTime orderDate = dataReader.GetDateTime(1);
    DateTime shipDate = dataReader.GetDateTime(2);
    string shipName = dataReader.GetString(3);
    string shipAddress = dataReader.GetString(4);
    string shipCity = dataReader.GetString(5);
    string shipCountry = dataReader.GetString(6);
    Console.WriteLine(
        "Order: {0}\nPlaced: {1}\nShipped: {2}\n" +
        "To Address: {3}\n{4}\n{5}\n{6}\n\n", orderId, orderDate,
        shipDate, shipName, shipAddress, shipCity, shipCountry);
}
```

This block of code shows how you read the data from the database by using a *SqlDataReader* object. A *SqlDataReader* object contains the most recent row retrieved from the database. You can use the *GetXXX* methods to extract the information from each column in the row—there is a *GetXXX* method for each common type of data. For example, to read an *int* value, you use the *GetInt32* method; to read a string, you use the *GetString* method; and you can probably guess how to read a *DateTime* value. The *GetXXX* methods take a parameter indicating which column to read: 0 is the first column, 1 is the second column, and so on. The preceding code reads the various columns from the current *Orders* row, stores the values in a set of variables, and then prints out the values of these variables.

Firehose Cursors

One of the major drawbacks in a multiuser database application is locked data. Unfortunately, it is common to see applications retrieve rows from a database and keep those rows locked to prevent another user from changing the data while the application is using them. In some extreme circumstances, an application can even prevent other users from reading data that it has locked. If the application retrieves a large number of rows, it locks a large proportion of the table. If there are many users running the same application at the same time, they can end up waiting for one another to release locks and it all leads to a slow-running and frustrating mess.

The *SqlDataReader* class has been designed to remove this drawback. It fetches rows one at a time and does not retain any locks on a row after it has been retrieved. It is wonderful for improving concurrency in your applications. The *SqlDataReader* class is sometimes referred to as a *firehose cursor* because it pours data out as quickly as possible. (The term *cursor* is an acronym that stands for "current set of rows.")

When you have finished using a database, it's good practice to close your connection and release any resources you have been using.

Disconnect from the database, and test the application

1. Add the statement shown next in bold after the *while* loop in the *try* block:

    ```
    try
    {
        ...
        while(dataReader.Read())
        {
            ...
        }

        dataReader.Close();
    }
    ```

    This statement closes the *SqlDataReader* object. You should always close a *SqlDataReader* object when you have finished with it because you will not able to use the current *SqlConnection* object to run any more commands until you do. It is also considered good practice to do it even if all you are going to do next is close the *SqlConnection*.

    > **Note** If you activate multiple active result sets (MARS) with SQL Server 2008, you can open more than one *SqlDataReader* object against the same *SqlConnection* object and process multiple sets of data. MARS is disabled by default. To learn more about MARS and how you can activate and use it, consult SQL Server 2008 Books Online.

2. After the *catch* block, add the following *finally* block:

    ```
    catch(SqlException e)
    {
        ...
    }
    finally
    {
        dataConnection.Close();
    }
    ```

    Database connections are scarce resources. You need to ensure that they are closed when you have finished with them. Putting this statement in a *finally* block guarantees that the *SqlConnection* will be closed, even if an exception occurs; remember that the code in the *finally* block will be executed after the *catch* handler has finished.

> **Tip** An alternative approach to using a *finally* block is to wrap the code that creates the *SqlDataConnection* object in a *using* statement, as shown in the following code. At the end of the block defined by the *using* statement, the *SqlConnection* object is closed automatically, even if an exception occurs:
>
> ```
> using (SqlConnection dataConnection = new SqlConnection())
> {
>     try
>     {
>         SqlConnectionStringBuilder builder = new SqlConnectionStringBuilder();
>         ...
>     }
>     catch (SqlException e)
>     {
>         Console.WriteLine("Error accessing the database: {0}", e.Message);
>     }
> }
> ```

3. On the *Debug* menu, click *Start Without Debugging* to build and run the application.

4. At the customer ID prompt, type the customer ID **VINET**, and press Enter.

   The SQL SELECT statement appears, followed by the orders for this customer, as shown in the following image:

   ```
   C:\Windows\system32\cmd.exe
   Please enter a customer ID (5 characters): VINET
   About to find orders for customer VINET

   Order: 10248
   Placed: 04/07/1996 00:00:00
   Shipped: 16/07/1996 00:00:00
   To Address: Vins et alcools Chevalier
   59 rue de l'Abbaye
   Reims
   France

   Order: 10274
   Placed: 06/08/1996 00:00:00
   Shipped: 16/08/1996 00:00:00
   To Address: Vins et alcools Chevalier
   59 rue de l'Abbaye
   Reims
   France

   Order: 10295
   Placed: 02/09/1996 00:00:00
   Shipped: 10/09/1996 00:00:00
   ```

   You can scroll back through the console window to view all the data. Press the Enter key to close the console window when you have finished.

5. Run the application without debugging, and then type **BONAP** when prompted for the customer ID.

   Some rows appear, but then an error occurs and a message box is displayed with the message "ReportOrders has stopped working." If the message "Do you want to send more information about the problem?" appears, click *Cancel*.

An error message containing the text "Unhandled Exception: System.Data.SqlTypes. SqlNullValueException: Data is Null. This method or property cannot be called on Null values" appears in the console window.

The problem is that relational databases allow some columns to contain null values. A null value is a bit like a null variable in C#: it doesn't have a value, but if you try to read it, you get an error. In the *Orders* table, the *ShippedDate* column can contain a null value if the order has not yet been shipped. You should also note that this is a *SqlNullValueException* and consequently is not caught by the *SqlException* handler.

6. Press Enter to close the console window and return to Visual Studio 2010.

Closing Connections

In many older applications, you might notice a tendency for the application to open a connection when the application starts and not close the connection until the application terminates. The rationale behind this strategy was that opening and closing database connections were expensive and time-consuming operations. This strategy had an impact on the scalability of applications because each user running the application had a connection to the database open while the application was running, even if the user went to lunch for a few hours. Most databases limit the number of concurrent connections that they allow. (Sometimes this is because of licensing, but usually it's because each connection consumes resources on the database server that are not infinite.) Eventually, the database would hit a limit on the number of users that could operate concurrently.

Most .NET Framework data providers (including the SQL Server provider) implement *connection pooling*. Database connections are created and held in a pool. When an application requires a connection, the data access provider extracts the next available connection from the pool. When the application closes the connection, it is returned to the pool and made available for the next application that wants a connection. This means that opening and closing database connections are no longer expensive operations. Closing a connection does not disconnect from the database; it just returns the connection to the pool. Opening a connection is simply a matter of obtaining an already-open connection from the pool. Therefore, you should not hold on to connections longer than you need to—open a connection when you need it, and close it as soon as you have finished with it.

You should note that the *ExecuteReader* method of the *SqlCommand* class, which creates a *SqlDataReader*, is overloaded. You can specify a *System.Data.CommandBehavior* parameter that automatically closes the connection used by the *SqlDataReader* when the *SqlDataReader* is closed, like this:

```
SqlDataReader dataReader =
    dataCommand.ExecuteReader(System.Data.CommandBehavior.CloseConnection);
```

When you read the data from the *SqlDataReader* object, you should check that the data you are reading is not null. You'll see how to do this next.

Handle null database values

1. In the *Main* method of the *Report* class, change the code in the body of the *while* loop to contain an *if ... else* block, as shown here in bold:

```
while (dataReader.Read())
{
    int orderId = dataReader.GetInt32(0);
    if (dataReader.IsDBNull(2))
    {
        Console.WriteLine("Order {0} not yet shipped\n\n", orderId);
    }
    else
    {
        DateTime orderDate = dataReader.GetDateTime(1);
        DateTime shipDate = dataReader.GetDateTime(2);
        string shipName = dataReader.GetString(3);
        string shipAddress = dataReader.GetString(4);
        string shipCity = dataReader.GetString(5);
        string shipCountry = dataReader.GetString(6);
        Console.WriteLine(
            "Order {0}\nPlaced {1}\nShipped{2}\n" +
            "To Address {3}\n{4}\n{5}\n{6}\n\n", orderId, orderDate,
            shipDate, shipName, shipAddress, shipCity, shipCountry);
    }
}
```

The *if* statement uses the *IsDBNull* method to determine whether the *ShippedDate* column (column 2 in the table) is null. If it is null, no attempt is made to fetch it (or any of the other columns, which should also be null if there is no *ShippedDate* value); otherwise, the columns are read and printed as before.

2. Build and run the application again.

3. Type **BONAP** for the customer ID when prompted.

    This time you do not get any errors, but you receive a list that includes orders that have not yet been shipped.

4. When the application finishes, press Enter and return to Visual Studio 2010.

Querying a Database by Using LINQ to SQL

In Chapter 20, "Querying In-Memory Data by Using Query Expressions," you saw how to use LINQ to examine the contents of enumerable collections held in memory. LINQ provides query expressions, which use SQL-like syntax for performing queries and generating a result set that you can then step through. It should come as no surprise that you can use an extended form of LINQ, called LINQ to SQL, for querying and manipulating the contents of a database. LINQ to SQL is built on top of ADO.NET. LINQ to SQL provides a high level of abstraction, removing the need for you to worry about the details of constructing an ADO.NET *Command* object, iterating through a result set returned by a *DataReader* object, or fetching data column by column using the various *GetXXX* methods.

Defining an Entity Class

You saw in Chapter 20 that using LINQ requires the objects that you are querying to be enumerable; they must be collections that implement the *IEnumerable* interface. LINQ to SQL can create its own enumerable collections of objects based on classes you define and that map directly to tables in a database. These classes are called *entity classes*. When you connect to a database and perform a query, LINQ to SQL can retrieve the data identified by your query and create an instance of an entity class for each row fetched.

The best way to explain LINQ to SQL is to see an example. The *Products* table in the Northwind database consists of columns that contain information about the different aspects of the various products that Northwind Traders sells. The instnwnd.sql script that you ran in the first exercise in this chapter includes a *CREATE TABLE* statement that looks similar to this (some of the columns, constraints, and other details have been omitted):

```
CREATE TABLE "Products" (
    "ProductID" "int" NOT NULL ,
    "ProductName" nvarchar (40) NOT NULL ,
    "SupplierID" "int" NULL ,
    "UnitPrice" "money" NULL,
    CONSTRAINT "PK_Products" PRIMARY KEY CLUSTERED ("ProductID"),
    CONSTRAINT "FK_Products_Suppliers" FOREIGN KEY ("SupplierID")
        REFERENCES "dbo"."Suppliers" ("SupplierID")
)
```

You can define an entity class that corresponds to the *Products* table like this:

```
[Table(Name = "Products")]
public class Product
{
    [Column(IsPrimaryKey = true, CanBeNull = false)]
    public int ProductID { get; set; }

    [Column(CanBeNull = false)]
    public string ProductName { get; set; }
```

```
    [Column]
    public int? SupplierID { get; set; }

    [Column(DbType = "money")]
    public decimal? UnitPrice { get; set; }
}
```

The *Product* class contains a property for each of the columns in which you are interested in the *Products* table. You don't have to specify every column from the underlying table, but any columns that you omit will not be retrieved when you execute a query based on this entity class. The important points to note are the *Table* and *Column* attributes.

The *Table* attribute identifies this class as an entity class. The *Name* parameter specifies the name of the corresponding table in the database. If you omit the *Name* parameter, LINQ to SQL assumes that the entity class name is the same as the name of the corresponding table in the database.

The *Column* attribute describes how a column in the *Products* table maps to a property in the *Product* class. The *Column* attribute can take a number of parameters. The ones shown in this example and described in the following list are the most common:

■ The *IsPrimaryKey* parameter specifies that the property makes up part of the primary key. (If the table has a composite primary key spanning multiple columns, you should specify the *IsPrimaryKey* parameter for each corresponding property in the entity class.)

■ The *DbType* parameter specifies the type of the underlying column in the database. In many cases, LINQ to SQL can detect and convert data in a column in the database to the type of the corresponding property in the entity class, but in some situations you need to specify the data type mapping yourself. For example, the *UnitPrice* column in the *Products* table uses the SQL Server *money* type. The entity class specifies the corresponding property as a *decimal* value.

 Note The default mapping of *money* data in SQL Server is to the *decimal* type in an entity class, so the *DbType* parameter shown here is actually redundant. However, I wanted to show you the syntax.

■ The *CanBeNull* parameter indicates whether the column in the database can contain a null value. The default value for the *CanBeNull* parameter is *true*. Notice that the two properties in the *Product* class that correspond to columns that permit null values in the database (*SupplierID* and *UnitPrice*) are defined as nullable types in the entity class.

Note You can also use LINQ to SQL to create new databases and tables based on the definitions of your entity classes by using the *CreateDatabase* method of the *DataContext* object. LINQ to SQL uses the definition of the *DbType* parameter to specify whether a column should allow null values. If you are using LINQ to SQL to create a new database, you should specify the nullability of each column in each table in the *DbType* parameter, like this:

```
[Column(DbType = "NVarChar(40) NOT NULL", CanBeNull = false)]
public string ProductName { get; set; }
...
[Column(DbType = "Int NULL", CanBeNull = true)]
public int? SupplierID { get; set; }
```

Like the *Table* attribute, the *Column* attribute provides a *Name* parameter that you can use to specify the name of the underlying column in the database. If you omit this parameter, LINQ to SQL assumes that the name of the column is the same as the name of the property in the entity class.

Creating and Running a LINQ to SQL Query

After you have defined an entity class, you can use it to fetch and display data from the *Products* table. The following code shows the basic steps for performing this task:

```
SqlConnectionStringBuilder builder = new SqlConnectionStringBuilder();
builder.DataSource = ".\\SQLExpress";
builder.InitialCatalog = "Northwind";
builder.IntegratedSecurity = true;

DataContext db = new DataContext(builder.ConnectionString);

Table<Product> products = db.GetTable<Product>();
var productsQuery = from p in products
                    select p;

foreach (var product in productsQuery)
{
    Console.WriteLine("ID: {0}, Name: {1}, Supplier: {2}, Price: {3:C}",
                product.ProductID, product.ProductName,
                product.SupplierID, product.UnitPrice);
}
```

Note Remember that the keywords *from*, *in*, and *select* in this context are C# identifiers and are not elements of SQL syntax. You must type them in lowercase.

The *DataContext* class is responsible for managing the relationship between your entity classes and the tables in the database. You use it to establish a connection to the database and create collections of the entity classes. The *DataContext* constructor expects a connection string as a parameter, specifying the database that you want to use. This connection string is exactly the same as the connection string that you would use when connecting through an ADO.NET *Connection* object. (The *DataContext* class actually creates an ADO.NET connection behind the scenes.)

The generic *GetTable<TEntity>* method of the *DataContext* class expects an entity class as its *TEntity* type parameter. This method constructs an enumerable collection based on this type and returns the collection as a *Table<TEntity>* type. You can perform LINQ to SQL queries over this collection. The query shown in this example simply retrieves every object from the *Products* table.

> **Note**   If you need to recap your knowledge of LINQ query expressions, turn back to Chapter 20.

The *foreach* statement iterates through the results of this query and displays the details of each product. The following image shows the results of running this code. (The prices shown are per case, not per individual item.)

```
C:\Windows\system32\cmd.exe
ID: 1, Name: Chai, Supplier: 1, Price: £18.00
ID: 2, Name: Chang, Supplier: 1, Price: £19.00
ID: 3, Name: Aniseed Syrup, Supplier: 1, Price: £10.00
ID: 4, Name: Chef Anton's Cajun Seasoning, Supplier: 2, Price: £22.00
ID: 5, Name: Chef Anton's Gumbo Mix, Supplier: 2, Price: £21.35
ID: 6, Name: Grandma's Boysenberry Spread, Supplier: 3, Price: £25.00
ID: 7, Name: Uncle Bob's Organic Dried Pears, Supplier: 3, Price: £30.00
ID: 8, Name: Northwoods Cranberry Sauce, Supplier: 3, Price: £40.00
ID: 9, Name: Mishi Kobe Niku, Supplier: 4, Price: £97.00
ID: 10, Name: Ikura, Supplier: 4, Price: £31.00
ID: 11, Name: Queso Cabrales, Supplier: 5, Price: £21.00
ID: 12, Name: Queso Manchego La Pastora, Supplier: 5, Price: £38.00
ID: 13, Name: Konbu, Supplier: 6, Price: £6.00
ID: 14, Name: Tofu, Supplier: 6, Price: £23.25
ID: 15, Name: Genen Shouyu, Supplier: 6, Price: £15.50
ID: 16, Name: Pavlova, Supplier: 7, Price: £17.45
ID: 17, Name: Alice Mutton, Supplier: 7, Price: £39.00
ID: 18, Name: Carnarvon Tigers, Supplier: 7, Price: £62.50
ID: 19, Name: Teatime Chocolate Biscuits, Supplier: 8, Price: £9.20
ID: 20, Name: Sir Rodney's Marmalade, Supplier: 8, Price: £81.00
ID: 21, Name: Sir Rodney's Scones, Supplier: 8, Price: £10.00
ID: 22, Name: Gustaf's Knäckebröd, Supplier: 9, Price: £21.00
ID: 23, Name: Tunnbröd, Supplier: 9, Price: £9.00
ID: 24, Name: Guaraná Fantástica, Supplier: 10, Price: £4.50
ID: 25, Name: NuNuCa Nuß-Nougat-Creme, Supplier: 11, Price: £14.00
```

The *DataContext* object controls the database connection automatically; it opens the connection immediately prior to fetching the first row of data in the *foreach* statement and then closes the connection after the last row has been retrieved.

The LINQ to SQL query shown in the preceding example retrieves every column for every row in the *Products* table. In this case, you can actually iterate through the *products* collection directly, like this:

```
Table<Product> products = db.GetTable<Product>();

foreach (Product product in products)
{
    ...
}
```

When the *foreach* statement runs, the *DataContext* object constructs a SQL SELECT statement that simply retrieves all the data from the *Products* table. If you want to retrieve a single row in the *Products* table, you can call the *Single* method of the *Products* entity class. *Single* is an extension method that itself takes a method that identifies the row you want to find and returns this row as an instance of the entity class (as opposed to a collection of rows in a *Table* collection). You can specify the method parameter as a lambda expression. If the lambda expression does not identify exactly one row, the *Single* method returns an *InvalidOperationException*. The following code example queries the Northwind database for the product with the *ProductID* value of 27. The value returned is an instance of the *Product* class, and the *Console.WriteLine* statement prints the name of the product. As before, the database connection is opened and closed automatically by the *DataContext* object.

```
Product singleProduct = products.Single(p => p.ProductID == 27);
Console.WriteLine("Name: {0}", singleProduct.ProductName);
```

Deferred and Immediate Fetching

An important point to emphasize is that by default, LINQ to SQL retrieves the data from the database only when you request it and not when you define a LINQ to SQL query or create a *Table* collection. This is known as *deferred fetching*. In the example shown earlier that displays all of the products from the *Products* table, the *productsQuery* collection is populated only when the *foreach* loop runs. This mode of operation matches that of LINQ when querying in-memory objects; you will always see the most up-to-date version of the data, even if the data changes after you have run the statement that creates the *productsQuery* enumerable collection.

When the *foreach* loop starts, LINQ to SQL creates and runs a SQL SELECT statement derived from the LINQ to SQL query to create an ADO.NET *DataReader* object. Each iteration of the *foreach* loop performs the necessary *GetXXX* methods to fetch the data for that row. After the final row has been fetched and processed by the *foreach* loop, LINQ to SQL closes the database connection.

Deferred fetching ensures that only the data an application actually uses is retrieved from the database. However, if you are accessing a database running on a remote instance of SQL Server, fetching data row by row does not make the best use of network bandwidth. In this scenario, you can fetch and cache all the data in a single network request by forcing immediate evaluation of the LINQ to SQL query. You can do this by calling the *ToList* or *ToArray* extension methods, which fetch the data into a list or array when you define the LINQ to SQL query, like this:

```
var productsQuery = from p in products.ToList()
                    select p;
```

In this code example, *productsQuery* is now an enumerable list, populated with information from the *Products* table. When you iterate over the data, LINQ to SQL retrieves it from this list rather than sending fetch requests to the database.

Joining Tables and Creating Relationships

LINQ to SQL supports the *join* query operator for combining and retrieving related data held in multiple tables. For example, the *Products* table in the Northwind database holds the ID of the supplier for each product. If you want to know the name of each supplier, you have to query the *Suppliers* table. The *Suppliers* table contains the *CompanyName* column, which specifies the name of the supplier company, and the *ContactName* column, which contains the name of the person in the supplier company that handles orders from Northwind Traders. You can define an entity class containing the relevant supplier information like this (the *SupplierID* column in the database is mandatory, but the *ContactName* allows null values):

```
[Table(Name = "Suppliers")]
public class Supplier
{
    [Column(IsPrimaryKey = true, CanBeNull = false)]
    public int SupplierID { get; set; }

    [Column(CanBeNull = false)]
    public string CompanyName { get; set; }

    [Column]
    public string ContactName { get; set; }
}
```

You can then instantiate *Table<Product>* and *Table<Supplier>* collections and define a LINQ to SQL query to join these tables together, like this:

```
DataContext db = new DataContext(...);
Table<Product> products = db.GetTable<Product>();
Table<Supplier> suppliers = db.GetTable<Supplier>();
var productsAndSuppliers = from p in products
                           join s in suppliers
                           on p.SupplierID equals s.SupplierID
                           select new { p.ProductName, s.CompanyName, s.ContactName };
```

When you iterate through the *productsAndSuppliers* collection, LINQ to SQL will execute a SQL SELECT statement that joins the *Products* and *Suppliers* tables in the database over the *SupplierID* column in both tables and fetches the data.

However, with LINQ to SQL you can specify the relationships between tables as part of the definition of the entity classes. LINQ to SQL can then fetch the supplier information for each product automatically without requiring that you construct a potentially complex and error-prone *join* statement. Returning to the products and suppliers example, these tables have a many-to-one relationship in the Northwind database; each product is supplied by a single supplier, but a single supplier can supply several products. Phrasing this relationship slightly differently, a row in the *Products* table can reference a single row in the *Suppliers* table through the *SupplierID* columns in both tables, but a row in the *Suppliers* table can reference a whole set of rows in the *Products* table. LINQ to SQL provides the *EntityRef<TEntity>* and *EntitySet<TEntity>* generic types to model this type of relationship. Taking the *Product* entity class first, you can define the "one" side of the relationship with the *Supplier* entity class by using the *EntityRef<Supplier>* type, as shown here in bold:

```
[Table(Name = "Products")]
public class Product
{
    [Column(IsPrimaryKey = true, CanBeNull = false)]
    public int ProductID { get; set; }
    ...
    [Column]
    public int? SupplierID { get; set; }
    ...
    private EntityRef<Supplier> supplier;
    [Association(Storage = "supplier", ThisKey = "SupplierID", OtherKey = "SupplierID")]
    public Supplier Supplier
    {
        get { return this.supplier.Entity; }
        set { this.supplier.Entity = value; }
    }
}
```

The private *supplier* field is a reference to an instance of the *Supplier* entity class. The public *Supplier* property provides access to this reference. The *Association* attribute specifies how LINQ to SQL locates and populates the data for this property. The *Storage* parameter identifies the *private* field used to store the reference to the *Supplier* object. The *ThisKey* parameter indicates which property in the *Product* entity class LINQ to SQL should use to locate the *Supplier* to reference for this product, and the *OtherKey* parameter specifies which property in the *Supplier* table LINQ to SQL should match against the value for the *ThisKey* parameter. In this example, the *Product* and *Supplier* tables are joined across the *SupplierID* property in both entities.

> **Note** The *Storage* parameter is actually optional. If you specify it, LINQ to SQL accesses the corresponding data member directly when populating it rather than going through the *set* accessor. The *set* accessor is required for applications that manually fill or change the entity object referenced by the *EntityRef<TEntity>* property. Although the *Storage* parameter is actually redundant in this example, it is recommended practice to include it.

The *get* accessor in the *Supplier* property returns a reference to the *Supplier* entity by using the *Entity* property of the *EntityRef<Supplier>* type. The *set* accessor populates this property with a reference to a *Supplier* entity.

You can define the "many" side of the relationship in the *Supplier* class with the *EntitySet<Product>* type, like this:

```
[Table(Name = "Suppliers")]
public class Supplier
{
    [Column(IsPrimaryKey = true, CanBeNull = false)]
    public int SupplierID { get; set; }
    ...
    private EntitySet<Product> products = null;
    [Association(Storage = "products", OtherKey = "SupplierID", ThisKey = "SupplierID")]
    public EntitySet<Product> Products
    {
        get { return this.products; }
        set { this.products.Assign(value); }
    }
}
```

> **Tip** It is conventional to use a singular noun for the name of an entity class and its properties. The exception to this rule is that *EntitySet<TEntity>* properties typically take the plural form because they represent a collection rather than a single entity.

This time, notice that the *Storage* parameter of the *Association* attribute specifies the private *EntitySet<Product>* field. An *EntitySet<TEntity>* object holds a collection of references to entities. The *get* accessor of the public *Products* property returns this collection. The *set* accessor uses the *Assign* method of the *EntitySet<Product>* class to populate this collection.

So, by using the *EntityRef<TEntity>* and *EntitySet<TEntity>* types you can define properties that can model a one-to-many relationship, but how do you actually fill these properties with data? The answer is that LINQ to SQL fills them for you when it fetches the data. The following code creates an instance of the *Table<Product>* class and issues a LINQ to SQL query to fetch the details of all products. This code is similar to the first LINQ to SQL example you saw earlier. The difference is in the *foreach* loop that displays the data.

```
DataContext db = new DataContext(...);
Table<Product> products = db.GetTable<Product>();

var productsAndSuppliers = from p in products
                           select p;

foreach (var product in productsAndSuppliers)
{
    Console.WriteLine("Product {0} supplied by {1}",
        product.ProductName, product.Supplier.CompanyName);
}
```

The *Console.WriteLine* statement reads the value in the *ProductName* property of the product entity as before, but it also accesses the *Supplier* entity and displays the *CompanyName* property from this entity. If you run this code, the output looks like this:

As the code fetches each *Product* entity, LINQ to SQL executes a second, deferred, query to retrieve the details of the supplier for that product so that it can populate the *Supplier* property, based on the relationship specified by the *Association* attribute of this property in the *Product* entity class.

When you have defined the *Product* and *Supplier* entities as having a one-to-many relationship, similar logic applies if you execute a LINQ to SQL query over the *Table<Supplier>* collection, like this:

```
DataContext db = new DataContext(...);
Table<Supplier> suppliers = db.GetTable<Supplier>();
var suppliersAndProducts = from s in suppliers
                           select s;

foreach (var supplier in suppliersAndProducts)
{
    Console.WriteLine("Supplier name: {0}", supplier.CompanyName);
    Console.WriteLine("Products supplied");
    foreach (var product in supplier.Products)
    {
        Console.WriteLine("\t{0}", product.ProductName);
    }
    Console.WriteLine();
}
```

In this case, when the *foreach* loop fetches a supplier, it runs a second query (again deferred) to retrieve all the products for that supplier and populate the *Products* property. This time, however, the property is a collection (an *EntitySet<Product>*), so you can code a nested *foreach* statement to iterate through the set, displaying the name of each product. The output of this code looks like this:

Deferred and Immediate Fetching Revisited

Earlier in this chapter, I mentioned that LINQ to SQL defers fetching data until the data is actually requested but that you could apply the *ToList* or *ToArray* extension method to retrieve data immediately. This technique does not apply to data referenced as *EntitySet<TEntity>* or *EntityRef<TEntity>* properties; even if you use *ToList* or *ToArray*, the data will still be fetched only when accessed. If you want to force LINQ to SQL to query and fetch referenced data immediately, you can set the *LoadOptions* property of the *DataContext* object as follows:

```
DataContext db = new DataContext(...);
Table<Supplier> suppliers = db.GetTable<Supplier>();
DataLoadOptions loadOptions = new DataLoadOptions();
loadOptions.LoadWith<Supplier>(s => s.Products);
db.LoadOptions = loadOptions;
var suppliersAndProducts = from s in suppliers
                           select s;
```

The *DataLoadOptions* class provides the generic *LoadWith* method. By using this method, you can specify whether an *EntitySet<TEntity>* property in an instance should be loaded when the instance is populated. The parameter to the *LoadWith* method is a lambda expression that identifies the related data to retrieve when the data for a table is fetched. The example shown here causes the *Products* property of each *Supplier* entity to be populated as soon as the data for each *Supplier* entity is fetched rather than being deferred. If you specify the *LoadOptions* property of the *DataContext* object together with the *ToList* or *ToArray* extension method of a *Table* collection, LINQ to SQL will load the entire collection as well as the data for the referenced properties for the entities in that collection into memory as soon as the LINQ to SQL query is evaluated.

> **Tip** If you have several *EntitySet<TEntity>* properties, you can call the *LoadWith* method of the
> same *LoadOptions* object several times, each time specifying the *EntitySet<TEntity>* to load.

Defining a Custom *DataContext* Class

The *DataContext* class provides functionality for managing databases and database
connections, creating entity classes, and executing commands to retrieve and update data
in a database. Although you can use the raw *DataContext* class provided with the .NET
Framework, it is better practice to use inheritance and define your own specialized version
that declares the various *Table<TEntity>* collections as public members. For example, here is
a specialized *DataContext* class that exposes the *Products* and *Suppliers Table* collections as
public members:

```
public class Northwind : DataContext
{
    public Table<Product> Products;
    public Table<Supplier> Suppliers;

    public Northwind(string connectionInfo) : base(connectionInfo)
    {
    }
}
```

Notice that the *Northwind* class also provides a constructor that takes a connection string as
a parameter. You can create a new instance of the *Northwind* class and then define and run
LINQ to SQL queries over the *Table* collection classes it exposes like this:

```
Northwind nwindDB = new Northwind(...);

var suppliersQuery = from s in nwindDB.Suppliers
                     select s;

foreach (var supplier in suppliersQuery)
{
    ...
}
```

This practice makes your code easier to maintain. Using an ordinary *DataContext* object,
you can instantiate any entity class by using the *GetTable* method, regardless of the database to which the *DataContext* object connects. You find out that you have used the wrong
DataContext object and have connected to the wrong database only at run time, when you
try to retrieve data. With a custom *DataContext* class, you reference the *Table* collections
through the *DataContext* object. (The *base DataContext* constructor uses a mechanism called
reflection to examine its members, and it automatically instantiates any members that are
Table collections—the details of how reflection works are outside the scope of this book.)

It is obvious to which database you need to connect to retrieve data for a specific table; if IntelliSense does not display your table when you define the LINQ to SQL query, you have picked the wrong *DataContext* class, and your code will not compile.

Using LINQ to SQL to Query Order Information

In the following exercise, you will write a version of the console application that you developed in the preceding exercise that prompts the user for a customer ID and displays the details of any orders placed by that customer. You will use LINQ to SQL to retrieve the data. You will then be able to compare LINQ to SQL with the equivalent code written by using ADO.NET.

Define the *Order* entity class

1. Using Visual Studio 2010, create a new project called **LINQOrders** by using the *Console Application* template. Save it in the \Microsoft Press\Visual CSharp Step By Step\Chapter 25 folder under your Documents folder.

2. In *Solution Explorer*, change the name of the file Program.cs to **LINQReport.cs**. In the *Microsoft Visual Studio* message box, click *Yes* to change all references of the *Program* class to *LINQReport*.

3. On the *Project* menu, click *Add Reference*. In the *Add Reference* dialog box, click the *.NET* tab, select the *System.Data.Linq* assembly, and then click *OK*.

   This assembly holds the LINQ to SQL types and attributes.

4. In the *Code and Text Editor* window, add the following *using* statements to the list at the top of the file:

   ```
   using System.Data.Linq;
   using System.Data.Linq.Mapping;
   using System.Data.SqlClient;
   ```

5. Add the *Order* entity class to the LINQReport.cs file after the *LINQReport* class. Tag the *Order* class with the *Table* attribute, as follows:

   ```
   [Table(Name = "Orders")]
   public class Order
   {
   }
   ```

   The table is called *Orders* in the Northwind database. Remember that it is common practice to use the singular noun for the name of an entity class because an entity object represents one row from the database.

6. Add the property shown here in bold to the *Order* class:

```
[Table(Name = "Orders")]
public class Order
{
    [Column(IsPrimaryKey = true, CanBeNull = false)]
    public int OrderID { get; set; }
}
```

The *OrderID* column is the primary key for this table in the Northwind database.

7. Add the following properties shown in bold type to the *Order* class:

```
[Table(Name = "Orders")]
public class Order
{
    ...
    [Column]
    public string CustomerID { get; set; }

    [Column]
    public DateTime? OrderDate { get; set; }

    [Column]
    public DateTime? ShippedDate { get; set; }

    [Column]
    public string ShipName { get; set; }

    [Column]
    public string ShipAddress { get; set; }

    [Column]
    public string ShipCity { get; set; }

    [Column]
    public string ShipCountry { get; set; }
}
```

These properties hold the customer ID, order date, and shipping information for an order. In the database, all of these columns allow null values, so it is important to use the nullable version of the *DateTime* type for the *OrderDate* and *ShippedDate* properties. (Note that *string* is a reference type that automatically allows null values.) Notice that LINQ to SQL automatically maps the SQL Server *NVarChar* type to the .NET Framework *string* type and the SQL Server *DateTime* type to the .NET Framework *DateTime* type.

8. Add the following *Northwind* class to the LINQReport.cs file after the *Order* entity class:

```
public class Northwind : DataContext
{
    public Table<Order> Orders;

    public Northwind(string connectionInfo)
        : base (connectionInfo)
    {
    }
}
```

The *Northwind* class is a *DataContext* class that exposes a *Table* property based on the *Order* entity class. In the next exercise, you will use this specialized version of the *DataContext* class to access the *Orders* table in the database.

Retrieve order information by using a LINQ to SQL query

1. In the *Main* method of the *LINQReport* class, add the code shown next in bold type, which creates a *Northwind* object:

```
static void Main(string[] args)
{
    SqlConnectionStringBuilder builder = new SqlConnectionStringBuilder();
    builder.DataSource = ".\\SQLExpress";
    builder.InitialCatalog = "Northwind";
    builder.IntegratedSecurity = true;

    Northwind northwindDB = new Northwind(builder.ConnectionString);
}
```

The connection string constructed by using the *SqlConnectionStringBuilder* object is exactly the same as in the earlier exercise. The *northwindDB* object uses this string to connect to the Northwind database.

2. After the code added in the previous step, add a *try/catch* block to the *Main* method:

```
static void Main(string[] args)
{
    ...
    try
    {
        // You will add your code here in a moment
    }
    catch (SqlException e)
    {
        Console.WriteLine("Error accessing the database: {0}", e.Message);
    }
}
```

As when using ordinary ADO.NET code, LINQ to SQL raises a *SqlException* if an error occurs when accessing a SQL Server database.

3. Replace the comment in the *try* block with the following code shown in bold type:

```
try
{
    Console.Write("Please enter a customer ID (5 characters): ");
    string customerId = Console.ReadLine();
}
```

These statements prompt the user for a customer ID and save the user's response in the string variable *customerId*.

4. Type the statement shown here in bold type after the code you just entered:

```
try
{
    ...
    var ordersQuery = from o in northwindDB.Orders
                      where String.Equals(o.CustomerID, customerId)
                      select o;
}
```

This statement defines the LINQ to SQL query that will retrieve the orders for the specified customer.

5. Add the *foreach* statement and *if...else* block shown next in bold type after the code you added in the previous step:

```
try
{
    ...
    foreach (var order in ordersQuery)
    {
        if (order.ShippedDate == null)
        {
            Console.WriteLine("Order {0} not yet shipped\n\n", order.OrderID);
        }
        else
        {
            // Display the order details
        }
    }
}
```

The *foreach* statement iterates through the orders for the customer. If the value in the *ShippedDate* column in the database is *null*, the corresponding property in the *Order* entity object is also *null*, and then the *if* statement outputs a suitable message.

6. Replace the comment in the *else* part of the *if* statement you added in the preceding step with the code shown here in bold type:

```
if (order.ShippedDate == null)
{
    ...
}
else
{
    Console.WriteLine("Order: {0}\nPlaced: {1}\nShipped: {2}\n" +
                      "To Address: {3}\n{4}\n{5}\n{6}\n\n", order.OrderID,
                      order.OrderDate, order.ShippedDate, order.ShipName,
                      order.ShipAddress, order.ShipCity,
                      order.ShipCountry);
}
```

7. On the *Debug* menu, click *Start Without Debugging* to build and run the application.

8. In the console window displaying the message "Please enter a customer ID (5 characters):", type **VINET**.

The application should display a list of orders for this customer. When the application has finished, press Enter to return to Visual Studio 2010.

9. Run the application again. This time type **BONAP** when prompted for a customer ID.

The final order for this customer has not yet shipped and contains a null value for the *ShippedDate* column. Verify that the application detects and handles this null value. When the application has finished, press Enter to return to Visual Studio 2010.

In this chapter, you have seen the basic elements that LINQ to SQL provides for querying information from a database. LINQ to SQL has many more features that you can employ in your applications, including the ability to modify data and update a database. You will look briefly at some of these aspects of LINQ to SQL in the next chapter.

- If you want to continue to the next chapter

  Keep Visual Studio 2010 running, and turn to Chapter 26.

- If you want to exit Visual Studio 2010 now

  On the *File* menu, click *Exit*. If you see a *Save* dialog box, click *Yes* and save the project.

Chapter 25 Quick Reference

To	Do this
Connect to a SQL Server database by using ADO.NET	Create a *SqlConnection* object, set its *ConnectionString* property with details specifying the database to use, and call the *Open* method.
Create and execute a database query by using ADO.NET	Create a *SqlCommand* object. Set its *Connection* property to a valid *SqlConnection* object. Set its *CommandText* property to a valid SQL SELECT statement. Call the *ExecuteReader* method to run the query, and create a *SqlDataReader* object.
Fetch data by using an ADO.NET *SqlDataReader* object	Ensure that the data is not null by using the *IsDBNull* method. If the data is not null, use the appropriate *GetXXX* method (such as *GetString* or *GetInt32*) to retrieve the data.
Define an entity class	Define a class with public properties for each column. Prefix the class definition with the *Table* attribute, specifying the name of the table in the underlying database. Prefix each property with the *Column* attribute, and specify parameters indicating the name, type, and nullability of the corresponding column in the database.
Create and execute a query by using LINQ to SQL	Create a *DataContext* object, and specify a connection string for the database. Create a *Table* collection based on the entity class corresponding to the table you want to query. Define a LINQ to SQL query that identifies the data to be retrieved from the database and returns an enumerable collection of entities. Iterate through the enumerable collection to retrieve the data for each row and process the results.

Chapter 26

Displaying and Editing Data by Using the Entity Framework and Data Binding

After completing this chapter, you will be able to:

- Use the ADO.NET Entity Framework to generate entity classes.

- Use data binding in a Microsoft Windows Presentation Foundation (WPF) application to display and maintain data retrieved from a database.

- Update a database by using the Entity Framework.

- Detect and resolve conflicting updates made by multiple users.

In Chapter 25, "Querying Information in a Database," you learned the essentials of using Microsoft ADO.NET and LINQ to SQL for executing queries against a database. The primary purpose of LINQ to SQL is to provide a LINQ interface to Microsoft SQL Server. However, the underlying model used by LINQ to SQL is extensible, and some third-party vendors have built data providers that can access different database management systems.

Visual Studio 2010 also provides a technology called the Entity Framework that you can use for querying and manipulating databases. However, where LINQ to SQL generates code that closely resembles the database structure, you can use the Entity Framework to generate a logical model of a database called an entity data model, and you can write your code against this logical model. By using the Entity Framework, you can construct classes that map the items in the logical model (or *entities*) to the physical tables in the database. This mapping layer can help to insulate your applications against any changes that might occur in the structure of your database at a later date, and it can also be used to provide a degree of independence from the technology used to implement the database. For example, you can build an application that uses the Entity Framework to access data in an Oracle database, and later migrate the database to SQL Server. The logic in your application should not need to change; all you need to do is to update the way in which the logical entities are implemented in the mapping layer.

The Entity Framework can operate with a variant of LINQ called *LINQ to Entities*. By using LINQ to Entities, you can query and manipulate data through an entity object model through LINQ syntax.

In this chapter, you will learn how to use the Entity Framework to generate a logical data model, and then write applications that use data binding to display and modify data through this model.

 Note This chapter provides only a brief introduction to the Entity Framework and LINQ to Entities. For more information, consult the documentation provided with Microsoft Visual Studio 2010, or visit the ADO.NET Entity Framework page on the Microsoft Web site at *http://msdn. microsoft.com/en-us/library/bb399572(VS.100).aspx.*

Using Data Binding with the Entity Framework

You first encountered the idea of data binding in a WPF application in Chapter 24, "Performing Validation," when you used this technique to associate the properties of controls on a WPF form with properties in an instance of a class. You can adopt a similar strategy and bind properties of controls to entity objects so that you can display and maintain data held in a database by using a graphical user interface. First, however, you need to define the entity classes that map to the tables in the database.

In Chapter 25, you used LINQ to SQL to construct a series of entity classes and a context class. The Entity Framework operates in a similar but more expansive manner, and many of the concepts that you learned in Chapter 25 are still applicable. The Entity Framework provides the ADO.NET Entity Data Model template and wizards that can generate entity classes from the database. (You can also define an entity model manually and use it to create a database.) The Entity Framework also generates a custom context class that you can use to access the entities and connect to the database.

In the first exercise, you will use the ADO.NET Entity Data Model template to generate a data model for managing products and suppliers in the Northwind database.

 Important The exercises in this chapter assume that you have created and populated the Northwind database. For more information, see the exercise in the section "Creating the Database" in Chapter 25.

Granting Access to a SQL Server 2008 Database File—Visual C# 2010 Express Edition

If you are using Microsoft Visual C# 2010 Express Edition, when you define a Microsoft SQL Server database connection for the entity wizard, you connect directly to the SQL Server database file. Visual C# 2010 Express Edition starts its own instance of SQL Server Express, called a *user instance* for accessing the database. The user instance runs using the credentials of the user executing the application. If you are using Visual C# 2010 Express Edition, you must detach the database from the SQL Server Express default instance because it will not allow a user instance to connect to a database that it is currently using. The following procedures describe how to perform these tasks.

Detach the Northwind database

1. On the Windows Start menu, click *All Programs*, click *Accessories*, and then click *Command Prompt* to open a command prompt window.

2. In the command prompt window, type the following command to move to the \Microsoft Press\Visual CSharp Step By Step\Chapter 26 folder under your Documents folder. Replace *Name* with your user name.

    ```
    cd "\Users\Name\Documents\Microsoft Press\Visual CSharp Step By Step\Chapter 26"
    ```

3. In the command prompt window, type the following command:

    ```
    sqlcmd -S.\SQLExpress -E -idetach.sql
    ```

> **Note** The *detach.sql* script contains the following SQL Server command, which detaches the Northwind database from the SQL Server instance:
>
> ```
> sp_detach_db 'Northwind'
> ```

4. When the script finishes running, close the command prompt window.

> **Note** If you need to rebuild the Northwind database, you can run the *instnwnd.sql* script as described in Chapter 25. However, if you have detached the Northwind database, you must first delete the Northwind.mdf and Northwind_log.ldf files in the C:\Program Files\ Microsoft SQL Server\MSSQL10.SQLEXPRESS\MSSQL\DATA folder. Otherwise, the script will fail.

After you have detached the database from SQL Server, you must grant your login account access to the folder holding the database and grant Full Control over the database files themselves. The next procedure shows how to do this.

Grant access to the Northwind database file

1. Log on to your computer using an account that has administrator access.

2. Using Windows Explorer, move to the folder C:\Program Files\Microsoft SQL Server\MSSQL10.SQLEXPRESS\MSSQL.

> **Note** If you are using a 64-bit version of Windows Vista or Windows 7, replace all references to the C:\Program Files folder in these instructions with C:\Program Files (x86).

3. If a message box appears displaying the message "You don't currently have permission to access this folder," click *Continue*. In the *User Account Control* message that follows, click *Continue* again.

4. Move to the DATA folder, right-click the Northwind file, and then click *Properties*.

5. In the *Northwind Properties* dialog box, click the *Security* tab.

6. If the *Security* page contains the message "Do you want to continue?", click *Continue*. In the *User Account Control* message box, click *Continue*.

   If the *Security* page contains the message "To change permissions, click Edit", click *Edit*. If a *User Account Control* message box appears, click *Continue*.

7. If your user account is not listed in the *Group or user names* list box, in the *Permissions for Northwind* dialog box, click *Add*. In the *Select Users or Groups* dialog box, enter the name of your user account, and then click *OK*.

8. In the *Permissions for Northwind* dialog box, in the *Group or user names* list box, click your user account.

9. In the *Permissions for Account* list box (where *Account* is your user account name), select the *Allow* check box for the *Full Control* entry, and then click *OK*.

10. In the *Northwind Properties* dialog box, click *OK*.

11. Repeat steps 4 through 10 for the Northwind_log file in the DATA folder.

Generate an Entity Data Model for the *Suppliers* and *Products* tables

1. Start Visual Studio 2010 if it is not already running.

2. Create a new project by using the *WPF Application* template. Name the project **Suppliers**, and save it in the \Microsoft Press\Visual CSharp Step By Step\Chapter 26 folder in your Documents folder.

> **Note** If you are using Visual C# 2010 Express Edition, you can specify the location for saving your project when you click *Save Suppliers* on the *File* menu.

3. In *Solution Explorer*, right-click the Suppliers project, point to *Add*, and then click *New Item*.

4. In the *Add New Item – Suppliers* dialog box, in the left pane expand *Visual C#* if it is not already expanded. In the middle pane, scroll down and click the *ADO.NET Entity Data Model* template, type **Northwind.edmx** in the *Name* box, and then click *Add*.

   The *Entity Data Model Wizard* dialog box appears. You can use this window to specify the tables in the Northwind database for which you want to create entity classes, select the columns that you want to include, and define the relationships between them.

5. In the *Entity Data Model Wizard* dialog box, choose *Generate from database* and then click *Next*.

   The *Entity Data Model Wizard* requires you to configure a connection to a database, and the *Choose Your Data Connection* page appears.

6. If you are using Visual Studio 2010 Standard Edition or Visual Studio 2010 Professional Edition, perform the following tasks:

   6.1. Click New Connection.

      If the *Choose Data Source* dialog box appears, in the *Data source* list box, click *Microsoft SQL Server*. In the *Data provider* drop-down list box, select *.NET Framework Data Provider for SQL Server* if it is not already selected and then click *Continue*.

> **Note** If you have already created database connections previously, this dialog box might not appear and the *Connection Properties* dialog box will be displayed. In this case, click the *Change* button adjacent to the *Data source* text box. The *Change Data Source* dialog box appears, which is the same as the *Choose Data Source* dialog box except that the *Continue* button has the legend *OK* instead.

   6.2. In the *Connection Properties* dialog box, in the *Server name* combo box type **.\SQLExpress**. In the *Log on to the server* section of the dialog box, choose the *Use Windows Authentication* radio button. In the *Connect to a database* section of the dialog box, in the *Select or enter a database name* combo box type **Northwind**, and then click *OK*.

7. If you are using Visual C# 2010 Express Edition, perform the following tasks:

   7.1. Click *New Connection*.

   If the *Choose Data Source* dialog box appears, in the *Data source* list box, click *Microsoft SQL Server Database File*. In the *Data provider* drop-down list box, select *.NET Framework Data Provider for SQL Server* if it is not already selected and then click *Continue*.

> **Note** If you have already created database connections previously, this dialog box might not appear and the *Connection Properties* dialog box will be displayed. In this case, click the *Change* button adjacent to the *Data source* text box. The *Change Data Source* dialog box appears, which is the same as the *Choose Data Source* dialog box except that the *Continue* button has the legend *OK* instead.

   7.2. In the *Connection Properties* dialog box, in the *Database file name* text click **Browse**.

   7.3. In the *Select SQL Server Database File* dialog box, move to the folder C:\Program Files\Microsoft SQL Server\MSSQL10.SQLEXPRESS\MSSQL\DATA, click the Northwind database file, and then click *Open*.

   7.4. In the *Log on to the server* section of the dialog box, choose the *Use Windows Authentication* radio button and then click *OK*.

8. On the *Choose Your Data Connection* page of the *Entity Data Model Wizard*, select the *Save entity connection settings in App.Config as* check box, type **NorthwindEntities** (this is the default name), and then click *Next*.

   If you are using Visual C# 2010 Express Edition, a message box appears asking whether you want to add the database file to your project. Click *No*.

9. On the *Choose Your Database Objects* page, verify that the *Pluralize or singularize generated object names* and *Include foreign key columns in the model* check boxes are both selected. In the *Which database objects do you want to include in your model?* list box, expand *Tables* and then click the *Products (dbo)* and *Suppliers (dbo)* tables. In the *Model Namespace* text box, type **NorthwindModel** (this is the default namespace). The following image shows the completed page.

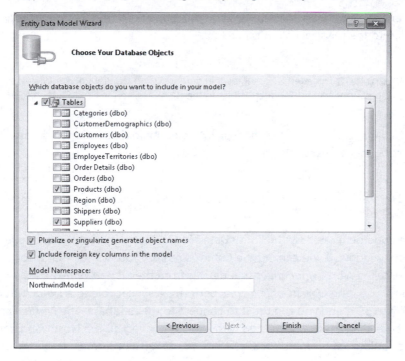

10. Click *Finish*.

The Entity Data Model Wizard generates entity classes called *Supplier* and *Product* based on the *Suppliers* and *Products* tables, with property fields for each column in the tables, as shown in the following image. The data model also defines navigation properties that link the two entities together and maintain the relationship between them. In this case, a single *Supplier* entity can be related to many *Product* entities.

You can modify the properties of an entity class by selecting the class and changing the property values in the *Properties* window. You can also use the *Mapping Details* pane that appears at the bottom of the window to select and edit the fields that appear in an entity class. This is how you change the mapping from the logical properties in an entity to the physical columns in a table.

> **Important** This exercise assumes that you are using the default entity classes generated for the Suppliers and Products tables in the database, so please do not change anything!

11. In *Solution Explorer*, expand the Northwind.edmx folder, and then double-click *Northwind.designer.cs*.

> **Tip** If Solution Explorer is not visible, on the *View* menu click *Solution Explorer*.

The code generated by the Entity Data Model Wizard appears in the *Code and Text Editor* window. If you expand the *Contexts* region, you will see that it contains a class called *NorthwindEntities* that derives from the *ObjectContext* class. In the Entity Framework, the *ObjectContext* class performs a similar role to a *DataContext* class in LINQ to SQL, and you can use it to connect to the database. The *NorthwindEntities* class extends the *ObjectContext* class with logic to connect to the Northwind database, and to populate *Supplier* and *Product* entities (just like a custom *DataContext* class in LINQ to SQL).

The information concerning the connection you specified before creating the two entity classes is saved in an application configuration file. Storing the connection string in a configuration file enables you to modify the connection string without rebuilding the application; you simply edit the application configuration file. You'll find it useful if you envisage ever needing to relocate or rename the database, or switching from using a local development database to a production database that has the same set of tables.

The code for the two entity classes is located in the *Entities* region of the file. These entity classes are a little more complicated than the classes that you created manually in Chapter 25, but the general principles are similar. The additional complexity is the result of the entity classes indirectly implementing the *INotifyPropertyChanging* and *INotifyPropertyChanged* interfaces, and the navigational properties used to link related entities together. The *INotifyPropertyChanging* and *INotifyPropertyChanged* interfaces define events that the entity classes raise when their property values change. The various user interface controls in the WPF library subscribe to these events to detect any changes to data and ensure that the information displayed on a WPF form is up to date.

> **Note** The entity classes inherit from the *System.Data.Objects.DataClasses.EntityObject* class, which in turn inherits from the *System.Data.Objects.DataClasses.StructuralObject* class. The *StructuralObject* class implements the the *INotifyPropertyChanging* and *INotifyPropertyChanged* interfaces.

Using an Application Configuration File

An application configuration file provides a useful mechanism enabling a user to modify some of the resources used by an application without rebuilding the application itself. The connection string used for connecting to a database is an example of just such a resource.

When you use the Entity Data Model Wizard to generate entity classes, a new file is added to your project called App.config. This is the source for the application configuration file, and it appears in the *Solution Explorer* window. You can examine the contents of the App.config file by double-clicking it. You will see that it is an XML file, as shown here (the text has been reformatted to fit on the printed page):

```
<?xml version="1.0" encoding="utf-8"?>
<configuration>
  <connectionStrings>
    <add name="NorthwindEntities" connectionString="metadata=res://*/Northwind.
csdl|res://*/Northwind.ssdl|res://*/Northwind.msl;provider=System.Data.
SqlClient;provider connection string=&quot;Data Source=.\SQLExpress;Initial
Catalog=Northwind;Integrated Security=True;MultipleActiveResultSets=True&quot;"
providerName="System.Data.EntityClient" />
  </connectionStrings>
</configuration>
```

The connection string is held in the *<connectionStrings>* element of the file. This string contains a set of elements in the form `property=value`. The elements are separated by a semi-colon character. The key properties are the *Data Source*, *Initial Catalog*, and *Integrated Security* elements, which you should recognize from earlier exercises.

When you build the application, the C# compiler copies the app.config file to the folder holding the compiled code and renames it as *application*.exe.config, where *application* is the name of your application. When your application connects to the database, it should read the connection string value from the configuration file rather than using values that are hard-coded in your C# code. You will see how to do this when using generated entity classes later in this chapter.

You should deploy the application configuration file (the *application*.exe.config file) with the executable code for the application. If you need to connect to a different database, you can edit the configuration file by using a text editor to modify the *<connectionString>* attribute of the *<connectionStrings>* element. When the application runs, it will use the new value automatically.

Be aware that you should take steps to protect the application configuration file and prevent a user from making inappropriate changes.

Now that you have created the entity model for the application, you can build the user interface that can display the information retrieved by using data binding.

Create the user interface for the Suppliers application

1. In *Solution Explorer*, right-click the MainWindow.xaml file, click *Rename*, and rename the file as SupplierInfo.xaml.

2. Double-click the App.xaml file to display it in the *Design View* window. In the *XAML* pane, change the *StartupUri* element to "SupplierInfo.xaml", as shown next in bold type:

```
<Application x:Class="Suppliers.App"
    xmlns="http://schemas.microsoft.com/winfx/2006/xaml/presentation"
    xmlns:x="http://schemas.microsoft.com/winfx/2006/xaml"
    StartupUri="SupplierInfo.xaml">
    ...
</Application>
```

3. In *Solution Explorer*, double-click the SupplierInfo.xaml file to display it in the *Design View* window. In the *XAML* pane, as shown in bold type in the following code snippet, change the value of the *x:Class* element to "Suppliers.SupplierInfo", set the *Title* to "Supplier Information", set the *Height* to"362", and set the *Width* to "614":

```
<Window x:Class="Suppliers.SupplierInfo"
    xmlns="http://schemas.microsoft.com/winfx/2006/xaml/presentation"
    xmlns:x="http://schemas.microsoft.com/winfx/2006/xaml"
    Title="Supplier Information" Height="362" Width="614">
    ...
</Window>
```

4. Display the SupplierInfo.xaml.cs file in the *Code and Text Editor* window. Change the name of the *MainWindow* class to *SupplierInfo*, and change the name of the constructor, as shown next in bold type:

```
public partial class SupplierInfo : Window
{
    public SupplierInfo()
    {
        InitializeComponent();
    }
}
```

5. In *Solution Explorer*, double-click the SupplierInfo.xaml file to display it in the *Design View* window. From the *Common WPF Controls* section of the *Toolbox*, add a *ComboBox* control and a *Button* control to the form. (Place them anywhere on the form.) From the *All WPF Controls* section of the *Toolbox*, add a *ListView* control to the form.

6. Using the *Properties* window, set the properties of these controls to the values specified in the following table.

Control	Property	Value
comboBox1	Name	suppliersList
	Height	23
	Width	Auto
	Margin	40,16,42,0
	VerticalAlignment	Top
	HorizontalAlignment	Stretch
listView1	Name	productsList
	Height	Auto
	Width	Auto
	Margin	40,44,40,60
	VerticalAlignment	Stretch
	HorizontalAlignment	Stretch
button1	Name	saveChanges
	Content	Save Changes
	IsEnabled	False (clear the check box)
	Height	23
	Width	90
	Margin	40,0,0,10
	VerticalAlignment	Bottom
	HorizontalAlignment	Left

The Supplier Information form should look like this in the *Design View* window:

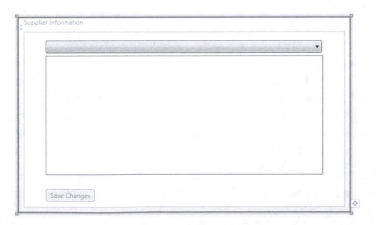

7. In the *XAML* pane, add the *Window.Resources* element shown next in bold type to the *Window* element, above the *Grid* element:

```
<Window x:Class="Suppliers.SupplierInfo"
...>
    <Window.Resources>
        <DataTemplate x:Key="SuppliersTemplate">
            <StackPanel Orientation="Horizontal">
                <TextBlock Text="{Binding Path=SupplierID}" />
                <TextBlock Text=" : " />
                <TextBlock Text="{Binding Path=CompanyName}" />
                <TextBlock Text=" : " />
                <TextBlock Text="{Binding Path=ContactName}" />
            </StackPanel>
        </DataTemplate>
    </Window.Resources>
    <Grid>
    ...
    </Grid>
</Window>
```

You can use a *DataTemplate* to specify how to display data in a control. You will apply this template to the *suppliersList* combo box in the next step. This template contains five *TextBlock* controls organized horizontally by using a *StackPanel*. The first, third, and fifth *TextBlock* controls will display the data in the *SupplierID*, *CompanyName*, and *ContactName* properties, respectively, of the *Supplier* entity object to which you will bind later. The other *TextBlock* controls just display a ":" separator.

8. In the *XAML* pane, modify the definition of the *suppliersList* combo box and specify the *IsSynchronizedWithCurrentItem*, *ItemsSource*, and *ItemTemplate* properties, as shown next in bold type:

```
<ComboBox ... Name="suppliersList" IsSynchronizedWithCurrentItem="True"
    ItemsSource="{Binding}" ItemTemplate="{StaticResource SuppliersTemplate}" />
```

 Tip If you prefer, you can also set these properties by using the Properties window for the *suppliersList* combo box.

You will display the data for each supplier in the *suppliersList* control. Recall from Chapter 25 that LINQ to SQL used *Table<T>* collection classes to hold the rows for a table. The Entity Framework follows a similar approach, but it holds the rows in an *ObjectSet<T>* collection class. Setting the *IsSynchronizedWithCurrentItem* property ensures that the *SelectedItem* property of the control is kept synchronized with the current item in the collection. If you don't set this property to *True*, when the application starts up and establishes the binding with the collection, the combo box will not automatically display the first item in this collection.

ItemsSource currently has an empty binding. In Chapter 24, you defined an instance of a class as a static resource and specified that resource as the binding source. If you do not specify a binding source, WPF binds to an object specified in the *DataContext* property of the control. (Do not confuse the *DataContext* property of a control with a *DataContext* object used by LINQ to SQL to communicate with a database; it is unfortunate that they happen to have the same name.) You will set the *DataContext* property of the control to an *ObjectSet<Supplier>* collection object in code.

The *ItemTemplate* property specifies the template to use to display data retrieved from the binding source. In this case, the *suppliersList* control will display the *SupplierID*, *CompanyName*, and *ContactName* fields from the binding source.

9. Modify the definition of the *productsList* ListView, and specify the *IsSynchronizedWithCurrentItem* and *ItemsSource* properties:

```
<ListView ... Name="productsList" IsSynchronizedWithCurrentItem="True"
    ItemsSource="{Binding}" />
```

The *Supplier* entity class contains an *EntityCollection<Product>* property that references the products the supplier can provide. (The *EntityCollection<T>* class is very similar to the *EntitySet<T>* class in LINQ to SQL.) You will set the *DataContext* property of the *productsList* control to the *Products* property of the currently selected *Supplier* object in code. In a later exercise, you will also provide functionality enabling the user to add and remove products. This code will modify the list of products acting as the binding source. Setting the *IsSynchronizedWithCurrentItem* property to *True* ensures that the newly created product is selected in the list when the user adds a new one or that an existing item is selected if the user deletes one. (If you set this property to *False*, when you delete a product, no item in the list will be selected afterwards, which can cause problems in your application if your code attempts to access the currently selected item.)

10. Add the *ListView.View* child element shown next in bold type, which contains a *GridView* and column definitions, to the *productsList* control. Be sure to replace the closing delimiter (/>) of the *ListView* element with an ordinary delimiter (>) and add a terminating </ListView> element.

```
<ListView ... Name="productsList" ...>
    <ListView.View>
        <GridView>
            <GridView.Columns>
                <GridViewColumn Width="75" Header="Product ID"
                    DisplayMemberBinding="{Binding Path=ProductID}" />
                <GridViewColumn Width="225" Header="Name"
                    DisplayMemberBinding="{Binding Path=ProductName}" />
                <GridViewColumn Width="135" Header="Quantity Per Unit"
                    DisplayMemberBinding="{Binding Path=QuantityPerUnit}" />
                <GridViewColumn Width="75" Header="Unit Price"
                    DisplayMemberBinding="{Binding Path=UnitPrice}" />
            </GridView.Columns>
        </GridView>
    </ListView.View>
</ListView>
```

You can make a *ListView* control display data in various formats by setting the *View* property. This Extensible Application Markup Language (XAML) code uses a *GridView* component. A *GridView* displays data in a tabular format; each row in the table has a fixed set of columns defined by the *GridViewColumn* properties. Each column has its own header that displays the name of the column. The *DisplayMemberBinding* property of each column specifies the data that the column should display from the binding source.

The data for the *UnitPrice* column is a *Decimal* property in the *Product* entity class. WPF will convert this information to a string and apply a default numeric format. Ideally, the data in this column should be displayed as a currency value. You can reformat the data in a *GridView* column by creating a *converter* class. You first encountered converter classes in Chapter 24 when converting an enumeration to a string. This time, the converter class will convert a *decimal?* value to a *string* containing a representation of a currency value.

11. Switch to the *Code and Text Editor* window displaying the SupplierInfo.xaml.cs file. Add the *PriceConverter* class shown next to this file, after the *SupplierInfo* class:

```
[ValueConversion(typeof(string), typeof(Decimal))]
class PriceConverter : IValueConverter
{
    public object Convert(object value, Type targetType, object parameter,
                          System.Globalization.CultureInfo culture)
    {
        if (value != null)
            return String.Format("{0:C}", value);
        else
            return "";
    }

    public object ConvertBack(object value, Type targetType, object parameter,
                              System.Globalization.CultureInfo culture)
    {
        throw new NotImplementedException();
    }
}
```

The *Convert* method calls the *String.Format* method to create a string that uses the local currency format of your computer. The user will not actually modify the unit price in the list view, so there is no need to implement the *ConvertBack* method to convert a *string* back to a *Decimal* value.

12. Return to the *Design View* window displaying the SupplierInfo.xaml form. Add the following XML namespace declaration to the *Window* element, and define an instance of the *PriceConverter* class as a Window resource, as shown next in bold type:

```
<Window x:Class="Suppliers.SupplierInfo"
...
xmlns:app="clr-namespace:Suppliers"
...>
    <Window.Resources>
        <app:PriceConverter x:Key="priceConverter" />
```

```
        ...
    </Window.Resources>
    ...
</Window>
```

> **Note** The Design View window caches the definitions of controls and other user interface items, and does not always recognize new namespaces that have been added to a form immediately. If this statement causes an error in the Design View window, on the *Build* menu click *Build Solution*. This will refresh the WPF cache and should clear the errors.

13. Modify the definition of the Unit Price *GridViewColumn*, and apply the converter class to the binding, as shown next in bold type:

```
<GridViewColumn ... Header ="Unit Price" DisplayMemberBinding=
    "{Binding Path=UnitPrice, Converter={StaticResource priceConverter}}" />
```

You have now laid out the form. Next, you need to write some code to retrieve the data displayed by the form, and you must set the *DataContext* properties of the *suppliersList* and *productsList* controls so that the bindings function correctly.

Write code to retrieve supplier information and establish the data bindings

1. In the SupplierInfo.xaml file, change the definition of the *Window* element and add a *Loaded* event method called *Window_Loaded*. (This is the default name of this method, generated when you click *<New Event Handler>*.) The XAML code for the Window element should look like this:

```
<Window x:Class="Suppliers.SupplierInfo"
    ...
    Title="Supplier Information" ... Loaded="Window_Loaded">
    ...
</Window>
```

2. In the *Code and Text Editor* window displaying the SupplierInfo.xaml.cs file, add the following *using* statements to the list at the top of the file:

```
using System.ComponentModel;
using System.Collections;
```

3. Add the three private fields shown next in bold type to the *SupplierInfo* class:

```
public partial class SupplierInfo : Window
{
    private NorthwindEntities northwindContext = null;
    private Supplier supplier = null;
    private IList productsInfo = null;
    ...
}
```

You will use the *northwindContext* variable to connect to the Northwind database and retrieve the data from the *Suppliers* table. The *supplier* variable holds the data for the current supplier displayed in the *suppliersList* control. The *productsInfo* variable holds the products provided by the currently displayed supplier. It will be bound to the *productsList* control.

You might be wondering about this definition of the *productsInfo* variable; after all, you learned in the previous exercise that the *Supplier* class has an *EntityCollection<Product>* property that you can use to access the products supplied by a supplier. You can actually bind this *EntityCollection<Product>* property to the *productsList* control, but there is one important problem with this approach. I mentioned earlier that the *Supplier* and *Product* entity classes indirectly implement the *INotifyPropertyChanging* and *INotifyPropertyChanged* interfaces through the *EntityObject* and *StructuralObject* classes. When you bind a WPF control to a data source, the control automatically subscribes to the events exposed by these interfaces to update the display when the data changes. However, the *EntityCollection<Product>* class does not implement these interfaces, so the list view control will not be updated if any products are added to, or removed from, the supplier. (It will be updated if an existing product changes, however, because each item in *EntityCollection<Product>* is a *Product* object, which does send the appropriate notifications to the WPF controls to which it is bound.)

4. Add the following code shown in bold to the *Window_Loaded* method:

```
private void Window_Loaded(object sender, RoutedEventArgs e)
{
    this.northwindContext = new NorthwindEntities();
    suppliersList.DataContext = this.northwindContext.Suppliers;
}
```

When the application starts and loads the window, this code creates a *NorthwindEntities* variable that connects to the Northwind database. Remember that the Entity Data Model Wizard created this class earlier. The default constructor for this class reads the database connection string from the application configuration file. The method then sets the *DataContext* property of the *suppliersList* combo box to the *Suppliers ObjectSet* collection property of the *northwindContext* variable. This action resolves the binding for the combo box, and the data template used by this combo box displays the values in the *SupplierID*, *CompanyName*, and *ContactName* for each *Supplier* object in the collection.

Note If a control is a child of another control—for example, a *GridViewColumn* in a *ListView*—you need to set the *DataContext* property only of the parent control. If the *DataContext* property of a child control is not set, the WPF runtime uses the *DataContext* of the parent control instead. This technique makes it possible for you to share a data context between several child controls and a parent control.

If the immediate parent control does not have a data context, the WPF runtime examines the grandparent control, and so on, all the way up to the *Window* control defining the form. If no data context is available, any data bindings for a control are ignored.

5. Return to the *Design View* window. Double-click the *suppliersList* combo box. This action creates the *suppliersList_SelectionChanged* event method, which runs whenever the user selects a different item in the combo box.

6. In the *Code and Text Editor* window, add the statements shown next in bold type to the *suppliersList_SelectionChanged* method:

```
private void suppliersList_SelectionChanged(object sender,
SelectionChangedEventArgs e)
{
    this.supplier = suppliersList.SelectedItem as Supplier;
    this.northwindContext.LoadProperty<Supplier>(this.supplier, s => s.Products);
    this.productsInfo = ((IListSource)supplier.Products).GetList();
    productsList.DataContext = this.productsInfo;
}
```

This method obtains the currently selected supplier from the combo box and copies the data in the *EntityCollection<Product>* property for this supplier to the *productsInfo* variable. The *EntityCollection<Product>* class implements the *IListSource* interface, which provides the *GetList* method for copying the data in the entity set into an *IList* object. Like LINQ to SQL, any data related to an entity is not retrieved automatically when an entity is instantiated. In this case, this means that whenever the application fetches the data for a *Supplier* entity from the database, it does not automatically retrieve the data for the products related to that supplier. You saw in Chapter 25 that LINQ to SQL provides the *LoadWith* method of *DataLoadOptions* class to specify related data that should be retrieved when a row is read from the database. The Entity Framework provides the generic *LoadProperty<T>* method of the *ObjectContext* class, which performs much the same task. The second statement in the preceding code causes the Entity Framework to retrieve the products associated with a supplier each time a supplier is fetched.

Finally, the code sets the *DataContext* property of the *productsList* control to this list of products. This statement enables *productsList* control to display the items in the list of products.

7. On the *Debug* menu, click *Start Without Debugging* to build and run the application.

When the form runs, it should display the products for the first supplier—Exotic Liquids. The form should look like the following image.

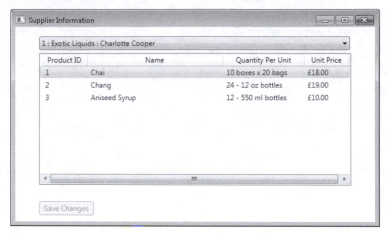

8. Select a different supplier from the combo box, and verify that the list view displays the products for that supplier. When you have finished browsing the data, close the form and return to Visual Studio 2010.

Using LINQ to Entities to Query Data

The previous exercise used data binding to fetch and display information through the Entity Framework rather than explicitly creating and running LINQ queries. However, as mentioned previously, you can also retrieve information from a data model built by using the Entity Framework by using LINQ to Entities. The syntax is similar to that of LINQ to SQL, with the principal difference being that you base a LINQ to Entities query on an *ObjectQuery<T>* object, where *T* is an *EntityObject* type.

For example, you can retrieve a list of product names from the *Products ObjectSet* in the *NorthwindEntities ObjectContext* shown in the previous examples and display them like this:

```
NorthwindEntities northwindContext = new NorthwindEntities();
ObjectQuery<Product> products = northwindContext.Products;

var productNames = from p in products
                   select p.ProductName;

foreach (var name in productNames)
{
    Console.WriteLine("Product name: {0}", name);
}
```

> **Note** Strictly speaking, the *Products* property of the *NorthwindEntities* class has the type *ObjectSet<Products>*. However, the *ObjectSet<T>* type inherits from *ObjectQuery<T>*, so you can safely assign the *Products* property to an *ObjectQuery<Products>* variable.

LINQ to Entities supports most of the standard LINQ query operators, although there are a few exceptions described in the documentation supplied with Visual Studio 2010. You can join data from multiple tables, order the results, and perform operations such as grouping data and calculating aggregate values. For more information, refer back to Chapter 20, "Querying In-Memory Data by Using Query Expressions."

The next step in the Suppliers application is to provide functionality enabling the user to modify the details of products, remove products, and create new products. Before you can do that, you need to learn how to use the Entity Framework to update data.

Using Data Binding to Modify Data

The Entity Framework provides a two-way communication channel with a database. You have seen how to use data binding with the Entity Framework to fetch data, but you can also modify the information you have retrieved and send these changes back to the database.

Updating Existing Data

When you retrieve data by using an *ObjectContext* object, the objects created from this data are held in an in-memory cache within the application. You can change the values of objects held in this cache in exactly the same way that you change the values in any ordinary object—by setting their properties. However, updating an object in memory does not update the database. To persist changes to the database, you need to generate the appropriate SQL UPDATE commands and arrange for them to be executed by the database server. You can do this quite easily with the Entity Framework. The following code fragment shows a LINQ to Entities query that fetches product number 14. The code then changes the name of the product to "Bean Curd" (product 14 was originally named "Tofu" in the Northwind database) and sends the change back to the database:

```
NorthwindEntities northwindContext = new NorthwindEntities();
Product product = northwindContext.Products.Single(p => p.ProductID == 14);
product.ProductName = "Bean Curd";
northwindContext.SaveChanges();
```

The key statement in this code example is the call to the *SaveChanges* method of the *ObjectContext* object. (Remember that *NorthwindEntities* inherits from *ObjectContext*.) When you modify the information in an entity object that was populated by running a query, the *ObjectContext* object managing the connection that was used to run the original query tracks the changes you make to the data. The *SaveChanges* method propagates these changes back to the database. Behind the scenes, the *ObjectContext* object constructs and executes a SQL UPDATE statement.

If you fetch and modify several products, you need to call *SaveChanges* only once, after the final modification. The *SaveChanges* method batches all of the updates together. The *ObjectContext* object creates a database transaction and performs all of the SQL UPDATE statements within this transaction. If any of the updates fail, the transaction is aborted, all the changes made by the *SaveChanges* method are rolled back in the database, and the *SaveChanges* method throws an exception. If all the updates succeed, the transaction is committed, and the changes become permanent in the database. You should note that if the *SaveChanges* method fails, only the database is rolled back; your changes are still present in the entity objects in memory. The exception thrown when the *SaveChanges* method fails provides some information on the reason for the failure. You can attempt to rectify the problem and call *SaveChanges* again.

The *ObjectContext* class also provides the *Refresh* method. With this method, you can repopulate *EntityObject* collections in the cache from the database and discard any changes you have made. You use it like this:

```
northwindContext.Refresh(RefreshMode.StoreWins, northwindContext.Products);
```

The first parameter is a member of the *System.Data.Objects.RefreshMode* enumeration. Specifying the value *RefreshMode.StoreWins* forces the data to be refreshed from the database. The second parameter is the entity in the cache to be refreshed.

> **Tip** Change tracking is a potentially expensive operation for an *ObjectContext* object to perform. If you know that you are not going to modify data (if for example your application generates a read-only report), you can disable change tracking for an *EntityObject* object by setting the *MergeOption* property to *MergeOption.NoTracking*, like this:
>
> ```
> northwindContext.Suppliers.MergeOption = MergeOption.NoTracking;
> ```
>
> You can make changes to an entity that has change tracking disabled, but these changes will not be saved when you call *SaveChanges*, and they will be lost when the application exits.

Handling Conflicting Updates

There could be any number of reasons why an update operation fails, but one of the most common causes is conflicts occurring when two users attempt to update the same data simultaneously. If you think about what happens when you run an application that uses the Entity Framework, you can see that there is plenty of scope for conflict. When you retrieve data through an *ObjectContext* object, it is cached in the memory of your application. Another user could perform the same query and retrieve the same data. If you both modify the data and then you both call the *SaveChanges* method, one of you will overwrite the changes made by the other in the database. This phenomenon is known as a *lost update*.

This phenomenon occurs because the Entity Framework implements optimistic concurrency. In other words, when it fetches data from a database it does not lock that data in the database. This form of concurrency enables other users to access the same data at the same time, but it assumes that the probability of two users changing the same data is small (hence the term *optimistic concurrency.*)

The opposite of optimistic concurrency is *pessimistic concurrency*. In this scheme, all data is locked in the database as it is fetched and no other concurrent users can access it. This approach guarantees that you will not lose any changes, but it is somewhat extreme.

The Entity Framework does not directly support pessimistic concurrency. Instead, it provides a middle ground. Each item in an *EntityObject* class has a property called *Concurrency Mode*. By default, the *Concurrency Mode* is set to *None*, but you can change it to *Fixed* by using the Entity Framework designer. The following image shows the entity model you built earlier. The user has clicked the *ProductName* item in the *Product* entity and has changed the *Concurrency Mode* property to *Fixed* in the *Properties* window.

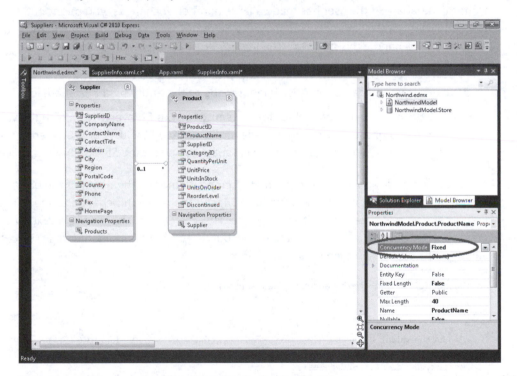

When an application modifies the value in the *ProductName* property in an instance of the *Products EntityObject* class, the Entity Framework keeps a copy of the original value of this property in the cache. When you set the *Concurrency Mode* for a property, when the application calls the *SaveChanges* method of the *ObjectContext* object, the Entity Framework uses the cached copy of the original value to verify that the column in the corresponding row in the database has not been changed by another user since it was fetched. If it has not, the row is updated. If the column has changed, the *SaveChanges* method stops and throws an *OptimisticConcurrencyException* exception. When this happens, all changes made by the

SaveChanges method in the database are undone, although the changes still remain in the cache in your application.

When an *OptimisticConcurrencyException* exception arises, you can determine which entity caused the conflict by examining the *StateEntries* property of the exception object. This property holds a collection of *ObjectStateEntry* objects. The *ObjectStateEntry* class itself contains a number of properties. The most important are the *Entity* property, which contains a reference to the entity that caused the conflict; the *CurrentValues* property, which contains the modified data for the entity; and the *OriginalValues* property, which contains the data for the entity originally retrieved from the database.

The recommended approach to resolving conflicts is to use the *Refresh* method to reload the cache from the database and call *SaveChanges* again. The *Refresh* method repopulates the *original* values for a specified entity (passed as the second parameter) with up-to-date values from the database. If the user has made a large number of changes, you might not want to force the user to rekey them. Fortunately, the *RefreshMode* parameter of the *Refresh* method enables you to handle this situation. The *RefreshMode* enumeration defines two values:

- **StoreWins**   The *current* values for the entity will be overwritten with the up-to-date values from the database. Any changes made to the entity by the user are lost.

- **ClientWins**   The *current* values for the entity will not be overwritten with the values from the database. Any changes made to the entity by the user are retained in the cache and will be propagated to the database the next time *SaveChanges* is called.

The following code shows an example that attempts to modify the name of the product in the *Products ObjectSet* with the *ProductID* of 14, and then save this change to the database. If another user has already modified this same data, the *OptimisticConcurrencyException* handler refreshes the *original* values in the cache, but it retains the modified data in the *current* values in the cache, and then calls *SaveChanges* again.

```
NorthwindEntities northwindContext = new NorthwindEntities();

try
{
    Product product = northwindContext.Products.Single(p => p.ProductID == 14);
    product.ProductName = "Bean Curd";
    northwindContext.SaveChanges();
}
catch (OptimisticConcurrencyException ex)
{
    northwindContext.Refresh(RefreshMode.ClientWins, northwindContext.Products);
    northwindContext.SaveChanges();
}
```

> **Important** The Entity Framework stops and throws the *OptimisticConcurrencyException* exception when it detects the first conflict. If you have changed multiple rows, subsequent calls to the *SaveChanges* method might detect further conflicts.
>
> Additionally, there is a small possibility that another user might have changed the data between the calls to *Refresh* and *SaveChanges* in the *OptimisticConcurrencyException* exception handler. In a commercial application, you should be prepared to catch this exception as well.

Adding and Deleting Data

As well as modifying existing data, the Entity Framework enables you to add new items to an *ObjectSet* collection and remove items from an *ObjectSet* collection.

When you use the Entity Framework to generate an entity model, the definition of each entity includes a factory method called *CreateXXX* (where *XXX* is the name of the entity class), which you can use to create a new entity. This method expects you to provide parameters for each of the mandatory (non-NULL) columns in the underlying database. You can set the values of additional columns by using the properties exposed by the entity class. You add the new entity to an *ObjectSet* collection by using the *AddObject* method. To save the new entity to the database, call the *SaveChanges* method on the *ObjectContext* object.

The following code example creates a new *Product* entity and adds it to the list of products in the collection maintained by the *NorthwindEntities* context object. The code also adds a reference to the new object to the supplier with the *SupplierID* of 1. (The *Add* method is provided by the Entity Framework to help maintain the relationships between entities.) The *SaveChanges* method inserts the new product into the database.

```
NorthwindEntities northwindContext = new NorthwindEntities();

Product newProduct = Product.CreateProduct(0, "Fried Bread", false);
newProduct.UnitPrice = 55;
newProduct.QuantityPerUnit = "10 boxes";

ObjectSet<Product> products = northwindContext.Products;
products.AddObject(newProduct);

Supplier supplier = northwindContext.Suppliers.Single(s => s.SupplierID == 1);
supplier.Products.Add(newProduct);
northwindContext.SaveChanges();
```

> **Note** In this example, the first parameter to the *CreateProduct* method is the *ProductID*. In the Northwind database, the *ProductID* is an IDENTITY column. When you call *SaveChanges*, SQL Server generates its own unique value for this column and discards the value that you specified.

Deleting an entity object from an *ObjectSet* collection is straightforward. You call the *DeleteObject* method and specify the entity to be deleted. The following code deletes all products with a *ProductID* greater than or equal to 79. The products are removed from the database when the *SaveChanges* method runs.

```
NorthwindEntities northwindContext = new NorthwindEntities();

var productList = from p in northwindContext.Products
                  where p.productID >= 79
                  select p;

ObjectSet<Product> products = northwindContext.Products;
foreach (var product in productList)
{
    products.DeleteObject(product);
}

northwindContext.SaveChanges();
```

Be careful when deleting rows in tables that have relationships to other tables because such deletions can cause referential integrity errors when you update the database. For example, in the Northwind database, if you attempt to delete a supplier that currently supplies products, the update will fail. You must first remove all products from the supplier. You can achieve this by using the *Remove* method of the *Supplier* class. (Like the *Add* method, the *Remove* method is also provided by the Entity Framework.)

If an error occurs while saving changes after adding or deleting data, the *SaveChanges* method throws an *UpdateException* exception. You should be prepared to catch this exception.

You now have enough knowledge to complete the Suppliers application.

Write code to modify, delete, and create products

1. Return to the Suppliers application in Visual Studio 2010, and display the SupplierInfo. xaml file in the *Design View* window.

2. In the *XAML* pane, modify the definition of the *productsList* control to trap the *KeyDown* event and invoke an event method called *productsList_KeyDown*. (This is the default name of the event method.)

3. In the *Code and Text Editor* window, add the following code shown in bold type to the *productsList_KeyDown* method:

```
private void productsList_KeyDown(object sender, KeyEventArgs e)
{
    switch (e.Key)
    {
        case Key.Enter: editProduct(this.productsList.SelectedItem as Product);
            break;
```

```
        case Key.Insert: addNewProduct();
            break;

        case Key.Delete: deleteProduct(this.productsList.SelectedItem as Product);
            break;
    }
}
```

This method examines the key pressed by the user. If the user presses the Enter key, the code calls the *editProduct* method, passing in the details of the product as a parameter. If the user presses the Insert key, the code calls the *addNewProduct* method to create and add a new product to the list for the current supplier, and if the user presses the Delete key, the code calls the *deleteProduct* method to delete the product. You will write the *editProduct*, *addNewProduct*, and *deleteProduct* methods in the next few steps.

4. Return to the *Design View* window. In the *XAML* pane, modify the definition of the *productsList* control to trap the *MouseDoubleClick* event and invoke an event method called *productsList_MouseDoubleClick*. (Again, this is the default name of the event method.)

5. In the *Code and Text Editor* window, add the following statement shown in bold type to the *productsList_MouseDoubleClick* method:

```
private void productsList_MouseDoubleClick(object sender, KeyEventArgs e)
{
    editProduct(this.productsList.SelectedItem as Product);
}
```

This method simply calls the *editProducts* method. It is a convenience for users, who naturally expect to edit data by double-clicking on it.

6. Add the *deleteProduct* method to the *SupplierInfo* class, as follows:

```
private void deleteProduct(Product product)
{
    MessageBoxResult response = MessageBox.Show(
        String.Format("Delete {0}", product.ProductName),
        "Confirm", MessageBoxButton.YesNo, MessageBoxImage.Question,
        MessageBoxResult.No);
    if (response == MessageBoxResult.Yes)
    {
        this.northwindContext.Products.DeleteObject(product);
        saveChanges.IsEnabled = true;
    }
}
```

This method prompts the user to confirm that she really does want to delete the currently selected product. The *if* statement calls the *DeleteObject* method of the *Products ObjectSet* collection. Finally, the method activates the *saveChanges* button. In a later step, you will add functionality to this button to send the changes made to the *Products ObjectSet* collection back to the database.

7. On the *Project* menu, click *Add Class*. In the *Add New Items – Suppliers* dialog box, select the *Window (WPF)* template, type **ProductForm.xaml** in the *Name* box, and then click *Add*.

There are several approaches you can use for adding and editing products. The columns in the *ListView* control are read-only text items, but you can create a customized list view that contains text boxes or other controls that enable user input. However, the simplest strategy is to create another form that enables the user to edit or add the details of a product.

8. In the *Design View* window, click the *ProductForm* form, and in the *Properties* window, set the *ResizeMode* property to *NoResize*, set the *Height* property to *225*, and set the *Width* property to *515*.

9. Add three *Label* controls, three *TextBox* controls, and two *Button* controls anywhere on the form. Using the *Properties* window, set the properties of these controls to the values shown in the following table.

Control	Property	Value
label1	Content	Product Name
	Height	23
	Width	120
	Margin	17,20,0,0
	VerticalAlignment	Top
	HorizontalAlignment	Left
label2	Content	Quantity Per Unit
	Height	23
	Width	120
	Margin	17,60,0,0
	VerticalAlignment	Top
	HorizontalAlignment	Left
label3	Content	Unit Price
	Height	23
	Width	120
	Margin	17,100,0,0
	VerticalAlignment	Top
	HorizontalAlignment	Left
textBox1	Name	productName
	Height	21
	Width	340
	Margin	130,24,0,0

Control	Property	Value
	VerticalAlignment	Top
	HorizontalAlignment	Left
textBox2	Name	quantityPerUnit
	Height	21
	Width	340
	Margin	130,64,0,0
	VerticalAlignment	Top
	HorizontalAlignment	Left
textBox3	Name	unitPrice
	Height	21
	Width	120
	Margin	130,104,0,0
	VerticalAlignment	Top
	HorizontalAlignment	Left
button1	Name	ok
	Content	OK
	Height	23
	Width	75
	Margin	130,150,0,0
	VerticalAlignment	Top
	HorizontalAlignment	Left
button2	Name	cancel
	Content	Cancel
	Height	23
	Width	75
	Margin	300,150,0,0
	VerticalAlignment	Top
	HorizontalAlignment	Left

The form should look like this in the *Design View* window:

10. Double-click the *OK* button to create an event handler for the *click* event. In the *Code and Text Editor* window displaying the ProductForm.xaml.cs file, add the following code shown in bold type:

```
private void ok_Click(object sender, RoutedEventArgs e)
{
    if (String.IsNullOrEmpty(this.productName.Text))
    {
        MessageBox.Show("The product must have a name", "Error",
            MessageBoxButton.OK, MessageBoxImage.Error);
        return;
    }

    decimal result;
    if (!Decimal.TryParse(this.unitPrice.Text, out result))
    {
        MessageBox.Show("The price must be a valid number", "Error",
            MessageBoxButton.OK, MessageBoxImage.Error);
        return;
    }

    if (result < 0)
    {
        MessageBox.Show("The price must not be less than zero", "Error",
            MessageBoxButton.OK, MessageBoxImage.Error);
        return;
    }

    this.DialogResult = true;
}
```

The application will display this form by calling the *ShowDialog* method. This method displays the form as a modal dialog box. When the user clicks a button on the form, it closes automatically if the code for the *click* event sets the *DialogResult* property. If the user clicks *OK*, this method performs some simple validation of the information entered by the user. The *Quantity Per Unit* column in the database accepts *null* values, so the user can leave this field on the form empty. If the user enters a valid product name and price, the method sets the *DialogResult* property of the form to *true*. This value is passed back to the *ShowDialog* method call.

11. Return to the *Design View* window displaying the ProductForm.xaml file. Select the *Cancel* button, and in the *Properties* window, set the *IsCancel* property to *true*. (Select the check box.)

    If the user clicks the *Cancel* button, it automatically closes the form and returns a *DialogResult* value of *false* to the *ShowDialog* method.

12. Switch to the *Code and Text Editor* window displaying the SupplierInfo.xaml.cs file. Add the *addNewProduct* method shown here to the *SupplierInfo* class:

    ```
    private void addNewProduct()
    {
        ProductForm pf = new ProductForm();
        pf.Title = "New Product for " + supplier.CompanyName;
        if (pf.ShowDialog().Value)
        {
            Product newProd = new Product();
            newProd.ProductName = pf.productName.Text;
            newProd.QuantityPerUnit = pf.quantityPerUnit.Text;
            newProd.UnitPrice = Decimal.Parse(pf.unitPrice.Text);
            this.supplier.Products.Add(newProd);
            this.productsInfo.Add(newProd);
            saveChanges.IsEnabled = true;
        }
    }
    ```

    The *addNewProduct* method creates a new instance of the *ProductForm* form, sets the *Title* property of this form to contain the name of the supplier, and then calls the *ShowDialog* method to display the form as a modal dialog box. If the user enters some valid data and clicks the *OK* button on the form, the code in the *if* block creates a new *Product* object and populates it with the information from the *ProductForm* instance. The method then adds it to the *Products* collection for the current supplier and also adds it to the list displayed in the list view control on the form. Finally, the code activates the *Save Changes* button. In a later step, you will add code to the *click* event handler for this button so that the user can save changes back to the database.

13. Add the *editProduct* method shown here to the *SupplierInfo* class:

    ```
    private void editProduct(Product product)
    {
        ProductForm pf = new ProductForm();
        pf.Title = "Edit Product Details";
        pf.productName.Text = product.ProductName;
        pf.quantityPerUnit.Text = product.QuantityPerUnit;
        pf.unitPrice.Text = product.UnitPrice.ToString();

        if (pf.ShowDialog().Value)
        {
            product.ProductName = pf.productName.Text;
            product.QuantityPerUnit = pf.quantityPerUnit.Text;
            product.UnitPrice = Decimal.Parse(pf.unitPrice.Text);
            saveChanges.IsEnabled = true;
        }
    }
    ```

The *editProduct* method also creates an instance of the *ProductForm* form. This time, as well as setting the *Title* property, the code also populates the fields on the form with the information from the currently selected product. When the form is displayed, the user can edit these values. If the user clicks the *OK* button to close the form, the code in the *if* block copies the new values back to the currently selected product before activating the *Save Changes* button. Notice that this time you do not need to update the current item manually in the *productsInfo* list because the *Product* class notifies the list view control of changes to its data automatically.

14. Return to the *Design View* window displaying the SupplierInfo.xaml file. Double-click the *Save Changes* button to create the *click* event handler method.

15. In the *Code and Text Editor* window, add the following *using* statements to the list at the top of the file:

```
using System.Data;
using System.Data.Objects;
```

These namespaces contain many of the types used by the Entity Framework.

16. Find the *saveChanges_Click* method, and add the code shown here in bold type to this method:

```
private void saveChanges_Click(object sender, RoutedEventArgs e)
{
    try
    {
        this.northwindContext.SaveChanges();
        saveChanges.IsEnabled = false;
    }
    catch (OptimisticConcurrencyException)
    {
        this.northwindContext.Refresh(RefreshMode.ClientWins,
                                      northwindContext.Products);
        this.northwindContext.SaveChanges();
    }
    catch (UpdateException uEx)
    {
        MessageBox.Show(uEx.InnerException.Message, "Error saving changes");
        this.northwindContext.Refresh(RefreshMode.StoreWins,
                                      northwindContext.Products);
    }
    catch (Exception ex)
    {
        MessageBox.Show(ex.Message, "Error saving changes");
        this.northwindContext.Refresh(RefreshMode.StoreWins,
                                      northwindContext.Products);
    }
}
```

This method calls the *SaveChanges* method of the *ObjectContext* object to send all the changes back to the database. The exception handlers catch any exceptions that might occur. The *OptimisticConcurrencyException* handler uses the strategy described earlier to refresh the cache and save the changes again. The *UpdateException* handler reports the error to the user and then refreshes the cache from the database by speci-fying the *RefreshMode.StoreWins* parameter. (This causes the changes made by the user to be discarded.) Note that the most meaningful data for this exception is held in the *InnerException* property of the exception (although you might not want to display this type of information to a user!). If any other type of exception occurs, the *Exception* handler displays a simple message and refreshes the cache from the database.

Test the Suppliers application

1. On the *Debug* menu, click *Start Without Debugging* to build and run the application. When the form appears displaying the products supplied by Exotic Liquids, click prod-uct 3 (Aniseed Syrup) and then press Enter or double-click the row. The *Edit Product Details* form should appear. Change the value in the *Unit Price* field to **12.5**, and then click *OK*. Verify that the new price is copied back to the list view.

2. Press the Insert key. The *New Product for Exotic Liquids* form should appear. Enter a product name, quantity per unit, and price, and then click *OK*. Verify that the new product is added to the list view.

   The value in the *Product ID* column should be 0. This value is an identity column in the database, so SQL Server will generate its own unique value for this column when you save the changes.

3. Click *Save Changes*. After the data is saved, the ID for the new product is displayed in the list view.

4. Click the new product, and then press the Delete key. In the *Confirm* dialog box, click *Yes*. Verify that the product disappears from the form. Click *Save Changes* again, and verify that the operation completes without any errors.

   Feel free to experiment by adding, removing, and editing products for other suppliers. You can make several modifications before clicking *Save Changes*—the *SubmitChanges* method saves all changes made since the data was retrieved or last saved.

> **Tip** If you accidentally delete or overwrite the data for a product that you want to keep, close the application without clicking *Save Changes*. Note that the application as written does not warn the user if the user tries to exit without first saving changes.
>
> Alternatively, you can add a *Discard Changes* button to the application that calls the *Refresh* method of the *northwindContext ObjectContext* object to repopulate its tables from the database, as shown in the exception handlers in the previous exercise.

5. Close the form, and return to Visual Studio 2010.

In this chapter, you learned how to use the Entity Framework to generate an entity model for a database. You saw how to use the entity model from a WPF application by binding controls to collections of entities. You also saw how to use LINQ to Entities to access data through an entity model.

- If you want to continue to the next chapter

  Keep Visual Studio 2010 running, and turn to Chapter 27.

- If you want to exit Visual Studio 2010 now

  On the *File* menu, click *Exit*. If you see a *Save* dialog box, click *Yes* and save the project.

Chapter 26 Quick Reference

To	Do this
Create entity classes by using the Entity Framework	Add a new class to the project by using the *ADO.NET Entity Data Model* template. Use the Entity Model Wizard to connect to the database containing the tables that you want to model, and select the tables that you require.
Display data from an entity object or collection in a WPF control	Define a binding for the appropriate property of the control. If the control displays a list of objects, set the *DataContext* property of the control to a collection of entity objects. If the control displays the data for a single object, set the *DataContext* property of the control to an entity object and specify the property of the entity object to display in the *Path* attribute of the binding.
Modify information in a database by using the Entity Framework	First do one of the following: ■ To update a row in a table in the database, fetch the data for the row into an entity object, and assign the new values to the appropriate properties of the entity object. ■ To insert a new row into a table in the database, create a new instance of the corresponding entity object by using the CreateXXX factory method generated for this entity class (where XXX is the name of the entity). Set its properties, and then call the AddObject method of the appropriate ObjectSet collection, specifying the new entity object as the parameter. ■ To remove a row from a table in the database, call the DeleteObject method of the appropriate ObjectSet collection, specifying the entity object to be removed as the parameter. Then, after making all your changes, call the *SaveChanges* method of the *ObjectContext* object to propagate the modifications to the database.
Handle conflicts when updating a database by using the Entity Framework	Provide a handler for the *OptimisticConcurrencyException*. In the exception handler, call the *Refresh* method of the *ObjectContext* object to retrieve the most recent data from the database for the *original* values in the cache, and then call *SaveChanges* again.

Part VI

Building Professional Solutions with Visual Studio 2010

Chapter 27
Introducing the Task Parallel Library

After completing the chapter, you will be able to

- Describe the benefits that implementing parallel operations in an application can bring.

- Explain how the Task Parallel Library provides an optimal platform for implementing applications that can take advantage of multiple processor cores.

- Use the *Task* class to create and run parallel operations in an application.

- Use the *Parallel* class to parallelize some common programming constructs.

- Use tasks with threads to improve responsiveness and throughput in graphical user interface (GUI) applications.

- Cancel long-running tasks, and handle exceptions raised by parallel operations.

You have now seen how to use Microsoft Visual C# to build applications that provide a graphical user interface and that can manage data held in a database. These are common features of most modern systems. However, as technology has advanced so have the requirements of users, and the applications that enable them to perform their day-to-day operations need to provide ever-more sophisticated solutions. In the final part of this book, you will look at some of the advanced features introduced with the .NET Framework 4.0. In particular, in this chapter you will see how to improve concurrency in an application by using the Task Parallel Library. In the next chapter, you will see how the parallel extensions provided with the .NET Framework can be used in conjunction with Language Integrated Query (LINQ) to improve the throughput of data access operations. And in the final chapter, you will meet Windows Communication Foundation for building distributed solutions that can incorporate services running on multiple computers. As a bonus, the appendix (provided on the CD) describes how to use the Dynamic Language Runtime to build C# applications and components that can interoperate with services built by using other languages that operate outside of the structure provided by the .NET Framework, such as Python and Ruby.

In the bulk of the preceding chapters in this book, you learned how to use C# to write programs that run in a single-threaded manner. By "single-threaded," I mean that at any one point in time, a program has been executing a single instruction. This might not always be the most efficient approach for an application to take. For example, you saw in Chapter 23, "Gathering User Input," that if your program is waiting for the user to click a button on a Windows Presentation Foundation (WPF) form, there might be other work that it can perform while it is waiting. However, if a single-threaded program has to perform a lengthy, processor-intensive calculation, it cannot respond to the user typing in data on a form or clicking a menu item. To the user, the application appears to have frozen. Only when the calculation has completed does the user interface start responding again. Applications that can perform multiple tasks at the same time can make far better use of the resources available on a computer, can run more quickly, and can be more responsive. Additionally, some individual tasks might run more quickly if you can divide them into parallel paths of execution that can run concurrently. In Chapter 23, you saw how WPF can take advantage of threads to improve responsiveness in a graphical user interface. In this chapter, you will learn how to use the Task Parallel Library to implement a more generic form of multitasking in your programs that can apply to computationally intensive applications and not just those concerned with managing user interfaces.

Why Perform Multitasking by Using Parallel Processing?

As mentioned in the introduction, there are two principle reasons why you might want to perform multitasking in an application:

- **To improve responsiveness**   You can give the user of an application the impression that the program is performing more than one task at a time by dividing the program up into concurrent threads of execution and allowing each thread to run in turn for a short period of time. This is the conventional co-operative model that many experienced Windows developers are familiar with. However, it is not true multitasking because the processor is shared between threads, and the co-operative nature of this approach requires that the code executed by each thread behaves in an appropriate manner. If one thread dominates the CPU and resources available at the expense of other threads, the advantages of this approach are lost. It is sometimes difficult to write well-behaved applications that follow this model consistently.

- **To improve scalability**   You can improve scalability by making efficient use of the processing resources available and using these resources to reduce the time required to execute parts of an application. A developer can determine which parts of an application can be performed in parallel and arrange for them to be run concurrently. As more computing resources are added, more tasks can be run in parallel. Until recently, this model was suitable only for systems that either had multiple CPUs or were able to spread the processing across different computers networked together. In both cases, you had to use a model that arranged for coordination between parallel tasks. Microsoft provides a specialized version of Windows called High Performance Compute (HPC) Server 2008, which enables an organization to build clusters of servers that can distribute and execute tasks in parallel. Developers can use the Microsoft implementation of the Message Passing Interface (MPI), a well-known language-independent communications protocol, to build applications based on parallel tasks that coordinate and cooperate with each other by sending messages. Solutions based on Windows HPC Server 2008 and MPI are ideal for large-scale, compute-bound engineering and scientific applications, but they are expensive for smaller scale, desktop systems.

From these descriptions, you might be tempted to conclude that the most cost-effective way to build multitasking solutions for desktop applications is to use the cooperative multithreaded approach. However, the multithreaded approach was simply intended as a mechanism to provide responsiveness—to enable computers with a single processor to ensure that each task got a fair share of the processor. It is not well-suited for multiprocessor machines because it is not designed to distribute the load across processors and, consequently, does not scale well. While desktop machines with multiple processors were expensive (and consequently relatively rare), this was not an issue. However, this situation is changing, as I will briefly explain.

The Rise of the Multicore Processor

Ten years ago, the cost of a decent personal computer was in the range of $500 to $1000. Today, a decent personal computer still costs about the same, even after ten years of price inflation. The specification of a typical PC these days is likely to include a processor running at a speed of between 2 GHz and 3 GHz, 500 GB of hard disk storage, 4 GB of RAM, high-speed and high-resolution graphics, and a rewritable DVD drive. Ten years ago, the processor speed for a typical machine was between 500 MHz and 1 GHz, 80 GB was a big hard drive, Windows ran quite happily with 256 MB or less of RAM, and rewritable CD drives cost well over $100. (Rewritable DVD drives were rare and extremely expensive.) This is the joy of technological progress: ever faster and more powerful hardware at cheaper and cheaper prices.

This is not a new trend. In 1965, Gordon E. Moore, co-founder of Intel, wrote a paper titled "Cramming more components onto integrated circuits," which discussed how the increasing miniaturization of components enabled more transistors to be embedded on a silicon chip, and how the falling costs of production as the technology became more accessible would lead economics to dictate squeezing as many as 65,000 components onto a single chip by 1975. Moore's observations lead to the dictum frequently referred to as "Moore's Law," which basically states that the number of transistors that can be placed inexpensively on an integrated circuit will increase exponentially, doubling approximately every two years. (Actually, Gordon Moore was more optimistic than this initially, postulating that the volume of transistors was likely to double every year, but he later modified his calculations.) The ability to pack transistors together led to the ability to pass data between them more quickly. This meant we could expect to see chip manufacturers produce faster and more powerful microprocessors at an almost unrelenting pace, enabling software developers to write ever more complicated software that would run more quickly.

Moore's Law concerning the miniaturization of electronic components still holds, even after more than 40 years. However, physics has started to intervene. There comes a limit when it is not possible transmit signals between transistors on a single chip any more quickly, no matter how small or densely packed they are. To a software developer, the most noticeable result of this limitation is that processors have stopped getting faster. Six years ago, a fast processor ran at 3 GHz. Today, a fast processor still runs at 3 GHz.

The limit to the speed at which processors can transmit data between components has caused chip companies to look at alternative mechanisms for increasing the amount of work a processor can do. The result is that most modern processors now have two or more *processor cores*. Effectively, chip manufacturers have put multiple processors on the same chip and added the necessary logic to enable them to communicate and coordinate with each other. Dual-core processors (two cores) and quad-core processors (four cores) are now common. Chips with 8, 16, 32, and 64 cores are available, and the price of these is expected to fall sharply in the near future. So, although processors have stopped speeding up, you can now expect to get more of them on a single chip.

What does this mean to a developer writing C# applications?

In the days before multicore processors, a single-threaded application could be sped up simply by running it on a faster processor. With multicore processors, this is no longer the case. A single-threaded application will run at the same speed on a single-core, dual-core, or quad-core processor that all have the same clock frequency. The difference is that on a dual-core processor, one of the processor cores will be sitting around idle, and on a quad-core processor, three of the cores will be simply ticking over waiting for work. To make the best use of multicore processors, you need to write your applications to take advantage of multitasking.

Implementing Multitasking in a Desktop Application

Multitasking is the ability to do more than one thing at the same time. It is one of those concepts that is easy to describe but that, until recently, has been difficult to implement.

In the optimal scenario, an application running on a multicore processor performs as many concurrent tasks as there are processor cores available, keeping each of the cores busy. However, there are many issues you have to consider to implement concurrency, including the following:

- How can you divide an application into a set of concurrent operations?

- How can you arrange for a set of operations to execute concurrently, on multiple processors?

- How can you ensure that you attempt to perform only as many concurrent operations as there are processors available?

- If an operation is blocked (such as while it is waiting for I/O to complete), how can you detect this and arrange for the processor to run a different operation rather than sit idle?

- How can you determine when one or more concurrent operations have completed?

- How can you synchronize access to shared data to ensure that two or more concurrent operations do not inadvertently corrupt each other's data?

To an application developer, the first question is a matter of application design. The remaining questions depend on the programmatic infrastructure—Microsoft provides the Task Parallel Library (TPL) to help address these issues.

In Chapter 28, "Performing Parallel Data Access," you will see how some query-oriented problems have naturally parallel solutions, and how you can use the *ParallelEnumerable* type of PLINQ to parallelize query operations. However, sometimes you need a more imperative approach for more generalized situations. The TPL contains a series of types and operations that enable you to more explicitly specify how you want to divide an application into a set of parallel tasks.

Tasks, Threads, and the *ThreadPool*

The most important type in the TPL is the *Task* class. The *Task* class is an abstraction of a concurrent operation. You create a *Task* object to run a block of code. You can instantiate multiple *Task* objects and start them running in parallel if sufficient processors or processor cores are available.

 Note From now on, I will use the term "processor" to refer to either a single-core processor or a single processor core on a multicore processor.

Internally, the TPL implements tasks and schedules them for execution by using *Thread* objects and the *ThreadPool* class. Multithreading and thread pools have been available with the .NET Framework since version 1.0, and you can use the *Thread* class in the *System. Threading* namespace directly in your code. However, the TPL provides an additional degree of abstraction that enables you to easily distinguish between the degree of parallelization in an application (the tasks) and the units of parallelization (the threads). On a single-processor computer, these items are usually the same. However, on a computer with multiple processors or with a multicore processor, they are different. If you design a program based directly on threads, you will find that your application might not scale very well; the program will use the number of threads you explicitly create, and the operating system will schedule only that number of threads. This can lead to overloading and poor response time if the number of threads greatly exceeds the number of available processors, or to inefficiency and poor throughput if the number of threads is less than the number of processors.

The TPL optimizes the number of threads required to implement a set of concurrent tasks and schedules them efficiently according to the number of available processors. The TPL uses a set of threads provided by the .NET Framework, called the *ThreadPool*, and implements a queuing mechanism to distribute the workload across these threads. When a program creates a *Task* object, the task is added to a global queue. When a thread becomes available, the task is removed from the global queue and is executed by that thread. The *ThreadPool* implements a number of optimizations and uses a work-stealing algorithm to ensure that threads are scheduled efficiently.

 Note The *ThreadPool* was available in previous editions of the .NET Framework, but it has been enhanced significantly in the .NET Framework 4.0 to support *Tasks*.

You should note that the number of threads created by the .NET Framework to handle your tasks is not necessarily the same as the number of processors. Depending on the nature of the workload, one or more processors might be busy performing high-priority work for other applications and services. Consequently, the optimal number of threads for your application might be less than the number of processors in the machine. Alternatively, one or more threads in an application might be waiting for long-running memory access, I/O, or a network operation to complete, leaving the corresponding processors free. In this case, the optimal number of threads might be more than the number of available processors. The .NET Framework follows an iterative strategy, known as a *hill-climbing* algorithm, to dynamically determine the ideal number of threads for the current workload.

The important point is that all you have to do in your code is divide your application into tasks that can be run in parallel. The .NET Framework takes responsibility for creating the appropriate number of threads based on the processor architecture and workload of your computer, associating your tasks with these threads and arranging for them to be run efficiently. It does not matter if you divide your work into too many tasks because the .NET Framework will attempt to run only as many concurrent threads as is practical; in fact, you are encouraged to *overpartition* your work because this will help to ensure that your application scales if you move it onto a computer that has more processors available.

Creating, Running, and Controlling Tasks

The *Task* object and the other types in the TPL reside in the *System.Threading.Tasks* namespace. You can create *Task* objects by using the *Task* constructor. The *Task* constructor is overloaded, but all versions expect you to provide an *Action* delegate as a parameter. Remember from Chapter 23 that an *Action* delegate references a method that does not return a value. A *task* object uses this delegate to run the method when it is scheduled. The following example creates a *Task* object that uses a delegate to run the method called *doWork* (you can also use an anonymous method or a lambda expression, as shown by the code in the comments):

```
Task task = new Task(new Action(doWork));
// Task task = new Task(delegate { this.doWork(); });
// Task task = new Task(() => { this.doWork(); });
...
private void doWork()
{
    // The task runs this code when it is started
    ...
}
```

> **Note** In many cases, you can let the compiler infer the *Action* delegate type itself and simply specify the method to run. For example, you can rephrase the first example just shown as follows:
>
> ```
> Task task = new Task(doWork);
> ```
>
> The delegate inference rules implemented by the compiler apply not just to the *Action* type, but anywhere you can use a delegate. You will see many more examples throughout the remainder of this book.

The default *Action* type references a method that takes no parameters. Other overloads of the *Task* constructor take an *Action<object>* parameter representing a delegate that refers to a method that takes a single *object* parameter. These overloads enable you to pass data into the method run by the task. The following code shows an example:

```
Action<object> action;
action = doWorkWithObject;
object parameterData = ...;
Task task = new Task(action, parameterData);
...
private void doWorkWithObject(object o)
{
    ...
}
```

After you create a *Task* object, you can set it running by using the *Start* method, like this:

```
Task task = new Task(...);
task.Start();
```

The *Start* method is also overloaded, and you can optionally specify a *TaskScheduler* object to control the degree of concurrency and other scheduling options. It is recommended that you use the default *TaskScheduler* object built into the .NET Framework, or you can define your own custom *TaskScheduler* class if you want to take more control over the way in which tasks are queued and scheduled. The details of how to do this are beyond the scope of this book, but if you require more information look at the description of the *TaskScheduler* abstract class in the .NET Framework Class Library documentation provided with Visual Studio.

You can obtain a reference to the default *TaskScheduler* object by using the static *Default* property of the *TaskScheduler* class. The *TaskScheduler* class also provides the static *Current* property, which returns a reference to the *TaskScheduler* object currently used. (This *TaskScheduler* object is used if you do not explicitly specify a scheduler.) A task can provide hints to the default *TaskScheduler* about how to schedule and run the task if you specify a value from the *TaskCreationOptions* enumeration in the *Task* constructor. For more information about the *TaskCreationOptions* enumeration, consult the documentation describing the .NET Framework Class Library provided with Visual Studio.

When the method run by the task completes, the task finishes, and the thread used to run the task can be recycled to execute another task.

Normally, the scheduler arranges to perform tasks in parallel wherever possible, but you can also arrange for tasks to be scheduled serially by creating a *continuation*. You create a continuation by calling the *ContinueWith* method of a *Task* object. When the action performed by the *Task* object completes, the scheduler automatically creates a new *Task* object to run the action specified by the *ContinueWith* method. The method specified by the continuation expects a *Task* parameter, and the scheduler passes in a reference to the task that completed to the method. The value returned by *ContinueWith* is a reference to the new *Task* object. The following code example creates a *Task* object that runs the *doWork* method and specifies a continuation that runs the *doMoreWork* method in a new task when the first task completes:

```
Task task = new Task(doWork);
task.Start();
Task newTask = task.ContinueWith(doMoreWork);
...
private void doWork()
{
    // The task runs this code when it is started
    ...
}
...
private void doMoreWork(Task task)
{
    // The continuation runs this code when doWork completes
    ...
}
```

The *ContinueWith* method is heavily overloaded, and you can provide a number of parameters that specify additional items, such as the *TaskScheduler* to use and a *TaskContinuationOptions* value. The *TaskContinuationOptions* type is an enumeration that contains a superset of the values in the *TaskCreationOptions* enumeration. The additional values available include

- **NotOnCanceled and OnlyOnCanceled**   The *NotOnCanceled* option specifies that the continuation should run only if the previous action completes and is not canceled, and the *OnlyOnCanceled* option specifies that the continuation should run only if the previous action is canceled. The section "Canceling Tasks and Handling Exceptions" later in this chapter describes how to cancel a task.

- **NotOnFaulted and OnlyOnFaulted**   The *NotOnFaulted* option indicates that the continuation should run only if the previous action completes and does not throw an unhandled exception. The *OnlyOnFaulted* option causes the continuation to run only if the previous action throws an unhandled exception. The section "Canceling Tasks and Handling Exceptions" provides more information on how to manage exceptions in a task.

- **NotOnRanToCompletion and OnlyOnRanToCompletion**   The *NotOnRanToCompletion* option specifies that the continuation should run only if the previous action does not complete successfully; it must either be canceled or throw an exception. *OnlyOnRanToCompletion* causes the continuation to run only if the previous action completes successfully.

The following code example shows how to add a continuation to a task that runs only if the initial action does not throw an unhandled exception:

```
Task task = new Task(doWork);
task.ContinueWith(doMoreWork, TaskContinuationOptions.NotOnFaulted);
task.Start();
```

If you commonly use the same set of *TaskCreationOptions* values and the same *TaskScheduler* object, you can use a *TaskFactory* object to create and run a task in a single step. The constructor for the *TaskFactory* class enables you to specify the task scheduler, task creation options, and task continuation options that tasks constructed by this factory should use. The *TaskFactory* class provides the *StartNew* method to create and run a *Task* object. Like the *Start* method of the *Task* class, the *StartNew* method is overloaded, but all of them expect a reference to a method that the task should run.

The following code shows an example that creates and runs two tasks using the same task factory:

```
TaskScheduler scheduler = TaskScheduler.Current;
TaskFactory taskFactory = new TaskFactory(scheduler, TaskCreationOptions.None,
    TaskContinuationOptions.NotOnFaulted);
Task task = taskFactory.StartNew(doWork);
Task task2 = taskFactory.StartNew(doMoreWork);
```

Even if you do not currently specify any particular task creation options and you use the default task scheduler, you should still consider using a *TaskFactory* object; it ensures consistency, and you will have less code to modify to ensure that all tasks run in the same manner if you need to customize this process in the future. The *Task* class exposes the default *TaskFactory* used by the TPL through the static *Factory* property. You can use it like this:

```
Task task = Task.Factory.StartNew(doWork);
```

A common requirement of applications that invoke operations in parallel is to synchronize tasks. The *Task* class provides the *Wait* method, which implements a simple task coordination method. It enables you to suspend execution of the current thread until the specified task completes, like this:

```
task2.Wait(); // Wait at this point until task2 completes
```

You can wait for a set of tasks by using the static *WaitAll*, and *WaitAny* methods of the *Task* class. Both methods take a *params* array containing a set of *Task* objects. The *WaitAll* method waits until all specified tasks have completed, and *WaitAny* stops until at least one of the specified tasks has finished. You use them like this:

```
Task.WaitAll(task, task2); // Wait for both task and task2 to complete
Task.WaitAny(task, task2); // Wait for either of task or task2 to complete
```

Using the Task Class to Implement Parallelism

In the next exercise, you will use the *Task* class to parallelize processor-intensive code in an application, and you will see how this parallelization reduces the time taken for the application to run by spreading the computations across multiple processor cores.

The application, called GraphDemo, comprises a WPF form that uses an *Image* control to display a graph. The application plots the points for the graph by performing a complex calculation.

Note The exercises in this chapter are intended to run on a computer with a multicore processor. If you have only a single-core CPU, you will not observe the same effects. Also, you should not start any additional programs or services between exercises because these might affect the results that you see.

Examine and run the GraphDemo single-threaded application

1. Start Microsoft Visual Studio 2010 if it is not already running.

2. Open the GraphDemo solution, located in the \Microsoft Press\Visual CSharp Step By Step\Chapter 27\GraphDemo folder in your Documents folder.

3. In Solution Explorer, in the GraphDemo project, double-click the file GraphWindow. xaml to display the form in the *Design View* window.

   The form contains the following controls:

   - An *Image* control called *graphImage*. This image control displays the graph rendered by the application.

   - A *Button* control called *plotButton*. The user clicks this button to generate the data for the graph and display it in the *graphImage* control.

   - A *Label* control called *duration*. The application displays the time taken to generate and render the data for the graph in this label.

4. In Solution Explorer, expand GraphWindow.xaml, and then double-click GraphWindow. xaml.cs to display the code for the form in the *Code and Text Editor* window.

   The form uses a *System.Windows.Media.Imaging.WriteableBitmap* object called *graphBitmap* to render the graph. The variables *pixelWidth* and *pixelHeight* specify the horizontal and vertical resolution, respectively, for the *WriteableBitmap* object; the variables *dpiX* and *dpiY* specify the horizontal and vertical density, respectively, of the image in dots per inch:

```
public partial class GraphWindow : Window
{
    private static long availableMemorySize = 0;
    private int pixelWidth = 0;
    private int pixelHeight = 0;
    private double dpiX = 96.0;
    private double dpiY = 96.0;
    private WriteableBitmap graphBitmap = null;
    ...
}
```

5. Examine the *GraphWindow* constructor. It looks like this:

```
public GraphWindow()
{
    InitializeComponent();

    PerformanceCounter memCounter = new PerformanceCounter("Memory", "Available
Bytes");
    availableMemorySize = Convert.ToUInt64(memCounter.NextValue());

    this.pixelWidth = (int)availablePhysicalMemory / 20000;
    if (this.pixelWidth < 0 || this.pixelWidth > 15000)
        this.pixelWidth = 15000;
```

```
    this.pixelHeight = (int)availablePhysicalMemory / 40000;
    if (this.pixelHeight < 0 || this.pixelHeight > 7500)
        this.pixelHeight = 7500;
}
```

To avoid presenting you with code that exhausts the memory available on your computer and generates *OutOfMemory* exceptions, this application creates a *PerformanceCounter* object to query the amount of available physical memory on the computer. It then uses this information to determine appropriate values for the *pixel-Width* and *pixelHeight* variables. The more available memory you have on your computer, the bigger the values generated for *pixelWidth* and *pixelHeight* (subject to the limits of 15,000 and 7500 for each of these variables, respectively) and the more you will see the benefits of using the TPL as the exercises in this chapter proceed. However, if you find that the application still generates *OutOfMemory* exceptions, increase the divisors (20,000 and 40,000) used for generating the values of *pixelWidth* and *pixelHeight*.

If you have a lot of memory, the values calculated for *pixelWidth* and *pixelHeight* might overflow. In this case, they will contain negative values and the application will fail with an exception later on. The code in the constructor checks this case and sets the *pixelWidth* and *pixelHeight* fields to a pair of useful values that enable the application to run correctly in this situation.

6. Examine the code for the *plotButton_Click* method:

```
private void plotButton_Click(object sender, RoutedEventArgs e)
{
    if (graphBitmap == null)
    {
        graphBitmap = new WriteableBitmap(pixelWidth, pixelHeight, dpiX, dpiY,
PixelFormats.Gray8, null);
    }
    int bytesPerPixel = (graphBitmap.Format.BitsPerPixel + 7) / 8;
    int stride = bytesPerPixel * graphBitmap.PixelWidth;
    int dataSize = stride * graphBitmap.PixelHeight;
    byte [] data = new byte[dataSize];

    Stopwatch watch = Stopwatch.StartNew();
    generateGraphData(data);

    duration.Content = string.Format("Duration (ms): {0}", watch.ElapsedMilliseconds);
    graphBitmap.WritePixels(
        new Int32Rect(0, 0, graphBitmap.PixelWidth, graphBitmap.PixelHeight),
        data, stride, 0);
    graphImage.Source = graphBitmap;
}
```

This method runs when the user clicks the *plotButton* button. The code instantiates the *graphBitmap* object if it has not already been created by the user clicking the *plotButton* button previously, and it specifies that each pixel represents a shade of gray, with 8 bits per pixel. This method uses the following variables and methods:

- The *bytesPerPixel* variable calculates the number of bytes required to hold each pixel. (The *WriteableBitmap* type supports a range of pixel formats, with up to 128 bits per pixel for full-color images.)

- The *stride* variable contains the vertical distance, in bytes, between adjacent pixels in the *WriteableBitmap* object.

- The *dataSize* variable calculates the number of bytes required to hold the data for the *WriteableBitmap* object. This variable is used to initialize the *data* array with the appropriate size.

- The *data* byte array holds the data for the graph.

- The *watch* variable is a *System.Diagnostics.Stopwatch* object. The *StopWatch* type is useful for timing operations. The static *StartNew* method of the *StopWatch* type creates a new instance of a *StopWatch* object and starts it running. You can query the running time of a *StopWatch* object by examining the *ElapsedMilliseconds* property.

- The *generateGraphData* method populates the *data* array with the data for the graph to be displayed by the *WriteableBitmap* object. You will examine this method in the next step.

- The *WritePixels* method of the *WriteableBitmap* class copies the data from a byte array to a bitmap for rendering. This method takes an *Int32Rect* parameter that specifies the area in the *WriteableBitmap* object to populate, the data to be used to copy to the *WriteableBitmap* object, the vertical distance between adjacent pixels in the *WriteableBitmap* object, and an offset into the *WriteableBitmap* object to start writing the data to.

> **Note** You can use the *WritePixels* method to selectively overwrite information in a *WriteableBitmap* object. In this example, the code overwrites the entire contents. For more information about the *WriteableBitmap* class, consult the .NET Framework Class Library documentation installed with Visual Studio 2010.

- The *Source* property of an *Image* control specifies the data that the *Image* control should render. This example sets the *Source* property to the *WriteableBitmap* object.

7. Examine the code for the *generateGraphData* method:

```
private void generateGraphData(byte[] data)
{
    int a = pixelWidth / 2;
    int b = a * a;
    int c = pixelHeight / 2;

    for (int x = 0; x < a; x ++)
    {
        int s = x * x;
        double p = Math.Sqrt(b - s);
        for (double i = -p; i < p; i += 3)
        {
            double r = Math.Sqrt(s + i * i) / a;
            double q = (r - 1) * Math.Sin(24 * r);
            double y = i / 3 + (q * c);
            plotXY(data, (int)(-x + (pixelWidth / 2)), (int)(y + (pixelHeight / 2)));
            plotXY(data, (int)(x + (pixelWidth / 2)), (int)(y + (pixelHeight / 2)));
        }
    }
}
```

This method performs a series of calculations to plot the points for a rather complex graph. (The actual calculation is unimportant—it just generates a graph that looks attractive!) As it calculates each point, it calls the *plotXY* method to set the appropriate bytes in the *data* array that correspond to these points. The points for the graph are reflected around the X axis, so the *plotXY* method is called twice for each calculation: once for the positive value of the X coordinate, and once for the negative value.

8. Examine the *plotXY* method:

```
private void plotXY(byte[] data, int x, int y)
{
    data[x + y * pixelWidth] = 0xFF;
}
```

This is a simple method that sets the appropriate byte in the *data* array that corresponds to X and Y coordinates passed in as parameters. The value 0xFF indicates that the corresponding pixel should be set to white when the graph is rendered. Any pixels left unset are displayed as black.

9. On the *Debug* menu, click *Start Without Debugging* to build and run the application.

10. When the *Graph Demo* window appears, click *Plot Graph*, and wait.

Please be patient. The application takes several seconds to generate and display the graph. The following image shows the graph. Note the value in the *Duration (ms)* label in the following figure. In this case, the application took 4478 milliseconds (ms) to plot the graph.

Note The application was run on a computer with 2 GB of memory and an Intel® Core 2 Duo Desktop Processor E6600 running at 2.40 GHz. Your times might vary if you are using a different processor or a different amount of memory. Additionally, you might notice that it seems to take longer initially to display the graph than the reported time. This is because of the time taken to initialize the data structures required to actually display the graph as part of the *WritePixels* method of the *graphBitmap* control rather than the time taken to calculate the data for the graph. Subsequent runs do not have this overhead.

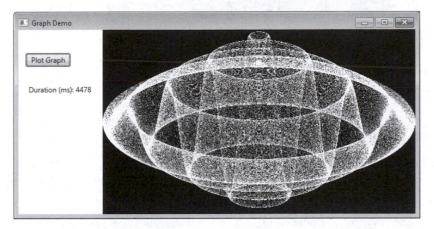

11. Click *Plot Graph* again, and take note of the time taken. Repeat this action several times to get an average value.

12. On the desktop, right-click an empty area of the taskbar, and then in the pop-up menu click *Start Task Manager*.

 Note Under Windows Vista, the command in the pop-up menu is called *Task Manager*.

13. In the Windows Task Manager, click the *Performance* tab.

14. Return to the *Graph Demo* window and then click *Plot Graph*.

15. In the Windows Task Manager, note the maximum value for the CPU usage while the graph is being generated. Your results will vary, but on a dual-core processor the CPU utilization will probably be somewhere around 50–55 percent, as shown in the following image. On a quad-core machine, the CPU utilization will likely be below 30 percent.

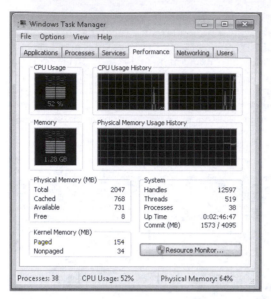

16. Return to the *Graph Demo* window, and click *Plot Graph* again. Note the value for the CPU usage in the Windows Task Manager. Repeat this action several times to get an average value.

17. Close the *Graph Demo* window, and minimize the Windows Task Manager.

You now have a baseline for the time the application takes to perform its calculations. However, it is clear from the CPU usage displayed by the Windows Task Manager that the application is not making full use of the processing resources available. On a dual-core machine, it is using just over half of the CPU power, and on a quad-core machine it is employing a little over a quarter of the CPU. This phenomenon occurs because the application is single-threaded, and in a Windows application, a single thread can occupy only a single core on a multicore processor. To spread the load over all the available cores, you need to divide the application into tasks and arrange for each task to be executed by a separate thread running on a different core.

Modify the GraphDemo application to use parallel threads

1. Return to the Visual Studio 2010, and display the GraphWindow.xaml.cs file in the *Code and Text Editor* window if it is not already open.

2. Examine the *generateGraphData* method.

If you think about it carefully, the purpose of this method is to populate the items in the *data* array. It iterates through the array by using the outer *for* loop based on the *x* loop control variable, highlighted in bold here:

```
private void generateGraphData(byte[] data)
{
    int a = pixelWidth / 2;
    int b = a * a;
    int c = pixelHeight / 2;


    for (int x = 0; x < a; x ++)
    {
        int s = x * x;
        double p = Math.Sqrt(b - s);
        for (double i = -p; i < p; i += 3)
        {
            double r = Math.Sqrt(s + i * i) / a;
            double q = (r - 1) * Math.Sin(24 * r);
            double y = i / 3 + (q * c);
            plotXY(data, (int)(-x + (pixelWidth / 2)), (int)(y + (pixelHeight / 2)));
            plotXY(data, (int)(x + (pixelWidth / 2)), (int)(y + (pixelHeight / 2)));
        }
    }
}
```

The calculation performed by one iteration of this loop is independent of the calculations performed by the other iterations. Therefore, it makes sense to partition the work performed by this loop and run different iterations on a separate processor.

3. Modify the definition of the *generateGraphData* method to take two additional *int* parameters called *partitionStart* and *partitionEnd*, as shown in bold here:

```
private void generateGraphData(byte[] data, int partitionStart, int partitionEnd)
{
    ...
}
```

4. In the *generateGraphData* method, change the outer *for* loop to iterate between the values of *partitionStart* and *partitionEnd*, as shown in bold here:

```
private void generateGraphData(byte[] data, int partitionStart, int partitionEnd)
{
    ...

    for (int x = partitionStart; x < partitionEnd; x ++)
    {
        ...
    }
}
```

5. In the *Code and Text Editor* window, add the following *using* statement to the list at the top of the GraphWindow.xaml.cs file:

```
using System.Threading.Tasks;
```

6. In the *plotButton_Click* method, comment out the statement that calls the *generateGraphData* method and add the statement shown next in bold that creates a *Task* object by using the default *TaskFactory* object and starts it running:

```
...
Stopwatch watch = Stopwatch.StartNew();
// generateGraphData(data);
Task first = Task.Factory.StartNew(() => generateGraphData(data, 0, pixelWidth / 4));
...
```

The task runs the code specified by the lambda expression. The values for the *partitionStart* and *partitionEnd* parameters indicate that the *Task* object calculates the data for the first half of the graph. (The data for the complete graph consists of points plotted for the values between 0 and *pixelWidth / 2*.)

7. Add another statement that creates and runs a second *Task* object on another thread, as shown in bold here:

```
...
Task first = Task.Factory.StartNew(() => generateGraphData(data, 0, pixelWidth / 4));
Task second = Task.Factory.StartNew(() => generateGraphData(data, pixelWidth / 4,
pixelWidth / 2));
...
```

This *Task* object invokes the *generateGraph* method and calculates the data for the values between *pixelWidth / 4* and *pixelWidth / 2*.

8. Add the following statement that waits for both *Task* objects to complete their work before continuing:

```
Task.WaitAll(first, second);
```

9. On the *Debug* menu, click *Start Without Debugging* to build and run the application.

10. Display the Windows Task Manager, and click the Performance tab if it is not currently displayed.

11. Return to the *Graph Demo* window, and click *Plot Graph*. In the Windows Task Manager, note the maximum value for the CPU usage while the graph is being generated. When the graph appears in the *Graph Demo* window, record the time taken to generate the graph. Repeat this action several times to get an average value.

12. Close the *Graph Demo* window, and minimize the Windows Task Manager.

This time you should see that the application runs significantly quicker than previously. On my computer, the time dropped to 2682 milliseconds—a reduction in time of about 40 percent. Additionally, you should see that the application uses more cores of the CPU. On a dual-core machine, the CPU usage peaked at 100 percent. If you have a quad-core computer, the CPU utilization will not be as high. This is because two of the cores will not be occupied. To rectify this and reduce the time further, add two further *Task* objects and divide the work into four chunks in the *plotButton_Click* method, as shown in bold here:

```
...
Task first = Task.Factory.StartNew(() => generateGraphData(data, 0, pixelWidth / 8));
Task second = Task.Factory.StartNew(() => generateGraphData(data, pixelWidth / 8,
pixelWidth / 4));
Task third = Task.Factory.StartNew(() => generateGraphData(data, pixelWidth / 4,
pixelWidth * 3 / 8));
Task fourth = Task.Factory.StartNew(() => generateGraphData(data, pixelWidth * 3 / 8,
pixelWidth / 2));
Task.WaitAll(first, second, third, fourth);
...
```

If you have only a dual-core processor, you can still try this modification, and you should still notice a beneficial effect on the time. This is primarily because of efficiencies in the TPL and the algorithms in the .NET Framework optimizing the way in which the threads for each task are scheduled.

Abstracting Tasks by Using the Parallel Class

By using the *Task* class, you have complete control over the number of tasks your applica-tion creates. However, you had to modify the design of the application to accommodate the use of *Task* objects. You also had to add code to synchronize operations; the applica-tion can render the graph only when all the tasks have completed. In a complex application, synchronization of tasks can become a nontrivial process and it is easy to make mistakes.

The *Parallel* class in the TPL enables you to parallelize some common programming constructs without requiring that you redesign an application. Internally, the *Parallel* class creates its own set of *Task* objects, and it synchronizes these tasks automatically when they have completed. The *Parallel* class is located in the *System.Threading.Tasks* namespace and provides a small set of static methods you can use to indicate that code should be run in parallel if possible. These methods are as follows:

- **Parallel.For**   You can use this method in place of a C# *for* statement. It defines a loop in which iterations can run in parallel by using tasks. This method is heavily overloaded (there are nine variations), but the general principle is the same for each; you specify a start value, an end value, and a reference to a method that takes an integer parameter. The method is executed for every value between the start value and one below the end value specified, and the parameter is populated with an integer that specifies the current value. For example, consider the following simple *for* loop that performs each iteration in sequence:

```
for (int x = 0; x < 100; x++)
{
    // Perform loop processing
}
```

Depending on the processing performed by the body of the loop, you might be able to replace this loop with a *Parallel.For* construct that can perform iterations in parallel, like this:

```
Parallel.For(0, 100, performLoopProcessing);
...
private void performLoopProcessing(int x)
{
    // Perform loop processing
}
```

The overloads of the *Parallel.For* method enable you to provide local data that is private to each thread, specify various options for creating the tasks run by the *For* method, and create a *ParallelLoopState* object that can be used to pass state information to other concurrent iterations of the loop. (Using a *ParallelLoopState* object is described later in this chapter.)

- **Parallel.ForEach<T>**   You can use this method in place of a C# *foreach* statement. Like the *For* method, *ForEach* defines a loop in which iterations can run in parallel. You specify a collection that implements the *IEnumerable<T>* generic interface and a reference to a method that takes a single parameter of type *T*. The method is executed for each item in the collection, and the item is passed as the parameter to the method. Overloads are available that enable you to provide private local thread data and specify options for creating the tasks run by the *ForEach* method.

- **Parallel.Invoke**   You can use this method to execute a set of parameterless method calls as parallel tasks. You specify a list of delegated method calls (or lambda expressions) that take no parameters and do not return values. Each method call can be run on a separate thread, in any order. For example, the following code makes a series of method calls:

```
doWork();
doMoreWork();
doYetMoreWork();
```

You can replace these statements with the following code, which invokes these methods by using a series of tasks:

```
Parallel.Invoke(
    doWork,
    doMoreWork,
    doYetMoreWork
);
```

You should bear in mind that the .NET Framework determines the actual degree of parallelism appropriate for the environment and workload of the computer. For example, if you use *Parallel.For* to implement a loop that performs 1000 iterations, the .NET Framework does not necessarily create 1000 concurrent tasks (unless you have an exceptionally powerful processor with 1000 cores). Instead, the .NET Framework creates what it considers to be the optimal number of tasks that balances the available resources against the requirement to keep the processors occupied. A single task might perform multiple iterations, and the tasks coordinate with each other to determine which iterations each task will perform. An important consequence of this is that you cannot guarantee the order in which the iterations are executed, so you must ensure there are no dependencies between iterations; otherwise, you might get unexpected results, as you will see later in this chapter.

In the next exercise, you will return to the original version of the GraphData application and use the *Parallel* class to perform operations concurrently.

Use the *Parallel* class to parallelize operations in the GraphData application

1. Using Visual Studio 2010, open the *GraphDemo* solution, located in the \Microsoft Press\Visual CSharp Step By Step\Chapter 27\GraphDemo Using the Parallel Class folder in your Documents folder.

    This is a copy of the original GraphDemo application. It does not use tasks yet.

2. In Solution Explorer, in the GraphDemo project, expand the GraphWindow.xaml node, and then double-click GraphWindow.xaml.cs to display the code for the form in the *Code and Text Editor* window.

3. Add the following *using* statement to the list at the top of the file:

    ```
    using System.Threading.Tasks;
    ```

4. Locate the *generateGraphData* method. It looks like this:

    ```
    private void generateGraphData(byte[] data)
    {
        int a = pixelWidth / 2;
        int b = a * a;
        int c = pixelHeight / 2;

        for (int x = 0; x < a; x++)
        {
            int s = x * x;
            double p = Math.Sqrt(b - s);
            for (double i = -p; i < p; i += 3)
            {
                double r = Math.Sqrt(s + i * i) / a;
                double q = (r - 1) * Math.Sin(24 * r);
                double y = i / 3 + (q * c);
                plotXY(data, (int)(-x + (pixelWidth / 2)), (int)(y + (pixelHeight / 2)));
                plotXY(data, (int)(x + (pixelWidth / 2)), (int)(y + (pixelHeight / 2)));
            }
        }
    }
    ```

The outer *for* loop that iterates through values of the integer variable *x* is a prime candidate for parallelization. You might also consider the inner loop based on the variable *i*, but this loop takes more effort to parallelize because of the type of *i*. (The methods in the *Parallel* class expect the control variable to be an integer.) Additionally, if you have nested loops such as occur in this code, it is good practice to parallelize the outer loops first and then test to see whether the performance of the application is sufficient. If it is not, work your way through nested loops and parallelize them working from outer to inner loops, testing the performance after modifying each one. You will find that in many cases parallelizing outer loops has the most effect on performance, while the effects of modifying inner loops becomes more marginal.

5. Move the code in the body of the *for* loop, and create a new private *void* method called *calculateData* with this code. The *calculateData* method should take an integer parameter called *x* and a byte array called *data*. Also, move the statements that declare the local variables *a*, *b*, and *c* from the *generateGraphData* method to the start of the *calculateData* method. The following code shows the *generateGraphData* method with this code removed and the *calculateData* method (do not try and compile this code yet):

```
private void generateGraphData(byte[] data)
{
    for (int x = 0; x < a; x++)
    {
    }
}

private void calculateData(int x, byte[] data)
{
    int a = pixelWidth / 2;
    int b = a * a;
    int c = pixelHeight / 2;

    int s = x * x;
    double p = Math.Sqrt(b - s);
    for (double i = -p; i < p; i += 3)
    {
        double r = Math.Sqrt(s + i * i) / a;
        double q = (r - 1) * Math.Sin(24 * r);
        double y = i / 3 + (q * c);
        plotXY(data, (int)(-x + (pixelWidth / 2)), (int)(y + (pixelHeight / 2)));
        plotXY(data, (int)(x + (pixelWidth / 2)), (int)(y + (pixelHeight / 2)));
    }
}
```

6. In the *generateGraphData* method, change the *for* loop to a statement that calls the static *Parallel.For* method, as shown in bold here:

```
private void generateGraphData(byte[] data)
{
    Parallel.For (0, pixelWidth / 2, (int x) => { calculateData(x, data); });
}
```

This code is the parallel equivalent of the original *for* loop. It iterates through the values from 0 to pixelWidth / 2 – 1 inclusive. Each invocation runs by using a task. (Each task might run more than one iteration.) The *Parallel.For* method finishes only when all the tasks it has created complete their work. Remember that the *Parallel.For* method expects the final parameter to be a method that takes a single integer parameter. It calls this method passing the current loop index as the parameter. In this example, the *calculateData* method does not match the required signature because it takes two parameters: an integer and a byte array. For this reason, the code uses a lambda expression to define an anonymous method that has the appropriate signature and that acts as an adapter that calls the *calculateData* method with the correct parameters.

7. On the *Debug* menu, click *Start Without Debugging* to build and run the application.

8. Display the Windows Task Manager, and click the *Performance* tab if it is not currently displayed.

9. Return to the *Graph Demo* window, and click *Plot Graph*. In the Windows Task Manager, note the maximum value for the CPU usage while the graph is being generated. When the graph appears in the *Graph Demo* window, record the time taken to generate the graph. Repeat this action several times to get an average value.

10. Close the *Graph Demo* window, and minimize the Windows Task Manager.

You should notice that the application runs at a comparable speed to the previous version that used *Task* objects (and possibly slightly faster, depending on the number of CPUs you have available), and that the CPU usage peaks at 100 percent.

When Not to Use the Parallel Class

You should be aware that despite appearances and the best efforts of the Visual Studio development team at Microsoft, the *Parallel* class is not magic; you cannot use it without due consideration and just expect your applications to suddenly run significantly faster and produce the same results. The purpose of the *Parallel* class is to parallelize compute-bound, independent areas of your code.

The key phrases in the previous paragraph are *compute-bound* and *independent*. If your code is not compute-bound, parallelizing it might not improve performance. The next exercise shows you that you should be careful in how you determine when to use the *Parallel.Invoke* construct to perform method calls in parallel.

Determine when to use *Parallel.Invoke*

1. Return to Visual Studio 2010, and display the GraphWindow.xaml.cs file in the *Code and Text Editor* window if it is not already open.

2. Examine the *calculateData* method.

The inner *for* loop contains the following statements:

```
plotXY(data, (int)(-x + (pixelWidth / 2)), (int)(y + (pixelHeight / 2)));
plotXY(data, (int)(x + (pixelWidth / 2)), (int)(y + (pixelHeight / 2)));
```

These two statements set the bytes in the *data* array that correspond to the points specified by the two parameters passed in. Remember that the points for the graph are reflected around the X axis, so the *plotXY* method is called for the positive value of the X coordinate and also for the negative value. These two statements look like good candidates for parallelization because it does not matter which one runs first, and they set different bytes in the *data* array.

3. Modify these two statements, and wrap them in a *Parallel.Invoke* method call, as shown next. Notice that both calls are now wrapped in lambda expressions, and that the semicolon at the end of the first call to *plotXY* is replaced with a comma and the semi-colon at the end of the second call to *plotXY* has been removed because these statements are now a list of parameters:

```
Parallel.Invoke(
    () => plotXY(data, (int)(-x + (pixelWidth / 2)), (int)(y + (pixelHeight / 2))),
    () => plotXY(data, (int)(x + (pixelWidth / 2)), (int)(y + (pixelHeight / 2)))
);
```

4. On the *Debug* menu, click *Start Without Debugging* to build and run the application.

5. In the *Graph Demo* window, click *Plot Graph*. Record the time taken to generate the graph. Repeat this action several times to get an average value.

   You should find, possibly unexpectedly, that the application takes significantly longer to run. It might be up to 20 times slower than it was previously.

6. Close the *Graph Demo* window.

The questions you are probably asking at this point are, "What went wrong? Why did the application slow down so much?" The answer lies in the *plotXY* method. If you take another look at this method, you will see that it is very simple:

```
private void plotXY(byte[] data, int x, int y)
{
    data[x + y * pixelWidth] = 0xFF;
}
```

There is very little in this method that takes any time to run, and it is definitely not a compute-bound piece of code. In fact, it is so simple that the overhead of creating a task, running this task on a separate thread, and waiting for the task to complete is much greater than the cost of running this method directly. The additional overhead might account for only a few milliseconds each time the method is called, but you should bear in mind the number of times that this method runs; the method call is located in a nested loop and is executed thousands of times, so all of these small overhead costs add up. The general rule is to use

Parallel.Invoke only when it is worthwhile. Reserve *Parallel.Invoke* for operations that are computationally intensive.

As mentioned earlier in this chapter, the other key consideration for using the *Parallel* class is that operations should be independent. For example, if you attempt to use *Parallel.For* to parallelize a loop in which iterations are not independent, the results will be unpredictable. To see what I mean, look at the following program:

```csharp
using System;
using System.Threading;
using System.Threading.Tasks;

namespace ParallelLoop
{
    class Program
    {
        private static int accumulator = 0;

        static void Main(string[] args)
        {
            for (int i = 0; i < 100; i++)
            {
                AddToAccumulator(i);
            }
            Console.WriteLine("Accumulator is {0}", accumulator);
        }

        private static void AddToAccumulator(int data)
        {
            if ((accumulator % 2) == 0)
            {
                accumulator += data;
            }
            else
            {
                accumulator -= data;
            }
        }
    }
}
```

This program iterates through the values from 0 to 99 and calls the *AddToAccumulator* method with each value in turn. The *AddToAccumulator* method examines the current value of the *accumulator* variable, and if it is even it adds the value of the parameter to the *accumulator* variable; otherwise, it subtracts the value of the parameter. At the end of the program, the result is displayed. You can find this application in the ParallelLoop solution, located in the \Microsoft Press\Visual CSharp Step By Step\Chapter 27\ParallelLoop folder in your Documents folder. If you run this program, the value output should be –100.

To increase the degree of parallelism in this simple application, you might be tempted to replace the *for* loop in the *Main* method with *Parallel.For*, like this:

```
static void Main(string[] args)
{
    Parallel.For (0, 100, AddToAccumulator);
    Console.WriteLine("Accumulator is {0}", accumulator);
}
```

However, there is no guarantee that the tasks created to run the various invocations of the *AddToAccumulator* method will execute in any specific sequence. (The code is also not thread-safe because multiple threads running the tasks might attempt to modify the *accumulator* variable concurrently.) The value calculated by the *AddToAccumulator* method depends on the sequence being maintained, so the result of this modification is that the application might now generate different values each time it runs. In this simple case, you might not actually see any difference in the value calculated because the *AddToAccumulator* method runs very quickly and the .NET Framework might elect to run each invocation sequentially by using the same thread. However, if you make the following change shown in bold to the *AddToAccumulator* method, you will get different results:

```
private static void AddToAccumulator(int data)
{
    if ((accumulator % 2) == 0)
    {
        accumulator += data;
        Thread.Sleep(10); // wait for 10 milliseconds
    }
    else
    {
        accumulator -= data;
    }
}
```

The *Thread.Sleep* method simply causes the current thread to wait for the specified period of time. This modification simulates the thread, performing additional processing and affects the way in which the .NET Framework schedules the tasks, which now run on different threads resulting in a different sequence.

The general rule is to use *Parallel.For* and *Parallel.ForEach* only if you can guarantee that each iteration of the loop is independent, and test your code thoroughly. A similar consideration applies to *Parallel.Invoke*; use this construct to make method calls only if they are independent and the application does not depend on them being run in a particular sequence.

Returning a Value from a Task

So far, all the examples you have seen use a *Task* object to run code that performs a piece of work but does not return a value. However, you might also want to run a method that calculates a result. The TPL includes a generic variant of the *Task* class, *Task<TResult>*, that you can use for this purpose.

You create and run a *Task<TResult>* object in a similar way as a *Task* object. The main difference is that the method run by the *Task<TResult>* object returns a value, and you specify the type of this return value as the type parameter, *T*, of the *Task* object. For example, the method *calculateValue* shown in the following code example returns an integer value. To invoke this method by using a task, you create a *Task<int>* object and then call the *Start* method. You obtain the value returned by the method by querying the *Result* property of the *Task<int>* object. If the task has not finished running the method and the result is not yet available, the *Result* property blocks the caller. What this means is that you don't have to perform any synchronization yourself, and you know that when the *Result* property returns a value the task has completed its work.

```
Task<int> calculateValueTask = new Task<int>(() => calculateValue(...));
calculateValueTask.Start(); // Invoke the calculateValue method
...
int calculatedData = calculateValueTask.Result; // Block until calculateValueTask completes
...
private int calculateValue(...)
{
    int someValue;
    // Perform calculation and populate someValue
    ...
    return someValue;
}
```

Of course, you can also use the *StartNew* method of a *TaskFactory* object to create a *Task<TResult>* object and start it running. The next code example shows how to use the default *TaskFactory* for a *Task<int>* object to create and run a task that invokes the *calculateValue* method:

```
Task<int> calculateValueTask = Task<int>.Factory.StartNew(() => calculateValue(...));
...
```

To simplify your code a little (and to support tasks that return anonymous types), the *TaskFactory* class provides generic overloads of the *StartNew* method and can infer the type returned by the method run by a task. Additionally, the *Task<TResult>* class inherits from the *Task* class. This means that you can rewrite the previous example like this:

```
Task calculateValueTask = Task.Factory.StartNew(() => calculateValue(...));
...
```

The next exercise gives a more detailed example. In this exercise, you will restructure the GraphDemo application to use a *Task<TResult>* object. Although this exercise seems a little academic, you might find the technique that it demonstrates useful in many real-world situations.

Modify the GraphDemo application to use a *Task<TResult>* object

1. Using Visual Studio 2010, open the *GraphDemo* solution, located in the \Microsoft Press\Visual CSharp Step By Step\Chapter 27\GraphDemo Using Tasks that Return Results folder in your Documents folder.

   This is a copy of the GraphDemo application that creates a set of four tasks that you saw in an earlier exercise.

2. In Solution Explorer, in the GraphDemo project, expand the GraphWindow.xaml node, and then double-click GraphWindow.xaml.cs to display the code for the form in the *Code and Text Editor* window.

3. Locate the *plotButton_Click* method. This is the method that runs when the user clicks the *Plot Graph* button on the form. Currently, it creates a set of *Task* objects to perform the various calculations required and generate the data for the graph, and it waits for these *Task* objects to complete before displaying the results in the *Image* control on the form.

4. Underneath the *plotButton_Click* method, add a new method called *getDataForGraph*. This method should take an integer parameter called *dataSize* and return a *byte* array, as shown in the following code:

```
private byte[] getDataForGraph(int dataSize)
{
}
```

   You will add code to this method to generate the data for the graph in a *byte* array and return this array to the caller. The *dataSize* parameter specifies the size of the array.

5. Move the statement that creates the data array from the *plotButton_Click* method to the *getDataForGraph* method as shown here in bold:

```
private byte[] getDataForGraph(int dataSize)
{
    byte[] data = new byte[dataSize];
}
```

6. Move the code that creates, runs, and waits for the *Task* objects that populate the *data* array from the *plotButton_Click* method to the *getDataForGraph* method, and add a return statement to the end of the method that passes the *data* array back to the caller. The completed code for the *getDataForGraph* method should look like this:

```
private byte[] getDataForGraph(int dataSize)
{
    byte[] data = new byte[dataSize];
    Task first = Task.Factory.StartNew(() => generateGraphData(data, 0, pixelWidth /
8));
    Task second = Task.Factory.StartNew(() => generateGraphData(data, pixelWidth / 8,
pixelWidth / 4));
    Task third = Task.Factory.StartNew(() => generateGraphData(data, pixelWidth / 4,
```

```
pixelWidth * 3 / 8));
    Task fourth = Task.Factory.StartNew(() => generateGraphData(data, pixelWidth * 3 /
8, pixelWidth / 2));
    Task.WaitAll(first, second, third, fourth);
    return data;
}
```

> **Tip** You can replace the code that creates the tasks and waits for them to complete with the following *Parallel.Invoke* construct:
>
> ```
> Parallel.Invoke(
>     () => generateGraphData(data, 0, pixelWidth / 8),
>     () => generateGraphData(data, pixelWidth / 8, pixelWidth / 4),
>     () => generateGraphData(data, pixelWidth / 4, pixelWidth * 3 / 8),
>     () => generateGraphData(data, pixelWidth * 3 / 8, pixelWidth / 2)
> );
> ```

7. In the *plotButton_Click* method, after the statement that creates the *Stopwatch* variable used to time the tasks, add the statement shown next in bold that creates a *Task<byte[]>* object called *getDataTask* and uses this object to run the *getDataForGraph* method. This method returns a *byte* array, so the type of the task is *Task<byte []>*. The *StartNew* method call references a lambda expression that invokes the *getDataForGraph* method and passes the *dataSize* variable as the parameter to this method.

```
private void plotButton_Click(object sender, RoutedEventArgs e)
{
    ...
    Stopwatch watch = Stopwatch.StartNew();
    Task<byte[]> getDataTask = Task<byte[]>.Factory.StartNew(() =>
getDataForGraph(dataSize));
    ...
}
```

8. After creating and starting the *Task<byte []>* object, add the following statements shown in bold that examine the *Result* property to retrieve the data array returned by the *getDataForGraph* method into a local byte array variable called *data*. Remember that the *Result* property blocks the caller until the task has completed, so you do not need to explicitly wait for the task to finish.

```
private void plotButton_Click(object sender, RoutedEventArgs e)
{
    ...
    Task<byte[]> getDataTask = Task<byte[]>.Factory.StartNew(() =>
getDataForGraph(dataSize));
    byte[] data = getDataTask.Result;
    ...
}
```

> **Note** It might seem a little strange to create a task and then immediately wait for it to complete before doing anything else because it only adds overhead to the application. However, in the next section, you will see why this approach has been adopted.

9. Verify that the completed code for the *plotButton_Click* method looks like this:

```
private void plotButton_Click(object sender, RoutedEventArgs e)
{
    if (graphBitmap == null)
    {
        graphBitmap = new WriteableBitmap(pixelWidth, pixelHeight, dpiX, dpiY,
PixelFormats.Gray8, null);
    }
    int bytesPerPixel = (graphBitmap.Format.BitsPerPixel + 7) / 8;
    int stride = bytesPerPixel * pixelWidth;
    int dataSize = stride * pixelHeight;

    Stopwatch watch = Stopwatch.StartNew();
    Task<byte[]> getDataTask = Task<byte[]>.Factory.StartNew(() =>
getDataForGraph(dataSize));
    byte[] data = getDataTask.Result;

    duration.Content = string.Format("Duration (ms): {0}", watch.ElapsedMilliseconds);
    graphBitmap.WritePixels(new Int32Rect(0, 0, pixelWidth, pixelHeight), data,
stride, 0);
    graphImage.Source = graphBitmap;
}
```

10. On the *Debug* menu, click *Start Without Debugging* to build and run the application.

11. In the *Graph Demo* window, click *Plot Graph*. Verify that the graph is generated as before and that the time taken is similar to that seen previously. (The time reported might be marginally slower because the data array is now created by the task, whereas previously it was created before the task started running.)

12. Close the *Graph Demo* window.

Using Tasks and User Interface Threads Together

The section "Why Perform Multitasking by Using Parallel Processing?" at the start of this chapter highlighted the two principal reasons for using multitasking in an application—to improve throughput and increase responsiveness. The TPL can certainly assist in improving throughput, but you need to be aware that using the TPL alone is not the complete solution to improving responsiveness, especially in an application that provides a graphical user interface. In the GraphDemo application used as the basis for the exercises in this chapter, although the time taken to generate the data for the graph is reduced by the effective use of tasks, the application itself exhibits the classic symptoms of many GUIs that perform processor-intensive computations—it is not responsive to user input while these computations are being performed. For example, if you run the *GraphDemo* application from the previous exercise, click *Plot Graph*, and then try and move the Graph Demo window by clicking and dragging the title bar, you will find that it does not move until after the various tasks used to generate the graph have completed and the graph is displayed.

In a professional application, you should ensure that users can still use your application even if parts of it are busy performing other tasks. This is where you need to use threads as well as tasks.

In Chapter 23, you saw how the items that constitute the graphical user interface in a WPF application all run on the same user interface (UI) thread. This is to ensure consistency and safety, and it prevents two or more threads from potentially corrupting the internal data structures used by WPF to render the user interface. Remember also that you can use the WPF *Dispatcher* object to queue requests for the UI thread, and these requests can update the user interface. The next exercise revisits the *Dispatcher* object and shows how you can use it to implement a responsive solution in conjunction with tasks that ensure the best available throughput.

Improve responsiveness in the GraphDemo application

1. Return to Visual Studio 2010, and display the GraphWindow.xaml.cs file in the *Code and Text Editor* window if it is not already open.

2. Add a new method called *doPlotButtonWork* below the *plotButton_Click* method. This method should take no parameters and not return a result. In the next few steps, you will move the code that creates and runs the tasks that generate the data for the graph to this method, and you will run this method on a separate thread, leaving the UI thread free to manage user input.

    ```
    private void doPlotButtonWork()
    {
    }
    ```

3. Move all the code except for the *if* statement that creates the *graphBitmap* object from the *plotButton_Click* method to the *doPlotButtonWork* method. Note that some of these statements attempt to access user interface items; you will modify these statements to use the *Dispatcher* object later in this exercise. The *plotButton_Click* and *doPlotButtonWork* methods should look like this:

    ```
    private void plotButton_Click(object sender, RoutedEventArgs e)
    {
        if (graphBitmap == null)
        {
            graphBitmap = new WriteableBitmap(pixelWidth, pixelHeight, dpiX, dpiY,
    PixelFormats.Gray8, null);
        }
    }
    ```

```
private void doPlotButtonWork()
{
    int bytesPerPixel = (graphBitmap.Format.BitsPerPixel + 7) / 8;
    int stride = bytesPerPixel * pixelWidth;
    int dataSize = stride * pixelHeight;

    Stopwatch watch = Stopwatch.StartNew();
    Task<byte[]> getDataTask = Task<byte[]>.Factory.StartNew(() =>
getDataForGraph(dataSize));
    byte[] data = getDataTask.Result;

    duration.Content = string.Format("Duration (ms): {0}", watch.ElapsedMilliseconds);
    graphBitmap.WritePixels(new Int32Rect(0, 0, pixelWidth, pixelHeight), data,
stride, 0);
    graphImage.Source = graphBitmap;
}
```

4. In the *plotButton_Click* method, after the *if* block, create an *Action* delegate called *doPlotButtonWorkAction* that references the *doPlotButtonWork* method, as shown here in bold:

```
private void plotButton_Click(object sender, RoutedEventArgs e)
{
    ...
    Action doPlotButtonWorkAction = new Action(doPlotButtonWork);
}
```

5. Call the *BeginInvoke* method on the *doPlotButtonWorkAction* delegate. The *BeginInvoke* method of the *Action* type executes the method associated with the delegate (in this case, the *doPlotButtonWork* method) on a new thread.

> **Note** The *Action* type also provides the *Invoke* method, which runs the delegated method on the current thread. This behavior is not what we want in this case because it blocks the user interface and prevents it from being able to respond while the method is running.

The *BeginInvoke* method takes parameters you can use to arrange notification when the method finishes, as well as any data to pass to the delegated method. In this example, you do not need to be notified when the method completes and the method does not take any parameters, so specify a *null* value for these parameters as shown in bold here:

```
private void plotButton_Click(object sender, RoutedEventArgs e)
{
    ...
    Action doPlotButtonWorkAction = new Action(doPlotButtonWork);
    doPlotButtonWorkAction.BeginInvoke(null, null);
}
```

The code will compile at this point, but if you try and run it, it will not work correctly when you click *Plot Graph*. This is because several statements in the *doPlotButtonWork* method attempt to access user interface items, and this method is not running on the UI thread. You met this issue in Chapter 23, and you also saw the solution at that time—use the *Dispatcher* object for the UI thread to access UI elements. The following steps amend these statements to use the *Dispatcher* object to access the user interface items from the correct thread.

6. Add the following *using* statement to the list at the top of the file:

```
using System.Windows.Threading;
```

The *DispatcherPriority* enumeration is held in this namespace. You will use this enumeration when you schedule code to run on the UI thread by using the *Dispatcher* object.

7. At the start of the *doPlotButtonWork* method, examine the statement that initializes the *bytesPerPixel* variable:

```
private void doPlotButtonWork()
{
    int bytesPerPixel = (graphBitmap.Format.BitsPerPixel + 7) / 8;
    ...
}
```

This statement references the *graphBitmap* object, which belongs to the UI thread. You can access this object only from code running on the UI thread. Change this statement to initialize the *bytesPerPixel* variable to zero, and add a statement to call the *Invoke* method of the *Dispatcher* object, as shown in bold here:

```
private void doPlotButtonWork()
{
    int bytesPerPixel = 0;
    plotButton.Dispatcher.Invoke(new Action(() =>
        { bytesPerPixel = (graphBitmap.Format.BitsPerPixel + 7) / 8; }),
        DispatcherPriority.ApplicationIdle);
    ...
}
```

Recall from Chapter 23 that you can access the *Dispatcher* object through the *Dispatcher* property of any UI element. This code uses the *plotButton* button. The *Invoke* method expects a delegate and an optional dispatcher priority. In this case, the delegate references a lambda expression. The code in this expression runs on the UI thread. The *DispatcherPriority* parameter indicates that this statement should run only when the application is idle and there is nothing else more important going on in the user interface (such as the user clicking a button, typing some text, or moving the window).

8. Examine the final three statements in the *doPlotButtonWork* method. They look like this:

```
private void doPlotButtonWork()
{
    . . .
    duration.Content = string.Format("Duration (ms): {0}", watch.ElapsedMilliseconds);
    graphBitmap.WritePixels(new Int32Rect(0, 0, pixelWidth, pixelHeight), data,
stride, 0);
    graphImage.Source = graphBitmap;
}
```

These statements reference the *duration*, *graphBitmap*, and *graphImage* objects, which are all part of the user interface. Consequently, you must change these statements to run on the UI thread.

9. Modify these statements, and run them by using the *Dispatcher.Invoke* method, as shown in bold here:

```
private void doPlotButtonWork()
{
    . . .
    plotButton.Dispatcher.Invoke(new Action(() =>
    {
        duration.Content = string.Format("Duration (ms): {0}", watch.
ElapsedMilliseconds);
        graphBitmap.WritePixels(new Int32Rect(0, 0, pixelWidth, pixelHeight), data,
stride, 0);
        graphImage.Source = graphBitmap;
    }), DispatcherPriority.ApplicationIdle);
}
```

This code converts the statements into a lambda expression wrapped in an *Action* delegate, and then invokes this delegate by using the *Dispatcher* object.

10. On the *Debug* menu, click *Start Without Debugging* to build and run the application.

11. In the Graph Demo window, click *Plot Graph* and before the graph appears quickly drag the window to another location on the screen. You should find that the window responds immediately and does not wait for the graph to appear first.

12. Close the Graph Demo window.

Canceling Tasks and Handling Exceptions

Another common requirement of applications that perform long-running operations is the ability to stop those operations if necessary. However, you should not simply abort a task because this could leave the data in your application in an indeterminate state. Instead, the TPL implements a cooperative cancellation strategy. Cooperative cancellation enables a task to select a convenient point at which to stop processing and also enables it to undo any work it has performed prior to cancellation if necessary.

The Mechanics of Cooperative Cancellation

Cooperative cancellation is based on the notion of a *cancellation token*. A cancellation token is a structure that represents a request to cancel one or more tasks. The method that a task runs should include a *System.Threading.CancellationToken* parameter. An application that wants to cancel the task sets the Boolean *IsCancellationRequested* property of this parameter to *true*. The method running in the task can query this property at various points during its processing. If this property is set to *true* at any point, it knows that the application has requested that the task be canceled. Also, the method knows what work it has done so far, so it can undo any changes if necessary and then finish. Alternatively, the method can simply ignore the request and continue running if it does not want to cancel the task.

> **Tip** You should examine the cancellation token in a task frequently, but not so frequently that you adversely impact the performance of the task. If possible, you should aim to check for cancellation at least every 10 milliseconds, but no more frequently than every millisecond.

An application obtains a *CancellationToken* by creating a *System.Threading.CancellationTokenSource* object and querying the *Token* property of this object. The application can then pass this *CancellationToken* object as a parameter to any methods started by tasks that the application creates and runs. If the application needs to cancel the tasks, it calls the *Cancel* method of the *CancellationTokenSource* object. This method sets the *IsCancellationRequested* property of the *CancellationToken* passed to all the tasks.

The following code example shows how to create a cancellation token and use it to cancel a task. The *initiateTasks* method instantiates the *cancellationTokenSource* variable and obtains a reference to the *CancellationToken* object available through this variable. The code then creates and runs a task that executes the *doWork* method. Later on, the code calls the *Cancel* method of the cancellation token source, which sets the cancellation token. The *doWork* method queries the *IsCancellationRequested* property of the cancellation token. If the property is set the method terminates; otherwise, it continues running.

```
public class MyApplication
{
    ...
    // Method that creates and manages a task
    private void initiateTasks()
    {
        // Create the cancellation token source and obtain a cancellation token
        CancellationTokenSource cancellationTokenSource = new CancellationTokenSource();
        CancellationToken cancellationToken = cancellationToken.Token;
```

```
        // Create a task and start it running the doWork method
        Task myTask = Task.Factory.StartNew(() => doWork(cancellationToken));
        ...
        if (...)
        {
            // Cancel the task
            cancellationTokenSource.Cancel();
        }
        ...
    }

    // Method run by the task
    private void doWork(CancellationToken token)
    {
        ...
        // If the application has set the cancellation token, finish processing
        if (token.IsCancellationRequested)
        {
            // Tidy up and finish
            ...
            return;
        }
        // If the task has not been canceled, continue running as normal
        ...
    }
}
```

As well as providing a high degree of control over the cancellation processing, this approach is scalable across any number of tasks. You can start multiple tasks and pass the same *CancellationToken* object to each of them. If you call *Cancel* on the *CancellationTokenSource* object, each task will see that the *IsCancellationRequested* property has been set and can react accordingly.

You can also register a callback method with the cancellation token by using the *Register* method. When an application invokes the *Cancel* method of the corresponding *CancellationTokenSource* object, this callback runs. However, you cannot guarantee when this method executes; it might be before or after the tasks have performed their own cancellation processing, or even during that process.

```
...
cancellationToken,Register(doAdditionalWork);
...
private void doAdditionalWork()
{
    // Perform additional cancellation processing
}
```

In the next exercise, you will add cancellation functionality to the GraphDemo application.

Add cancellation functionality to the GraphDemo application

1. Using Visual Studio 2010, open the *GraphDemo* solution, located in the \Microsoft Press\Visual CSharp Step By Step\Chapter 27\GraphDemo Canceling Tasks folder in your Documents folder.

   This is a completed copy of the GraphDemo application from the previous exercise that uses tasks and threads to improve responsiveness.

2. In Solution Explorer, in the GraphDemo project, double-click GraphWindow.xaml to display the form in the *Design View* window.

3. From the *Toolbox*, add a *Button* control to the form under the *duration* label. Align the button horizontally with the *plotButton* button. In the *Properties* window, change the *Name* property of the new button to *cancelButton*, and change the *Content* property to *Cancel*.

   The amended form should look like the following image.

4. Double-click the *Cancel* button to create a *Click* event handling method called *cancelButton_Click*.

5. In the GraphWindow.xaml.cs file, locate the *getDataForGraph* method. This method creates the tasks used by the application and waits for them to complete. Move the declaration of the *Task* variables to the class level for the *GraphWindow* class as shown in bold in the following code, and then modify the *getDataForGraph* method to instantiate these variables:

```
public partial class GraphWindow : Window
{
    ...
    private Task first, second, third, fourth;
    ...
    private byte[] getDataForGraph(int dataSize)
```

```
        {
            byte[] data = new byte[dataSize];
            first = Task.Factory.StartNew(() => generateGraphData(data, 0, pixelWidth /
8));
            second = Task.Factory.StartNew(() => generateGraphData(data, pixelWidth / 8,
pixelWidth / 4));
            third = Task.Factory.StartNew(() => generateGraphData(data, pixelWidth / 4,
pixelWidth * 3 / 8));
            fourth = Task.Factory.StartNew(() => generateGraphData(data, pixelWidth * 3 /
8, pixelWidth / 2));
            Task.WaitAll(first, second, third, fourth);
            return data;
        }
    }
```

6. Add the following *using* statement to the list at the top of the file:

```
using System.Threading;
```

The types used by cooperative cancellation live in this namespace.

7. Add a *CancellationTokenSource* member called *tokenSource* to the *GraphWindow* class, and initialize it to null, as shown here in bold:

```
public class GraphWindow : Window
{
    ...
    private Task first, second, third, fourth;
    private CancellationTokenSource tokenSource = null;
    ...
}
```

8. Find the *generateGraphData* method, and add a *CancellationToken* parameter called *token* to the method definition:

```
private void generateGraphData(byte[] data, int partitionStart, int partitionEnd,
CancellationToken token)
{
    ...
}
```

9. In the *generateGraphData* method, at the start of the inner *for* loop, add the code shown next in bold to check whether cancellation has been requested. If so, return from the method; otherwise, continue calculating values and plotting the graph.

```
private void generateGraphData(byte[] data, int partitionStart, int partitionEnd,
CancellationToken token)
{
    int a = pixelWidth / 2;
    int b = a * a;
    int c = pixelHeight / 2;

    for (int x = partitionStart; x < partitionEnd; x ++)
    {
        int s = x * x;
```

```
    double p = Math.Sqrt(b - s);
    for (double i = -p; i < p; i += 3)
    {
        if (token.IsCancellationRequested)
        {
            return;
        }

        double r = Math.Sqrt(s + i * i) / a;
        double q = (r - 1) * Math.Sin(24 * r);
        double y = i / 3 + (q * c);
        plotXY(data, (int)(-x + (pixelWidth / 2)), (int)(y + (pixelHeight / 2)));
        plotXY(data, (int)(x + (pixelWidth / 2)), (int)(y + (pixelHeight / 2)));
    }
  }
}
```

10. In the *getDataForGraph* method, add the following statements shown in bold that in-stantiate the *tokenSource* variable and retrieve the *CancellationToken* object into a vari-able called *token*:

```
private byte[] getDataForGraph(int dataSize)
{
    byte[] data = new byte[dataSize];
    tokenSource = new CancellationTokenSource();
    CancellationToken token = tokenSource.Token;
    ...
}
```

11. Modify the statements that create and run the four tasks, and pass the *token* variable as the final parameter to the *generateGraphData* method:

```
first = Task.Factory.StartNew(() => generateGraphData(data, 0, pixelWidth / 8,
token));
second = Task.Factory.StartNew(() => generateGraphData(data, pixelWidth / 8,
pixelWidth / 4, token));
third = Task.Factory.StartNew(() => generateGraphData(data, pixelWidth / 4, pixelWidth
* 3 / 8, token));
fourth = Task.Factory.StartNew(() => generateGraphData(data, pixelWidth * 3 / 8,
pixelWidth / 2, token));
```

12. In the *cancelButton_Click* method, add the code shown here in bold:

```
private  void cancelButton_Click(object sender, RoutedEventArgs e)
{
    if (tokenSource != null)
    {
        tokenSource.Cancel();
    }
}
```

This code checks that the *tokenSource* variable has been instantiated; if it has been, the code invokes the *Cancel* method on this variable.

13. On the *Debug* menu, click *Start Without Debugging* to build and run the application.

14. In the GraphDemo window, click *Plot Graph*, and verify that the graph appears as it did before.

15. Click *Plot Graph* again, and then quickly click *Cancel*.

If you are quick and click *Cancel* before the data for the graph is generated, this action causes the methods being run by the tasks to return. The data is not complete, so the graph appears with holes, as shown in the following figure. (The size of the holes depends on how quickly you clicked *Cancel*.)

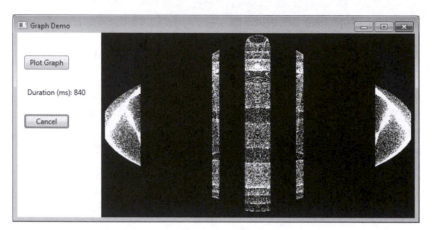

16. Close the GraphDemo window, and return to Visual Studio.

You can determine whether a task completed or was canceled by examining the *Status* property of the *Task* object. The *Status* property contains a value from the *System.Threading.Tasks.TaskStatus* enumeration. The following list describes some of the status values that you might commonly encounter (there are others):

- **Created**   This is the initial state of a task. It has been created but has not yet been scheduled to run.

- *WaitingToRun*   The task has been scheduled but has not yet started to run.

- *Running*   The task is currently being executed by a thread.

- *RanToCompletion*   The task completed successfully without any unhandled exceptions.

- *Canceled*   The task was canceled before it could start running, or it acknowledged cancellation and completed without throwing an exception.

- *Faulted*   The task terminated because of an exception.

In the next exercise, you will attempt to report the status of each task so that you can see when they have completed or have been canceled.

Canceling a Parallel *For* or *ForEach* Loop

The *Parallel.For* and *Parallel.ForEach* methods don't provide you with direct access to the *Task* objects that have been created. Indeed, you don't even know how many tasks are running—the .NET Framework uses its own heuristics to work out the optimal number to use based on the resources available and the current workload of the computer.

If you want to stop the *Parallel.For* or *Parallel.ForEach* method early, you must use a *ParallelLoopState* object. The method you specify as the body of the loop must include an additional *ParallelLoopState* parameter. The TPL creates a *ParallelLoopState* object and passes it as this parameter into the method. The TPL uses this object to hold information about each method invocation. The method can call the *Stop* method of this object to indicate that the TPL should not attempt to perform any iterations beyond those that have already started and finished. The following example shows the *Parallel. For* method calling the *doLoopWork* method for each iteration. The *doLoopWork* method examines the iteration variable; if it is greater than 600, the method calls the *Stop* method of the *ParallelLoopState* parameter. This causes the *Parallel.For* method to stop running further iterations of the loop. (Iterations currently running might continue to completion.)

> **Note** Remember that the iterations in a *Parallel.For* loop are not run in a specific sequence. Consequently, canceling the loop when the iteration variable has the value 600 does not guarantee that the previous 599 iterations have already run. Equally, some iterations with values greater than 600 might already have completed.

```
Parallel.For(0, 1000, doLoopWork);
...
private void doLoopWork(int i, ParallelLoopState p)
{
    ...
    if (i > 600)
    {
        p.Stop();
    }
}
```

Display the status of each task

1. In Visual Studio, in the *Code and Text Editor* window, find the *getDataForGraph* method.

2. Add the following code shown in bold to this method. These statements generate a string that contains the status of each task after they have finished running, and they display a message box containing this string.

```
private byte[] getDataForGraph(int dataSize)
{
    ...
    Task.WaitAll(first, second, third, fourth);

    String message = String.Format("Status of tasks is {0}, {1}, {2}, {3}",
        first.Status, second.Status, third.Status, fourth.Status);
    MessageBox.Show(message);

    return data;
}
```

3. On the *Debug* menu, click *Start Without Debugging*.

4. In the GraphDemo window, click *Plot Graph* but do not click *Cancel*. Verify that the following message box appears, which reports that the status of the tasks is *RanToCompletion* (four times), and then click *OK*. Note that the graph appears only after you have clicked *OK*.

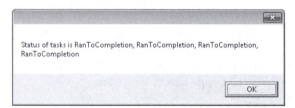

5. In the GraphDemo window, click *Plot Graph* again and then quickly click *Cancel*.

   Surprisingly, the message box that appears still reports the status of each task as *RanToCompletion*, even though the graph appears with holes. This is because although you sent a cancellation request to each task by using the cancellation token, the methods they were running simply returned. The .NET Framework runtime does not know whether the tasks were actually canceled or whether they were allowed to run to completion and simply ignored the cancellation requests.

6. Close the GraphDemo window, and return to Visual Studio.

So how do you indicate that a task has been canceled rather than allowed to run to completion? The answer lies in the *CancellationToken* object passed as a parameter to the method that the task is running. The *CancellationToken* class provides a method called *ThrowIfCancellationRequested*. This method tests the *IsCancellationRequested* property of a cancellation token; if it is true, the method throws an *OperationCanceledException* exception and aborts the method that the task is running.

The application that started the thread should be prepared to catch and handle this exception, but this leads to another question. If a task terminates by throwing an exception, it actually reverts to the *Faulted* state. This is true, even if the exception is an *OperationCanceledException* exception. A task enters the *Canceled* state only if it is canceled without throwing an exception. So how does a task throw an *OperationCanceledException* without it being treated as an exception?

The answer lies in the task itself. For a task to recognize that an *OperationCanceledException* is the result of canceling the task in a controlled manner and not just an exception caused by other circumstances, it has to know that the operation has actually been canceled. It can do this only if it can examine the cancellation token. You passed this token as a parameter to the method run by the task, but the task does not actually look at any of these parameters. (It considers them to be the business of the method and is not concerned with them.) Instead, you specify the cancellation token when you create the task, either as a parameter to the *Task* constructor or as a parameter to the *StartNew* method of the *TaskFactory* object you are using to create and run tasks. The following code shows an example based on the GraphDemo application. Notice how the *token* parameter is passed to the *generateGraph-Data* method (as before), but also as a separate parameter to the *StartNew* method:

```
Task first = null;
tokenSource = new CancellationTokenSource();
CancellationToken token = tokenSource.Token;
...
first = Task.Factory.StartNew(() => generateGraphData(data, 0, pixelWidth / 8, token),
token);
```

Now when the method being run by the task throws an *OperationCanceledException* exception, the infrastructure behind the task examines the *CancellationToken*. If it indicates that the task has been canceled, the infrastructure handles the *OperationCanceledException* exception, acknowledges the cancelation, and sets the status of the task to *Canceled*. The infrastructure then throws a *TaskCanceledException*, which your application should be prepared to catch. This is what you will do in the next exercise, but before you do that you need to learn a little more about how tasks raise exceptions and how you should handle them.

Handling Task Exceptions by Using the *AggregateException* Class

You have seen throughout this book that exception handling is an important element in any commercial application. The exception handling constructs you have met so far are straightforward to use, and if you use them carefully it is a simple matter to trap an exception and determine which piece of code raised it. However, when you start dividing work into multiple concurrent tasks, tracking and handling exceptions becomes a more complex problem. The issue is that different tasks might each generate their own exceptions, and you need a way to catch and handle multiple exceptions that might be thrown concurrently. This is where the *AggregateException* class comes in.

An *AggregateException* acts as a wrapper for a collection of exceptions. Each of the exceptions in the collection might be thrown by different tasks. In your application, you can catch the *AggregateException* exception and then iterate through this collection and perform any necessary processing. To help you, the *AggregateException* class provides the *Handle* method. The *Handle* method takes a *Func<Exception, bool>* delegate that references a method. The referenced method takes an *Exception* object as its parameter and returns a *Boolean* value. When you call *Handle*, the referenced method runs for each exception in the collection in the *AggregateException* object. The referenced method can examine the exception and take the appropriate action. If the referenced method handles the exception, it should return *true*. If not, it should return *false*. When the *Handle* method completes, any unhandled exceptions are bundled together into a new *AggregateException* and this exception is thrown; a subsequent outer exception handler can then catch this exception and process it.

In the next exercise, you will see how to catch an *AggregateException* and use it to handle the *TaskCanceledException* exception thrown when a task is canceled.

Acknowledge cancellation, and handle the *AggregateException* exception

1. In Visual Studio, display the GraphWindow.xaml file in the *Design View* window.

2. From the Toolbox, add a *Label* control to the form underneath the *cancelButton* button. Align the left edge of the *Label* control with the left edge of the *cancelButton* button.

3. Using the Properties window, change the *Name* property of the *Label* control to *status*, and remove the value in the *Content* property.

4. Return to the *Code and Text Editor* window displaying the GraphWindow.xaml.cs file, and add the following method below the *getDataForGraph* method:

```
private bool handleException(Exception e)
{
    if (e is TaskCanceledException)
    {
        plotButton.Dispatcher.Invoke(new Action(() =>
        {
            status.Content = "Tasks Canceled";
        }), DispatcherPriority.ApplicationIdle);
        return true;
    }
    else
    {
        return false;
    }
}
```

This method examines the *Exception* object passed in as a parameter; if it is a *TaskCanceledException* object, the method displays the text "Tasks Canceled" in the *status* label on the form and returns *true* to indicate that it has handled the exception; otherwise, it returns false.

5. In the *getDataForGraph* method, modify the statements that create and run the tasks and specify the *CancellationToken* object as the second parameter to the *StartNew* method, as shown in bold in the following code:

```
private byte[] getDataForGraph(int dataSize)
{
    byte[] data = new byte[dataSize];
    tokenSource = new CancellationTokenSource();
    CancellationToken token = tokenSource.Token;

    ...
    first = Task.Factory.StartNew(() => generateGraphData(data, 0, pixelWidth / 8,
token), token);
    second = Task.Factory.StartNew(() => generateGraphData(data, pixelWidth / 8,
pixelWidth / 4, token), token);
    third = Task.Factory.StartNew(() => generateGraphData(data, pixelWidth / 4,
pixelWidth * 3 / 8, token), token);
    fourth = Task.Factory.StartNew(() => generateGraphData(data, pixelWidth * 3 / 8,
pixelWidth / 2, token), token);
    Task.WaitAll(first, second, third, fourth);
    ...
}
```

6. Add a *try* block around the statements that create and run the tasks, and wait for them to complete. If the wait is successful, display the text "Tasks Completed" in the *status* label on the form by using the *Dispatcher.Invoke* method. Add a *catch* block that handles the *AggregateException* exception. In this exception handler, call the *Handle* method of the *AggregateException* object and pass a reference to the *handleException* method. The code shown next in bold highlights the changes you should make:

```
private byte[] getDataForGraph(int dataSize)
{
    byte[] data = new byte[dataSize];
    tokenSource = new CancellationTokenSource();
    CancellationToken token = tokenSource.Token;

    try
    {
        first = Task.Factory.StartNew(() => generateGraphData(data, 0, pixelWidth / 8,
token), token);
        second = Task.Factory.StartNew(() => generateGraphData(data, pixelWidth / 8,
pixelWidth / 4, token), token);
        third = Task.Factory.StartNew(() => generateGraphData(data, pixelWidth / 4,
pixelWidth * 3 / 8, token), token);
        fourth = Task.Factory.StartNew(() => generateGraphData(data, pixelWidth * 3 /
8, pixelWidth / 2, token), token);
        Task.WaitAll(first, second, third, fourth);
```

```
        plotButton.Dispatcher.Invoke(new Action(() =>
        {
            status.Content = "Tasks Completed";
        }), DispatcherPriority.ApplicationIdle);
    }
    catch (AggregateException ae)
    {
        ae.Handle(handleException);
    }

    String message = String.Format("Status of tasks is {0}, {1}, {2}, {3}",
        first.Status, second.Status, third.Status, fourth.Status);
    MessageBox.Show(message);

    return data;
}
```

7. In the *generateDataForGraph* method, replace the *if* statement that examines the *IsCancellationProperty* of the *CancellationToken* object with code that calls the *ThrowIfCancellationRequested* method, as shown here in bold:

```
private void generateDataForGraph(byte[] data, int partitionStart, int partitionEnd,
CancellationToken token)
{
    ...
    for (int x = partitionStart; x < partitionEnd; x++);
    {
        ...
        for (double i = -p; I < p; i += 3)
        {
            token.ThrowIfCancellationRequested();
            ...
        }
    }
    ...
}
```

8. On the *Debug* menu, click *Start Without Debugging*.

9. In the Graph Demo window, click *Plot Graph* and verify that the status of every task is reported as *RanToCompletion*, the graph is generated, and the *status* label displays the message "Tasks Completed".

10. Click *Plot Graph* again, and then quickly click *Cancel*. If you are quick, the status of one or more tasks should be reported as *Canceled*, the *status* label should display the text "Tasks Canceled", and the graph should be displayed with holes. If you are not quick enough, repeat this step to try again!

11. Close the Graph Demo window, and return to Visual Studio.

Using Continuations with Canceled and Faulted Tasks

If you need to perform additional work when a task is canceled or raises an unhandled exception, remember that you can use the *ContinueWith* method with the appropriate *TaskContinuationOptions* value. For example, the following code creates a task that runs the method *doWork*. If the task is canceled, the *ContinueWith* method specifies that another task should be created and run the method *doCancellationWork*. This method can perform some simple logging or tidying up. If the task is not canceled, the continuation does not run.

```
Task task = new Task(doWork);
task.ContinueWith(doCancellationWork, TaskContinuationOptions.OnlyOnCanceled);
task.Start();
...
private void doWork()
{
    // The task runs this code when it is started
    ...
}
...
private void doCancellationWork(Task task)
{
    // The task runs this code when doWork completes
    ...
}
```

Similarly, you can specify the value *TaskContinuationOptions.OnlyOnFaulted* to specify a continuation that runs if the original method run by the task raises an unhandled exception.

In this chapter, you learned why it is important to write applications that can scale across multiple processors and processor cores. You saw how to use the Task Parallel Library to run operations in parallel, and how to synchronize concurrent operations and wait for them to complete. You learned how to use the *Parallel* class to parallelize some common program-ming constructs, and you also saw when it is inappropriate to parallelize code. You used tasks and threads together in a graphical user interface to improve responsiveness and through-put, and you saw how to cancel tasks in a clean and controlled manner.

- If you want to continue to the next chapter

  Keep Visual Studio 2010 running, and turn to Chapter 28.

- If you want to exit Visual Studio 2010 now

  On the *File* menu, click *Exit*. If you see a *Save* dialog box, click *Yes* and save the project.

Chapter 27 Quick Reference

To	Do this

Create a task and run it	Either use the *StartNew* method of a *TaskFactory* object to create and run the task in a single step:
	
	``
	Task task = taskFactory.StartNew(doWork());
	...
	private void doWork()
	{
	    // The task runs this code when it is started
	    ...
	}
	``
	
	Or create a new *Task* object that references a method to run and call the *Start* method:
	
	``
	Task task = new Task(doWork);
	task.Start();
	``

Wait for a task to finish	Call the *Wait* method of the *Task* object:
	
	``
	Task task = ...;
	...
	task.Wait();
	``

Wait for several tasks to finish	Call the static *WaitAll* method of the *Task* class, and specify the tasks to wait for: ``` Task task1 = ...; Task task2 = ...; Task task3 = ...; Task task4 = ...; ... Task.WaitAll(task1, task2, task3, task4); ```
Specify a method to run in a new task when a task has completed	Call the *ContinueWith* method of the task, and specify the method as a continuation: ``` Task task = new Task(doWork); task.ContinueWith(doMoreWork, TaskContinuationOptions.NotOnFaulted); ```

Return a value from a task	Use a *Task<TResult>* object to run a method, where the type parameter *T* specifies the type of the return value of the method. Use the *Result* property of the task to wait for the task to complete and return the value:
	
	``
	Task<int> calculateValueTask = new Task<int>(() =>
	calculateValue(...));
	calculateValueTask.Start(); // Invoke the calculateValue method
	...
	int calculatedData = calculateValueTask.Result; // Block until
	calculateValueTask completes
	``

To	Do this
Perform loop iterations and statement sequences by using parallel tasks	Use the *Parallel.For* and *Parallel.ForEach* methods to perform loop iterations by using tasks:

```
Parallel.For(0, 100, performLoopProcessing);
...
private void performLoopProcessing(int x)
{
    // Perform loop processing
}
```

Use the *Parallel.Invoke* method to perform concurrent method calls by using separate tasks:

```
Parallel.Invoke(
    doWork,
    doMoreWork,
    doYetMoreWork
);
```

To	Do this
Handle exceptions raised by one or more tasks	Catch the *AggregateException* exception. Use the *Handle* method to specify a method that can handle each exception in the *AggregateException* object. If the exception-handling method handles the exception, return *true*; otherwise, return *false*:

```
try
{
    Task task = Task.Factory.StartNew(...);
    ...
}
catch (AggregateException ae)
{
    ae.Handle(new Func<Exception, bool> (handleException));
}
...
private bool handleException(Exception e)
{
    if (e is TaskCanceledException)
    {
        ...
        return true;
    }
    else
    {
        return false;
    }
}
```

To	Do this
Support cancellation in a task	Implement cooperative cancellation by creating a *CancellationTokenSource* object and using a *CancellationToken* parameter in the method run by the task. In the task method, call the *ThrowIfCancellationRequested* method of the *CancellationToken* parameter to throw an *OperationCanceledException* exception and terminate the task: ```\nprivate void generateGraphData(..., CancellationToken token)\n{\n ...\n token.ThrowIfCancellationRequested();\n ...\n}\n```

Chapter 28
Performing Parallel Data Access

After completing this chapter, you will be able to:

- Use PLINQ to parallelize time-consuming LINQ queries.

- Use the parallel concurrent collection classes to maintain collections of data in a thread-safe manner.

- Use the parallel synchronization primitives to coordinate access to data being manipulated by concurrent tasks.

In Chapter 27, "Introducing the Task Parallel Library," you saw how to exploit the new features of the .NET Framework to perform operations in parallel. Earlier chapters also showed you how you can access data in a declarative manner by using Language Integrated Query (LINQ). A typical LINQ query generates an enumerable result set, and you can iterate serially through this set to retrieve the data. If the data source used to generate the result set is large, running a LINQ query can take a long time. Many database management systems faced with the issue of optimizing queries address this issue by using algorithms that break down the process of identifying the data for a query into a series of tasks, and then running these tasks in parallel, combining the results when the tasks have completed to generate the completed result set. The designers of the Task Parallel Library (TPL) decided to provide LINQ with a similar facility, and the result is Parallel LINQ, or PLINQ. You will study PLINQ in the first part of this chapter.

However, PLINQ is not always the most appropriate technology to use for an application. If you create your own tasks manually, you need to ensure that the concurrent threads that run the tasks coordinate their activities correctly. The TPL provides methods that enable you to wait for tasks to complete, and you can use these methods to coordinate tasks at a very coarse level. But consider what happens if two tasks attempt to access and modify the same data. If both tasks run at the same time, their overlapping operations might corrupt the data. This situation can lead to bugs that are difficult to correct, primarily because of their unpredictability. Since version 1.0, the Microsoft .NET Framework has provided primitives that you can use to lock data and coordinate threads, but to use them effectively you must have a good understanding of the way in which threads interact. The TPL includes some variations to these primitives, and it includes specialized collection classes that can synchronize access to data across tasks. These classes hide much of the complexity involved in coordinating data access. You will see how to use some of these new synchronization primitives and collection classes in the second half of this chapter.

Using PLINQ to Parallelize Declarative Data Access

In earlier chapters, you saw how powerful LINQ is for retrieving data from an enumerable data structure. In the .NET Framework 4.0, LINQ has been extended by using the technology available as part of the TPL to help you boost performance and parallelize some query operations. These extensions are PLINQ.

PLINQ works by dividing a data set into partitions, and then using tasks to retrieve the data that matches the criteria specified by the query for each partition in parallel. The results retrieved for each partition are combined into a single enumerable result set when the tasks have completed. PLINQ is ideal for scenarios that involve data sets with large numbers of elements, or if the criteria specified for matching data involve complex, expensive operations.

A primary aim of PLINQ is to be as nonintrusive as possible. If you have a lot of existing LINQ queries, you don't want to have to modify your code to enable them to run with the latest build of the .NET Framework. To achieve this, the .NET Framework includes the extension method *AsParallel* that you can use with an enumerable object. The *AsParallel* method returns a *ParallelQuery* object that acts in a similar manner to the original enumerable object except that it provides parallel implementations of many of the LINQ operators, such as *join* and *where*. These new implementations of the LINQ operators are based on the TPL and use various algorithms to try and run parts of your LINQ query in parallel wherever possible.

As ever in the world of parallel computing, the *AsParallel* method is not magic. You cannot guarantee that your code will speed up; it all depends on the nature of your LINQ queries and whether the tasks they are performing lend themselves to parallelization. To understand how PLINQ works and the situations in which it is useful, it helps to see some examples. The exercises in the following sections demonstrate a pair of simple scenarios.

Using PLINQ to Improve Performance While Iterating Through a Collection

The first scenario is simple. Consider a LINQ query that iterates through a collection and retrieves elements from the collection based on a processor-intensive calculation. This form of query can benefit from parallel execution as long as the calculations are independent. The elements in the collection can be divided into a number of partitions; the exact number depends on the current load of the computer and the number of CPUs available. The elements in each partition can be processed by a separate thread. When all the partitions have been processed, the results can be merged. Any collection that supports access to elements through an index, such as an array or a collection that implements the *IList<T>* interface, can be managed in this way.

> **Note** If the calculations require access to shared data, you must synchronize the threads. This can impose an overhead and might negate the benefits of parallelizing the query.

Parallelize a LINQ query over a simple collection

1. Using Microsoft Visual Studio 2010, open the PLINQ solution, located in the \Microsoft Press\Visual CSharp Step By Step\Chapter 28\PLINQ folder in your Documents folder.

2. In Solution Explorer, double-click Program.cs to display the file in the *Code and Text Editor* window.

    This is a console application. The skeleton structure of the application has already been created for you. The *Program* class contains two methods called *Test1* and *Test2* that illustrate a pair of common scenarios. The *Main* method calls each of these test methods in turn.

    Both test methods have the same general structure; they create a LINQ query, run it, and display the time taken. The code for each of these methods is almost completely separate from the statements that actually create and run the queries. You will add these statements as you progress through this set of exercises.

3. Locate the *Test1* method. This method creates a large array of integers and populates it with a set of random numbers between 0 and 200. The random number generator is seeded, so you should get the same results every time you run the application. You will add a LINQ query that retrieves all the numbers in this array that have a value greater than 100.

4. After the first *TO DO* comment in this method, add the LINQ query shown here in bold:

    ```
    // TO DO: Create a LINQ query that retrieves all numbers that are greater than 100
    var over100 = from n in numbers
                    where TestIfTrue(n > 100)
                    select n;
    ```

    The test *n > 100* is not computationally intensive enough by itself to show the benefits of parallelizing this query, so the code calls a method named *TestIfTrue*, which slows it down a little by performing a *SpinWait* operation. The *SpinWait* method causes the processor to continually execute a loop of special "no operation" instructions for a short period of time, keeping the processor busy but not actually doing any work. (This is known as *spinning*.) The *TestIfTrue* method looks like this:

    ```
    public static bool TestIfTrue(bool expr)
    {
        Thread.SpinWait(1000);
        return expr;
    }
    ```

5. After the second *TO DO* comment in the *Test1* method, add the following code shown in bold:

```
// TO DO: Run the LINQ query, and save the results in a List<int> object
List<int> numbersOver100 = new List<int>(over100);
```

Remember that LINQ queries use deferred execution, so they do not run until you retrieve the results from them. This statement creates a *List<int>* object and populates it with the results of running the *over100* query.

6. After the third *TO DO* comment in the *Test1* method, add the following statement shown in bold:

```
// TO DO: Display the results
Console.WriteLine("There are {0} numbers over 100.", numbersOver100.Count);
```

7. On the *Debug* menu, click *Start Without Debugging*. Note the time taken to run Test 1 and the number of items in the array that are greater than 100.

8. Run the application several times, and take an average for the time. Verify that the number of items greater than 100 is the same each time. Return to Microsoft Visual Studio when you have finished.

9. Each item returned by the LINQ query is independent of all the other rows, and this query is an ideal candidate for partitioning. Modify the statement that defines the LINQ query, and specify the *AsParallel* extension method to the *numbers* array, as shown here in bold:

```
var over100 = from n in numbers.AsParallel()
              where TestIfTrue(n > 100)
              select n;
```

10. On the *Debug* menu, click *Start Without Debugging*. Verify that the number of items reported by Test 1 is the same as before, but that the time taken to perform the test has decreased significantly. Run the test several times, and take an average of the duration required for the test. If you are running on a dual-core processor (or a twin-processor computer), you should see the time reduced by 40 to 45 percent. If you have more processor cores, the decrease should be even more dramatic.

11. Close the application, and return to Visual Studio.

The preceding exercise shows the performance improvement you can get by making a small change to a LINQ query. However, bear in mind that you will see results such as this only if the calculations performed by the query require significant CPU time. I cheated a little by spinning the processor. Without this overhead, the parallel version of the query is actually slower than the serial version. In the next exercise, you will see a LINQ query that joins two arrays in memory. This time, the exercise uses more realistic data volumes, so there is no need to slow down the query artificially.

Parallelize a LINQ query that joins two collections

1. In the *Code and Text Editor* window, locate the *CustomersInMemory* class.

   This class contains a public *string* array called *Customers*. Each *string* in the *Customers* array holds the data for a single customer, with the fields separated by commas; this format is typical of data that an application might read in from a text file that uses comma-separated fields. The first field contains the customer ID, the second field is the name of the company that the customer represents, and the remaining fields hold the address, city, country, and postal code.

2. Find the *OrdersInMemory* class.

   This class is similar to the *CustomersInMemory* class except that it contains a string array called *Orders*. The first field in each string is the order number, the second field is the customer ID, and the third field is the date that the order was placed.

3. Find the *OrderInfo* class. This class contains four fields that hold the customer ID, company name, order ID, and order date for an order. You will use a LINQ query to populate a collection of *OrderInfo* objects from the data in the *Customers* and *Orders* arrays.

4. Locate the *Test2* method in the *Program* class. In this method, you will create a LINQ query that joins the *Customers* and *Orders* arrays over the customer ID. The query will store each row of the result in an *OrderInfo* object.

5. In the *try* block in this method, add the code shown next in bold after the first TO DO comment:

```
// TO DO: Create a LINQ query that retrieves customers and orders from arrays
// Store each row returned in an OrderInfo object
var orderInfoQuery = from c in CustomersInMemory.Customers
                     join o in OrdersInMemory.Orders
                     on c.Split(',')[0] equals o.Split(',')[1]
                     select new OrderInfo
                     {
                         CustomerID = c.Split(',')[0],
                         CompanyName = c.Split(',')[1],
                         OrderID = Convert.ToInt32(o.Split(',')[0]),
                         OrderDate = Convert.ToDateTime(o.Split(',')[2], new
CultureInfo("en-US"))
                     };
```

This statement defines the LINQ query. Notice that it uses the *Split* method of the *String* class to split each string into an array of strings. The strings are split on the comma character. (The commas are stripped out.) One complication is that the dates in the array are held in US English format, so the code that converts them into *DateTime* objects in the *OrderInfo* object specifies the US English formatter. If you use the default formatter for your locale, the dates might not parse correctly.

6. In the *Test2* method, add the following code shown in bold after the second TO DO statement:

```
// TO DO: Run the LINQ query, and save the results in a List<OrderInfo> object
List<OrderInfo> orderInfo = new List<OrderInfo>(orderInfoQuery);
```

This statement runs the query and populates the *orderInfo* collection.

7. Add the statement shown here in bold after the third TO DO statement:

```
// TO DO: Display the results
Console.WriteLine("There are {0} orders", orderInfo.Count);
```

8. On the Debug menu, click *Start Without Debugging*.

Verify that Test 2 retrieves 830 orders, and note the duration of the test. Run the application several times to obtain an average duration and then return to Visual Studio.

9. In *theTest2* method, modify the LINQ query and add the *AsParallel* extension method to the *Customers* and *Orders* arrays, as shown here in bold:

```
var orderInfoQuery = from c in CustomersInMemory.Customers.AsParallel()
                     join o in OrdersInMemory.Orders.AsParallel()
                     on c.Split(',')[0] equals o.Split(',')[1]
                     select new OrderInfo
                     {
                         CustomerID = c.Split(',')[0],
                         CompanyName = c.Split(',')[1],
                         OrderID = Convert.ToInt32(o.Split(',')[0]),
                         OrderDate = Convert.ToDateTime(o.Split(',')[2], new
CultureInfo("en-US"))
                     };
```

> **Note** When you join two data sources in this way, they must both be *IEnumerable* objects or *ParallelQuery* objects. This means that if you specify the *AsParallel* method for one source you should also specify *AsParallel* for the other. If you fail to do this, the runtime will not parallelize the query and you will not gain any benefits.

10. Run the application several times again. Notice that the time taken for Test 2 should be significantly less than it was previously. PLINQ can make use of multiple threads to optimize join operations by fetching the data for each part of the join in parallel.

11. Close the application, and return to Visual Studio.

These two simple exercises have shown you the power of the *AsParallel* extension method and PLINQ. However, PLINQ is an evolving technology, and the internal implementation is very likely to change over time. Additionally, the volumes of data and the amount of processing you perform in a query also have a bearing on the effectiveness of using PLINQ. Therefore, you should not regard these exercises as defining fixed rules you should always follow. Rather, they illustrate the point that you should carefully measure and assess the likely performance or other benefits of using PLINQ with your own data in your own environment.

Specifying Options for a PLINQ Query

The *ParallelEnumerable* object returned by the *AsParallel* method exposes a number of methods you can use to influence the way in which a query is parallelized. For example, you can specify the number of tasks that you feel is optimal and override any decisions made by the runtime by using the *WithDegreeOfParallelism* method, like this:

```
var orderInfoQuery =
    from c in CustomersInMemory.Customers.AsParallel().WithDegreeOfParallelism(4)
    join o in OrdersInMemory.Orders.AsParallel()
    on ...
```

The value you specify applies across the entire query. Consequently, you should specify *WithDegreeOfParallelism* only once in a query. In the example just shown, the degree of parallelism applies to the *Customers* and the *Orders* objects.

On occasion, there might be instances when the runtime decides, by using its own heuristics, that parallelizing a query might be of little benefit. If you are certain this is not the case, you can use the *WithExecutionMode* method of the *ParallelQuery* class and force the runtime to parallelize the query. The following code shows an example:

```
var orderInfoQuery =
    from c in CustomersInMemory.Customers.AsParallel().WithExecutionMode(ParallelExecutionMo
de.ForceParallelism)
    join o in OrdersInMemory.Orders.AsParallel()
    on ...
```

Again, you can use *WithExecutionMode* only once in a query.

When you parallelize queries, you might affect the sequence in which data is returned. If ordering is important, you can specify the *AsOrdered* extension method of the *ParallelQuery* class. For example, if you want to return only the first few results from a query, it might be important to preserve the order to ensure that the query returns consistent results each time it runs, as shown in the following example, which uses the *Take* method to return the first 10 matching items from a data set:

```
var over100 = from n in numbers.AsParallel().AsOrdered().Take(10)
              where ...
              select n;
```

This will likely slow down the query, and you need to consider the tradeoffs between performance and ordering when implementing queries such as this.

Canceling a PLINQ Query

Unlike ordinary LINQ queries, a PLINQ query can be canceled. To do this, you specify a *CancellationToken* object from a *CancellationTokenSource* and use the *WithCancellation* extension method of the *ParallelQuery*.

```
CancellationToken tok = ...;
...
var orderInfoQuery =
    from c in CustomersInMemory.Customers.AsParallel().WithCancellation(tok)
    join o in OrdersInMemory.Orders.AsParallel()
    on ...
```

You specify *WithCancellation* only once in a query. Cancellation applies to all sources in the query. If the *CancellationTokenSource* object used to generate the *CancellationToken* is canceled, the query stops with an *OperationCanceledException* exception.

Synchronizing Concurrent Imperative Data Access

The TPL supplies a powerful framework that enables you to design and build applications that can take advantage of multiple CPU cores to perform tasks in parallel. However, as I alluded to in the introduction to this chapter, you need to be careful when building solutions that perform concurrent operations, especially if those operations share access to the same data.

The issue is that you have little control over how parallel operations are scheduled, or even the degree of parallelism that the operating system might provide to an application constructed by using the TPL. These decisions are left as run-time considerations and depend on the workload and hardware capabilities of the computer running your application. This level of abstraction was a deliberate design decision on the part of the development team within Microsoft, and it removes the need for you to understand the low-level threading and scheduling details when you build applications that require concurrent tasks. But this abstraction comes at a cost. Although it all appears to work magically, you must make some effort to understand how your code runs; otherwise, you can end up with applications that exhibit unpredictable (and erroneous) behavior, as shown in the following example:

```
using System;
using System.Threading;

class Program
{
    private const int NUMELEMENTS = 10;

    static void Main(string[] args)
    {
        SerialTest();
    }
```

```
static void SerialTest()
{
    int[] data = new int[NUMELEMENTS];
    int j = 0;

    for (int i = 0; i < NUMELEMENTS; i++)
    {
        j = i;
        doAdditionalProcessing();
        data[i] = j;
        doMoreAdditionalProcessing();
    }

    for (int i = 0; i < NUMELEMENTS; i++)
    {
        Console.WriteLine("Element {0} has value {1}", i, data[i]);
    }
}

static void doAdditionalProcessing()
{
    Thread.Sleep(10);
}

static void doMoreAdditionalProcessing()
{
    Thread.Sleep(10);
}
}
```

The *SerialTest* method populates an integer array with a set of values (in a rather long-winded way), and then iterates through this list, printing the index of each item in the array together with the value of the corresponding item. The *doAdditionalProcessing* and *doMore-AdditionalProcessing* methods simply simulate performing long-running operations as part of the processing that might cause the runtime to yield control of the processor. The output of the program method is shown here:

```
Element 0 has value 0
Element 1 has value 1
Element 2 has value 2
Element 3 has value 3
Element 4 has value 4
Element 5 has value 5
Element 6 has value 6
Element 7 has value 7
Element 8 has value 8
Element 9 has value 9
```

Now consider the *ParallelTest* method shown next. This method is the same as the *SerialTest* method except that it uses the *Parallel.For* construct to populate the *data* array by running concurrent tasks. The code in the lambda expression run by each task is identical to that in the initial *for* loop in the *SerialTest* method.

```
using System.Threading.Tasks;
...

static void ParallelTest()
{
    int[] data = new int[NUMELEMENTS];
    int j = 0;

    Parallel.For (0, NUMELEMENTS, (i) =>
    {
        j = i;
        doAdditionalProcessing();
        data[i] = j;
        doMoreAdditionalProcessing();
    });

    for (int i = 0; i < NUMELEMENTS; i++)
    {
        Console.WriteLine("Element {0} has value {1}", i, data[i]);
    }
}
```

The intention is for the *ParallelTest* method to perform the same operation as the *SerialTest* method, except that it uses concurrent tasks and (hopefully) runs a little faster as a result. The problem is that it might not always work as expected. Some sample output generated by the *ParallelTest* method is shown here:

```
Element 0 has value 1
Element 1 has value 1
Element 2 has value 4
Element 3 has value 8
Element 4 has value 4
Element 5 has value 1
Element 6 has value 4
Element 7 has value 8
Element 8 has value 8
Element 9 has value 9
```

The values assigned to each item in the *data* array are not always the same as the values generated by using the *SerialTest* method. Additionally, further runs of the *ParallelTest* method can produce different sets of results.

If you examine the logic in the *Paralell.For* construct, you should see where the problem lies. The lambda expression contains the following statements:

```
j = i;
doAdditionalProcessing();
data[i] = j;
doMoreAdditionalProcessing();
```

The code looks innocuous enough. It copies the current value of the variable *i* (the index variable identifying which iteration of the loop is running) into the variable *j*, and later on it stores the value of *j* in the element of the data array indexed by *i*. If *i* contains 5, then *j* is assigned the value 5, and later on the value of *j* is stored in *data[5]*. The problem is that between assigning the value to *j* and then reading it back, the code does more work; it calls the *doAdditionalProcessing* method. If this method takes a long time to execute, the runtime might suspend the thread and schedule another task. A concurrent task running another iteration of the *Parallel.For* construct might run and assign a new value to *j*. Consequently, when the original task resumes, the value of *j* it assigns to *data[5]* is not the value it stored, and the result is data corruption. More troublesome is that sometimes this code might run as expected and produce the correct results, and at other times it does not; it all depends on how busy the computer is and when the various tasks are scheduled. Consequently, these types of bugs can lie dormant during testing and then suddenly manifest themselves in a production environment.

The variable *j* is shared by all the concurrent tasks. If a task stores a value in *j* and later reads it back, it has to ensure that no other task has modified *j* in the meantime. This requires synchronizing access to the variable across all concurrent tasks that can access it. One way in which you can achieve synchronized access is to lock data.

Locking Data

The C# language provides locking semantics through the *lock* keyword, which you can use to guarantee exclusive access to resources. You use the *lock* keyword like this:

```
object myLockObject = new object();
...
lock (myLockObject)
{
    // Code that requires exclusive access to a shared resource
    ...
}
```

The *lock* statement attempts to obtain a mutual-exclusion lock over the specified object (you can actually use any reference type, not just *object*), and it blocks if this same object is currently locked by another thread. When the thread obtains the lock, the code in the block following the *lock* statement runs. At the end of this block, the lock is released. If another thread is blocked waiting for the lock, it can then grab the lock and continue its processing.

If an object is locked, what should a thread do while waiting for the lock to be released? There are at least two answers. The thread can be put to sleep until the lock becomes available. This requires the runtime to perform a significant amount of work, including saving the state of the thread and queuing the thread for later execution when the lock becomes available. If the lock is held only for a small duration, the overhead of suspending, rescheduling, and resuming the thread can exceed the time taken for the lock to become available, which in turn affects the performance of your application. An alternative strategy is to let the thread spin the processor (in the style of the *Thread.SpinWait* method you saw earlier in this chapter) until the lock is released, at which point it can quickly obtain the lock and continue. This mechanism avoids the overhead of suspending and resuming the thread; however, if the wait is lengthy, this action can occupy the processor and consume resources while doing no useful work, and this will also impact the performance of your application.

Internally, the *lock* statement uses the *System.Threading.Monitor* class to lock the specified object. The *Monitor* class follows an intelligent algorithm to minimize the potential overhead associated with locking an object and waiting for the lock to be released. When a thread requests a lock, if the same object is currently locked by another thread, the waiting thread spins the processor for a small number of iterations. If the lock is not obtained during this period, the thread is then put to sleep and suspended. The thread is resumed when the lock is released. In this way, short waits are very responsive while longer waits do not impact the performance of other threads too drastically.

The *lock* keyword is fine for many simple scenarios, but there are situations in which you might have more complex requirements. The TPL includes a number of additional synchronization primitives you can use to address these situations. The following sections summarize some of these primitives. The primitives have been designed to operate not only with the TPL, but with any multithreaded code. They are all located in the *System.Threading* namespace.

Note The .NET Framework has included a good set of synchronization primitives ever since its initial release. The following section describes only the new primitives added as part of the TPL. There is some overlap between the new primitives and those provided previously. Where overlapping functionality exists, you should use the primitives in the TPL because they have been designed and optimized for computers with multiple CPUs.

Detailed discussion of the theory of all the possible synchronization mechanisms available for building multithreaded applications is outside the scope of this book. For more information about the general theory of multiple threads and synchronization, see the topic "Synchronizing Data for Multithreading" in the .NET Framework Developers Guide, provided as part of the documentation with Visual Studio 2010.

Important You should not use locking and the synchronization primitives as a substitute for good design or proper programming practice. The .NET Framework provides many other mechanisms you can use to maximize parallelism while reducing the potential overhead associated with locking data. For example, if multiple tasks must update common information in a collection, you can use thread-local storage (TLS) to hold the data used by the threads running each task. To create a variable in TLS, declare the variable as a static class member and then prefix it with the *ThreadStatic* attribute, like this:

```
[ThreadStatic]
static Hashtable privateDataForThread;
```

Although the *Hashtable* variable is declared as static, it is not shared by all instances of the class in which it is defined. Instead, a copy of the static variable is held in TLS. If two concurrent tasks access this variable, they each get their own copy in TLS. When the tasks have completed, they can return their copy of the static data and you can aggregate these results together. Detailed discussion of TLS is outside the scope of this book, but for more information see the documentation provided with Visual Studio 2010.

Synchronization Primitives in the Task Parallel Library

Most synchronization primitives take the form of locking mechanisms that restrict access to a resource while a thread holds the lock. The TPL supports a variety of locking techniques you can use to implement different styles of concurrent access, ranging from simple exclusive locks (where a single thread has sole access to a resource) to semaphores (where multiple threads can access a resource simultaneously, but in a controlled manner) to reader/writer locks that enable different threads to share read-only access to a resource while guaranteeing exclusive access to a thread that needs to modify the resource.

The *ManualResetEventSlim* Class

The *ManualResetEventSlim* class provides functionality that enables one or more threads to wait for an event. A *ManualResetEventSlim* object can be in one of two states: *signaled* (true) and *unsignaled* (false). A thread creates a *ManualResetEventSlim* object and specifies its initial state. Other threads can wait for the *ManualResetEventSlim* object to be signaled by calling the *Wait* method. If the *ManualResetEventSlim* object is in the unsignaled state, the *Wait* method blocks the threads. Another thread can change the state of the *ManualResetEventSlim* object to *signaled* by calling the *Set* method. This action releases all threads waiting on the *ManualResetEventSlim* object, which can then resume running. The *Reset* method changes the state of a *ManualResetEventSlim* object back to unsignaled.

When a thread waits for an event, it spins. However, if the wait exceeds a number of spin cycles, the thread is suspended and yields the processor in a manner similar to that of the *Monitor* class described earlier. You can specify the number of spin cycles that occur before suspending the thread in the constructor for a *ManualResetEventSlim* object, and you can determine how many spin cycles will be performed before the thread is suspended by querying the *SpinCount* property. You can ascertain the state of a *ManualResetEventSlim* object by examining the Boolean *IsSet* property.

The following example creates two tasks that access the integer variable *i*. The first task uses a *do/while* loop to repeatedly display the value of *i* and increment it until the value of *i* reaches 10. The second task waits for the first task to finish updating *i*; it then reads the value of *i* and displays it. The tasks use a *ManualResetEventSlim* object to coordinate their activities. The *ManualResetEventSlim* object is initialized to the *unsignaled* state (false), and it specifies that a thread waiting on this object can spin 100 times before it is suspended. The first task signals the *ManualResetEventSlim* object at the end of the loop. The second task waits for the *ManualResetEventSlim* object to be signaled. In this way, the second task reads *i* only when it has reached 10.

```
ManualResetEventSlim resetEvent = new ManualResetEventSlim(false, 100);
int i = 0;

Task t1 = Task.Factory.StartNew(() =>
    {
        do
        {
            Console.WriteLine("Task t1. i is {0}", i);
            i++;
        } while (i < 10);
        resetEvent.Set();
    });

Task t2 = Task.Factory.StartNew(() =>
    {
        resetEvent.Wait();
        Console.WriteLine("Task t2. i is {0}", i);
    });

Task.WaitAll(t1, t2);
```

The output from this code looks like this:

```
Task t1. i is 0
Task t1. i is 1
Task t1. i is 2
Task t1. i is 3
Task t1. i is 4
Task t1. i is 5
Task t1. i is 6
Task t1. i is 7
Task t1. i is 8
Task t1. i is 9
Task t2. i is 10
```

The *SemaphoreSlim* Class

You can use the *SemaphoreSlim* class to control access to a pool of resources. A *SemaphoreSlim* object has an initial value (a non-negative integer) and an optional maximum value. Typically, the initial value of a *SemaphoreSlim* object is the number of resources in the pool. Threads accessing the resources in the pool first call the *Wait* method. This method attempts to decrement the value of the *SemaphoreSlim* object, and if the result is non-zero the thread is allowed to continue and can take a resource from the pool. When it has finished, the thread should call the *Release* method on the *SemaphoreSlim* object. This action increments the value of the *Semaphore*.

If a thread calls the *Wait* method and the result of decrementing the value of the *SemaphoreSlim* object would result in a negative value, the thread waits until another thread calls *Release*. The thread spins initially, but the thread is suspended if the waiting time is too long.

The *SemaphoreSlim* class also provides the *CurrentCount* property, which you can use to determine whether a *Wait* operation is likely to succeed immediately or will result in blocking. The following example shows how to create a *SemaphoreSlim* object to protect a pool of three shared resources. Concurrent tasks can call the *Wait* method before they access a resource from this pool, and they call the *Release* method when they have finished. In this way, no more than three tasks can use a resource at any one time—the fourth task will be blocked until one of the first three calls *Release*.

```
// SemaphoreSlim object shared by threads
SemaphoreSlim semaphore = new SemaphoreSlim(3);
...
Task t1 = Task.Factory.StartNew(() =>
    {
        semaphore.Wait();
        // Access a resource from the pool
        semaphore.Release();
    });

Task t2 = Task.Factory.StartNew(() =>
    {
        semaphore.Wait();
        // Access a resource from the pool
        semaphore.Release();
    });

Task t3 = Task.Factory.StartNew(() =>
    {
        semaphore.Wait();
        // Access a resource from the pool
        semaphore.Release();
    });
```

```
Task t4 = Task.Factory.StartNew(() =>
    {
        // This task will be blocked until one of the previous three calls Release
        semaphore.Wait();
        // Access a resource from the pool
        semaphore.Release();
    });

Task.WaitAll(t1, t2, t3, t4);
```

The *CountdownEvent* Class

You can think of the *CountdownEvent* class as a cross between the inverse of a semaphore and a manual reset event. When a thread creates a *CountdownEvent* object, it specifies an initial value (a non-negative integer). One or more threads can call the *Wait* method of the *CountdownEvent* object, and if its value is non-zero the threads are blocked. (The thread spins initially and is then suspended.) *Wait* does not decrement the value of the *CountdownEvent* object; instead, other threads can call the *Signal* method to reduce the value. When the value of the *CountdownEvent* object reaches zero, all blocked threads are signaled and can resume running.

A thread can set the value of a *CountdownEvent* object back to the value specified in its constructor by using the *Reset* method, and a thread can increase the value by calling the *AddCount* method. You can query the value of a *CountdownEvent* object and determine whether a call to *Wait* is likely to block by examining the *CurrentCount* property. The following code creates a *CountdownEvent* object that must be signaled five times before threads blocked waiting for it can continue. The *countDownWaitTask* waits on this object, and the task *countDownSignalTask* signals it five times.

```
CountdownEvent countDown = new CountdownEvent(5);

Task countDownWaitTask = Task.Factory.StartNew(() =>
    {
        countDown.Wait();
        Console.WriteLine("CountdownEvent has been signaled 5 times");
    });

Task countDownSignalTask = Task.Factory.StartNew(() =>
    {
        for (int i = 0; i < 5; i++)
        {
            Console.WriteLine("Signaling CountdownEvent");
            countDown.Signal();
        }
    });

Task.WaitAll(countDownWaitTask, countDownSignalTask);
```

The output from this code is shown here:

```
Signaling CountdownEvent
Signaling CountdownEvent
Signaling CountdownEvent
Signaling CountdownEvent
Signaling CountdownEvent
CountdownEvent has been signaled 5 times
```

The *ReaderWriterLockSlim* Class

The *ReaderWriterLockSlim* class is an advanced synchronization primitive that supports a single writer and multiple readers. The idea is that modifying (writing) to a resource requires exclusive access, but reading a resource does not; multiple readers can access the same resource at the same time.

A thread that wants to read a resource calls the *EnterReadLock* method of a *ReaderWriterLockSlim* object. This action grabs a read lock on the object. When the thread has finished with the resource, it calls the *ExitReadLock* method, which releases the read lock. Multiple threads can read the same resource at the same time, and each thread obtains its own read lock.

If a thread wants to modify the resource, it calls the *EnterWriteLock* method of the same *ReaderWriterLockSlim* object to obtain a write lock. If one or more threads currently have a read lock for this object, the *EnterWriteLock* method blocks until they are all released. The thread can then modify the resource and call the *ExitWriteLock* method to release the write lock. A *ReaderWriterLockSlim* object has only a single write lock. If another thread attempts to obtain the write lock, it is blocked until the first thread releases the write lock.

To ensure that writing threads are not blocked indefinitely, as soon as a thread requests the write lock all subsequent calls to *EnterReadLock* are blocked until the write lock has been obtained and released.

The blocking mechanism is similar to that used by the other primitives described in this section; it spins the processor for a number of cycles before suspending the thread if it is still blocked.

The following code creates a *ReaderWriterLockSlim* object to protect a shared resource and then creates three tasks. Two of the tasks obtain a read lock over the object, and the third obtains a write lock. The two tasks *readerTask1* and *readerTask2* can access the shared resource simultaneously, but the task *writerTask* can access the resource only when *readerTask1* and *readerTask2* have both released their read locks.

```
ReaderWriterLockSlim readerWriterLock = new ReaderWriterLockSlim();

Task readerTask1 = Task.Factory.StartNew(() =>
    {
        readerWriterLock.EnterReadLock();
        // Read shared resource
        readerWriterLock.ExitReadLock();
    });

Task readerTask2 = Task.Factory.StartNew(() =>
    {
        readerWriterLock.EnterReadLock();
        // Read shared resource
        readerWriterLock.ExitReadLock();
    });

Task writerTask = Task.Factory.StartNew(() =>
    {
        readerWriterLock.EnterWriteLock();
        // Write to shared resource
        readerWriterLock.ExitWriteLock();
    });

Task.WaitAll(readerTask1, readerTask2, writerTask);
```

The *Barrier* Class

The *Barrier* class enables you to temporarily halt the execution of a set of threads at a particular point in an application and continue only when all threads have reached this point. It is useful for synchronizing threads that need to perform a series of concurrent operations in step with each other.

When a thread creates a *Barrier* object, it specifies the number of threads in the set that will be synchronized. You can think of this value as a thread counter maintained internally inside the *Barrier* class. This value can be amended later by calling the *AddParticipant* or *RemoveParticipant* methods. When a thread reaches a synchronization point, it calls the *SignalAndWait* method of the *Barrier* object, which decrements the thread counter inside the *Barrier* object. If this counter is greater than zero, the thread is blocked. Only when the counter reaches zero are all the threads waiting on the *Barrier* object released and only then can they continue running.

The *Barrier* class provides the *ParticipantCount* property, which specifies the number of threads that it synchronizes, and the *ParticipantsRemaining* property, which indicates how many threads need to call *SignalAndWait* before the barrier is raised and blocked threads can continue running.

You can also specify a delegate in the *Barrier* constructor. This delegate can refer to a method that runs when all the threads have arrived at the barrier. The *Barrier* object is passed in as a parameter to this method. The barrier is not raised and the threads are not released until this method completes.

The following example creates a *Barrier* object that synchronizes three threads and provides a lambda expression that runs when the *Barrier* is signaled. The tasks *t1*, *t2*, and *t3* all call *SignalAndWait* on this barrier. The tasks can continue only when all three have signaled the barrier and the delegate specified by the *Barrier* object has completed.

```
Barrier barrier = new Barrier(3, (x) =>
{
    Console.WriteLine("All tasks have reached the barrier");
});

Task t1 = Task.Factory.StartNew(() =>
    {
        Console.WriteLine("Task t1 starting");
        barrier.SignalAndWait();
        Console.WriteLine("Task t1 continuing after the barrier");
    });

Task t2 = Task.Factory.StartNew(() =>
    {
        Console.WriteLine("Task t2 starting");
        barrier.SignalAndWait();
        Console.WriteLine("Task t2 continuing after the barrier");
    });

Task t3 = Task.Factory.StartNew(() =>
    {
        Console.WriteLine("Task t3 starting");
        barrier.SignalAndWait();
        Console.WriteLine("Task t3 continuing after the barrier");
    });

Task.WaitAll(t1, t2, t3);
```

The output from this code looks like this (the order in which the tasks start and resume after the barrier has been raised can vary):

```
Task t1 starting
Task t2 starting
Task t3 starting
All tasks have reached the barrier
Task t3 continuing after the barrier
Task t1 continuing after the barrier
Task t2 continuing after the barrier
```

Cancellation and the Synchronization Primitives

The *ManualResetEventSlim*, *SemaphoreSlim*, *CountdownEvent*, and *Barrier* classes all support cancellation by following the cancellation model described in Chapter 27. The wait operations for each of these classes can take an optional *CancellationToken* parameter, retrieved from a *CancellationTokenSource* object. If you call the *Cancel* method of the *CancellationTokenSource* object, each wait operation referencing a *CancellationToken* generated from this source is aborted with an *OperationCanceledException* exception.

> **Note** If the wait operation is being executed by a task, *OperationCanceledException* is wrapped in an *AggregateException*, as described in Chapter 27.

The following code shows how to invoke the *Wait* method of a *SemaphoreSlim* object and specify a cancellation token. If the wait operation is canceled, the *OperationCanceledException* catch handler runs.

```
CancellationTokenSource cancellationTokenSource = new CancellationTokenSource();
CancellationToken cancellationToken = cancellationTokenSource.Token;
...
// Semaphore that protects a pool of 3 resources
SemaphoreSlim semaphoreSlim = new SemaphoreSlim(3);
...
// Wait on the semaphore, and catch the OperationCanceledException if
// another thread calls Cancel on cancellationTokenSource
try
{
    semaphoreSlim.Wait(cancellationToken);
}
catch (OperationCanceledException e)
{
    ...
}
```

The Concurrent Collection Classes

A common requirement of many multithreaded applications is to store and retrieve data in a collection. The standard collection classes provided with the .NET Framework are not thread-safe by default, although you can use the synchronization primitives described in the previous section to wrap code that adds, queries, and removes elements in a collection. However, this process is potentially error-prone and not very scalable, so the .NET Framework 4.0 Class Library includes a small set of thread-safe collection classes and interfaces in the *System.Collections.Concurrent* namespace that are designed specifically for use with the TPL. The following table briefly summarizes these types.

Class	Description
ConcurrentBag<T>	This is a general-purpose class for holding an unordered collection of items. It includes methods to insert (*Add*), remove (*TryTake*), and examine (*TryPeek*) items in the collection. These methods are thread-safe. The collection is also enumerable, so you can iterate over its contents by using a *foreach* statement.
ConcurrentDictionary<TKey, TValue>	This class implements a thread-safe version of the generic *Dictionary<TKey, TValue>* collection class described in Chapter 18, "Introducing Generics." It provides the methods *TryAdd*, *ContainsKey*, *TryGetValue*, *TryRemove*, and *TryUpdate*, which you can use to add, query, remove, and modify items in the dictionary.
ConcurrentQueue<T>	This class provides a thread-safe version of the generic *Queue<T>* class described in Chapter 18. It includes the methods *Enqueue*, *TryDequeue*, and *TryPeek*, which you can use to add, remove, and query items in the queue.
ConcurrentStack<T>	This is a thread-safe implementation of the generic *Stack<T>* class, also described in Chapter 18. It provides methods such as *Push*, *TryPop*, and *TryPeek*, which you can use to push, pop, and query items on the stack.
IProducerConsumerCollection<T>	This interface defines methods for implementing classes that exhibit producer/consumer behavior. A producer adds items to a collection, and a consumer reads (and possibly removes) items from the same collection. It is frequently used to define types that work with the *BlockingCollection<T>* class described next in this table.
	The *IProducerConsumerCollection* interface defines methods to add (*TryAdd*) items to a collection, remove (*TryTake*) items from a collection, and obtain an enumerator (*GetEnumerator*) to enable an application to iterate through a collection. (The interface defines other methods and properties as well.) You can implement this interface and create your own custom concurrent collection classes. The *ConcurrentBag<T>*, *ConcurrentQueue<T>*, and *ConcurrentStack<T>* classes all implement this interface.
BlockingCollection<T>	This class is useful for building applications based on producers and consumers that access the same collection. The *type* parameter references a type that implements the *IProducerConsumerCollection<T>* interface and adds blocking capabilities to it.
	It achieves this feat by acting as a thread-safe adapter; it provides methods such as *Add* and *Take* that wrap calls to the *TryAdd* and *TryTake* methods in the underlying collection by using code that creates and uses the synchronization primitives described earlier. The *BlockingCollection<T>* class can also limit the number of items held in the underlying collection.

The following code shows how to use a *BlockingCollection<T>* object to wrap an instance of a user-defined type called *MyCollection<T>* that implements the *IProducerConsumerCollection* interface. It limits the number of items in the underlying collection to 1000.

```
class MyCollection<T> : IProducerConsumerCollection<T>
{
    // Implementation details not shown
    ...
}

...

// Create an instance of MyCollection<T>,
// and wrap it in a BlockingCollection<T> object
MyCollection<int> intCollection = new MyCollection<int>();
BlockingCollection<int> collection = new BlockingCollection<int>(myCollection, 1000);
```

> **Note** You can also instantiate a *BlockingCollection<T>* object without specifying a collection class. In this case, the *BlockingCollection<T>* object creates a *ConcurrentQueue<T>* object internally.

Adding thread-safety to the methods in a collection class imposes additional runtime overhead, so these classes are not as fast as the regular collection classes. You need to bear this fact in mind when deciding whether to parallelize a set of operations that require access to a shared collection.

Using a Concurrent Collection and a Lock to Implement Thread-Safe Data Access

In the following set of exercises, you will implement an application that calculates PI by using a geometric approximation. Initially, you will perform the calculation in a single-threaded manner; then you will change the code to perform the calculation by using parallel tasks. In the process, you will uncover some data synchronization issues you need to address and that you will solve by using a concurrent collection class and a lock to ensure that the tasks coordinate their activities correctly.

The algorithm you will implement calculates PI based on some simple mathematics and statistical sampling. If you draw a circle of radius *r* and draw a square with sides that touch the circle, the sides of the square are *2 * r* in length as shown in the following image:

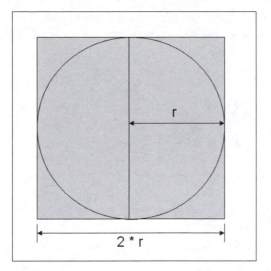

The area of the square, *S*, is calculated as follows:

*(2 * r) * (2 * r)*

or

*4 * r * r*

The area of the circle, *C*, is calculated as follows:

*PI * r * r*

Using these areas, you can calculate PI as follows:

*4 * C / S*

The trick is to determine the value of the ratio *C / S*. This is where the statistical sampling comes in.

To do this, generate a set of random points that lie within the square and count how many of these points also fall within the circle. If you have generated a sufficiently large and random sample, the ratio of points that lie within the circle to the points that lie within the square (and also in the circle) approximates the ratio of the areas of the two shapes, *C / S*. All you have to do is count them.

How do you determine whether a point lies within the circle? To help visualize the solution, draw the square on a piece of graph paper with the center of the square at the origin, point (0, 0). You can then generates pairs of values, or coordinates, that lie within the range (*-r, -r*) to (*+r, +r*). You can determine whether any set of coordinates *(x, y)* lie within the circle by applying Pythagoras' theorem to determine the distance *d* of these coordinates from the origin.

You can calculate *d* as the square root of *((x * x) + (y * y))*. If *d* is less than or equal to *r*, the radius of the circle, then the coordinates *(x, y)* specify a point within the circle, as shown in the following diagram:

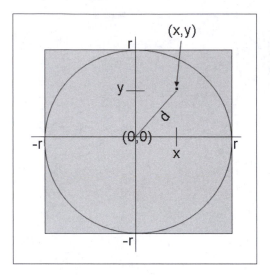

You can simplify matters further by generating only coordinates that lie in the upper right quadrant of the graph so that you only have to generate pairs of random numbers between 0 and *r*. This is the approach you will take in the exercises.

> **Note** The exercises in this chapter are intended to run on a computer with a multicore processor. If you have only a single-core CPU, you will not observe the same effects. Also, you should not start any additional programs or services between exercises because these might affect the results you see.

Calculate PI by using a single thread

1. Start Microsoft Visual Studio 2010 if it is not already running.

2. Open the CalculatePI solution, located in the \Microsoft Press\Visual CSharp Step By Step\Chapter 28\CalculatePI folder in your Documents folder.

3. In Solution Explorer, double-click Program.cs to display the file in the *Code and Text Editor* window.

    This is a console application. The skeleton structure of the application has already been created for you.

4. Scroll to the bottom of the file, and examine the *Main* method. It looks like this:

```
static void Main(string[] args)
{
    double pi = SerialPI();
    Console.WriteLine("Geometric approximation of PI calculated serially: {0}", pi);

    Console.WriteLine();
    pi = ParallelPI();
    Console.WriteLine("Geometric approximation of PI calculated in parallel: {0}",
pi);
}
```

This code calls the *SerialPI* method, which will calculate PI by using the geometric algorithm described before this exercise. The value is returned as a *double* and displayed. The code then calls the *ParallelPI* method, which will perform the same calculation but by using concurrent tasks. The result displayed should be exactly the same as that returned by the *SerialPI* method.

5. Examine the *SerialPI* method.

```
static double SerialPI()
{
    List<double> pointsList = new List<double>();
    Random random = new Random(SEED);
    int numPointsInCircle = 0;
    Stopwatch timer = new Stopwatch();
    timer.Start();

    try
    {
        // TO DO: Implement the geometric approximation of PI
        return 0;
    }
    finally
    {
        long milliseconds = timer.ElapsedMilliseconds;
        Console.WriteLine("SerialPI complete: Duration: {0} ms", milliseconds);
        Console.WriteLine("Points in pointsList: {0}. Points within circle: {1}",
pointsList.Count, numPointsInCircle);
    }
}
```

This method will generate a large set of coordinates and calculates the distances of each set of coordinates from the origin. The size of the set is specified by the constant *NUMPOINTS* at the top of the *Program* class. The bigger this value is, the greater the set of coordinates and the more accurate is the value of PI calculated by this method. If you have sufficient memory, you can increase the value of *NUMPOINTS*. Similarly, if you find that the application throws *OutOfMemoryException* exceptions when you run it, you can reduce this value.

You store the distance of each point from the origin in the *pointsList List<double>* collection. The data for the coordinates is generated by using the *random* variable. This is a *Random* object, seeded with a constant to generate the same set of random numbers each time you run the program. (This helps you determine that it is running correctly.) You can change the *SEED* constant at the top of the *Program* class if you want to seed the random number generator with a different value.

You use the *numPointsInCircle* variable to count the number of points in the *pointsList* collection that lie within the bounds of the circle. The radius of the circle is specified by the *RADIUS* constant at the top of the *Program* class.

To help you compare performance between this method and the *ParallelPI* method, the code creates a *Stopwatch* variable called *timer* and starts it running. The *finally* block determines how long the calculation took and displays the result. For reasons that will be described later, the *finally* block also displays the number of items in the *pointsList* collection and the number of points that it found that lay within the circle.

You will add the code that actually performs the calculation to the *try* block in the next few steps.

6. In the *try* block, delete the comment and remove the *return* statement. (This statement was provided only to ensure that the code compiles.) Add the *for* block and statements shown next in bold to the *try* block:

```
try
{
    for (int points = 0; points < NUMPOINTS; points++)
    {
        int xCoord = random.Next(RADIUS);
        int yCoord = random.Next(RADIUS);
        double distanceFromOrigin = Math.Sqrt(xCoord * xCoord + yCoord * yCoord);
        pointsList.Add(distanceFromOrigin);
        doAdditionalProcessing();
    }
}
```

This block of code generates a pair of coordinate values that lie in the range 0 to *RADIUS*, and it stores them in the *xCoord* and *yCoord* variables. The code then uses Pythagoras' theorem to calculate the distance of these coordinates from the origin and adds the result to the *pointsList* collection.

Note Although there is a little bit of computational work performed by this block of code, in a real-world scientific application you are likely to include far more complex calculations that will keep the processor occupied for longer. To simulate this situation, this block of code calls another method, *doAdditionalProcessing*. All this method does is occupy a number of CPU cycles as shown in the following code sample. I opted to follow this approach to better demonstrate the data synchronization requirements of multiple tasks rather than have you write an application that performs a highly complex calculation such as a Fast Fourier Transform to keep the CPU occupied:

```
private static void doAdditionalProcessing()
{
    Thread.SpinWait(SPINWAITS);
}
```

SPINWAITS is another constant defined at the top of the *Program* class.

7. In the *SerialPI* method, in the *try* block, add the *foreach* statement shown next in bold after the *for* block:

```
try
{
    for (int points = 0; points < NUMPOINTS; points++)
    {
        ...
    }

    foreach (double datum in pointsList)
    {
        if (datum <= RADIUS)
        {
            numPointsInCircle++;
        }
    }
}
```

This code iterates through the *pointsList* collection and examines each value in turn. If the value is less than or equal to the radius of the circle, it increments the *numPointsIn-Circle* variable. At the end of this loop, *numPointsInCircle* should contain the total number of coordinates that were found to lie within the bounds of the circle.

8. Add the following statements shown in bold to the *try* block, after the *foreach* block:

```
try
{
    for (int points = 0; points < NUMPOINTS; points++)
    {
        ...
    }

    foreach (double datum in pointsList)
    {
        ...
    }

    double pi = 4.0 * numPointsInCircle / NUMPOINTS;
    return pi;
}
```

These statements calculate PI based on the ratio of the number of points that lie within the circle to the total number of points, using the formula described earlier. The value is returned as the result of the method.

9. On the Debug menu, click *Start Without Debugging*.

The program runs and displays its approximation of PI, as shown in the following image. (It took just over 46 seconds on my computer, so be prepared to wait for a little while.) The time taken to calculate the result is also displayed. (You can ignore the results from the *ParallelPI* method because you have not written the code for this method yet.)

```
C:\Windows\system32\cmd.exe
SerialPI complete: Duration: 46180 ms
Points in pointsList: 10000000. Points within circle: 7853722
Geometric approximation of PI calculated serially: 3.1414888

ParallelPI complete: Duration: 0 ms
Points in pointsList: 0. Points within circle: 0
Geometric approximation of PI calculated in parallel: 0
Press any key to continue . . . _
```

 Note Apart from the timing, your results should be the same unless you have changed the *NUMPOINTS*, *RADIUS*, or *SEED* constants.

10. Close the console window, and return to Visual Studio.

In the *SerialPI* method, the code in the *for* loop that generates the points and calculates their distance from the origin is an obvious area that can parallelized. This is what you will do in the next exercise.

Calculate PI by using parallel tasks

1. In Solution Explorer, double-click Program.cs to display the file in the *Code and Text Editor* window if it is not already open.

2. Locate the *ParallelPI* method. It contains exactly the same code as the initial version of the *SerialPI* method before you added the code to the *try* block to calculate PI.

3. In the *try* block, delete the comment and remove the *return* statement. Add the *Parallel.For* statement shown next in bold to the *try* block:

```
try
{
    Parallel.For (0, NUMPOINTS, (x) =>
    {
        int xCoord = random.Next(RADIUS);
        int yCoord = random.Next(RADIUS);
        double distanceFromOrigin = Math.Sqrt(xCoord * xCoord + yCoord * yCoord);
```

```
        pointsList.Add(distanceFromOrigin);
        doAdditionalProcessing();
    });
}
```

This construct is the parallel analog of the code in the *for* loop in the *SerialPI* method. The body of the original *for* loop is wrapped in a lambda expression.

4. Add the following code shown in bold to the *try* block after the *Parallel.For* statement. This code is exactly the same as the corresponding statements in the *SerialPI* method.

```
try
{
    Parallel.For (...
    );

    foreach (double datum in pointsList)
    {
        if (datum <= RADIUS)
        {
            numPointsInCircle++;
        }
    }

    double pi = 4.0 * numPointsInCircle / NUMPOINTS;
    return pi;
}
```

5. On the Debug menu, click *Start Without Debugging*.

   The program runs. The following image shows the typical output:

The value calculated by the *SerialPI* method should be exactly the same as before. However, the result of the *ParallelPI* method looks somewhat suspect. The random number generator is seeded with the same value as that used by the *SerialPI* method, so it should produce the same sequence of random numbers with the same result and the same number of points within the circle. Another curious point is that the *point-sList* collection in the *ParallelPI* method seems to contain fewer points than the same collection in the *SerialPI* method.

 Note If the *pointsList* collection actually contains the expected number of items, run the application again. You should find that it contains fewer items than expected in most (but not necessarily all) runs.

6. Close the console window, and return to Visual Studio.

So what went wrong with the parallel calculation? A good place to start is the number of items in the *pointsList* collection. This collection is a generic *List<double>* object. However, this type is not thread-safe. The code in the *Parallel.For* statement calls the *Add* method to append a value to the collection, but remember that this code is being executed by tasks running as concurrent threads. Consequently, given the number of items being added to the collection, it is highly probable that some of the calls to *Add* will interfere with each other and cause some corruption. A solution is to use one of the collections from the *System.Collections.Concurrent* namespace because these collections are thread-safe. The generic *ConcurrentBag<T>* class in this namespace is probably the most suitable collection to use for this example.

Use a thread-safe collection

1. In Solution Explorer, double-click Program.cs to display the file in the *Code and Text Editor* window if it is not already open.

2. Locate the *ParallelPI* method. At the start of this method, replace the statement that instantiates the *List<double>* collection with code that creates a *ConcurrentBag<double>* collection, as shown here in bold:

```
static double ParallelPI()
{
    ConcurrentBag<double> pointsList = new ConcurrentBag <double>();
    Random random = ...;
    ...
}
```

3. On the Debug menu, click *Start Without Debugging*.

The program runs and displays its approximation of PI by using the *SerialPI* and *ParallelPI* methods. The following image shows the typical output.

This time, the *pointsList* collection in the *ParallelPI* method contains the correct number of points, but the number of points within the circle still appears to be very high; it should be the same as that reported by the *SerialPI* method.

You should also note that the time taken by the *ParallelPI* method has increased significantly. This is because the methods in the *ConcurrentBag<T>* class have to lock and unlock data to guarantee thread safety, and this process adds to the overhead of calling these methods. You need to bear this in mind when considering whether it is appropriate to parallelize an operation.

4. Close the console window, and return to Visual Studio.

You now have the correct number of points in the *pointsList* collection, but the values of these points is now suspect. The code in the *Parallel.For* construct calls the *Next* method of a *Random* object, but like the methods in the generic *List<T>* class this method is not thread-safe. Sadly, there is no concurrent version of the *Random* class, so you must resort to using an alternative technique to serialize calls to the *Next* method. Because each invocation is relatively brief, it makes sense to use a lock to guard calls to this method.

Use a lock to serialize method calls

1. In Solution Explorer, double-click Program.cs to display the file in the *Code and Text Editor* window if it is not already open.

2. Locate the *ParallelPI* method. Modify the code in the lambda expression in the *Parallel.For* statement to protect the calls to *random.Next* by using a *lock* statement. Specify the *pointsList* collection as the subject of the lock, as shown here in bold:

```
static double ParallelPI()
{
    ...
    Parallel.For(0, NUMPOINTS, (x) =>
    {
        int xCoord;
        int yCoord;
```

```
            lock(pointsList)
            {
                xCoord = random.Next(RADIUS);
                yCoord = random.Next(RADIUS);
            }

            double distanceFromOrigin = Math.Sqrt(xCoord * xCoord + yCoord * yCoord);
            pointsList.Add(distanceFromOrigin);
            doAdditionalProcessing();
        });

    ...
}
```

3. On the Debug menu, click *Start Without Debugging*.

This time, the values of PI calculated by the *SerialPI* and *ParallelPI* methods are the same. The only difference is that the *ParallelPI* method runs more quickly.

4. Close the console window, and return to Visual Studio.

In this chapter, you learned a little about PLINQ and how you can use the *AsParallel* extension method to parallelize some LINQ queries. However, PLINQ is a big subject in its own right and this chapter has only shown you how to get started. For more information, see the topic "Parallel LINQ (PLINQ)" in the documentation provided with Visual Studio.

This chapter also showed you how to synchronize data access in concurrent tasks by using the synchronization primitives provided for use with the TPL. You also saw how to use the concurrent collection classes to maintain collections of data in a thread-safe manner.

- If you want to continue to the next chapter

  Keep Visual Studio 2010 running, and turn to Chapter 29.

- If you want to exit Visual Studio 2010 now

  On the *File* menu, click *Exit*. If you see a *Save* dialog box, click *Yes* and save the project.

Chapter 28 Quick Reference

To	Do this

Parallelize a LINQ query	Specify the *AsParallel* extension method with the data source in the query. For example:
	
	``
	var over100 = from n in numbers.AsParallel()
	              where ...
	              select n;
	``

Enable cancellation in a PLINQ query	Use the *WithCancellation* method of the *ParallelQuery* class in the PLINQ query, and specify a cancellation token. For example:
	
	``
	CancellationToken tok = ...;
	...
	var orderInfoQuery =
	    from c in CustomersInMemory.Customers.AsParallel().
	WithCancellation(tok)
	    join o in OrdersInMemory.Orders.AsParallel()
	    on ...
	``

Synchronize one or more tasks to implement thread-safe exclusive access to shared data	Use the *lock* statement to guarantee exclusive access to the data. For example:
	
	``
	object myLockObject = new object();
	...
	lock (myLockObject)
	{
	    // Code that requires exclusive access to a shared resource
	    ...
	}
	``

Synchronize threads, and make them wait for an event	Use a *ManualResetEventSlim* object to synchronize an indeterminate number of threads. Use a *CountdownEvent* object to wait for an event to be signaled a specified number of times. Use a *Barrier* object to coordinate a specified number of threads and synchronize them at a particular point in an operation.

Synchronize access to a shared pool of resources	Use a *SemaphoreSlim* object. Specify the number of items in the pool in the constructor. Call the *Wait* method prior to accessing a resource in the shared pool. Call the *Release* method when you have finished with the resource. For example:
	
	``
	SemaphoreSlim semaphore = new SemaphoreSlim(3);
	...
	semaphore.Wait();
	// Access a resource from the pool
	...
	semaphore.Release();
	``

To	Do this
Provide exclusive write access to a resource, but shared read access	Use a *ReaderWriterLockSlim* object. Prior to reading the shared resource, call the *EnterReadLock* method. Call the *ExitReadLock* method when you have finished. Before writing to the shared resource, call the *EnterWriteLock* method. Call the *ExitWriteLock* method when you have completed the write operation. For example:

```
ReaderWriterLockSlim readerWriterLock = new ReaderWriterLockSlim();

Task readerTask = Task.Factory.StartNew(() =>
    {
        readerWriterLock.EnterReadLock();
        // Read shared resource
        readerWriterLock.ExitReadLock();
    });

Task writerTask = Task.Factory.StartNew(() =>
    {
        readerWriterLock.EnterWriteLock();
        // Write to shared resource
        readerWriterLock.ExitWriteLock();
    });
```

To	Do this
Cancel a blocking wait operation	Create a cancellation token from a *CancellationTokenSource* object, and specify this token as a parameter to the wait operation. To cancel the wait operation, call the *Cancel* method of the *CancellationTokenSource* object. For example:

```
CancellationTokenSource cancellationTokenSource = new
CancellationTokenSource();
CancellationToken cancellationToken = cancellationTokenSource.Token;
...
// Semaphore that protects a pool of 3 resources
SemaphoreSlim semaphoreSlim = new SemaphoreSlim(3);
...
// Wait on the semaphore, and throw an OperationCanceledException if
// another thread calls Cancel on cancellationTokenSource
semaphore.Wait(cancellationToken);
```

To	Do this
Create a thread-safe collection object	Depending on the functionality required for the collection, either use one of the classes in the in the *System.Collections.Concurrent* namespace (*ConcurrentBag<T>*, *ConcurrentDictionary<TKey, TValue>*, *ConcurrentQueue<T>*, or *ConcurrentStack<T>*) or create your own class that implements the *IProducerConsumerCollection<T>* interface and wrap an instance of this type in a *BlockingCollection<T>* object. For example:

```
class MyCollection<T> : IProducerConsumerCollection<T>
{
    // Implementation details not shown
    ...
}
...
// Create an instance of MyCollection<T>,
// and wrap it in a BlockingCollection<T> object
MyCollection<int> intCollection = new MyCollection<int>();
BlockingCollection<int> collection = new BlockingCollection<int>(myCo
llection, 1000);
```

Chapter 29
Creating and Using a Web Service

After completing this chapter, you will be able to:

- Create SOAP and REST Web services that expose simple Web methods.

- Display the description of a SOAP Web service by using Internet Explorer.

- Design classes that can be passed as parameters to a Web method and returned from a Web method.

- Create proxies for SOAP and REST Web services in a client application.

- Invoke a REST Web method by using Internet Explorer.

- Invoke Web methods from a client application.

The previous chapters showed you how to build desktop applications that can perform a variety of tasks. However, in this day and age, very few systems operate in isolation. An organization performs business operations and, as such, frequently has existing applications that support this business functionality. An increasingly common requirement is to build new solutions that can reuse much of this functionality and protect the investment the organization has made in building or buying the underlying software components. These components and services might be constructed by using an assortment of technologies and programming languages, and running on a collection of computers connected together over a network. Additionally, now that we are in the Internet age, an organization can elect to compose solutions that incorporate various third-party services. The challenge is to establish how to combine these pieces to enable them to communicate and cooperate in a seamless manner.

Web services provide one possible solution. By using Web services, you can build distributed systems from elements that are spread across the Internet—databases, business services, and so on. Components and services are hosted by a Web server that receives requests from a client application, parses them, and sends the corresponding command to the component or service. The response is routed back through the Web server to the client application.

The aim of this chapter is to show you how to design, build, and test Web services that can be accessed over the Internet and integrated into distributed applications. You'll also learn how to construct a client application that uses the methods exposed by a Web service.

 Note The purpose of this chapter is to provide a basic introduction to Web services and Microsoft Windows Communication Foundation (WCF). If you want detailed information about how WCF works and how to build secure services by using WCF, you should consult a book such as *Microsoft Windows Communication Foundation Step by Step* (Microsoft Press, 2007).

What Is a Web Service?

A Web service is a business component that provides some useful, reusable functionality to clients or consumers. A Web service can be thought of as a component with truly global accessibility—if you have the appropriate access rights, you can make use of a Web service from anywhere in the world as long as your computer is connected to the Internet. Web services use a standard, accepted, and well-understood protocol—Hypertext Transfer Protocol (HTTP)—to transmit data and a portable data format that is based on XML. HTTP and XML are both standardized technologies that can be used by other programming environments outside the Microsoft .NET Framework. With Microsoft Visual Studio 2010, you can build Web services by using Microsoft Visual C++, Microsoft Visual C#, or Microsoft Visual Basic. However, as far as a client application is concerned, the language used to create the Web service, and even how the Web service performs its tasks, is not important. Client applications running in a totally different environment, such as Java, can use them. The reverse is also true: you can build Web services by using Java and write client applications in C#.

The Role of Windows Communication Foundation

Windows Communication Foundation, or WCF, emerged as part of version 3.0 of the .NET Framework. Visual Studio provides a set of templates you can use for building Web services by using WCF. However, Web services are just one technology you can use to create distributed applications for the Windows operating systems. Others include Enterprise Services, .NET Framework Remoting, and Microsoft Message Queue (MSMQ). If you are building a distributed application for Windows, which technology should you use, and how difficult will it be to switch later if you need to? The purpose of WCF is to provide a unified programming model for many of these technologies so that you can build applications that are as independent as possible from the underlying mechanism being used to connect services and applications. (Note that WCF applies as much to services operating in non-Web environments as it does to the World Wide Web.) It is very difficult, if not impossible, to completely divorce the programmatic structure of an application or service from its communications infrastructure, but WCF lets you come very close to achieving this aim much of the time.

To summarize, if you are considering building distributed applications and services for Windows, you should use WCF. The exercises in this chapter will show you how.

Web Service Architectures

There are two common architectures that organizations use for implementing Web services; services based on the Simple Object Access Protocol (SOAP), and services based on the Representational State Transfer (REST) model. Both architectures rely on the ubiquitous HTTP protocol (the protocol used by the Web to send and receive HTML pages) and the addressing scheme used by the Internet, but they use it in different ways. If you are building solutions that incorporate Web services hosted by third-party organizations, they might implement these Web services by using either of these models, so it helps to have a good understanding of both. The following sections briefly describe these architectures.

SOAP Web Services

A SOAP Web service exposes functionality by using the traditional procedural model; the principal difference from an ordinary desktop application is that the procedures run remotely on the Web server. A client application's view of a Web service is of an interface that exposes a number of well-defined methods, known as Web methods. The client application sends requests to these Web methods by using standard Internet protocols, passing parameters in an XML format and receiving responses also in an XML format. SOAP Web methods can query and modify data.

The Role of SOAP

SOAP is the protocol used by client applications for sending requests to and receiving responses from Web services. SOAP is built on top of HTTP. SOAP defines an XML grammar for specifying the names of Web methods that a consumer can invoke on a Web service, for defining the parameters and return values, and for describing the types of parameters and return values. When a client calls a Web service, it must specify the method and parameters by using this XML grammar.

SOAP is an industry standard. Its function is to improve cross-platform interoperability. The strength of SOAP is its simplicity and also the fact that it is based on other industry-standard technologies, such as HTTP and XML. The SOAP specification defines a number of things. The most important are the following:

- The format of a SOAP message
- How data should be encoded
- How to send messages
- How to process replies

Descriptions of the exact details of how SOAP works and the internal format of a SOAP message are beyond the scope of this book. It is highly unlikely you will ever need to create and format SOAP messages manually because many development tools, including Visual Studio 2010, automate this process, presenting a programmer-friendly API to developers building Web services and client applications.

What Is the Web Services Description Language?

The body of a SOAP message is an XML document. When a client application invokes a Web method, the Web server expects the client to use a particular set of tags for encoding the parameters for the method. How does a client know which tags, or XML schema, to use? The answer is that, when asked, a Web service is expected to supply a description of itself. The Web service response is another XML document that describes the Web service. Unsurprisingly, this document is known as the Web Service Description. The XML schema used for this document has been standardized and is called Web Services Description Language (WSDL). This description provides enough information for a client application to construct a SOAP request in a format that the Web server should understand. Again, the details of WSDL are beyond the scope of this book, but Visual Studio 2010 contains tools that can parse the WSDL for a Web service in a mechanical manner. Visual Studio 2010 then uses the information to define a proxy class that a client application can use to convert ordinary method calls on this proxy class to SOAP requests that the proxy sends over the Web. This is the approach you will use in the exercises in this chapter.

Nonfunctional Requirements of Web Services

The initial efforts to define Web services and their associated standards concentrated on the functional aspects for sending and receiving SOAP messages. Not long after Web services became a mainstream technology for integrating distributed services, it became apparent that there were issues that SOAP and HTTP alone could not address. These issues concern many nonfunctional requirements that are important in any distributed environment, but much more so when using the Internet as the basis for a distributed solution. They include the following items:

- **Security**   How do you ensure that SOAP messages that flow between a Web service and a consumer have not been intercepted and changed on their way across the Internet? How can you be sure that a SOAP message has actually been sent by the consumer or Web service that claims to have sent it, and not some "spoof" site that is trying to obtain information fraudulently? How can you restrict access to a Web service to specific users? These are matters of message integrity, confidentiality, and authentication and are fundamental concerns if you are building distributed applications that make use of the Internet.

  In the early 1990s, a number of vendors supplying tools for building distributed systems formed an organization that later became known as the Organization for the Advancement of Structured Information Standards (OASIS). As the shortcomings of the early Web services infrastructure became apparent, members of OASIS pondered these problems (and other Web services issues) and produced what became known as the WS-Security specification. The WS-Security specification describes how to protect the messages sent by Web services. Vendors that subscribe to WS-Security provide their own implementations that meet this specification, typically by using technologies such as encryption and certificates.

- **Policy**   Although the WS-Security specification defines how to provide enhanced security, developers still need to write code to implement it. Web services created by different developers often vary in how stringent the security mechanism is that they have elected to implement. For example, a Web service might use only a relatively weak form of encryption that can easily be broken. A consumer sending highly confidential information to this Web service would probably insist on a higher level of security. This is one example of policy. Other examples include the quality of service and reliability of the Web service. A Web service can implement varying degrees of security, quality of service, and reliability and charge the client application accordingly. The client application and the Web service can negotiate which level of service to use based on the requirements and cost. However, this negotiation requires that the client and the Web service have a common understanding of the policies available. The WS-Policy specification provides a general-purpose model and corresponding syntax to describe and communicate the policies that a Web service implements.

- **Routing and addressing**   It is useful for a Web server to be able to reroute a Web service request to one of a number of computers hosting instances of the service. For example, many scalable systems make use of load balancing, in which requests sent to a Web server are actually redirected by that server to other computers to spread the load across those computers. The server can use any number of algorithms to try to balance the load. The important point is that this redirection is transparent to the client making the Web service request, and the server that ultimately handles the request must know where to send any responses that it generates. Redirecting Web service requests is also useful if an administrator needs to shut down a computer to perform maintenance. Requests that would otherwise have been sent to this computer can be rerouted to one of its peers. The WS-Addressing specification describes a framework for routing Web service requests.

Note Developers refer to the WS-Security, WS-Policy, WS-Addressing, and other "WS-" specifications collectively as the WS-* specifications.

REST Web Services

In contrast to SOAP Web services, the REST model of Web services uses a navigational scheme to represent business objects and resources over a network. For example, an organization might provide access to employee information, exposing the details of each employee as a single resource, by using a scheme similar to this:

```
http://northwind.com/employees/7
```

Accessing this URL causes the Web service to retrieve the data for employee 7. This data can be returned in a number of formats, but for portability the most common formats include

XML (sometimes referred to as "Plain Old XML" or POX) and JavaScript Object Notation (or JSON). If the Northwind Traders organization chooses to use POX, the result returned by querying the URL shown earlier might be something like this:

```
<Employee>
    <EmployeeID>
        7
    </EmployeeID>
    <LastName>
        King
    </LastName>
    <FirstName>
        Robert
    </FirstName>
    <Title>
        Sales Representative
    </Title>
</Employee>
```

The key to designing a REST-based solution is to understand how to divide a business model into a set of resources. In some cases, such as employees, this might be straightforward, but in other situations this might be more of a challenge.

The REST model relies on the application that accesses the data sending the appropriate HTTP verb as part of the request used to access the data. For example, the simple request shown previously should send an HTTP GET request to the Web service. HTTP supports other verbs as well, such as POST, PUT, and DELETE, which you can use to create, modify, and remove resources, respectively. Using the REST model, you can exploit these verbs and build Web services that can update data.

In contrast to SOAP, the messages sent and received by using the REST model tend to be much more compact. This is primarily because REST does not provide the same routing, policy, or security facilities provided by the WS-* specifications, and you have to rely on the underlying infrastructure provided by the Web server to protect REST Web services. However, this minimalist approach means that a REST Web service is usually much more efficient than the equivalent SOAP Web service when transmitting and receiving messages.

Building Web Services

Using WCF, you can build Web services that follow the REST or SOAP models. However, the SOAP mechanism is the more straightforward of the two schemes to implement by using WCF, so you will concentrate on this model for the initial exercises in this chapter. Later in this chapter, you will see how to build a REST Web service.

In this chapter, you will create two Web services:

- The ProductInformation Web service. This is a SOAP Web service that enables the user to calculate the cost of buying a specified quantity of a particular product in the Northwind database

- The ProductDetails Web service. This is a REST Web service that enables a user to query the details of products in the Northwind database.

Creating the ProductInformation SOAP Web Service

In the first exercise, you will create the ProductInformation Web service and examine the sample code generated by Visual Studio 2010 whenever you create a new WCF service project. In subsequent exercises, you will define and implement the *HowMuchWillItCost* Web method and then test the Web method to ensure that it works as expected.

> **Important** You cannot build Web services by using Microsoft Visual C# 2010 Express. Instead, you should use Microsoft Visual Web Developer 2010 Express. You can download Visual Web Developer 2010 Express free of charge from the Microsoft Web site.

Create the SOAP Web service, and examine the sample code

1. Start Visual Studio 2010 if it is not already running, or start Visual Web Developer 2010 Express.

2. If you are using Visual Studio 2010 Professional or Enterprise, on the *File* menu, point to *New*, and then click *Web Site*.

3. If you are using Visual Web Developer 2010 Express, on the *File* menu, click *New Web Site*. Make sure that you select *Visual C#* under *Installed Templates* in the left pane.

4. In the *New Web Site* dialog box, click the *WCF Service* template. Select *File System* in the *Location* drop-down list box, specify the \Microsoft Press\Visual CSharp Step By Step\Chapter 29\ProductInformationService folder under your Documents folder, and then click *OK*.

   Visual Studio 2010 generates a Web site hosted by using the Development Web Server provided with Visual Studio and Visual Web Developer. You can also host Web services by using Microsoft Internet Information Services (IIS) if you have it available, although the details for doing this are outside the scope of this chapter. The Web site contains folders called App_Code and App_Data, a file called Service.svc, and a configuration file called Web.config. The code for an example Web service is defined in the *Service* class, stored in the file Service.cs in the App_Code folder, and displayed in the *Code and Text Editor* window. The *Service* class implements a sample interface called *IService*, stored in the file IService.cs in the App_Code folder.

Note The solution file for a Web site project is located under the Visual Studio 2010\ Projects folder in your Documents folder rather than in the folder that contains the files for the Web site. You can open an existing Web Site project either by finding and opening the appropriate solution file, or by using the *Open Web Site* command on the *File* menu and then specifying the folder that contains the files for the Web site. You can also copy the solution file for a Web site to the folder holding the files for the Web site, but this is not recommended in a production environment, for security purposes.

5. Click the C:\...\ProductInformationService\ project. In the *Properties* window, set the *Use dynamic ports* property to *False* and set the *Port number* property to *4500*.

Note You might need to wait a few seconds after setting the *Use dynamic ports* property to *False* before you can set the *Port number* property.

A port specifies the location that the Web server listens on for incoming requests from client applications. By default, the Development Web server picks a port at random to reduce the chances of clashing with any other ports used by other network services running on your computer. This feature is useful if you are building and testing Web sites (as opposed to Web services) in a development environment prior to copying them to a production server such as IIS. However, when building a Web service, it is more useful to use a fixed port number because client applications need to be able to connect to it.

Note When you close a Web site and reopen it by using Visual Studio or by using Visual Web Developer, the *Use dynamic ports* property frequently reverts to *True* and the *Port number* property is set to a random port. In this case, reset these properties to the values described in this step.

6. In *Solution Explorer*, expand the App_Code folder if it is not already open, right-click the Service.cs file, and then click *Rename*. Change the name of the file to **ProductInformation.cs**.

7. Using the same technique, change the name of the IService.cs file to **IProductInformation.cs**.

8. Double-click the IProductInformation.cs file to display it in the *Code and Text Editor* window.

This file contains the definition of an interface called *IService*. At the top of the IProductInformation.cs file, you will find *using* statements referencing the *System*, *System.Collections.Generic*, and *System.Text* namespaces (which you have met before), and three additional statements referencing the *System.ServiceModel*, *System. ServiceModel.Web*, and *System.Runtime.Serialization* namespaces.

The *System.ServiceModel* and *System.ServiceModel.Web* namespaces contain the classes used by WCF for defining services and their operations. WCF uses the classes in the *System.Runtime.Serialization* namespace to convert objects to a stream of data for transmission over the network (a process known as *serialization*) and to convert a stream of data received from the network back to objects (*deserialization*). You will learn a little about how WCF serializes and deserializes objects later in this chapter.

The primary contents of the IProductInformation file are the *IService* interface and a class called *CompositeType*. The *IService* interface is prefixed with the *ServiceContract* attribute, and the *CompositeType* class is tagged with the *DataContract* attribute. Because of the structure of a WCF service, you can adopt a "contract-first" approach to development. When performing contract-first development, you define the interfaces, or *contracts*, that the service will implement, and then you build a service that conforms to these contracts. This is not a new technique, and you have seen examples of this strategy throughout this book. The point behind using contract-first development is that you can concentrate on the design of your service. If necessary, it can quickly be reviewed to ensure that your design does not introduce any dependencies on specific hardware or software before you perform too much development; remember that in many cases client applications might not be built using WCF and might not even be running on Windows.

The *ServiceContract* attribute marks an interface as defining methods that the class implementing the Web service will expose as Web methods. The methods themselves are tagged with the *OperationContract* attribute. The tools provided with Visual Studio 2010 use these attributes to help generate the appropriate WSDL document for the service. Any methods in the interface not marked with the *OperationContract* attribute will not be included in the WSDL document and therefore will not be accessible to client applications using the Web service.

If a Web method takes parameters or returns a value, the data for these parameters and values must be converted to a format that can be transmitted over the network and then converted back again to objects—this is the process known as serialization and deserialization mentioned earlier. The various Web services standards define mechanisms for specifying the serialized format of simple data types, such as numbers and strings, as part of the WSDL description for a Web service. However, you can also define your own complex data types based on classes and structures. If you make use of these types in a Web service, you must provide information on how to serialize and deserialize them. If you look at the definition of the *GetDataUsingDataContract* method in the *IService* interface, you can see that it expects a parameter of the type *CompositeType*. The *CompositeType* class is marked with the *DataContract* attribute, which specifies that the class must define a type that can be serialized and deserialized as an XML stream as part of a SOAP request or response message. Each member that you want to include in the serialized stream sent over the network must be tagged with the *DataMember* attribute.

9. Double-click the ProductInformation.cs file to display it in the *Code and Text Editor* window.

   This file contains a class called *Service* that implements the *IService* interface and provides the *GetData* and *GetDataUsingDataContract* methods defined by this interface. This class is the Web service. When a client application invokes a Web method in this Web service, it generates a SOAP request message and sends it to the Web server hosting the Web service. The Web server creates an instance of this class and runs the corresponding method. When the method completes, the Web server constructs a SOAP response message, which it sends back to the client application.

10. Double-click the Service.svc file to display it in the *Code and Text Editor* window.

   This is the service file for the Web service; it is used by the host environment (IIS, in this case) to determine which class to load when it receives a request from a client application.

   The *Service* property of the *@ ServiceHost* directive specifies the name of the Web service class, and the *CodeBehind* property specifies the location of the source code for this class.

 Tip If you don't want to deploy the source code for your WCF service to the Web server, you can provide a compiled assembly instead. You can then specify the name and location of this assembly by using the *@ Assembly* directive. For more information, search for *"@ Assembly"* in the documentation provided with Visual Studio 2010.

Now that you have seen the structure of a WCF service, you can define the interface that specifies the service contract for the ProductInformation Web service and then create a class that implements this service contract.

Define the contract for the ProductInformation Web service

1. Display the IProductInformation.cs file in the *Code and Text Editor* window.

2. In the line of code that defines the *IService* interface, double-click the name *IService* to highlight it. On the *Refactor* menu, click *Rename*. In the *Rename* dialog box, type **IProductInformation** in the *New name* text box, deselect the *Preview reference changes* check box, and then click *OK*.

   This action changes the name of the interface from *IService* to *IProductInformation* and also changes all references to *IService* to *IProductInformation* in all files in the project. The line that defines the interface in the *Code and Text Editor* window should look like this:

```
public interface IProductInformation
{
    ...
}
```

3. In the *IProductInformation* interface, remove the definitions of the *GetData* and
   GetDataUsingDataContract methods and replace them with the *HowMuchWillItCost*
   method shown next in bold. Make sure you retain the *OperationContract* attribute in
   the Web method.

```
[ServiceContract]
public interface IProductInformation
{
    [OperationContract]
    decimal HowMuchWillItCost(int productID, int howMany);
}
```

The *HowMuchWillItCost* method takes a product ID and a quantity and returns a
decimal value specifying the amount this quantity will cost.

4. Remove the *CompositeType* class, including the *DataContract* attribute, from
   the IProductInformation.cs file. The file should contain only the definition of the
   IProductInformation interface.

The next stage is to define the *ProductInformation* class, which implements the
IProductInformation interface. The *HowMuchWillItCost* method in this class will retrieve the
price of the product from the database by performing a simple ADO.NET query.

Note The Web services that you build in this chapter require access to the Northwind database.
If you have not already done so, you can create this database by following the steps in the section "Creating the Database" in Chapter 25, "Querying Information in a Database." Additionally,
if you have previously been using Visual C# 2010 Express, you cannot use the detached version of the Northwind database for the exercises in this chapter. Instead, you should delete the
Northwind.mdf and Northwind_log.ldf files from the C:\Program Files\Microsoft SQL Server\
MSSQL10.SQLEXPRESS\MSSQL\DATA folder and then rebuild the Northwind database by running
the instwnd.sql script as described in Chapter 25.

Implement the *IProductInformation* interface

1. Display the code for the ProductInformation.cs file in the *Code and Text Editor* window.

2. Add the following *using* statements to the list at the top of the file:

```
using System.Data;
using System.Data.SqlClient;
```

You should recall from Chapter 25 that these namespaces contain the types necessary
to access a Microsoft SQL Server database and query data.

3. In the line of code that defines the *Service* class, double-click the name *Service* to
   highlight it. On the *Refactor* menu, click *Rename*. In the *Rename* dialog box, type
   ProductInformation in the *New name* text box and then click *OK*.

As in the previous exercise, this action changes the name of the class from *Service* to
ProductInformation and also changes all references to *Service* to *ProductInformation* in

all files in the project. The line that defines the class in the *Code and Text Editor* window should look like this:

```
public class ProductInformation : IProductInformation
{
    ...
}
```

4. Remove the *GetData* and *GetDataUsingDataContract* methods from the *ProductInformation* class.

5. Add the *HowMuchWillItCost* method to the *ProductInformation* class, shown here in bold:

```
public class ProductInformation : IProductInformation
{
    public decimal HowMuchWillItCost(int productID, int howMany)
    {
        SqlConnection dataConnection = new SqlConnection();
        decimal totalCost = 0;

        try
        {
            SqlConnectionStringBuilder builder = new SqlConnectionStringBuilder();
            builder.DataSource = ".\\SQLExpress";
            builder.InitialCatalog = "Northwind";
            builder.IntegratedSecurity = true;
            dataConnection.ConnectionString = builder.ConnectionString;
            dataConnection.Open();

            SqlCommand dataCommand = new SqlCommand();
            dataCommand.Connection = dataConnection;
            dataCommand.CommandType = CommandType.Text;
            dataCommand.CommandText = "SELECT UnitPrice FROM  Products WHERE ProductID
= @ProductID";

            SqlParameter productIDParameter = new SqlParameter("@ProductID",
SqlDbType.Int);
            productIDParameter.Value = productID;
            dataCommand.Parameters.Add(productIDParameter);

            decimal? price = dataCommand.ExecuteScalar() as decimal?;
            if (price.HasValue)
            {
                totalCost = price.Value * howMany;
            }
        }
        finally
        {
            dataConnection.Close();
        }

        return totalCost;
    }
}
```

This method connects to the database and executes an ADO.NET query to retrieve the price of the product matching the supplied product ID from the Northwind database. If the price returned is not null, the method calculates the total cost of the request and returns it; otherwise, the method returns the value 0. The code is similar to that shown in Chapter 25, except that it uses the *ExecuteScalar* method to read the value of the *UnitPrice* column from the database. The *ExecuteScalar* method provides a very efficient mechanism for running queries that return a single, scalar value (and is much more efficient than opening a cursor and reading data from the cursor). The value returned by *ExecuteScalar* is an object, so you must cast it to the appropriate type before using it.

> **Important** This method performs no validation of the input parameters. For example, you can specify a negative value for the *howMany* parameter. In a production Web service, you would trap errors such as this, log them, and return an exception. However, transmitting meaningful reasons for an exception back to a client application has security implications in a WCF service. The details are beyond the scope of this book. For more information, see *Microsoft Windows Communication Foundation Step by Step*.

Before you can use the Web service, you must update the configuration in the Service.svc file to refer to the *ProductInformation* class in the ProductInformation.cs file. The Web server uses information in the Web.config file created with the project to hold information about how to publish the service and make it available to client applications. You must modify the Web.config file and add the details of the Web service.

Configure the Web service

1. In *Solution Explorer*, double-click the Service.svc file to display it in the *Code and Text Editor* window. Update the *Service* and *CodeBehind* attributes of the *ServiceHost* directive, as shown here in bold:

   ```
   <%@ ServiceHost Language="C#" Debug="true" Service="ProductInformation"
       CodeBehind="~/App_Code/ProductInformation.cs" %>
   ```

2. In *Solution Explorer*, double-click the Web.config file. In the *Code and Text Editor* window, locate the *<system.serviceModel>* element. You use this element to specify the configuration of a WCF service. This element currently contains a *<behaviors>* element, which you can ignore for the moment.

3. In the Web.config file, add the *<services>* element and child elements shown next in bold to the *<system.serviceModel>* element, before the *<behaviors>* element:

   ```
   <system.serviceModel>
     <services>
       <service name="ProductInformation">
         <endpoint address="" binding="wsHttpBinding" contract="IProductInformation"/>
       </service>
   ```

```
    </services>
    <behaviors>
        ...
    </behaviors>
</system.serviceModel>
```

This configuration specifies the name of the class that implements the Web service (*ProductInformation*). WCF uses the notion of endpoints to associate a network address with a specific Web service. If you are hosting a Web service by using IIS or the Development Web Server, you should leave the *address* property of your endpoint blank because these servers listen for incoming requests on an address specified by their own configuration information. You can build your own custom host applications if you don't want to use IIS or the Development Server. In these situations, you must specify an address for the service as part of the endpoint definition. The *binding* parameter indicates the network protocol that the server uses to receive requests and transmit responses.

For more information about endpoints, custom hosts, and bindings see *Microsoft Windows Communication Foundation Step by Step*, published by Microsoft Press.

4. On the *File* menu, click *Save All*.

5. In *Solution Explorer*, right-click *Service.svc*, and then click *View in Browser*.

Internet Explorer starts and displays the following page, confirming that you have successfully created and deployed the Web service and providing helpful information about how to create a simple client application that can access the Web service.

Note If you click the link shown on the Web page (*http://localhost:4500/ ProductInformationService/Service.svc?wsdl*), Internet Explorer displays a page containing the WSDL description of the Web service. This is a long and complicated piece of XML, but Visual Studio 2010 can take the information in this description and use it to generate a class that a client application can use to communicate with the Web service.

6. Close Internet Explorer, and return to Visual Studio 2010.

SOAP Web Services, Clients, and Proxies

A SOAP Web service uses the SOAP protocol to transmit data between a client application and a service. SOAP uses XML to format the data being transmitted, which rides on top of the HTTP protocol used by Web servers and browsers. This is what makes Web services so powerful—SOAP, HTTP, and XML are well understood (in theory anyway) and are the subjects of several standards committees. Any client application that "talks" SOAP can communicate with a Web service. So how does a client "talk" SOAP? There are two ways: the difficult way and the easy way.

Talking SOAP: The Difficult Way

In the difficult way, the client application performs a number of steps. It must do the following:

1. Determine the URL of the Web service running the Web method.

2. Perform a Web Services Description Language (WSDL) inquiry using the URL to obtain a description of the Web methods available, the parameters used, and the values returned. You saw how to do this by using Internet Explorer in the preceding exercise.

3. Parse the WSDL document, convert each operation to a Web request, and serialize each parameter into the format described by the WSDL document.

4. Submit the request, along with the serialized data, to the URL by using HTTP.

5. Wait for the Web service to reply.

6. Using the formats specified by the WSDL document, deserialize the data returned by the Web service into meaningful values that your application can then process.

This is a lot of work just to invoke a method, and it is potentially error-prone.

Talking SOAP: The Easy Way

The bad news is that the easy way to use SOAP is not much different from the difficult way. The good news is that the process can be automated because it is largely mechanical. As mentioned earlier, many vendors, including Microsoft, supply tools that can generate a proxy class based on a WSDL description. The proxy hides the complexity of using SOAP and exposes a simple programmatic interface based on the methods published by the Web service. The client application calls Web methods by invoking methods with the same name in the proxy. The proxy converts these local method calls to SOAP requests and sends them to the Web service. The proxy waits for the reply, deserializes the data, and then passes it back to the client just like the return from any simple method call. This is the approach you will take in the exercises in this section.

Consuming the ProductInformation SOAP Web Service

You have created a SOAP Web service call that exposes a Web method called *HowMuchWillItCost* to determine the cost of buying *n* items of product *x* from Northwind Traders. In the following exercises, you will use this Web service and create an application that consumes this method.

Open the Web service client application

1. Start another instance of Visual Studio 2010. This is important. The Development Server used to host the Web service stops if you close the ProductInformationService Web service project, meaning that you won't be able to access it from the client. (An alternative approach you can use if you are running Visual Studio 2010 and not Visual Web Developer 2010 Express is to create the client application as a project in the same solution as the Web service.) When you host a Web service in a production environment by using IIS, this problem does not arise because IIS runs independently of Visual Studio 2010.

> **Important** If you have been using Visual Web Developer 2010 Express for the exercises in this part of the book, start Visual C# 2010 Express rather than a second instance of Visual Web Developer 2010 Express. (Leave Visual Web Developer 2010 Express running.)

2. In the second instance of Microsoft Visual Studio 2010, open the ProductClient solution in the \Microsoft Press\Visual CSharp Step By Step\Chapter 29\ProductClient folder in your Documents folder.

3. In *Solution Explorer*, double-click the file ProductClient.xaml to display the form in the *Design View* window. The form looks like this:

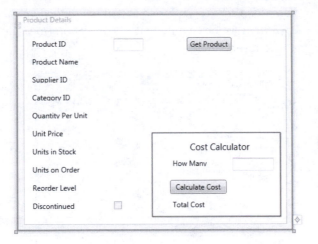

The form enables the user to specify a product ID and retrieve the details of the product from the Northwind database. (You will implement this functionality in a later exercise by using a REST Web service.) The user can also provide a quantity and retrieve a price for buying that quantity of the product. Currently, the buttons on the form do nothing. In the following steps, you will add the necessary code to invoke the *HowMuchWillItCost* method from the ProductInformation Web service to obtain the cost and then display it.

Add code to call the Web service in the client application

1. On the *Project* menu, click *Add Service Reference*.

   The *Add Service Reference* dialog box opens. In this dialog box, you can browse for Web services and examine the Web methods that they provide.

2. In the *Address* text box, type **http://localhost:4500/ProductInformationService/Service.svc** and then click *Go*.

   The ProductInformation service appears in the *Services* box.

3. Expand the *ProductInformation* service, and then click the *IProductInformation* interface that appears. In the *Operations* list box, verify that the operation *HowMuchWillItCost* appears, as shown in the following image:

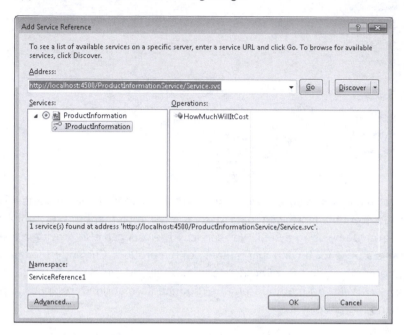

4. Change the value in the *Namespace* text box to **ProductInformationService** and then click *OK*.

A new folder called *Service References* appears in *Solution Explorer*. This folder contains an item called ProductInformationService.

5. Click the *Show All Files* button on the *Solution Explorer* toolbar. Expand the ProductInformationService folder, and then expand the Reference.svcmap folder. Double-click the Reference.cs file and examine its contents in the *Code and Text Editor* window.

This file contains several classes and interfaces, including a class called *ProductInformationClient* in a namespace called *ProductClient.ProductInformationService*. The *ProductInformationClient* is the proxy class generated by Visual Studio 2010 from the WSDL description of the *ProductInformation* Web service. It contains a number of constructors, as well as a method called *HowMuchWillItCost*. The following code shows some highlights of this file, formatted to make it slightly more readable:

```
namespace ProductClient.ProductInformationService {
    ...
    [System.ServiceModel.ServiceContractAttribute(...)]
    public interface IProductInformation {
```

```
        [System.ServiceModel.OperationContractAttribute(...)]
        decimal HowMuchWillItCost(int productID, int howMany);
    }
    ...
    ...
    public partial class ProductInformationClient :
System.ServiceModel.ClientBase<ProductClient.ProductInformationService.
IProductInformation>,
ProductClient.ProductInformationService.IProductInformation {

        public ProductInformationClient() {
        }

        public ProductInformationClient(string endpointConfigurationName) :
            base(endpointConfigurationName) {
        }

        public ProductInformationClient(string endpointConfigurationName, string
remoteAddress) :
            base(endpointConfigurationName, remoteAddress) {
        }

        public ProductInformationClient(string endpointConfigurationName,
                System.ServiceModel.EndpointAddress remoteAddress) :
            base(endpointConfigurationName, remoteAddress) {
        }

        public ProductInformationClient(System.ServiceModel.Channels.Binding binding,
                System.ServiceModel.EndpointAddress remoteAddress) :
            base(binding, remoteAddress) {
        }

        public decimal HowMuchWillItCost(int productID, int howMany) {
            return base.Channel.HowMuchWillItCost(productID, howMany);
        }
    }
}
```

The *IProductInformation* interface is similar to the interface you defined in the Web service, except that some of the attributes specify additional parameters. (The purpose of these parameters is beyond the scope of this chapter.) The *ProductInformation* class implements this interface, as well as inheriting from the generic *ClientBase* class. The *ClientBase* class in the *System.ServiceModel* namespace provides the basic communications functionality that a client application requires to communicate with a Web service. The type parameter specifies the interface that the class implements. The *ClientBase* class provides the *Channel* property, which encapsulates an HTTP connection to a Web service. The various constructors for the *ProductInformationClient* class configure the channel to connect it to the endpoint that the Web service is listening on.

The client application can instantiate the *ProductInformationClient* class, specifying the endpoint to connect to, and then call the *HowMuchWillItCost* method. When this happens, the channel in the underlying *ClientBase* class packages up the information supplied as parameters into a SOAP message that it transmits to the Web service. When the Web service replies, the information returned is unpacked from the SOAP response and passed back to the client application. In this way, the client application can call a method in a Web service in exactly the same way as it would call a local method.

 Note You might have noticed that the interface is tagged with *ServiceContractAttribute* rather than simply *ServiceContract*, and the operation is tagged with *OperationContractAttribute* rather than *OperationContract*. In fact, all attributes have the *Attribute* suffix to their name. The C# compiler recognizes this naming convention, and consequently it allows you to omit the *Attribute* suffix in your own code.

6. Display the ProductClient.xaml form in the *Design View* window. Double-click the *Calculate Cost* button to generate the *calcCost_Click* event handler method for this button.

7. In the *Code and Text Editor* window, add the following *using* statements to the list at the top of the ProductClient.xaml.cs file:

```
using ProductClient.ProductInformationService;
using System.ServiceModel;
```

8. In the *calcCost_Click* method, add the following code shown in bold:

```
private void calcCost_Click(object sender, RoutedEventArgs e)
{
    ProductInformationClient proxy = new ProductInformationClient();
}
```

This statement creates an instance of the *ProductInformationClient* class that your code will use to call the *HowMuchWillItCost* Web method.

9. Add the code shown next in bold to the *calcCost_Click* method. This code extracts the product ID and the number required from the *How Many* text box on the form, executes the *HowMuchWillItCost* Web method by using the *proxy* object, and then displays the result in the *totalCost* label.

```
private void calcCost_Click(object sender, RoutedEventArgs e)
{
    ProductInformationClient proxy = new ProductInformationClient();
    try
    {
        int prodID = Int32.Parse(productID.Text);
        int numberRequired = Int32.Parse(howMany.Text);
        decimal cost = proxy.HowMuchWillItCost(prodID, numberRequired);
        totalCost.Content = String.Format("{0:C}", cost);
    }
    catch (Exception ex)
    {
        MessageBox.Show("Error obtaining cost: " + ex.Message,
            "Error", MessageBoxButton.OK, MessageBoxImage.Error);
```

```
        }
        finally
        {
            if (proxy.State == CommunicationState.Faulted)
                proxy.Abort();
            else
                proxy.Close();
        }
}
```

You are probably aware of how unpredictable networks are, and this applies doubly to the Internet. The *try/catch* block ensures that the client application catches any network exceptions that might occur. It is also possible that the user might not enter a valid integer into the *ProductID* text box on the form. The *try/catch* block also handles this exception.

The *finally* block examines the state of the proxy object. If an exception occurred in the Web service (which could be caused by the user supplying a nonexistent product ID, for example), the proxy will be in the *Faulted* state. In this case, the *finally* block calls the *Abort* method of the proxy to acknowledge the exception and close the connection; otherwise, it calls the *Close* method. The *Abort* and *Close* methods both close the communications channel with the Web service and release the resources associated with this instance of the *ProductInformationClient* object.

Test the application

1. On the *Debug* menu, click *Start Without Debugging*.

2. When the Product Details form appears, type **3** in the *Product ID* text box, type **5** in the *How Many* text box, and then click *Calculate Cost*.

   After a short delay while the client instantiates the proxy and builds a SOAP request containing the product ID, the proxy sends the request to the Web service. The Web service deserializes the SOAP request to extract the product ID, reads the unit price of the product from the database, calculates the total cost, wraps it up as XML in a SOAP response message, and then sends this response message back to the proxy. The proxy deserializes the XML data and then passes it to your code in the *calcCost_Click* method. The cost for 5 units of product 3 appears on the form (50 currency units).

 Tip If you get an exception with the message "Error obtaining cost: There was no endpoint listening at http://localhost:4500/ProductInformationService/Service.svc that could accept the message," the Development Server has probably stopped running. (It shuts down if it is inactive for a time.) To restart it, switch to the Visual Studio 2010 instance for the ProductInformation Web service, right-click *Service.svc* in *Solution Explorer*, and then click *View in Browser*. Close Internet Explorer when it appears.

3. Experiment by typing the IDs of other products. Notice that if you enter an ID for a product that does not exist, the Web service returns the value 0 for the total cost.

4. When you have finished, close the form and return to Visual Studio.

Creating the ProductDetails REST Web Service

In the previous section, you built and used a SOAP Web service to implement a small piece of procedural functionality. In the next set of exercises, you will build the *ProductDetails* Web service that enables a user to retrieve the details of products. This form of Web service is naturally navigational, so you will implement it by using the REST model. You will start by creating a data contract for transmitting *Product* objects over the network.

You can access a REST Web service from a client application in a similar manner to a SOAP Web service—by using a proxy object that hides the complexity of sending a message over a network from the client application. However, Visual Studio does not currently support generating proxy classes for REST Web services automatically, so you will create the proxy class manually. Also, it is not necessarily good practice to duplicate code such as service contracts across Web services and clients because it can make maintenance difficult. For these reasons, you will adopt a slightly different approach to building the Web service.

Create the data contract for the REST Web service

1. If you are using Visual Studio 2010 Standard or Visual Studio 2010 Professional, perform the following tasks to create a new class library project:

   1.1. In the instance of Visual Studio that you used to edit the client application, on the *File* menu, point to *New*, and then click *Project*.

   1.2. In the *New Project* dialog box, in the left pane, under *Visual C#*, click *Windows*.

   1.3. In the middle pane, select the *Class Library* template.

   1.4. In the *Name* text box, type **ProductDetailsContracts**.

   1.5. In the *Location* text box, specify the *Microsoft Press\\Visual CSharp Step By Step\\ Chapter 29* folder under your Documents folder.

   1.6. Click *OK*.

2. If you are using Microsoft Visual C# 2010 Express, perform the following tasks to create a new class library project:

   2.1. Start Visual C# 2010 Express if it is not already running.

   2.2. On the *File* menu, click *New Project*.

   2.3. In the *New Project* dialog box, in the middle pane select the *Class Library* template.

2.4. In the *Name* text box, type **ProductDetailsContracts**.

2.5. Click *OK*.

2.6. On the *File* menu, click *Save ProductDetailsContracts*.

2.7. In the *Save Project* dialog box, in the *Location* text box specify the *\Microsoft Press\Visual CSharp Step By Step\Chapter 29* folder under your Documents folder.

2.8. Click *Save*.

3. On the *Project* menu, click *Add Reference*.

4. In the *Add Reference* dialog box, click the *.NET* tab. Select the *System.Data.Linq*, *System.ServiceModel*, *System.ServiceModel.Web*, and *System.Runtime.Serialization* assemblies and then click *OK*.

5. In *Solution Explorer*, right-click the Class1.cs file and then click *Rename*. Change the name of the file to **Product.cs**. Allow Visual Studio to change all references to *Class1* to *Product* when prompted.

6. Double-click the Product.cs file to display it in the *Code and Text Editor* window if it is not already open.

7. In the Product.cs file, add the following using statements to the list at the top:

```
using System.Runtime.Serialization;
using System.Data.Linq.Mapping;
```

8. Prefix the *Product* class with the *Table* and *DataContract* attributes, as shown here in bold:

```
[Table (Name="Products")]
[DataContract]
public class Product
{
}
```

You will use LINQ to SQL to retrieve the data from the Northwind database. Recall from Chapter 25 that the *Table* attribute marks the class as an *Entity* class. The table is called Products in the Northwind database.

9. Add the properties shown next in bold to the *Product* class. Make sure that you prefix each property with the *Column* and *DataMember* attributes. Notice that some of these properties are nullable.

```
[DataContract]
public class Product
{
    [Column]
    [DataMember]
    public int ProductID { get; set; }

    [Column]
```

```
    [DataMember]
    public string ProductName { get; set; }

    [Column]
    [DataMember]
    public int? SupplierID { get; set; }

    [Column]
    [DataMember]
    public int? CategoryID { get; set; }

    [Column]
    [DataMember]
    public string QuantityPerUnit { get; set; }

    [Column]
    [DataMember]
    public decimal? UnitPrice { get; set; }

    [Column]
    [DataMember]
    public short? UnitsInStock { get; set; }

    [Column]
    [DataMember]
    public short? UnitsOnOrder { get; set; }

    [Column]
    [DataMember]
    public short? ReorderLevel { get; set; }

    [Column]
    [DataMember]
    public bool Discontinued { get; set; }
}
```

The next step is to define the service contract for the ProductDetails Web service.

Create the service contract for the REST Web service

1. On the *Project* menu, click *Add Class*.

2. In the *Add Class* dialog box, in the middle pane select the *Class* template. In the *Name* text box, type **IProductDetails.cs**, and then click *Add*.

3. In the *Code and Text Editor* window displaying the IProductDetails.cs file, add the following *using* statements to the list at the top of the file:

```
using System.ServiceModel;
using System.ServiceModel.Web;
```

4. Change the *IProductDetails* class into a public interface, and prefix it with the *ServiceContract* attribute, as shown here in bold:

```
[ServiceContract]
public interface IProductDetails
{
}
```

5. Add the *GetProduct* method definition shown next in bold to the *IProductsDetails* interface:

```
[ServiceContract]
public interface IProductDetails
{
    [OperationContract]
    [WebGet(UriTemplate = "products/{productID}")]
    Product GetProduct(string productID);
}
```

The *GetProduct* method takes a product ID and will return a *Product* object for the product that has this ID. The *OperationContract* attribute indicates that this method should be exposed as a Web method. (If you omit the *OperationContract* attribute, the method is not accessible to client applications.) The *WebGet* attribute indicates that this is a logical retrieve operation, and the *UriTemplate* parameter specifies the format of the URL you provide to invoke this operation, relative to the base address of the Web service. In this case, you can specify the following URL to retrieve the product with *productID* 7:

```
http://host/service/products/7
```

The terms *host* and *service* represent the address of your Web server and the name of the Web service. The element of the *UriTemplate* in curly braces denotes the data that is passed as the parameter to the *GetProduct* method. The identifier in the curly braces must match the name of the parameter.

6. On the *Build* menu, click *Build Solution* and verify that the class library compiles without any errors. The project creates an assembly called ProductDetailsContracts.dll.

Now that you have built an assembly that defines the data contract and service contract for the Web service, you can build the Web service itself.

Create the REST Web service

1. Open another instance of Visual Studio or Visual Web Developer Express.

 Important Do not use the instance you used to create the SOAP Web service because this copy of Visual Studio must remain running to keep the Development Web Server hosting the SOAP Web service open.

2. If you are using Visual Studio 2010 Professional or Enterprise, on the *File* menu, point to *New*, and then click *Web Site*.

3. If you are using Visual Web Developer 2010 Express, on the *File* menu, click *New Web Site*.

4. In the *New Web Site* dialog box, click the *WCF Service* template. Select *File System* in the *Location* drop-down list box, and specify the \Microsoft Press\Visual CSharp Step By Step\Chapter 29\ProductDetailsService folder under your Documents folder and then click *OK*.

5. Click the C:\...\ProductDetailsService\ project. In the *Properties* window, set the *Use dynamic ports* property to *False* and set the *Port number* property to *4600*.

> **Note** It is important to specify a different port from the ProductInformationService Web service; otherwise, the two Web services will conflict.

6. On the *Website* menu, click *Add Reference*. In the *Add Reference* dialog box, click the *Browse* tab. In the toolbar, click the *Up One Level* button, browse to the folder ProductDetailsContracts\ProductDetailsContracts\bin\Debug folder, select the *ProductDetailsContracts.dll* assembly, and then click *OK*.

7. In *Solution Explorer*, expand the App_Code folder if it is not already open, right-click the file Service.cs, and then click *Rename*. Change the name of the file to ProductDetails.cs.

8. In the App_Code folder, delete the file IService.cs. This file is not needed by the Web service.

9. Double-click the ProductDetails.cs file to display it in the *Code and Text Editor* window.

10. Add the following using statements to the list at the top of the file:

```
using System.Data.Linq;
using System.Data.SqlClient;
using ProductDetailsContracts;
```

11. Modify the definition of the *Service* class, change the name to *ProductDetails*, and specify that it implements the *IProductDetails* interface, as shown next in bold. Remove the *GetData* and *GetDataUsingDataContract* methods from the *ProductDetails* class:

```
public class ProductDetails : IProductDetails
{

}
```

12. Add the *GetProduct* method shown next in bold to the *ProductDetails* class:

```
public class ProductDetails : IProductDetails
{
    public Product GetProduct(string productID)
```

```
    {
        int ID = Int32.Parse(productID);

        SqlConnectionStringBuilder builder =
            new SqlConnectionStringBuilder();
        builder.DataSource = ".\\SQLExpress";
        builder.InitialCatalog = "Northwind";
        builder.IntegratedSecurity = true;
        DataContext productsContext =
            new DataContext(builder.ConnectionString);

        Product product = (from p in productsContext.GetTable<Product>()
                            where p.ProductID == ID
                            select p).First();

        return product;
    }
}
```

The product ID is passed to the method as a string, so the first statement converts it to an integer and stores the result in the variable *ID*. The code then creates a *DataContext* object that connects to the Northwind database. The LINQ query retrieves all rows that have a product ID that matches the value in the *ID* variable. There should be at most one matching product. Usually, you must iterate through the results of a LINQ to SQL query to fetch each row in turn, but if there is only a single row you can use the *First* extension method to retrieve the data immediately. The *Product* object retrieved by the query is returned as the result of the method.

The next step is to configure the REST Web service to provide the connection string that the *ProductDetailsContract* assembly uses to connect to the database, and then specify the protocol and endpoint that client applications can use to communicate with the Web service.

Configure the Web service

1. In *Solution Explorer*, double-click the *Web.config* file to display it in the *Code and Text Editor* window.

2. Add the *<services>* element and child elements shown next in bold to the *<system.serviceModel>* element, before the *<behaviors>* element. Also, add the *<endpointBehaviors>* element also shown in bold as a child of the *<behaviors>* element. Notice that you must fully qualify the name of the interface that provides the service contract with the *ProductDetailsContracts* namespace.

```
<?xml version="1.0"?>
<configuration>
  <system.web>
    <compilation debug="false" targetFramework="4.0" />
  </system.web>
  <system.serviceModel>
    <services>
```

```
       <service name="ProductDetails">
         <endpoint address="" binding="webHttpBinding"
                   contract="ProductDetailsContracts.IProductDetails"
                   behaviorConfiguration="WebBehavior"/>
       </service>
     </services>
     <behaviors>
       <endpointBehaviors>
         <behavior name="WebBehavior">
           <webHttp/>
         </behavior>
       </endpointBehaviors>
       <serviceBehaviors>
         <behavior>
           <!-- To avoid disclosing metadata information, set the value below
to false and remove the metadata endpoint above before deployment -->
           <serviceMetadata httpGetEnabled="true"/>
           <!-- To receive exception details in faults for debugging
purposes, set the value below to true.  Set to false before deployment to
avoid disclosing exception information -->
           <serviceDebug includeExceptionDetailInFaults="false"/>
         </behavior>
       </serviceBehaviors>
     </behaviors>
   </system.serviceModel>
</configuration>
```

This Web service uses a different binding from the ProductInformation Web service—
webHttpBinding. The *webHttpBinding* binding and the *WebBehavior* behavior indicate
that the Web service expects requests to be sent following the REST style, encoded in
the URL, and that it should return response messages as plain XML (POX).

3. In *Solution Explorer*, double-click the Service.svc file to display it in the *Code and
Text Editor* window. Update the *Service* and *CodeBehind* elements to refer to the
ProductsDetails class in the ProductDetails.cs file, as shown here in bold:

```
<%@ ServiceHost Language="C#" Debug="true" Service="ProductDetails"
CodeBehind="~/App_Code/ProductDetails.cs" %>
```

4. On the *Build* menu, click *Build Web Site*.

5. In *Solution Explorer*, right-click Service.svc, and then click *View in Browser*.

Internet Explorer appears displaying the page for the ProductDetails service.

6. In the address bar, specify the following URL and then press Enter:

```
http://localhost:4600/ProductDetailsService/Service.svc/products/5
```

This URL invokes the *GetProduct* method in the ProductDetails Web service and
specifies product 5. The *GetProduct* method fetches the data for product 5 from the
Northwind database and returns the information as a *Product* object, serialized as XML.
Internet Explorer should display the XML representation of this product.

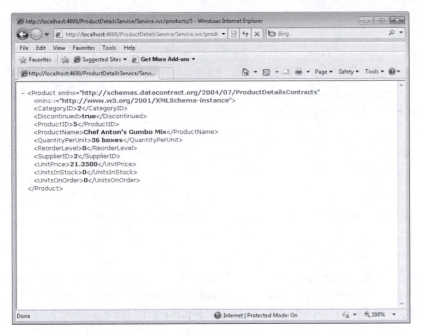

7. Close Internet Explorer.

Consuming the ProductDetails REST Web Service

You have seen that you can invoke a REST Web service quite easily from a Web browser simply by specifying an appropriate URL. To call methods in a REST Web service from an application, you can construct a proxy class, similar to that used by a client application connecting to a SOAP Web service. As mentioned earlier, Visual Studio does not provide functionality that can generate a proxy class for a REST Web service. Fortunately, it is not difficult to create a simple REST proxy class manually; you can use the same generic *ClientBase* class that a SOAP proxy class uses.

In the final exercise, you will return to the ProductClient application and add functionality to call the *GetProduct* method in the REST Web service.

Invoke the REST Web service from the client application

1. Return to the instance of Visual Studio or Visual C# Express that you used to create the service contract for the REST Web service.

2. Open the ProductClient solution in the \Microsoft Press\Visual CSharp Step By Step\ Chapter 29\ProductClient folder in your Documents folder. This is the client application that you used to test the SOAP Web service earlier in this chapter.

3. On the *Project* menu, click *Add Reference*. In the *Add Reference* dialog box, click the *Browse* tab. In the toolbar, click the *Up One Level* button twice, browse to the folder ProductDetailsContracts\ProductDetailsContracts\bin\Debug folder, select the *ProductDetailsContracts* assembly, and then click *OK*.

4. On the *Project* menu, click *Add Reference* again. In the *Add Reference* dialog box, click the *.NET* tab. Select the *System.Data.Linq* assembly, and then click *OK*.

5. On the *Project* menu, click *Add Class*. In the *Add New Item – ProductClient* dialog box, in the middle pane click the *Class* template. In the *Name* text box, type **ProductClientProxy.cs**, and then click *Add*.

6. In the *Code and Text Editor* window displaying the ProductClientProxy.cs file, add the following *using* statements to the list at the top of the file:

```
using System.ServiceModel;
using ProductDetailsContracts;
```

7. Modify the definition of the *ProductClientProxy* class so that it inherits from the generic *ClientBase* class and implements the *IProductDetails* interface. Specify the *IProductDetails* interface as the type parameter for the *ClientBase* class. The *ProductClientProxy* class should look like the following code example:

```
class ProductClientProxy : ClientBase<IProductDetails>, IProductDetails
{
}
```

8. Add the *GetProduct* method shown next in bold to the *ProductClientProxy* class. This method follows the same pattern as that used by the SOAP proxy shown earlier in this chapter; it forwards the request from the client to the communications channel.

```
class ProductClientProxy : ClientBase<IProductDetails>, IProductDetails
{
    public Product GetProduct(string productID)
    {
        return this.Channel.GetProduct(productID);
    }
}
```

9. Display the ProductClient.xaml file in the *Design View* window.

10. Double-click the *Get Product* button to generate the *getProduct_Click* event handler method for this button.

11. In the *Code and Text Editor* window, add the following *using* statement to the list at the top of the ProductClient.xaml.cs file:

```
using ProductDetailsContracts;
```

12. In the *getProduct_Click* method, add the following code shown in bold:

```
private void getProduct_Click(object sender, RoutedEventArgs e)
{
    ProductClientProxy proxy = new ProductClientProxy();
    try
    {
        Product product = proxy.GetProduct(productID.Text);
        productName.Content = product.ProductName;
        supplierID.Content = product.SupplierID.Value;
        categoryID.Content = product.CategoryID.Value;
        quantityPerUnit.Content = product.QuantityPerUnit;
        unitPrice.Content = String.Format("{0:C}", product.UnitPrice.Value);
        unitsInStock.Content = product.UnitsInStock.Value;
        unitsOnOrder.Content = product.UnitsOnOrder.Value;
        reorderLevel.Content = product.ReorderLevel.Value;
        discontinued.IsChecked = product.Discontinued;
    }
    catch (Exception ex)
    {
        MessageBox.Show("Error fetching product details: " + ex.Message,
            "Error", MessageBoxButton.OK, MessageBoxImage.Error);
    }
    finally
    {
        if (proxy.State == CommunicationState.Faulted)
        {
            proxy.Abort();
        }
        else
        {
            proxy.Close();
        }
    }
}
```

This code creates an instance of the *ProductClientProxy* class and uses it to call the *GetProduct* method in the REST Web service. The data in the *Product* object returned is displayed in the labels on the form.

13. In *Solution Explorer*, double-click the *app.config* file. This is the configuration file for the application. It was generated automatically when you created the SOAP Web service proxy in an earlier exercise. It contains a *<system.serviceModel>* element that describes the endpoint for the SOAP Web service, including the URL that the application should connect to.

14. Locate the *<client>* element, and add the *<endpoint>* element shown here in bold above the existing *<endpoint>* section:

```
<client>
  <endpoint address="http://localhost:4600/ProductDetailsService/Service.svc"
          binding="webHttpBinding" contract="ProductDetailsContracts.
IProductDetails"
          behaviorConfiguration="WebBehavior">
  </endpoint>
```

```
<endpoint address="http://localhost:4500/ProductInformationService/Service.svc"
          binding="wsHttpBinding" bindingConfiguration="WSHttpBinding_
IProductInformation"
          contract="ProductInformationService.IProductInformation"
          name="WSHttpBinding_IProductInformation">
  <identity>
    <userPrincipalName value="YourComputer\YourName" />
  </identity>
</endpoint>
</client>
```

15. After the closing *</client>* tag, add the *<behaviors>* section shown here in bold:

```
<client>
  ...
</client>
<behaviors>
  <endpointBehaviors>
    <behavior name="WebBehavior">
      <webHttp />
    </behavior>
  </endpointBehaviors>
</behaviors>
```

This code defines the *WebBehavior* behavior referenced by the client endpoint. It specifies that the client should connect to the Web service by using the *webHttp* behavior expected by the REST Web service.

16. On the *Debug* menu, click *Start Without Debugging*.

17. When the *Product Details* form appears, in the *Product ID* text box type **10**; in the *How Many* text box, type **5**; and then click *Calculate Cost*. The total cost should be displayed (155 currency units). This verifies that the SOAP Web service is still working.

18. Click *Get Product*. The details for *Ikura* should appear in the labels on the form, as shown in the following image:

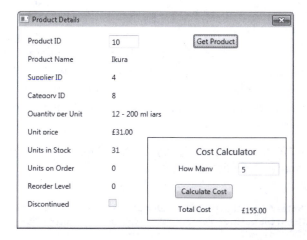

19. Experiment with other product IDs. Note that if you specify a product ID that does not exist, the Web service returns a "Bad Request" exception.

20. Close the Product Details form when you have finished.

In this chapter, you saw how to use Visual Studio to build two different styles of Web service: SOAP and REST. You also saw how to build client applications that can consume these different styles of Web service.

You have now completed all the exercises in this book. Hopefully, you are thoroughly conversant with the C# language and understand how to use Visual Studio 2010 to build professional applications. However, this is not the end of the story. You have jumped the first hurdle, but the best C# programmers learn from continued experience, and you can gain this experience only by building C# applications. As you do so, you will discover new ways to use the C# language and the many features available in Visual Studio 2010 that I have not had space to cover in this book. Also, remember that C# is an evolving language. Back in 2001, when we wrote the first edition of this book, C# introduced the syntax and semantics necessary for you to build applications that made use of .NET Framework 1.0. Some enhancements were added to Visual Studio and .NET Framework 1.1 in 2003, and then in 2005, C# 2.0 emerged with support for generics and .NET Framework 2.0. C# 3.0 added numerous features such as anonymous types, lambda expressions, and most significantly, LINQ. And now C# 4.0 has extended the language further with support for named arguments, optional parameters, contra and covariant interfaces, and integration with dynamic languages. What will the next version of C# bring? Watch this space!

Chapter 29 Quick Reference

To	Do this
Create a SOAP Web service	Use the WCF Service template. Define a service contract that specifies the Web methods exposed by the Web service by creating an interface with the *ServiceContract* attribute. Tag each method with the *OperationContract* attribute. Create a class that implements this interface.
	Configure the service to use the *wsHttpBinding* binding.
Create a REST Web service	Use the WCF Service template. Define a service contract that specifies the Web methods exposed by the Web service by creating an interface with the *ServiceContract* attribute. Tag each method with the *OperationContract* attribute and the *WebGet* attribute, which specifies the URI template for invoking the method. Create a class that implements this interface.
	Configure the service to use the *webHttpBinding*, and specify the *webHttp* behavior for the service endpoint.

To	Do this
Display the description of a SOAP Web service	Right-click the .svc file in *Solution Explorer*, and click *View in Browser*. Internet Explorer runs, moves to the Web service URL, and displays a page describing how to create a client application that can access the Web service. Click the WSDL link to display the WSDL description of the Web service.
Pass complex data as Web method parameters and return values	Define a class to hold the data, and tag it with the *DataContract* attribute. Ensure that each item of data is accessible either as a public field or through a public property that provides *get* and *set* access. Ensure that the class has a default constructor (which might be empty).
Create a proxy class for a SOAP Web service in a client application	On the *Project* menu, click *Add Service Reference*. Type the URL of the Web service in the *Address* text box at the top of the dialog box, and then click *Go*. Specify the namespace for the proxy class, and then click *OK*.
Create a proxy class for a REST Web service in a client application	Create a class that inherits from the *ClientBase* generic class, and specify the interface that defines the service contract as the type parameter. Implement this interface, and use the *Channel* property inherited from the *ClientBase* class to send requests to the Web service.
Invoke a Web method	Create an instance of the proxy class. Call the Web method by using the proxy class.

Appendix
Interoperating with Dynamic Languages

After completing this chapter, you will be able to:

- Explain the purpose of the Dynamic Language Runtime.

- Use the *dynamic* keyword to reference objects implemented by using dynamic languages, and invoke methods on these objects.

Interoperability between code written by using managed languages has been a key feature of the Microsoft .NET Framework ever since its inception. The idea is that you can build a component using the language of your choice, compile it into an assembly, reference the assembly from your application, and then access the component from code in your application. Your application might be built by using a different language from the component, but this does not matter. The compilers for each of the managed languages (Visual C#, Visual Basic, Visual C++, Visual F#, and so on) all convert code written by using these languages into another language called MSIL, or Microsoft Intermediate Language. When you run an application, the .NET Framework runtime converts the MSIL code into machine instructions and then runs them. The result is that the .NET Framework does not actually know, nor even care, what language you originally used. If you really want to, you can write your applications by using MSIL rather than C#, although this would be a real shame!

However, not all modern computer languages are compiled. There are a large number of interpreted scripting languages currently in use. Two of the most common examples that have appeared outside of the Microsoft domain are Ruby and Python. In earlier releases of the .NET Framework, it was never a straightforward matter to incorporate code written by using languages such as these into managed applications, and the result was often applications that were difficult to understand and maintain. The .NET Framework 4.0 has addressed this issue with the Dynamic Language Runtime, which is the subject of this brief appendix.

 Note This appendix assumes you are familiar with either Ruby or Python. It does not attempt to teach you about these languages. Additionally, this appendix does not contain any exercises. If you want to run the code shown in this chapter, you must download and install the most recent builds of IronRuby or IronPython from the CodePlex Web site at *http://www.codeplex.com*. IronPython and IronRuby are full implementations of the Python and Ruby languages that include extensions enabling them to instantiate objects defined in the .NET Framework. They are fully compatible with the most recent open source versions of these languages, and you can use them to run existing Python and Ruby scripts unchanged.

What Is the Dynamic Language Runtime?

C# is a strongly typed language. When you create a variable, you specify the type of that variable, and you can invoke only methods and access members defined by that type. If you try and call a method that the type does not implement, your code will not compile. This is good because it catches a large number of possible errors early, before you even run your code.

However, this strong typing becomes a problem if you want to create objects defined by languages such as Ruby and Python that are interpreted and not compiled. It is very difficult, if not impossible, for the C# compiler to verify that any members you access in your C# code actually exist in these objects. Additionally, if you call a method on a Ruby or Python object, the C# compiler cannot check that you have passed the correct number of parameters and that each parameter has the appropriate type.

There is another issue. The types defined by C# and the .NET Framework by and large have a different internal representation from those used by Ruby and Python. Therefore, if you call a Ruby method that returns an integer, for example, somehow this integer has to be converted from the representation used by Ruby to that expected by C#. A similar problem arises if you pass an integer as a parameter from a C# application into a Ruby method; the integer must be converted from the C# representation to that of Ruby.

The process of converting data between formats is known as *marshaling*, and it is an age-old problem familiar to developers who have ever had to build applications that invoke COM components. The solution is to use an intermediary layer. In the .NET Framework 4.0, this intermediary layer is called the Dynamic Language Runtime, or DLR.

As well as marshaling data between languages, the DLR also provides many of the services provided by the compiler when using a strongly typed language. For example, when you invoke a method on a Ruby or Python object, the DLR checks that this method call is valid.

The DLR is not tied to a specific set of languages; it implements an architecture based on language binders as shown in the following image:

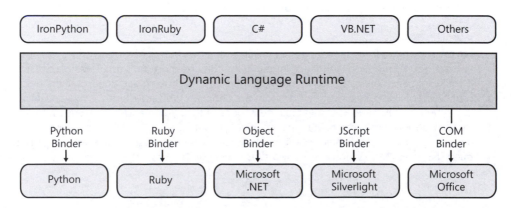

A language binder is a component that slots into the DLR and understands how to invoke methods in a specified language, and how to marshal and unmarshal data between the format expected by the language and the .NET Framework. The binder also performs a certain amount of checking, such as verifying that an object does actually expose a method being invoked, and that the parameters and return types are valid.

The .NET Framework 4.0 provides binders for IronPython, IronRuby, COM (which you can use to access COM components, such as those in Microsoft Office), and Jscript, as well as the .NET Framework itself. Furthermore, the .NET Framework 4.0 enables you to write your own binders for other languages by using the types and interfaces in the *System.Dynamic* namespace. (The details of how to do this are outside the scope of this appendix.) Additionally, IronPython and IronRuby can themselves use the DLR to access objects built by using other technologies and languages.

The DLR performs its work at runtime. This means that any type-checking for objects referenced through the DLR is deferred until your application executes. How do you indicate in a C# application that type-checking for an object should be deferred in this way? The answer lies in the *dynamic* keyword.

The *dynamic* Keyword

The *dynamic* keyword is new in C# 4.0. You use it in exactly the same way that you use a type. For example, the following statement creates a variable called *rubyObject* using the *dynamic* type:

```
dynamic rubyObject;
```

There is actually no such thing as the *dynamic* type in C#. All this statement does is create a variable of type *object*, but with type-checking deferred until runtime. You can assign a value to this variable and call methods using it. At runtime, the DLR uses the appropriate binder to validate your code, instantiate objects, and invoke methods. The internal details of the DLR are subject to change, so discussion of how this works is beyond the scope of this appendix. Suffice to say, that the DLR knows how to call a binder to create objects, invoke methods, and marshal and unmarshal data.

There is one small caveat. Because the type-checking is deferred until runtime, Visual Studio IntelliSense cannot help you by providing the names of members exposed through a dynamic object reference. If you attempt to call an invalid method or reference a nonexistent field in a dynamic object, you will not know about it until runtime, when it will throw a *RuntimeBinderException* exception.

Example: IronPython

The following example shows a Python script called CustomerDB.py. This class contains four items:

- **A class called Customer.** This class contains three fields, which contain the ID, name, and telephone number for a customer. The constructor initializes these fields with values passed in as parameters. The _str_ method formats the data in the class as a string so that it can be output.

- **A class called CustomerDB.** This class contains a dictionary called *customerDatabase*. The *storeCustomer* method adds a customer to this dictionary, and the *getCustomer* method retrieves a customer when given the customer ID. The _str_ method iterates through the customers in the dictionary and formats them as a string. For simplicity, none of these methods include any form of error checking.

- **A function called GetNewCustomer.** This is a factory method that constructs a *Customer* object using the parameters passed in and then returns this object.

- **A function called GetCustomerDB.** This is another factory method that constructs a *CustomerDB* object and returns it.

```python
class Customer:
  def __init__(self, id, name, telephone):
    self.custID = id
    self.custName = name
    self.custTelephone = telephone

  def __str__(self):
    return str.format("ID: {0}\tName: {1}\tTelephone: {2}",
                      self.custID, self.custName, self.custTelephone)



class CustomerDB:
  def __init__(self):
    self.customerDatabase = {}

  def storeCustomer(self, customer):
   self.customerDatabase[customer.custID] = customer

  def getCustomer(self, id):
    return self.customerDatabase[id]

  def __str__(self):
    list = "Customers\n"
    for id, cust in self.customerDatabase.iteritems():
      list += str.format("{0}", cust) + "\n"
    return list
```

```
def GetNewCustomer(id, name, telephone):
  return Customer(id, name, telephone)



def GetCustomerDB():
  return CustomerDB()
```

The following code example shows a simple C# console application that tests these items. You can find this application in the \Microsoft Press\Visual CSharp Step By Step\Appendix\ PythonInteroperability folder under your Documents folder. It references the IronPython assemblies, which provide the language binding for Python. These assemblies are included with the IronPython download and are not part of the .NET Framework Class Library.

> **Note** This sample application was built using the version of IronPython that was current when the book went to press. If you have a later build of IronPython, you should replace the references to the IronPython and Microsoft.Scripting assemblies in this application with those provided with your installation of IronPython.

The static *CreateRuntime* method of the *Python* class creates an instance of the Python runtime. The *UseFile* method of the Python runtime opens a script containing Python code, and it makes the items in this script accessible.

> **Note** In this example, the script CustomerDB.py is located in the Appendix folder, but the executable is built under the Appendix\PythonInteroperability\PythonInteroperability\bin\ Debug folder, which accounts for the path to the CustomerDB.py script shown in the parameter to the *UseFile* method.

In this code, notice that the *pythonCustomer* and *pythonCustomerDB* variables reference Python types, so they are declared as *dynamic*. The *python* variable used to invoke the *GetNewCustomer* and *GetCustomerDB* functions is also declared as *dynamic*. In reality, the type returned by the *UseFile* method is a *Microsoft.Scriping.Hosting.ScriptScope* object. However, if you declare the *python* variable using the *ScriptScope* type, the code will not build because the compiler, quite correctly, spots that the *ScriptScope* type does not contain definitions for the *GetNewCustomer* and *GetCustomerDB* methods. Specifying *dynamic* causes the compiler to defer its checking to the DLR at runtime, by which time the *python* variable refers to an instance of a Python script, which does include these functions.

The code calls the *GetNewCustomer* Python function to create a new *Customer* object with the details for Fred. It then calls *GetCustomerDB* to create a *CustomerDB* object, and then invokes the *storeCustomer* method to add Fred to the dictionary in the *CustomerDB* object. The code creates another *Customer* object for a customer called Sid, and adds this customer to the *CustomerDB* object as well. Finally, the code displays the *CustomerDB* object. The *Console.WriteLine* method expects a string representation of the *CustomerDB* object.

Consequently, the Python runtime invokes the *__str__* method to generate this representation, and the *WriteLine* statement displays a list of the customers found in the Python dictionary.

```
using System;
using IronPython.Hosting;

namespace PythonInteroperability
{
    class Program
    {
        static void Main(string[] args)
        {
            // Creating IronPython objects
            Console.WriteLine("Testing Python");
            dynamic python =
                Python.CreateRuntime().UseFile(@"..\..\..\..\CustomerDB.py");
            dynamic pythonCustomer = python.GetNewCustomer(100, "Fred", "888");
            dynamic pythonCustomerDB = python.GetCustomerDB();
            pythonCustomerDB.storeCustomer(pythonCustomer);
            pythonCustomer = python.GetNewCustomer(101, "Sid", "999");
            pythonCustomerDB.storeCustomer(pythonCustomer);
            Console.WriteLine("{0}", pythonCustomerDB);
        }
    }
}
```

The following image shows the output generated by this application:

Example: IronRuby

For completeness, the following code shows a Ruby script called CustomerDB.rb, which contains classes and functions that exhibit similar functionality to those in the Python script demonstrated previously.

Note The *to_s* method in a Ruby class returns a string representation of an object, just like the *__str__* method in a Python class.

```ruby
class Customer
  attr_reader :custID
  attr_accessor :custName
  attr_accessor :custTelephone

  def initialize(id, name, telephone)
    @custID = id
    @custName = name
    @custTelephone = telephone
  end

  def to_s
    return "ID: #{custID}\tName: #{custName}\tTelephone: #{custTelephone}"
  end
end


class CustomerDB
  attr_reader  :customerDatabase

  def initialize
    @customerDatabase ={}
  end

  def storeCustomer(customer)
   @customerDatabase[customer.custID] = customer
 end

  def getCustomer(id)
    return @customerDatabase[id]
  end

  def to_s
    list = "Customers\n"
    @customerDatabase.each {
        |key, value|
        list = list + "#{value}" + "\n"
    }
    return list
  end
end


def GetNewCustomer(id, name, telephone)
  return Customer.new(id, name, telephone)
end


def GetCustomerDB
  return CustomerDB.new
end
```

The following C# program uses this Ruby script to create two *Customer* objects, store them in a *CustomerDB* object, and then print the contents of the *CustomerDB* object. It operates in the same way as the Python interoperability application described in the previous section, and it uses the *dynamic* type to define the variables for the Ruby script and the Ruby objects. You can find this application in the \Microsoft Press\Visual CSharp Step By Step\Appendix\ RubyInteroperability folder under your Documents folder. It references the IronRuby assemblies, which provide the language binding for Ruby. These assemblies are part of the IronRuby download.

> **Note** This sample application was built using the version of IronRuby that was current when the book went to press. If you have a later build of IronRby, you should replace the references to the IronRuby, IronRuby.Libraries, and Microsoft.Scripting assemblies in this application with those provided with your installation of IronRuby.

```
using System;
using IronRuby;

namespace RubyInteroperability
{
    class Program
    {
        static void Main(string[] args)
        {
            // Creating IronRuby objects
            Console.WriteLine("Testing Ruby");
            dynamic ruby =
                Ruby.CreateRuntime().UseFile(@"..\..\..\..\CustomerDB.rb");
            dynamic rubyCustomer = ruby.GetNewCustomer(100, "Fred", "888");
            dynamic rubyCustomerDB = ruby.GetCustomerDB();
            rubyCustomerDB.storeCustomer(rubyCustomer);
            rubyCustomer = ruby.GetNewCustomer(101, "Sid", "999");
            rubyCustomerDB.storeCustomer(rubyCustomer);
            Console.WriteLine("{0}", rubyCustomerDB);
            Console.WriteLine();
        }
    }
}
```

The following image shows the output of this program:

Summary

This appendix has provided a brief introduction to using the DLR to integrate code written with scripting languages such as Ruby and Python into a C# application. The DLR provides an extensible model that can support any language or technology that has a binder. You can write a binder by using the types in the System.Dynamic namespace.

The C# language includes the dynamic type. When you declare a variable as dy-namic, C# type-checking is disabled for this variable. The DLR performs type-checking at runtime, dispatches method calls, and marshals data.

Index

Symbols

−= compound assignment operator, 92, 332, 344
+= compound assignment operator, 92, 331, 343
? modifier, 157, 171, 174
−− operator, 44, 425
* operator, 36, 170
*= operator, 92
/= operator, 92
%= operator, 37, 92
++ operator, 43, 425

A

About Box windows template, 488
about event methods, 488–489
abstract classes, 232, 253, 269–271
  creating, 272–274, 277
abstract keyword, 270, 276, 277
abstract methods, 270–271, 277
access, protected, 242
accessibility
  of fields and methods, 132–133
  of properties, 301
access keys for menu items, 480
accessors, *get* and *set*, 298
Action delegates, 604–605
  creating, 508
  invoking, 632
Action type, 630
add_Click method, 472
AddCount method, 664
AddExtension property, 496
addition operator, 36
  precedence of, 41, 77
Add method, 208, 214, 217, 587
<Add New Event> command, 476
AddObject method, 596
AddParticipant method, 666
addValues method, 50, 52
Add Window command, 457
Administrator privileges, for exercises, 535–537

ADO.NET, 535
  connecting to databases with, 564
  LINQ to SQL and, 549
  querying databases with, 535–548, 564
ADO.NET class library, 535
ADO.NET Entity Data Model template, 566, 569, 596
ADO.NET Entity Framework, 566–583
AggregateException class, 642–644
  Handle method, 642
AggregateException exceptions, 647
AggregateException handler, 642–644
anchor points of controls, 447–448
AND (&) operator, 316
anonymous classes, 147–148
anonymous methods, 341
anonymous types in arrays, 194–195, 197
APIs, 300
App.config (application configuration) file, 8, 573
  connection strings, storing in, 572, 573
ApplicationException exceptions, 517
Application objects, 457
application programming interfaces, 330
applications
  building, 26
  multitasking in, 602–628
  parallelization in, 603
  responsiveness of, 498–507
  running, 26
Application.xaml.cs files, 24
App.xaml files, code in, 24
ArgumentException class, 220
ArgumentException exceptions, 205, 225
argumentList, 51
ArgumentOutOfRangeException class, 121
arguments
  in methods, 52
  modifying, 159–162
  named, ambiguities with, 66–71

omitting, 66
passing to methods, 159
positional, 66
arithmetic operations, 36–43
  results type, 37
arithmetic operators
  checked and unchecked, 119
  precedence, 41–42
  using, 38–41
array arguments, 220–226
array elements
  accessing, 195, 218
  types of, 192
array indexes, 195, 218
  integer types for, 201
array instances
  copying, 197–198
  creating, 192–193, 218
ArrayList class, 208–209, 217
  number of elements in, 209
arrays, 191–206
  associative, 212
  card playing application, 199–206
  cells in, 198
  vs. collections, 214
  copying, 197–198
  implicitly typed, 194–195
  initializing elements of, 218
  inserting elements, 208
  of *int* variables, 207
  iterating through, 195–197, 218
  keys arrays, 212, 213
  length of, 218
  multidimensional, 198–199
  of objects, 207
  params arrays, 219–220
  removing elements from, 208
  resizing, 208
  size of, 192–193
  zero-length arrays, 223
array variables
  declaring, 191–192, 218
  initializing, 193–194
  naming conventions, 192
as operator, 169, 236
AsOrdered method, 655
AsParallel method, 650, 681
  specifying, 652
assemblies, 361
  definition of, 16
  namespaces and, 16
  uses of, 8

About the Author

John Sharp is a principal technologist at Content Master, part of CM Group Ltd, a technical authoring and consulting company. An expert on developing applications by using the Microsoft .NET Framework and other technologies, John has produced numerous tutorials, white papers, and presentations on distributed systems, SOA and Web services, the C# language, and interoperability issues. John has helped to develop a large number of courses for Microsoft Training (he co-wrote the first C# programming course for them) and he is also the author of several popular books, including *Microsoft Windows Communication Foundation Step by Step*.

For C# Developers

Microsoft® Visual C#® 2008 Express Edition: Build a Program Now!

Patrice Pelland

ISBN 9780735625426

Build your own Web browser or other cool application—no programming experience required! Featuring learn-by-doing projects and plenty of examples, this full-color guide is your quick start to creating your first applications for Windows®. DVD includes Express Edition software plus code samples.

Microsoft Visual C# 2008 Step by Step

John Sharp

ISBN 9780735624306

Teach yourself Visual C# 2008—one step at a time. Ideal for developers with fundamental programming skills, this practical tutorial delivers hands-on guidance for creating C# components and Windows–based applications. CD features practice exercises, code samples, and a fully searchable eBook.

Learn Programming Now! Microsoft XNA® Game Studio 2.0

Rob Miles

ISBN 9780735625228

Now you can create your own games for Xbox 360® and Windows—as you learn the underlying skills and concepts for computer programming. Dive right into your first project, adding new tools and tricks to your arsenal as you go. Master the fundamentals of XNA Game Studio and Visual C#—no experience required!

Programming Microsoft Visual C# 2008: The Language

Donis Marshall

ISBN 9780735625402

Get the in-depth reference, best practices, and code you need to master the core language capabilities in Visual C# 2008. Fully updated for Microsoft .NET Framework 3.5, including a detailed exploration of LINQ, this book examines language features in detail—and across the product life cycle.

Windows via C/C++, Fifth Edition

Jeffrey Richter, Christophe Nasarre

ISBN 9780735624245

Jeffrey Richter's classic guide to C++ programming—now fully revised for Windows XP, Windows Vista®, and Windows Server® 2008. Learn to develop more-robust applications with unmanaged C++ code—and apply advanced techniques—with comprehensive guidance and code samples from the experts.

CLR via C#, Second Edition

Jeffrey Richter

ISBN 9780735621633

Dig deep and master the intricacies of the common language runtime (CLR) and the .NET Framework. Written by programming expert Jeffrey Richter, this guide is ideal for developers building any kind of application—ASP.NET, Windows Forms, Microsoft SQL Server®, Web services, console apps—and features extensive C# code samples.

ALSO SEE

Microsoft Visual C# 2005 Step by Step
ISBN 9780735621299

Programming Microsoft Visual C# 2005: The Language
ISBN 9780735621817

Debugging Microsoft .NET 2.0 Applications
ISBN 9780735622029

For Visual Basic Developers

Microsoft® Visual Basic® 2008 Express Edition: Build a Program Now!
Patrice Pelland
ISBN 9780735625419

Build your own Web browser or other cool application—no programming experience required! Featuring learn-by-doing projects and plenty of examples, this full-color guide is your quick start to creating your first applications for Windows®. DVD includes Express Edition software plus code samples.

Microsoft Visual Basic 2008 Step by Step
Michael Halvorson
ISBN 9780735625372

Teach yourself the essential tools and techniques for Visual Basic 2008—one step at a time. No matter what your skill level, you'll find the practical guidance and examples you need to start building applications for Windows and the Web. CD features practice exercises, code samples, and a fully searchable eBook.

Programming Microsoft Visual Basic 2005: The Language
Francesco Balena
ISBN 9780735621831

Master the core capabilities in Visual Basic 2005 with guidance from well-known programming expert Francesco Balena. Focusing on language features and the Microsoft .NET Framework 2.0 base class library, this book provides pragmatic instruction and examples useful to both new and experienced developers.

Programming Windows Services with Microsoft Visual Basic 2008
Michael Gernaey
ISBN 9780735624337

The essential guide for developing powerful, customized Windows services with Visual Basic 2008. Whether you're looking to perform network monitoring or design a complex enterprise solution, this guide delivers the right combination of expert advice and practical examples to accelerate your productivity.

ALSO SEE

Microsoft Visual Basic 2005 Express Edition: Build a Program Now!
Patrice Pelland
ISBN 9780735622135

Microsoft Visual Basic 2005 Step by Step
Michael Halvorson
ISBN 9780735621312

Microsoft ADO.NET 2.0 Step by Step
Rebecca Riordan
ISBN 9780735621640

Microsoft ASP.NET 3.5 Step by Step
George Shepherd
ISBN 9780735624269

Programming Microsoft ASP.NET 3.5
Dino Esposito
ISBN 9780735625273

Debugging Microsoft .NET 2.0 Applications
John Robbins
ISBN 9780735622029

Microsoft® Press

microsoft.com/mspress

Best Practices for Software Engineering

Software Estimation: Demystifying the Black Art
Steve McConnell
ISBN 9780735605350

Amazon.com's pick for "Best Computer Book of 2006"! Generating accurate software estimates is fairly straight-forward—once you understand the art of creating them. Acclaimed author Steve McConnell demystifies the process—illuminating the practical procedures, formulas, and heuristics you can apply right away.

Code Complete, Second Edition
Steve McConnell
ISBN 9780735619678

Widely considered one of the best practical guides to programming—fully updated. Drawing from research, academia, and everyday commercial practice, McConnell synthesizes must-know principles and techniques into clear, pragmatic guidance. Rethink your approach—and deliver the highest quality code.

Agile Portfolio Management
Jochen Krebs
ISBN 9780735625679

Agile processes foster better collaboration, innovation, and results. So why limit their use to software projects—when you can transform your entire business? This book illuminates the opportunities—and rewards—of applying agile processes to your overall IT portfolio, with best practices for optimizing results.

Simple Architectures for Complex Enterprises
Roger Sessions
ISBN 9780735625785

Why do so many IT projects fail? Enterprise consultant Roger Sessions believes complex problems require simple solutions. And in this book, he shows how to make simplicity a core architectural requirement—as critical as performance, reliability, or security—to achieve better, more reliable results for your organization.

The Enterprise and Scrum
Ken Schwaber
ISBN 9780735623378

Extend Scrum's benefits—greater agility, higher-quality products, and lower costs—beyond individual teams to the entire enterprise. Scrum cofounder Ken Schwaber describes proven practices for adopting Scrum principles across your organization, including that all-critical component—managing change.

ALSO SEE

Software Requirements, Second Edition
Karl E. Wiegers
ISBN 9780735618794

More About Software Requirements: Thorny Issues and Practical Advice
Karl E. Wiegers
ISBN 9780735622678

Software Requirement Patterns
Stephen Withall
ISBN 9780735623989

Agile Project Management with Scrum
Ken Schwaber
ISBN 9780735619937

microsoft.com/mspress

What do you think of this book?

We want to hear from you!

To participate in a brief online survey, please visit:

microsoft.com/learning/booksurvey

...and enter this book's ISBN number (appears above barcode on back cover).

Tell us how well this book meets your needs—what works effectively, and what we can do better. Your feedback will help us continually improve our books and learning resources for you.

Thank you in advance for your input!

Where to find the ISBN on back cover

Example only. Each book has unique ISBN.

Stay in touch!

To subscribe to the *Microsoft Press® Book Connection Newsletter*—for news on upcoming books, events, and special offers—please visit:

microsoft.com/learning/books/newsletter